Lecture Notes in Computer Science 11066

Commenced Publication in 1973
Founding and Former Series Editors:
Gerhard Goos, Juris Hartmanis, and Jan van Leeuwen

Editorial Board

More information about this series at http://www.springer.com/series/7409

Xingming Sun · Zhaoqing Pan
Elisa Bertino (Eds.)

Cloud Computing
and Security

4th International Conference, ICCCS 2018
Haikou, China, June 8–10, 2018
Revised Selected Papers, Part IV

 Springer

Editors
Xingming Sun ⓘ
Nanjing University of Information Science
and Technology
Nanjing
China

Elisa Bertino ⓘ
Department of Computer Science
Purdue University
West Lafayette, IN
USA

Zhaoqing Pan ⓘ
Nanjing University of Information Science
and Technology
Nanjing
China

ISSN 0302-9743   ISSN 1611-3349 (electronic)
Lecture Notes in Computer Science
ISBN 978-3-030-00014-1   ISBN 978-3-030-00015-8 (eBook)
https://doi.org/10.1007/978-3-030-00015-8

Library of Congress Control Number: 2018952646

LNCS Sublibrary: SL3 – Information Systems and Applications, incl. Internet/Web, and HCI

This Springer imprint is published by the registered company Springer Nature Switzerland AG
The registered company address is: Gewerbestrasse 11, 6330 Cham, Switzerland

Preface

The 4th International Conference on Cloud Computing and Security (ICCCS 2018) was held in Haikou, China, during June 8–10, 2018, and hosted by the School of Computer and Software at the Nanjing University of Information Science and Technology. ICCCS is a leading conference for researchers and engineers to share their latest results of research, development, and applications in the field of cloud computing and information security.

We made use of the excellent Tech Science Press (TSP) submission and reviewing software. ICCCS 2018 received 1743 submissions from 20 countries and regions, including USA, Canada, UK, Italy, Ireland, Japan, Russia, France, Australia, South Korea, South Africa, India, Iraq, Kazakhstan, Indonesia, Vietnam, Ghana, China, Taiwan, and Macao. The submissions covered the areas of cloud computing, cloud security, information hiding, IOT security, multimedia forensics, and encryption, etc. We thank our Technical Program Committee members and external reviewers for their efforts in reviewing papers and providing valuable comments to the authors. From the total of 1743 submissions, and based on at least two reviews per submission, the Program Chairs decided to accept 386 papers, yielding an acceptance rate of 22.15%. The volume of the conference proceedings contains all the regular, poster, and workshop papers.

The conference program was enriched by six keynote presentations, and the keynote speakers were Mauro Barni, University of Siena, Italy; Charles Ling, University of Western Ontario, Canada; Yunbiao Guo, Beijing Institute of Electronics Technology and Application, China; Yunhao Liu, Michigan State University, USA; Nei Kato, Tokyo University, Japan; and Jianfeng Ma, Xidian University, China. We thank them very much for their wonderful talks.

There were 42 workshops organized in conjunction with ICCCS 2018, covering all the hot topics in cloud computing and security. We would like to take this moment to express our sincere appreciation for the contribution of all the workshop chairs and their participants. In addition, we would like to extend our sincere thanks to all authors who submitted papers to ICCCS 2018 and to all PC members. It was a truly great experience to work with such talented and hard-working researchers. We also appreciate the work of the external reviewers, who assisted the PC members in their particular areas of expertise. Moreover, we would like to thank our sponsors: Nanjing University of Information Science and Technology, Springer, Hainan University, IEEE Nanjing Chapter, ACM China, Michigan State University, Taiwan Cheng Kung University, Taiwan Dong Hwa University, Providence University, Nanjing University of Aeronautics and Astronautics, State Key Laboratory of Integrated Services Networks, Tech Science Press, and the National Nature Science Foundation of China. Finally, we would like to thank all attendees for their active participation and the organizing team, who nicely managed this conference. Next year, ICCCS will be renamed as the International Conference on Artificial Intelligence and Security (ICAIS). We look forward to seeing you again at the ICAIS.

July 2018   Xingming Sun
                                                                Zhaoqing Pan
                                                                Elisa Bertino

Organization

General Chairs

Xingming Sun   Nanjing University of Information Science
and Technology, China
Han-Chieh Chao   Taiwan Dong Hwa University, Taiwan, China
Xingang You   China Information Technology Security Evaluation
Center, China
Elisa Bertino   Purdue University, USA

Technical Program Committee Chairs

Aniello Castiglione   University of Salerno, Italy
Yunbiao Guo   China Information Technology Security Evaluation
Center, China
Zhangjie Fu   Nanjing University of Information Science
and Technology, China
Xinpeng Zhang   Fudan University, China
Jian Weng   Jinan University, China
Mengxing Huang   Hainan University, China
Alex Liu   Michigan State University, USA

Workshop Chair

Baowei Wang   Nanjing University of Information Science
and Technology, China

Publication Chair

Zhaoqing Pan   Nanjing University of Information Science
and Technology, China

Publicity Chair

Chuanyou Ju   Nanjing University of Information Science
and Technology, China

Local Arrangement Chair

Jieren Cheng   Hainan University, China

Website Chair

Wei Gu   Nanjing University of Information Science
and Technology, China

Technical Program Committee Members

Saeed Arif	University of Algeria, Algeria
Zhifeng Bao	Royal Melbourne Institute of Technology University, Australia
Lianhua Chi	IBM Research Center, Australia
Bing Chen	Nanjing University of Aeronautics and Astronautics, China
Hanhua Chen	Huazhong University of Science and Technology, China
Jie Chen	East China Normal University, China
Xiaofeng Chen	Xidian University, China
Ilyong Chung	Chosun University, South Korea
Jieren Cheng	Hainan University, China
Kim-Kwang Raymond Choo	University of Texas at San Antonio, USA
Chin-chen Chang	Feng Chia University, Taiwan, China
Robert H. Deng	Singapore Management University, Singapore
Jintai Ding	University of Cincinnati, USA
Shaojing Fu	National University of Defense Technology, China
Xinwen Fu	University of Central Florida, USA
Song Guo	Hong Kong Polytechnic University, Hong Kong, China
Ruili Geng	Spectral MD, USA
Russell Higgs	University College Dublin, Ireland
Dinh Thai Hoang	University of Technology Sydney, Australia
Robert Hsu	Chung Hua University, Taiwan, China
Chih-Hsien Hsia	Chinese Culture University, Taiwan, China
Jinguang Han	Nanjing University of Finance & Economics, China
Debiao He	Wuhan University, China
Wien Hong	Nanfang College of Sun Yat-Sen University, China
Qiong Huang	South China Agricultural University, China
Xinyi Huang	Fujian Normal University, China
Yongfeng Huang	Tsinghua University, China
Zhiqiu Huang	Nanjing University of Aeronautics and Astronautics, China
Mohammad Mehedi Hassan	King Saud University, Saudi Arabia
Farookh Hussain	University of Technology Sydney, Australia
Hai Jin	Huazhong University of Science and Technology, China
Sam Tak Wu Kwong	City University of Hong Kong, China
Patrick C. K. Hung	University of Ontario Institute of Technology, Canada

Krzysztof Szczypiorski	Warsaw University of Technology, Poland
Frank Y. Shih	New Jersey Institute of Technology, USA
Arun Kumar Sangaiah	VIT University, India
Jing Tian	National University of Singapore, Singapore
Cezhong Tong	Washington University in St. Louis, USA
Shanyu Tang	University of West London, UK
Tsuyoshi Takagi	Kyushu University, Japan
Xianping Tao	Nanjing University, China
Yoshito Tobe	Aoyang University, Japan
Cai-Zhuang Wang	Ames Laboratory, USA
Xiaokang Wang	St. Francis Xavier University, Canada
Jie Wang	University of Massachusetts Lowell, USA
Guiling Wang	New Jersey Institute of Technology, USA
Ruili Wang	Massey University, New Zealand
Sheng Wen	Swinburne University of Technology, Australia
Jinwei Wang	Nanjing University of Information Science and Technology, China
Ding Wang	Peking University, China
Eric Wong	University of Texas at Dallas, USA
Pengjun Wan	Illinois Institute of Technology, USA
Jian Wang	Nanjing University of Aeronautics and Astronautics, China
Honggang Wang	University of Massachusetts-Dartmouth, USA
Liangmin Wang	Jiangsu University, China
Xiaojun Wang	Dublin City University, Ireland
Q. M. Jonathan Wu	University of Windsor, Canada
Shaoen Wu	Ball State University, USA
Yang Xiao	The University of Alabama, USA
Haoran Xie	The Education University of Hong Kong, China
Zhihua Xia	Nanjing University of Information Science and Technology, China
Yang Xiang	Deakin University, Australia
Naixue Xiong	Northeastern State University, USA
Shuangkui Xia	Beijing Institute of Electronics Technology and Application, China
Fan Yang	University of Maryland, USA
Kun-Ming Yu	Chung Hua University, Taiwan, China
Xiaoli Yue	Donghua University, China
Ming Yin	Harvard University, USA
Aimin Yang	Guangdong University of Foreign Studies, China
Qing Yang	University of North Texas, USA
Ching-Nung Yang	Taiwan Dong Hwa University, Taiwan, China
Ming Yang	Southeast University, China
Qing Yang	Montana State University, USA
Xinchun Yin	Yangzhou University, China

Yong Yu	University of Electronic Science and Technology of China, China
Guomin Yang	University of Wollongong, Australia
Wei Qi Yan	Auckland University of Technology, New Zealand
Shaodi You	Australian National University, Australia
Yanchun Zhang	Victoria University, Australia
Mingwu Zhang	Hubei University of Technology, China
Wei Zhang	Nanjing University of Posts and Telecommunications, China
Weiming Zhang	University of Science and Technology of China, China
Yan Zhang	Simula Research Laboratory, Norway
Yao Zhao	Beijing Jiaotong University, China
Linna Zhou	University of International Relations, China

Organization Committee Members

Xianyi Chen	Nanjing University of Information Science and Technology, China
Yadang Chen	Nanjing University of Information Science and Technology, China
Beijing Chen	Nanjing University of Information Science and Technology, China
Chunjie Cao	Hainan University, China
Xianyi Chen	Hainan University, China
Xianmei Chen	Hainan University, China
Fa Fu	Hainan University, China
Xiangdang Huang	Hainan University, China
Zhuhua Hu	Hainan University, China
Jielin Jiang	Nanjing University of Information Science and Technology, China
Zilong Jin	Nanjing University of Information Science and Technology, China
Yan Kong	Nanjing University of Information Science and Technology, China
Jingbing Li	Hainan University, China
Jinlian Peng	Hainan University, China
Zhiguo Qu	Nanjing University of Information Science and Technology, China
Le Sun	Nanjing University of Information Science and Technology, China
Jian Su	Nanjing University of Information Science and Technology, China
Qing Tian	Nanjing University of Information Science and Technology, China
Tao Wen	Hainan University, China
Xianpeng Wang	Hainan University, China

Lizhi Xiong   Nanjing University of Information Science
                             and Technology, China
Chunyang Ye   Hainan University, China
Jiangyuan Yao   Hainan University, China
Leiming Yan   Nanjing University of Information Science
                             and Technology, China
Yu Zhang   Hainan University, China
Zhili Zhou   Nanjing University of Information Science
                             and Technology, China

Contents – Part IV

IOT Security

Encryption

The Research of Cryptosystem Recognition Based on Randomness Test's Return Value

Zhicheng Zhao[1]($\boxtimes$), Yaqun Zhao[1], and Fengmei Liu[2]

[1] State Key Laboratory of Mathematical Engineering and Advanced Computing,
Zhengzhou, China
zhicheng_zhao1@sina.com
[2] Science and Technology on Information Assurance Laboratory, Beijing, China

Abstract. Feature extraction of ciphertext is a key procedure in cryptosystem recognition task. Varieties of ciphertext's features are proposed in exited literatures, while feature based on randomness test has derived little attention. In this paper, by segmenting ciphertexts and changing parameter of randomness test, we propose 54 features of ciphertext based on NIST's 15 randomness tests. As a measure of these features, we choose support vector machine as classifier algorithm to verify its performance in cryptosystem recognition. In experimental settings, we consider 15 situations of 6 cryptosystems' one to one recognition. The experimental results demonstrate that the application of randomness test in cryptosystem recognition is feasible and necessary. Most of proposed features reach better recognition accuracies than random recognition, which indicates that randomness tests are applicable for cryptosystem recognition applications. And we also conduct further analysis: (a) analyze some features' recognition performance, and find the relation of some feature's recognition accuracies and cryptosystem. (b) compared with existed features, part of new features maintain high recognition accuracy with lower dimension and smaller data storage space.

Keywords: Cryptosystem recognition · Block cipher · Randomness test
Feature extraction · Support vector machine

1 Introduction

The research of cryptosystem recognition is tightly related to cryptanalysis. Cryptanalysis is a type of passive attack approach, which means that attacker tries to obtain secret information without knowing decryption key and any details of encryption algorithm used by both side. The Kerchoffs' assumption thinks that the awareness to encryption algorithm shouldn't influence the security of plaintext and decryption key [1, 2]. The designers of many existed cryptosystems want to achieve security assurance based on this assumption. Interestingly, most of existed cryptanalysis research is conducted by supposing that the attacker knows the exact cryptosystem of ciphertext, and this form a contradiction—it not only prompts both the design and analysis of cryptosystems, but also leads the recognition of cryptosystem towards a significant issue in real-world cryptanalysis situations, since we usually cannot easily find out the exact cryptosystem of ciphertext when facing chaotic network flows.

© Springer Nature Switzerland AG 2018
X. Sun et al. (Eds.): ICCCS 2018, LNCS 11066, pp. 3–15, 2018.
https://doi.org/10.1007/978-3-030-00015-8_1

For its quickly speed in encryption and convenient execution in hardware or software, block ciphers have wildly application in information security, they are usually used as core cryptographic algorithms in data encryption, message identification, authentication and so on. Meanwhile, the recognition of block cipher is becoming a main area of cryptosystem recognition. There are two major directions of cryptosystem recognition research: Statistical approaches and machine learning based approaches. Statistical methods usually utilize the frequency of occurrence of elements of alphabets and their n-grams [3, 4]. In machine learning based methods, the task of identification of the encryption algorithm is considered as a pattern classification problem. Researchers extract features from ciphertexts, the data of features are then submitted into a specific classifier to get the classification results.

Machine learning based cryptosystem recognition usually complete its task by classification algorithm, obtaining identification results by processing the feature of the target. Since ciphertext always has strong randomness, extracting effective features becomes a key segment in recognition task. In current public research, the features of ciphertexts could be approximately divided into 4 categories: (1) entropy based features: the entropy of some bit string in ciphertext, such as the entropy of alphabets 'A' or bit string '00000' [3, 5]; (2) probability based features: the probability of some bit string in ciphertext, such as the probability of alphabets 'A' or bit string '00000' [3, 5]; (3) randomness test based features: the return value of some randomness test [6]; (4) document vector based features, which is derived by considering ciphertext as fixed or vary length vector [7]; (5) combined features, which is derived by combining some of the above mentioned features [5].

In fact, a block cipher could be considered as a pseudorandom generator, the designers hope that the statistical property of plaintext can be hidden after encryption. As a kind of tools that measure the performance of pseudorandom number generators, randomness tests are developed to test the randomness of their produced binary sequences [8]. Currently, there are different sets of randomness test in cryptology such as DIEHARD [9, 10], Crypt-XS [11] and NIST [8]. Since all of these tests have its limitations, the unified standards aren't built. NIST's SP800-22 document discussed and advised 15 kinds of statistical tests. The statistical experiment's results show that the correlations between 15 tests are extremely low [7], that is to say these 15 criteria could characterize the randomness of binary sequence from different aspects. These tests are widely applied into the randomness test of pseudorandom generator and cipher [12, 13]. The initial study on ciphertext features based on randomness test was done by Wu [6], based on randomness test, they designed 3 kinds of features and achieved good results in block ciphers' recognition.

In this paper, we'll carry out a more complete research about features' extraction based on randomness test for block cipher's recognition. To the best of our knowledge, this is the first work that studies the effectiveness of randomness test based features in cryptosystem recognition. In our research, 54 kinds of features based on NIST's randomness tests are proposed. We extract features from ciphertexts encrypted by AES, DES, 3DES, IDEA, Blowfish, Camellia in ECB mode, and implement machine learning based classification experiments of ciphertext, the feasibility and effectiveness of randomness tests are verified. A series of features which have good performance in classification experiments are found, differences between ciphertexts encrypted by different cryptosystems are also explored. The rest of this paper is organized as follows. In Sect. 2, the recent related works about cryptosystem recognition are discussed. We introduce the main method, the settings about experiments and the scheme of recognition task in Sect. 3. The reason and methods of extract ciphertext's features are presented in Sect. 4. Section 5 presents and analyses our experimental results. Finally, Sect. 6 concludes.

2 Related Work

The original work in the study of cryptosystem recognition is classical cryptosystem. based on the frequency of alphabets in ciphertext, Pooja designed a recognition scheme, which analyzed classical cipher including substitution ciphers, transposition ciphers and Vigenère cipher [4]. However, modern cryptosystems possess higher level of security. By utilizing machine learning classification algorithm, researchers proposed some cryptosystem recognition schemes. In the work done by De Souza W, a neural network based method is used to classify the final round of candidate AES algorithm [14]. Wu et al. presented a method based on k-means cluster algorithm to classify AES, Camellia, DES, 3DES and SMS4 [6]. In 2006, Dileep et al. [8] put forward a scheme based on support vector machines to identify the cryptosystems including AES, DES, 3DES, Blowfish, RC5. Researchers also studied cryptosystem recognition with different modes of operation. To classify AES, DES, 3DES, Blowfish and RC5 in ECB mode and CBC mode, Negireddy combined support vector machine with recognition task [15]. Another support vector machine based scheme for identification of DES and AES in ECB mode and CBC mode is discussed in [5], this method is successful in ECB mode but failed in CBC mode. Some researchers analyzed the performance of 8 different machine learning techniques, the simulation result shows that, the ensemble classification algorithm Rotation Forest classifier performs better than other 7 kinds of classifiers [16, 17]. In [18], Huang et al. gave a definition system for cryptosystem recognition problem, which naturally unifies single-stage and two-stage recognition problems and schemes under its framework. Experiments show that their two-stage scheme outperforms the best compared existed single stage schemes.

The focus of cryptosystem recognition is spreading from block cipher to wider fields. In 2011, Manjula et al. in their paper presented a recognition scheme with decision tree classifier, and classified 11 kinds of cryptosystems covering classical ciphers, stream ciphers, block ciphers and public key ciphers [3]. Constructed on random mappings, Turan et al. proposed a new framework of randomness testing, they experimentally observed some statistical weakness in Pomaranch among Phase III Candidates of eSTREAM project [19]. The classification between IDEA and RSA has been investigated by Rao [20].

Currently, researchers usually focus on the classification algorithms and target cryptosystem. Lots of works didn't specially study the approach of ciphertext's feature extraction, and just adopted existed features (e.g., those mentioned in Sect. 1). The existed feature extraction methods are usually simple, which are not very closely connected to cryptosystem's structure. Some features have high dimension which are harmful to large data processing. Randomness test initially used to measure the

6   Z. Zhao et al.

ciphertext's randomness, the result of the test is associate with cryptosystem's security. Though some features based on randomness test have already been proposed in [6], but in public research, just a few kinds of randomness tests are discussed, the remaining tests in NIST are waited to be researched, and that's what we'll discuss in this paper.

3 Method Introduction

3.1 Methodology Overview

Although our work mainly focus on the recognition of block ciphers, to work efficiently, some related work also need to be done. The cryptosystem recognition scheme involved in this paper can be divided into 5 stages. In the first stage, ciphertexts which are going to be recognized are collected. Extracting ciphertexts features and dividing them into training dataset and test dataset at the second stage. Then we choose classifier. In the fourth stage, we utilize the training dataset to construct classification model. Finally, test dataset will be put into classifier. The specific flowchart of the cryptosystem recognition scheme is shown in Fig. 1:

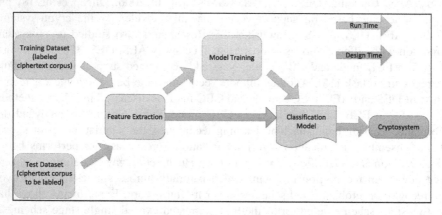

Fig. 1. Flowchart of cryptosystems recognition scheme.

3.2 Ciphertext Collection

To collect ciphertexts, the plaintexts are generated by splicing the pictures which were randomly chosen from digital image library [21]. We averagely divide it into 1000 portions with equal size of 512 KB, which named as plaintext segments. The encryption was achieved by using OpenSSL. 6 cryptosystems such as AES, DES, 3DES, IDEA, Blowfish and Camellia are used to encrypt plaintexts [22]. For the plaintexts encrypted by the same cryptosystem, we use fixed cipher key respectively.

3.3   Features' Extraction Based on NIST's Randomness Testing

The model's accurate construction of a learning task depends on whether we can extract meaningful features from dataset. In machine learning based cryptosystem recognition research, researchers have studied several methods, including the features based on NIST's randomness tests, to extract ciphertexts' features [5–7, 16, 17]. As a statistical package, the NIST Test Suite, consisting of 15 tests, is developed to test the randomness of binary sequences with finite length [8]. These tests mainly focus on a variety of different types of non-randomness that could exist in a sequence, such as the balance of 0 and 1, the distribution of specific length of sequence and so on. The range of sequence's length and block are defined detailedly in instructions, so we choose appropriate parameter to get the available result. In this paper, to explore the potential of randomness tests, 15 randomness tests are considered. We extract 51 different ciphertext's features by partitioning the cipher text, modifying some parameters of randomness tests. Besides, we also choose 7 ciphertext's features, proposed by public literature, as reference. The details of features' description and extraction are discussed in Sect. 4.

3.4   Recognition Algorithm

We choose support vector machine algorithm (SVM, also support vector networks) to construct the classifier of recognition research in our work. As mentioned in related work [5, 7], some experiments had already shown this algorithm's performance in cryptosystem recognition outperforms other algorithms. Support vector machine algorithm's application is mature and its performance is more robust in practice. Support vector machine algorithm was firstly proposed by Cortes and Vapnik in 1995 [23, 24]. In addition to performing linear classification, SVM can efficiently perform a non-linear classification using the kernel trick [23], implicitly mapping their inputs into high-dimensional feature spaces.

3.5   Experimental Protocol

In our experiment, Cryptosystem algorithms are implemented in OpenSSL, all features' extraction codes are written by C language, and SVM algorithm is implemented by RStudio. In the training phase and testing phase, we take experiments by repeating random sub-sampling validation. In each sampling, training dataset is collected by doing the random sampling of 75% of the feature dataset, and the remaining features dataset is used for test dataset. A 10-fold cross-validations was used as a test mode, the average of the accuracy in test dataset is taken as recognition accuracy of the corresponding cryptosystem. 6 different cryptosystems' 15 kinds of one to one recognition task are implemented.

4 Features Extraction

In the fields of machine learning, the quality of model depends on the feature which we use [25]. Researchers always try to extract some excellent features of ciphertext. As mentioned in Sect. 1, there are four main feature's extraction ways. Block ciphers encrypt data by confusion and diffusion, the ability of confusion and diffusion vary depending on the cipher's structure [2]. In fact, ciphertexts can't be totally random, the difference between different ciphers' structure will influence the randomness of ciphertexts. In [26], the experiments results show that the randomness of different versions of lower round Camellia exist differences. The performances of lower round version of AES, Camellia and SMS4 are also different from each other [27]. Features based on randomness test really get good performance in cryptosystem recognition. In [6], the randomness tests were utilized to extract features of the ciphertexts, and got good results in some block ciphers' recognition tasks, which indicates the variant levels of randomness of ciphertexts produced by different cryptosystems could be reflected by certain kinds of randomness tests. Since we mainly think about extracting features based on randomness tests, the detail of features' extraction will be discussed in this section.

Specifically, in the prerequisite of keeping the validity of the results about randomness tests, 15 randomness tests in NIST are implemented [8]. By modifying the parameters or partitioning ciphertexts, we get a series of features with different dimensions. For example, when we extract features based on *the Non-Overlapping Template Matching test* [8], by choosing different parameters of window length (e.g. m = 5,6,7,8), the test will return result values with the number of 20, 40, 74, 148. we take these results as ciphertext's features. For another example, when we extract features based on *the Run test* [8], we'll divide ciphertext into 32, 64, 128, 256 blocks, then run the test on these blocks, and the test will return result of each block, we consider these results as ciphertext's features.

According to the dimensions of derived features and the corresponding randomness tests, we divide the features into 51 kinds. The introduction of the randomness test and features' construction are presented as follows:

(1). Features based on *the cumulative sums test*: Divide the ciphertext into 16, 32, 64, 128, 256 blocks, running this test respectively, we can get five features with dimension of 16, 32, 64, 128 and 256, which named as Cus16, Cus32, Cus64, Cus128 and Cus256.

(2). Feature based on *the Linear complexity test*: Divide the ciphertext into 4 blocks, by running this test, we can get feature with dimension of 4, which named as Lc4.

(3). Features based on *the Longest run of ones test*: Divide the ciphertext into 32, 64 and 128 blocks, for each block respectively, by running this test, we can get three features with dimension of 32, 64 and 128. Those features are named as Lro32, Lro64 and Lro128.

(4). Features based on *the Overlapping template matchings test*: Both this test and the Non-Overlapping Template Matching test use an m-bit window to search for a specific m-bit pattern. Divide the ciphertext into 4 blocks, by choosing m = 9 and

10, run this test respectively, we can get two features with dimension of 4 which named as Otm4-1 and Otm4-2.

(5). Features based on *the Random Excursions test*: Divide the ciphertext into 1, 2, 3, 4 blocks, run this test for each block respectively, we can get four features with dimension of 8, 16,24 and 24. Those features are named as Re8, Re16, Re24 and Re32.

(6). Feature based on *the Random Excursions variant test*: Divide the ciphertext into 1, 2, 3, 4 blocks, for each block, run this test, we can get feature with dimension of 18,36,54,72. The feature is named as Rev18, Rev36, Rev54, Rev72.

(7). Features based on *the Approximate entropy test*: Divide the ciphertext into 1, 2, 4, 6, 7 blocks, for each block, run this test respectively, we can get five features with dimension of 12, 14, 48, 72 and 84. Those features are named as Aet12, Aet24, Aet48, Aet72 and Aet84.

(8). Features based on *the Universal statistical test*: Divide the ciphertext into 2, 4, 8 blocks, for each block, run this test, we can get three features with dimension of 2,4,8. Those features are named as Us2, Us4, Us8.

(9). Features based on *the Discrete Fourier Transform test*: Divide the ciphertext into 32, 64, 128, 256 blocks, for each block, we can get four features with dimension of 32, 64, 128, 256. We named those features as Dft32, Dft64, Dft128 and Dft256.

(10). Features based on *the Serial test*: Divide the ciphertext into 32, 64, 128 blocks, for each block, run this test, we can get three features with dimension of 32, 64, 128. Those features are named as St32, St64 and St128.

(11). Features based on *the Binary Matrix Rank test*: Divide the ciphertext into 32, 64, 96 blocks, for each block, run this test, we can get three features with dimension of 32, 64, 96. Those features are named as Rt32, Rt64 and Rt96.

(12). Features based on *the Non-Overlapping Template Matching test*: In this test, an m-bit window is used to search for a specific m-bit pattern. Set the length of window m = 5, 6, 7, 8 and 9, run this test respectively, We can get five features with dimension of 12, 20, 40, 74 and 148, which named as Nt12, Nt20, Nt40, Nt74 and Nt148.

(13). Features based on *the Block Frequency test*: Divide the ciphertext into 32, 64, 128, 256 blocks, for each block, run this test respectively, we get four features with dimension of 32, 64, 128 and 256, which named as Bf32, Bf64, Bf128 and Bf256.

(14). Features based on *the Frequency test*: Divide the ciphertext into 32, 64, 128 and 256 blocks, for each block, we get four features with dimension of 32, 64, 128, 256. Those features are named as Fre32, Fre64, Fre128 and Fre256.

(15). Features based on *the Run test*: Divide the ciphertext into 32, 64, 128 and 256 blocks, for each block, by running this test, we can get four features with dimension of 32, 64, 128 and 256, which named as Run32, Run64, Run128 and Run256.

To analyse the performance of proposed features and other frequently employed features, we choose some typical feature extraction method which built with entropy and probability [5, 16, 17], these features are listed as follows:

(1). Divide the ciphertexts into 56bits blocks, 128bits blocks and 256bits blocks, then compute every bit position's entropy of 0 and 1 in each block, we can get features with dimensions of 56, 128, 256. and named those features as F-56b, F-128b, F-256b.

(2). Divide the ciphertexts into 8-bits blocks, 9-bits blocks, 10-bits blocks, 11-bits blocks, by extracting 8-bits histogram, 9-bits histogram, 10-bits histogram, 11-bits histogram respectively, we get the features with dimensions of 256, 512, 1024, 2048, and named those features as F-256, F-512, F-1024, F-2048.

5 Experiments' Results and Analysis

5.1 The Recognition Results Based on Randomness Tests

The recognition experiments of 54 features are carried out. Each features' recognition average accuracy, in 15 recognition situations, are listed in the Table 1 and Fig. 2 as follows. Besides, to compare the performance of different features, we also list each feature's recognition accuracy's standard deviation in Table 1. As we can see in the Table 1, the recognition accuracies vary from feature to feature. Most of the features' recognition accuracies are higher than random recognition accuracy. In all 54 features, the average recognition accuracies of 42 features are higher than 50% (the black imaginary line in Fig. 2), 12 features' recognition accuracies are higher than 60%. It shows that some random test's return values can reflect the differences of these ciphertexts which encrypted by different cryptosystems. (Hereinafter, Dimension of feature is abbreviated as Dim, Average recognition accuracy is abbreviated as Accuracy, Standard deviation of recognition accuracy is abbreviated as SD).

Table 1. The recognition performance of 54 features based on random tests

Feature	Dim	Accuracy	SD	Feature	Dim	Accuracy	SD
Cus16	16	52.01	4.79	Dft128	128	49.93	26.57
Cus32	32	53.33	9.97	Dft256	256	49.98	14.43
Cus64	64	53.42	9.25	St32	32	50.99	37.37
Cus128	128	54.34	22.86	St64	64	51.56	45.71
Cus256	256	56.23	32.96	St128	128	52.40	38.05
Lc4	4	51.12	0.92	Rt32	32	52.53	61.06
Lro32	32	51.44	8.53	Rt64	64	53.23	59.72
Lro64	64	52.25	8.38	Rt96	96	51.74	39.18
Lro128	128	53.31	13.85	Nt12	12	82.85	2.38
Otm4-1	4	51.99	2.89	Nt20	20	84.50	1.77
Otm4-2	4	50.60	1.63	Nt40	40	75.60	264.5
Re8	8	56.37	3.64	Nt74	74	62.10	5.35
Re16	16	59.20	2.44	Nt148	148	64.79	1.00

(*continued*)

Table 1. (*continued*)

Feature	Dim	Accuracy	SD	Feature	Dim	Accuracy	SD
Re24	24	61.04	5.97	Bf32	32	57.66	61.88
Re32	32	63.40	3.71	Bf64	64	59.42	83.45
Aet12	12	54.10	11.67	Bf128	128	65.27	105.7
Aet24	24	54.93	13.70	Bf256	256	68.53	76.49
Aet48	48	53.91	23.13	Fre32	32	53.87	18.28
Aet72	72	53.52	35.91	Fre64	64	54.43	29.39
Aet84	84	52.80	45.17	Fre128	128	55.71	30.76
Us2	2	55.73	16.06	Fre256	256	58.74	72.01
Us4	4	56.60	24.21	Run32	32	53.18	19.57
Us8	8	58.90	100.38	Run64	64	55.24	11.32
Dft32	32	48.84	11.02	Run128	128	56.61	18.16
Dft64	64	48.47	10.03	Run256	256	58.72	32.95
Rev18	18	54.41	2.12	Rev54	54	58.49	1.13
Rev36	36	57.90	1.68	Rev72	72	60.28	2.27

The varying amplitudes of some features' recognition accuracies are bigger than other features' in Fig. 2. By analyzing the performance of these features in each recognition situation, we find that some features is appropriate to recognize special cryptosystems. As shown in Table 2, part of the features' recognition accuracy is actually related to the cryptosystem. Bf-128 is good at recognizing the ciphertext encrypted by 3DES or IDEA, Us8 is good at recognizing the ciphertext encrypted Camellia, Fre256 is good at recognizing the ciphertext encrypted by 3DES etc.

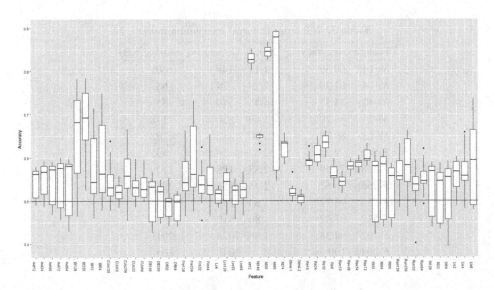

Fig. 2. The boxplot of 54 features' recognition accuracies

Table 2. The recognition results of part features in different situations (%)

	Bf-128	Us-8	Fre-256	Nt-40
AES-Blowfish	55.88	61.58	53.42	89.07
AES-Camellia	46.43	59.46	47.54	84.32
AES-DES	65.57	60.92	53.08	89.31
AES-3DES	72.84	58.52	67.71	89.41
AES-IDEA	59.20	61.20	56.32	88.53
Blowfish-Camellia	52.42	73.58	53.14	89.53
Blowfish- DES	72.44	49.68	54.24	55.40
Blowfish-3DES	76.56	48.45	73.12	54.54
Blowfish- IDEA	53.18	47.83	48.27	56.48
Camellia- DES	68.23	72.52	53.18	89.27
Camellia-3DES	73.18	71.28	67.27	88.13
Camellia- IDEA	57.22	72.88	56.14	87.87
DES-3DES	74.22	47.87	67.39	58.06
DES- IDEA	73.58	48.35	58.04	57.30
3DES- IDEA	78.22	49.47	72.24	56.84

5.2   Comparison of Features

As we can see in Table 2 and Fig. 2, Nt series features' recognition accuracy and stability are better than any other features. To analyze the recognition performance of the features above, 12 features' average recognition accuracy and standard deviation are listed in Table 3. Nt-20's average accuracy is higher than any other features in the Table 1, its standard deviation and dimension are lower than most of the features.

Table 3. NT series features' recognition results

Feature	Accuracy(%)	SD	Dimension	Storage(KB)
Nt-148	64.39	1.11	148	1405
Nt-74	61.20	2.23	74	653
Nt-40	74.37	16.45	40	354
Nt-20	83.20	1.69	20	178
Nt-12	80.69	2.00	12	108
F-56b	79.33	2.67	56	495
F-128b	72.59	2.33	128	1129
F-256b	70.62	2.45	256	2255
F-256	95.37	1.65	256	2255
F-512	91.92	1.80	512	4507
F-1024	94.38	1.86	1024	9011
F-2048	100	0	2048	18062

Furthermore, we do recognition experiments on 7 features that are F-56b, F-128b, F-256b, F-256, F-512, F-1024, F-2048. The results of three features are shown in Table 3, which shows that the accuracy of Nt-20 is higher than entropy based features with lower standard deviation, dimension and storage. We also make a comparison between the Nt series features and probability based features, although probability based features' accuracy is higher than Nt series features, while the latter have smaller data storage space and dimension. Especially, Nt-20 keeps a high accuracy and stability with lower dimension and data storage space.

6 Conclusion and Future Works

In this paper, we study the features' extraction and machine learning based classifier's application in cryptosystem recognition. First, for the first time, we propose 54 new features of ciphertext based on randomness test. Second, by constructing SVM classifier, we conduct one to one recognition experiments on 6 block ciphers. Third, following our experiments' results, we analyze the performance of different features in recognition task, and demonstrate the effectiveness of features based on randomness test. The experimental results show that most of the features based on randomness test can reflect the difference between cryptosystems. Compared to existed researches, some features proposed by us achieve high accuracy with lower dimension, we believe that these features still have the enhanced space. Besides, the performance of SVM algorithm indicates that it is suitable to carry out block ciphers' cryptosystem recognition task.

Our next work will focus on: (i) the evaluation of the reasonableness of features' construction; (ii) the generalization of these features on more complex and diverse cryptosystem recognition task; (iii) the choice of classification algorithms and its influence on recognition performance; (iv) the trade-off between the features' recognition accuracy and computational complexity.

Acknowledgments. This work was partially supported by the State Key Laboratory of Information Assurance Technology (No. KJ-15-008), by the Foundation of Science and Technology on Information Assurance Laboratory (No. KJ-15-008), by the National Key Research and Development Program 2016–2018 under Grant No. 2016YFE0100600.

References

1. Shannon, C.E.: Communication theory of secrecy systems. Bell Labs Tech. J. **28**(4), 656–715 (1949)
2. Schneier, B.: Applied Cryptography: Protocols, Algorithms, and Source Code in C, 2nd edn. Wiley, New York (1996)
3. Manjula, R., Anitha, R.: Identification of encryption algorithm using decision tree. Adv. Comput. **133**, 237–246 (2011)
4. Maheshwari, P.: Classification of Ciphers. Indian Institute of Technology, Kanpur (2001)

5. Chou, J.W., Lin, S.D., Cheng, C.M.: On the effectiveness of using state-of-the-art machine learning techniques to launch cryptographic distinguishing attacks. In: Proceedings of the 5th ACM Workshop on Security and Artificial Intelligence, pp. 105–110. ACM, New York (2012)
6. Wu, Y., Wang, T., Xing, M.: Block ciphers identification scheme based on the distribution character of randomness test values of ciphertext. J. Commun. 36(4), 146–155 (2015)
7. Dileep, A.D., Sekhar, C.C.: Identification of block ciphers using support vector machines. In: Proceedings of the International Joint Conference on Neural Networks (IJCNN 2006), pp. 2696–2701. IEEE, Gulf Islands (2006)
8. Rukhin, A., Soto, J., Nechvatal, J.: A statistical test suite for random and pseudorandom number generators for cryptographic applications. Appl. Phys. Lett. 22(7), 1645–1798 (2015)
9. Marsaglia, G.: The Marsaglia Random Number CDROM Including the DIEHARD Battery of Tests of Randomness (1996). http://stat.fsu.edu/pub/diehard
10. Gustafson, H., Dawson, E., Nielsen, L.: A computer package for measuring the strength of encryption algorithms. Comput. Secur. 13(8), 687–697 (1994)
11. Gustafson, H.M., Dawson, E.P., Golić, J.D.: Randomness measures related to subset occurrence. In: Dawson, E., Golić, J. (eds.) CPA 1995. LNCS, vol. 1029, pp. 132–143. Springer, Heidelberg (1996). https://doi.org/10.1007/BFb0032353
12. Lozach, F., Ben-Romdhane, M., Graba, T.: FPGA design of an open-loop true random number generator. In: Proceedings of 2013 Euromicro Conference on Digital System Design (DSD), pp. 615–622. IEEE, Los Alamitos (2013)
13. Alabaichi, A., Mahmod, R., Ahmad, F.: Randomness analysis of 128 bits blowfish block cipher on ECB and CBC modes. Int. J. Digital Content Technol. Appl. 7(15), 77 (2013)
14. Souza, W.A., Tomlinson, A.: A distinguishing attack with a neural network. In: Proceedings of the IEEE 13th International Conference on Data Mining Workshops (ICDMW 2013), Dallas, pp. 154–161 (2013)
15. Nagireddy, S.: A Pattern Recognition Approach to Block Cipher Identification. Indian Institute of Technology, Madras (2008)
16. Sharif, S.O., Mansoor, S.P.: Performance evaluation of classifiers used for identification of encryption algorithms. ACEEE Int. J. Netw. Secur. 2(04), 42–45 (2011)
17. Sharif, S.O., Kuncheva, L.I., Mansoor, S.P.: Classifying encryption algorithms using pattern recognition techniques. In: Proceedings of the IEEE International Conference on Information Theory and Information Security (ICITIS), Beijing, China, pp. 1168–1172 (2010)
18. Huang, L.T., Zhao, Z.C., Zhao, Y.Q.: A two-stage cryptosystem recognition scheme based on random forest. Chin. J. Comput. 41(2), 382–399 (2018)
19. Sönmez Turan, M., Çalık, Ç., Saran, N.B., Doğanaksoy, A.: New distinguishers based on random mappings against stream ciphers. In: Golomb, S.W., Parker, M.G., Pott, A., Winterhof, A. (eds.) SETA 2008. LNCS, vol. 5203, pp. 30–41. Springer, Heidelberg (2008). https://doi.org/10.1007/978-3-540-85912-3_3
20. Rao, M.B.: Classification of RSA and IDEA Ciphers. Indian Institute of Technology, Kanpur (2003)
21. Griffin, G., Holub, A., Perona, P.: Caltech-256 Object Category Dataset. California Institute of Technology, Pasadedna (2007)
22. Wu, W., Feng, D., Zhang, W.: Design and Analysis of Block Cipher, 2nd edn. Tsinghua University Press, Beijing (2009)

23. Cortes, C., Vapnik, V.: Support-vector networks. Mach. Learn. **20**(3), 273–297 (1995)
24. Benhur, A.: Support vector clustering. J. Mach. Learn. Res. **2**(2), 125–137 (2002)
25. Flach, P.: Machine Learning: The Art and Science of Algorithms that Make Sense of Data. Cambridge University Press, New York (2012)
26. Shi, G.D., Kang, F., Gu, H.W.: Research and implementation of randomness tests. Comput. Eng. **35**(20), 145–146 (2009)
27. Chen, H., Feng, D.G., Fan, L.M.: A new statistical test on block ciphers. Chin. J. Comput. **32** (4), 595–601 (2009)

Threshold Proxy Re-encryption
and Its Application in Blockchain

Xi Chen[1], Yun Liu[1(✉)], Yong Li[1,2,3(✉)], and Changlu Lin[3]

[1] Key Laboratory of Communication and Information Systems,
Beijing Municipal Commission of Education, Beijing Jiaotong University,
Beijing 100044, People's Republic of China
{xi_chen,liuyun,liyong}@bjtu.edu.cn
[2] Guangxi Key Laboratory of Cryptography and Information Security,
Guilin University of Electronic Technology, Guilin 541004, China
[3] Fujian Provincial Key Laboratory of Network Security and Cryptology,
Fujian Normal University, Fuzhou 350007, People's Republic of China

Abstract. Since the proxy re-encryption has the limitation of distributed applications and the security risk of collusion attacks in semi-trusted distributed environments (e.g. cloud computing), the novel definition of threshold proxy re-encryption is proposed based on secret sharing and proxy re-encryption. According to the definition, the threshold proxy re-encryption scheme can be flexibly created with the standard cryptographic prototype. An efficient, secure, and implementable unidirectional threshold proxy re-encryption scheme is constructed by the combination of Shamir's secret sharing, and is proved secure by using the intractability of discrete logarithms. This paper presents a consortium blockchain access permission scheme, which is built on the threshold proxy re-encryption scheme. When a new node joins a consortium blockchain, an access permission is achieved by the agreement on other existing nodes, instead of a centralized CA.

Keywords: Proxy re-encryption · Threshold secret sharing · Blockchain

1 Introduction

The concept of proxy re-encryption was first proposed by Blaze, Bleumer, and Strauss in article [1]. In this mechanism, a semi-trusted proxy converts Alice (delegator)'s ciphertext to Bob's, which can be decrypted with Bob(delegatee)'s private key. During the authorization process, neither the message nor the private key of either party is revealed. As the essential cryptographic tools for encrypted date storage and sharing, proxy re-encryption has been widely applied for protecting the confidentiality of data stored in third party, for example, Cloud storage, Electric healthy records, Digital rights management. etc.

With the continuous expansion of data scale, the security of proxy re-encryption with single proxy is challenged, how to defend against collusion attacks becomes a focus. Without the consent of the delegator, it is possible for the only semi-trusted proxy and malicious users to use a re-encryption key in combination for conversion of

© Springer Nature Switzerland AG 2018
X. Sun et al. (Eds.): ICCCS 2018, LNCS 11066, pp. 16–25, 2018.
https://doi.org/10.1007/978-3-030-00015-8_2

arbitrary ciphertext of the delegator, which may result in confusion of authorization. Meanwhile, with the rapid development of cloud computing, Internet of things, block chain and other distributed systems, the number of proxies increase manifold, the traditional proxy re-encryption is no longer able to meet the performance and security requirements under the new situation.

Threshold proxy re-encryption including multi proxies, is put forward under the background. Its main goal is to keep from colluding between a single proxy and the delegatee through multiple proxies, prevent third-party servers from converting arbitrary files against the wishes of the licensor. When individual proxy servers are paralyzed, dishonest, or damaged, it can provide normal service for ensuring the safety and reliability of the system. These features make multi-proxies re-encryption have great application potential in cloud storage, cloud data sharing, block chain and other scenarios. Therefore, it is of great practical significance to study threshold proxy re-encryption scheme.

The proxy re-encryption including multi-proxy has attracted academic attention. Shengming et al. [7] combined proxy re-encryption, threshold cipher and identity-based cipher and proposed the first ID-based threshold multi-proxy re-encryption scheme in 2010. However, the scheme remains under threat of collusion. In 2017, Li et al. [8] combined proxy re-encryption and resplitable threshold cipher on the lattices to construct a re-separating threshold multi-broker proxy re-encryption scheme. That gave a wider range of choices to the boundaries of noise, and proved that the scheme is indistinguishable from IND-Uni RTPRE-CPA under the selected plaintext attack. [4] However, each ciphertext fragment in this scheme needs to be verified, which will inevitably result in a large amount of computing overhead and reduce the scalability of the system. Song [9] proposed the definition of multi proxy re-encryption technology based on the quorum controlled (quorum-controlled) asymmetric proxy re-encryption. Due to the use of bilinear pairs with high complexity in constructing schemes, a large amount of computational consumption [6] will be generated, and the efficiency of the scheme will be reduced.

In order to solve the problem of collusion attack and high computational load, a threshold proxy re-encryption scheme is proposed in this paper. The scheme includes several proxies that work independently, and there is no interaction between them. Third party proxies can be prevent from converting arbitrary files against collusion attacks from malicious delegatees and semi-trusted proxies. In addition, the proposed threshold proxy re-encryption can support a variety of cryptographic prototypes, flexible construction of a variety of schemes, improve operational efficiency without sacrificing its security. Threshold proxy re-encryption is also applied to the access permission mechanism of consortium blockchain nodes, and it has flexible adaptability to multi-party collaboration scenarios such as consortium blockchain.

The rest of this article is structured as follows: Sect. 2 introduces the premise of our work. In Sect. 3, the definition, security model and constructed scheme of threshold proxy re-encryption are given. In Sect. 4, we compare the threshold proxy re-encryption scheme with other similar schemes in performance and prove the security of proposed scheme. Section 5 represents an application of threshold proxy re-encryption in the blockchain. Section 6 gives the conclusion.

2 Preliminaries

2.1 Threshold Secret Sharing

The (t, n) secret sharing scheme [3, 5] is a method of sharing secrets. It divides the secrets and is held by the participants. The secret can be restored only when there are at least one participant present. We review the (t, n) threshold secret sharing scheme proposed by Shamir [2]:

Assume a group of n participants $(p_1, p_2, \ldots, p_n)$. p is a large prime number in Z_p^*. The dealer randomly picks a polynomial $f(x) = s + \sum_{j=1}^{k-1} a_j x^j$ of $(k-1)$ degrees, where s is a constant in $f(x)$. Each participant p_i is assigned a unique domain element b_i and receives the corresponding secret share $s_i = f(b_i)$ through the privacy channel. If at least t participants in the group $(p_1, p_2, \ldots, p_n)$ are present, the participants can recover secrets by s:

$$f(x) = \sum_{j=1}^{k} f(b_j) \lambda_{ij} \tag{1}$$

where $\lambda_{ij} = \prod_{\substack{l=1 \\ l \neq i}}^{k} \frac{x - b_l}{b_i - b_l}$, and $s = f(0)$.

If less than t participants are present, the participants cannot recover secrets because they cannot derive any information about the polynomial $f(x)$.

2.2 Discrete Logarithm Problem

Given a prime number p, a $\mathbb{Z}_p^*$ generator α and an element $\beta \in \mathbb{Z}_p^*$, its goal is to find an integer x, $0 \leq x \leq p - 2$, that satisfies $\alpha^x \equiv \beta \pmod{p}$.

3 Unidirectional Threshold Proxy Re-encryption

3.1 Definitions of Unidirectional Threshold Proxy Re-encryption

Definition 1. Unidirectional threshold proxy re-encryption (UTPR) contains a series of algorithms: *Setup, KeyGen, Encryption, Decryption*, Re *KeyGen, SharePRe Enc, Combine*, where:

- *Setup(k)* is the initialization algorithm with security parameter k as the input, then generates global parameter *params*. Here the assumption is *params* contains the Plaintext space M.
- *(KeyGen, Encryption, Decryption)* includes standard key generation, encryption, and decryption algorithms. *KeyGen(params)* generates a set of secret key pairs

respectively, (sk_A, pk_A) for user A, and (sk_B, pk_B) for user B. It also produces secret keys (sk_{P_i}, pk_{P_i}) for proxy P, here P is the collective name of each proxy $P_i, i = 1, 2, \ldots, n$. For convenience, the rest of inputs are all implied to includes the global parameter *params*.

- Re *KeyGen* is a re-encryption key generation algorithm for the proxies. The user A inputs the secret key sk_A and the public key pk_B to generate the re-encryption secret key $rk_{A->B}^i, i = 1, 2, \ldots, n$, for proxies P_i.
- *ShareP* Re *Enc* is the re-encryption algorithm of the proxies $P_i, i = 1, 2, \ldots, n$. Proxy P_i uses a re-encryption key $rk_{A->B}^i, i = 1, 2, \ldots, n$, the ciphertext C_A generated from *Encryption* and other parameters as input to output a re-encrypted ciphertext $C_B^i, i = 1, 2, \ldots, n$. The algorithm *Combine* makes ciphertexts to generate a complete re-encrypted ciphertext C_B.

Note: The algorithm Re *KeyGen* shows that the threshold proxy re-encryption is non-interactive. Specifically, the proxy re-encryption key is generated by the delegator (user A) through the public key of the delegatee (user B) and unnecessary to be produced by the interaction or a third party.

Definition 2. Correctness of UTPR

It usually makes sense in the threshold proxy re-encryption, that user A holding the secret key sk_A is supposed to have the ability to decrypt the ciphertext encrypted on message m with the public key pk_A, and user B is able to decrypt the ciphertext C_B with the secret key sk_B. In this process, the encrypted plaintext m needs to be consistent, namely, the user B is supposed to receive the original text sent by the user A accurately.

For the message $m \in M$, a key pair $(sk, pk) \leftarrow KeyGen(1^k)$, re-encryption keys $rk_{A \rightarrow B}^i \leftarrow ReKeyGen(1^k)$, set $C_A \leftarrow Encryption(pk_A, m)$, $C_B^i \leftarrow ReEnc(rk_{A \rightarrow B}^i, C_A)$, $i = 1, 2, \ldots, n$, then, the correctness must satisfy the equation as follows:

$$Decryption(sk_A, C_A) = m \tag{2}$$

$$Decryption(sk_B, Combine(C_B^i)) = m \tag{3}$$

3.2 Security Model

In this security model, it is possible for a delegator to be challenged by the collusion between multiple proxies and the delegatee. The security discussed in this paper is for the delegator, even if the proxies colluded with the delegatee, the delegator's secret key still can't be recovery. In a threshold proxy re-encryption scheme, an attacker would steal a secret key to decrypt ciphertexts or uses a public key for forgery of a ciphertext. Three kinds of adversaries are defined based on different scenes. Att_1 represents an external attacker, Att_2 represents a malicious proxy within the system, Att_3 represents a malicious proxy and dishonest delegatee. Att_1, Att_2, Att_3 are defined for unidirectional threshold proxy re-encryption.

Definition 3. The unidirectional threshold proxy re-encryption scheme is unforgeable if no polynomial bounded adversaries Att_i, $i = 1, 2, 3$ have a non-negligible advantage in the following game.

To simulate these different adversaries, we define the oracles. There are two types of oKeyGen.

- *opKeyGen:* Produce a new key pair $(sk', pk') \leftarrow KeyGen(params)$. The attacker Att_1, Att_2, Att_3 are given delegator's public key pk'.
- *oqKeyGen:* Produce a new key pair $(sk', pk') \leftarrow KeyGen(params)$. The attacker Att_3 is given pk' and sk'. pk' is the delegator's public key.
- oRe$KeyGen$: The attacker inputs sk'_A and pk_B, and uses oRe$KeyGen$ to produce a share of partial re-encryption key $(rk^i_{A \to B})' \leftarrow$ Re$KeyGen$ (sk', pk_B), $i = 1, 2, \ldots, n$. The attacker Att_2, Att_3 are given $(rk^i_{A \to B})'$.
- *oEncryption* : The attacker inputs sk'_A and a message m' to produce the ciphertext $C'_A = Encryption(sk'_A, m')$.
- *oShare*PRe Enc : The attacker uses the re-encryption key share $(rk^i_{A \to B})'$, C'_A and other parameters for generating the re-encryption ciphertexts $(C^i_B)'$, $i = 1, 2, \ldots, n$.
- *oDecryption* : The attacker uses sk'_B and *Combine* for decryption, and outputs $oDecryption\left(sk'_B, Combine(C^i_B)'\right) = m'$.

Here is the attacker's challenge game:

Init phase. The attacker outputs a set $R \subset \{1, 2, \ldots, n\}$ of $t - 1$ proxies to corrupt.
Query phase. The attacker adaptively issues queries.
Forgery phase. The attacker outputs a message m', a private key sk' and a string σ'. The attackers succeeds if the following equation holds: $Adv_{Att_i} = \Pr[Att_i succeeds]$.

Remark: The advantage of attackers $Att_i (i = 1, 2, 3)$ in the above game is defined to be $Adv_{Att_i} = \Pr[Att_i succeeds]$, where the probability is taken oven all coin tosses made by the challenger and the attackers.

3.3   Unidirectional Threshold Proxy Re-encryption Scheme

In this section, a specific unidirectional threshold proxy re-signature scheme is proposed under the definitions presented in Sect. 3.1.

Suppose that user B (the delegatee) is authorized to share the data from user A (the delegator). The proxies cooperate with each other to convert data encrypted with user $A's$ public key into being decrypted by user B, even not owning user $A's$ private key, and not vice versa.

We assume that there is a group of proxies P_i, $i = 1, 2, \ldots, n$, and there exists a dealer D, who is responsible for selecting and distributing the secret keys for all the participants, the shadows for all the proxies and the security parameters related to different phases. All the messages are supposed to be transferred in a dedicated broadcast channel, which is accessed by all participants.

In the initialization phase, the dealer D firstly selects three public parameters p, q and g. p is a large prime modulus in the range of $(2^{511}, 2^{512})$; q is a prime divisor of p in the range of $(2^{159}, 2^{160})$; g is a generator with order q in $GF(p)$. There is $g = h^{(p-1)/q}(\bmod\, p)$, where h is a random integer, with the range of $(1, p-1)$ such that $h^{(p-1)/q}(\bmod\, p) > 1$. What's more, the dealer D also needs to select a series of integers $a_i, i = 0, \ldots, t-1$, as the secret coefficients of $f(x) = a_0 + a_1 x + \cdots + a_{t-1} x^{t-1}$. It should be pointed out that according to Lemma 1 [10], if g is a generator with order q in $GF(p)$, then $g^r(\bmod\, p) = g^{r(\bmod\, q)}(\bmod\, p)$, for any nonnegative integer r.

- *KeyGen* : Two numbers a and b are randomly selected by D, then the two key pairs separately, $pk_A = g^a$, $sk_a = a$, for A; $pk_B = g^b$, $sk_B = b$, for B.
- *ReKeyGen* : User A authorizes user B by calculating $rk_{A \to B} = g^{b/a} \in G_1$, with inputs of $B's$ public key pk_B and $A's$ private key sk_A. According to the formula that

$$f(x) = \sum_{i=1}^{k} f(x_i) \lambda_{ij}, \quad \lambda_{ij} = \prod_{\substack{l=1 \\ l \neq j}}^{k} \frac{x - x_l}{x_i - x_l},$$ the re-encryption key share hold by each proxy

is $rk_{p_i} = g^{f(x_i)} \bmod q, i = 1, 2, \ldots, n$, and x_i is the secret number related to each proxy P_i.
- *Level$_1$Enc* : The inputs of the first level encryption algorithm are pk_B and $m \in G_2$. The output is $C_B = (Z^{br}, mZ^r)(\bmod\, p)$, $Z = e(g, g)$, which can be decrypted by sk_B.
- *Level$_2$Enc* : The inputs of the second level encryption algorithm are pk_A and $m \in G_2$. The output is $C_A = (g^{ar}, mZ^r)(\bmod\, p)$, $Z = e(g, g)$, which can be decrypted by sk_A. It is possible for ciphertext C_A to be converted into the first level ciphertext C_B, which is decrypted by the delegatee B.
- *SharePReEnc* : This algorithm permit t out of n proxies convert the second level ciphertext C_A into the first level ciphertext C_B with the re-encryption key $rk_{p_i} = g^{f(x_i)}(\bmod\, q), i = 1, 2, \ldots, n$.
  According to $C_A = (g^{ar}, mZ^r)(\bmod\, p)$, where r is a random coefficient, calculate:

$$e\left(g^{ar}, \left(rk_{p_i}\right)^{\lambda_i}\right) = e\left(g^{ar}, g^{[\lambda_i f(x_i)]}\right) = Z^{ar[\lambda_i f(x_i)]}. \tag{4}$$

And the output is:

$$C_{b_i} = \left(Z^{ar[\lambda_i f(x_i)]}, mZ^r\right). \tag{5}$$

- *Combine* : After re-encryption by the re-encryption key, the ciphertext C_{b_i} would be combined to the first level ciphertext C_B, which is related to the delegatee B:

$$\prod_{i=1}^{k} Z^{ar[\lambda_i f(x_i)]} = Z^{ar \sum_{i=1}^{k} \lambda_i f(x_i)} = Z^{ar \cdot b/a} = Z^{br}, \tag{6}$$

then $C_B = (Z^{br}, mZ^r) \pmod q$.

- *Decryption*(C_A, C_B) : The algorithm $Level_1Dec$ is to decrypt the first level ciphertext $C_B = (\alpha, \beta)$ with sk_B, the output of which is $m = \beta/\alpha^{1/sk_B}$. The algorithm $Level_2Dec$ is to decrypt the second level ciphertext $C_A = (\alpha, \beta)$ with sk_A, the output of which is $m = \beta/e(\alpha, g)^{1/sk_A}$.

4 The Analysis

4.1 Security Analysis

The details of security analysis is presented in the full version.

4.2 Efficiency Analysis

To evaluate the performance of the proposed scheme, we make a comparison with another multi-proxy re-encryption scheme [6] on efficiency, which is measured by the runtime of algorithms. The more details of efficiency analysis is given in the full version.

5 Consortium Blockchain Access Permission Scheme Based on Threshold Proxy Re-encryption

5.1 Application Background

Currently, The original scheme for a new node joining a consortium blockchain is by authentication with a licence from CA (Certificate Authority). When starting to communicate with other nodes in the blockchain networks, the new node sends a message with the licence to identify itself. But the disadvantages of centralized CA are obvious, if the security of CA is threatened or fraudulent practices happen in CA, the authorized consortium blockchain will be also at risk. On the other side, since the licence directory needs to be progressing online, and the authentication reliability depends on the certificate chain and root certificate, centralized CA is easy to be the performance and security bottleneck, when applied in distributed consortium blockchains. Therefore, we introduce threshold proxy re-encryption to a novel method for access permission, when a new node taking part in the consortium blockchain.

5.2 Proposed Scheme

In the node access license model using threshold proxy re-encryption, there are three parties, W bank is marked as node A; other cooperative banks are marked as $P_i, i = 1, 2, \ldots, n - 1$; the new bank is marked as node B, which is applying for joining a consortium blockchain. Node A is the delegator, and other cooperative bank nodes $P_i, i = 1, 2, \ldots, n - 1$ are proxies. Firstly, node A would accept $B's$ blockchain admission. Meanwhile, it would send the proxy $P_i, i = 1, 2, \ldots, n - 1$, a secret message including ID, which represents the identity of members in the consortium blockchain. If the proxy node agrees the entrance of the new node B, it will broadcast the share of re-encrypted ciphertext to B. When there are at least t out of n nodes reach a consensus, node B will receive consortium blockchain ID, and the licence will be valid.

Figure 1 is shown that W bank and other cooperative banks establish a interbank reconciliation platform based on consortium blockchain, where the transaction details between banks and capital flow generated by core accounting would be stored for enquiries from institutions. W bank and cooperative banks operate different nodes separately. There are n nodes in the consortium blockchain.

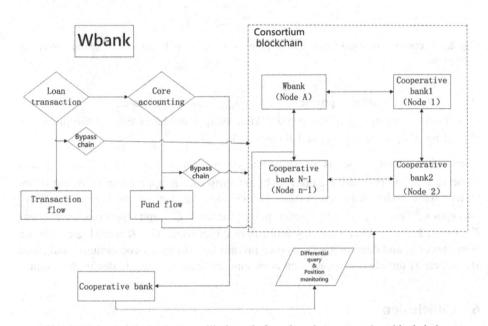

Fig. 1. A basic interbank reconciliation platform based on consortium blockchain

As shown in Fig. 2, when a new cooperative bank is added to the reconciliation platform, it is expressed that the new node joins in the consortium blockchain. According to the consensus, when a new organization applies, if and only if at least t out of n existing organizations agree the proposal, the application would be adopted.

Initialization Phase. After network initialization, nodes in the consortium blockchain generates the public and private keys by themselves. Every node knows others' public keys. We assume that each node in the system uses a different public key for encryption.

Application Phase. The new node B sends node A the application for entrance of the consortium blockchain firstly. At the same time, B also sends the public key pk'_b and the merkle tree's root message R_b to A. When A confirm that the root message R_b is on the chain, it would permit the entrance. Then, A would encrypt the consortium blockchain

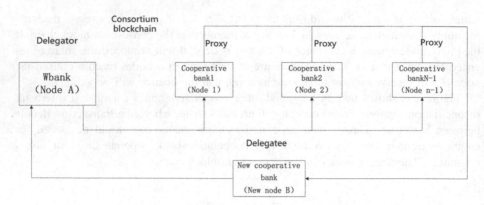

Fig. 2. A consortium blockchain access permission scheme based on threshold proxy re-encryption

ID with its own private key sk'_a, and generate the ciphertext $C' = Encryption(m) = Encryption(ID)$. After that, A produces the re-encryption key $rk'_{A \to B}$, by $A's$ private key sk'_a and $B's$ public key pk'_b.

Permission Phase. A sends proxy re-encryption key $rk^i_{A \to B}$, $i=1, 2, \ldots, n-1$ and ciphertext C' to cooperative bank P_i. On agreeing on the application of B, the cooperative bank nodes in the consortium blockchain will use the received share of re-encryption key $rk^i_{A \to B}$ to re-encrypt ciphertext C' and generate ciphertext $C^i_B, i = 1, 2, \ldots, n$. After receiving more than t ciphertext C^i_B, B would generate the ciphertext C_B, and decrypt it with its own private key sk_B to get consortium blockchain ID, which as the identification when communicate with existing nodes in the chain.

6 Conclusion

In this paper, we propose a new definition and security model of threshold proxies. Unlike previous studies, we used a standard cryptographic prototype to build a solution. This extends the application scope of the threshold proxy re-encryption. We propose a one-way threshold proxy re-encryption and verify its security based on discrete logarithm problem, and compare performance with related schemes. And we apply the threshold proxy re-encryption scheme to the block chain domain to solve the problem of the access license of the federated chain node.

Acknowledgments. We appreciate all helpful comments given by the reviewers. This research has been supported by Beijing Natural Science Foundation (Grant No. 4132057), the National Natural Science Foundation of China (Grant No. 61472032, No. 61572132; U1705264), Guangxi Key Laboratory of Cryptography and Information Security (No. GCIS201609), and Fujian Provincial Key Laboratory of Network Security and Cryptology Research Fund (Fujian Normal University) (No. 15007).

References

1. Blaze, M., Bleumer, G., Strauss, M.: Divertible protocols and atomic proxy cryptography. In: Nyberg, K. (ed.) EUROCRYPT 1998. LNCS, vol. 1403, pp. 127–144. Springer, Heidelberg (1998). https://doi.org/10.1007/BFb0054122
2. Shamir, A.: How to share a secret. Commun. ACM **22**(11), 612–613 (1979)
3. Blakley, G.R.: Safeguarding cryptographic keys. In: Proceedings of National Computer Conference, pp. 313–317. AFIPS Press, Montvale (1979)
4. Asmuth, C., Bloom, J.: A modular approach to key safeguarding. IEEE Trans. Inf. Theor. **29** (2), 208–210 (1983)
5. Karnin, E.D., Greene, J.W., Helman, M.E.: On sharing secret system. IEEE Trans. Inf. Theor. **29**, 208–210 (1983)
6. Nikov, V., Nikova, S., Preneel, B.: On the size of monotone span programs. In: Blundo, C., Cimato, S. (eds.) SCN 2004. LNCS, vol. 3352, pp. 249–262. Springer, Heidelberg (2005). https://doi.org/10.1007/978-3-540-30598-9_18
7. Sheng, M.L., Cao, Z.F.: ID-based proxy re-encryption with threshold multi-proxies. J. Nat. Sci. Hei Long Jiang Univ. **27**(2), 151–156 (2010)
8. Li, J.-Y., Ma, C.-G., Zhao, Q.: Resplittable threshold multi-broker proxy re-encryption scheme from lattices. J. Commun. **5**, 157–164 (2017)
9. Song, Y.-J.: Threshold delegation scheme based on multi-proxy re-encryption. Int. J. Secur. Appl. **10**(7), 355–362 (2016)
10. NIST: The digital signature standard. Commun. ACM **35**(7), 36–40 (1992)

Trace Representation of the Sequences Derived from Polynomial Quotient

Liping Zhao[1($\boxtimes$)], Xiaoni Du[1], and Chenhuang Wu[2]

[1] Northwest Normal University, Lanzhou 730070, Gansu, People's Republic of China
marching666@126.com, ymLdxn@126.com
[2] Putian University, Putian 351100, Fujian, People's Republic of China
wuchenhuang2008@126.com

Abstract. The discrete Fourier transform and trace representation of certain sequences can help generate the sequences efficiently and analyse their cryptographic properties. In this paper, we first determine the defining pairs of the binary sequences derived from a class of polynomial quotient modulo an odd prime p and the Legendre symbol. We then derive the discrete Fourier transform and the trace representation of this class of sequences.

Keywords: Polynomial quotient · Trace representation
Fourier transform · Defining pairs · Binary sequence

1 Introduction

Sequences with certain good pseudorandom properties have been widely used in communication systems, ranging systems, coding theory and stream ciphers [11,16]. The trace representation of sequences is useful for implementing the sequences and analysing their pseudorandom properties [16]. Thus, it is of great interest to represent sequences by the trace function (see [2,8,9,14,15] and the references therein).

Cyclotomic sequences over finite fields form a class of important sequences due to their nice pseudorandom properties, such as high linear complexity and low correlation, in addition to their easiness of implementation [9,14,15]. Legendre sequences [14] and Hall's sequences [15] are the well known and important classical cyclotomic sequences with period of an odd prime p [9]. Jacobi sequences are a class of generalized cyclotomic sequences with period pq, where p, q are distinct odd primes [8]. Fermat quotient, the p-th power residues modulo p^2, plays a very important role in a variety of number theoretic problems (see [10] and references therein). In 2011, Igor Shparlinski [12] proposed an application of Fermat quotient in cryptography. After that, the analysis of pseudorandom sequences derived from Fermat quotient has been an interesting research direction. A number of related theoretic and cryptographic problems as well as measures of pseudorandomness have been studied (for example, see [3,4,6]). Chen [2]

X. Sun et al. (Eds.): ICCCS 2018, LNCS 11066, pp. 26–37, 2018.
https://doi.org/10.1007/978-3-030-00015-8_3

derived the trace representation of the sequence derived from Fermat quotient by determining the defining pairs of the sequences with character set being the cyclotomic cosets of order p modulo p^2. In this article, we will determine the discrete Fourier transform and the trace representation of the binary sequences proposed by Chen in [5]. Our method is the based on a further partition of the cyclotomic cosets of order p modulo p^2, which is different from that of [2].

The rest of this paper is organized as follows. Section 2 introduces the sequences proposed by Chen [5] and some notation. Section 3 determines the discrete Fourier transform of the sequences. Section 4 derives the trace representations of the sequences. Section 5 concludes this paper. For convenience, we adopt the following notation unless otherwise stated in this paper.

- $\left(\frac{u}{p}\right)$ denotes the Legendre symbol for u modulo an odd prime p.
- $\mathbf{Z}_N = \{0, 1, \ldots, N-1\}$ denotes the residue class ring modulo N, and $\mathbf{Z}_N^*$ denotes the unit group of $\mathbf{Z}_N$ for integer $N > 1$.
- $Q = \{u \in \mathbf{Z}_p^* : \left(\frac{u}{p}\right) = 1\}$, $N = \{u \in \mathbf{Z}_p^* : \left(\frac{u}{p}\right) = -1\}$.
- g is a (fixed) primitive root modulo p^2.
- $\mathbf{F}_2 = \{0, 1\}$ denotes the binary field and $\overline{\mathbf{F}}_2$ denotes the algebraic closure of $\mathbf{F}_2$.
- $\beta \in \overline{\mathbf{F}}_2$ is a primitive p^2-th root of unity and α is an element in $\overline{\mathbf{F}}_2$ satisfying $\alpha + \alpha^2 = 1$.
- $\delta(j) = \begin{cases} 0, \text{ if } j \equiv 0 \pmod{2}, \\ p, \text{ if } j \equiv 1 \pmod{2}, \end{cases}$ and $\epsilon = \begin{cases} 1, \text{ if } 2^{p-1} \not\equiv 1 \pmod{p^2}, \\ 0, \text{ if } 2^{p-1} \equiv 1 \pmod{p^2}. \end{cases}$
- $\lambda := ord_p(2)$ is the smallest positive integer satisfying $2^\lambda \equiv 1 \pmod{p}$.

2   Preliminaries

For an odd prime p and an integer u with $\gcd(u, p) = 1$, the *Fermat quotient* $q_p(u)$ modulo p is defined as the unique integer with

$$q_p(u) \equiv \frac{u^{p-1} - 1}{p} \pmod{p}, \quad 0 \le q_p(u) < p,$$

and we also define $q_p(kp) = 0$ for all $k \in \mathbf{Z}$. An equivalent definition is

$$q_p(u) \equiv \frac{u^{p-1} - u^{p(p-1)}}{p} \pmod{p}. \tag{1}$$

In particular, for all integers $w > 0$ and $u \ge 0$, Chen et al. extended (1) to define

$$q_{p,w}(u) \equiv \frac{u^w - u^{wp}}{p} \pmod{p}, \quad 0 \le q_{p,w}(u) < p, \tag{2}$$

which is called a *polynomial quotient* in [6]. In fact $q_{p,p-1}(u) = q_p(u)$. Obviously,

$$q_{p,w}(u) \equiv \begin{cases} -u^w w q_p(u) \pmod{p}, & \text{if } \gcd(u, p) = 1, \\ 0, & \text{if } p | u \text{ and } w \ge 2, \\ k \pmod{p}, & \text{if } u \equiv kp \pmod{p^2} \text{ and } w = 1. \end{cases} \tag{3}$$

In [5], based on the Legendre symbol $\left(\frac{\cdot}{p}\right)$, Chen *et al.* constructed the binary sequence (e_u) from polynomial quotient by defining

$$(-1)^{e_u} = \begin{cases} \left(\frac{aq_{p,w}(u)}{p}\right), & \text{if } \gcd(q_{p,w}(u),p) = 1, \\ 1, & \text{otherwise}, \end{cases} \tag{4}$$

for fixed $1 \leq a, w < p$, and also determined the linear complexity of the sequence. We note that (e_u) is p^2-periodic [4] since

$$q_{p,w}(v + kp) \equiv q_{p,w}(v) + kv^{w-1} \pmod{p}, \ 0 < v < p. \tag{5}$$

Below we will investigate the trace representation of (e_u) defined in (4) with w odd since that of (e_u) with w even was presented in [2]. For our purpose, we need to describe (e_u) in an equivalent way.

Motivated by (3), we write

$$H_{a,w}(u) \equiv \begin{cases} -awq_p(u) \pmod{p}, & \text{if } \gcd(u,p) = 1, \\ 0, & \text{if } p|u \text{ and } w \geq 2, \\ ak \pmod{p}, & \text{if } u \equiv kp \pmod{p^2} \text{ and } w = 1. \end{cases} \tag{6}$$

We will use the theory of cyclotomy, since $H_{a,w} : \mathbf{Z}_{p^2}^* \to \mathbf{Z}_p$ is a group homomorphism

$$H_{a,w}(uv) \equiv H_{a,w}(u) + H_{a,w}(v) \pmod{p}, \quad \gcd(uv,p) = 1, \tag{7}$$

by the fact that $q_p(uv) \equiv q_p(u) + q_p(v) \pmod{p}$ for $\gcd(uv,p) = 1$.

Define

$$D_l = \{u : 0 \leq u < p^2, \ \gcd(u,p) = 1, \ H_{a,w}(u) = l\}$$

for $l = 0, 1, \ldots, p - 1$. With the definition of g, by (7) we have

$$D_0 = \{g^{kp} \pmod{p^2} : 0 \leq k < p\}.$$

In the following, for convenience, we will choose g such that $g \in D_1$, that is, $H_{a,w}(g) = 1$. And we claim that such g always exists. Since otherwise if $H_{a,w}(g) = s$, then $g^{s^{-1}}$ will be the desired. Hence, for $l = 0, 1, \ldots, p - 1$, we have $D_l = g^l D_0$ and each D_l has the cardinality $|D_l| = p - 1$. Naturally $D_0, D_1, \ldots, D_{p-1}$ form a partition of $\mathbf{Z}_{p^2}^*$. We define

$$Q_l = \left\{u \in D_l : \left(\frac{u}{p}\right) = 1\right\} \text{ and } N_l = \left\{u \in D_l : \left(\frac{u}{p}\right) = -1\right\}, \text{ for } 0 \leq l < p.$$

Here and hereafter, we suppose that the subscripts of D, Q and N are all performed modulo p.

Let $P = \{kp : 0 \leq k < p\}$. For odd $w \geq 3$, (e_u) can be equivalently defined by

$$e_u = \begin{cases} 0, \text{ if } u \in \cup_{l \in Q} Q_l \cup \cup_{l \in N} N_l \cup D_0 \cup P, \\ 1, \text{ if } u \in \cup_{l \in Q} N_l \cup \cup_{l \in N} Q_l. \end{cases}$$

For $w = 1$, (e_u) can be equivalently defined by

$$e_u = \begin{cases} 0, \text{ if } u \in \cup_{l \in Q} Q_l \cup \cup_{l \in N} N_l \cup D_0 \cup \{0\} \cup \{lp : l \in Q\}, \\ 1, \text{ if } u \in \cup_{l \in Q} N_l \cup \cup_{l \in N} Q_l \cup \{lp : l \in N\}, \end{cases}$$

if $\left(\frac{a}{p}\right) = 1$, and otherwise

$$e_u = \begin{cases} 0, \text{ if } u \in \cup_{l \in Q} Q_l \cup \cup_{l \in N} N_l \cup D_0 \cup \{0\} \cup \{lp : l \in N\}, \\ 1, \text{ if } u \in \cup_{l \in Q} N_l \cup \cup_{l \in N} Q_l \cup \{lp : l \in Q\}. \end{cases}$$

We note that $|Q| = |N| = (p-1)/2$.

Define the *binary characteristic sequences* with respect to the coset Q_l ($l = 0, 1, \ldots, p-1$) and the set pQ respectively by

$$s_u^{(l)} = \begin{cases} 1, \text{ if } u \in Q_l, \\ 0, \text{ otherwise,} \end{cases} \quad and \quad s_u' = \begin{cases} 1, \text{ if } u \in pQ, \\ 0, \text{ otherwise,} \end{cases}$$

In the following, we will represent (e_u) defined in (4) as a sum of trace functions via determining the *defining pair* (see Sect. 3 for the definition) of the sequences $(s_u^{(l)})$ and (s_u'). We should mention that most of the calculations in the article are performed over $\mathbf{F}_2$.

3   Discrete Fourier Transform

For a binary sequence (s_u) over $\mathbf{F}_2$ of odd period T, there exist a primitive T-th root $\beta \in \overline{\mathbf{F}}_2$ of unity and a polynomial $g(x) = \sum_{0 \leq i < T} \rho_i x^i \in \overline{\mathbf{F}}_2[x]$ such that $s_u = g(\beta^u)$, $u \geq 0$, see [1,13, Theorem 6.8.2]. We call the pair $(g(x), \beta)$ a *defining pair* of (s_u) and $g(x)$ the *defining polynomial* of (s_u) corresponding to β [1,8,9]. Note that for a given β, $g(x)$ is uniquely determined [9, Lemma 2]. The relation between (s_u) and (ρ_i) is given as $s_u = \sum_{0 \leq i < T} \rho_i \beta^{iu} \Longleftrightarrow \rho_i = \sum_{0 \leq u < T} s_u \beta^{-iu}$. The right hand side is referred to as the *discrete Fourier transform* of (s_u) [1].

We use the notation $uD_l = \{uv \pmod{p^2} : v \in D_l\}$. By [4,5], for all $0 \leq l, l' < p$, we have the following basic facts:

(I) If $u \in D_{l'}$, then $uD_l = D_{l+l'}$.
(II) If $u \in Q_{l'}$, then $uQ_l = Q_{l+l'}$ and $uN_l = N_{l+l'}$.
(III) If $u \in N_{l'}$, then $uQ_l = N_{l+l'}$ and $uN_l = Q_{l+l'}$.
(IV) $\{u \pmod p : u \in D_l\} = \{1, 2, \ldots, p-1\}$, $|Q_l| = |N_l| = (p-1)/2$.
(V) $Q_0 = \{g^{2kp} \pmod{p^2} : 0 \leq k < (p-1)/2\}$, $N_0 = g^p Q_0$.

For all $0 \leq l < p$, we define the following polynomials in $\mathbf{F}_2[x]$ as

$$D_l(x) = \sum_{u \in D_l} x^u, \quad Q_l(x) = \sum_{u \in Q_l} x^u, \quad N_l(x) = \sum_{u \in N_l} x^u,$$

$$Q(x) = \sum_{u \in Q} x^u, \quad N(x) = \sum_{u \in N} x^u.$$

We see that $D_l(x) = Q_l(x) + N_l(x)$.

Lemma 1. *[3,4] With the same notation as above, we have*

(i) $\sum_{l=0}^{p-1} D_l(\beta^n) = 0$, *for all* $n \in \mathbf{Z}_{p^2}^*$.

(ii) $\sum_{l=0}^{p-1} Q_l(\beta^n) = \sum_{l=0}^{p-1} N_l(\beta^n) = 0$, *for all* $n \in \mathbf{Z}_{p^2}^*$.

(iii) $D_l(\beta^{kp}) = \begin{cases} 0, & \text{if } k \equiv 0 \pmod{p}, \\ 1, & \text{otherwise}, \end{cases}$ *for all* $0 \le l < p$.

(iv) $Q_l(\beta^{kp}) = Q(\beta^{kp})$ *and* $N_l(\beta^{kp}) = N(\beta^{kp})$, *for all* $0 \le l < p$ *and* $k \in \mathbf{Z}$.

Define p-tuples

$$\mathcal{A}_i = (Q_i(\beta), Q_{i+1}(\beta), \dots, Q_{i+p-1}(\beta)), \quad \mathcal{B}_i = (N_i(\beta), N_{i+1}(\beta), \dots, N_{i+p-1}(\beta)).$$

In the following lemma, we will compute

$$\mathcal{A}_i \cdot \mathcal{A}_j^{\mathrm{T}} + \mathcal{B}_i \cdot \mathcal{B}_j^{\mathrm{T}} \quad \text{and} \quad \mathcal{A}_i \cdot \mathcal{B}_j^{\mathrm{T}} + \mathcal{B}_i \cdot \mathcal{A}_j^{\mathrm{T}}$$

where $i, j \in \{0, 1, \dots, p-1\}$ and C^T is the transpose of the vector C.

Lemma 2. *For all* $0 \le i, j < p$, *we have*

(i) $\mathcal{A}_i \cdot \mathcal{A}_j^{\mathrm{T}} + \mathcal{B}_i \cdot \mathcal{B}_j^{\mathrm{T}} = \begin{cases} 1, & \text{if } i \ne j \text{ and } p \equiv 1 \pmod 4, \\ 0, & \text{otherwise}, \end{cases}$

(ii) $\mathcal{A}_i \cdot \mathcal{B}_j^{\mathrm{T}} + \mathcal{B}_i \cdot \mathcal{A}_j^{\mathrm{T}} = \begin{cases} 1, & \text{if } i \ne j \text{ and } p \equiv 3 \pmod 4, \\ 0, & \text{otherwise}. \end{cases}$

Proof. We only prove (i) here, since the other case can be proved in the same way. By Facts (II), (III) and (V), we have

$$N_l = g^p Q_l = g^{l+\delta(l+1)} Q_0, \quad Q_l = g^p N_l = g^{l+\delta(l)} Q_0. \tag{8}$$

Firstly, for $i + j \equiv 0 \pmod 2$, denote $\gamma_r = \beta^{g^{i-j}+r}$, we have

$$\mathcal{A}_i \cdot \mathcal{A}_j^{\mathrm{T}} + \mathcal{B}_i \cdot \mathcal{B}_j^{\mathrm{T}} = \sum_{k=0}^{p-1} \left(\sum_{u \in Q_0} \beta^{ug^{i+k}} \sum_{v \in Q_0} \beta^{vg^{j+k}} + \sum_{u \in Q_0} \beta^{ug^{i+k+p}} \sum_{v \in Q_0} \beta^{vg^{j+k+p}} \right)$$

$$= \sum_{k=0}^{p-1} \sum_{u \in Q_0} \left(\beta^{ug^{i+k}} \sum_{r \in Q_0} \beta^{urg^{j+k}} + \beta^{ug^{i+k+p}} \sum_{r \in Q_0} \beta^{urg^{j+k+p}} \right) \text{ (here } v = ur)$$

$$= \sum_{r \in Q_0} \sum_{k=0}^{p-1} \sum_{u \in Q_0} (\gamma_r^{ug^{j+k}} + \gamma_r^{ug^{j+k+p}}) = \sum_{r \in Q_0} \sum_{k=0}^{p-1} D_{j+k}(\gamma_r)$$

$$= \sum_{r \in Q_0} \sum_{z \in \mathbf{Z}_{p^2}^*} \gamma_r^z.$$

Thus, for those $r \in Q_0$ with $\gcd(g^{i-j} + r, p) = 1$, we see that γ_r is a primitive p^2-th root of unity. Hence we have by Lemma 1(i)

$$\sum_{z \in \mathbf{Z}_{p^2}^*} \gamma_r^z = \sum_{l=0}^{p-1} D_l(\gamma_r) = 0.$$

For $r \in Q_0$ with $\gcd(g^{i-j} + r, p) = p$, we claim that there is exactly one $r \in Q_0$ satisfying it if $p \equiv 1 \pmod 4$. Since $-1 \in Q$ when $p \equiv 1 \pmod 4$ [7], so by Fact (V), there exists some $0 \le k_0 < (p-1)/2$ such that $p | g^{i-j}(g^{2k_0 p + j - i} + 1)$.

In particular, if $i = j$ we see that $k_0 = (p-1)/4$, and hence $\gamma_r = 1$. So we have $\sum_{z \in \mathbf{Z}_{p^2}^*} \gamma_r^z = p(p-1) \equiv 0 \pmod 2$. However, if $i \ne j$, we see that γ_r is a primitive p-th root of unity. So by Lemma 1(iii), we have

$$\sum_{z \in \mathbf{Z}_{p^2}^*} \gamma_r^z = \sum_{l=0}^{p-1} D_l(\gamma_r) = p \equiv 1 \pmod 2.$$

Then, for $i + j \equiv 1 \pmod 2$, by (8), similarly we have

$$\mathcal{A}_i \cdot \mathcal{A}_j^{\mathrm{T}} + \mathcal{B}_i \cdot \mathcal{B}_j^{\mathrm{T}}$$

$$= \sum_{k=0}^{p-1} \left(\sum_{u \in Q_0} \beta^{u g^{i+k}} \sum_{v \in Q_0} \beta^{v g^{j+k+p}} + \sum_{u \in Q_0} \beta^{u g^{i+k+p}} \sum_{v \in Q_0} \beta^{v g^{2p} g^{j+k}} \right)$$

$$= \sum_{r \in Q_0} \sum_{k=0}^{p-1} \sum_{u \in Q_0} (\theta_r^{u g^{j+k+p}} + \theta_r^{u g g^{j+k}}) \quad \text{(we use } \theta_r = \beta^{g^{i-j-p}+r})$$

$$= \sum_{r \in Q_0} \sum_{k=0}^{p-1} D_{j+k}(\theta_r) = \sum_{r \in Q_0} \sum_{z \in \mathbf{Z}_{p^2}^*} \theta_r^z.$$

Thus $\mathcal{A}_i \cdot \mathcal{A}_j^{\mathrm{T}} + \mathcal{B}_i \cdot \mathcal{B}_j^{\mathrm{T}} = 1$ iff $p \equiv 1 \pmod 4$.

Summarizing all the conclusions above, we finish the proof of (i).

Lemma 3. *[8] There exists a primitive p^2-th root of unity $\beta \in \overline{\mathbf{F}}_2$ such that*

$$(Q(\beta^p), N(\beta^p)) = \begin{cases} (1, 0), & \text{if } p \equiv \pm 1 \pmod 8, \\ (\alpha, \alpha^2), & \text{if } p \equiv \pm 3 \pmod 8. \end{cases}$$

From now on, we always suppose that $\beta \in \overline{\mathbf{F}}_2$ is a primitive p^2-th root of unity satisfying Lemma 3. Below we denote $\Gamma_{l,k}(x) = Q_{l+k}(\beta)Q_k(x) + N_{l+k}(\beta)N_k(x)$ and $\Gamma_{l,k}'(x) = Q_{l+k}(\beta)N_k(x) + N_{l+k}(\beta)Q_k(x)$.

Theorem 1. *Let $w > 1$.*

(i) If $p \equiv 1 \pmod 4$, then $G(x) = \sum_{k=0}^{p-1} \left(\sum_{l \in N} \Gamma_{l,k}(x) + \sum_{l \in Q} \Gamma_{l,k}'(x) \right)$.

(ii) If $p \equiv 3 \pmod 4$, then $G(x) = \sum_{j=1}^{p-1} x^{jp} + \sum_{k=0}^{p-1} \left(\sum_{l \in N} \Gamma_{l,k}'(x) + \sum_{l \in Q} \Gamma_{l,k}(x) \right)$.

Proof. First, we claim that the defining pair of $(s_u^{(i)})$ is $(G_i(x), \beta)$ with

(a1) $G_i(x) = \sum_{j \in Q} x^{jp} + \sum_{k=0}^{p-1} \Gamma_{i,k}(x)$ if $p \equiv 1 \pmod 8$, (a2) $G_i(x) = 1 + \sum\limits_{j \in N} x^{jp} + \sum\limits_{k=0}^{p-1} \Gamma'_{i,k}(x)$ if $p \equiv 7 \pmod 8$,

(a3) $G_i(x) = \alpha \sum\limits_{j \in Q} x^{jp} + \alpha^2 \sum\limits_{j \in N} x^{jp} + \sum\limits_{k=0}^{p-1} \Gamma_{i,k}(x)$ if $p \equiv 5 \pmod 8$,

(a4) $G_i(x) = 1 + \alpha^2 \sum\limits_{j \in Q} x^{jp} + \alpha \sum\limits_{j \in N} x^{jp} + \sum\limits_{k=0}^{p-1} \Gamma'_{i,k}(x)$, if $p \equiv 3 \pmod 8$.

Here we only verify (a1) holds since the other three cases can be similarly proved. For $u = 0$ we have

$$G_i(\beta^u) = G_i(1) = (p-1)/2 + (p-1)/2 \sum_{j=0}^{p-1} [Q_{i+j}(\beta) + N_{i+j}(\beta)] = 0 = s_u^{(i)}.$$

For $u = lp$ with $1 \le l < p$, by Lemma 1(ii), (iv) and Lemma 2 we have

$$G_i(\beta^u) = \sum_{j \in Q} \beta^{jlp^2} + \sum_{j=0}^{p-1} \Gamma_{l,k}(\beta^{lp}) = Q(\beta^{lp}) \sum_{j=0}^{p-1} Q_j(\beta) + N(\beta^{lp}) \sum_{j=0}^{p-1} N_j(\beta) = 0.$$

For $u \in Q_k$ with $0 \le k < p$, by Lemmas 1(iv), 2 and 3, we have

$$G_i(\beta^u) = 1 + \sum_{j=0}^{p-1} [Q_{i+j}(\beta) Q_{k+j}(\beta) + N_{i+j}(\beta) N_{k+j}(\beta)]$$

$$= 1 + \mathcal{A}_i \cdot \mathcal{A}_k^{\mathrm T} + \mathcal{B}_i \cdot \mathcal{B}_k^{\mathrm T} = \begin{cases} 1, \text{ if } i = k, \\ 0, \text{ otherwise,} \end{cases} = s_u^{(i)}$$

For $u \in N_k$ with $0 \le k < p$, by Lemmas 2 and 3 we have

$$G_i(\beta^u) = \sum_{j \in N} \beta^{jp} + \sum_{j=0}^{p-1} [Q_{i+j}(\beta) N_{k+j}(\beta) + N_{i+j}(\beta) Q_{k+j}(\beta)]$$

$$= 0 + \mathcal{A}_i \cdot \mathcal{B}_k^{\mathrm T} + \mathcal{B}_i \cdot \mathcal{A}_k^{\mathrm T} = 0 = s_u^{(i)}$$

That is, $s_u^{(i)} = G_i(\beta^u)$ for all $u \ge 0$. Thus, it is easy to see that $(G(x), \beta)$ is the defining pair of (e_u) with $w > 1$ when $p \equiv 1 \pmod 8$, where

$$G(x) = \sum_{l \in N} G_l(x) + \sum_{l \in Q} G_l(x^{g^p}) = \sum_{k=0}^{p-1} \left(\sum_{l \in N} \Gamma_{l,k}(x) + \sum_{l \in Q} \Gamma'_{l,k}(x) \right).$$

This completes the proof.

Theorem 2. *For $w = 1$ and $\left(\frac{a}{p}\right) = 1$, the defining pair $(G(x), \beta)$ of (e_u) is given as follows.*

(i) If $p \equiv 1 \pmod 8$, then $G(x) = \sum\limits_{j \in N} x^j \sum\limits_{j=0}^{p-1} x^{jp} + \sum\limits_{k=0}^{p-1} \left(\sum\limits_{l \in N} \Gamma_{l,k}(x) + \sum\limits_{l \in Q} \Gamma'_{l,k}(x) \right).$

(ii) *If $p \equiv 7 \pmod 8$, then*

$$G(x) = 1 + \sum_{j \in Q} x^j \sum_{j=0}^{p-1} x^{jp} + \sum_{k=0}^{p-1} \left(\sum_{l \in N} \Gamma'_{l,k}(x) + \sum_{l \in Q} \Gamma_{l,k}(x) \right).$$

(iii) *If $p \equiv 5 \pmod 8$, then*

$$G(x) = \left(\alpha \sum_{j \in N} x^j + \alpha^2 \sum_{j \in Q} x^j \right) \sum_{j=0}^{p-1} x^{jp} + \sum_{k=0}^{p-1} \left(\sum_{l \in N} \Gamma_{l,k}(x) + \sum_{l \in Q} \Gamma'_{l,k}(x) \right).$$

(iv) *If $p \equiv 3 \pmod 8$, then*

$$G(x) = 1 + \left(\alpha^2 \sum_{j \in N} x^j + \alpha \sum_{j \in Q} x^j \right) \sum_{j=0}^{p-1} x^{jp} + \sum_{k=0}^{p-1} \left(\sum_{l \in N} \Gamma'_{l,k}(x) + \sum_{l \in Q} \Gamma_{l,k}(x) \right).$$

Proof. First, we prove that the defining pair of (s'_u) is $(G'(x), \beta)$ with

(b1) $G'(x) = \sum_{j \in Q} x^j \sum_{j=0}^{p-1} x^{pj}$, if $p \equiv 1 \pmod 8$,

(b2) $G'(x) = \left(\sum_{j \in N} x^j + 1 \right) \sum_{j=0}^{p-1} x^{pj}$, if $p \equiv 7 \pmod 8$,

(b3) $G'(x) = \left(\alpha \sum_{j \in Q} x^j + \alpha^2 \sum_{j \in N} x^j \right) \sum_{j=0}^{p-1} x^{pj}$, if $p \equiv 5 \pmod 8$,

(b4) $G'(x) = \left(\alpha^2 \sum_{j \in Q} x^j + \alpha \sum_{j \in N} x^j + 1 \right) \sum_{j=0}^{p-1} x^{pj}$, if $p \equiv 3 \pmod 8$.

Note that

$$\sum_{k=0}^{p-1} \beta^{pu} = \begin{cases} 1, & \text{if } u \in P, \\ 0, & \text{otherwise.} \end{cases}$$

Thus, for $p \equiv 1 \pmod 8$, we have with the choice of β that

$$\sum_{j \in Q} \beta^{ju} \sum_{j=0}^{p-1} \beta^{pju} = 1$$

iff $u \in pQ$. By Theorem 1, we get the desired result. The other three cases can be similarly proved.

4   Trace Representation

The trace function from $\mathbf{F}_{2^n}$ to its subfield $\mathbf{F}_{2^k}$ $(k|n)$ is defined by

$$\mathrm{Tr}^n_k(x) = x + x^{2^k} + x^{2^{2k}} + \ldots + x^{2^{(n/k-1)k}}.$$

For $a, b \in \mathbf{F}_{2^k}$ and $x, y \in \mathbf{F}_{2^n}$, we have $\mathrm{Tr}_k^n(ax + by) = a\mathrm{Tr}_k^n(x) + b\mathrm{Tr}_k^n(y)$. We refer the reader to [16] for details on the trace function.

From Theorems 1 and 2, we only need to represent $\sum_{j=1}^{p-1} x^{jp}$, $Q(x)$, $N(x)$, $Q_j(x)$ and $N_j(x)$ $(0 \leq j < p)$ via trace functions.

Lemma 4. *For all $0 \leq j < p$, we have the following.*

(i) $\displaystyle\sum_{i=1}^{p-1} x^{ip} = \sum_{k=0}^{\frac{p-1}{\lambda}-1} \mathrm{Tr}_1^\lambda(x^{pg^k})$.

(ii) $\displaystyle Q(x) = \sum_{k=0}^{\frac{p-1}{2\lambda}-1} \mathrm{Tr}_1^\lambda(x^{g^{2k}})$, $\displaystyle Q_j(x) = \sum_{k=0}^{\frac{p-1}{2\lambda}-1} \mathrm{Tr}_{p^\epsilon}^{\lambda p^\epsilon}(x^{g^{2kp+j+\delta(j)}})$,

$\displaystyle N(x) = \sum_{k=0}^{\frac{p-1}{2\lambda}-1} \mathrm{Tr}_1^\lambda(x^{g^{2k+1}})$, $\displaystyle N_j(x) = \sum_{k=0}^{\frac{p-1}{2\lambda}-1} \mathrm{Tr}_{p^\epsilon}^{\lambda p^\epsilon}(x^{g^{2kp+j+\delta(j+1)}})$,

if $p \equiv \pm1 \pmod 8$.

(iii) $\displaystyle Q(x) = \sum_{k=0}^{\frac{p-1}{\lambda}-1} \mathrm{Tr}_2^\lambda(x^{g^{2k}})$, $\displaystyle Q_j(x) = \sum_{k=0}^{\frac{p-1}{\lambda}-1} \mathrm{Tr}_{2p^\epsilon}^{\lambda p^\epsilon}(x^{g^{2kp+j+\delta(j)}})$,

$\displaystyle N(x) = \sum_{k=0}^{\frac{p-1}{\lambda}-1} \mathrm{Tr}_2^\lambda(x^{g^{2k+1}})$, $\displaystyle N_j(x) = \sum_{k=0}^{\frac{p-1}{\lambda}-1} \mathrm{Tr}_{2p^\epsilon}^{\lambda p^\epsilon}(x^{g^{2kp+j+\delta(j+1)}})$,

if $p \equiv \pm3 \pmod 8$.

Proof. See [2] and [14] for the proof of (i), $Q(x)$ and $N(x)$ in (ii), respectively. Below we only prove the trace representation of $Q_j(x)$ in (ii), $Q(x)$ and $Q_j(x)$ in (iii), since the rest can be obtained from (8).

(ii) If $p \equiv \pm1 \pmod 8$, then $2 \in Q$. If $2^{p-1} \not\equiv 1 \pmod{p^2}$, then the order of 2 modulo p^2 is λp. We find that a power of 2 modulo p^2 belonging to Q_0 is of the form 2^{ip} $(0 \leq i < \lambda)$, all of which are generated by 2^p $(= g^{\frac{p-1}{\lambda}p})$ modulo p^2 and form a subgroup of Q_0. So we have

$$Q_0 = \cup_{k=0}^{\frac{p-1}{2\lambda}-1} g^{2kp}\langle 2^p\rangle \text{ and } Q_j = \cup_{k=0}^{\frac{p-1}{2\lambda}-1} g^{2kp+j+\delta(j)}\langle 2^p\rangle$$

by (8). Hence we deduce that

$$Q_j(x) = \sum_{u \in Q_j} x^u = \sum_{k=0}^{\frac{p-1}{2\lambda}-1} \mathrm{Tr}_p^{\lambda p}(x^{g^{2kp+j+\delta(j)}}).$$

If $2^{p-1} \equiv 1 \pmod{p^2}$, we see that $2 \in Q_0$ and $\langle 2 \rangle = \{1, 2, 2^2, \ldots, 2^{\lambda-1}\}$ generated by 2 modulo p^2 is a subgroup of Q_0. Then one can similarly get

$$Q_j = \cup_{k=0}^{\frac{p-1}{2\lambda}-1} g^{2kp+j+\delta(j)}\langle 2\rangle \text{ and } Q_j(x) = \sum_{k=0}^{\frac{p-1}{2\lambda}-1} \mathrm{Tr}_1^\lambda(x^{g^{2kp+j+\delta(j)}}).$$

(iii) If $p \equiv \pm 3 \pmod 8$, then $2 \in N$. Thus $\langle 2^2 \rangle = \{1, 2^2, \dots, 2^{\lambda-2}\}$ generated by 4 modulo p is a subgroup of Q. So we have

$$Q = \cup_{k=0}^{\frac{p-1}{\lambda}-1} g^{2k} \langle 2^2 \rangle \ and \ Q(x) = \sum_{k=0}^{\frac{p-1}{\lambda}-1} \mathrm{Tr}_2^{\lambda}(x^{g^{2k}}).$$

If $2^{p-1} \not\equiv 1 \pmod{p^2}$, note that $\langle 2^{2p} \rangle$ is a subgroup of Q_0, then similarly we deduce

$$Q_0 = \cup_{k=0}^{\frac{p-1}{\lambda}-1} g^{2kp} \langle 2^{2p} \rangle \ and \ Q_j(x) = \sum_{k=0}^{\frac{p-1}{\lambda}-1} \mathrm{Tr}_{2p}^{\lambda p}(x^{g^{2kp+j+\delta(j)}}).$$

If $2^{p-1} \equiv 1 \pmod{p^2}$, we see that $2 \in N_0$ and $\langle 2^2 \rangle = \{1, 2^2, \dots, 2^{\lambda-2}\}$ generated by 4 modulo p^2 is a subgroup of Q_0. Similarly, we have

$$Q_j(x) = \sum_{k=0}^{\frac{p-1}{\lambda}-1} \mathrm{Tr}_2^{\lambda}(x^{g^{2kp+j+\delta(j)}}).$$

Denote

$$\rho_k^{(i)} = \sum_{l \in g^i Q} Q_{l+k}(\beta), \quad \eta_k^{(i)} = \sum_{l \in g^i Q} N_{l+k}(\beta), \quad i = 0, 1.$$

We present the trace representation of (e_u) in the following Theorems 3 and 4 without proof since both are immediate results of Lemma 4, Theorems 1 and 2, respectively.

Theorem 3. *Let $\theta = \beta^{u g^{2ip+k+\delta(k+1+j)}}, \xi = \beta^{u g^{2ip+k+\delta(k+j)}}$ and $w > 1$. Then,*

$$e_u = \begin{cases} \sum_{j=0}^{p-1} \sum_{k=0}^{\frac{p-1}{\lambda}-1} \sum_{i=0}^{\frac{p-1}{2\lambda}-1} [\rho_k^{(j)} \mathrm{Tr}_{p^e}^{\lambda p^e}(\theta) + \eta_k^{(j)} \mathrm{Tr}_{p^e}^{\lambda p^e}(\xi)], & p \equiv 1 \pmod 8, \\[2em] \sum_{k=0}^{\frac{p-1}{\lambda}-1} \mathrm{Tr}_1^{\lambda}(\beta^{u p g^k}) + \sum_{j=0}^{p-1} \sum_{k=0}^{\frac{p-1}{\lambda}-1} \sum_{i=0}^{\frac{p-1}{2\lambda}-1} [\rho_k^{(j)} \mathrm{Tr}_{p^e}^{\lambda p^e}(\xi) + \eta_k^{(j)} \mathrm{Tr}_{p^e}^{\lambda p^e}(\theta)], \\ & p \equiv 7 \pmod 8, \\[2em] \sum_{j=0}^{p-1} \sum_{k=0}^{\frac{p-1}{\lambda}-1} \sum_{i=0}^{\frac{p-1}{2\lambda}-1} [\rho_k^{(j)} \mathrm{Tr}_{2p^e}^{\lambda p^e}(\theta) + \eta_k^{(j)} \mathrm{Tr}_{2p^e}^{\lambda p^e}(\xi)], & p \equiv 5 \pmod 8, \\[2em] \sum_{k=0}^{\frac{p-1}{\lambda}-1} \mathrm{Tr}_1^{\lambda}(\beta^{u p g^k}) + \sum_{j=0}^{p-1} \sum_{k=0}^{\frac{p-1}{\lambda}-1} \sum_{i=0}^{\frac{p-1}{\lambda}-1} [\rho_k^{(j)} \mathrm{Tr}_{2p^e}^{\lambda p^e}(\xi) + \eta_k^{(j)} \mathrm{Tr}_{2p^e}^{\lambda p^e}(\theta)], \\ & p \equiv 3 \pmod 8. \end{cases}$$

Theorem 4. *Let $w = 1$ and $\left(\frac{a}{p}\right) = 1$.*

(i) If $p \equiv 1 \pmod 8$, then $e_u = \sum_{i=0}^{\frac{p-1}{2\lambda}-1} \mathrm{Tr}_1^{\lambda}(x^{g^{2i+1}})[\sum_{k=0}^{\frac{p-1}{\lambda}-1} \mathrm{Tr}_1^{\lambda}(\beta^{u p g^k}) + 1]

$$+ \sum_{j=0}^{p-1} \sum_{k=0}^{\frac{p-1}{2\lambda}-1} \sum_{i=0}^{\frac{p-1}{\lambda}-1} [\rho_k^{(j)} \mathrm{Tr}_{p^e}^{\lambda p^e}(\theta) + \eta_k^{(j)} \mathrm{Tr}_{p^e}^{\lambda p^e}(\xi)].$$

(ii) If $p \equiv 7 \pmod 8$, then $e_u = 1 + \sum\limits_{i=0}^{\frac{p-1}{2\lambda}-1} \mathrm{Tr}_1^\lambda(x^{g^{2i}})[\sum\limits_{k=0}^{\frac{p-1}{\lambda}-1} \mathrm{Tr}_1^\lambda(\beta^{upg^k}) + 1]$

$+ \sum\limits_{j=0}^{1} \sum\limits_{k=0}^{p-1} \sum\limits_{i=0}^{\frac{p-1}{2\lambda}-1} [\rho_k^{(j)}\mathrm{Tr}_{p^\epsilon}^{\lambda p^\epsilon}(\xi) + \eta_k^{(j)}\mathrm{Tr}_{p^\epsilon}^{\lambda p^\epsilon}(\theta)].$

(iii) If $p \equiv 5 \pmod 8$, then

$$e_u = \sum\limits_{i=0}^{\frac{p-1}{\lambda}-1} [\alpha\mathrm{Tr}_2^\lambda(x^{g^{2i+1}}) + \alpha^2\mathrm{Tr}_2^\lambda(x^{g^{2i}})][\sum\limits_{k=0}^{\frac{p-1}{\lambda}-1} \mathrm{Tr}_1^\lambda(\beta^{upg^k}) + 1]$$

$$+ \sum\limits_{j=0}^{1} \sum\limits_{k=0}^{p-1} \sum\limits_{i=0}^{\frac{p-1}{\lambda}-1} [\rho_k^{(j)}\mathrm{Tr}_{2p^\epsilon}^{\lambda p^\epsilon}(\theta) + \eta_k^{(j)}\mathrm{Tr}_{2p^\epsilon}^{\lambda p^\epsilon}(\xi)].$$

(iv) If $p \equiv 3 \pmod 8$, then

$$e_u = 1 + \sum\limits_{i=0}^{\frac{p-1}{\lambda}-1} [\alpha^2\mathrm{Tr}_2^\lambda(x^{g^{2i+1}}) + \alpha\mathrm{Tr}_2^\lambda(x^{g^{2i}})][\sum\limits_{k=0}^{\frac{p-1}{\lambda}-1} \mathrm{Tr}_1^\lambda(\beta^{upg^k}) + 1]$$

$$+ \sum\limits_{j=0}^{1} \sum\limits_{k=0}^{p-1} \sum\limits_{i=0}^{\frac{p-1}{\lambda}-1} [\rho_k^{(j)}\mathrm{Tr}_{2p^\epsilon}^{\lambda p^\epsilon}(\xi) + \eta_k^{(j)}\mathrm{Tr}_{2p^\epsilon}^{\lambda p^\epsilon}(\beta^{ug^{2ip+k+\delta(k+j+1)}})].$$

Note: For $w = 1$ and $\left(\frac{a}{p}\right) = -1$, similar to that of $\left(\frac{a}{p}\right) = 1$, one can obtain the defining pair $(G(x), \beta)$ of (e_u) and thus their trace representations.

5   Concluding Remarks

The discrete Fourier transform is a very useful tool for studying the linear complexity of sequences. In this paper, we described the discrete Fourier transform and the trace representation of three families of binary sequences derived from polynomial quotient. From Blahut's theorem [1], one can see that the linear complexity of a binary periodic sequence is equal to the Hamming weight of its discrete Fourier transform [16]. Hence we can get the linear complexity immediately by determining the values of $\eta_j^{(i)}$ and $\rho_j^{(i)}$ for $0 \le j < p$ and $i = 0, 1$. We should mention that the linear complexity of the sequence was presented in [5].

We finally remark that our method can be applied to derive the trace representation and thus the linear complexity of many classes of sequences derived from polynomial quotient. For example, the sequences

$$f_u = \begin{cases} 0, & \text{if } 0 \le q_{p,w}(u) < p/2, \\ 1, & \text{otherwise,} \end{cases}$$

defined in [4] for $w = \frac{p-1}{2}$.

Acknowledgement. X. N. Du was partially supported by the National Natural Science Foundation of China (grants No. 61462077 and 61772022). C. Wu is partially supported by the National Natural Science Foundation of China (grant No. 61772292) and 2016 Development Program for Distinguished Young Scientific Research Talent of Universities in Fujian Province.

References

1. Blahut, R.E.: Transform techniques for error control codes. IBM J. Res. Develop. **23**, 299–315 (1979). https://doi.org/10.1147/rd.233.0299
2. Chen, Z.: Trace representation and linear complexity of binary sequences derived from Fermat quotient. Sci. China Inf. Sci. **57**, 1–10 (2014). https://doi.org/10.1007/s11432-014-5092-x
3. Chen, Z., Du, X.: On the linear complexity of binary threshold sequences derived from Fermat quotient. Des. Codes Cryptogr. **67**, 317–323 (2013). https://doi.org/10.1007/s10623-012-9608-3
4. Chen, Z., Gómez-Pérez, D.: Linear complexity of binary sequences derived from polynomial quotients. In: Helleseth, T., Jedwab, J. (eds.) SETA 2012. LNCS, vol. 7280, pp. 181–189. Springer, Heidelberg (2012). https://doi.org/10.1007/978-3-642-30615-0_17
5. Chen, Z.: Linear complexity of Legendre-polynomial quotient. arXiv:1705.01380
6. Chen, Z., Winterhof, A.: Additive character sums of polynomial quotient. Contemp. Math., Amer. Math. Soc., Providence, RI. **579**, 67–73 (2012). https://doi.org/10.1090/conm/579/11519
7. Cusick, T., Ding, C., Renvall, A.: Stream ciphers and number theory, North-Holland Mathematical Library, vol. 55 (1998)
8. Dai, Z., Gong, G., Song, H.Y.: A trace representation of binary Jacobi sequences. Discrete Math. **309**, 1517–1527 (2009). https://doi.org/10.1016/j.disc.2008.02.024
9. Dai, Z., Gong, G., Song, H., Ye, D.: Trace representation and linear complexity of binary e-th power residue sequences of period p. IEEE Trans. Inform. Theory **57**, 1530–1547 (2011). https://doi.org/10.1109/TIT.2010.2103757
10. Ernvall, R., Metsänkylä, T.: On the p-divisibility of Fermat quotient. Math. Comp. **66**, 1353–1365 (1997). https://doi.org/10.1090/S0025-5718-97-00843-0
11. Golomb, S.W.: Shift Register Sequences, Holden-Day, CA, San Francisco (1967). Revised edition: Aegean Park, CA, Laguna Hills (1982)
12. Shparlinski, I.E.: Character sums with Fermat quotient. Q. J. Math. **62**(4), 1031–1043 (2011)
13. Jungnickel, D.: Finite Fields, Structure and Arithmetics, Bibliographisches Institut, Mannheim (1993)
14. Kim, J.H., Song, H.Y.: Trace representation of Legendre sequences. Des. Codes Cryptogr. **24**, 343–348 (2001). https://doi.org/10.1023/A:1011287607979
15. Kim, J.H., Song, H.Y., Gong, G.: Trace representation of Hall's sextic residue sequences of period $p \equiv 7 \pmod 8$. In: Mathematical Properties of Sequences and Other Combinatorial Structures 2002, Int'l Series in Engineering and Computer Science, vol. 579, pp. 23–32. Springer, Boston (2003). https://doi.org/10.1007/978-1-4615-0304-04
16. Lidl, R., Niederreiter, H.: Finite Fields. Cambridge University Press, Cambridge (1997)

Unified Quantum No-Go Theorems
of Pure States

Hui-Ran Li[1], Ming-Xing Luo[1(✉)], and Hong Lai[2]

[1] Information Security and National Computing Grid Laboratory,
Southwest Jiaotong University, Chengdu 610031, China
luomxgg@163.com
[2] School of Computer and Information Science,
Southwest University, Chongqing 400715, China

Abstract. Various results of the no-cloning theorem and no-superposing theorem in quantum mechanics have been proved using the superposition principle and the linearity of quantum operations. In this paper, we investigate general transformations forbidden by quantum mechanics in order to unify these theorems. We prove that any useful information cannot be created from an unknown pure state which is randomly chosen from a Hilbert space according to the Harr measure. And then, we propose a unified no-go theorem based on a generalized no-superposing result. The new theorem includes various no-go theorems of the no-cloning theorem, no-anticloning theorem, no-splitting theorem as a special case.

Keywords: Quantum no-go theorem · Quantum no-cloning theorem
Quantum operations · Pure states

1 Introduction

In physics, the no-cloning theorem forbids creating an identical copy of an unknown pure state randomly chosen from a state space according to the Harr measure [1,2]. Since its appearance, it has been generalized in several directions. Although the unitary transformation cannot create duplicated states of non orthogonal states, Yuen [3] showed that the photon amplifier is possible [4]. Barnum et al. extended it to the no-broadcast theorem for mixed states [5–7]. Piani et al. [8] proved the no locally broadcasting theorem for correlations of quantum bipartite state which was further extended to the no-unilocal broadcasting theorem [9,10]. Lindblad [11] investigated the invariant elements of operators that are abstract generalizations in a Hilbert space. In [12,13], the generic probabilistic models are explored to treat both classical and quantum theory. Beyond these generalizations with finite-dimensional models and complete positive (CP) mapping, some researchers consider the von Neumann algebra on a Hilbert space [14]. The main difference of them is that the Schwarz mapping on a von Neumann algebra has no related Kraus operator representation [15–17].

© Springer Nature Switzerland AG 2018
X. Sun et al. (Eds.): ICCCS 2018, LNCS 11066, pp. 38–47, 2018.
https://doi.org/10.1007/978-3-030-00015-8_4

The completely positive quantum operations and superposition principle are essential for the no-cloning theorem [1]. If the quantum operations are restricted to unitary, the inverse of a cloning operation is also impossible, which states that an unknown quantum state randomly chosen from a Hilbert space cannot be transformed into a known state using a universal unitary machine. It is named as the no-deleting theorem [18]. Similar to these results, there does not exist a universal quantum machine to superpose two unknown states [19,20] or an unknown state randomly chosen from a Hilbert space and a fixed state [21]. Although these theorems are assumed to be no relationships, Luo et al. have presented some generalized theorems which include them as special cases [21].

Our motivation in this paper is to investigate general forms of these no-go theorems. We firstly present a unified no-go theorem forbidden by a completely positive mapping. The theorem is based on the nothing-not-identity lemma, which guarantees any nontrivial information cannot be created from an unknown state randomly chosen from any subspace of a Hilbert space if the input state is perfectly protected. The new result includes previous quantum no-go theorems as special cases [1, 19–25]. Moreover, it can imply new forbidden statements such as the no-rotation superposing theorem, no-orthogonalizing theorem, no-conjugate theorem or no-entry-splitting theorem. In particular, some results hold for both real and complex Hilbert spaces while others are only for a complex Hilbert space.

The rest of the paper is organized as follows. In Sect. 2, we firstly prove two lemmas. One is used to perfectly protect an unknown state randomly chosen from a Hilbert space of finite dimension while the other is to generalize the non superposing theorem. From these lemmas, we present the first unified theorem which may include various quantum no-go theorems as special cases. In Sect. 3, we propose some new results that are derived from the unified no-go theorem.

2   Preliminaries

In this subsection we present some well-known facts for convenience. Denote the complex or real Hilbert space by $\mathbb{H}$. Let $\{|j\rangle|j = 0, 1, \cdots, d-1\}$ be a normalized basis of a d-dimensional Hilbert space $\mathbb{H}$. Denote $\mathbb{H}^m$ as the tensor space $\mathbb{H}^{\otimes m}$.

In quantum mechanics, a pure state provides a probability distribution for a set of observable. In mathematical formulation, it corresponds to a ray in a Hilbert space from Riesz representation theorem [26] while each observable quantity is associated with a self-adjoint (or Hermitian) and positive semi-definite operator. Here, the ray is a set of nonzero vectors up to a global scalar factor. A unit vector is usually used to represent a pure state while its phase factor can be freely chosen.

In what follows, our consideration is focus on pure states on a Hilbert space of finite dimension, i.e., $\dim(\mathbb{H}) = d \geq 2$ if there is no special statement. The density matrix of a normalized pure state is denoted as $\rho_\psi = |\psi\rangle\langle\psi|$ that is unique, where $|\psi\rangle$ is the representative vector of ρ_ψ. Denote $|\psi\rangle \propto |\phi\rangle$ as $|\psi\rangle = e^{i\theta}|\phi\rangle$ for some phase θ, where ρ_ψ and ρ_ϕ are physically undiscriminating. In the following explanations, we take use of the vector representative of pure state.

Let $\mathcal{M}(\mathbb{H}_1, \mathbb{H}_2)$ be the set of nonzero mappings (or their representative operators) which transform finite-dimensional Hilbert space $\mathbb{H}_1$ into finite-dimensional Hilbert space $\mathbb{H}_2$. Denote $\mathcal{F} : |\psi\rangle \mapsto |\phi\rangle$ as the equivalent form of $\mathcal{F}(|\psi\rangle) = |\phi\rangle$ for $|\psi\rangle$ in $\mathbb{H}_1$ and $|\phi\rangle$ in $\mathbb{H}_2$. Denote $\mathcal{M}(\mathbb{H}, \mathbb{H})$ as $\mathcal{M}(\mathbb{H})$ for short. $\mathcal{CP}(\mathbb{H}_1, \mathbb{H}_2)$ denotes the set of completely positive (CP) mappings which transform pure states on Hilbert space $\mathbb{H}_1$ into pure states in Hilbert space $\mathbb{H}_2$. Note that all CP mappings are physically available in quantum mechanics [15–17]. All unitary mappings of Hilbert space $\mathbb{H}$, denoted as $SU(\mathbb{H})$, are surjective CP mappings and preserving the inner product of $\mathbb{H}$. Note that $SU(\mathbb{H}) \subseteq \mathcal{CP}(\mathbb{H}) \subseteq \mathcal{M}(\mathbb{H})$. Denote $SA(\mathbb{H})$ as all the affine mappings on Hilbert space $\mathbb{H}$ with representative operators $\mathbb{1} + c$ (up to a global factor), where $\mathbb{1}$ denotes the identity operator and c is a nonzero constant.

For each CP mapping $\mathcal{F} \in \mathcal{CP}(\mathbb{H}_1, \mathbb{H}_2)$, it may be represented by $\mathcal{F}(\rho_\psi) = F\rho_\psi F^\dagger$ for all pure states $\rho_\psi \in \mathbb{H}_1$, where F is the representative of $\mathcal{F}$. If the vector representative of a pure state is used, we can rewrite the CP mapping into $\mathcal{F}(|\psi\rangle) \propto F|\psi\rangle$. From the Stinespring's Theorem [15], for each CP mapping $\mathcal{F} \in \mathcal{CP}(\mathbb{H}_1, \mathbb{H}_2)$, there exist a unitary mapping $\mathcal{U} \in SU(\mathbb{H}_1 \otimes \mathbb{H}_2 \otimes \mathbb{H}_P)$ and a projective mapping $\mathcal{P} \in \mathcal{CP}(\mathbb{H}_1 \otimes \mathbb{H}_2 \otimes \mathbb{H}_P, \mathbb{H}_1 \otimes \mathbb{H}_2)$ such that $\mathcal{F} = \mathcal{P} \circ \mathcal{U}$, where $\mathbb{H}_2$ is an ancillary Hilbert space and $\mathbb{H}_P$ is another ancillary Hilbert space used for defining projective mapping $\mathcal{P}$ (named as the probe space for simplicity).

Definition 1. *A nonzero mapping $\mathcal{G} \in \mathcal{M}(\mathbb{H})$ is degenerate if there exists a pure state $|\phi\rangle \in \mathbb{H}$ such that $\mathcal{G}(|\psi\rangle) \propto |\phi\rangle$ for all pure states $|\psi\rangle$ in $\mathbb{H}$. Otherwise, $\mathcal{G}$ is non-degenerate.*

Definition 1 has not restricted the mapping to be linear. This is important for the following statements.

For any two mappings $\mathcal{G}_1, \mathcal{G}_2 \in \mathcal{M}(\mathbb{H}_1, \mathbb{H}_2)$, $\mathcal{G}_1 \propto \mathcal{G}_2$ means that there exists some nonzero constant c satisfying $\mathcal{G}_1(|\phi\rangle) = c\mathcal{G}_2(|\phi\rangle)$ for all pure states $|\phi\rangle$ on $\mathbb{H}_1$.

3 Unified No-Go Theorem with CP Mappings

In this section, we explore a general form of the no-cloning theorem [1], no-superposing theorem [27,28] and no-encoding theorem [29] using CP mappings.

3.1 Generalized No-Go Theorem

Lemma 1. *Let $\mathcal{G}$ be a non-degenerate mapping in $\mathcal{M}(\mathbb{H})$. There does not exist CP mapping $\mathcal{F} \in \mathcal{CP}(\mathbb{H}, \mathbb{H}^2)$ for all pure states $|\psi\rangle$ in complex or real Hilbert $\mathbb{H}$ such that*

$$\mathcal{F}(|\psi\rangle) \propto |\psi\rangle|\varphi\rangle, \tag{1}$$

where $|\varphi\rangle = r\mathcal{G}(|\psi\rangle)$ with a normalization constant r.

Proof. Note that $\mathbb{R}^2 \subset \mathbb{R}^n$ and $\mathbb{R}^2 \subset \mathbb{C}^2 \subset \mathbb{C}^n$. It is sufficient to prove the result for real qubit space $\mathbb{H} = \mathbb{R}^2$. Assume that there exists a CP mapping $\mathcal{F} \in CP(\mathbb{H}, \mathbb{H}^2)$ satisfying Eq. (1). From the Stinespring's Theorem [15], there exist an ancillary state $|\Omega\rangle$ in Hilbert space $\mathbb{H}_A$ with $\dim(\mathbb{H}_A) > 2d$, two orthogonal states $|P_0\rangle$ and $|P_1\rangle$ in Hilbert space $\mathbb{H}_P \subset \mathbb{H}_A$ with $\dim(\mathbb{H}_P) > d$, and a unitary mapping $\mathcal{U} \in SU(\mathbb{H} \otimes \mathbb{H}_A)$ such that

$$\mathcal{U}(|\psi\rangle|\Omega\rangle) \propto p(a,b)|\psi\rangle\mathcal{G}(|\psi\rangle)|P_0\rangle + q(a,b)|\Psi\rangle|P_1\rangle, \tag{2}$$

where the vector representative $|\psi\rangle$ is given by $|\psi\rangle \propto a|0\rangle + b|1\rangle$ with $a^2 + b^2 = 1$. In Eq. (2), $|\Psi\rangle$ is the vector representative of failure state in $\mathbb{H}^2$. $p(a,b)$ and $q(a,b)$ are positive probability functions depending on a and b, and satisfy $p(a,b)^2 + q(a,b)^2 = 1$ for all a, b. In particular, for classical states $|0\rangle$ and $|1\rangle$, it follows that

$$\mathcal{U}(|0\rangle|\Omega\rangle) \propto p_0|0\rangle\mathcal{G}(|0\rangle)|P_0\rangle + q_0|\Psi_0\rangle|P_1\rangle, \tag{3}$$
$$\mathcal{U}(|1\rangle|\Omega\rangle) \propto p_1|1\rangle\mathcal{G}(|1\rangle)|P_0\rangle + q_1|\Psi_1\rangle|P_1\rangle. \tag{4}$$

In Eq. (3), $|\Psi_0\rangle$ is the vector representative of failure state for transforming pure state $|0\rangle$ with probability $q_0 > 0$. $p_0 > 0$ is the corresponding success probability. In Eq. (4), $|\Psi_1\rangle$ is the vector representative of failure state for transforming pure state $|1\rangle$ with probability $q_1 > 0$. $p_1 > 0$ is the corresponding success probability.

Now, from the linearity of unitary mapping, we obtain that

$$\mathcal{U}(|\psi\rangle|\Omega\rangle) \propto |\Phi_0\rangle|P_0\rangle + |\Phi_1\rangle|P_1\rangle, \tag{5}$$

where the vectors $|\Phi_0\rangle$ and $|\Phi_1\rangle$ are respectively given by $|\Phi_0\rangle = ap_0|0\rangle\mathcal{G}(|0\rangle) + bp_1|1\rangle\mathcal{G}(|1\rangle)$ and $|\Phi_1\rangle = ap_0|\Psi_0\rangle + bp_1|\Psi_1\rangle$. Combined with Eq. (2), we obtain

$$ap_0|0\rangle\mathcal{G}(|0\rangle) + bp_1|1\rangle\mathcal{G}(|1\rangle) \propto p(a,b)|\psi\rangle\mathcal{G}(|\psi\rangle) \tag{6}$$

Since $\mathcal{U}$ is continuous on the compact set $\{(a,b) \in \mathbb{R}^2 : a^2 + b^2 = 1\}$ and $p(a,b)$ is assumed to be positive for all a, b, then $p(a,b) \geq c_0$ with a fixed constant $c_0 > 0$. Moreover, the right side of Eq. (6) is a product state for all a, b, it follows that $\mathcal{G}(|0\rangle) \propto \mathcal{G}(|1\rangle)$. Otherwise, decompose $\mathcal{G}(|1\rangle)$ into $\mathcal{G}(|1\rangle) = c\mathcal{G}(|0\rangle) + d\mathcal{G}(|0\rangle)^\perp$ with $d \neq 0$, the left side of Eq. (6) is entangled by using the following equality $ap_0|0\rangle\mathcal{G}(|0\rangle) + bp_1|1\rangle\mathcal{G}(|1\rangle) = ap_0|0\rangle\mathcal{G}(|0\rangle) + bcp_1|1\rangle\mathcal{G}(|0\rangle) + bdp_1|1\rangle\mathcal{G}(|0\rangle)^\perp$ using the Schmidt decomposition for $abp_0p_1d \neq 0$, where $\mathcal{G}(|0\rangle)$ and $\mathcal{G}(|0\rangle)^\perp$ are orthogonal states. Furthermore, $\mathcal{U}$ in Eq. (2) is analytic on open set $|a| < 1$ or $|b| < 1$, we obtain that $p(a,b)|\psi\rangle\mathcal{G}_2(|\psi\rangle)$ is analytic on the same set. In particular, the left side of Eq. (6) is a homogeneous linear function of variables a and b, where the constants p_0, p_1, and the vectors $\mathcal{G}(|0\rangle), \mathcal{G}(|1\rangle)$ are independent of a and b. It follows that $p(a,b)\mathcal{G}(|\psi\rangle)$ is a constant function independent of two variables a and b because $|\psi\rangle$ is a homogeneous linear function of a, b. Hence, $\mathcal{G}(|\psi\rangle) = \frac{1}{p(a,b)}(c_1, c_2)^T \propto (c_1, c_2)^T$ for some constants c_1 and c_2, where T denotes the transpose of a vector. $\mathcal{G}$ is degenerate which is a contradiction to the assumption of $\mathcal{G}$. $\square$

Denote $\mathcal{S}$ as the splitting mapping of complex vector, i.e, $\mathcal{S} : |\psi\rangle \mapsto |\varphi\rangle$ for all vectors $|\psi\rangle = \sum_{j=0}^{d-1} r_j e^{i\theta_j} |j\rangle \in \mathbb{C}^d$, where $|\varphi\rangle = \sum_{j=0}^{d-1} r_j \in \mathbb{R}^d$ (the amplitude vector of $|\varphi\rangle$) or $|\varphi\rangle = \frac{1}{\sqrt{d}} \sum_{j=0}^{d-1} e^{i\theta_j} |j\rangle \in [0, 2\pi)^{\times d}$ (the phase vector of $|\varphi\rangle$). Lemma 1 implies the no-partial-cloning theorem as follows:

Corollary 1 *(No-partial-cloning theorem). There does not exist CP mapping $\mathcal{F} \in CP(\mathbb{H}, \mathbb{H}^2)$ for all pure states $|\psi\rangle$ in complex Hilbert space $\mathbb{H}$ such that*

$$\mathcal{F}(|\psi\rangle) \propto |\psi\rangle |\mathcal{S}(|\psi\rangle)\rangle. \tag{7}$$

If the mapping $\mathcal{G}$ is non-degenerate, combined with the quantum state discrimination it easily follows that the universal cloning is possible for classical systems (Theorem 2 in [13]). If the post-selection of a quantum measurement is available, the universal cloning holds for linearly independent states [29].

Lemma 2. *Let α, β be complex constants satisfying $|\alpha|^2 + |\beta|^2 = 1$ and $|\alpha| \neq 1$, and $\mathcal{G}$ be a mapping on complex or real Hilbert space $\mathbb{H}$. Then there does not exist CP mapping $\mathcal{F} \in CP(\mathbb{H})$ for all pure states $|\psi\rangle$ on $\mathbb{H}$ such that*

$$\mathcal{F}(|\psi\rangle) \propto |\varphi\rangle \tag{8}$$

if $\mathcal{G}$ satisfies one of the following conditions:

(i) $\mathcal{G} \notin CP(\mathbb{H})$ when $\alpha = 0$;
(ii) $\mathcal{G}$ is nonlinear (not homogeneous linear) when $\alpha \neq 0$;

where the vector representative $|\varphi\rangle \propto r(\alpha|\psi\rangle + \beta\mathcal{G}(|\psi\rangle))$ with a normalization constant r.

The proof is similar to that of Lemma 1.

Theorem 1. *Let α_j, β_j be complex constants satisfying $|\alpha_j|^2 + |\beta_j|^2 = 1$, and $\mathcal{G}_j$ be a mapping on complex or real Hilbert space $\mathbb{H}$, $j = 1, 2, \cdots, m$. Then there does not exist CP mapping $\mathcal{F} \in CP(\mathbb{H}, \mathbb{H}^m)$ for all pure states $|\psi\rangle \in \mathbb{H}$ such that*

$$\mathcal{F}(|\psi\rangle) \propto \otimes_{j=1}^{m} |\varphi_j\rangle \tag{9}$$

if $\mathcal{G}_1, \mathcal{G}_2, \cdots, \mathcal{G}_m$ satisfy one of the following conditions:

(i) there exist two mappings $\mathcal{G}_i$ and $\mathcal{G}_j$ such that they are not affine mappings in $AF(\mathbb{H})$ or non-identity mappings;
(ii) there exists a nonlinear mapping $\mathcal{G}_j$ when $\alpha_j \neq 0$ and $\beta_j \neq 0$;
(iii) there exists a mapping $\mathcal{G}_j \notin CP(\mathbb{H})$ when $\alpha_i = 0$ for all $i = 1, 2, \cdots, m$;

where the vector representative $|\varphi_j\rangle \propto \alpha_j|\psi\rangle + \beta_j\mathcal{G}_j(|\psi\rangle)$, $j = 1, 2, \cdots, m$.

Proof. Similar to the proof in Ref. [1], it is easy to prove the no-cloning result for all real states. Moreover, from Lemmas 1 and 2, we only need to prove the first case (i). For the simplicity, assume that exists a CP mapping $\mathcal{F} \in \mathcal{CP}(\mathbb{H}, \mathbb{H}^2)$ for all states $|\psi\rangle \in \mathbb{H}$ such that

$$\mathcal{F}(|\psi\rangle) \propto |\varphi_1\rangle|\varphi_2\rangle, \tag{10}$$

where the vector representative $|\varphi_j\rangle \propto r_j(\alpha_j|\psi\rangle + \beta_j\mathcal{G}_j(|\psi\rangle))$ with normalization constant r_j, and $\mathcal{G}_j$ is non-degenerate mapping, $j = 1, 2$.

If one mapping $\mathcal{G}_j$ is proportional to the identity mapping, i.e., $\mathcal{G}_j \propto \mathbb{1}$, it contradicts to Lemma 1. In general, it is sufficient to prove the result for qubit space $\mathbb{H} := \mathbb{R}^2$ (or $\mathbb{C}^2$). From the Stinespring Theorem [15], there exist an ancillary state $|\Omega\rangle$ on Hilbert space $\mathbb{H}_A$, two orthogonal states $|P_0\rangle, |P_1\rangle$ in Hilbert space $\mathbb{H}_P \subset \mathbb{H}_A$, and a unitary mapping $\mathcal{U} \in SU(\mathbb{H} \otimes \mathbb{H}_A)$ such that

$$\mathcal{U}(|\psi\rangle|\Omega\rangle) \propto p(a, b)|\varphi_1\rangle|\varphi_2\rangle|P_0\rangle + q(a, b)|\Psi\rangle|P_1\rangle \tag{11}$$

where the vector representative $|\psi\rangle \propto a|0\rangle + b|1\rangle$ with $a^2 + b^2 = 1$. $|\Psi\rangle$ is the vector representative of failure state in Hilbert space $\mathbb{H}^2$. $p(a, b)$ and $q(a, b)$ are positive probability functions of variables a and b, and satisfy $p(a, b)^2 + q(a, b)^2 = 1$ for all a, b. In particular, for classical states $|0\rangle$ and $|1\rangle$, it follows that

$$\mathcal{U}(|0\rangle|\Omega\rangle) \propto p_0|\varphi_{10}\rangle|\varphi_{20}\rangle|P_0\rangle + q_0|\Psi_0\rangle|P_1\rangle, \tag{12}$$

$$\mathcal{U}(|1\rangle|\Omega\rangle) \propto p_1|\varphi_{11}\rangle|\varphi_{21}\rangle|P_0\rangle + q_1|\Psi_1\rangle|P_1\rangle, \tag{13}$$

where $|\varphi_{ij}\rangle \propto r_{ij}(\alpha_j|j\rangle + \beta_j\mathcal{G}_i(|j\rangle))$ with normalization constant r_{ij}, $i = 1, 2$ and $j = 0, 1$. In Eq. (12), $|\Psi_0\rangle$ is the vector representative of failure state for transforming pure state $|0\rangle$ with probability $q_0 > 0$. $p_0 > 0$ is the corresponding success probability. In Eq. (13), $|\Psi_1\rangle$ is the vector representative of failure state for transforming pure state $|1\rangle$ with probability $q_1 > 0$. $p_1 > 0$ is the corresponding success probability.

From the linearity of unitary mapping, we obtain that

$$\mathcal{U}(|\psi\rangle|\Omega\rangle) \propto |\Phi_0\rangle|P_0\rangle + |\Phi_1\rangle|P_1\rangle, \tag{14}$$

where $|\Phi_0\rangle$ and $|\Phi_2\rangle$ are respectively given by $|\Phi_0\rangle = ap_0|\varphi_{10}\rangle|\varphi_{20}\rangle + bp_1|\varphi_{11}\rangle|\varphi_{21}\rangle$ and $|\Phi_1\rangle = ap_0|\Psi_0\rangle + bp_1|\Psi_1\rangle$. Combined with Eqs. (10) and (11), we obtain

$$ap_0|\varphi_{10}\rangle|\varphi_{20}\rangle + bp_1|\varphi_{11}\rangle|\varphi_{21}\rangle \propto p(a, b)|\varphi_1\rangle|\varphi_2\rangle \tag{15}$$

Since the right side of Eq. (15) is a product state for all a, b, it follows that $|\varphi_{10}\rangle \propto |\varphi_{11}\rangle$ or $|\varphi_{20}\rangle \propto |\varphi_{21}\rangle$. Otherwise, the left side of Eq. (15) is entangled. For convenience, assume that $|\varphi_{10}\rangle \propto |\varphi_{11}\rangle$, i.e, $\mathcal{G}_1(|j\rangle) \propto |j\rangle$, $j = 0, 1$. Note that the left side of Eq. (15) is a homogeneous linear function of two variables a and b because the vectors $|\varphi_{10}\rangle, |\varphi_{11}\rangle, |\varphi_{20}\rangle$ and $|\varphi_{21}\rangle$ are independent of a, b. It means that $p(a, b)|\varphi_1\rangle|\varphi_2\rangle$ should be a homogeneous linear function of two variables a and b. Since $\mathcal{U}$ is continuous on compact set $\{(a, b) | |a|^2 + |b|^2 = 1\}$,

$p(a, b) \geq c_0$ with a fixed constant $c_0 > 0$, where $p(a, b)$ is assumed to be positive for all values of a and b with $|a|^2 + |b|^2 = 1$. So, we obtain that $|\varphi_1\rangle|\varphi_2\rangle \propto \frac{1}{p(a,b)}|\varphi_{10}\rangle(ap_0|\varphi_{20}\rangle + bp_1|\varphi_{21}\rangle)$ for all a, b. It follows that $|\varphi_1\rangle \propto |\varphi_{10}\rangle$ and $|\varphi_2\rangle \propto ap_0|\varphi_{20}\rangle + bp_1|\varphi_{21}\rangle$. Hence, from the definitions of $|\varphi_1\rangle$ and $|\varphi_2\rangle$, we obtain $\mathcal{G}_1 \propto \mathbb{1} + c$ with a constant c (i.e, $\mathcal{G}_1 \in AF(\mathbb{H})$) and $\mathcal{G}_2 \propto \mathbb{1}$. This contradicts to the assumption of $\mathcal{G}_1$. $\square$

If assume that all mappings $\mathcal{G}_j$s are identity mapping, i.e., $\mathcal{G}_j \propto \mathbb{1}$ for all $j = 1, 2, \cdots, m$, Theorem 1 reduces to the quantum no-cloning theorem [1]. If $\alpha_j = 0$ and $\mathcal{G}_j$ is orthogonalization mapping for all $j = 1, 2, \cdots, m$, Theorem 1 implies the quantum no-anticloning theorem [30]. In order to prove the quantum no-splitting theorem [31], we can let $|\phi_1\rangle$ and $|\phi_2\rangle$ be the split states of an unknown state $|\psi\rangle$. It can be completed by assuming $r_j(\alpha_j|\psi\rangle + \beta_j\mathcal{G}_j(|\psi\rangle)) \propto |\phi_j\rangle$, $j = 1, 2$. Similarly, Theorem 1 may yield to the no-partial erasure theorem [31] or the no-encoding theorem [29] which includes the no-superposing theorem [27] as a special case.

3.2   New No-Go Theorems

In Sect. 3.1, a unified no-go theorem has been proved. In this section, we present new results inspired by Theorem 1. If all the mappings $\mathcal{G}_1$, $\mathcal{G}_2, \cdots, \mathcal{G}_m$ are restricted to be rotation mappings of d-dimensional Hilbert space $\mathbb{H}$, Theorem 1 reduces to the nonexistence of the rotation-superposing theorem as follows.

Corollary 2 *(The no-rotation-superposing theorem). Let α_j, β_j be complex constants satisfying $|\alpha_j|^2 + |\beta_j|^2 = 1$, $\mathcal{G}_j$ be a rotation mapping with representative $G_j \in SU(\mathbb{H})$ for complex Hilbert space $\mathbb{H}$ (or orthogonal matrix $G_j \in SO(\mathbb{H})$ for real Hilbert space $\mathbb{H}$), $j = 1, 2, \cdots, m$. Then there does not exist CP mapping $\mathcal{F} \in \mathcal{CP}(\mathbb{H}, \mathbb{H}^m)$ with $m \geq 2$ for all pure states $|\psi\rangle \in \mathbb{H}$ such that*

$$\mathcal{F}(|\psi\rangle) \propto \otimes_{j=1}^{m}|\phi_j\rangle, \qquad (16)$$

where the vector representative $|\phi_j\rangle \propto r_j(\alpha_j|\psi\rangle + \beta_j G_j|\psi\rangle)$ with the normalization constant r_j, and $j = 1, 2, \cdots, m$.

Note that when $m = 1$, the matrix $\alpha_1 I + \beta_1 G_1$ can induce a CP mapping for all nonzero constants α_1, β_1 and matrix G_1. In particular, when $\alpha = 0$, the corollary reduces to the no-rotation-cloning theorem as follows.

Corollary 3 *(The no-rotation-superposing theorem). Let α_j, β_j be complex constants satisfying $|\alpha_j|^2 + |\beta_j|^2 = 1$, $j = 1, 2, \cdots, m$. Then there does not exist CP mapping $\mathcal{F} \in \mathcal{CP}(\mathbb{H}, \mathbb{H}^m)$ with $m \geq 2$ for all pure states $|\psi\rangle$ in Hilbert space $\mathbb{H}$ such that*

$$\mathcal{F}(|\psi\rangle) \propto \otimes_{j=1}^{m}(G_j|\phi_j\rangle) \qquad (17)$$

where $G_j \in SU(\mathbb{H})$ for complex Hilbert space $\mathbb{H}$ (or $G_j \in SO(\mathbb{H})$ for real Hilbert space $\mathbb{H}$), $j = 1, 2, \cdots, m$.

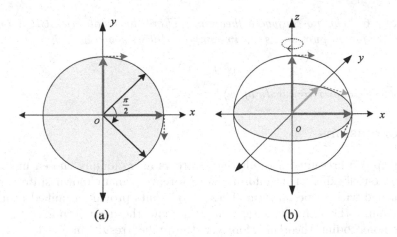

(a)   (b)

Fig. 1. The schematic orthogonalization of qubit states randomly chosen from a Hilbert space according to the Harr measure in terms of their vector representatives. (a) Qubit states in $\mathbb{R}^2$. (b) Qubit states in $\mathbb{C}^2$. (Color figure online)

The corollary implies the no-cloning theorem [1]. Moreover, when $\mathcal{G}$ is orthogonalization mapping, i,e., $\mathcal{G} : |\psi\rangle \mapsto |\psi^\perp\rangle$), Theorem 1 reduces to the following no-orthogonal cloning theorem, where $|\psi^\perp\rangle$ is orthogonal to $|\psi\rangle$.

Corollary 4 *(The no-orthogonal-cloning theorem). There does not exist CP mapping $\mathcal{F} \in \mathcal{CP}(\mathbb{H}, \mathbb{H}^m)$ for all pure states $|\psi\rangle$ in complex Hilbert space $\mathbb{H}$ such that*

$$\mathcal{F}(|\psi\rangle) \propto |\psi^\perp\rangle^{\otimes m}, \tag{18}$$

where $|\psi^\perp\rangle$ is orthogonal to $|\psi\rangle$.

When $m = 1$, Corollary 4 reduces to the no-orthogonalizing theorem, i.e, the orthogonalization mapping of all pure states with complex vector representatives is physically unavailable (Fig. 1).

Corollary 5 *(The no-orthogonalizing theorem). There does not exist CP mapping $\mathcal{F} \in \mathcal{CP}(\mathbb{H})$ for all pure states $|\psi\rangle$ in complex Hilbert space $\mathbb{H}$ such that*

$$\mathcal{F}(|\psi\rangle) \propto |\psi^\perp\rangle, \tag{19}$$

where $|\psi^\perp\rangle$ is orthogonal to $|\psi\rangle$.

Note that $\mathbb{C}^n$ is equivalent to $\mathbb{R}^{2n-1}$ up to a global phase. The proposition implies the non-orthogonalizing theorem. Let U be the matrix representative of $\mathcal{U} \in \mathcal{CP}(\mathbb{H})$. Define $r(|\psi\rangle) = |\langle\psi|U|\psi\rangle|$ for each vector $|\psi\rangle$. From the proof above, we obtain that $r(|\psi\rangle)$ cannot be constant. In fact, r has pole or peak around each eigenvector of U. In detail, let λ be an eigenvalue and $|\varphi\rangle$ be its corresponding eigenvector. For each vector $|\phi\rangle = |\varphi\rangle + \varepsilon|\psi\rangle$ with $0 < \varepsilon \ll 1$ and $|\psi\rangle$ being normalized vector, we obtain that $r(|\phi\rangle) \approx |\lambda| + O(\varepsilon)$.

46   H.-R. Li et al.

Corollary 6 *(The no-conjugate theorem).* *There does not exist CP mapping* $\mathcal{F} \in \mathcal{CP}(\mathbb{H})$ *for all pure states* $|\psi\rangle$ *in complex Hilbert space* $\mathbb{H}$ *such that*

$$\mathcal{F}(|\psi\rangle) \propto |\overline{\psi}\rangle, \tag{20}$$

where $|\overline{\psi}\rangle$ *is complex conjugate of* $|\psi\rangle$.

4 Conclusions

To sum up, we presented a result that protects an randomly chosen unknown state without leaking of its information. Moreover, an unknown state cannot be disturbed with a special form. These two results provide a unified result of the no-cloning theorem, the no-splitting theorem, the no-superposing theorem and the no-encoding theorem. Moreover, the unified result implies lots of new no-go theorems. All of these results hold for pure states. It remains unknown for a unified form of mixed state (the continuous variable) or correlations of multipartite entanglements.

Acknowledgements. This work was supported by the National Natural Science Foundation of China (Nos. 61772437, 61702427), Sichuan Youth Science and Technique Foundation (No. 2017JQ0048), and Fundamental Research Funds for the Central Universities (Nos.2018GF07, XDJK2016C043).

References

1. Wootters, W.K., Zurek, W.H.: A single quantum cannot be cloned. Nature **299**, 802 (1982)
2. Diecks, D.: Communication by EPR devices. Phys. Lett. A **92**, 271 (1982)
3. Yuen, H.P.: Amplification of quantum states and noiseless photon amplifiers. Phys. Lett. A **113**, 405–407 (1986)
4. Peres, A.: Quantum Theory: Concepts and Methods. Kluwer Academic Publishers, Boston (1995)
5. Barnum, H., Caves, C.M., Fuchs, C.A., Jozsa, R., Schumacher, B.: Noncommuting mixed states cannot be broadcast. Phys. Rev. Lett. **76**, 2818–2821 (1996)
6. Barnum, H., Barrett, J., Leifer, M., Wilce, A.: Generalized no-broadcasting theorem. Phys. Rev. Lett. **99**, 240501 (2007)
7. Kalev, A., Hen, I.: No-broadcasting theorem and its classical counterpart. Phys. Rev. Lett. **100**, 210502 (2008)
8. Piani, M., Horodecki, P., Horodecki, R.: No-local-broadcasting theorem for multipartite quantum correlations. Phys. Rev. Lett. **100**, 090502 (2008)
9. Luo, S.L.: On quantum no-broadcasting. Lett. Math. Phys. **92**, 143 (2010)
10. Luo, S.L., Sun, W.: Decomposition of bipartite states with applications to quantum no-broadcasting theorems. Phys. Rev. A **82**, 012338 (2010)
11. Lindblad, G.: A general no-cloning theorem. Lett. Math. Phys. **47**, 189 (1999)
12. Barnum, H., Barrett, J., Leifer, M., Wilce, A.: Cloning and broadcasting in generic probabilistic theories, arXiv:quant-ph/0611295 (2006)
13. Barnum, H., Barrett, J., Leifer, M., Wilce, A.: Generalized no-broadcasting theorem. Phys. Rev. Lett. **99**, 240501 (2007)

14. Kaniowski, K., Lubnauer, K., Łuczak, A.: Multicloning and multibroadcasting in operator algebras. Quart. J. Math. **66**, 191–192 (2015)

15. Stinespring, W.F.: Positive functions on C^*-algebras. Proc. Am. Math. Soc. **6**, 211–216 (1955)

16. Choi, M.-D.: Completely positive maps on complex matrices. Linear Algebra Appl. **10**, 285–290 (1975)

17. Kraus, K.: States, Effects and Operations: Fundamental Notions of Quantum Theory. Springer, New York (1983)

18. Miyadera, T., Imai, H.: No-cloning theorem on quantum logics. J. Math. Phys. **50**, 1063 (2009)

19. Niestegge, G.: Non-classical conditional probability and the quantum no-cloning theorem. Phys. Scr. **90**, 095101 (2015)

20. D'Ariano, G.M., Perinotti, P.: Quantum no-stretching: a geometrical interpretation of the no-cloning theorem. Phys. Lett. A **373**, 2416–2419 (2009)

21. Abramsky, S.: Semantic Techinques in Quantum Computation. In: Gay, S., Mackie, I. (ed.), pp. 1–28. Cambridge University Press, Cambridge (2010)

22. Bennett, C.H., Brassard, G.: Proceedings of IEEE International Conference on Computers, Systems and Signal Processing, Bangalore, India, p. 175. IEEE, New York (1984)

23. Shor, P.W., Preskill, J.: Simple proof of security of the BB84 quantum key distribution protocol. Phys. Rev. Lett. **85**, 441 (2000)

24. Lo, H.-K., Chau, H.F.: Unconditional security of quantum key distribution over arbitrarily long distances. Science **283**, 2050–2056 (1999)

25. Cerf, N.J., Bourennane, M., Karlsson, A., Gisin, N.: Security of quantum key distribution using d-level systems. Phys. Rev. Lett. **88**(12), 127902 (2002)

26. Riesz, F.C.: Sur les operations fonctionelles lineaires. R. Acad. Sci. Paris. **149**, 974–977 (1909)

27. Oszmaniec, M., Grudka, A., Horodecki, M., Wójcik, A.: Creation of superposition of unknown quantum states. Phys. Rev. Lett. **116**, 110403 (2016)

28. Alvarez-Rodriguez, U., Sanz, M., Lamata, L., Solano, E.: The forbidden quantum adder. Sci. Rep. **5**, 11983 (2015)

29. Luo, M.L., Li, H.R., Lai, H., Wang, X.: Unified quantum no-go theorems and transforming of quantum pure states in a restricted set. Quantum Inf. Process. **16**, 297 (2017)

30. Pati, A.K.: General impossible operations in quantum information. Phys. Rev. A **66**, 062319 (2002)

31. Pati, A.K., Sanders, B.C.: No-partial erasure of quantum information. Phys. Lett. A **359**, 31–36 (2006)

VideoChain: Trusted Video Surveillance Based on Blockchain for Campus

Mingda Liu$^{(\boxtimes)}$ ⓘ, Jing Shang$^{(\boxtimes)}$ ⓘ, Peng Liu$^{(\boxtimes)}$ ⓘ,
Yijuan Shi$^{(\boxtimes)}$ ⓘ, and Mian Wang$^{(\boxtimes)}$ ⓘ

Jiangnan Institute of Computing Technology, Wuxi 214083, China
happyliumd@163.com

Abstract. We are living in the age that crisis events happen everywhere and every day. Video evidence plays an important role in restoring the truth of the incident. The credibility of video evidence is gradually declining. On the one hand, the credibility of the government has been questioned. On the other hand, malicious attackers will distort the video and publish it on the Internet to mislead public. Inspired by the blockchain, this paper proposes a model based on blockchain to ensure the credibility of video evidence, which is called Video-Chain. VideoChain is essentially a blockchain system, but different from digital currency such as Bitcoin. It records the hash of the surveillance video. This paper takes the campus Video Surveillance as an example to describe the architecture and operation of VideoChain. We also give a consensus protocol based on the proof of stake according to the application scenario. The analysis shows that VideoChain is traceable and non-tampering, which can effectively ensure the credibility of video surveillance data. It also has good operational efficiency. This research is of great significance to enhance the trust between the government and citizens, which will improve the credibility of the government.

Keywords: Blockchain · Video evidence · Trust

1 Introduction

Recent years, the development of the mobile Internet has broken the limits of using Internet from both time and space [1]. The public can access information on the Internet anytime, anywhere, and express their opinions. However, just as every coin, network technology also has two sides. When sudden public events occur, people's emotions to the events can quickly spread and interact with each other online. The government occupies a dominant position in the governance of public opinion. When fails, the government even becomes the object of public opinion attacking. Regrettably, due to the long-term accumulation of emotions, the government's credibility has shown a downward trend. This is realistic and unavoidable.

Taking the "Red-Yellow-Blue" kindergarten incident in China in 2017 as an example [2]. At the beginning, government has only responsibility for the ineffective supervision. However, because there are still flaws in public services, the government has not established an effective communication mechanism with the public. The status of investigations is not transparent and the public cannot know the progress. In

X. Sun et al. (Eds.): ICCCS 2018, LNCS 11066, pp. 48–58, 2018.
https://doi.org/10.1007/978-3-030-00015-8_5

addition, the ability of the public to screen false information on the Internet is insufficient, so it is vulnerable to malicious misdirection. This eventually leads to overwhelming sentiment on the Internet.

AS the most direct evidence in public emergencies, Surveillance video can restore the truth of public events and effectively calm public emotions. In the public emergency, there is no effective mutual trust communication mechanism between government and public. Besides, the time at which video surveillance announced is often the time when the public is most "angered". Two reasons cause the credibility of the video is often questioned. At this time, the two sides usually lack effective evidence to prove themselves. The government officials will be helpless "The result is clear and why they don't believe it." The public is dominated by the Internet sentiment. They think that "evidence must have been tampered with and must be deceiving us." Now there is no technical solution. This paper aims to start with a technical perspective, to find a suitable method of building a mutual trust bridge between the government and the public.

Inspired by blockchain [3], we propose a credible video surveillance system for campus video surveillance to solve the above problems. The Bitcoin system was proposed by Satoshi Nakamoto in 2008 as a decentralized database. Its underlying technology blockchain has received extensive attention from researchers due to its decentralized, non-tampering, and traceable features. Blockchain is an combination of traditional technologies such as distributed database, P2P, consensus protocol, and encryption algorithms [4–6]. In a blockchain system, there is no trusted center. Only when more than half of users jointly modify the database can it take effect. Note that only the leader node's modifications to the blockchain will be accepted. The algorithm that elects the leader is called the consensus protocol. In short, any data written into the blockchain system can be basically regarded as non-tampering and traceable when most participating users are trusted.

With the development of blockchain, the Public Blockchain represented by Bitcoin has exposed a series of defects, such as low transaction rate and poor privacy protection. At the same time, the completely decentralized model is not suitable for all application scenarios. For example, in the financial sector, the authority of banks and stock exchanges is obviously higher than ordinary users. Driven by application, the Consortium Blockchain [7] came into being. Consortium Blockchain refers to a blockchain in which several agencies participate in the management. It runs multiple "big nodes", which cause the degree of decentralization reduced, while sacrificing security. However, security and efficiency are contradictory. The Consortium Blockchain can effectively simplify consensus protocols and greatly increase the transaction rate of the blockchain. There is an admission mechanism that could help overcome the privacy issue of Public blockchain [8–11]. Introducing blockchain into credible video surveillance system is not an easy task. Challenges as follows:

- Store evidence and original data.

In a credible video surveillance system, data is divided into two types. One is the original video data. The amount of original data is huge. It usually requires to store at least two weeks. The other is the integrity evidence of surveillance video, which is essentially the hash. As we all know, the amount of hash data is small. The current blockchain architecture is not suitable for huge data such as video. We need to design a special storage structure according to both data.

- Special consensus protocol.

In the application scenario of this paper, the purpose of blockchain is to enhance the credibility of video evidence and make users believe the integrity evidence has not been tampered. So we are more concerned about the blockchain against tampering. Because special application scenario determines special consensus protocol, the number of participating nodes, the power and responsibility, and the transaction rate are all important factors affecting the consensus protocol. We need to design a consensus protocol which is consistent with the application scenario.

- Complex authority of data.

Different characters have different permissions to different data. Especially in the campus scene, the issue of privacy protection for minors will be involved. The original video can only be viewed by the parents of the students, which shouldn't be spread. Evidence data on the blockchain is expected to be seen by more people. Because the more participating nodes, the stronger the ability of tamper resistance, which is determined by the technical principle of the blockchain.

In this paper, to solve the challenges discussed above, we propose a trusted video surveillance based on blockchain for campus, called **VideoChain**. **VideoChain** is developed based on a four-layer blockchain architecture, the same as traditional architecture, but we simplify it.

The following are contributions:

- As far as we know, this is the first work that introduces blockchain into video surveillance system. It could ensure the official and the public agree on the credibility of the video evidence, at the technical level.
- Propose a method of combining blockchain with traditional data storage. We designed an efficient storage structure, storing original data in traditional databases, while video integrity evidence on blockchain. For complex data permissions, we design two core parts of blockchain system: *Update Blockchain* and *Verify Evidence on Blockchain*.
- Propose a high transaction rate consensus protocol for video surveillance application scenarios.
- We analyze the security and efficiency of VideoChain in theory.

2   Problem Statement

2.1   System Model

As can be seen in Fig. 1, there are four kinds of participant in VideoChain: admin, school, parent, and ordinary man. Admin and every school hold a storage sever, which response for store blockchain and original data. Participants and ordinary man also need storage, but the amount of data they hold is small, their PC is enough. Now we describe the participant in details.

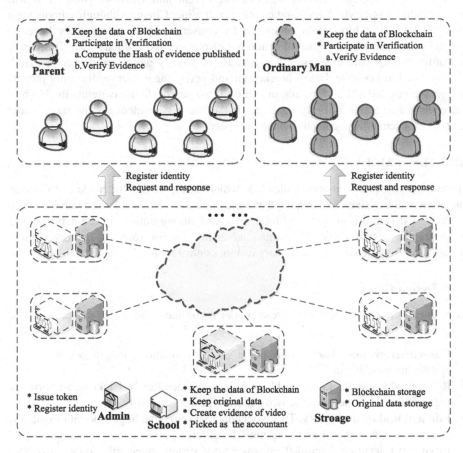

Fig. 1. Framework of **VideoChain**

VideoChain is a kind of Consortium blockchain, everyone must register a legal identity, and then get a token which is used to represent his identity. Admin take this responsibility. In the campus video surveillance scene, admin can be played by government or police office.

School have four duties: (1) Create the evidence of video. In fact, cameras are placed across every corner of the campus. So, school is the birthplace of video. When cameras create new video, the sever will compute the hash of video per 10 min as example. (2) Keep original data and blockchain. Especially for original data, only school have the ability to store. (3) Picked as the leader. Just as Bitcoin, blockchain system always needs leader to update it. The school itself can play the role. On the one hand, school don't have the motivation to tamper the evidence at beginning, because the we need these video as evidence at least one hour later. Integrity evidence has been already written into blockchain. On the other hand, Consortium blockchain need "big node" to be the leader, which is more trusted than ordinary node.

There two different users in VideoChain, Parent and Ordinary Man, who will register their identity via Admin and connect with VideoChain. Although schools have the right to update blockchain controlled by consensus protocol, but they have no method to tamper, owing to the huge number of parents and ordinary men. But parent and ordinary man hold different duties, because of privacy protection for minors. Both of them need to keep the data of blockchain and verify the evidence. But only parents can get the original video when admin publish it, so parent should compute the Hash of video published as the integrity evidence. If the integrity evidence is the same as the data on blockchain, it means the video is trusted.

2.2 Threat Model

There is a Certificate Authority, called CA, which is responsible for create certificate as the token of the system. We assume that an active adversary is able to control the web traffic, and it can also tamper, and forge message among entities in the network. For cryptographic assumptions, we assume adversary cannot forge signatures without private key. And the strongest adversary cannot control more 51% nodes in blockchain.

2.3 Design Goals

According to system model and thread model mentioned above, we put forward our design goals.

- **Consensus fairness.** Each school has a similar probability to generate blocks for update the blockchain.
- **Reliable storage.** The data on blockchain don't need extra backups, the original video data should be stored at two different places randomly.
- **Efficient update and verify.** This blockchain system have huge amount of data, the process of updating and verifying must be efficient.
- **Intrusion tolerance.** Even if there was a very strong adversary, we can also get a real result.

3 Architecture of VideoChain

3.1 Overview of VideoChain

In this paper, we design a trusted video surveillance system based on a four-layer blockchain architecture that includes data layer, network layer, extension layer, and application layer. The architecture of VideoChain is described in Fig. 2. In *data layer*, to combine two types of data, we design a new data storage structure called **TVES** (Trusted Video Evidence Storage), proposing a valid strategy to decide the storage location. In *network layer*, this layer provides the basic channel of communication. It might be an obstacle for our system, because there is also original video data transferring via this layer. We will design special mechanism to alleviate it. In *extension layer*, we design a high transaction rate consensus protocol, called **VCCP** (VideoChain consensus protocol). In *application layer*, we propose two core processes of VideoChain: Update and Verify.

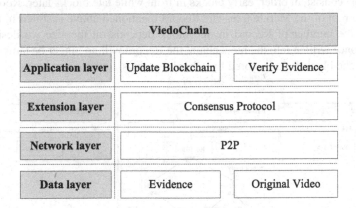

Fig. 2. Architecture of **VideoChain**

3.2 Data Layer

1. Original video data

Original video data will occupy huge amount of storage resource, but a reliable storage system always needs three copies, it seems very hard to balance. We solve this problem by three steps:

i. *Create integrity evidence.* The camera collect video and cut it per 10 min as a part. As we all know, original video from camera is always huge, so we must compress it while making sure identifiable. It is a mature technology. Note that, the original video data refers to the compressed video data in our paper. After compressing, the sever compute the hash of this piece of video, as the integrity evidence.

ii. Backup original video data. We implement backup mechanism at two level. On the one hand, video-generated schools need to have dual backup, it is a conventional practice. On the other hand, a remote node will be picked randomly to store the video, which will improve the reliability.

iii. Report to blockchain agent. The sever will send useful information to the blockchain agent, which runs on the same school and provides blockchain related service. Useful information means it can accurately describe the integrity evidence of the video clip, including Timestamp, Integrity Evidence, Location, and Nonce. We call the data set about one video clip as a Record, which is similar to a transaction record in Bitcoin.

2. Blockchain

Blockchain is a chained data structure, so as VideoChain, the hash structure shown in the Fig. 3. Every block has a head and a body. The block head include PrevBlockHash, Leader, and Root Hash. PrevBlockHash is the hash of the previous block, which is used to ensure the consistent order, early blocks in front while late blocks later. Root Hash is actually the root of the Merkle tree. The Record mentioned above is stored in the block body, and the number of Record in one block depends on the size we designed. In summary, once written into the blockchain, the Record will no longer be tampered with by others. The blockchain is stored by schools, parents, and ordinary men.

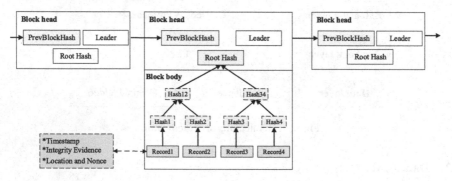

Fig. 3. The basic hash structure of **VideoChain**

3.3 Extension Layer

Consensus protocol is the core of Extension layer. We design our consensus protocol based on Pos [13], which is a provably secure proofs of stake. The basic idea of Snow White is a mechanism called Check Point, but we just refer to it not copy. In Extension layer, we describe the block and blockchain, consensus protocol.

1. **Block and blockchain:** At first, we give definitions about some issue concepts.

*Definition 1: **Genesis block**.* The genesis block B_0 is created by the **Admin**, which is the head of the whole blockchain.

*Definition 2: **Authority block**.* It is a new kind of concept, which is used to contain the list of legal school nodes identified by their public keys $\{PK_1, PK_2, PK_3, \ldots, PK_n\}$ and other auxiliary information ρ. When new school node registers the system, Admin create an authority block to record this data and update the blockchain. Every node in the system identifies the admin by its public key.

*Definition 3: **Block**.* A block B_i is shown in the Fig. 3, we have described above. The relationship among genesis block, authority and block is described in Fig. 4. Compared with block, the number of authority block is little, while there is only one genesis block.

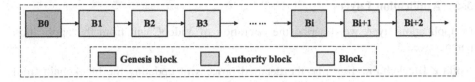

Fig. 4. The relationship among genesis block, authority and block

Definition 4: Blockchain. A blockchain is a sequence of $B_0, B_1, \ldots, B_n$. The length of a blockchain $len(C)$ is its number of blocks.

2. **The nonce based consensus protocol:** The consensus protocol in blockchain always designed to solve two problems. One is to elect the leader of every age during which a new will be written into the blockchain. The other is to solve the problem called fork. But in our design, there will be no possibility of fork owing to special method of electing leader. So our main focus is on the process of selecting leader.

Definition 5: Leader Selection. If the school node's number taking part in the system is N, a school S_i is selected as the leader with the probability P_i, while $P_i = 1/N$. In other words, each node is selected as a leader with the same probability. We cleverly use the nonce of each Record in block. The core idea is that the leader of one age is decided by the Record in the last block. As described in Sect. 3.2, there are several Records in a block, assuming the number is M. And each record contains one nonce. At first, we compute the hash of nonce: $H = Hash(\{Nonce_1, Nonce_2, \ldots, Nonce_M\})$.

And then get the number $L = HmodN$. So the leader of next age is NO.L node. This is simple and valid.

Nonce based consensus protocol

This is a protocol run by blockchain agent support by admin A and schools $S_1, S_2, \ldots, S_n$. The protocol proceeds as follows:

(1) **Initialization.** When protocol starts, A create the genesis block B_0 and the first authority block B_1. Then A broadcasts B_0 and B_1 to every node in the blockchain, including registered parents and ordinary men.

(2) **Chain extension.** Before the latest block is generated,no one knows who is the next leader. But after the latest block generated, everyone will know the certain leader according to the number L mentioned above. Every school S_i performs the following steps:

   i. Collect all records received into a buffer, verifying whether the records are valid according to PK_i. If valid, the record will be put into a set $\mathbb{C}$.

   ii. If S_i is selected as the leader, it will pack $\mathbb{C}$, PrevBlockHash, the hash set of $\mathbb{C}$, and the signature of S_i,as the new block B. Then S_i broadcasts B.

3.4 Application Layer

In application layer, we describe the operation of VideoChain from the application perspective.

Update Blockchain. Describe the detailed process of updating the blockchain from the perspective of system operation. First, the camera captures raw video data and send to the sever to process. On the one hand, the server compresses the raw video data and sends it to local storage server. On the other hand, the server calculates the integrity evidence and sends it to the blockchain agent. The blockchain agent broadcasts integrity evidence to other nodes seeking to write it to the blockchain. Finally, the integrity evidence is written into the blockchain and the blockchain is updated. The implementation principle has been specifically described in the above two chapters.

Verify Evidence on Blockchain. The core strength of the blockchain database in this paper is its resistance to tampering and traceability. When an official surveillance video is published, it needs to verify whether the video is authentic. This process requires the participation of parents and ordinary men, while they have different duties. For the protection of the privacy of minors, only parents can watch the original video data. They will calculate the hash of the government's published video, and broadcast to all participating nodes. Users retrieve the blockchain and compares the hash value with the original record on the blockchain to determine whether the video is authentic.

4 Protocol Analysis

4.1 Correctness Analysis

This video system is different from traditional system which is not built on blockchain. So we can achieve the most important goal, ensuring the evidence trusted. In the original system, users can only believe that the published evidence is true, and when the publisher claims that the evidence is damaged, there is no way. However, in our system, each user can verify the authenticity of the evidence on their own, and the publisher cannot unilaterally delete the video evidence.

4.2 Security Analysis

Theorem 1: In VideoChain, the integrity evidence on the blockchain is true and trustworthy.
Proof: The integrity evidence is created by schools. When writing integrity evidence to the blockchain, school has no motivation to tamper. Because at the time of the video, the incident has not attracted attention. On the one hand, it takes a while for the incident to be noticed. It is entirely adequate for us to record video in intervals of ten minutes. On the other hand, consensus protocol for Consortium Blockchain are usually more efficient. Our algorithm can randomly select a leader without spending extra calculations. So the integrity evidence will be quickly written into the blockchain.

Theorem 2: VideoChain can tolerate the failure of defense mechanisms under the threat model in Sect. 2.2.

Proof: The main threat comes from the Sybil Attack, the adversary try his best to control user nodes and then throw an erroneous conclusion. His purpose is to mislead people, guide public opinion, and attack the government at the public opinion level. But And the adversary cannot control more 51% nodes in blockchain, so the final conclusion cannot be controlled by him.

Theorem 3: VideoChain has traceable and tamper-resistant security features.

Proof: (1) traceable. Traceability is determined by the characteristics of the blockchain itself, with a double meaning. On the one hand, the evidence written in the blockchain can be retrieved. On the other hand, the evidence traced back is credible and cannot be denied. (2) tamper-resistant. This feature also comes from two aspects. On the one hand, only privileged node has the potential to become leaders, that is, new blocks can be generated by it. On the other hand, the number of users is huge, no one can control more than half of the nodes to modify the entire blockchain database.

4.3 Efficiency Analysis

Scenario assumption: There are 100 different schools in the city. Each school has 200 cameras. It means, per ten minute, one school will create 200 records while the whole 20000records. One record is around 50B, and the sum is 50B*20000 = 1 MB. So, one block is sufficient to store it.

- **Consensus efficiency.**

    At the beginning of the production of PoS [12], it is to improve the PoW's inefficiency and high energy consumption. It has better efficiency in itself. This is also the basis on which VideoChain can theoretically achieve good efficiency. The consensus method in this article only needs to calculate the hash value without additional calculations and no additional communication overhead. So consensus efficiency will be high.

- **Storage efficiency.**

    The total storage of one age (every ten minutes) is just around 1 MB. For bigger city, the size of block will not be the limitation. In addition, the data type on the blockchain is single, and data storage performance can be optimized for the characteristics of the data.

- **Query efficiency.**

    Currently, there is usually a data processing unit in the node of the blockchain system, which preprocesses the entire blockchain database system to form a more easily searchable data structure. It depends on the specific design method. Note that, we do not need real-time queries. Existing methods are sufficient to ensure effective query efficiency.

5 Conclusion

This paper focus on how to enhance the credibility of the video surveillance system, and the mutual trust between the official and the public. Wet take the campus video surveillance application scenario as an example, propose a trusted video surveillance system based on blockchain called VideoChain. We propose a method of combining blockchain with traditional data storage and design two core parts of blockchain system: Update Blockchain and Verify Evidence on Blockchain. We also design a high transaction rate consensus protocol for video surveillance application scenarios. The security proof and efficiency analysis show that VideoChain is suitable in practice.

References

1. Wachter, M.: Mobile Internet. Springer Fachmedien Wiesbaden (2016). https://doi.org/10. 1007/978-3-658-06011-4
2. Red-Yellow-Blue kindergarten incident. https://www.huxiu.com/article/223234.html. Accessed 21 Mar 2018
3. Nakamoto, S.: Bitcoin: a peer-to-peer electronic cash system (2008). Consulted
4. Ametrano, F.M.: Bitcoin, Blockchain, and Distributed Ledger Technology. Social Science Electronic Publishing, Rochester (2016)
5. Yuan, Y., Wang, F.Y.: Blockchain: the state of the art and future trends. Acta Automatica Sinica **42**(4), 481–494 (2016)
6. Pu, H.E., Ge, Y.U., Zhang, Y.F., Bao, Y.B.: Survey on blockchain technology and its application prospect. Comput. Sci. **44**(4), 1–7(2017)
7. Types of blockchain. https://en.wikipedia.org/wiki/Types_of_blockchain. Accessed 19 Mar 2018
8. Halpin, H., Piekarska, M.: Introduction to security and privacy on the blockchain. In: IEEE European Symposium on Security and Privacy Workshops, pp. 1–3 (2017)
9. Zhu, L., Dong, H., Shen, M.: Privacy protection mechanism for blockchain transaction data. Big Data Res. **33**(3), 557–567(2018)
10. Andrychowicz, M., Dziembowski, S., Malinowski, D.: Secure Multiparty Computations on Bitcoin. In: IEEE Security & Privacy, pp. 76–84 (2014)
11. Liang, X., Shetty, S., Tosh, D., Kamhoua, C., Kwiat, K., Njilla, L.: Provchain: a blockchain-based data provenance architecture in cloud environment with enhanced privacy and availability. In: IEEE/ACM International Symposium on Cluster, Cloud and Grid Computing, pp. 468–477 (2017)
12. Kiayias, A., Russell, A., David, B., Oliynykov, R.: Ouroboros: a provably secure proof-of-stake blockchain protocol. In: Katz, J., Shacham, H. (eds.) CRYPTO 2017. LNCS, vol. 10401, pp. 357–388. Springer, Cham (2017). https://doi.org/10.1007/978-3-319-63688-7_12
13. Li, W., Andreina, S., Bohli, J.-M., Karame, G.: Securing proof-of-stake blockchain protocols. In: Garcia-Alfaro, J., Navarro-Arribas, G., Hartenstein, H., Herrera-Joancomartí, J. (eds.) ESORICS/DPM/CBT -2017. LNCS, vol. 10436, pp. 297–315. Springer, Cham (2017). https://doi.org/10.1007/978-3-319-67816-0_17

Information Hiding

A Blind Quantization Watermarking Scheme for Screen Content Image

Jun Wang[1], Wenbo Wan[1(✉)], Mingsheng Zhang[2], Liming Zou[1], and Jiande Sun[1]

[1] School of Information Science and Engineering, Shandong Normal University, Jinan, China
wanwenbo@sdnu.edu.cn
[2] Public Security Department of Shandon Province, Jinan, China

Abstract. With the development of the big data age, information security is becoming more and more important. Screen content image are composed of text, graphics and natural image. They present strong anisotropic features, especially on the text and graphics parts. It is well known that Spread Transform Dither Modulation(STDM) is more robust to re-quantization, such as JPEG compression, than regular Quantization Index Modulation(QIM). In this paper, we propose a novel watermarking scheme for screen content grayscale image in DCT domain. On the basis of STDM, combined with the characteristics of human visual system, we use the texture complexity effect factor on DCT domain to adjust the watermarking process. To evaluate the performance of our proposed scheme, we use the reference image from the SIQAD image database. The 20 reference SCIs were thoughtfully identified from the Internet, and they cover a wide variety of image contents, including texts, graphics, symbols, patterns, and natural images. Experiments show that our method has a good performance in term of robustness and better visual quality.

Keywords: Screen content image · STDM · DCT · Digital watermarking

1 Introduction

In the era of multimedia communications, mobile and cloud computing, and the Internet of things, the contents of digital images are no longer just limited to natural scenes. In fact, the contents of digital images nowadays can have a mixture of sources, such as natural scene, computer-generated graphics, texts, charts, maps, user's handwriting and -drawing, and even some special symbols or patterns (e.g., logo, bar code, QR code) imposed and rendered by an electronic device or a photo editing software. Such kind of images is denoted as the screen content images (SCIs) [1, 2], and they are frequently encountered in various multimedia applications and services, such as online news and advertisement, online education, electronic brochures, remote computing, cloud gaming, to name a few [3]. A variety of processing of screen content images, such as appropriate evaluation and compression coding, has been attracted the attention of many researchers. Furthermore, numerous solutions have been proposed to process SCIs, including segmentation and compression of SCIs [4–7]. Lately, MPEG/VCEG

X. Sun et al. (Eds.): ICCCS 2018, LNCS 11066, pp. 61–71, 2018.
https://doi.org/10.1007/978-3-030-00015-8_6

called for proposals to efficiently compress screen content image/videos as an extension of the HEVC standard, and many proposals have been reported to address this need [8].

In the past few decades, the digital watermarking algorithms of natural scene images emerge in an endless stream [9]. Much related works have been conducted over the years to understand different visual models being using for Spread transform dither modulation (STDM), which is a typical watermarking application owing to its advantages in implementation and computational flexibility, to obtain a better tradeoff between fidelity and robustness. In 2006, Cox et al. [10] first proposed a new STDM watermarking by using Watson's perceptual JND model [11]. In their framework, the projection vectors used in STDM were assigned as the slacks computed by Watson's perceptual model, so as to ensure that more changes were directed to coefficients with larger perceptual slacks. Subsequently, an improved method was proposed [12], where the perceptual model was used not only to determine the projection vector but also to select the quantization step size.

Methods are designed and validated on natural images, which do not always share the same properties of screen content. As showed in Fig. 1, typically, compared with the traditional natural image, the discontinuous-tone computer generated screen image is featured by sharp edges and thin lines with few colors [13], while natural images usually have continuous-tone, smoother edges, thicker lines and more colors. Different settings of brightness or contrast of screens would result in the contrast change of captured SCIs. Further consider that the HVS is highly sensitive to image contents that have strong edges and contours, the edge information extracted from the image can be utilized for the development of the digital watermarking.

In this paper, we propose a novel digital watermarking scheme based on the STDM in DCT domain. The key novelty of the proposed method lies in the extraction and use of edge information, since a typical SCI contains abundant of edge information, and the HVS is highly sensitive to such type of information. In Sect. 2, we briefly introduce the tradition STDM watermarking algorithm. Section 3 details our proposed watermarking scheme. Section 4 shows the experimental results by comparing the state-of-the-art natural scene images watermarking scheme. Section 5 draws the conclusion and feature work.

2 Spread Transform Dither Modulation

The basic quantization index modulation(QIM) algorithm quantizes each signal sample, x, using a quantizer, $Q(\cdot)$, that is chosen from a family of quantizers based on the message bit, m, that is to be embedded. The watermarked signal sample, y is given by:

$$y = Q(x, \Delta, m, \delta), \quad m \in (0, 1) \tag{1}$$

where Δ is a fixed quantization step size and δ is a random dither. The quantizers $Q(\cdot)$ is define as follow:

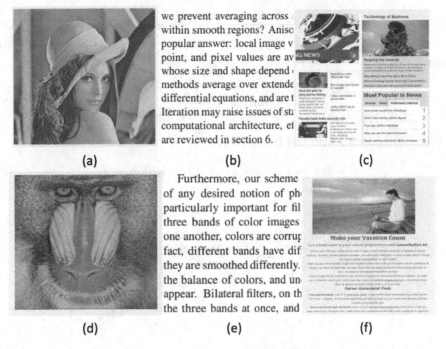

Fig. 1. Example of natural images, textual images and screen content images: **(a)** and **(d)** natural images; **(b)** and **(e)** text images; **(c)** and **(f)** screen content images.

$$Q(x, \Delta, m, \delta) = \Delta \cdot Round\left(\frac{x - \delta - m\frac{\Delta}{2}}{\Delta}\right) + \delta + m\frac{\delta}{2} \qquad (2)$$

At the detector, the received signal sample, z, a corrupted version of y, is re-quantized using the family of quantizers to determine the embedded message bit, i.e.

$$\hat{m} = arg \min_{b \in \{0,1\}} |z - Q(z, \Delta, b, \delta)| \qquad (3)$$

Note that the re-quantization at the detector is not a source of noise and does not refer to the re-quantization resulted by JPEG compression.

However, QIM and DM are also very sensitive to volumetric distortion. Therefore, Spread transform Dither Modulation has been proposed. STDM differs from regular QIM in that the signal, x is first projected onto a randomly generated vector, u, and the resulting scalar value is quantized before being added to the components of the signal that are orthogonal to u. The equation for embedding is thus:

$$y = x + \left(\frac{(Q(proj(x, u), \Delta, m, \delta) - proj(x, u))}{\|u\|_2} \right) u, \quad m \in \{0, 1\} \qquad (4)$$

where,

$$proj(x, u) = \frac{x^T u}{\|u\|_2} \qquad (5)$$

and the corresponding detection is given by:

$$\hat{m} = arg \min_{b \in \{0,1\}} |proj(\hat{x}, u) - Q(proj(\hat{x}, u), \Delta, b, \delta)| \qquad (6)$$

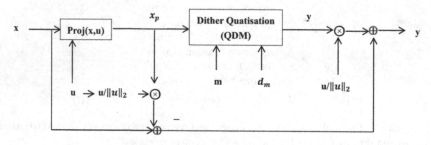

Fig. 2. Block diagram of spread transform dither modulation

Figure 2 illustrates the basic framework for spread transform dither modulation used in this paper.

3 Watermarking Scheme

3.1 Proposed Method

Generally, a watermarking scheme consists of three parts, the watermark message, the watermark embedding stage and the watermark detection stage. The watermark embedding algorithm incorporates the watermark message into the host image, whereas the verification algorithm extracts and authenticates the watermark determining the ownership of the image.

3.1.1 The DCT Transform

The discrete cosine transforms is a technique for converting a signal into elementary frequency components [14]. It represents an image as a sum of sinusoids of varying magnitudes and frequencies. With an input image, x, the DCT coefficients for the transformed output image, y, are computed according to Eq. 7 shown below.

$$y(u,v) = \sqrt{\frac{2}{M}}\sqrt{\frac{2}{M}}\alpha_u\alpha_v \sum_{u=0}^{M-1}\sum_{v=0}^{N-1} x(m,n)cos\left(\frac{(2m+1)u\pi}{2M}\right)cos\left(\frac{(2n+1)v\pi}{2N}\right)$$

$$(7)$$

where

$$\alpha_u = \begin{cases} \frac{1}{\sqrt{2}}, & u = 0 \\ 1, & u = 1,2,\ldots,N-1 \end{cases} \tag{8}$$

$$\alpha_v = \begin{cases} \frac{1}{\sqrt{2}}, & v = 0 \\ 1, & v = 1,2,\ldots,N-1 \end{cases} \tag{9}$$

The image is reconstructed by applying inverse DCT operation according to Eq. 10:

$$x(m,n) = \sqrt{\frac{2}{M}}\sqrt{\frac{2}{N}}\sum_{u=0}^{M-1}\sum_{v=0}^{N-1} \alpha_u\alpha_v cos\left(\frac{(2m+1)u\pi}{2M}\right)cos\left(\frac{(2n+1)v\pi}{2N}\right) \tag{10}$$

The popular block-based DCT transform segments an image non-overlapping blocks and applies DCT to each block.

3.1.2 Texture Complexity Effect

Visual sensitivities include amplitude sensitivity, motion sensitivity and flicker sensitivity, among which the amplitude sensitivity is the most widely studied [15]. The HVS decomposes the visual signals into channels of different spatial/temporal frequencies, colors and orientations. The texture complexity effects indicate that the HVS is less sensitive to distortion in highly textured regions than edge or plain regions. As discussed in [16], edge is the most important feature carrying most of the semantic information in an image, especially in the screen content image. For a given block, if it contains very sparse edge pixels, it can be considered as a flat block. On the other hand, if it contains many edge pixels, it means that this block has higher edge strength and more semantic information, thus it can be considered as a high detail block.

Considering that, we propose to use the *AC* coefficients $AC_{0,1}$, $AC_{1,0}$ and $AC_{1,1}$ (in which the subscripts refer to the row and column indices of the block), which have been regard as an effective measurement for the edge strength in both horizontal and vertical directions [17], to measure the contrast masking effects of the original image. Therefore, the contrast effect metric can be defined as,

$$E_{AC}(i,j) = |AC_{0,1}(i,j)| + |AC_{1,0}(i,j)| + |AC_{1,1}(i,j)| \tag{11}$$

Ngan [18] proposed an accurate block classification method based on edge pixel densities, which can be employed to measure texture complexities. Therefore, the

DCT-based modulation factor is modeled as a discontinuous function of texture complexity with three types: plane, edge, and texture, respectively. Here, the information contained in the screen content image and the natural scene image itself is completely different, and we classify the texture complexity TC according to its content. The block type is determined by:

$$TC = \begin{cases} 0.8, & plane\ block \quad for\ E_{AC} \leq 150 \\ 1.6, & edge\ block \quad for\ 150 < E_{AC} \leq 350 \\ 2.25, & texture\ block \qquad for\ others \end{cases} \tag{12}$$

Table 1. The contrast sensitivity function of the DCT domain

1.40	1.01	1.16	1.66	2.40	3.43	4.79	6.56
1.01	1.45	1.32	1.52	2.00	2.71	3.67	4.93
1.16	1.32	2.24	2.59	2.98	3.64	4.60	5.88
1.66	1.52	2.59	3.77	4.55	5.30	6.28	7.60
2.40	2.00	2.98	4.55	6.15	7.46	8.71	10.17
3.43	2.71	3.64	5.30	7.46	9.62	11.58	13.51
4.79	3.67	4.60	6.28	8.71	11.58	14.50	17.29
6.56	4.93	5.88	7.60	10.17	13.51	17.29	21.51

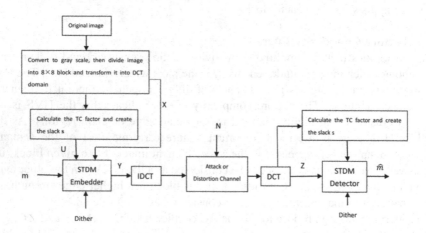

Fig. 3. The frame diagram of our method

Finally, inspired from JND model, the contrast sensitivity function C_{base} (showed in Table 1) of each 8×8 DCT block on the DCT domain was incorporated as a basic distortion threshold to form a slack vector s.

The values in the Table 1 are the basic distortion threshold which is corresponding to (i, j)-th location in each 8×8 DCT block. Based on this value, we further consider the impact of texture complexity for each DCT block, which can be defined as:

$$s = C_{base} \cdot TC \tag{13}$$

The frame diagram of our method is showed in Fig. 3.

3.2 Watermark Embedding Stage

1. First, we convert the screen content image into a grayscale map. Then, divided the carrier image into 8×8 non-overlapping blocks and perform a DCT transform for each block to determine the DCT coefficients. The coefficients are scanned by zig-zag arrangement. Then select the four to ten DCT coefficients (in zig-zag-scanned order after the eight by eight block DCT on each image) to form a single vector which is denoted as host vector x.
2. Calculate the texture complexity masking TC in the DCT domain according to Eq. (11), and get a block type map according to Eq. (12). And then, the type map is multiplied by the DCT domain contrast sensitive function according to Eq. (13) to form a perceptual slack vector s.
3. Then the host vector x and the perceptual slack vector s are projected onto the given projection vector u, which is set as the KEY, to generate the projections x_u and s_u. Then we can obtain the quantization step Δ via s_u, which can be multiplied by the embedding strength in practice.
4. One bit of watermark "m" is embedded in the host projection x_u.
5. Finally, the modified coefficient are transformed to obtain the watermarked image y.

3.3 Watermarking Detection Stage

Watermarked images are likely to be subjected to some signal processing attacks during propagation such as, Gaussian noise, and JPEG compression. At the detection, the specific steps of the watermark extraction process are as follows:

1. Divide the watermarked image into 8×8 blocks and perform DCT transform to determine the DCT coefficients. The coefficients are scanned by zig-zag arrangement. Then select the four to ten DCT coefficients (in zig-zag-scanned order after the eight by eight block DCT on each image) to form a single vector which denoted as the host vector x.
2. Calculate the texture complexity masking TC in the DCT domain according to Eq. (11), and get a block type map according to Eq. (12). And then, the type map is multiplied by the DCT domain contrast sensitive function according to Eq. (13) to form a perceptual slack vector s'.
3. Then the host vector x and the perceptual slack vector s' are projected onto the given projection vector u, which is set as the KEY, to generate the projections x'_u and s'_u. Then we can obtain the quantization step Δ via s'_u, which can be multiplied by the embedding strength in practice.
4. Use the STDM detector to extract the watermark message m' according to Eq. (6).

4 Experiments

To evaluate the performance of our proposed scheme, we used reference images from the SIQAD image database used in [19]. The 20 reference SCIs were thoughtfully identified from the Internet, and they cover a wide variety of image contents, including texts, graphics, symbols, patterns, and natural images. Before we did watermark in the DCT domain, we need to preprocess the original image into the size of the image that can be divided by 8. A 1024 bit random binary message was embedded into each image. Specially, we selected the four to ten DCT coefficients (in zig-zag-scanned order after the eight by eight block DCT on each image) to form the host vector and embedded one bit in it.

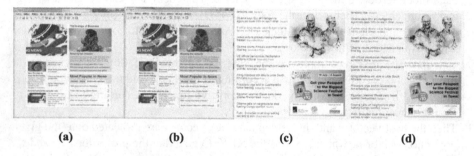

| (a) | (b) | (c) | (d) |

Fig. 4. (a) and (c) original image (cim1 and cim5); (b) and (d) their watermarked image

We explain the feasibility of the algorithm in the following two aspects: imperceptibility and robustness. Due to the difference between the natural image and the screen content image, at present, there is no watermark algorithm for screen content images, so we compared the scheme in this paper with two common natural image watermarking algorithms, marked as STDM-RW [10] and STDM-OptiWM [12]. Mean- while, two kinds of attacks (Gaussian noise with mean zero variance ranging from 0 to 15; JPEG compression, where the JPEG quality factor varies from 20 to 100 were used to verify the performance of the proposed models. The bit error rate (BER) was used to compare the robustness performance of other two watermarking schemes.

Furthermore, we used the quality evaluation method GSS of the screen content image obtained by using the gradient information in the literature [20] to control the quality of the image. Here, we kept the GSS as a fixed value (GSS = 0.1200), which can provide us with a good enough visual quality watermarking image and PSNR of test images are stable around 53 in the experiments. Some of the original and water- marked images in this article were showed in Fig. 4.

By observing the two original and their watermarked images in Fig. 4, we see that the watermarked images have a good visual quality compared with the original image. Meanwhile, we can not see any information that related with watermark message from the watermark image. So that the watermarked images have a very good hiding effect, called imperceptibly. This can greatly ensure the security of embedded information.

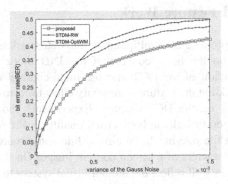

Fig. 5. BER comparisons of Gaussian noise

Figure 5 shows response to additive white Gaussian noise. The STDM-RW performs significantly worse because of the mismatch problem. The proposed method has obvious anti Gauss attack performance compared with the other two traditional algorithms and our proposed scheme has average BER values 8% lower than STDM-RM and STDM-OptiWM. It is known that the method STDM-RW and STDM-OptiWM both use a Watson perceptual model to guide watermarking process. Watson perceptual model considers the luminance and contrast masking from pixel domain which can reflect the JND threshold for natural image but is not suitable for screen content image. However, our method mainly uses the edge information in DCT domain to describe the texture complexity for image watermarking which could describe the characters of screen content images better than Watson perceptual model.

Furthermore, the sensitivity to JPEG compression is also demonstrated in Fig. 6. For the robustness, the curve of our algorithm is obviously lower than the other two algorithms, which shows that our algorithm has the best performance in term of robustness than others. The reason that we got a good performance is that we use the norm-2 of the random vector to process the dither modulation process. In this way, the quantization distortion is smaller and has better anti JPEG compression performance.

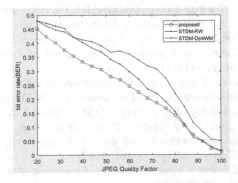

Fig. 6. BER comparisons of JPEG compression

5 Conclusion and Feature Work

In this paper, we first propose a novel quantization watermarking scheme for screen content image. Based on the basic concept of the JND model, we use the spatial contrast sensitivity function of the DCT and the multi-channel characteristics of the human visual system, adding the texture complexity effect to form a simple slack vector for image watermarking on the DCT domain. Experiments show that our proposed algorithm can achieve good results in both visual quality and robustness performance. In the feature work, on the one hand, we aim to find some more robustness features which can reflect the characters of a screen content image. On the other hand, we can use a JND model that can well reflect the human visual system to guide the watermark embedding when observing the maximum distortion threshold of the screen content image.

References

1. Yang, H., Fang, Y., Lin, W.: Perceptual quality assessment of screen content images. IEEE Trans. Image Process. 24(11), 4408–4421 (2015)
2. Wang, S., Ma, L., Fang, Y., Lin, W., Ma, S., Gao, W.: Just noticeable difference estimation for screen content images. IEEE Trans. Image Process. 25(8), 3838–3851 (2016)
3. Xu, J., Joshi, R., Cohen, R.A.: Overview of the emerging HEVC screen content coding extension. IEEE Trans. Circuits Syst. Video Technol. 26(1), 50–62 (2016)
4. Lin, T., Hao, P.: Compound image compression for real-time computer screen image transmission. IEEE Trans. Image Process. 14(8), 993–1005 (2005)
5. Lan, C., Shi, G., Wu, F.: Compress compound images in H.264/MPGE-4 AVC by exploiting spatial correlation. IEEE Trans. Image Process. 19(4), 946–957 (2010)
6. Yang, H., Lin, W., Deng, C.: Learning based screen image compression. In: Proceeding of the IEEE MMSP, pp. 77–82 (2012)
7. Pan, Z., Shen, H., Lu, Y., Li, S., Yu, N.: A low-complexity screen compression scheme for interactive screen sharing. IEEE Trans. Circuits Syst. Video Technol. 23(6), 949–960 (2013)
8. Requirements for an Extension of HEVC for Coding of Screen Content, document ISO/IEC JTC1/SC29/WG11 MPEG2013/N14174 (2014)
9. Tirkel, A.Z., Rankin, G.A., Van Schyndel, R.M., et al.: Electronic watermark. In: Digital Image Computing, Technology and Applications (DICTA 1993), pp. 666–673 (1993)
10. Li, Q., Doërr, G., Cox, I.J.: Spread transform dither modulation using a perceptual model. In: IEEE 8th Workshop on Multimedia Signal Processing, pp. 98–102 (2006)
11. Watson, A.B.: DCT quantization matrices visually optimized for individual images. In: Proceeding of the SPIE 1913(14) (1993)
12. Li, Q., Cox, I.J.: Improved spread transform dither modulation using a perceptual model: robustness to amplitude scaling and JPEG compression. In: IEEE International Conference on Acoustics, Speech and Signal Processing, ICASSP 2007, vol. 2, II-185 (2007)
13. Lin, Tao, Zhang, Peijun, Wang, Shuhui, Zhou, Kailun, Chen, Xianyi: Mixed chroma sampling-rate high efficiency video coding for full-chroma screen content. IEEE Trans. Circuits Syst. Video Technol. 23(1), 173–185 (2013)
14. Rao, K., Yip, P.: Discrete Cosine Transform: Algorithms, Advantages, Applications. Academic Press, Boston (1990)

15. Lu, Z., Lin, W., Yang, X., Ong, E., Susu, Y.: Modeling visual attention's modulatory aftereffects on visual sensitivity and quality evaluation. Image Process. IEEE Trans. **14**(11), 1928–1942 (2005)
16. Qi, H., Jiao, S., Lin, W., Tang, L., Shen, W.: Content-based image quality assessment using semantic information and luminance differences. Electron. Lett. **50**(20), 1435–1436 (2014)
17. Fang, Y., Lin, W., Chen, Z., Tsai, C.M., Lin, C.W.: A video saliency detection model in compressed domain. IEEE Trans. Circuits Syst. Video Technol. **24**(1), 27–38 (2014)
18. Wei, Z., Ngan, K.: Spatio-temporal just noticeable distortion profile for grey scale image/video in DCT domain. IEEE Trans. Circuits Systs. Video Technol. **20**(3), 337–346 (2009)
19. Gu, K., Qiao, J., Min, X., Yue, G., Weisi, L.I.N., Thalmann, D.: Evaluating quality of screen content images via structural variation analysis. IEEE Trans. Vis. Comput. Graph. **PP**(99), 1 (2017)
20. Ni, Z., Ma, L., Zeng, H., Cai, C., Ma, K.-K.: Gradient direction for screen content image quality assessment. IEEE Signal Process. Lett. **23**(10), 1394–1398 (2016)

A Comprehensive Analysis of Interval Based Network Flow Watermarking

Jin Shi[1(✉)], Li Zhang[2], Shuijun Yin[2], Weiwei Liu[1], Jiangtao Zhai[3],
Guangjie Liu[1], and Yuewei Dai[3]

[1] Nanjing University of Science and Technology, Nanjing 210094, China
shijin1011@163.com
[2] Wuhan Ship Communication Research Institute, Wuhan 430200, China
[3] Jiangsu University of Science and Technology, Zhenjiang 212003, China

Abstract. As the main active traffic analysis method, network flow watermarking (NFW) has been proven effective for flow correlation in anonymous communication system or stepping stone detection. In various types of network flow watermarking schemes, the interval-based ones can achieve significant better capability of resisting network interference. However, there still exists no work to give a comprehensive analysis of them, specifically on practicability as the implementation of NFW in Internet still remains a great challenge. In this paper, the existing interval-based NFW schemes are comparatively analyzed by benchmarking their performance on robustness, invisibility and practicability. Different from some prior work, we pay special attention to the practicability evaluation, which is related to time and storage overhead, communication and computation overhead, and the statistical model demand. Experimental results on CAIDA dataset give an overview of the existing interval-based NFW schemes.

Keywords: Anonymous communication system · Network flow watermarking
Practicability · Comparatively analysis

1 Introduction

With increasing number of users begin to employ anonymous communication systems to protect their privacy, some typical anonymous networks (e.g., Tor) and stepping stone strategies have made the network censorship more and more difficult [1–3]. Many attackers always make the malicious traffic passing through stepping stones or anonymous network to conceal their source IP address [4], which has become a significant challenge in the field of network flow tracing.

Traffic analysis technique can be used to identify whether an input flow is related to an output flow. There are two kinds of traffic analysis techniques [5], passive traffic analysis and active traffic analysis. Passive traffic analysis monitors network flows and determines if the observed flows are correlated based on the statistical characteristics of the flows, and it will not modify any characteristic of the target flows. The main drawback of passive traffic analysis is that it requires a long observing time and is vulnerable to network environment jitter, so it is not feasible for real-time environment

© Springer Nature Switzerland AG 2018
X. Sun et al. (Eds.): ICCCS 2018, LNCS 11066, pp. 72–84, 2018.
https://doi.org/10.1007/978-3-030-00015-8_7

due to the hysteresis. On the other hand, active traffic analysis, which is also known as NFW, makes a slice adjustment in certain fields of a data stream to embed watermark information. If the same or similar watermark information is detected in an observed flow, the flows can be regarded as a watermarked flow. NFW requires fewer packets than passive traffic analysis and is more suitable for flow tracing [6], thus it has attracted increasing attention of the researchers in the field of network flow traceback.

A network flow watermarking system contains a watermark encoder and a watermark decoder. The watermark encoder is used for embedding watermarks into a target flow, while the decoder observes the flow and extracts watermarks by analyzing the characteristics of the flow. Watermarks can be encoded in different fields of the flow. According to the carrier type, NFW can be classified into three types: content-based [7–9], rate-based [10] and timing-based [11–18]. Timing based NFW can be further divided into inter packet delay (IPD) based, interval packet counting based and interval centroid based.

Yu [10] proposed DSSS flow watermarking, a scheme based on direct sequence spread spectrum by modifying flow rate. DSSS assumes the carrier flow should be with long duration and stable flow rate. However, the stringent limits make it hard for implementation in practice. Wang [8] proposed sleepy watermark tracing (SWT), which utilizes packet payload as carriers to trace the source IP of the flow with the help of network router when an attack happens. Sleepy state means that watermarking system does not need external overhead when no attack occurs. However, SWT cannot be used in encrypted traffic and can be easily filtered. Then, Houmansadr [11] proposed the first non-blind watermarking named RAINBOW which decides whether the flow is watermarked by comparing the IPDs of the egress node with the IPDs of the ingress node that are stored in database. Only a few packets are needed for RAINBOW to make a decision. But RAINBOW assumes that traffic model follows some well-defined statistical patterns. Several interval-based NFWs will be further discussed in Sect. 2.

However, there still exist great obstacles for NFW to trace attackers in anonymous communication systems. Firstly, many NFWs are of low efficiency. NFW usually buffers hundreds of packets to embed watermarks. Secondly, the accuracy of them still needs to be enhanced. Network jitter and artificial interference may disturb NFW. Lastly, the invisibility of NFW remains a potential risk as the attacker will try to remove the watermark when they suspect the existence of NFW.

Interval-based NFW has become more and more popular due to its advantage on robustness. In this paper, we focus on the benchmarking of interval-based NFW, including interval packet counting based ones and interval centroid based ones. An evaluation mechanism is proposed to give a comprehensive analysis of NFW. Experiments are made for six typical NFWs, namely, IBW [13], BotMosaic [14], ICBW [15], DICBW [16], ICBSSW [17] and SWIRL [18]. Our experiments are based on real-world traffic captured by the center for applied internet data analysis (CAIDA). We use HTTP and SSH traffic traces which are extracted from the captures as overt carriers. We have considered the performance of these NFWs with respect to our evaluation mechanism.

The rest of this paper is organized as follows. In Sect. 2, the concerned interval-based NFW schemes are briefly introduced. In Sect. 3, an evaluation mechanism is proposed. The experimental results are given in Sect. 4, and the conclusions are made in the last section.

2 Related Work

In this paper, we consider following NFW schemes: IBW, ICBW, DICBW, ICBSSW, BOTMOSAIC and SWIRL. We list the NFW schemes with timeline and introduce the main features of them as follows: (1) the carrier type, (2) multiple-bit or zero-bit, (3) single-flow tracing or multi-flow tracing, (4) blind or not, (5) usage scenario, (6) relations among them (Fig. 1).

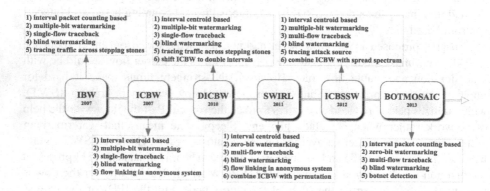

Fig. 1. Interval based NFWs

IPD based network flow watermarking does not work effectively when packet reassembly happens. To solve the problem, Pyun [13] proposed the first interval based watermarking (IBW). The duration of each flow is sliced into short fixed length intervals, and packet timing is adjusted to change the packet counting in two randomly selected intervals to embed the watermark. Let Y denotes the packet count difference of the selected interval pair, and IBW encodes a watermark bit by "load" and "clear" to increase or decrease Y. "Load" means shift the packets in previous interval to current interval and "clear" means delay the packets in current interval to next interval to change packet count in selected intervals.

Wang [15] proposed the first interval centroid based watermarking (ICBW). Interval centroid is defined as:

$$Cent(I_i) = \frac{1}{n_i} \sum_{j=0}^{n_i-1} \Delta t_i \qquad (1)$$

Whereas n_i is the number of packets in interval I_i, and Δt_i represents the offset of the i-th packet from the start of its interval. Starting from offset o, a duration is divided into intervals of equal length T. Intervals are randomly divided into two groups A and

B, and intervals in A and B are randomly selected to encode the watermark. Let A_i and B_i denotes the centroid of the selected intervals in group A and B, then $Y_i = A_i - B_i$. To encode a watermark bit '1', A_i is increased by delaying packets in selected intervals of group A so that Y_i will be positive. To encode a watermark bit '0', B_i is increased by delaying packets in selected intervals in group B so that Y_i will be negative.

To improve efficiency and invisibility of IBW, Wang [16] proposed double interval centroid based watermarking (DICBW). DICBW is similar to ICBW. However, there are two major differences between DICBW and ICBW. Firstly, the two intervals that used for embedding a watermark of DICBW are adjacent, whereas ICBW are randomly selected. Secondly, the methods of calculating centroid of an interval are different. ICBW is based on the "*offset*" of packets, whereas DICBW introduced the conception of "*complement offset*", which denotes "*T-offset*".

Luo [17] proposed interval centroid based spread spectrum watermark (ICBSSW), which combines ICBW modulation approach and spread spectrum coding technique. The original watermark is spread to generate spread watermark firstly by applying spread spectrum coding technique for achieving higher secrecy and efficiency.

BotMosaic [14] is a countermeasure to IRC-based botnets. BotMosaic relies on captured bots controlled by an encoder, who inserts a particular pattern into their network traffic. If this pattern can later be found in another instance's traffic, the two instances are in the same botnet. A duration is divided into fixed intervals with equal length. The intervals are randomly distributed into two groups A and B. The basic idea of the watermark is to send more packets in A interval compared to its corresponding B interval.

SWIRL [18] is a scalable watermark that is invisible and resilient to packet losses. SWIRL is an interval-based watermark, and the flow is divided into a collection of intervals of length T with an initial offset o. A base interval and a mark interval are selected to perform watermarking. The centroid of the base interval is used to decide which pattern to insert on the mark interval. The mark interval is subdivided into r subintervals of length T/r. The subintervals are then further subdivided into m slots. A slot in each subinterval is selected by applying a permutation, each packet is then delayed such that it falls in a selected slot.

3 Benchmarking System of Interval-Based NFW

Although many existing NFW schemes claim that they can achieve well robustness or invisibility. However, they are not benchmarked with a general criterion. In addition, no NFW schemes take practicability into account while the most significant challenge for the proposed NFW schemes at present is the gap between the real network and the experimental setup. Thus, we give a benchmarking system of interval-based NFW as follows.

As shown in Fig. 2, performance of a NFW can be evaluated with the benchmarking system with respect to robustness, invisibility and practicability. Robustness and invisibility are similar to that adopted in the prior works while practicability can be measured in several aspects on the overhead introduced by the NFW and the assumptions of the NFW. Robustness can be measured by the resistance to network jitter and flow transformations of the NFW. Invisibility can be evaluated by the similarity between original and watermarked flows, and whether it can survive the MFA. Practicability is evaluated from the aspect of time overhead, storage overhead, computation overhead, communication overhead and statistical model demand.

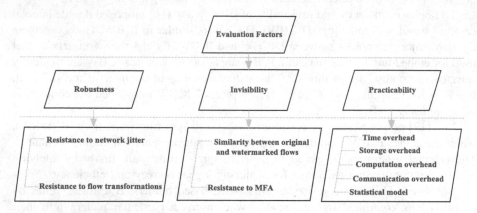

Fig. 2. Benchmarking system of interval-based NFW

3.1   Robustness

In a watermarking scheme, there exists probability that an encoded watermark bit cannot be extracted correctly by the decoder. That is, if a watermark bit is decoded as bit 0 whereas the real watermark bit is 1 and vice versa, the decoded watermark would not agree with the expected watermark. The failure on decoding may lead to a false traceback. The robustness of NFW is defined as the ability to resist normal network jitter and network flow transformations, which is measured by the probability that a watermark is decoded correctly under the above mentioned circumstances.

False positive rate (FPR) is used to measure the robustness of NFW. Let W denote a watermark with length l, and the decoder extracts a watermark W' using the optimum parameters. Then the hamming distance of W and W' can be denoted as l'. Then, FPR is calculated with Eq. (2).

$$\text{FPR} = \frac{l'}{l} \tag{2}$$

However, network condition has a great influence on the accuracy of NFW. Network jitter is the variation in the latency on a flow stream between two hosts. Network flow transformations contain intra-flow transformations and inter-flow transformations. Adding chaff, packet dropping and repacketization are common forms of intra-flow transformation. Flow mixing, flow split and flow merge are common forms of interflow transformation. Network jitter and flow transformation are inherent in anonymous networks or stepping stones. In [12], network jitter and flow transformations are summarized into three types: network noise, packets dropping and chaff packets. For a

NFW scheme, the lower the FPR is in diverse network environment, the more robust of a watermarking scheme is.

3.2 Invisibility

Invisibility means the undetectability of a NFW when the attackers analyze the watermarked flows with some typical statistical test tools. A visible watermarking scheme would be destroyed or removed by the attackers when it is found by the attacker. In this paper, invisibility is evaluated in two ways, one is to test the similarity of the original flow and watermarked flow by means of Kolmogorov-Smirnov test, the other is to test its resistance to multi-flow attack (MFA).

The Kolmogorov-Smirnov (K-S) test quantifies the distance between the empirical distribution functions of two samples. We use K-S test to measure the similarity of two packet timing distributions by calculating their distance. Let $t_u = t_{u1}, t_{u2}, \ldots, t_{un}$ denotes the IPDs of the original flow and $t_w = t_{w1}, t_{w2}, \ldots, t_{wm}$ denotes the IPDs of the watermarked flow. The cumulative distribution functions of the two sequences are denoted as $F_u(x)$ and $F_w(x)$. The test statistic D is defined in Eq. (3).

$$D = \max|F_u(x) - F_w(x)| \tag{3}$$

The value of D determines whether the two IPD sequences have the same distribution. If D falls below a pre-defined threshold, then the watermarked flow is in accordance with the original flow. The two hypotheses are described as follows.

H0 (null hypothesis): The distributions of the two IPD sequences are the same.
H1: The distributions of the two IPD sequences are different.

In *Matlab*, the test can be done conveniently using the *kstest2* function.

$$[H, P, KSSTAT] = kstest2(t_u, t_w, a, 0) \tag{4}$$

Where H is hypothesis test result, P is the probability of observing a test statistic as extreme as, or more extreme than, the observed value under the null hypothesis. The returned value $KSSTAT$ is D in Eq. (4). α is a scalar value in the range (0,1), which denotes the significance level of the hypothesis test. If $h = 1$, this indicates the rejection of the null hypothesis at the α significance level. This means the distribution of the two IPD sequences are different, and the NFW is visible. If $h = 0$, the NFW tends to be invisible.

Besides K-S test, multi-flow attack [19] is a typical network flow watermarking attack method. Multi-flow attack combines multiple watermarked flows, and thus magnifies the influences of network flow watermarking on the statistical characteristics of the flow. MFA can be used to detect the presence of a watermark, recover the secret parameters, and even remove the watermark from a flow. A countermeasure that defeats the MFA is to embed the watermark in randomly selected positions.

Encoder embeds watermarks in several flows simultaneously, which makes the watermarked flows relevant to each other. To detect the existence of the watermark, N watermarked flows are selected and combined. If periods of silence occur in the combined IPD sequences, watermarked is detected. Whereas the IPDs of common network flow tend to obey the normal distribution.

3.3 Practicability

Robustness and invisibility are commonly used to evaluate NFW while whether the NFW is suitable for applying in real network is not easy to evaluate. As described in Sect. 2, interval-based NFWs buffer packets for duration of length T_f and packet timings are adjusted to embed watermarks. The length of duration is different according to specified watermarking scheme. To achieve great robustness and invisibility, long duration may be selected to perform watermarking. However, long duration implies that much time overhead and storage overhead is introduced by a watermarking scheme. In addition, long duration may lead to TCP retransmission and normal communication disturbance, which would greatly reduce the feasibility of the NFW. To operate effectively in real network, NFW should try to balance the performance of watermarking and the influences on normal network traffic.

To analyze the performance of a NFW, we propose a novel evaluation factor—practicability, which refers to the measurement of resource demand of the NFW in real network. Resource consumption can be measured by time and storage overhead, communication and computation overhead, and statistical model.

3.3.1 Time and Storage Overhead

In a flow watermarking scheme, a duration of length T_f is selected and divided $2n$ intervals of length T, and l-bit watermark is encoded. However, given T_f, the watermark length differs in different watermarking schemes. Time overhead refers to how many delays will be introduced in for a successful traceback at least and it can be measured by delays introduced by each bit of watermark (*deb*). Obviously, smaller delays mean less time overhead. Storage overhead refers to the demand memory for storing buffered packets in a successful traceback at least and it can be measured by memory used by each bit of watermark (*meb*). Let $\overline{ipd}$ denote the average inter packet delay in a flow during length T_f and $\overline{ps}$ denote the average packet size in a flow during length T_f, *deb* and *meb* are defined with following equations.

$$deb = \frac{T_f}{l} \times \overline{ipd} \tag{5}$$

$$meb = \frac{T_f}{l} \times \overline{ps} \tag{6}$$

It is apparent that well-designed NFW should be with low time overhead and storage overhead. Excessive overhead will result in a failed traceback in real anonymous systems.

3.3.2 Communication and Computation Overhead

Besides time and storage overhead, communication and computation overhead are also important factors that influence the performance of NFW. Communication overhead refers to the cost due to the continuous communication among detectors. Computation overhead refers to the cost due to comparing the suspect flows with the original flows.

Considering a network environment with m input stream and output stream in a non-blind scheme. Decoders at the output nodes communicate with each other continuously, which requires $O(n)$ communication overhead for each decoder. As a result, a detector should compare each output stream with every input stream causing $O(mn)$ computation overhead.

However, blind schemes provide better scalability than non-blind schemes. Blind schemes share key before watermarking and no more cost is required while transmitting, which causing $O(1)$ communication overhead. Decoders in a blind scheme process a output stream individually, thus having $O(n)$ computation overhead. Generally speaking, blind watermarking is more effective than non-blind watermarking. Therefore, a majority of watermarking schemes are blind.

3.3.3 Statistical Model

In addition, assumptions in some flow watermarking schemes are not in accordance with real network. Some NFW schemes can only work when the statistical model of the carrier flow obeys certain distribution which is not true in real environment. Therefore, NFW schemes requiring flow statistical model are limited to specific environmental conditions.

4 Experiment and Analysis

In this section, experiments are made to test the performance of the NFWs described in Sect. 2: IBW, ICBW, DICBW, ICBSSW, BOTMISAIC and SWIRL. We simulated the six watermarking schemes in Matlab.

4.1 Experimental Setup

We use traces collected by the CAIDA project in the PCAP.GZ trace file format from the equinix-sanjose monitor, and all our experiments are performed on SSH flows. 4327 SSH flows (port 22) are extracted from the equinix-sanjose.dirA.20140619-131200.UTC.anon.pcap.gz file. Flows are selected with at least 1000 IPDs and the flows should be smooth. The cumulative distribution function of the timestamps in a flow is shown in Fig. 3.

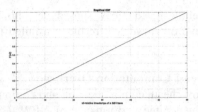

Fig. 3. CDF of a SSH flow

A watermark is generated using the random number generators. In every run of the simulation, a SSH flow is randomly selected from the database and they are watermarked using the designated watermark key.

Network noise is simulated with additive white noise and amplitude uniformly distributed white noise. Chaff packets are simulated with adding packets randomly and periodically. Dropping packets are simulated with dropping packets randomly and periodically. Mixed flow transformations are simulated under all the three circumstances. The parameters of each experiment are shown in Table 1.

Table 1. Parameters of network flow transformations (NFT)

NFT	1	2	3	4	5	6	7	8	9	10
Noise-1	5	8	11	14	17	20	23	26	29	32
Noise-2	0.001	0.002	0.003	0.004	0.005	0.006	0.007	0.008	0.009	0.01
Chaff-1	0.05	0.1	0.15	0.2	0.25	0.3	0.35	0.4	0.45	0.5
Chaff-2	5	10	15	20	25	30	35	40	45	50
Drop-1	0.05	0.1	0.15	0.2	0.25	0.3	0.35	0.4	0.45	0.5
Drop-2	5	10	15	20	25	30	35	40	45	50

4.2   Experimental Results

4.2.1   Robustness

See Fig. 4

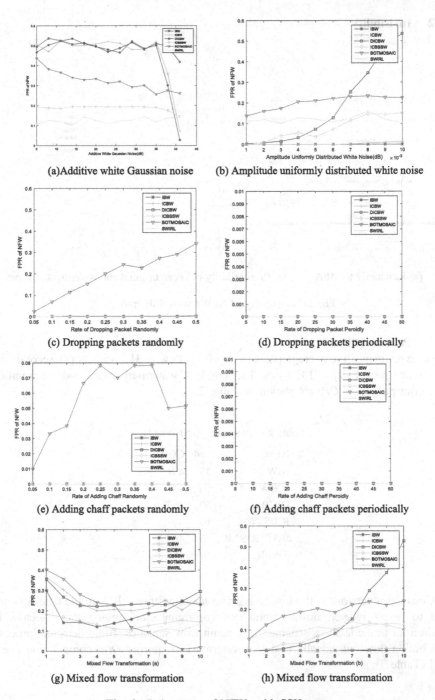

(a)Additive white Gaussian noise

(b) Amplitude uniformly distributed white noise

(c) Dropping packets randomly

(d) Dropping packets periodically

(e) Adding chaff packets randomly

(f) Adding chaff packets periodically

(g) Mixed flow transformation

(h) Mixed flow transformation

Fig. 4. Robustness of NFWs with SSH traces

4.2.2   Invisibility
See Fig. 5

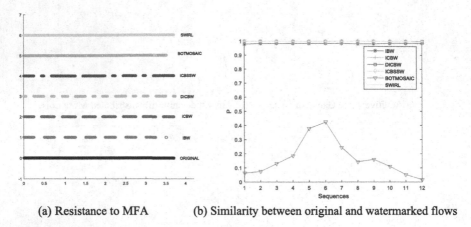

(a) Resistance to MFA   (b) Similarity between original and watermarked flows

Fig. 5. Invisibility of NFWs with SSH traces

4.2.3   Practicability
In our experiments, the average packet rate of the flow is 312 packets per second and the average packet size is 132 bytes. The length of watermarks (*LM*) and the count of the carrier packets (*CCP*) are shown in Table 2.

Table 2. Overhead of NFWs (1)

NFW	LM	CCP
IBW	33	491
ICBW	50	497
DICBW	50	497
ICBSSW	10	497
BOTMOSAIC	50	464
SWIRL	50	497

Consider a network with m incoming and n outing flows. If multiple detectors are used to detect relayed flows, continuous communication among the detectors is required for traffic analysis schemes to transmit flow statistics. Blind detectors process each outing flow individually to detect watermarks requiring $O(n)$ computation overhead (Table 3).

Table 3. Overhead of NFWs (2)

NFW	Time	Storage	Communication	Computation	Statistical model
IBW	0.048	1964	$O(n)$	$O(mn)$	no
ICBW	0.031	1312	$O(n)$	$O(mn)$	no
DICBW	0.031	1312	$O(n)$	$O(mn)$	no
ICBSSW	0.159	6560	$O(n)$	$O(mn)$	no
BOTMOSAIC	0.030	1224	$O(n)$	$O(mn)$	no
SWIRL	0.031	1312	$O(n)$	$O(mn)$	no

4.3 Overall Performance Comparison

See Table 4

Table 4. Performance comparison Robustness: Resistance to Network Jitter (RNJ), Resistance to Packets Dropping (RPD), Resistance to Chaff Packets (RCP), Resistance to Mixed Flow Transformations (RMFT). Invisibility: Similarity between Original and Watermarked Flows (SOWF), Resistance to MFA (RMFA). Practicability: Time Overhead (TO), Storage Overhead (SO), Computation Overhead (CPO), Communication Overhead (CMO), Statistical Model (SM).

NFW	Robustness				Invisibility		Practicability				
	RNJ	RPD	RCP	RMFT	SOWF	RMFA	TO	SO	CPO	CMO	SM
IBW	weak	strong	weak	weak	low	no	low	low	med	med	no
ICBW	weak	strong	weak	weak	low	no	low	low	med	med	no
DICBW	weak	weak	weak	weak	low	no	low	low	med	med	no
ICBSSW	strong	strong	strong	strong	low	no	high	high	med	med	no
BOTMOSAIC	weak	weak	weak	weak	low	yes	low	low	med	med	no
SWIRL	strong	strong	strong	strong	high	yes	low	low	med	med	no

5 Conclusion

NFW is an urgent technique for flow tracing in anonymous communication systems. In this paper, we investigate typical interval-based NFW schemes, and propose a benchmarking system for evaluating their performance comprehensively. In particular, we analyze the practicability by considering time overhead, storage overhead, computation overhead and communication overhead. The comparatively experimental results show that the practicability of NFW need to be further improved and should be paid special attention when designing NFW schemes.

Acknowledgments. This work was supported by the National Natural Science Foundation of China (Grants nos. 61602247, 61702235, 61472188, and U1636117), Natural Science Foundation of Jiangsu Province (Grants no. BK20160840 and BK20150472), CCF-VENUSTECH Foundation (Grant no. 2016011), and Fundamental Research Funds for the Central Universities (30920140121006 and 30915012208).

References

1. Dingledine, R., Mathewson, N., Syverson, P.F.: Tor: the second-generation onion router. Proc. Usenix Secur. Symp. **40**(3), 191–212(2004)
2. Egger, C., Schlumberger, J., Kruegel, C., Vigna, G.: Practical attacks against the I2P network. In: Stolfo, S.J., Stavrou, A., Wright, C.V. (eds.) RAID 2013. LNCS, vol. 8145, pp. 432–451. Springer, Heidelberg (2013). https://doi.org/10.1007/978-3-642-41284-4_22
3. Boyan, J,F.: The anonymizer: protecting user privacy on the web. Comput. Mediat. Commun. Mag. **4**(9), 7–13 (1997)
4. Wang, X., Reeves, D.F.: The traceback problem. In: Traceback and Anonymity, pp. 5–13 (2015)
5. Lu, T., Guo, R., Zhao, L., et al.: A systematic review of network flow watermarking in anonymity systems. Int. J. Secur. Appl. **10**(3), 129–138(2016)
6. Birth, O.C.: Correlated network flows detection. In: Network Architectures and Services, pp. 93–99 (2011)
7. Ramsbrock, D., Wang, X., Jiang, X.: A first step towards live botmaster traceback. In: Lippmann, R., Kirda, E., Trachtenberg, A. (eds.) RAID 2008. LNCS, vol. 5230, pp. 59–77. Springer, Heidelberg (2008). https://doi.org/10.1007/978-3-540-87403-4_4
8. Wang, X., Reeves, D.S., Wu, S.F., Yuill, J.: Sleepy watermark tracing: an active network-based intrusion response framework. In: Dupuy, M., Paradinas, P. (eds.) SEC 2001. IIFIP, vol. 65, pp. 369–384. Springer, Boston, MA (2002). https://doi.org/10.1007/0-306-46998-7_26
9. Lv, J., Zhang, T., Li, Z., et al.: Pacom: parasitic anonymous communication in the bittorrent network. Comput. Netw. **74**, 13–33 (2014)
10. Yu, W., Fu, X., Graham, S., et al.: DSSS-based flow marking technique for invisible traceback. In: Security and Privacy, pp. 18–32(2007)
11. Houmansadr, A., Kiyavash, N., Borisov, N.F.: Non-blind watermarking of network flows. IEEE Trans. Netw. **22**(4), 1232–1244 (2014)
12. Wang, X., Reeves, D.F.: Robust correlation of encrypted attack traffic through stepping stones by flow watermarking. IEEE Trans. Dependable Secure Comput. **8**(3), 434–449 (2011)
13. Pyun, Y.J., Park, Y.H., Wang, X., et al.: Tracing traffic through intermediate hosts that repacketize flows. In: INFOCOM, pp. 634–642 (2007)
14. Houmansadr, A., Borisov, N.: F.: BotMosaic: collaborative network watermark for the detection of IRC-based botnets. J. Syst. Softw. **86**(3), 707–715 (2013)
15. Wang, X., Chen, S., Jajodia, S.C.: Network flow watermarking attack on low latency anonymous communication systems, pp. 116–130. IEEE Computer Society (2007)
16. Wang, X., Luo, J., Yang, M.C.: A double interval centroid based watermark for network flow traceback. In: Computer Supported Cooperative Work, pp. 146–151 (2010)
17. Luo, J., Wang, X., Yang, M.F.: An interval centroid based spread spectrum watermarking scheme for multi-flow traceback. J. Netw. Comput. Appl. **35**(1), 60–71 (2010)
18. Houmansadr, A., Borisov, N.C.: SWIRL: a scalable watermark to detect correlated network flows. In: Network and Distributed System Security Symposium (2011)
19. Kiyavash, N., Houmansadr, A., Borisov, N.C.: Multi-flow attacks against network flow watermarking schemes. In: Usenix Security Symposium, pp. 307–320 (2008)

A Covert Communication Model Based on IPv6 Multicast

Yazhou Kong[1]([mark]) [ID], Liancheng Zhang[1], Zhenxing Wang[1] [ID],
Yi Guo[1], and Wen Guo[2]

[1] State Key Laboratory of Mathematical Engineering and Advanced Computing,
Zhengzhou 450002, China
coyote0916@163.com
[2] National Airspace Management Center, Beijing 100094, China

Abstract. Covert communication using Internet Protocol version 6 (IPv6) header fields can be easily detected. By thoroughly exploring the characteristics of IPv6 multicast, this study proposes a novel covert communication model based on IPv6 multicast (MCv6). In this model, a multicast group, containing a large number of members across different subnets, is created to hide the receiver's network ID, thereby achieving covert communications. To ensure the security of this covert communication, a random key generation algorithm, based on the chaotic sequence, is proposed to encrypt communication packets. To ensure the legitimacy of covert communications, a multicast source authentication mechanism based on hash comparison is proposed to verify the legitimacy of communication source nodes. To ensure the integrity of covert communications, a two-stage error control mechanism is proposed to control the possible packet-loss and other errors. Theoretical analysis and simulation results show that the proposed MCv6 model can provide good IPv6-based covert communications, efficiently reducing the probability of detection, and ensuring the security and reliability of the IPv6-based medium.

Keywords: IPv6 · Multicast · Covert communication · Network security

1 Introduction

A covert channel is a public communication channel known only by the receiver. Network covert communication is a means of transferring secret information via multiple network data streams. This falls into two types: storage-based covert communications and time-based covert communications. In storage-based covert communications, secret information is embedded in some reserved bits or payloads of network packets. In time-based covert communications, secret information is modulated into the characteristics of network packets (e.g., sending interval, sending rate, and sending sequence) [1].

The Transmission Control Protocol (TCP)/Internet Protocol (IP) suite, based on IP version 4 (IPv4), contains a large number of covert channels. Jankowski et al. [2] proposed a method of using the Ethernet address resolution protocol and TCP for covert transmissions. David et al. [3] proposed a method of using IP and Ethernet

© Springer Nature Switzerland AG 2018
X. Sun et al. (Eds.): ICCCS 2018, LNCS 11066, pp. 85–98, 2018.
https://doi.org/10.1007/978-3-030-00015-8_8

frames to encode information into the payload header. [4–8] described a method of using the TCP extension header for covert communications. [9–12] argued that the TCP/IP header could be used as a covert channel.

With the exhaustion of the IPv4 address space, IPv6, the core protocol of the next generation internet, has begun to be widely deployed and applied. The internet is being migrated on a large scale to the IPv6 network. IPv6 supports unicast and anycast, and also provides mechanisms for sending and receiving multicast traffic. Multicast support is optional in IPv4 but is mandatory in IPv6. This study proposes a novel covert communication model based on IPv6 multicast (MCv6). In this model, a multicast group, containing a large number of members across multiple different subnets, is created to hide the receiver network ID, thereby achieving covert communications. To ensure the security of covert communications, a random key generation algorithm, based on the chaotic sequence, is proposed to encrypt communication packets. To ensure the legitimacy of covert communications, a multicast source authentication mechanism based on hash comparison (MSVHC) is proposed to verify the legitimacy of communication source nodes. To ensure the integrity of covert communications, a two-stage error control (TSEC) mechanism is proposed to control the possible packet-loss and other errors.

The rest of this paper is organized as follows. Section 2 reviews related literature, Sect. 3 describes the MCv6 model. Section 4 presents the theoretical analysis and simulation test of the MCv6 model. Section 5 provides a summary.

2 Literature Review

Regarding IPv4-based covert communication, Handel and Sandford [13] found that covert channels can be constructed using the unused type-of-service field, or flag field, in the TCP/IP header. Ahsa et al. [6] used the "Don't Fragment" bit of the flag field as a covert channel. Hintz [14] proposed a method of using the "Urgent" pointer in the TCP header to send covert data. Rowland [15] proposed a method of composing the IP ID by multiplying each byte of each field in the TCP/IPv4 header by 256. Rutkowska [16] proposed a method of encrypting the data in the Linux ISX field to achieve covert communications. Dunigan [17] implemented the covert channel proposed by Rowland in the Open Systems Interconnection model.

Regarding IPv6-based covert communications, Trabelsi [18] and Lucena et al. [19] proposed various methods of using fields, such as traffic class, flow label, and hop-by-hop in the IPv6 header, to create covert channels. [20] mentioned that an attacker could exploit IPv6 allocation and tunneling techniques to avoid network protection monitoring to complete the covert transmission. Gobbi et al. [21] showed that an attacker could use Internet Control Message Protocol version 6 (ICMPv6) to transmit data or initiate distributed denial-of-service attacks. Graf [22] found that the "Destination Options" header had no practical use in certain cases, and would not be changed by a router. He therefore proposed a method of using option data fields to create covert channels. Mumrphy [23] demonstrated using IPv6/ICMPv6-based covert channels to attack VoodooNet on the defense readiness condition system, arguing that such channels could penetrate most network protection systems.

Based on a comprehensive analysis of IPv4 and IPv6-based covert communications, this study proposes a MCv6 model.

3   MCv6 Model

Multicast is unidirectional communication. Its addresses cannot be used as source addresses. Therefore, multicast technology can only be used for unidirectional transmission from senders to receivers, and cannot meet the requirements of bidirectional communication. That is why the conventional IPv6 multicast technology cannot provide covert communication. To address this problem, this study proposes a MCv6 model. Based on hierarchical and reliable IPv6 multicast, this model creates a multicast group that contains a large number of members across multiple subnets to achieve covert communications. The following parts are described in detail: basic structure, communication process, multicast group creation policy, random key generation algorithm, and reliable multicast mechanism of MCv6.

3.1   Basic Structure of MCv6

All routers and hosts involved in MCv6 are network nodes that support IPv6 multicast.

Before describing the basic structure of MCv6, this paper first defines several important concepts:

Definition 3-1. Sender: the initiator of communication.

Definition 3-2. Agent Node (AN): located in different IPv6 subnets. Each subnet selects only one host as the AN. The AN of a subnet joins the agent multicast group to receive the covert data transmitted by senders through multicast and transfers the data to all global nodes in the subnet.

Definition 3-3. Global Node (GN): multiple host nodes located in different IPv6 subnets, which join the same global multicast group as the receiver.

Definition 3-4. Receiver: the recipient of communication. By joining the global multicast group, the receiver can receive packets transmitted by the AN through multicast, and can recover the original data through reassembly and decryption.

Definition 3-5. Edge Router (ER): a router on the edge of the sender's IPv6 network.

Definition 3-6. Access Router (AR): a router located at the edge of the receiver's IPv6 network. It connects hosts in the subnet to provide internet access services.

Definition 3-7. Receiver Network (RN): the IPv6 subnet where the receiver is located.

MCv6 uses hierarchical multicast (i.e., agent and global layers). The basic structure of MCv6 is shown in Fig. 1.

An Agent Group (AG) is a multicast group composed of multiple ANs, having a unique multicast address.

A Global Group (GG) is a multicast group composed of multiple GNs, also having a unique multicast address.

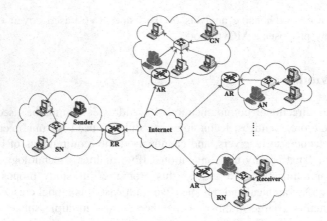

Fig. 1. Basic structure of MCv6

3.2 Multicast Group Creation Policy

To concisely describe the creation rules, this study uses the node IP address and group address to identify a multicast group member (i.e., a binary group $< IP, M\_add >$). Combined with the analysis of improving the MCv6 covert communication capability, the basic rules for creating a multicast group can be described as follows.

Assume that the set, $D1 = \{ < IP, M\_add >_i | M\_add = AM\_add, i \in (1, \ldots n), n \in N^* \}$, represents the set of all ANs, and the subset, $D2 = \{ < IP, GM\_add >_i | IP_{Prefix} \text{ is the same}, i \in (1, \ldots n), n \in N^* \}$, represents the members of the GGs in different subnets.

M_add represents the multicast group address. AM_add represents the AG address. GM_add represents the GG address.

(a) $|A1| \geq 2$; the same AG must have as many ANs (at least two) located in different subnets.

(b) $A1 \neq \emptyset$; the number of global nodes in the same subnet should as many as possible (at least one, excluding zero).

Random Key Generation Algorithm

During MCv6 data transmission, packets should be encrypted to guarantee data security. Chaotic mapping is an efficient encryption method, characterized by randomness, speed, simplicity, and high efficiency. Therefore, this study uses the chaotic mapping method to generate pseudo-random binary sequences as keys.

This study uses the typical logistic iterative formula of chaotic mapping to generate session keys. The logistic formula is $X_{n+1} = \lambda X_n (1 - X_n)$ ($0 < \lambda \leq 4, 0 < x \leq 1, n = 0, 1, 2 \ldots$). After logistic mapping, the last 128 values are compared with 0.5. Values less than or equal to 0.5 are set to 1, whereas values greater than 0.5 are set to 0, forming a 128-bit key. Then an exclusive-OR operation is performed between the calculated 128-bit key and the 16-byte data to generate encrypted data.

Reliable Multicast Mechanism

In this study, the network application scenario poses very high demand for the correctness and completeness of the received data during data transmission. Therefore, this study proposes two reliable multicast mechanisms: MSVHC and TSEC.

The two reliable multicast mechanisms are described in detail below.

(i) MSVHC

MSVHC is a multicast source verification mechanism based on hash comparison. This mechanism allows the sender to generate source verification data in real time when sending data. After receiving a packet, the receiver can immediately verify it to ensure correctness and security.

This mechanism uses two one-way hash functions: H_1 and H_2. The output lengths of H_1 and H_2 are N and M bits, respectively, where $M = L \times K$. M and L are chosen by considering the overall mechanism performance and the security of the source verification mechanism.

(a) Sender

First, the sender selects 2^K N-bit random integers, $E_i^0 (i = 1, 2 \ldots 2^K)$. The sender uses H_1 to generate 2^K hash function value chains, as shown in Fig. 2. The lengths of the function value chains are n.

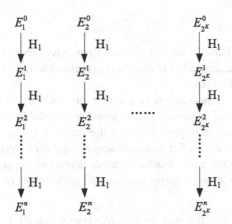

Fig. 2. One-way hash function value chains

Then, the sender uses n, which is the length of the hash function value chains of $E_1^n, E_2^n, \ldots, E_{2^K}^n$, and the signature applied to data using the private key to generates a multicast packet. After receiving this packet, the receiver uses the sender's public key to verify the packet. If the packet passes verification, the receiver receives the packet and uses it to perform source verification for the subsequent multicast packets received from the sender. Assume that the sequence of multicast packets sent by the sender is $P_0, P_1, \ldots, P_{n-1}$. When the sender attempts to send the jth packet P_j, the following source verification data is generated.

- Step number of the hash function value chain used in source verification: $n-j-1$.
- Hash value of P_j and n-j-1, which can be calculated using H_2. The sender sets this hash value to HP_j. Then, the sender divides HP_j into L fields with K bits, and regards the bit fields as binary integers, marks $(B_1, \ldots, B_L)$ as L integers obtained, and chooses $(E_{B1}^{n-j-1}, \ldots, E_{BL}^{n-j-1})$ from $(E_1^{n-j-1}, \ldots, E_{2^K}^{n-j-1})$.

Finally, the sender appends $n-j-1$ and $(E_{B1}^{n-j-1}, \ldots, E_{BL}^{n-j-1})$ as the source verification data of M_j at the end of packet, M_j.

(b) Receiver

The receiver uses H_2 to perform a hash operation on the received packet and the step number of the hash function value chain. The receiver also divides the generated message digest into L bit fields, and regards them as L binary integers. Then the receiver marks L integers as $(A1, A_L)$. Assume that the received source verification data is $(E_{A1}^{n-j-1}, \ldots, E_{AL}^{n-j-1})$. The receiver only needs to verify whether $H_1^{j+1}\left(E_{A1}^{n-j-1}\right)$ is equal to E_{Ai}^n. If all of the L equations hold, the packet is from the sender. Otherwise, the packet is from another unknown node. If the source verification is successful, the receiver will record n-j-1, the step number of the hash function value chain. The step number of the hash function value chain contained in the packets subsequently coming from the sender must be smaller than n-j-1. Otherwise, the receiver directly determines that the verification fails.

(ii) TSEC

Although many reliable multicast mechanisms have been proposed by existing literature, they do not adapt well to IPv6 covert communications. To this end, this study proposes a TSEC mechanism.

In MCv6, the TSEC mechanism is enabled only when the receiver experiences packet-loss. This mechanism combines the tree-based reliable multicast protocol and the automatic retransmission request based on the receiver's negative acknowledgment (NACK), and includes two packet-recovery stages: agent recovery and source recovery. If a packet fails at the agent recovery stage, it goes to the source recovery stage.

The retransmission request steps in case of packet-loss of the receiver are as follows.

(a) The receiver requests the AN in the receiver's subnet to retransmit packets. The AN will retransmit packets if it can. Otherwise, the procedure goes to (b).
(b) The AN sends a request to other ANs in the AG to query whether any AN' receives this packet. If "yes," the procedure goes to (d). If "no," the procedure goes to (c).
(c) Some ANs in the AG sends a retransmission request to the sender.
(d) When receiving this packet, AN sends it to the AN of the subnet where the receiver is located. Then this AN forwards the packet to the receiver.

This study involves two types of NACK packets.

(a) NACK packet initiated by the receiver. When the receiver experiences packet-loss, it sends a NACK to the AN of the receiver's subnet.
(b) NACK packet initiated by the AN. If no AN can complete packet retransmission, the AN sends a NACK to the sender.

4 MCv6 Model Analysis

A theoretical analysis of MCv6 performance, including covert communication capability and transmission performance, is described below.

4.1 Analysis of the Covert Communication Capability

(i) Covert communication capability of the subnet

Assume that attackers can check the existence of covert communicators through remote detection only. Attackers can detect the host nodes in the receiver's subnet by randomly sending packet, with the destination address of each packet being different. Let p represent the probability of attackers correctly detecting the active nodes in the RN through packets. The mean value of p can be given by

$$E(p) = \frac{m \cdot r \cdot k}{v \cdot T},$$ (1)

where m represents the number of nodes detected by an attacker; r represents the number of detection packets sent per second; v represents the number of subnets where all multicast group members are located (if $v = 1$, all multicast group members are located in the same subnet as the receiver); k represents the number of surviving nodes in the same subnet as the receiver; and T represents the number of host interface identifiers available in the destination network (in IPv6, this value is 2^{64}).

It can be seen from the derived equation that the number of detection packets that attackers successfully send to the surviving nodes in the RN is related to the number of subnets where all multicast group members are located, v, and the number of surviving hosts in the RN, k. The greater the v, the smaller the k, and the less probable the receiver is of being detected.

Conclusion 1: An MCv6 multicast group resides across a large number of different subnets, thereby reducing the probability of receivers being detected by attackers and improving the covert communication capability. The degree of such improvement is related to the number of subnets where all multicast group members and the surviving hosts in the RN are located.

(ii) Non-detectability of the subnet

Assume that an attacker detects the existence of covert communication, monitors all communication links, and analyzes and intercepts the packets to check the existence of the RN. Because the AG has a large number of ANs having similar communication behaviors and are located in different subnets, it is difficult for attackers to find the RN.

This study investigates the subnet non-detectability of MCv6 by calculating the probability of attackers successfully detecting the RN. This issue can be modeled as a classical ballot issue. This study uses the ball-fetching model to describe this issue. Assume there are n balls in a bag. n represents the number of subnets where all multicast group members are located, among which there is only one red ball representing the RN. Then the following calculations are made:

The probability of attackers obtaining the real RN after one analysis is given by

$$P_1 = \frac{1}{m}. \tag{2}$$

The probability of attackers obtaining the real RN after the second analysis (indicating that the first analysis fails) is given by

$$P_2 = \frac{A_{m-1}^1}{A_m^2} = \frac{1}{m}. \tag{3}$$

In the same manner, the probability of attackers obtaining the real RN after the ith analysis is given by

$$P_i = \frac{A_{m-1}^{i-1}}{A_m^i} = \frac{1}{m} \tag{4}$$

It can be seen from the above analysis that the probability of attackers successfully detecting the RN is related to the number of subnets where all multicast group members are located, m. In particular, the greater the m, the less probable the RN is of being detected.

Conclusion 2: MCv6 reduces the probability of the RN being detected by attackers and improves the covert communication capability. The degree of such improvement is positively correlated to the number of subnets where all multicast group members are located.

4.2   Transmission Performance Analysis

Packet Restoration Delay

The TSEC mechanism includes two data recovery stages: agent recovery and source recovery. The data recovery delay differs during each stage. This section analyzes the MCv6 packet-recovery delay from two aspects: the agent recovery delay and the source recovery delay.

This study uses a receipt vector as long as L, $\{X_L|L = 1, 2, 3\ldots\}$, to represent the receipt of all packets, with 0 indicating packet-loss and 1 indicating successful receipt of packets. For example, 10010 indicates that No. 1 and No. 4 packets are successfully received whereas No. 2, No. 3, and No. 5 packets are lost. Assume that all packets are lost at the same probability. For any multicast packet, the probability of correct receipt of receivers is p, each bit, $\{b_i|i = 1, 2, 3\ldots L\}$, in the receipt vector, $\{X_L|L = 1, 2, 3\ldots\}$, is the random variable of the value range, $M = \{0, 1\}$.

b_i obeys the distribution from 0 to 1. Its probability distribution is presented in Table 1.

Table 1. b_i probability distribution

b_i	0	1
Probability	$1-p$	p

Because packet-loss on nodes is independent and identically distributed, the value of each bit and receipt vector are also independent and identically distributed. Therefore, for any positive integer, L, and values, $x_1, x_2, \ldots x_n, x_{n+1}$,

$$P(X_{n+1} = X_{n+1}|X_1 = X_1, X_2 = X_2, X_n = X_n) = P(X_{n+1} = X_{n+1}|X_n = X_n). \quad (5)$$

That is, the receipt vector at time, $n + 1$, is only related to that at time, n. The following theorem is thus deduced.

Theorem 1. The receipt vector, $\{X_L|L = 1, 2, 3\ldots\}$, is a homogeneous Markov chain.

The receiver will not initiate the retransmission request until all packets are received or the timer expires. For the convenience of description, the case of sending two consecutive data packets is used as an example. That is, the length of the receipt vector is 2.

(i) Probability of successful AN recovery

Assume that the receiver experiences packet-loss and requests retransmission from the AN. Because the receipt vector is a homogeneous Markov chain, the state of any time, a, can be obtained by multiplying the absolute probability at time, b, and the state transition matrix, P^k, in which $k = a-b$.

The state space is $\Omega = \{00, 01, 10, 11\}$. The transition matrix of AN recovery P is

$$P = \begin{pmatrix} 1 & 0 & 0 & 0 \\ 1 - \sum_{w=0}^{v-1} p^w(1-p)^{v-w} & \sum_{w=0}^{v-1} p^w(1-p)^{v-w} & 0 & 0 \\ 1 - \sum_{w=0}^{v-1} p^w(1-p)^{v-w} & 0 & \sum_{w=0}^{v-1} p^w(1-p)^{v-w} & 0 \\ 1 - 2\sum_{w=0}^{v-1} p^w(1-p)^{v-w} - (1-p)^{2v} & \sum_{w=0}^{v-1} p^w(1-p)^{v-w} & \sum_{w=0}^{v-1} p^w(1-p)^{v-w} & (1-p)^{2v} \end{pmatrix}$$

where v represents the number of ANs, and w represents the number of ANs, of which, the receipt vector is $\{11\}$.

Obviously, P is a lower triangular matrix, from which a probability distribution, $\pi = \{1, 0, 0, 0\}$, can be detected to make $\pi = \pi P$, and $\pi = \{1, 0, 0, 0\}$ a steady distribution of a homogeneous Markov chain. This indicates that the receiver will eventually stay in the $\{11\}$ state: a stable state in which packet-recovery is successful.

Therefore, the probability of the receiver successfully recovering lost packets can be obtained.

$$
\begin{aligned}
P_D &= \pi_0(n+1)P \\
&= 2p^2 - 2p + 1 - (1-2p)^{2v+2} + 2(2p-1)(1-p)\sum_{w=0}^{v-1} p^w (1-p)^{v-w}
\end{aligned}
\tag{6}
$$

(ii) Probability of successful sender recovery

If the AN cannot recover lost packets, the sender retransmit them. At that time, the probability of the sender successfully recovering lost packets is

$$
P_S = p^2(1 - P_D)
\tag{7}
$$

The average recovery delay, $E(T)$, can be obtained using Eqs. (6) and (7).

$$
E(T) = (P_D + P_S) \cdot T_{NACK} \cdot v + (1 - p^2) \cdot T_w
\tag{8}
$$

where T_{NACK} represents the time required for transmitting a NACK packet, and T_w represents the delay of the backhaul.

It can be seen from the above analyses that, in MCv6, the average delay of successful packet-recovery is related to the number of ANs, the number of ANs that successfully receive packets, the NACK transmission time, and the delay of the backhaul. The number of ANs is equivalent to the number of different subnets, where all multicast group members are located. The number of ANs that successfully receive packets depends on the packet-loss rate of the link. The backhaul delay is related to the number of transmitted packets.

4.3   Simulation Analysis

To verify the MCv6 transmission performance and covert ability, this study carries out a simulation analysis. Generally, the global routing prefix has 48 bits, and the number of available networks is 2^{48}. The subnet identifier has 16 bits, and the number of available subnet identifiers in a network is 2^{16}. For the convenience of calculation and analysis, this study assumes that there are 200 networks, each having 300 available subnet IDs. Only one of these networks is a real receiver network.

MCv6 Covert Communication Capability

The number of different subnets where AG members are located has an important impact on the covert communication capabilities of MCv6. The larger the number of different subnets where AG members are located is, the more difficult the receiver network is of being detected by attackers.

It can be seen from Fig. 3 that, as the number of available subnets increases, the probability of the RN being found by the attacker decreases. When there is only one available subnet (i.e., all the nodes are in the same subnet), the probability of the RN being found by attackers is the highest.

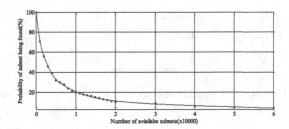

Fig. 3. Changes of probability of the RN being found with the number of subnets

MCv6 Transmission Performance

Assume that each link has the same packet-loss rate and the NACK transmission time remains unchanged. To test the MCv6 transmission performance, this study simulates and analyzes the impacts of the number of different subnets where the AG members are located, v, and the number of sent packets, L, on the average recovery delay and packet-delivery rate.

Average recovery delay is the total average time required from the loss of a packet to the successful recovery of the packet.

Packet-delivery rate is the percentage of the number of packets successfully received by the receiver in the total number of packets sent by the sender.

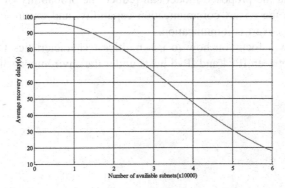

Fig. 4. Changes of the average recovery delay with the number of subnets

Figure 4 shows the simulation results of the changes of the average recovery delay with the number of subnets, v. Figure 5 shows the simulation results of the changes of the packet-delivery rate with the number of packets, L, under different numbers of available subnets. It can be seen from the results that when the number of transmitted packets, L, remains the same as v increases, the average recovery delay decreases, and the packet-delivery rate and MCv6 transmission performance increase.

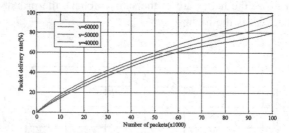

Fig. 5. Changes of the packet-delivery rate with the number of subnets

5 Summary

In existing studies, IPv6 covert communication mainly uses fields in the basic header or extended header, causing communications to be easily detected. By thoroughly exploiting IPv6 multicast characteristics, this study proposes an MCv6 model. In this model, a multicast group consisting of a large number of members across multiple different subnets was created based on the technological concept of hierarchical and reliable IPv6 multicast to hide IPv6 addresses of receivers, thereby achieving covert communication. To ensure the security of covert communication, a random key generation algorithm based on the chaotic sequence was proposed to encrypt communication packets. To ensure the legitimacy of covert communication, an MSVHC mechanism was proposed to verify the legitimacy of communication source nodes. To ensure the integrity of covert communication, a TSEC mechanism was proposed to control possible packet-loss and other errors. The theoretical analysis and simulation results showed that the proposed model can reduce the probability of receivers being detected, improve the covert communication capability, and ensure the security and reliability of IPv6 covert communication.

Future work will focus on how to use multicast characteristics to realize covert communication between IPv4 and IPv6 hosts under the environment of IPv4 and IPv6 coexistence.

References

1. Huang, Y., Li, S.: Network covert communication and its detection technology, pp. 13–14, Tsinghua University Press, Beijing (2016)
2. Jankowski, B., Mazurczyk, W., Szczypiorski, K.: Information hiding using improper frame padding. In: Telecommunications and Network Strategy and Planning Symposium (NETWORKS), pp. 1–6. IEEE (2010)
3. Anthony, D., et al.: A behavior based covert channel within anti-virus updates. In: Proceedings of the International Conference on Security and Management (SAM), p. 1. The Steering Committee of The World Congress in Computer Science, Computer Engineering and Applied Computing (WorldComp) (2012)
4. Murdoch, S.J.: Covert channel vulnerabilities in anonymity systems. No. UCAM-CL-TR-706. University of Cambridge, Computer Laboratory (2007)
5. Johnson, N.F., Duric, Z., Jajodia, S.: Information Hiding: Steganography and Watermarking-Attacks and Countermeasures: Steganography and Watermarking: Attacks and Counter-measures, vol. 1. Springer Science & Business Media, New York (2001). https://doi.org/10.1007/978-1-4615-4375-6
6. Ahsan, K., Kundur, D.: Practical data hiding in TCP/IP. In: Proceedings Workshop on Multimedia Security at ACM Multimedia, vol. 2. No. 7 (2002)
7. Frikha, L., Trabelsi, Z., Tabbane, S.: Simulation, optimisation and integration of Covert Channels, Intrusion Detection and packet filtering systems. In: Information Infrastructure Symposium, GIIS 2009. Global. IEEE (2009)
8. Allix, P.: Covert channels analysis in TCP/IP networks. IFIPS School of Engineering, University of Paris-Sud XI, Orsay, France (2007)
9. Zander, S., Armitage, G., Branch, P.: A survey of covert channels and countermeasures in computer network protocols. IEEE Commun. Surv. Tutorials 9(3), 44–57 (2007)
10. Supriyanto, R.K.M., Ramadass, S.: Review on ipv6 security vulnerability issues and mitigation methods. Int. J. Netw. Secur. Appl. 4(6), 173 (2012)
11. Zagar, D., Grgic, K.: IPv6 security threats and possible solutions. In: Automation Congress, WAC 2006. World, pp. 1–7. IEEE (2006)
12. Abley, J., Savola, P., Neville-Neil, G.: Deprecation of type 0 routing headers in ipv6. draft-ietf-ipv6-deprecate-rh0-01 (2007)
13. Handel, T.G., Sandford, M.T.: Hiding data in the OSI network model. In: Anderson, R. (ed.) IH 1996. LNCS, vol. 1174, pp. 23–38. Springer, Heidelberg (1996). https://doi.org/10.1007/3-540-61996-8_29
14. Hintz, A.: Covert channels in TCP and IP headers. Presentation at DEFCON 10 (2002)
15. Rowland, C.H.: Covert channels in the TCP/IP protocol suite. First Monday 2(5), (1997)
16. Rutkowska, J.: The implementation of passive covert channels in the Linux kernel. In: Chaos Communication Congress, Chaos Computer Club eV (2004)
17. Tom, D.: Internet steganography. Technical report, Oak Ridge National Laboratory (Contract No. DE-AC05-96OR22464), Oak Ridge, Tennessee (1998)
18. Trabelsi, Z., Jawhar, I.: Covert file transfer protocol based on the IP record route option. J. Inf. Assur. Secur. 5(1), 64–73 (2010)
19. Lucena, N.B., Lewandowski, G., Chapin, S.J.: Covert Channels in IPv6. In: Danezis, G., Martin, D. (eds.) PET 2005. LNCS, vol. 3856, pp. 147–166. Springer, Heidelberg (2006). https://doi.org/10.1007/11767831_10

20. Plonka, D., Berger, A.: kIP: a Measured Approach to IPv6 Address Anonymization. arXiv preprint arXiv:1707.03900 (2017)
21. Ryan Giobbi Homepage: Filtering ICMPv6 Using Host-Based Firewalls. https://www.cert.org/blogs/vuls/2008/11/icmpv6_types_and_hostbased_fir.html. Accessed 21 Dec 2017
22. Graf, T.: Messaging over IPv6 destination options (2003)
23. Murphy, R.P.: IPv6/ICMPv6 Covert Channels. Defcon, Las Vegas (2006)

A Data Hiding Scheme with High Quality for H.264/AVC Video Streams

Yi Chen[1], Hongxia Wang[1(✉)], Hanzhou Wu[2], Yanli Chen[1], and Yong Liu[1]

[1] School of Information Science and Technology, Southwest Jiaotong University,
Chengdu 611756, People's Republic of China
yichen.research@gmail.com, yanli_027@163.com
[2] Chinese Academy of Sciences (CAS), Institute of Automation, Beijing 100190,
People's Republic of China
hxwang@swjtu.edu.cn, wuhanzhou_2007@126.com,
liuymy@my.swjtu.edu.cn

Abstract. Visual quality and bit-rate increase are two main metrics of evaluation for many researchers to evaluate the marked videos that additional data is embedded into. In this paper, we combine matrix embedding with several assumptions to propose a novel data hiding method in H.264/AVC video stream. The assumptions can be exploited to analyse the propagation of intra-frame distortion. Namely, both matrix embedding and the given assumptions are used for improving the quality of marked videos. Therefore, although the proposed scheme cannot completely avoid the intra-frame distortion drift, it can keep a few degradations in terms of visual quality and keep a small variation in bit-rate increase. Experimental results have verified that the proposed method has no significant degradation in terms of visual quality (i.e., PSNR and SSIM) and indeed obtains a very small variation in bit-rate increase.

Keywords: Data hiding · Matrix embedding · Visual quality
Bit-rate increase · H.264/AVC

1 Introduction

Data hiding (DH) [1,2], also called as information hiding, is an important technology to embed/hide additional data into the host by slightly changing its insignificant component for covert communication [3,4]. In general, encryption [5] is another successful technology to protect confidentiality of important message/data. With the technology of encryption, the important information is encrypted and the unauthorized users without the decryption key cannot decrypt the encrypted information correctly and know the content of the original information. However, the unauthorized users they can make sure that there exists some data transmitted in communication. Therefore, the unauthorized users can destroy the transmitted data during the procedure of communication so that the authorized users cannot obtain the complete encrypted data. Even they

© Springer Nature Switzerland AG 2018
X. Sun et al. (Eds.): ICCCS 2018, LNCS 11066, pp. 99–110, 2018.
https://doi.org/10.1007/978-3-030-00015-8_9

can decrypt the destroyed information, they may not know the content of the original information correctly. Moreover, communication may be stopped when it is found. Based on the description mentioned above, therefore, the technology of DH is commonly used for protecting the to-be-transmitted information by embedding it into hosts because the technology makes unauthorized users hard to observe there exists data to be transmitted. Up to now, the technology of DH has attracted an increasing interest from many researchers.

For instance, Wu *et al.* proposed a DH scheme for covert communication in [6]. They first obtain the prediction errors of the pixels to be embedded according to their neighboring pixels. After that, the prediction-error of prediction error of a pixel is taken use of to carry the secret data. Actually, the technology of DH is exploited in many applications for different purposes, such as privacy protection, video authentication, copyright protection, broadcast monitoring, playback control, fingerprinting, and online location [7]. For example, Ma *et al.* propose a DH method for region-of-interest privacy protection in surveillance videos [8]. In this scheme, they introduce the concept of lossless region-of-interest privacy protection where the authorized users can recover the unaltered original compressed video bitstream. Therefore, the recovered/descrambled video can pass complete authentication to be adopted as evidence, which makes the authorized users benefit. In addition, the authors in [9] proposed a watermarking scheme satisfying the requirement of the copyright protection and content authentication. In their scheme, robust watermarking and fragile watermarking are embedded into the feature points and the non-feature point of vector maps, respectively. The robust watermarking is used for copyright protection and the fragile watermarking is used for content authentication because they are independent. In this paper, we propose a DH method with good visual quality for covert communication.

Generally speaking, PSNR, SSIM and variation of bit-rate are three commonly used metrics to evaluate the performance of the DH method. PSNR and SSIM are exploited to judge the visual quality on marked video sequences and the bit-rate variation is exploited to evaluate the coding efficiency of the data embedding encoder. In 2006, Zhang and Wang [10] proposed a data hiding algorithm by Exploiting Modification Directions (EMD). The main idea of this algorithm is that each secret digit in a $(2n+1)$-ary notational system is carried by n cover pixels, and at most only one pixel is increased or decreased by 1. It is a successful algorithm to reduce the distortion and achieve satisfactory visual quality after embedding data. Based on this work, Chen *et al.* proposed an adaptive DH for H.264/AVC video streams [11]. This scheme makes use of middle and high frequency coefficients (according to zig-zag scanning order) combined with EMD to realize a video DH scheme with low bit-rate growth. Recently, Fallahpour *et al.* also proposed to take advantage of high frequency coefficients to carry additional data in videos [12]. In their scheme, the parity of the position of the last nonzero coefficients in the embeddable blocks is modified for DH. Therefore, their scheme can guarantee good visual quality and slight bit-rate increase. Additionally, Ma *et al.* exploited several coefficient-pairs combined with intra-frame predictions to propose a DH scheme without intra-frame distortion drift in [13]. It is noted that these coefficients are fixedly paired two by two and only the correct coefficient-pairs combined with intra-frame modes can avoid the distortion caused by DH spreading in intra-frames. Thus, this scheme can achieve a good visual quality and small bit-rate variation of marked videos. Alternatively, the technology of matrix embedding [14] is a successful way to reduce the distortion caused by DH. Thus, we give a probability analysis of the intra-frame distortion drift caused by DH in the current luma block of intra-frames. After that, based on the analysis, we select the embeddable blocks and use matrix embedding to propose a DH scheme with good visual quality and slight variation in bit-rate in this paper.

The remainder of the paper is organized as follows. The proposed scheme, involving *Selection of Blocks for Data Hiding, Data Embedding* and *Data extraction*, is presented in Sect. 2. Experimental results and analysis are given in Sect. 3. Finally, we draw some conclusions in Sect. 4.

2 Proposed Scheme

Three parts, i.e., *Selection of Blocks for Data Hiding, Data Embedding* and *Data extraction*, are given in this Section. We first give an analysis of probability about the intra-frame distortion drift in Subsect. 2.1. *Data Embedding* and *Data Extraction* are given in Subsects. 2.2 and 2.3, respectively.

2.1 Selection of Blocks for Data Hiding

In 2010, Ma *et al.* first found the intra-frame prediction modes, which referred to three conditions, i.e., *Condition 1, Condition 2* and *Condition 3*, could be exploited to avoid the intra-frame distortion drift and thus obtain good visual quality in terms of marked videos [13]. Based on their work, we will address how to select blocks for our proposed scheme in this subsection. Without loss of generality, we will first give some assumptions as follows.

Assumption 1: For every 4×4 luma block, the probability of using intra-frame 4×4 predictions or intra-frame 16×16 predictions is equal. In other words, $P(Intra4 \times 4) = P(Intra16 \times 16) = \frac{1}{2}$, where Intra4×4 and Intra16 × 16 are short of intra-frame 4×4 prediction and intra-frame 16×16 prediction, respectively.

Assumption 2: For every 4×4 luma block, the probability of using any one of the intra-frame 4×4 prediction modes is identical. Namely, $P(Intra4 \times 4_0) = P(Intra4 \times 4_1) = ... = P(Intra4 \times 4_8) = \frac{1}{9}$, which are corresponding to the 9 intra-frame 4×4 prediction modes [15], respectively.

Assumption 3: Likewise, for every 4×4 luma block, the probability of using any one of the intra-frame 16×16 prediction modes is identical. Namely, $P(Intra16 \times 16_0) = P(Intra16 \times 16_1) = ... = P(Intra16 \times 16_3) = \frac{1}{4}$, which are corresponding to the 4 intra-frame 16×16 prediction modes [15], respectively.

In general, the above-mentioned conditions are combined with some properties or/and technologies for DH. For example, several coefficient-pairs and the conditions are exploited to embed additional data into the videos in [13] while averting the intra-frame distortion drift. Moreover, histogram shifting and the conditions are used for DH in this scheme of [16] while averting the intra-frame distortion drift. In this paper, we combine matrix embedding with the selected embeddable blocks to propose a novel DH scheme with good visual quality. Although the proposed method cannot completely avoid the intra-frame distortion drift, it can keep a low degradation in terms of visual quality and a low increase in bit-rate.

Before the selection of blocks for DH, we first calculate the probability of meeting *Condition* 1, *Condition* 2 and *Condition* 3, which are as follows:

$$
\begin{aligned}
P(Condition\ 1) &= P(Intra4 \times 4)P(Intra4 \times 4_*)_{C1} \\
&+ P(Intra16 \times 16)P(Intra16 \times 16_*)_{C1}
\end{aligned}
\tag{1}
$$

where $P(Intra4 \times 4_*)_{C1}$ and $P(Intra16 \times 16_*)_{C1}$ represent the probabilities of meeting the *Condition* 1 in the intra-frame 4×4 luma prediction modes and the intra-frame 16×16 luma prediction modes, respectively. Thus, We can know $P(Intra4 \times 4_*)_{C1} = \frac{3}{9}$, $P(Intra16 \times 16_*)_{C1} = \frac{1}{4}$ and $P(Condition\ 1) = \frac{1}{2} \times \frac{3}{9} + \frac{1}{2} \times \frac{1}{4} = \frac{7}{24}$.

Similarly, we can obtain $P(Condition\ 2)$ and $P(Condition\ 3)$ as follows.

$$
\begin{aligned}
P(Condition\ 2) &= P(Intra4 \times 4)P(Intra4 \times 4_*)_{C2-UL} \\
&\quad ((P(Intra4 \times 4)P(Intra4 \times 4_*)_{C2-U} \\
&+ P(Intra16 \times 16)P(Intra16 \times 16_*)_{C2-U})) \\
&+ P(Intra16 \times 16)P(Intra16 \times 16_*)_{C2-UL} \\
&\quad ((P(Intra4 \times 4)P(Intra4 \times 4_*)_{C2-U} \\
&+ P(Intra16 \times 16)P(Intra16 \times 16_*)_{C2-U}))
\end{aligned}
\tag{2}
$$

where $P(Intra4 \times 4_*)_{C2-UL}$ and $P(Intra16 \times 16_*)_{C2-UL}$ denote the probabilities of meeting the *Condition* 2 in the intra-frame 4×4 luma prediction modes and the intra-frame 16×16 luma prediction modes of *the under-left-block*, respectively. Likewise, $P(Intra4 \times 4_*)_{C2-U}$ and $P(Intra16 \times 16_*)_{C2-U}$ denote the probabilities of meeting the *Condition* 2 in the intra-frame 4×4 luma prediction modes and the intra-frame 16×16 luma prediction modes of *the under-block*, respectively. Therefore, $P(Condition\ 2) = \frac{17}{81}$.

$$
\begin{aligned}
P(Condition\ 3) &= P(Intra4 \times 4)P(Intra4 \times 4_*)_{C3} \\
&+ P(Intra16 \times 16)P(Intra16 \times 16_*)_{C3}
\end{aligned}
\tag{3}
$$

Obviously, we can obtain $P(Condition\ 3) = \frac{5}{6}$. Thus, for a given block, the probability of meeting *Condition* 1 and *Condition* 2 at the same time but not considering *Condition* 3 is that $P(NoIntraFrameDrift) = P(Condition\ 1)P(Condition\ 2) = \frac{7}{24} \times \frac{17}{81} = \frac{119}{1944} \approx 0.0612$. Similarly, the probability of meeting *Condition* 1 and *Condition* 2 but not meeting *Condition* 3 is $P(IntraFrameDrift) = P(Condition\ 1)P(Condition\ 2)P(\overline{Condition\ 3}) = \frac{119}{11664} \approx 0.0102$. In other words, the probabilities mentioned above are very close

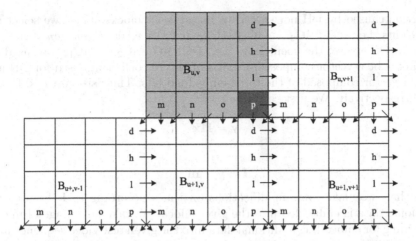

Fig. 1. The distortion caused by DH in the current block propagates to its neighboring blocks. Namely, the modifications of the pixels, i.e., d, h, l, m, n, o and p, will lead to the intra-frame distortion drift due to the intra-frame prediction.

and embedding data into the current block causes a low distortion while meeting *Condition* 1 and *Condition* 2 but not *Condition* 3. Therefore, the current block is selected as the embeddable block if it meets *Condition* 1 and *Condition* 2 at the same time in the proposed scheme. That is to say, we do not consider that the modification on the pixel "p" (shown in Fig. 1) causes a distortion.

2.2 Data Embedding

To improve the visual quality of marked videos, we take advantage of matrix embedding [14] combined with the selected blocks according to Subsect. 2.1 for DH. It is noted that the selected block must meet the value of the DC coefficient is nonzero. In the proposed method, the parity check matrix $\mathbf{H}$ is with the size of 4×15. Therefore, we only need 15 coefficients to carry additional data. For a given block (shown as Fig. 2), we try to keep AC_{15} unchanged and make the

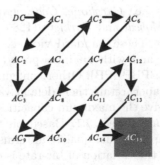

Fig. 2. A 4×4 luma block containing 16 coefficients.

distortion caused by DH not spread to its adjacent blocks. Thus, we select the coefficients, i.e., $AC_1, AC_2, ..., AC_{14}, AC_{15}$, for DH when *Condition* 3 are not satisfied. Otherwise, the coefficients, i.e., DC, $AC_1, AC_2, ..., AC_{14}$, are used for DH. Let **x** be a vector composed of LSBs of the 15 coefficients used for DH and **m** be a vector composed of the to-be-embedded bits. Their size are 1×15 and 1×4, respectively. We first calculate

$$\mathbf{y} = \mathbf{Hx} \tag{4}$$

and

$$\mathbf{I} = \mathbf{y} - \mathbf{m}. \tag{5}$$

After that, we make some modifications on the **x** according to **I**. Finally, the additional data is embedded into the given block. We take advantage of matrix embedding for embedding additional data into the given test video sequence until the test video sequence is embedded data into completely. The readers want to know more details about matrix embedding and they can refer to [14].

2.3 Data Extraction

The procedure of extracting data is simple and is addressed as follows.

We can obtain the embeddable blocks and carrier coefficients according to Subsect. 2.1. Thus, we can extract the embedded data by

$$\mathbf{m}' = \mathbf{Hx}' \tag{6}$$

where $\mathbf{x}'$ is a vector composed of LSBs of the 15 coefficients corresponding to the corresponding block at encoder side. In other words, $\mathbf{x}'$ carries the embedded data. $\mathbf{m}'$ is the embedded bits. Similarly, we do the operation mentioned above until all the embedded bits are extracted out completely.

3   Experimental Results

Experiments are performed on the H.264/AVC reference software JM12.0 with Main profile [17]. To evaluate the performance of the proposed method objectively, the 7 video sequences, i.e., *Carphone, Coastguard, Foreman, Hall, Mobile* (176×144 pixels/frame), *Mobcal* and *Parkrun* (1280×720 pixels/frame) [18], are used to be test samples. These standard video sequences are encoded into 300 frames at 15 frames/s and with an intra-period of 10 (group of picture (GOP):IBPBPBPBPBPBPBPBPBPB). Other configuration parameters, which are not mentioned in this paper, retain their default values.

In this section, we first give the maximum capacities of the proposed method on the 7 video sequences in Subsect. 3.1. Based on the maximum capacities aforementioned, we evaluate the visual quality in terms of PSNR and SSIM [19] in Subsect. 3.2. In addition, the variation of bit-rate is evaluated in Subsect. 3.3.

Table 1. Maximum embedding capacity (bits) on the video sequences

Sequences	QP = 26			QP = 28		
	[13]	*Thr = 13* [12]	Proposed	[13]	*Thr = 13* [12]	Proposed
Carphone	1023	1370	1288	999	879	1272
Coastguard	1743	2483	2296	1434	1533	1900
Foreman	1242	1143	1576	1092	537	1368
Hall	1413	1694	1836	1290	1206	1700
Mobile	1998	10260	2556	1860	7866	2412
Mobcal	51084	57997	68112	46821	32989	62428
Parkrun	65496	199558	87328	59583	142672	79444

3.1 Embedding Capacity

The maximum embedding capacities on the 7 video sequences are shown in Table 1. For each video sequence mentioned above, it is with resolution of 176×144 or 1280×720. For the method in [12], the parameter "*Thr*" is fixed at 13. Under such case that $QP = 26$ and $QP = 28$, the maximum embedding capacities are obtained on the video sequence *Parkrun* at the same time and they are 199558 and 142672 bits, respectively. However, the minimum embedding capacities are 1143 and 537 bits and they are obtained on the video sequence *Foreman*. For Ma et al.'s scheme [13], we use three coefficient-pairs, i.e., $\{\widetilde{Y}_{01}, \widetilde{Y}_{21}\}$, $\{\widetilde{Y}_{02}, \widetilde{Y}_{22}\}$ and $\{\widetilde{Y}_{03}, \widetilde{Y}_{23}\}$, for DH in this paper. Likewise, the corresponding maximum and minimum embedding capacities are 65496, 87328, 1023 and 999 bits. With our proposed scheme, moreover, the maximum embedding capacities are also obtained on the video sequence *Parkrun* at the same time and they are 87328 and 79444 bits. Instead, the minimum embedding of our proposed scheme are 1143 and 1273 bits and they are respectively obtained on the video sequences *Foreman* and *Carphone*.

Clearly, the embedding capacity of the scheme in [12] is affected easier when compared to our schemes. The differences between the maximum embedding capacities or the minimum embedding are very large when $QP = 26$ and $QP = 28$. For our proposed scheme, however, they are very little under same case. In other words, the maximum embedding capacities or the minimum embedding capacities are very close. Actually, we can know that the embedding capacity of [12] mainly depends on the position of the last nonzero coefficient of the embeddable 4×4 blocks according to [12]. *Mobile* and *Parkrun* are the video sequence with more detailed texture that leads to larger embedding capacity obtained compared with other video sequences. Using the same video sequence (like *Carphone* or *Mobile*) as test example, however, the differences between the embedding capacities are also larger when QP (e.g., $QP = 26$ and $QP = 28$ shown in Table 1) are different. In contrast, the embedding capacities on each video sequence are very close using our proposed scheme and Ma et al.'s scheme [13] even though the parameter QP is changed from 26 to 28. As shown in

Table 1, our proposed scheme has higher embedding capacity compared with [13]. In practice, therefore, our proposed scheme is more suitable to be applied because of high compression rate for communication.

In addition, since the additional data is only embedded into intra frames of each video sequence mentioned above, the value of the maximum embedding capacity is relatively few for a whole video sequence. For the embedded frames of a video sequence, the maximum embedding capacity is relatively positive. In fact, the low payloads is useful in practical applications [20].

3.2 Visual Quality

In this subsection, we will make use of PSNR and SSIM [19] to evaluate the visual quality of marked video sequences objectively. Before that, we first give some original and marked video frames to subjectively compare visual quality for the proposed scheme. As shown in Figs. 3 and 4, there is no significant degradation in terms of perceptual quality that can be observed when the marked video frames are compared with the original video frames. In other words, we cannot easily find the differences between them by our eyes.

To further better evaluate visual quality of the proposed scheme, Tables 2 and 3 are given and the data of them is obtained corresponding to the embedding capacities (shown as Table 1). From Table 2, we can know that PSNR values of the proposed scheme and Ma et al.'s scheme on the 7 video sequences are very close whenever $QP = 26$ or $QP = 28$: Clearly, the difference for each video sequence is not greater than 0.3 dB. However, the maximum differences between our proposed scheme and [12] are obtained on *Mobcal* and they are up to 5.507 and 5.868 dB.

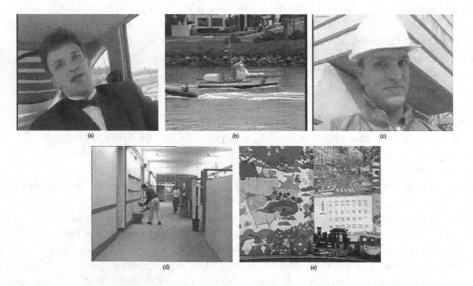

Fig. 3. Original video frames (100th frame, $QP = 26$). (a) Carphone. (b) Coastguard. (c) Foreman. (d) Hall. (e) Mobile.

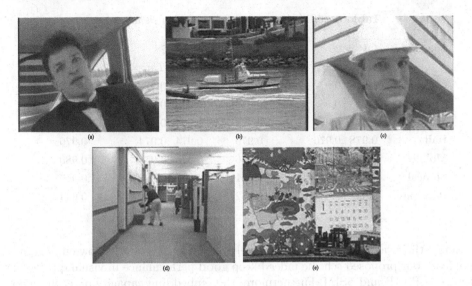

Fig. 4. Marked video frames corresponding to Fig. 3 (100th frame, $QP = 26$). (a) Carphone: 39.149 dB. (b) Coastguard: 36.741 dB. (c) Foreman: 38.321 dB. (d) Hall: 39.429 dB. (e) Mobile: 35.952 dB.

In general, the embedding capacity is much higher that leads to more significant distortion. Combined with Table 1, it seems so for *Mobile* and *Parkrun* when using the scheme in [12]. Instead, the embedding capacity using the method of [12] on each video sequences (except for *Mobile* and *Parkrun*) is less than or close to that of the proposed scheme, which still results in more significant degradation in terms of PSNR.

Additionally, we also give Table 3, also corresponding to Table 1, to compare visual quality in terms of SSIM. As shown in Table 3, although the scheme in [12] has more serious impact while compared to our proposed scheme and Ma et al.'s

Table 2. PSNR comparison on the video sequences.

Sequences	QP = 26			QP = 28		
	[13]	*Thr = 13* [12]	Proposed	[13]	*Thr = 13* [12]	Proposed
Carphone	39.096	38.316	39.149	37.649	37.199	37.717
Coastguard	36.653	35.908	36.741	35.140	34.976	35.234
Foreman	38.275	37.843	38.321	36.881	36.784	36.941
Hall	39.201	37.370	39.429	38.018	37.125	38.183
Mobile	35.883	32.940	35.952	34.183	31.966	34.251
Mobcal	35.735	30.183	35.690	34.083	28.197	34.065
Parkrun	36.593	34.255	36.564	35.523	33.468	35.504

108   Y. Chen et al.

Table 3. SSIM comparison on the video sequences.

Sequences	QP = 26			QP = 28		
	[13]	*Thr = 13* [12]	Proposed	[13]	*Thr = 13* [12]	Proposed
Carphone	0.978	0.977	0.978	0.972	0.972	0.972
Coastguard	0.958	0.958	0.959	0.943	0.943	0.943
Foreman	0.972	0.972	0.973	0.964	0.964	0.964
Hall	0.978	0.976	0.979	0.974	0.974	0.976
Mobile	0.986	0.981	0.986	0.975	0.975	0.980
Mobcal	0.961	0.947	0.961	0.947	0.930	0.947
Parkrun	0.952	0.943	0.952	0.944	0.939	0.944

scheme, their values are very close. Totally, under such case with low embedding payload, our proposed scheme indeed keep good performance in visual quality in terms of PSNR and SSIM. Furthermore, the embedding capacity on each video sequence changes small with the variation of parameter set (such as QP).

3.3 Bit-Rate Variation

Bit-rate variation is given as Table 4, also corresponding to Table 1, to compare the impact caused by DH at the coder side and relative descriptions are as follows.

Generally, the operation of DH must make some slight modifications on the host for embedding additional data that may lead to increase the redundancy to the host. Compared with the schemes in [12,13], the bit-rate of marked video sequences using our proposed scheme is very close according to Table 4. For the method of [12], although the bit-rate increase is less than that of our proposed scheme respectively corresponding to *Foreman* and *Hall* when $QP = 16$ and *Coastguard* and *Hall* when $QP = 28$, the differences is very small. In addition,

Table 4. Comparison of bit-rate variation.

Sequences	QP = 26			QP = 28		
	[13]	*Thr = 13* [12]	Proposed	[13]	*Thr = 13* [12]	Proposed
Carphone	110.44	110.38	110.35	85.25	85.20	85.15
Coastguard	154.01	154.03	153.89	114.73	114.39	114.62
Foreman	96.86	96.64	96.77	75.70	75.79	75.70
Hall	49.91	49.79	49.81	39.50	39.40	39.41
Mobile	260.36	261.01	260.29	194.55	194.94	194.48
Mobcal	2951.67	2952.98	2948.32	1843.54	1841.19	1840.08
Parkrun	14930.55	14934.85	14926.82	10812.26	10812.26	10808.38

the bit-rate increase using our proposed scheme is always less than or equal to that of Ma et al.'s scheme. Combined with Subsects. 3.1 and 3.2, our proposed scheme indeed keeps good performance of distortion and bit-rate increase.

4 Conclusions

The distortion is one of the most commonly used metric to evaluate the performance of a DH scheme. In this paper, we combine matrix embedding with several conditions preventing distortion propagating to propose a DH scheme. Based on matrix embedding and the conditions given, we select a 4×4 luma block for DH in the proposed scheme when the value of a DC coefficient in the current block is nonzero. Therefore, we can obtain marked videos with good visual quality in terms of PSNR and SSIM. Moreover, the variation of bit-rate before and after embedding additional data into video sequences is significantly slight. Although the embedding capacity using the proposed scheme is low, it is useful in practical applications.

Acknowledgment. The authors would like to thank the reviewers for their insightful comments and helpful suggestions. This work was supported by the National Natural Science Foundation of China (NSFC) under the grant No. U1536110.

References

1. Petitcolas, F.A.P., Anderson, R.J., Kuhn, M.G.: Information hiding-a survey. Proc. IEEE **87**(7), 1062–1078 (1999)
2. Xu, D., Wang, R., Shi, Y.Q.: Data hiding in encrypted H.264/AVC video streams by codeword substitution. IEEE Trans. Inf. Forensics Secur. **9**(4), 596–606 (2014)
3. Cao, Y., Zhang, H., Zhao, X., Yu, H.: Covert communication by compressed videos exploiting the uncertainty of motion estimation. IEEE Commun. Lett. **19**(2), 203–206 (2015)
4. Bloch, M.R.: Covert communication over noisy channels: a resolvability perspective. IEEE Trans. Inf. Theory **62**(5), 2334–2354 (2016)
5. Goldwasser, S., Micali, S.: Probabilistic encryption. J. Comput. Syst. Sci. **28**(2), 270–299 (1984)
6. Wu, H.Z., Wang, H.X., Shi, Y.Q.: PPE-based reversible data hiding. In: Proceedings of the 4th ACM Workshop on Information Hiding and Multimedia Security, New York, NY, USA, pp. 187–188. ACM (2016)
7. Asikuzzaman, M., Pickering, M.R.: An overview of digital video watermarking. IEEE Trans. Circuits Syst. Video Technol. **PP**(99), 1 (2017)
8. Ma, X., Zeng, W.K., Yang, L.T., Zou, D., Jin, H.: Lossless ROI privacy protection of H.264/AVC compressed surveillance videos. IEEE Trans. Emerg. Top. Comput. **4**(3), 349–362 (2016)
9. Peng, Y., Lan, H., Yue, M., Xue, Y.: Multipurpose watermarking for vector map protection and authentication. Multimed. Tools Appl. **77**, 7239–7259 (2017)
10. Zhang, X., Wang, S.: Efficient steganographic embedding by exploiting modification direction. IEEE Commun. Lett. **10**(11), 781–783 (2006)

11. Chen, Y., Wang, H., Wu, H., Liu, Y.: An adaptive data hiding algorithm with low bitrate growth for H.264/AVC video stream. Multimed. Tools Appl. **77**, 1–19 (2017)
12. Fallahpour, M., Shirmohammadi, S., Ghanbari, M.: A high capacity data hiding algorithm for H.264/AVC video. Secur. Commun. Netw. **8**(16), 2947–2955 (2015)
13. Ma, X., Li, Z., Tu, H., Zhang, B.: A data hiding algorithm for H.264/AVC video streams without intra-frame distortion drift. IEEE Trans. Circuits Syst. Video Technol. **20**(10), 1320–1330 (2010)
14. Fridrich, J., Soukal, D.: Matrix embedding for large payloads. IEEE Trans. Inf. Forensics Secur. **1**(3), 390–395 (2006)
15. Wiegand, T., Sullivan, G.J., Bjontegaard, G., Luthra, A.: Overview of the H.264/AVC video coding standard. IEEE Trans. Circuits Syst. Video Technol. **13**(7), 560–576 (2003)
16. Liu, Y., Chen, L., Hu, M., Jia, Z., Jia, S., Zhao, H.: A reversible data hiding method for H.264 with shamirs (t, n)-threshold secret sharing. Neurocomputing **188**, 63–70 (2016)
17. H.264/AVC Reference Software JM12.0. http://iphome.hhi.de/suehring/tml/download/old_jm/
18. H.264/AVC Reference Video Sequences. https://media.xiph.org/video/derf/
19. Lie, A., Klaue, J.: Evalvid-RA: trace driven simulation of rate adaptive MPEG-4 VBR video. Multimed. Syst. **14**(1), 33–50 (2008)
20. Yu, J., Li, F., Cheng, H., Zhang, X.: Spatial steganalysis using contrast of residuals. IEEE Signal Process. Lett. **23**(7), 989–992 (2016)

A Domain Name Model of Anonymous Network Hidden Service

Yitong Meng, Jinlong Fei[✉], Yan Chen, and Yuefei Zhu

State Key Laboratory of Mathematical Engineering and Advanced Computing,
Zhengzhou 450001, Henan, China
myt518@sina.com, feijinlong@126.com

Abstract. Tor hidden services have grown too rapidly so that anonymous users cannot verify the authenticity of Hidden Services. Meanwhile, there are many unsafe factors in the centralized directory management mode, and the service content and configuration can be detected and monitored by automated scripts. Faced with the above problems, this paper based on the current Tor domain name communication management model, proposed a new Hidden Service Domain Name System—HSDNS, which using SOR node decentralized management, then replace the top-level domain name as ".hs" to increase the anti-scanning property of the original domain name, introduces the PoW competition mechanism to enable registrants to get readable unique domain name among the whole network. On this basis, the random number provided by the BTC blockchain guarantees random competition and enhances the anti-registration attack, in the meantime, Merkle Tree hash detection mechanism is used to open verification service of domain authenticity, and finally verify model analysis results through the ExperimenTor simulation platform, and it shows that HSDNS model has decentralized management, service anti-scanning, domain name uniqueness and authenticity verification and so on.

Keywords: HSDNS · PoW · Merkle Tree

1 Introduction

Tor [1] is by far the most popular anonymous communication system, it can resist various network attacks, and has the perfect forward security, congestion control, end-to-end integrity detection and other security performances. The proposal of Hidden Service protocol complements the lack which Tor anonymous communication system provides anonymous protection in the service terminal.

Many studies or systems have improved Tor domain name system, such as Shallot [2] allows registrants to create customized ".onion" addresses for their own hidden service, nevertheless there is no way to control the size of the secret key space and management. Simon [3] uses the special world-list that the two sides have reached to improve the space, but at the expense of a lot of security and anonymity. Nolen [4] built a OnionDNS model to provide some service and authentication mechanisms with the idea of the onion domain name. Although the mechanisms can be work, the threat of centralization has always existed.

© Springer Nature Switzerland AG 2018
X. Sun et al. (Eds.): ICCCS 2018, LNCS 11066, pp. 111–122, 2018.
https://doi.org/10.1007/978-3-030-00015-8_10

A new Hidden Service Domain Name System (HSDNS) is proposed in this paper, which forms a set of decentralized, safe, searchable and readable Tor Hidden Service Domain model. Any hidden service managers can declare a human as readable domain name address in HSDNS model, and under this circumstance without the need for loss of anonymity, the client will query and verify ".hs" top-level domain name in the form of privacy protection and verifiability, meantime, a set of distributed management database is formed by random SOR node, provide anonymous protection to maximally restrict malicious node attacks, and use Merkle Tree detection mechanism to provide authenticity verification for services, cooperate with proof-of-work (PoW) and BTC blockchain information to define a competition mechanism, finally, the service provider can get readable only domain name.

2 Target

2.1 Security Analysis of Hidden Service

Hidden services means that service sites which cannot be crawled by crawlers and anonymously provided, however, automated crawler scripting tools such as OnionScan, HSprobe and Ichidan are used to detect and monitor the content, web configuration, and proxy devices of hidden service sites in real time. OnionScan [5] except by detecting site inherent attributes, for example, found hidden service operation safety and dislocation configuration, the main purpose is to monitor and track the sensitive anonymous service sites, and scan a large number of ".onion" domain addresses by intervening the Tor network, and have the capability to quickly acquire the sensitive information content and customize the configuration of hidden service.

The attackers have ability to continuously detect, observe, attack and other malicious acts on onion routers. Because the scale of hidden service websites is smaller than the external network data stream, it is more static than the ordinary websites, and the data stream will be isolated from various autonomous domains, finally, the attackers carry out compromise attack on hidden services by controlling the transmission node and analyzing anonymous data stream, and constantly threaten the servers. Furthermore, because the hidden service website can not verify the authenticity, the phishing sites can be set up to carry out efficient phishing attacks and data access analysis, so that a large number of anonymous users' information is leaked.

2.2 Improvement Targets

The hidden service protocol [6] must provide a secure, reliable and efficient anonymous access service, which protects the identity information and communication relationship between the server and the user. It mainly seeks to build a highly efficient distributed system, not only to ensure the unique domain name address, but also to provide a verifiable domain detection mechanism. The following are some of the improvement targets that must be met for the anonymous service domain name system:

1. *Anonymous registration.* The system does not need to obtain any sensitive information from the hidden service registry. The hidden service release has no more
   important information than the public RSA key and a series of IP addresses.
2. *Users' anonymity.* Anonymous users are protected by anonymity, it is difficult to
   distinguish the current access users, the traceability host IP cannot be tracked, and
   integrate multiple protection methods to hide service queries.
3. *Verification protection.* The customers must be able to verify the authenticity of the
   domain address and their encryption guarantee. This improvement can provide an
   effective way to defend phishing attacks against malicious servers.
4. *Unique Domain name address.* The corresponding relationship between domain
   name servers' registration domain name addresses and domain key, the uniqueness
   of domain name can prevent domain name registration attacks, but also provide a
   new defense system for website phishing attacks.
5. *Decentralization management.* The system decentralizes the traditional centralized
   management control, so as to eliminate the single highest management mode of the
   system and decentralize the centralized node control management. The system
   centralization control easily leads to the high-authority intrusion and other problems
   to quickly destroy the integrity of the system.
6. *Low latency.* The hidden service protocol is highly sensitive to communication
   latency, so the system reduces the latency of communication link transmission and
   domain name query to enhance the anonymous user experience.

3 HSDNS Overview

3.1 System Design

HSDNS (Hidden Service Domain Name System) uses Tor to transmit network components, use existing onion router (OR), basic six-jump forward transmission link and
TLS security protocol, at the same time, use BitCoin (BTC) network to distribute
random number $N(t)$, maximize the key node and terminal key generation randomness,
and each point in real-time P2P links. Descriptors use the ".hs" top-level domain name,
while the ".onion" top-level domain name can be backward compatible. OR routers
except carry out traditional data forwarding functions, which are used to maintain
domain name system information database and respond to client OP's address query
function. Other key components are newly defined components and structures:

- *Senior Onion Router (SOR).* This type of router is an HS-port entry router, holds
  the complete database of current system; receives and handles the descriptive data
  information from the HS port.
- *Senior Onion Router Candidates (SORC).* This type of router set holds the copy of
  the database and provides a rotation candidate set for advanced onion routers.
- *Cryptographically Secure Pseudo-Random Number Generator (CSPRNG).* The
  structure can turn information into a fixed-length 128 binary random number, a
  random variable random function associated with the time element [7].

- **Descriptive Data (DD)**. The data is the basic information combination of service domain name addresses, including type, name, contact domain, random number, signature, and public key RSA.
- **Consensus Data (Consensus Data)**. The data is the unified consensus data information of the advanced onion node in the whole network, which can be trusted by the client to obtain the trusted Root Hash, which serves as an important basis for the client to hide the service inquiry.
- **Merkle Tree**. The structure can be fast and integrity checking of data. Get the file Merkle Tree from the trusted source. Once the Root Hash is obtained, Merkle Tree can be obtained from other sources that are never trusted.

The HSDNS model mainly uses the P2P communication mode, and the communication link between the terminals is established and the data transmission is conducted through the detection of the surrounding reliable nodes. The domain name system work (see Fig. 1), first of all, will be extracted from BTC block chain random number $N(t)$ for each important component, using the $CSPRNG(N(t))$ in the Tor network select a group of senior onion node (SOR). Second, hidden service (HS) sends a descriptive data (DD) to the SOR, which is also transmitted to the OR node via SOR. Each relay router maintains a Merkle Tree of descriptive data obtained from the SOR. Then, the client can query the OR node by describing the data information, and the OR node will decompose the descriptive data into Merkle Tree data blocks to return. Finally, the client verifies the Merkle Tree structure and cooperates with the consensus data (CD) published by the SOR, and determine the authenticity of the domain name information.

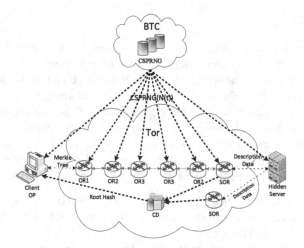

Fig. 1. Working diagram of HSDNS model.

The anonymous hidden server applies for a meaningful readable address name mainly by generating a descriptive data and Proof-of-Work (PoW). When the server address competition is successful, the only domain name that can be received is readable, and the domain database of SOR and OR node is updated. The descriptor record model specifies that a set of SOR nodes can handle one or more domain name visits during the activity week, but each round of access time is 24 h.

3.2 Protocol and Algorithm Design

Random Number Generation

Random number $N(t)$ is the basis of node key generation and domain name registration in domain name system, so $N(t)$ must have stable characteristics such as security, dispersion and random. The head of each block in the BTC blockchain contains a 80-byte header, size contains the version number, a father of hash value, timestamp, difficulty value, random number and Merkle Root, which is suitable for 32-bit work proves that the random nonce Root Hash by the hash value of the block [8]. Most of the information on the system block chain is relatively fixed. Only nonce and Merkle root have the largest randomness in the block information. One block can extract 32 bits of random numbers, because the blockchain's security depends on the dispersion of computing power, and the random number is used to build a $N(t)$ random number header:

$$N(t) = RAND(nonce \, || Merkle \, Root || \, H(t)) \tag{1}$$

In Formula 1, *nonce* is 32 bits random number, *Merkle Root* is Hash root, t is acquisition time for nearest block, *RAND* is an extraction function of random number.

Domain name system components can independently utilize three different methods to effectively obtain random number $N(t)$:

1. The first method is to download the block information from blockchain network center [3], extract the time of t acquisition, and calculate the random number $N(t)$ according to formula 1. This method is inefficient, but the data is more effective and safer.
2. The second method downloads the block header directly from a trusted block source, which is efficient, but security is low.
3. The third method is to find a trusted block from the main block chain and download the remaining blocks. This method is compared with the former two methods, only need a reliable source of initial seeds can satisfy the random number generation, keep the balance between the efficiency, safety and effectiveness, this acquisition method as the default configuration.

SOR Selection and Internal Data Collection

The SOR node has the security and authority tags, so it is not easy to intrude to protect the SOR node, and coordinate the timing rotation of the node with the candidate set of the SOR node. The SOR node is the entry node of the HS port, which requires a high performance guard entry node to meet the HSDNS model to deal with a large number of communication and query requirements, in addition, the SOR node always caches the latest information and data for the user to carry out the domain name verification and other subsequent operations.

The selection of entry nodes for high-performance guards use the bandwidth weighted random selection algorithm [9], such nodes are characterized by long online time, high bandwidth and stable state and so on. These characteristics are also the basic labels that the SOR candidate must hold, SOR nodes with high CPU or high bandwidth capacity, relative to the OR node will get a large proportion of the weight, this consensus weighting in the process of building the link would have made a significant impact on the choice of the router: weight, the higher the greater the chance of SOR is selected, the opposite is smaller.

In addition, SOR nodes hold the most complete and latest internal data. In order to make each OR node keep this standard, the Merkle Tree is recalculated through the record operation obtained within 24 h, and Root is stored in Contact field of the node descriptor, make the hash function appear in the consensus data CD, and ensure that OR nodes with the same hash function are selected first.

Each node and Tor client obtain $N(t)$ in the HSDNS model, which can check the current qualified SOR nodes. The client OP runs algorithm 1 to collect SOR nodes, where $Weight_f(a)$ is the consensus weight of router in each f group, and SORC has the maximum value of A in group f.

Algorithm 1: SOR collection algorithm.

Input: random number $N(t)$

Output: SOR node list

Steps:

Step 1: The client gets and verifies the consensus data CD;

Step 2: The client obtains secure and trusted $N(t)$ by default method;

Step 3: The client constructs a list A from the CD and selects the SOR candidate with high efficiency, stability and online logo;

Step 4: A is divided into several groups $A = \{f_1, f_2, f_3...\}$ according to performance, calculate $A = \sum_1^f weight_f(a)$;

Step 5: The client uses $CSPRNG(N(t))$ to select the SOR node from SORC, min(number(SORC), SOR), and select the SOR node: $P(SOR) = weight_{SORC}(SOR) / A$;

Step 6: The algorithm end.

Domain Name Registration

Algorithm 3: HSDNS domain name registration algorithm.

Input: registrant descriptive data $\{DD_i\}$.

Output: register the domain name $\{name\}$.

Steps:

Step 1: Hidden service registrant to generate its own DD, DD (type $\parallel$ name $\parallel$ contact $\parallel$ nonce $\parallel$ pubHSKey);

Step 2: The registrant generates a hash register: $register_i = H$ (type $\parallel$ name $\parallel$ contact $\parallel$ rand $\parallel$ nonce $\parallel$ public Key $\parallel$ signature);

Step 3: Proof-of-Work $v_{PoW} = H\left(signature \parallel nonce\right) \le v_{th}, v \le 2^{128}$;

Step 4: d_{th} is the threshold difficulty, d_{DD} is the actual difficulty, when $d_{th} = \left|\log_2\left(2^{128} / v_{th}\right)\right| > d_{DD} = \left|\log_2\left(2^{128} / v_{PoW}\right)\right|$ registrant can submit DD and $register_i$;

Step 5: The registrant publishes the information to all the SOR nodes, and all DD_i initially forms a competition pool;

Step 6: SOR nodes are recalculate $v_{PoW} = H\left(signature \parallel nonce\right)$ get the actual difficulties of each registrant PoW;

Step 7: Make a judgment to filter the complete DD_i:

    (1) if the hash of each field of if DD does not match $register_i$, jump to step 11;

    (2) if $v_{PoW} \ge v_{th}$, jump to step 11;

    (3) if signature, invalid or has any error, jump to step 11;

    (4) if name has already registered, jump to step 11;

    (5) if the information is complete, DD_i is stored in the competition pool.

Step 8: SOR nodes calculated $C_i = weight_i / \sum_{i=1}^n weight_i$ to select the winning $\{name\}$, weight is determined by the difficulty coefficient $weight_i = \left|2^{128} / H\left(signature \parallel nonce\right)\right|$;

Step 9: Determine that there are other competing names and the winning name, the same competitive name will be excluded from the competition pool directly, and jump to step 8 until the competition pool is empty;

Step 10: SOR nodes notify all the winning registrants through the contact field that they can use the application $\{name\}$, and SOR retain the winning registrar DD_i information and synchronizes DD information to OR node;

Step 11: The algorithm end.

In order to ensure the uniqueness of the address and prevent the malicious domain name registration attack, the HSDNS model needs to force hidden service registrants to make some efforts when occupy a domain address, and prevent the convenience and randomness of the registered domain name by introducing the PoW. PoW algorithm is characterized by constantly adjusting the nonce value to crack the equation, it is difficult to calculate and solve, but it is easy to verify. The PoW mechanism is proposed based on competition in HSDNS. The registrant wins a domain name registration right through the calculation of PoW in this mechanism, this mechanism forces the registrant to concentrate their computing power on a small domain name, and cannot register multiple domains at the same time. The competition mechanism is as follows: (1) it is necessary for each registrar to submit its own descriptive data DD and solve a PoW problem derived from DD data. The system will give different difficulty level and requirement to different registrants; (2) give effective DD to the final registrant ' needs based on weight ratio draw by lot, in which the weight division is mainly proportional to the amount of calculation spent by each registrant, specific algorithm as shown in algorithm 3. The specific explanation of the parameters in the algorithm, see Table 1:

Table 1. Specific expression of parameters.

Parameter	Content
Type	Descriptive Data
Name	Domain name address
Contact	PGP mail fingerprint.
Rand	Random number N (i)
Nonce	Coefficient of random difficulty
Public key	The registered user's RSA public key
Private key	The registry's RSA private key
Signature	S_{RSA} (type $\|$ name $\|$ contact $\|$ rand $\|$ nonce, private key)

Domain Authenticity Verification

In order to reduce the malicious hidden service, the HSDNS model can optionally fabricate a nonexistent domain name address, and then use phishing attack to easily get the vulnerability of anonymous users' information. The domain name model provides an anonymous user with a channel to verify the authenticity of the hidden service, through algorithm 4, all the OR nodes, including SOR nodes are carrying a Merkle Tree [10] authentication mechanism against malicious attacks, the client can use the Merkle Tree structure to verify whether hidden server using the correct DD response, OR if the customer query response to verify the integrity of the service address.

Algorithm 4: Merkle Tree verification algorithm.

Input: hidden service name: name; corresponding descriptive data: DDi.

Output: Merkle Tree verification results.

Steps:

Step 1: The OR/SOR nodes generate an array list B, $B = \{DD_i(name) \| H(DD_i)\}$, every data information DD_i obtained from the hidden service;

Step 2: OR/SOR nodes are classified by name in group B, and a Merkle Tree (MT) is constructed from B by category;

Step 3: The SOR node publish the Root Hash (RH) of MT in the consensus data CD;

Step 4: The client OP gets RH from CD;

Step 5: If the DD_i exists, the OR node returns MT, the leaf node contains the name, and all nodes from leaf node to root node and peer nodes; if DD_i does not exist, the OR node will return two adjacent leaf nodes left and right, $left(name) < n < right(name)$;

Step 6: The client verifies the authenticity of MT [(name included in the subtree or name is made, director of the child leaves) && (a Hash tree right) && (Root Hash with the Root of each SOR node release Hash matches)], when three conditions meet the DD_i for real, jump to step 8, otherwise jump to step 7;

Step 7: Merkle Tree verification results: "Address is false" feedback to the client OP, jump to step 9;

Step 8: Merkle Tree verification results: "Address is real" feedback to the client OP;

Step 9: The verification over, the algorithm ends.

---

4 Experiment and Assessment

4.1 Test Environment

ExperimenTor [11] platform for the Tor anonymity network transmission system basic components of liberalization can be deployed at the same time cooperate ModelNet network simulation system to simulate the real network traffic and user operation, used for HSDNS model performance test and the deployment environment detection. The platform built by independent Tor directory server and Tor routers with 1 GBPS bandwidth, run the new version Tor-0.3.1.8, because components support FreeBSD license certification, can run HSDNS protocols and algorithms in XML, base64 binary and C++, python code, blend in BTC block chain information, client access TCP normal simulation application service or the HS hidden service.

Experimental environment, the simulation of 100 relay points, three HS server and three Tor directory server, assign OR node address as 10.0.0.1-60, SOR node address is 10.0.0.61-100, hidden service descriptors domain for three: *nfmekwla872fvcld. onion, 12kdacnmgkdiwjdg.onion, uidajfnm75dfjcfg.onion*, corresponding HSDNS subdomain: test1.hs, test2.hs, test3.hs, and will generate the service descriptor upload directory server and SOR to domain name competition pool. When "*.hs" is requested in the Tor browser, the HSDNS proxy directly intercepts the ".hs" top-level domain request information, passes the domain query and can re-parse the data stream to the "*.onion" hidden service, realize the customized domain name access of hidden service.

4.2 Performance Test

First, verify the test addresses of "test1.hs, test2.hs, test3.hs" for the client and the OR node is performed, and detect the protocol overhead delay between the client and the OR node, respectively. By simulating the client and the OR node, by placing 200 testing data samples, the protocol overheads of XML, Hash, Signature (m, r) and total time were measured, respectively, the measurement results are shown in Table 2, it shows the feasibility and high efficiency of authentication.

Table 2. Domain name validation protocol overhead.

Agreement	Client (ms)	OR (ms)
XML	7.56	3.46
Hash	6.23	3.12
Signature (m, r)	8.44	4.89
Query time	22.23	11.47
Total query time	33.7	

The real network link attributes are simulate through ModelNet extension network platform, the main in HSDNS network is data flow (Round-Trip Time, RRT). It is determined by the message queue delay, processing delay, the length of the link among nodes and the number of forwarding hops. As shown in Fig. 2, the average latency of the hidden service communication link is 620 ms, the standard deviation is 224 ms, and the upper and lower edges are 445 ms and 912 ms, respectively.

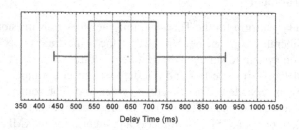

350 400 450 500 550 600 650 700 750 800 850 900 950 1000 1050
Delay Time (ms)

Fig. 2. Six-hop delay of transmission link.

Finally, the registrants upload the descriptive data to all SOR nodes in the domain name registration protocol. Descriptive data sets in order to avoid the possibility of information leak and must be uploaded in a short time. Considering the delay overhead of the previous six-hop circuit use the same settings as before, and the average uploaded time is measured by changing the number of SOR nodes and describing the data size.

The statistical results in Table 3 show that 40 SOR nodes upload 50 and need more than one minute. Based on these measurements, a 10-min upload timeout is released to reduce the probability which attacker invade the link to obtain descriptive data.

Table 3. Descriptive data uploaded to SOR node time.

SOR number	Transmission time (s)	Transmission size (KB)
5	5.36	50
10	11.02	50
20	21.82	50
40	44.34	50
5	7.55	100
10	16.36	100
20	36.96	100
40	80.13	100

4.3 Safety Assessment

SOR Node Management Mechanism

The SOR node bears the data information forwarding function of the original OR node, carries a decentralized database of the HSDNS system, which can receive and process the descriptive data information from the HS side, and effectively provides the client agent with consensus data CD and a Root Hash tree to verify the authenticity of the domain name address. The SOR node is resistant to being hijacked and maliciously controlled by the attacker; it modifies or replaces existing records during the SOR node data generation life cycle, and gives invalid information to the client. However, the malicious SOR node cannot effectively prevent the user from verifying the authenticity of the domain name information, the client can send the same query to other OR nodes and SOR nodes for query to check whether the records are the same, when can find trusted number from other trusted sources at different times.

PoW Mechanism

The weight that the registrant upload to the descriptive data DD and wins in the competition, which is directly proportional to the computing power of PoW. If the registrant wants to win the uploaded DD and the name information it contains, it needs to concentrate all the computing power to solve its own PoW formula. Each iteration result of PoW results is different, the output of the one-way, because signature (m, r) is a probability function, registration must give up again and again, and repeatedly recalculate PoW until conditions are met.

This mechanism can resist domain name registration attacks against hidden services. When the attackers try to block or occupy a large number of domain names, the attackers must spend a lot of calculation on the PoW problem to ensure that they have a certain attack probability, in order to simultaneously register multiple domain names at random, the attackers needs to expand the computing capacity, and at the same time, the difficulty threshold ensures that the registrant's winning probability leads to low weight for each name, and make the domain name registration attack invalid.

5 Conclusion

Hidden Service Domain Name System (HSDNS) is proposed in this paper, and through the decentralization of directory server, PoW proof mechanism, the domain name competition mechanism, BTC random number generation of BTC network and other mechanisms, communication security, scattered management, achieve a hidden service domain name system with secure communication, decentralized management and domain name can be queried, authenticity can be verified by minimum bandwidth overhead with the aid of Merkle Tree mechanism, and protect users from malicious means phishing attacks, etc. ExperimenTor platform simulation results show that this model has good performance in the domain name authentication, communication transmission, domain name registration, etc., and make the HSDNS model have safety, efficiency and feasibility.

Acknowledgements. Fund project: National key research and development program (2016YFB0801601).

References

1. Dingledine, R., Mathewson, N., Syverson, P.: Tor: the second-generation onion router. J. Franklin Inst., 135–139 (2004)
2. Katmagic and ericpaulbishop, Shallot (2012). https://github.com/katmagic/Shallot
3. Nicolussi, S.: Human-readable names for tor hidden services. Leopold–Franzens–Universitat Innsbruck, Institute for Computer Science (2011)
4. Scaife, N., Carter, H., Traynor, P.: OnionDNS: a seizure-resistant top-level domain. In: IEEE Conference on Communications and Network Security, pp. 379–387 (2017)
5. Hidden service script scan. OnionScan (2017). https://github.com/s-rah/onionscan. Accessed Feb 2017
6. Overlier, L., Syverson, P.: Locating hidden servers. In: 2006 IEEE Symposium on Security and Privacy, p. 15, 114. IEEE (2006)
7. Bonneau, J., Clark, J., Goldfeder, S.: On bitcoin as a public randomness source. IACR Cryptology ePrint Archive (2015)
8. Nakamoto, S.: Bitcoin: A peer-to-peer electronic cash system. Consulted (2008)
9. Goulet, D., Kadianakis, G.: Random number generation during tor voting (2015). https://gitweb.torproject.org/torspec.git/tree/proposals/250-commit-reveal-consensu.txt
10. Merkle, R.C.: A digital signature based on a conventional encryption function. In: Pomerance, C. (ed.) CRYPTO 1987. LNCS, vol. 293, pp. 369–378. Springer, Heidelberg (1988). https://doi.org/10.1007/3-540-48184-2_32
11. Bauer, K., et al.: ExperimenTor: a testbed for safe and realistic tor experimentation. In: Conference on Cyber Security Experimentation and Test USENIX Association, p. 7 (2011)

A Layered Steganography Model Based on User Interactions

Gao Quansheng(iD) and Wang Kaixi$^{(\boxtimes)}$(iD)

College of Computer Science and Technology, Qingdao University, Qingdao, China
kxwang@qdu.edu.cn

Abstract. The aim of steganography is to put a secret into carriers and only be seen by participants. This paper proposes a layered steganography model which helps to simplify the steganography design. The steganography model enables the two communication parties to interact with each other, which enables the receiving end to get data by data prediction, and optimizes the steganography mechanism to take full advantage of the existing methods to implement multi-carriers steganography. Herein, the interactive steganography action is decomposed into three basic interactive procedures, and the embedding and extracting procedures are implemented via these basic interactions, in which texts, pictures, voices or videos are used as carriers. With the features of language diversification, common media, real-time in an instant message communication, the proposed steganography in this paper is flexible, secure and reliable.

Keywords: Multi-carrier · Instant message · Interactive procedure
Layered steganography model

1 Introduction

Steganography has become a prominent research field in the information hiding discipline because of its ability to hide the very existence of a secret message in innocuous-looking cover media [1–3]. The most applications of steganography are: covert communications, digital watermarking, etc. Covert communication focuses on hiding a secret message in a carrier during the communication process, which enables the message to be secretly delivered in the open environment [4–6]. Digital watermarking is more concerned about ensuring the robustness of the watermark embedded in the carrier, that is, the availability and integrity of embedded watermarks should still be ensured when the carrier is destroyed, reconstructed, or it is incomplete [7–10]. In covert communication, the existing steganography methods are mostly based on the Prisoner model or its variants, in which a secret always be transformed from sender to receiver. The current researches hide information and improve their concealment by optimizing the embedding method. It is not enough only to focus on the optimization of the embedding process, but also it is needed to improve the entire communication process.

© Springer Nature Switzerland AG 2018
X. Sun et al. (Eds.): ICCCS 2018, LNCS 11066, pp. 123–134, 2018.
https://doi.org/10.1007/978-3-030-00015-8_11

Instant messaging is the first mobile Internet application, so the number of instant messaging users is very huge. Instant messaging has the features for the covert communication [11], which are analyzed as follows: (1) The diversity of medias enables an instant message system suitable for multi-carrier steganography; (2) The common used carriers can guarantee the security of covert communications; (3) The real-time feature can make the stego-objects less exposed to third party and enables the receiver to involve the steganography embedding process, which can guarantee the participants communicate with each other in a real-time way, and effectively ensures the consistency of the information transmitted by the covert communication and improves the security of the steganography system.

In a word, a simplex transmission mode makes the secret embedding (or extracting) operation isolated from the two sides of the communication parties. This mode is not compatible with the flexible information interaction mode in an instant messaging system. Combining the linguistic features in an instant messaging system, this paper proposes an interactive layered steganography model, which involve the receiving parties in sending the secret by prediction. This model can be effectively integrated into an instant messaging system. And this paper also presents a concrete steganography scheme, in which a secret message is segmented and serialized, and each fragment is sent via one of three basic processes. In addition, after the steganography method is selected, a secret message can be transmitted dynamically and securely by using different carriers in an instant messaging system, which is also called multi-carrier steganography.

2   The Steganography Model

2.1   The Classic Steganography Model

The classic steganography model is shown in Fig. 1. The covert communication consists of two parts: the embedding process and the extracting process. The embedding process is mainly to map a secret message into a carrier in an invisible way, that is to establish a mapping relationship between the plain cover space and the secret message space; the extracting process is the inverse process, namely to locate and extract the transmitted secret message from the stego-carrier.

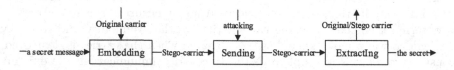

Fig. 1. Classic steganography model

2.2   Interactive Steganography Conversation Model

Different from the above traditional steganography model, an interactive steganography model is proposed in this paper. It matches the information interaction process such as in an instant messaging system. Just as the communication methods such as letters, telegrams, are gradually being replaced by the instant messaging based on the Internet, the covert communications should also adapt itself to the immediate interaction scenarios in the Internet.

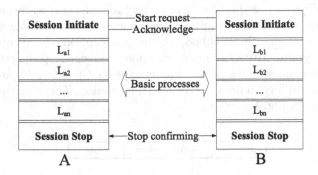

Fig. 2. Interactive steganography conversation model

In the interactive steganography conversation model illustrated in Fig. 2, the interaction process is mainly divided into three stages: Firstly, the two parties need to setup a covert communication session; then two parties communicate with each other, and finally the receiver acknowledges that it receives all the segmentation information $L_{a1} - L_{an}$ from the sender, which indicates that the entire covert communication process finishes. In the second stage, the interaction between two parties is in Question&Answer type. And any party can be used as either a sending end or a receiving end, so the interaction model can be performed bidirectional transmission. More details about these specific request-response processes will be given in Sect. 3.2.

3   The Steganography Algorithm

3.1   The Layered Steganography Model

A secret can be a natural language text, an image or other media. The secret is usually encrypted, segmented, serialized, encapsulated, and finally embedded into a carrier or be mapped to a carrier while being transmitted. In order to make the embedding process more clear, the layered steganography model is proposed by referring to TCP/IP network model in the following Fig. 3.

Herein, the presentation layer and the embedding layer are the main processes of steganography. The embedding layer will be introduced in Sect. 3.4.

Application layer		User messages	↑	Application layer
Encryption layer		Binary strings	Extracting	Encryption layer
Presentation layer	Embedding	Segment sequences		Presentation layer
Embedding layer	↓	Bit streams		Embedding layer
Communication layer		Carriers		Communication layer

Fig. 3. The layered steganography model

The functionalites in presentation layer mainly include: segmentation, serialization and encapsulation. The segmentation process is to break the integrity of a secret, and to reduce the likelihood of the interception of a complete secret. Generally, the granularity of the segmentation is inversely proportional to the security of a steganography system. Data encapsulation is to add packet header to each segment to form a data packet for transmission. The structure of a data packet is shown in Fig. 4.

3-bit Type	Serial number	Data

Fig. 4. Data packet structure

3-bit Types are defined to represent these procedures in Table 1. The serial number is the sequence number of the transmitted packet in the sending segment sequence, and its value range is [1, n], where n is the number of segments in the secret segment sequence. The data partition is to store a secret segment.

Table 1. The different types and their codes

Types		Codes
Signaling packets	Session initiation	000
	Session stop	001
	Acknowledgement	010
Data packets	Send data	011
	Predict data	100
	Request data	101
	Predict confirmation	110
	Predict correction	111

The serialization process is to change the order of the secret segments. It is to make it more difficult for the attacker to acquire the correct secret even if all secret segments are acquired. The receiver needs to take the right actions to restore the original segments according to the reordering rule in the sender.

3.2   Interaction Procedures

For covert communication, the first step is that two parties needs to setup an session via session setup procedure. After that, both the sender A and the receiver B can initiate data transmission. The sender and the receiver play different roles in the covert communication. For one thing, the sender is mainly responsible for reordering the fragments labeled L_{a1} to L_{an} in another sequence and sending them to the receiver. For another, the receiver not only can receive segments passively from the sender, but also can actively request a secret segment or predict the next segment. This transmission operation can be done actively, or can be performed passively when the receiver requests it. Therefore, the data transmission procedures are classified according to the transmission initiation party into three basic interaction procedures, which are defined in following Fig. 5.

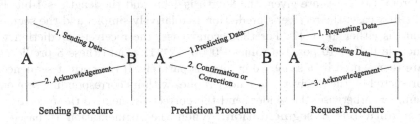

Fig. 5. Three basic interaction procedures

(1) The sending procedure is an normal action. In this procedure, the sender A sends a segment to the receiver B. When B receives a segment, it needs to make an acknowledgement to A.
(2) In the prediction procedure, the receiver will make a prediction of subsequent segment. The prediction can be made either randomly or based on semantics or the context. When the prediction is correct, the sender confirms it; otherwise, the sender correct the received data to the right data to the receiver.
(3) The request procedure is passive for the sender, and the receiver actively asks for a segment. After receiving a segment from the sender, the receiver will make an acknowledgement to the sender.

3.3   Segmentation and Prediction

Two segmentation methods are proposed here: Non-semantic and fixed-length segmentation (NSFL); Semantic-based and variable-length segmentation (SBVL).

(1) NSFL does not take the content of a secret into account. It is simply evenly divided into multiple segments after being encoded and encrypted. The simplest NSFL is to encode or encrypt a secret and each bit is viewed as a segment, but this segmentation is very low efficient. So the segmentation length should be longer, for example, 8 bits, or even more.

(2) SBVL first decomposes a secret based on semantic or syntactic structure, then performs encoding, encrypting, encapsulating data packets, serialization, and embedding. For example, a secret is split into many words, and each word is regarded as a segment.

Among three interaction procedures defined in Sect. 3.2, the prediction procedure is the core of the interactive steganography model. A secret is divided into at least two parts, one is sent actively and another is sent passively, which improves the security of the covert communication. The following describes the prediction procedure integrated with two segmentation methods.

(1) **Non-semantics based segmentation:** This method is only to evenly divide a binary string into many segments with the same length except the last one. Therefore, what to predict is a binary string with a fixed length. Herein, two cases are given, the length is 1-bit and the length is 4-bit. For the first case, the receiver's prediction is relatively simple, and the segment data is either '0' or '1'. For the second case, the receivers prediction will include half of 16 possible values ('0000' - '1111'), and these 8 predictions are represented by a sequence number separately. If the correct sequence is predicted by the receiver, the sender replies with its corresponding sequence number; otherwise, the sender send the correct segment to the receiver.

(2) **Semantic-based segmentation:** When the segmentation is based on semantics, the prediction procedure also will be based on semantics. For example, this prediction may utilize the natural language processing techniques, such as the N-gram model to predict the subsequent words.

3.4   Embedding or Mapping a Segment

The embedding layer is responsible for embedding a secret segment into a carrier or mapping a segment to an appropriate carrier. At this layer, multiple carriers or multiple methods can be used to achieve a high concealment of a steganography system. For embedding a secret segment, many existing methods can be fully employed. Many text steganography methods and multimedia methods are listed here as examples.

The approaches used in the text steganography methods:

1. Modify text formats, e.g.: font formats, word spacing, etc. [12].
2. Add null characters, invisible characters [13].
3. Replace words based on semantics or modify sentence structures [14].
4. Generate text carriers according to secret and rules [15].
5. Searching texts as carriers according to a secret [16].

Image steganography methods:
   Image LSB steganography [17,18].
Speech Steganography Methods:
   Audio Spread Spectrum Steganography [19].

At the same time, because multiple carriers may be used, it is necessary to specify the steganography method in every interaction procedure, and perform the corresponding extraction procedure. Here, after numbering the existing steganography methods, their unique IDs are transmitted in advanced.

The convergence of multiple methods can effectively improve the security of a steganography system. Before discussing the security of the convergent steganography mechanism, herein, the meaning of the symbols are given in the following table:

Table 2. The definition of the letters in formula

D	The degree of the covert communication concealment risks
R_{is}	Degree of content similarity of additional information and a secret
N_m	Modified bits in a carrier
D_d	The degree of embedding location scatter of a secret
N_i	Additional information
N_s	The number of steganography methods
R_{cs}	The degree of content similarity between a carrier and a secret
θ	The influence coefficient of additional information

Generally, the bigger the number of steganography methods are, the higher the security of steganography is, that is, while N_s increase, D decreases, the same as D_d. Additionally, the increase of R_{cs}, R_{is}, N_i, N_m and will increase D. Therefore, the concealment risk assessment function of a convergent steganography system can be defined as the following formula:

$$D = \frac{N_m * R_{cs} + \theta * N_i * R_{is}}{D_d * N_s}$$

The greater the value of D is, the greater the concealment risk of the convergence of these steganography methods is. The function of the risk assessment function is to assess the security risk of a steganography method and a carrier to be selected. The steganography method and the carrier with the lowest risk will be selected and used in this steganography mechanism.

4   The Operations of Embedding and Extracting

Corresponding to the two segmentation methods, two steganography approaches are proposed here. The non-semantic fixed-length segmentation corresponds to the non-semantic fixed-length steganography, and the semantic-based segmentation corresponds to the semantic-based variable-length steganography. The steganography model proposed in Sect. 3 is online interactive and the receiver can also involve in sending data, so that, the embedding and the extraction operations are mixed in one communication process instead of two separate processes.

4.1   The Non-semantic Fixed-Length Steganography

Step 1. Preprocess a secret. The secret will be encoded/encrypted as a binary string S by using the *UTF-8*, other encoding methods or encryption algorithms. The binary string S will be split into multiple segments with the same fixed length and an initial sequence number, which constructs the original sequence L_{send}. And then, the sequence L_{send} is reorder by hashing and got a new sequence La. The hash function has many choices, e.g.: $H(k) = x * k + y$, here, k is an element in L_{send} and x and y are a prime and their product will be the key sent to the receiving end as the additional side information.

Step 2. Start covert communication. Either the sender or the receiver can initiate the covert communication. But in fact, it is usually the sender that initiates the communication. As long as both sides are confirmed to each other, the covert communication starts. The items to be confirmed include:

(1) The identities with secret signals. Both communicating parties need to exchange their identity with secret signals.
(2) The sender A needs to specify the element number in the sequence L_a and the segment length L_{seg}.
(3) The product of x and y in the hash function.

Step 3. Prepare for receiving data. After confirming the communication, the receiver will calculate the position of each segment to be received in the original sequence according to the shared hash function, and then be ready to receive and/or predict each segment.

Step 4. Data exchange. The process of sending and receiving data includes multiple interactive procedures. The sender A can actively send data, and the receiver B can also actively request data or predict the next segment of a secret. The specific interaction procedures are described in Sect. 3.2. In addition to the above interaction procedures, the procedures also involves in embedding data and sending the selected carrier. The details about embedding data are described in Sects. 3.1, 3.3 and 3.4.

Step 5. Complete the communication. After receiving all the segments, the receiver will send an acknowledge notification to the sender to finish the communication and need be not acknowledged from the sender.

Step 6. Restore the original secret segment.

4.2   The Semantic-Based Variable-Length Steganography

The difference between the non-semantic fixed-length steganography and the semantic-based variable-length steganography is the procedure of preprocessing a secret. The procedure in the later is as follows:

Step 1. Preprocess a secret. The secret is segmented using a word segmentation tool, and these words the words are reordered according to the same hash function as in Step 1 of the non-semantic fixed-length steganography. And then, these words are encoded as a binary string using the *UTF-8*, other encoding methods or encryption algorithms separately.

Step 2-Step 5. Same as the **Step 2-Step 5** in the non-semantic fixed-length steganography.

5   Experiment and Performance Analysis

5.1   An Example of Covert Communication

Following is an example. The secret is a sentence in Chinese, and is sent from A to B. The Chinese characters were encoded, segmented and hashed, where the length of segment is 4.

In order to make the reordered sequence begin with 1, and be a continuous integer sequence, that is, the following conditions should hold true.

$$\text{Conditions}: \left\{ \begin{array}{l} H\left(k\right) \in [1,n] \\ H\left(k_1\right) \neq H\left(k_2\right) \ for \ k_1 \neq k_2 \end{array} \right. \quad k,\ k_1, k_2 \in [0,n)$$

A simple direct-address hash function with open addressing can satisfy the above demands as follows:

$$H\left(k\right) = \left(2 * k + 1\right) \ mod \ n + i$$

Herein, k is the sequence number in the original sequence segment, beginning with 0, n is the number of segments, and i is a non-negative integer, is value is determined by the existence H (k) in the $\{H(p)|0 < p < k-1\}$, and 0 if H (k) exists, otherwise 1.

In the receiver end, k is computed according the following inverse operation.

$$k = \left\{ \begin{array}{l} \frac{H(k)-1}{2}, \quad if \ H\left(k\right) \ is \ an \ odd \ number \\ \frac{H(k)-2+n}{2}, \quad if \ H\left(k\right) \ is \ an \ even \ number \end{array} \right.$$

All these operations are illustrated in Fig. 6.

Chinese	你				好				我			
Code	1100	0100	1110	0011	1011	1010	1100	0011	1100	1110	1101	0010
Number	0	1	2	3	4	5	6	7	8	9	10	11
Hash	1	3	5	7	9	11	13	15	17	19	21	23
Chinese	的				祖				国			
Code	1011	0101	1100	0100	1101	0111	1110	0110	1011	1001	1111	1010
Number	12	13	14	15	16	17	18	19	20	21	22	23
Hash	2	4	6	8	10	12	14	16	18	20	22	24

Fig. 6. An example of covert communication

Before A sends the secret, each party in the communication should send the following information to the peer: the identity with secret signals; the length of segment: 4; the numbers of segments: 24; the product 2.

After getting the above-mentioned data, the receiver B calculates the mapping between the sequence numbers in every segment and their original numbers and prepares to extract the secret information.

The packet header can be constructed according to the chosen interaction type, which is sending or requesting or predicting a secret segments. Here, the 23rd Hash segment is taken as an example in Fig. 6.

The sending packet: *011 10111 0010*.

The requesting packet: *101 10111*.

The acknowledgement packet: *011 10111 0010*.

The prediction packet: *100 10111 (random 8 four-bit binary strings, a total of 32 bits)*.

The prediction confirmation packet: *110 10111 (the correct serial number)*.

The prediction correction packet: *111 10111 (the correct segmentation)*.

Select appropriate steganography methods. Only three methods, namely adding spaces, synonyms substitution, and searching, are used to simplify the explanation. When we want to send the packet *011 0 00000 0010*, and the carrier text: *"Bob, the weather today is very good, let's go to travel far away!"* The three methods are illustrated as follows:

Adding spaces: *"Bob, (space) the weather today is very good, let's go to travel far (space) away!"*

Synonyms substitution: *"Bob, the clime today is very good, lets driving abroad!"*

Searching based on the parity of Chinese characters stroke numbers:

哇，今天天气十分好啊，不如玩呀！

The assessed risk can be calculated as follows:
Adding spaces:

$$D1 = 2*0.3 + 2*2*0.5/2*1 = 1.3$$

Synonyms substitution:

$$D2 = 6*0.3 + 0.5*2*0.5/2*1 = 1.15$$

Searching based on the parity of Chinese characters stroke numbers:

$$D3 = 0 + 0.5*2*0.5/4*1 = 0.125$$

The calculation results show that the searching method is better than others, so it will be chosen as the steganography method.

5.2   Security Analysis

The steganography model proposed in this paper is based on the user interaction in an instant messaging system, which make the steganography system can inherit the flexibility features of the communication method when it is well-integrated with an instant messaging system. The flexibility means that the steganography methods and the user interactions can be dynamically chosen, which make the steganography system more secure. The following is a detailed analysis for the security of the model.

(1) In an instant messaging system, the multiple user interactions implementing the steganography makes it difficult for attackers to get the original covers for a comparative analysis, which will makes system safer.

(2) The steganography model proposed in this paper is based on a question-and-answer process in the communication. Both parties can involve in sending data. And the secret segment is requested, or predicted and acknowledged to the sender, which may also improve the security of a covert communication.

(3) The data segments are sent after the secret is processed. It is difficult for an attacker to acquire the secret even if it is detected that it is susceptible, because that it is not known the complete data package structure. This can ensure the security of the content in an open channel.

(4) The variable steganography methods can be chosen in real time, which can effectively increase the concealment of a covert communication.

(5) In the embedded layer, multi-carrier can be used in the steganography model, which will help to make the steganography more safe and effective.

5.3   Robustness Analysis

In the transmission, a secret is segmented, and each segment is sent in a unified structure of data packages, and has a corresponding sequence number, and an acknowledgement is employed. All of these are useful to assure that a secret is safely sent to the receiver.

6   Conclusion

To make full advantage of instant messaging, this paper proposes a real-time interactive steganography model and describes three user interaction procedures. This model differs from the traditional steganography model in the following points: (1) A layered steganography model is helpful to simplify the understanding of a steganography design. (2) The sender and the receiver embed and extract a secret by the segment transmissions in a real time way, and each segment is transmitted based on the user interactions, which make the receiver involved in the segment sending. (3) The mode instantly supports multiple steganography methods and multi-carrier to transmit a secret. The dynamic selection method and the instant messaging can be well integrated, which improves the security of the steganography system.

Acknowledgment. This work was supported by NSFC-General Technical Research Foundation Joint Fund of China under Grant No. U1536113.

References

1. Johnson, N.F., Jajodia, S.: Exploring steganography: seeing the unseen. Computer **31**(2), 26–34 (1998)
2. Cachin, C.: An information-theoretic model for steganography. In: Aucsmith, D. (ed.) IH 1998. LNCS, vol. 1525, pp. 306–318. Springer, Heidelberg (1998). https://doi.org/10.1007/3-540-49380-8_21
3. Katzenbeisser, S., Petitcolas, F.: Information Hiding Techniques for Steganography and Digital Watermarking, 2nd edn. Artech house, Boston (2000)
4. Cachin, C.: An information-theoretic model for steganography. Inf. Comput. **192**(1), 41–56 (2004)
5. Cole, E.R.D.: Hiding in Plain Sight: Steganography and the Art of Covert Communication, 2nd edn. Wiley, New York (2003)
6. Hanafy, A.A., Salama, G.I., Mohasseb, Y.Z.: A secure covert communication model based on video steganography. In: Military Communications Conference 2009, pp. 1–6. IEEE, Milcom (2009)
7. Cox, I.J., Kilian, J., Leighton, F.T.: Secure spread spectrum watermarking for multimedia. IEEE Trans. Image Process. **6**(12), 1673–1687 (1997)
8. Hartung, F., Kutter, M.: Multimedia watermarking techniques. Proc. IEEE **87**(7), 1079–1107 (1999)
9. Luo, L., Chen, Z., Chen, M.: Reversible image watermarking using interpolation technique. IEEE Trans. Inf. Forensics Secur. **5**(1), 187–193 (2010)
10. Coltuc, D.: Low distortion transform for reversible watermarking. IEEE Trans. Image Process. Publ. IEEE Signal Process. Soc. **21**(1), 412–7 (2012)
11. Zielinska, E., Mazurczyk, W., Szczypiorski, K.: Trends in steganography. Commun. ACM **57**(3), 86–95 (2014)
12. Brassil, J.T., Low, S., Maxemchuk, N.F.: Copyright protection for the electronic distribution of text documents. Proc. IEEE **87**(7), 1181–1196 (1999)
13. Khairullah, M.: A novel text steganography system using font color of the invisible characters in microsoft word documents. In: Second International Conference on Computer and Electrical Engineering 2009, pp. 482–484. IEEE Computer Society (2009)
14. Bender, W., Gruhl, D., Morimoto, N.: Techniques for data hiding. IBM Syst. J. **35**(34), 313–336 (1995)
15. Majumder, A., Changder, S.: A novel approach for text steganography: generating text summary using reflection symmetry. Procedia Technol. **10**, 112–120 (2013)
16. Shi, S., Qi, Y., Huang, Y.: An approach to text steganography based on search in internet. In: Computer Symposium 2017, pp. 227–232. IEEE (2017)
17. Wang, R.Z., Lin, C.F., Lin, J.C.: Image hiding by optimal LSB substitution and genetic algorithm. Pattern Recognit. **34**(3), 671–683 (2001)
18. Jiang, W., Guo, Z., Wang, K., et al.: A self-contained steganography combining LSB substitution with MSB matching. In: International Conference on Computer Science and Network Technology 2016, pp. 635–640. IEEE (2017)
19. Cheng Q, Sorensen J.: Spread spectrum signaling for speech watermarking. In: 2001 IEEE International Conference on of the Acoustics, Speech, and Signal Processing 2001. Proceedings of the ICASSP 2001, pp. 1337–1340. IEEE (2001)

A Multiple Linear Regression Based High-Performance Error Prediction Method for Reversible Data Hiding

Bin Ma[1], Xiaoyu Wang[1(✉)], Bing Li[1], and Yunqing Shi[2]

[1] School of Information, Qilu University of Technology (Shandong Academy of Sciences), Jinan 250300, China
qluwxy@163.com
[2] Department of Electrical and Computer Engineering, New Jersey Institute of Technology, Newark, NJ 07102, USA

Abstract. In this paper, a high-performance error-prediction method based on Multiple Linear Regression (MLR) algorithm is first proposed to improve the performance of Reversible Data Hiding (RDH). The MLR matrix function that indicates the inner correlations between the pixels and its neighbors is established adaptively according to the consistency of pixels in local area of a natural image, and thus the object pixel is predicted accurately with the achieved MLR function that satisfies the consistency of the neighboring pixels. Compared with conventional methods that only predict the object pixel with fixed parameters predictors through simple arithmetic combination of its surroundings pixel, experimental results show that the proposed method can provide a sparser prediction-error image for data embedding, and thus improves the performance of RDH more effectively than those state-of-the-art error prediction algorithms.

Keywords: Multiple linear regression · Reversible data hiding
Prediction error · Embedded capacity

1 Introduction

Reversible data hiding (RDH) enables the embedding of secret message into a host image without loss of any original information. It considers not only extracting the hidden message correctly, but also recovering the original image exactly after data extraction [1]. Data hiding capacity and image fidelity are the two main important indicators of RDH algorithm. To improving the data embedding capacity and maintaining the quality of the marked images simultaneously is a big challenge in this area. At present, RDH based on difference expansion and RDH based on histogram shifting are two kinds of most prevalent methods being widely employed. In a difference expansion based RDH scheme, the secret messages are embedded by multiplying the difference between the object pixel and its predicted value (prediction-error); while, the RDH scheme based on histogram shifting achieves data embedding by translating the largest number of prediction errors. If the prediction-errors are small and distribute around "0" closely, the prediction-error image employed for data hiding would minimize the distortion of the marked image largely after data embedding.

© Springer Nature Switzerland AG 2018
X. Sun et al. (Eds.): ICCCS 2018, LNCS 11066, pp. 135–146, 2018.
https://doi.org/10.1007/978-3-030-00015-8_12

As the secret messages are hidden into the redundant information of the host image, accurate error prediction algorithm can obtain small prediction-errors and thus the histogram distributes steeper around "0", causing the data embedding capacity is enhanced at the same marked image quality. Therefore, the study of high performance error predictor to improve the prediction accuracy of object pixel attracts more and more attentions. Tian [2] presented the first difference expansion based RDH scheme, through which the secret data can be embedded and extracted exactly without damage the original image. Thodi and Rodríguez [3] firstly provided the prediction-error expansion based RDH scheme. This new technique exploited the inherent correlations between the object pixel and its neighbors better than Tian's difference-expansion scheme. Therefore, the prediction-error expansion method reduced the image distortion at low embedding capacity and mitigates the capacity control problem. Fallahpour *et al.* [4] illustrated a lossless data hiding method based on the technique of gradient-adjusted prediction (GAP), in which the prediction-errors are computed and slightly modified with histogram shifting method, so as to hided more secret message at high PSNR. Later on, Sachnev *et al.* [5] proposed the rhombus error prediction method to embed secret message into an image, and a sorting technique is employed to record the prediction-errors according to the magnitude of its local variance. The sorted prediction errors and a size reduced location map allowed more data can be embedded into the image with less distortion. Yang and Tsai [6] provided an interleaving error prediction method, in which the amount of predictive values are as many as the pixels, and all prediction-errors are transformed into image histogram to create higher peak bins to improve the embedding capacity. Recently, Dragoi and Coltuc [7] presented a local error prediction method and evaluated it with difference expansion based RDH scheme. For each pixel, a least square predictor is established from a square block centered on the pixel, and thus the smaller corresponding prediction-errors are obtained. The method is employed regardless of the predictor order or the prediction context, which enable it achieved higher reversible data hiding performance.

The pixels distribute differently from one region to another in a natural image [8]. Although many methods have been proposed to increase the prediction accuracy of the object pixels in host image, most of them estimate the object pixel with fixed parameter algorithm through simple arithmetic combination of its surroundings pixel, the inner correlation among adjacent pixels in the image can not be fully exploited, consequently, the prediction accuracy improved less. So, it is very instructive to explore more effective error prediction methods to improve the performance of reversible data hiding.

In this paper, we firstly proposed a machine learning method - multiple linear regression algorithm to adaptively estimate the object pixels. Unlike the conventional methods just employ the fixed parameters algorithm to estimate the objective pixel through simple arithmetical combinations of its neighbors, the proposed method explores the inner correlations among the object pixel and its neighborhoods. The method adaptively studies the inner relations among the object pixel and its neighbors, and then predicts the object pixel with the MLR function achieved from its neighboring pixels. According to the local consistency of the natural image, the prediction accuracy is highly improved and the value of the prediction-errors are minimized, which enable the image prediction-errors distribute around "0" closely and the histogram distribute steep. And thus, the performance of RDH scheme based on the proposed prediction-error image outperforms those state-of-the-art schemes based on conventional counterparts clearly.

The outline of the paper is as follows. The principle of MLR algorithm is introduced in Sect. 2. The error prediction method based on MLR algorithm for RDH is presented in Sect. 3. The experimental results of error prediction based on MLR algorithm are shown in Sect. 4. In Sect. 5, the comparisons of RDH performance based on the proposed prediction-error image and images from other state-of-the-art algorithms are demonstrated. Finally, conclusions are drawn in Sect. 6.

2 MLR Algorithm Based Error Prediction

MLR is a linear approach for modeling the relationship between a scalar dependent variable Y and independent variables denoted by X. The relationships are modeled with the linear predictor whose unknown model parameters are estimated from the data, and such models are called linear models. The basic purpose of MLR is utilizing the independent variables to estimate another dependent variable and its variability.

The general model of multiple linear regression is

$$y_i = \beta_0 + \beta_1 x_{i1} + \beta_2 x_{i2} + \cdots \beta_k x_{ik} \tag{1}$$

Where, $\beta_0, \beta_1, \beta_2, \cdots, \beta_k$ are $k+1$ unknown parameters, β_0 is regression constant, $\beta_1, \beta_2, \cdots, \beta_k$ are called regression coefficients and $x_1, x_2, \ldots, x_k$ are variables that can be accurately measured, and ε is random error.

In a multiple variable estimated system, where the variables comply with the same mapping regular, the MLR function can be expressed in matrix format as

$$Y = \beta X + \varepsilon \tag{2}$$

Where, Y, β, X, ε are as follows

$$Y = \begin{bmatrix} y_1 \\ y_2 \\ \vdots \\ y_n \end{bmatrix} \quad \beta = \begin{bmatrix} \beta_0 \\ \beta_1 \\ \vdots \\ \beta_n \end{bmatrix} \quad X = \begin{bmatrix} 1 & x_{11} & \cdots & x_{1k} \\ \vdots & \vdots & & \vdots \\ 1 & x_{n1} & \cdots & x_{nk} \end{bmatrix} \quad \varepsilon = \begin{bmatrix} \varepsilon_0 \\ \varepsilon_1 \\ \vdots \\ \varepsilon_n \end{bmatrix} \tag{3}$$

The above matrix equation can be solved with the Least-Square method, so that the MLR function is constructed with respect to the known and unknown variables, which enables the sum of the squared deviations between the estimated and observed values of the model is as small as possible, i.e. the sum of squared residuals is smallest. At last, the value of the regression coefficients β is calculated as formula (4), and the prediction of the object variables is achieved effectively.

$$\beta = (X^T X)^{-1} X^T Y \tag{4}$$

3 MLR Based Objective Pixel Error Prediction

According to the consistency of pixels in local area of natural image, the neighboring pixels generally have similar values, and the neighboring pixels and the object pixel from same local area usually have close relation. Thus, the object pixel can be predicted by exploiting the inner relation among its neighboring pixels.

Suppose the object pixel to be predicted is $x_{m,n}$, its neighboring pixels are chosen as the prediction samples, and the prediction result is $y_{m,n}$. The MLR predictor of the object pixel is

$$y_{m,n} = \beta_0 + \beta_1 x_{11} + \beta_2 x_{12} + \ldots + \beta_k x_{1k} + \varepsilon \tag{5}$$

Where, $x_{m-1,n-1}, x_{m,n-1}, \ldots, x_{m+i,n+j}$ are the neighbors of object pixel.

Considering the closely correlations of pixels distribute in local area of natural image, the object pixel and its neighbors usually comply with the same pixel prediction function, thus, the object pixel can be predicted with the same function of its neighboring pixels precisely. In the light of this principle, the object pixel is not predicted through simple arithmetical combinations with its neighboring pixels in our proposed scheme, but through the MLR function established from the neighboring pixels, and thus, the prediction accuracy of the object pixel is improved.

Let $x_{m,n}$ be the pixel to be predicted, choose 4 pixels around the object pixel as the prediction samples, at the same time, choose 4 neighboring pixels of each prediction sample as training samples. Construct the MLR matrix function with the training samples as variables X and the prediction samples as variable Y. The MLR coefficients that indicate the inner correlation of pixels in local area are obtained by least-square method. Then, the object pixel is predicted with the achieved MLR equation which indicates the consistency relations of neighboring pixels in local area.

In the first stage, choose the four pixels at the top left of the object pixel $x_{m,n-1}, x_{m-1,n-1}, x_{m-1,n}, x_{m-1,n+1}$ (shown as Table 1, the Euclidean distance to object pixel is less than 2 pixels) as prediction samples, and every four pixels located at the upper left corner of each prediction pixel is chosen as the training sample. Then, the MLR matrix function is established according to the relationship between the training samples and the training pixels, through which the parameters are obtained adaptively (shown as formula (6)).

$$\begin{bmatrix} x_{m,n-1} \\ x_{m-1,n-1} \\ x_{m-1,n} \\ x_{m-1,n+1} \end{bmatrix} = \begin{bmatrix} \beta_1 \\ \beta_2 \\ \beta_3 \\ \beta_4 \end{bmatrix} \begin{bmatrix} x_{m,n-2} & x_{m-1,n-2} & x_{m-1,n-1} & x_{m-1,n} \\ x_{m-1,n-2} & x_{m-2,n-1} & x_{m-1,n} & x_{m,n-1} \\ x_{m-1,n-1} & x_{m-2,n-1} & x_{m-2,n} & x_{m-1,n+1} \\ x_{m-1,n} & x_{m-2,n} & x_{m-2,n+1} & x_{m-1,n+2} \end{bmatrix} + \begin{bmatrix} \varepsilon_1 \\ \varepsilon_2 \\ \varepsilon_3 \\ \varepsilon_4 \end{bmatrix} \tag{6}$$

Table 1. Pixel chosen method.

	$x_{m-2,n-1}$	$x_{m-2,n}$	$x_{m-2,n+1}$	
$x_{m-1,n-2}$	$x_{m-1,n-1}$	$x_{m-1,n}$	$x_{m-1,n+1}$	$x_{m-1,n+2}$
$x_{m,n-2}$	$x_{m,n-1}$	$x_{m,n}$		

Where, the vector $[x_{m,n-1}, x_{m-1,n-1}, x_{m-1,n}, x_{m-1,n+1}]^T$ denotes Y in Eq. (2). The MLR coefficients are obtained with Least-Squares (LS) method. As the optimal resolutions of MLR matrix function enable to minimize the sum of squared residuals (the residual is the difference between the estimated and original pixels), the optimal coefficients of a MLR function composed by the similar neighboring pixels are achieved.

In the following stage, the obtained MLR function and the four pixels located at the upper left corner of the object pixel are employed to predict the object pixel value according to the formula (7).

$$\hat{x}_{m,n} = \beta_1 x_{m,n-1} + \beta_2 x_{m-1,n-1} + \beta_3 x_{m-1,n} + \beta_4 x_{m-1,n+1} \tag{7}$$

Finally, the prediction-error is obtained with the formula (8), where, the original pixel value is subtracted by its predicted value.

$$e(i,j) = round(x(m,n) - \hat{x}(m,n)) \quad example \tag{8}$$

In order to further reduce the influence of the sudden change of local pixel values on the prediction accuracy, we adjust the pixels that have a larger change in the training matrix. Remove the maximum and minimum values for each set of training samples to eliminate the influence of pixel mutations in the local area on the prediction results.

For example, for prediction sample $x_{m,n-1}$, maximum and minimum of its training sample are $x_{m-1,n-2}$ and $x_{m-1,n}$, its optimized training sample is $[x_{m,n-2} \quad x_{m-1,n-1}]$. The training sample is changed from 4 to 2, and the prediction sample used for predicting the target pixel value is also 2 (named 2×2). The other three training samples are optimized according to the above method, and example formula (9) is obtained. Using the optimized training samples to train linear regression coefficients can further improve the accuracy of error prediction.

$$\begin{bmatrix} x_{m,n-1} \\ x_{m-1,n-1} \\ x_{m-1,n} \\ x_{m-1,n+1} \end{bmatrix} = \begin{bmatrix} x_{m,n-2} & x_{m-1,n-1} \\ x_{m-1,n-2} & x_{m-2,n-1} \\ x_{m-1,n-1} & x_{m-2,n} \\ x_{m-1,n} & x_{m-2,n+1} \end{bmatrix} \begin{bmatrix} \beta_1 \\ \beta_2 \end{bmatrix} + \begin{bmatrix} \varepsilon_1 \\ \varepsilon_2 \end{bmatrix} \tag{9}$$

Prediction sample is optimized by removing the maximum and minimum. Formula (10) is obtained by the optimized prediction sample and the regression coefficient β trained according to formula (9).

$$\hat{x}_{m,n} = \beta_1 x_{m,n-1} + \beta_2 x_{m-1,n} \tag{10}$$

Apparently, the proposed method does not just rely on the simple arithmetical combination of pixels closely adjacent to the object pixel to predict the object pixel, but learns the inner correlations between the training samples and the prediction samples. According to the close relation of local pixels, the object pixel is predicted with the optimized MLR function established from its neighboring pixels. As the method adaptively learns the inner correlation of pixels distribute in local area, the accuracy of prediction is improved clearly compared with those coefficients fixed error prediction method.

4   Experimental Results and Discussion

To evaluate the performance of the proposed MLR based error prediction method, four well known standard 512×512 test images include Lena, Baboon, Airplane and Tiffany (see Fig. 1) from the image database of MISC are chosen to evaluate the performance of the proposed method. As image Lena and Tiffany have plenty of moderate frequency information, that is, it is moderate texture complexity; while image Baboon is high texture complexity, and image Airplane is with large uniform areas, experiments with these four images can evaluate the performance of the proposed error prediction method comprehensively.

Fig. 1.   Test images of Lena, Baboon, Airplane and Tiffany

In the experiment, the object pixel is predicted by its four neighboring pixels locate on its upper left corner which are defined as prediction samples. It is supposed that the data embedding is from the lower right corner to the upper left corner, so that the value of the prediction samples are consistent before and after data embedding, accordingly, high accurate pixel prediction is achieved. The training samples on the upper left corner of the prediction samples are employed to established the MLR function coefficients, and the objective pixel is predicted with the established MLR function and the four prediction samples.

Moreover, to enable the correct extraction of the embedded message and the lossless recovery of the original image, the left two columns as well as the top two rows of the image are not involved in the reversible data hiding process, however, they are reserved for additional information saving or other specific application. Therefore, the net amount of the pixels involved for RDH is 510×510 actually. Here, two kinds of MLR equations establish method (2 training instances and 4 training instances) are adopted to evaluate the performance of the proposed method. Meanwhile, we compare the proposed error prediction method with other state-of-the-art error prediction methods such as Yang et al. method and Sachnev et al. method. Yang et al. proposed the interleaving prediction methods, in which the number of prediction-errors are as many as the pixels, Sachnev et al. presented the rhombus error prediction method for RDH. They all have achieved excellent experimental results in the process of object pixel error prediction. The experimental results are shown in Fig. 2.

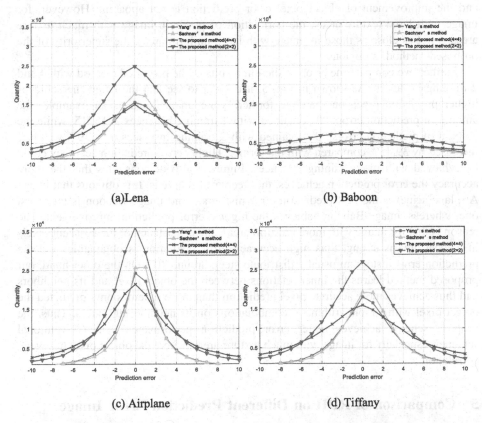

(a)Lena

(b) Baboon

(c) Airplane

(d) Tiffany

Fig. 2. The distribution of the prediction errors from −10 to 10 for image Lena, Baboon, Airplane, Tiffany.

Figure 2 shows that the proposed scheme with 2 training instances achieves higher performance than other state-of-the-art schemes clearly. the number of prediction-errors in the scope of $[-10, 10]$ obtained from the MLR algorithm is obviously better than from other algorithms. Take image *Lena* as an example, the total amount of pixels with prediction-errors belongs to $[-10, 10]$ is 229368 obtained from the proposed method (2×2), accounting for 87.5% of total image pixels; whereas, the total amount of prediction-errors whose absolute value less than 10 is 134732 with Sachnev *et al.* method, accounting for 47.6% of the total pixels; and the total number of prediction-errors in the scope of $[-10, 10]$ is only 121562 with Yang *et al.* method, accounting for 46.4% of the total pixels. The performance of the proposed predictor outperforms other two classical predictors clearly. Moreover, the results also demonstrate that the improvement of the error prediction accuracy partially depends on image content, namely, it is more significant for images with much texture areas than for ones with large uniform areas. The reasons is that the object pixel generally is more consistent with its adjacent pixels for image with large uniform areas than ones with much texture areas. Thus, its error prediction accuracy is high even with simple prediction method, and the improvement of object pixel error prediction is not apparent. However, for image with large texture areas, the correlation of pixels in image with much texture areas is not as close as those in image with large uniform areas, the superiority of the proposed method is obvious.

Further, we compare the error prediction results of the proposed method with 4 and 2 training instances. As shown in Fig. 3, it is clear to see that the latter one achieves higher prediction precision than the former. Take image Lena as an example, the amount of prediction-errors "0" obtained with 4 training instances is 15015, while the amount of prediction-errors "0" obtained with 2 training instances is 24797, which is increased by 39.45% compared with the former. Higher error prediction accuracy could be achieved with more training instances. Figure 3 also demonstrates that the more accuracy the error prediction achieves, the steeper the curve is. It is obvious that image Airplane achieves the best prediction-error histogram and image Baboon is the worst one, whereas, image Baboon achieves the highest error prediction improvement. The reason is that for image with more uniform areas, the consistency of the adjacent pixels in a local area is strong, thus high accuracy error prediction is obtainable, and the prediction-error histogram usually distribute steep around "0". On the other hand, our proposed method learns the inner relations between the object pixel and its neighbors and thus achieves more accurate pixel prediction than those schemes only predicted the object pixel with simple arithmetic combinations on its neighboring pixels. Thus, the propose scheme achieves better error prediction performance than conventional schemes, especially for image with much texture areas, where the object pixel has weak correlation.

5   Comparison of RDH on Different Prediction-Error Image

To further verify the superiority of the MLR based error prediction method, we compare the performance of difference expansion based RDH scheme on different prediction-error image formulated with Yang *et al.* method, Sachnev *et al.* method, Dragoi *et al.* method and the two proposed methods. Here, we choose difference

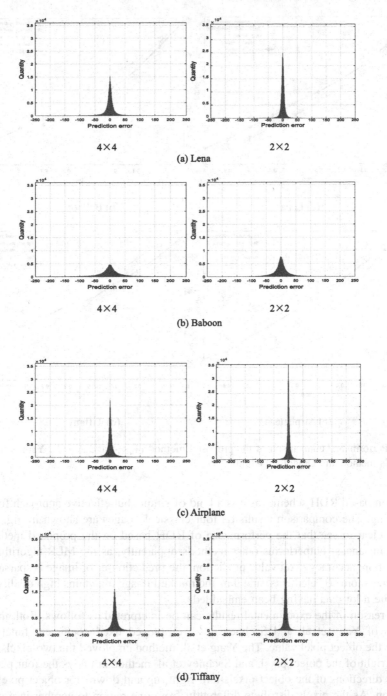

Fig. 3. The proposed method (4×4 and 2×2) generate predict error histogram on four images.

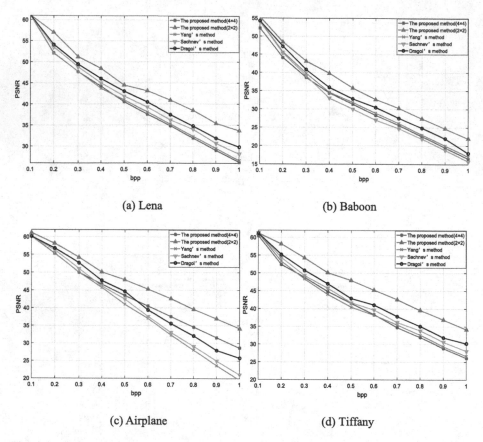

(a) Lena

(b) Baboon

(c) Airplane

(d) Tiffany

Fig. 4. Performance comparison of the proposed method (4 × 4 and 2 × 2), Yang's method, Sachnev's method and Dragoi's method

expansion based RDH scheme, as it is a kind of simple but effective approach for data embedding. The comparison results on four classical images are shown in Fig. 4.

It is clear to see that the performance of RDH based on the proposed method (2 training instances) outperforms other methods apparently, as the MLR algorithm can achieve more accuracy pixel value prediction, the prediction-error image is sparser than others (has more "0" elements) and thus the marked image maintains high quality even after quite a lot data having been embedded.

The reason of the experimental results can be interpreted as follows. Both the two methods of Yang et al. and Sachnev et al. employed fixed coefficient function to estimate the object pixel value. The Yang et al. method employed the two pixels at the left and right of the object pixel, and Sachnev et al. method employs the four pixels at the four directions of the object pixels(left, right, up and down) for object pixel error prediction. As the pixels distribute differently from one region to another in a natural image, the object pixel prediction accuracy different from one area to another. The more texture the host image has, the lower the prediction accuracy would be. Although

Drogia et al. method predict the object pixel adaptively with pixels distribute in a local area, the marked and the original pixels are both involved for error prediction, its prediction accuracy is decreased apparently. On the other hand, our proposed scheme not just estimates the object pixel directly with fixed parameters algorithm, it establishes the MLR function and deciding its coefficients firstly from the neighboring pixels closely adjacent to the object pixel, and then predicts the object pixel with the achieved MLR function and its surrounding pixels. According to the consistency of pixels in local area of natural image, the error prediction accuracy is improved effectively.

As the MLR based error prediction method adaptively estimates the object pixel according to its neighboring pixels, for image with large uniform areas, the accuracy of prediction-error is similar for the proposed algorithm and other classical algorithms. However, if the image is rich in texture areas, it achieves higher error prediction performance than those fixed coefficients error prediction methods. Thus, the performance of the reversible data hiding based on the proposed prediction-error image is highly improved than those state-of-the-art schemes, especially for image with much texture areas. Moreover, Fig. 4 also shows that the proposed scheme achieves higher performance than others at moderate to high data embedding capacity, that is, when the data embedding capacity is low, all kinds of error prediction algorithms can provide sufficient prediction-errors "0" for data embedding, but with the embedding capacity increase, the error image with less prediction-errors "0" brings more image distortion than others. The better the error prediction algorithm is, the more accuracy the error prediction would be, and the higher the RDH performance is achieved.

6 Conclusion

In this paper, a new kind of error prediction method based on MLR algorithm is presented. The object pixel is predicted with MLR function and its neighboring pixels, where, the MLR is established from the neighboring pixels distribute closely to the object pixel. According to the consistency of the pixels in local area of natural image, the object pixel is predicted accurately. The experimental results compared with some state-of-the-art schemes show that the MLR based error prediction scheme achieves higher performance than others clearly. Moreover, the prediction-error image achieves with the proposed method also has been employed for RDH, and the results demonstrate that the RDH on the proposed prediction-error image outperforms the counterparts apparently, especially for image with much texture areas. The MLR based adaptive error prediction method can increase the object pixel prediction accuracy (minimize the prediction-error) largely and then improve image RDH performance in great extent.

References

1. Shi, Y.Q., Li, X., Zhang, X., et al.: Reversible data hiding: advances in the past two decades. IEEE Access **2016**(4), 3210–3237 (2016)
2. Tian, J.: Reversible data embedding using a difference expansion. IEEE Trans. Circ. Syst. Video Technol. **13**(8), 890–896 (2003)
3. Thodi, D.M., Rodriguez, J.J.: Prediction-error based reversible watermarking. In: International Conference on Image Processing, ICIP 2004, vol. 3, pp. 1549–1552. IEEE (2004)
4. Fallahpour, M.: Reversible image data hiding based on gradient adjusted prediction. IEICE Electron. Express **5**(20), 870–876 (2008)
5. Sachnev, V., Kim, H.J., Nam, J., et al.: Reversible watermarking algorithm using sorting and prediction. IEEE Trans. Circ. Syst. Video Technol. **19**(7), 989–999 (2009)
6. Yang, C.H., Yang, M.H.: Improving histogram-based reversible data hiding by interleaving predictions. IET Image Proc. **4**(4), 223–234 (2010)
7. Dragoi, I.C., Coltuc, D.: Local-prediction-based difference expansion reversible watermarking. IEEE Trans. Image Process. **23**(4), 1779–1790 (2014). A Publication of the IEEE Signal Processing Society
8. Ma, B., Shi, Y.Q.: A reversible data hiding scheme based on code division multiplexing. IEEE Trans. Inf. Forensics Secur. **11**(9), 1914–1927 (2016)

A Multiple Watermarking Scheme for Content Authentication of OOXML Format Documents

Niandong Liao[1,2], Caixia Sun[2], Lingyun Xiang[1,2(✉)], and Feng Li[1,2]

[1] Hunan Provincial Key Laboratory of Intelligent Processing of Big Data on Transportation, Changsha University of Science and Technology, Changsha 410114, Hunan, China
[2] School of Computer and Communication Engineering, Changsha University of Science and Technology, Changsha 410114, Hunan, China
xiangly210@163.com

Abstract. The content of the document tends to be tampered and forged easily, and it may cause serious consequences in many important situations. Therefore, this paper proposes a multiple watermarking scheme for copyright protection and tamper detection of OOXML format documents. For an OOXML format document, we firstly embed a robust watermark by synonym substitutions, then embed double watermarks fragilely by utilizing the format characteristics of the document. The double fragile watermarks are embedded by the ways of modifying the word number in a text element defined by the main document body and modifying the values of revision identifiers. The embedding of multiple watermarks does not cause any visual impact on the content and format of the original document, which maintains the original meaning of the content basically. As shown by the experimental results, the watermarking method based on synonym substitutions has a strong robustness against the attacks on formats and the content. However, the double fragile watermarking methods can sensitively perceive tampers in the content and formats of the watermarked document, and predict the type of tampers with capability of locating the tampering.

Keywords: Digital watermarking · OOXML format document
Tamper detection and location · Synonyms substitution

1 Introduction

With the development of digital technology and the increasing use of the Internet, due to the characteristics of the digital products such as being easy to be copied or tampered, the infringements of copyright, tampering with maliciousness, illegal distribution and some other security issues have become the biggest problem of digital industry. Digital watermarking [7,9] emerged as an effective means of protecting copyright and data integrity. Many researchers have paid more attentions on text watermarking recently.

© Springer Nature Switzerland AG 2018
X. Sun et al. (Eds.): ICCCS 2018, LNCS 11066, pp. 147–159, 2018.
https://doi.org/10.1007/978-3-030-00015-8_13

Text watermarking methods are mainly divided into three categories in terms of ability to resist attacks:

(1) Robust watermarking [2]: the embedded watermarks can be extracted accurately even suffering malicious attacks. It is generally used for copyright identifications. To preserve the original meaning of the cover text, this kind of watermarking method embeds information by equivalent substitutions. A typical watermarking method is based on synonym substitution [1,8], which embeds watermark by making replacement operations among synonymous words. This method has strong robustness as long as the modified content does not involve the embedded watermark.

(2) Fragile watermark: This watermarking method can detect sensitively the subtle changes in watermarked carriers. It is generally used as content authentication, tamper detection, and even location of tampers. Watermarking methods based on word-shift, line-shift and font format [6,11] are all fragile, which embed watermark information by simple format transformations towards format documents. Absolutely, such methods are difficult to resist format attacks and have poor robustness. Sun et al. [5] proposed a watermarking based on text segmentation according to the characteristics of the OOXML format document. It embeds information by the number of displayed characters contained in the text element. However, the method is difficult to resist malicious attacks such as insertion and deletion. Xu et al. [13] combined the characteristics of OOXML format and then proposed a watermarking algorithm based on revision identifier, which embedded information by replacing or adding the attribute values of revision identifiers. This method is difficult to resist reformatting, content modification and format attacks.

(3) Semi-fragile watermark: this is a kind of watermarking whose processing operations remain to be robust watermark within certain range, but beyond the scope, the modifications can be detected. At present, there few researches of text Semi-fragile watermarking compared with image watermarking methods [3,10].

Although there are many research achievements in text watermarking, most watermarking method only have single objective of document copyright authentication or content authenticity authentication. They cannot implement tamper detection and tamper location simultaneously. To solve this problem, in this paper we propose a novel multiple watermarking scheme for OOXML format document. Firstly, the scheme uses synonym substitutions to embed the first watermark information for authenticating the copyright robustly. Then, the first fragile watermark is embedded by changing the number of characters in a text element, and the second fragile watermark is embedded by modifying attribute values of revision identifiers. Fragile watermarks are used for tampering detection of the content, format of documents and location of tampers. As shown in the experiments, the robust watermark based on synonym substitution has a strong robustness against the attacks on formats and content. However, the double fragile watermarks based on text segmentation and revision identifier modification can sensitively perceive the tampering of the content and format and judge tampering type. In a conclusion, it can be used for copyright protection, content authenticity authentication, tamper detection and location of OOXML format document.

2   The Proposed Scheme

2.1   General Framework

In order to achieve the multiple objectives such as copyright protection, tampering detection, and tampering location simultaneously, in this paper we propose a multiple watermarking scheme based on content and format. The overall framework of the proposed scheme is shown in Fig. 1.

The proposed scheme embeds the copyright owner's information as a watermark three times in different manners. The embedding process is as follows:

Step 1: Robust watermark embedding: The first watermark is embedded by substitutions among synonymous words. This watermarking has a strong robustness, and strong ability to resist tampering attacks.

Step 2: Text-field-based fragile watermark embedding: For the document with the first watermark, we read the display characters stored in the text element and segment the text element to embed the second watermark by adjusting the number of characters. The embedding of the second watermark is related to the storage of the document content, so its ability to resist the attack of document content editing and format modification is poor. It is very fragile and sensitive to document tampering.

Step 3: Format-field-based fragile watermark embedding: For the text element with text-field-based fragile watermark, the attribute value of the revision identifier in its parent node is modified to embed the third watermark information. Then, the final watermarked document is generated. When the watermarked document is tampered, format-field-based watermark and text-field-based watermark are detected to determine the type and location of tampers.

The embedding of fragile watermarks will not affect the embedded robust watermark, and it can effectively ensure the correct extraction of all kinds of watermark information when the watermarked document is untampered. When there are dispute or malicious tampers, the triple watermarks will be extracted and analyzed in turn to authenticate the copyright and integrity of the content of the document, then determine whether the OOXML document has been tampered. If do, the proposed scheme determines the type of tampers and locate their positions. The process of the watermark extraction and tamper detection is as follows:

Step 1: Robust watermark extraction: By decoding the synonyms in the watermarked document, the robust watermark A is extracted. If the watermark A is complete, the copyright is successfully authenticated, otherwise the document is pirated.

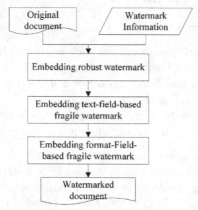

(a) Watermark embedding process

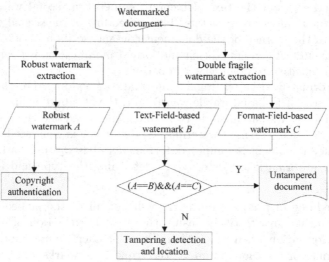

(b) Watermark detection process

Fig. 1. General framework of the proposed scheme

Step 2: Double fragile watermark extraction: read the text field and format field information in the main document, and extract the fragile watermark B based on the text segmentation according to the number of characters displayed in the text element. At the same time, the fragile watermark C is extracted according to the values of revision identifiers in the parent nodes of text elements.

Step 3: Tamper detection and location: The fragile watermarks B and C are compared with the watermark A in turn to authenticate the copyright and integrity of the document content. If the triple watermark information is identical, we can naturally come to a conclusion that the document has not been tampered. Otherwise, according to where the fragile watermarks B and C differ from the robust watermark A, and the location where the fragile watermark falls to be extracted, the type and the location of tampers will be determined.

2.2   Multiple Watermark Embedding

Microsoft Office 2007 and later versions all use Office Open XML [4] (OOXML) format for storage and typesetting. The multiple watermarking scheme proposed in this paper is performed in the main component document.xml of the OOXML format document. In document.xml, $<w:p>$, the element of paragraph, defines the content of a paragraph and its format attributes. The format attribute is defined with subelements $<w:pPr>$, and its content is defined by the run element $<w:r>$. The run element contains the corresponding format attribute information defined by subelements such as $<w:rPr>$, and the text characters are defined by the subelement $<w:t>$, i.e., the text element. The $<w:p>$ and $<w:r>$ also contain a special kind of attributes: the revision identifiers, such as w: rsidR, w: rsidRPr, w: rsidRDefaul, w: rsidP, and w: rsidRPr.

(1) Robust Watermarking Based on Synonym Substitution. For the content of the $<w:t>$ element, we use a synonym substitution method to embed a robust watermark. Its watermark embedding process is briefly described as follows:

Step 1: Preprocess the synonym database. This paper only selects the absolute synonym from the resources provided by WordNet 3.0 to construct a synonym database. According to the word frequency of the synonym [12], the two words with the relative largest frequencies in each synonym set form the final synonym set.

Step 2: Synonym encoding. In a synonym set, the synonym with higher word frequency is encoded as '0', and the other one is encoded as '1'.

Step 3: Watermark embedding. For the synonyms in the document, when the watermark bit to be embedded coincides with the coded value of the current synonym, no modification is made; otherwise, the current synonym is replaced by its synonymous word so that the encoded value of the replaced synonym is the same as the watermark bit. Particularly, 8-bit additional space is used to store the byte length of the watermark for extraction.

(2) Text-Field-Based Fragile Watermarking Based on Text Segmentation. The OOXML format allows a single run element to be split into multiple run elements without making any changes on the normal display and use of the document [8]. In view of this, the fragile watermark information can be embedded by the segmentation of the display characters contained in the text element. That is, the watermark information is represented by the number of displayed display characters, and the reliable binding between the watermark information and the text content is achieved. Once the text content is modified, tamper detection can be implemented sensitively. The text element segmentation watermarking process used in this paper is as follows:

Step 1: Run elements preprocessing. Traverses the main component, extracts the contents of the current run element, and removes any space-reserved mark in the run element. Then, calculate the number of characters in the text subelement ($<w : t>$ $</w : t>$) under the run element. If the number of characters is less than 4, the current run element is merged with the next run element until the number of characters of the text subelement in the current run element is greater than or equal to 4.

Step 2: Watermark embedding. Each text element, 2 watermark bits are embedded. The characters in the text element are divided according to the following rules, and the number of characters after the division indicates the corresponding watermark information.

(a) If the watermark information is '00', then the first word is split from the text element to create a new element. The same $<w : r>$ element and child elements $<w : rPr>$ and $<w : t>$ are synchronously created for it. At the same time, a space preserve tag [8] is added for each new $<w : t>$ element to mark the watermark position;

(b) If the watermark information is '01', the first two words are separated from the text element content, and the subsequent operations are similar;

(c) If the watermark information is '10', then the first three words are separated from the text element content, and the subsequent operations are similar;

(d) If the watermark information is '11', the first four words are separated from the text element content, and the subsequent operations are similar;

Step 3: The remaining characters in the split original text element are processed in the same way until all the run elements in the document have been processed.

It is worth noting that the fragile watermark is embedded repeatedly until all eligible run elements embed the watermark information.

(3) Format-Field-Based Fragile Watermarking Based on Revision Identifier. The special element attribute in the main partmodification identifier is mainly used to identify the modification of the document. Among them, the attribute w:rsidRPr in the run element is a character format modification identifier, and each time the modification of the text character format will change the attribute value of the corresponding character format modification identifier. Replacing the attribute value of the revision identifier does not affect the normal display and use of the document. Based on this, this paper modifies the attribute value of the revision identifier in the run element to embed the second fragile watermark information, which is used to track its child element(the change of the text character format stored in the text element).

Modifying the identifier modification rule is: while embedding a text field watermark in the segmented run element, the last two bits of the w:rsidRPr attribute are the two-bit watermark information to be embedded.

2.3 Tampering Detection and Location

In order to verify the copyright and the integrity of a document, we will check the watermark information by the following process.

Step 1: Robust watermark extraction. The synonym sequences appearing in the document will be identified, and the robust watermark information A will be extracted with the encoding value of the synonyms;

Step 2: Double fragile watermark extraction. The content of the run element and its child elements text element are extracted in turn. If the text element does not contain a space preserve tag, the run element is skipped; otherwise,

(a) Read characters in the text element and calculate the number of words. Then, the corresponding binary watermark B_i is obtained. If $W = 1$, B is 00; if $W = 2$, it is 01; if $W = 3$, it is 10; if $W = 4$, it is 11.

(b) Get the attribute value of the revision identifier of the run element of the parent node of the text element. After the interception, two bits are stored in the fragile watermark C_i.

Step 3: Step 2 is repeated until the text field watermark $\{B_i\}$ and the format field watermark $\{C_i\}$ contained in all run elements are extracted, and two complete watermark information strings B and C are serially concatenated.

Step 4: Compare and analyze the matching result of the robust watermark A and the fragile watermark strings B and C. If B is equal to C and repeated with A as the basic pattern, the document has not been tampered and A is used to determine the copyright of the document; otherwise, the document undergoes tampering. A large number of experiments have found that when editing an OOXML format document, the content in its main component is changed, causing the text content or format attribute stored in the run element to change.

The following analyzes the change rule of the run element structure when the document is subjected to tamper operations such as insertion, deletion, and format modification. Based on the fragile watermark of the text field and the fragile watermark extraction of the format field, the tampered type is detected, and the tampering position is located.

(1) Insert operation

(a) Insert occurs between two run elements. The newly inserted content will result in the generation of a new run element whose child elements $<w:t>$ will inherit the basic attributes of the previous run element, containing the space preserve tag and the newly inserted content. This element does not contain the w:rsidRPr and only includes a w:rsidR attribute that adds a modification identifier to track content additions. Therefore, when text-field-based watermark extracted from the run element is incorrect, and format-field-based watermark extraction fails, it can be determined that the document is subjected to tampering and the current run element is tampering content.

(b) Inserts occur inside the run element. The newly inserted content will cause the current run element to be split into two run elements with the same attributes and insert a newly generated run element in between. This run element contains a space preserve tag and newly added content, and contains the w:rsidR attribute. Therefore, when the text field extracted from the run element is watermarked incorrectly but the format field watermark is correct, and the next run element contains the w:rsidR attribute, the document can be judged to be tampered with and the next run element is tampered with. At this point, you need to skip the next run element to extract the fragile watermark.

(2) Delete operation

(a) Delete some of the text in the run element. In this case, only the text content stored in the run element's child text element will be changed, other formatting attributes will remain unchanged, and the next run element will not be affected. Therefore, when the text field in the run element is watermarked incorrectly and the format field watermark is correct, and the format field watermark in the next run element is correct, it can be determined that the document has been subjected to deletion tampering and the current run element is a tampering position.

(b) Delete the entire text in the run element. In this case, the run element will disappear and the corresponding text field and format field watermark information will not be extracted. Therefore, comparing the robust watermark A with the fragile watermark in the current run element, if there is a case where the watermark in the text field and the format field are missing at the same time, it can be determined that the document is subjected to deletion tamper and the starting position of the text content stored in the current run element is a tampering position.

(3) Format modification operation

(a) Modify the format of part text in the run element. The format here includes attributes such as character size, color, or font. In this case, the original run element will be split so that the characters of the same attribute are in the same run element. Unlike the insert operation, the format modification causes the new run element to include the w:rsidRPr attribute, but the attribute value is random, so the wrong text field and format field watermark information will be extracted from the new run element. The change of the format causes the first run element after the current run element is split to be a run element with the same format or a new run element with a changed format. Therefore, the tamper detection is divided into the following two cases:

Case 1: if the watermark information in the text field of the current run element is incorrect, the format field watermark information is correct, and the text field and format field watermark information in the next run element are all wrong. It can be determined that the document is subject to format tampering and the next run element is a tampered location. At this point, detect the next run element, if the text field watermark extraction fails, but the format field watermark is the same as the current run element, then the run element is affected by the format modification and the text field watermark extraction fails. It is not a partial deletion tampering.

Case 2: If the text field and format field watermarks in the current run element are extracted incorrectly, it can be determined that the document is subject to format tampering and the current run element is a tampering position. At this time, the next run element is detected. If the text field watermark extraction fails, but the format field watermark is extracted correctly, the run element is affected by the format modification and fails to extract the watermark in the text field, and is not partially deleted and tampered.

(b) Modify the format of all text content in the run element. At this point, changing some of the format attributes of the current run element causes the w:rsidRPr attribute value to change, but does not affect the text content in the run element. Therefore, when the watermark of the text field in the run element is correctly extracted and the format field watermark is extracted incorrectly, it can be determined that the document is subject to format tampering and the current run element is accurately located as a tampering position.

3   Experimental Results and Analysis

In this paper, 300 English OOXML format document are downloaded from the Internet as samples to conduct experiments, and the performance of various aspects of multiple watermarking scheme is analyzed and verified.

3.1   Analysis of Attack Resistance

The proposed scheme mainly relies on the robust watermarking algorithm based on synonym substitution to resist attacks for copyright authentication of the document. Therefore, this paper conducts experiments under attacks of content Insert, content deletion, format conversion, and save as to verify the anti-attack ability of the watermarked document based on synonym substitution. The results are shown in Table 1.

Table 1. Anti-attack ability

Attacks	Whether the watermark can be extracted correctly
Insert	Yes except inserting synonyms
Delete	Yes except deleting synonyms with watermark
Format modification	YES
Save as	YES

From Table 1, it can be seen that the synonym-substitution-based watermarking algorithm performs well against attacks. AS the synonyms carried watermark information do not generally appear densely, the probability that a synonym is attacked is low. A changed synonym can only change one bit of watermark information. We can consider combining text field and format field watermark information to recover damaged robust watermark information, and improve the anti-attack ability of robust watermark based on synonym substitution.

3.2 Tampering Detection and Location Analysis

For watermark documents generated by multiple watermarking schemes, this paper performs operations such as inserting, deleting, modifying and format transforming, then extracts multiple watermarks for analysis, and verifies the tamper-type detection and tamper-targeting capabilities of multiple watermarking methods.

(1) Insert attack

Figure 2 is an original watermark document that has not been subjected to any tampering. The embedded watermark information is "suncaixia". When new content is inserted in the document, such as when inserting new content "make" in front of "change usually" in the first line of paragraph 2. he multiple watermarking scheme can still extract the robust watermark information and the fragile watermark information "suncaixia" in the format field, but the extracted text field watermark information is "suncaixhX". The document was successfully detected as an insert attack, and the insert was accurately located as "make".

(2) Delete attack

A delete attack is performed on the document shown in Fig. 2, such as deleting the word "look forward to" in the first line of the first paragraph. The scheme of this paper correctly extracts the robust watermark and the format field fragile watermark "suncaixia", but the extracted text field watermark information is "puncaixia". At this point, the solution can successfully detect that the document is subject to a delete attack, and accurately locate the tampering that occurred before the "new".

(3) Format modification attack

When the document shown in Fig. 2 is subjected to a format modification attack. For example, the font size of the word "and" in the fourth line of the first paragraph is modified. This scheme correctly extracts the robust watermark and

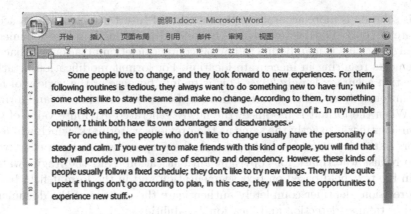

Fig. 2. Original watermarked document

text field watermark, but the extracted format field watermark information is garbled "sunc$xia". At this point, the solution can successfully detect that the document is subjected to format tampering, and accurately locating the error in extracting the format field watermark is a tampering position, that is, the position of "and".

300 documents with multiple watermarks were generated by embedding watermarks into 300 test samples, which are randomly and equally divided into three groups. We arbitrarily make Insert, delete or format modification to the watermarked document in the three sets. The proposed scheme is employed for detecting and locating tampering of the tampered documents. The experimental results are shown in Table 2.

Seen from Table 2, the watermarked document can basically extract robust watermark after encountering insert, delete and format modification attacks. Only if the deleted contents contain synonym, the extraction of the robust watermark is incorrect. The tamper detection relies on that the tampered document suffers from an erroneous extraction of the watermarks in the text field or the format field. Therefore, for the three types of attacks, the accuracy of tampering detection has reached 100%. However, when we try to locate the attacks, Insert attacks will destroy the text field and format field based watermark information. At the same time, it will introduce the added revision identifier $w : rsidR$.

Table 2. Tampering detection and location results under various tamper attacks

Attacks	Number of documents	Accuracy		
		Robust watermark	Tamper detection	Location
Insert	100	100%	100%	100%
Delete	100	99%	100%	93%
Format modification	100	100%	100%	79%

So, this solution is more accurate in the location of Insert attacks with an accuracy rate of 100%. For delete attacks, the deleted positions in a few documents is misaligned. This is mainly due to partial content deletion attacks on adjacent run elements resulting in inaccurate location. For format modification attacks, the location accuracy is only 79%. This is mainly because of the variety of format transformations, which greatly damages the watermarks in text and format fields. When the format is modified, the newly generated attribute value of the revision identifier is exactly the same as the previous watermark, which will lead to errors in the detection result. In general, the proposed scheme can effectively use the robust watermark for copyright authentication. And the fragile watermark in the text field based on text segmentation and in the format field based on the revision identifier completely authenticate the content of the document, and it has tamper detection and location capabilities.

4   Conclusion

In order to solve single function problem of the existing watermarking techniques for OOXML format documents, a multiple watermarking scheme for copyright protection and tamper detection is presented in this paper. This scheme robustly embeds the watermark information used for copyright authentication through the synonym substitution algorithm, while using the double fragile watermark to achieve tamper detection and location. The proposed scheme has a high application value, but there are still some shortcomings to be further improved, such as the robustness of robust watermarking, the accuracy of locating tamper when facing more complex attacks.

Acknowledgements. This project is supported by National Natural Science Foundation of China (No. 61202439), and partly supported by Scientific Research Fundation of Hunan Provincial Education Department of China (No. 16A008).

References

1. Chang, C.Y., Clark, S.: Practical linguistic steganography using contextual synonym substitution and a novel vertex coding method. Comput. Linguist. **40**(2), 403–448 (2014)
2. Cheng, W., Feng, H., Yang, C.: A robust text digital watermarking algorithm based on fragments regrouping strategy. In: 2010 IEEE International Conference on Information Theory and Information Security (ICITIS), pp. 600–603. IEEE (2010)
3. Duan, G.D., Zhao, X., Li, J.P., Liao, J.M.: A novel semi-fragile digital watermarking algorithm for image content authentication, localization and recovery. Dianzi Xuebao (Acta Electronica Sinica) **38**(4), 842–847 (2010)
4. ECMA International: Office open xml file formats-open packaging conventions. Dianzi Xuebao (Acta Electronica Sinica) **38**(4), 842–847 (2010)
5. Fu, Z., Sun, X., Liu, Y., Li, B.: Text split-based steganography in OOXML format documents for covert communication. Secur. Commun. Netw. **5**(9), 957–968 (2012)

6. He, Y.H.: Word spacing and character encoding based on a combination of text features digital watermarking algorithm. In: Applied Mechanics and Materials, vol. 401, pp. 2029–2032. Trans Tech Publ. (2013)
7. Hua, G., Huang, J., Shi, Y.Q., Goh, J., Thing, V.L.: Twenty years of digital audio watermarking a comprehensive review. Signal Process. **128**, 222–242 (2016)
8. Huanhuan, H., Xin, Z., Weiming, Z., Nenghai, Y.: Adaptive text steganography by exploring statistical and linguistical distortion. In: 2017 IEEE Second International Conference on Data Science in Cyberspace (DSC), pp. 145–150. IEEE (2017)
9. Kundur, D., Hatzinakos, D.: Digital watermarking for telltale tamper proofing and authentication. Proc. IEEE **87**(7), 1167–1180 (1999)
10. Li, C., Huang, J.W.: A semi-fragile image watermarking resisting to jpeg. J. Softw. **17**(2), 315–324 (2006)
11. Low, S.H., Maxemchuk, N.F., Brassil, J., O'Gorman, L.: Document marking and identification using both line and word shifting. In: INFOCOM 1995, Fourteenth Annual Joint Conference of the IEEE Computer and Communications Societies, Bringing Information to People, Proceedings, vol. 2, pp. 853–860. IEEE (1995)
12. Xiang, L., Sun, X., Luo, G., Xia, B.: Linguistic steganalysis using the features derived from synonym frequency. Multimed. Tools Appl. **71**(3), 1893–1911 (2014)
13. Xu, M., Wang, Y., Li, T.: A novel scheme of information hiding in word2007 document. J. Comput. Res. Dev. **46**, 112–116 (2009)

A Novel Framework of Robust Video Watermarking Based on Statistical Model

Li Li[1], Xin Li[1], Tong Qiao[2(✉)], Xiaoyu Xu[1], Shanqing Zhang[1],
and Chin-Chen Chang[3]

[1] School of Computer Science and Technology, Hangzhou Dianzi University,
Hangzhou 310018, China
[2] School of Cyberspace, Hangzhou Dianzi University, Hangzhou 310018, China
tong.qiao@hdu.edu.cn
[3] Department of Information Engineering and Computer Science, Feng Chia
University, Taichung, Taiwan

Abstract. This paper is to investigate a novel framework of robust video watermarking based on the statistical model with robustness against multiple attacks. The main contribution is threefold. First, the Laplacian distribution is proposed to model each naive video frame, referring to as the original frame; meanwhile the noisy frame, referring to as the one with adding Gaussian-distributed noise, is modeled using the Gaussian distribution. Second, we propose a novel mechanism of embedding watermark by artificially adding noise or not, corresponding to *watermark bit* 1 or 0. Third, it is proposed to cast the problem of watermark extraction into the framework of hypothesis testing theory. In the ideal context, with knowing all the model parameters, the Likelihood Ratio Test (LRT) is smoothly established with verifying the feasibility of the designed watermark extraction based on the statistical models. In the case of estimating model parameters, we propose to design the Generalized Likelihood Ratio Test (GLRT) to deal with the practical problem of watermark extraction. Finally, compared with some prior arts, extensive experimental results show that our proposed novel framework of robust video watermarking can achieve the high video quality with robustness against various attacks such as re-scaling, cropping, and compression.

Keywords: Robust video watermarking · Statistical model
Hypothesis testing · Parameter estimation

1 Introduction

With the remarkable development of social networking and Internet technology, digital videos become increasingly popular. Due to the fact that digital videos are possibly transmitted or shared by unauthorized users [26], the technique of video watermarking with dramatic advances, referring to as the art of embedding a marker into noise-tolerant signal such as a video, has been widely adopted in the community of multimedia security, such as copyright protection,

© Springer Nature Switzerland AG 2018
X. Sun et al. (Eds.): ICCCS 2018, LNCS 11066, pp. 160–172, 2018.
https://doi.org/10.1007/978-3-030-00015-8_14

broadcast monitoring, and content authentication. Without loss of generality, fragile video watermarking is utilized to detect tampering of the digital video while locating tampered areas; meanwhile robust video watermarking is aimed at protecting the copyright of the authorized video. However, most algorithms of robust video watermarking only perform the robustness with resisting against one typical attack. Besides, to our knowledge, few of current literature designs the watermarking technique based on the statistical model. To fill that gap, in this context, based on the statistical model, it is proposed to focus on investigating a novel framework of robust video watermarking with resistance against multiple attacks.

1.1 State of the Art

Many algorithms of the robust video watermarking have been proposed. In general, let us arbitrarily formulate those methodologies into two schemes: *frequency* domain-based and *spatial* domain-based digital watermarking, see [7] for a detailed review:

The scheme in the category of the frequency domain-based digital watermarking mainly relies on embedding the watermark in frequency domain. In frequency domain, the algorithms are implemented in the transform domain such as Discrete Cosine Transfer (DCT) and Discrete Wavelet Transfer (DWT) [8,21]. Cox et al. [5] proposed a watermarking technique by taking DCT of entire video. The method involves adding the watermark to the N lowest frequency non-dc coefficients of host video where N is the length of the watermark sequence with zero mean. This algorithm is one of the first attempts with providing video adaptability in the watermark embedding model.

The scheme in the category of the spatial domain-based digital watermarking is implemented by directly modifying each frame of video. In comparison with the frequency domain-based algorithms, the watermarking algorithms in this category slightly degrade the quality of videos while guaranteeing the robustness of the proposed methods. Besides, the scheme in this category has relevantly low cost of computation and is easily implemented (see [2,27]). Generally, the papers of [1,9,11,24] indeed improve the robustness of the spatial domain-based watermarking algorithm, but they are more complicated with requiring higher calculation cost. Besides, few of current robust watermarking algorithms study the statistical model-based scheme. Therefore, in this context, we propose to design a novel general framework of the robust video watermarking based on the proposed statistical model.

2 Statistical Model of Residual Noise from Naive Frame

In this section, we specifically describe the statistical model of extracted noise from the naive frame. Then, it is proposed to utilize the linear filter to deal with the problem of noise extraction. In the estimation of model parameters, the Maximum Likelihood Estimation (MLE) algorithm is proposed.

2.1   Establishment of the Proposed Model

Let us denote the naive frame $\mathbf{Z} = \{z_{i,j}\}, i \in \{1, \ldots, I\}, j \in \{1, \ldots, J\}$. In general, $z_{i,j}$ can be formulated by using its expectation $\mu_{i,j}$ and noise $n_{i,j}$:

$$z_{i,j} = \mu_{i,j} + n_{i,j} \tag{1}$$

where $\mu_{i,j}$ denotes an expected value of $z_{i,j}$, referring to as low frequency component of $\mathbf{Z}$, and $n_{i,j}$ denotes the noise of $z_{i,j}$, referring to as high frequency component. Immediately, $n_{i,j}$ can be defined as

$$n_{i,j} \equiv z_{i,j} - z_{i,j} \otimes H_{lp}(i,j) \tag{2}$$

where H_{lp} represents a low-pass linear filter, and $\otimes$ denotes two dimensional convolution in spatial domain. In this context, let us assume that addition noise $n_{i,j}$ follows the Laplacian distribution, which has been verified in [13, 20, 23]. Then, it is proposed to give the Probability Density Function (PDF) of the continuous Laplacian distribution:

$$P_{\boldsymbol{\theta}_0}[x] = \frac{1}{2b} \exp(\frac{-|x - e|}{b}), \forall x \in \mathbb{R} \tag{3}$$

where $\boldsymbol{\theta}_0 = (e, b)$, the location parameter e represents the expectation of the Laplacian distribution and b is the scale parameter; it is assumed that each observation x follows the proposed Laplacian model.

2.2   Parameter Estimation of the Proposed Model

For simplicity, in this context, MLE is used to estimate parameters of the Laplacian model (3). Thus, the likelihood function $L(x_i; \boldsymbol{\theta}_0), i \in \{1, \ldots, k\}$ can be described as:

$$L(x_i; \boldsymbol{\theta}_0) = \prod_{i=1}^{k} P_{\boldsymbol{\theta}_0}(x_i) = \frac{1}{(2b)^k} \exp(\frac{1}{b} \sum_{i=1}^{k} -|x_i - e|) \tag{4}$$

where k represents the total number of each observation; i denotes its corresponding index. For clarity, let us use the log of likelihood function (see (4)) to obtain the estimated parameters, which can be straightly formulated by:

$$\frac{\partial \ln L(x_i; \boldsymbol{\theta}_0)}{\partial b} = \frac{k}{b} + \frac{\sum_{i=1}^{k} -|x_i - e|}{b^2} = 0 \tag{5}$$

where the parameter $\boldsymbol{\theta}_0$ maximizes the probability of the function (4), leading to the establishment of the correlation between nuisance parameters represented by:

$$\hat{b} = \frac{1}{k} \sum_{i=1}^{k} |x_i - e| \tag{6}$$

where $\hat{b}$ denotes the estimate of the scale parameter b; $\hat{e}$ represent the estimate of e. Since the mean value of extracted noise from the naive frame approximately approaches to zero, let us assume that $\hat{e} \approx 0$. Then, the estimated $\hat{b}$ of the scale parameter can be straightly acquired by using (6).

3   Statistical Model of Residual Noise from Noisy Frame

In this section, let us mainly study the statistical model of extracted noise from the noisy frame. Then, it is proposed to utilize the linear filter to deal with the problem of noise extraction. The MLE algorithm is proposed to deal with the problem of parameter estimation.

3.1   Establishment of the Proposed Model

In our proposed framework, it is assumed that the residual noise extracted from the noisy frame (watermarked frame by bit 1) follows the Gaussian distribution. The embedding method is implemented by adding random noise with zero mean following the Gaussian statistical model into the noise-free naive frame. Then, each noisy frame $\mathbf{Z}' = \{z'_{i,j}\}, i \in \{1, \dots, I\}, j \in \{1, \dots, J\}$ can be formulated as follows:

$$\mathbf{Z}' = \mathbf{Z} \otimes \mathbf{H}_{lp} + \Omega \tag{7}$$

where $\Omega = \{\omega_{i,j}\}$ denotes the zero-mean Gaussian noise, $\mathbf{H}_{lp}$ represents the low-pass filter. By referring to (1) and (2), together with (7), the noise extracted from the noisy frame can be expressed as follows:

$$z'_{i,j} = \mu_{i,j} + \omega_{i,j} \tag{8}$$

Since, the linear transformation does not change the distribution characteristics, let us denote $w'_{i,j}$ the noise residuals from the noised frame, it can been defined as:

$$w'_{i,j} = z'_{i,j} \otimes H_{hp}(i,j) = \omega_{i,j} \otimes H_{hp}(i,j) \tag{9}$$

where H_{hp} represents the high-pass filter. It should be noted that in our assumption, we propose to ignore the noise residual generated from the expectation $\mu_{i,j}$ caused by the linear filter H_{hp} or H_{lp}. Immediately, the PDF of the assumed Gaussian model can be written as:

$$Q_{\theta_1}[x] = \frac{1}{\sigma\sqrt{2\pi}} \exp(-\frac{(x-m)^2}{2\sigma^2}) \tag{10}$$

where $\theta_1 = (m, \sigma)$, m denotes the expectation of the distribution, σ is the standard deviation controlling the intensity of noise.

3.2   Parameter estimation of the proposed model

For clarity, we also use MLE to estimate the model parameters of the Gaussian distribution (10) in this context. The likelihood function $L(x_i; \theta_1)$ is defined as follows:

$$L(x_i; \theta_1) = \prod_{i=1}^{k} f_{\theta_1}(x_i) = (\frac{1}{\sqrt{2\pi}\sigma})^k \exp(\sum_{i=1}^{k} \frac{(x_i - m)^2}{2\sigma^2}) \tag{11}$$

where k denotes the total number of each observation x_i; i represents its corresponding index. To obtain the estimated parameters, the log of likelihood function (see (11)) can be utilized. Immediately, by referring to the detailed deduction of (5), together with (11), we can smoothly estimate the model parameters by using the following formulations:

$$\hat{m} = \frac{1}{k}\sum_{i=1}^{k}x_i$$

$$\hat{\sigma}^2 = \frac{1}{k-1}\sum_{i=1}^{k}(x_i - \hat{m})^2 \tag{12}$$

where $\hat{\sigma}^2$ denotes the estimate of the variance σ^2; $\hat{m}$ represents the expectation of each observation. For simplicity, we assume that $\hat{m} \approx 0$. Then, the variance $\hat{\sigma}^2$ can be acquired by (12).

4   Proposed Watermark Embedding Algorithm

The main goal of embedding algorithm is to make the scheme robust against various attacks without degrading the visual quality of the video. The proposed watermark method embeds information into the video by adding the Gaussian-distributed noise to the noise-free naive frame, based on the proposed statistical model of Sects. 2 and 3. Since individual cones are less sensitive to green channel (or B channel in this context), in our proposed scheme, only the B channel of each frame is watermarked in spatial domain by considering the quality of the watermarked video.

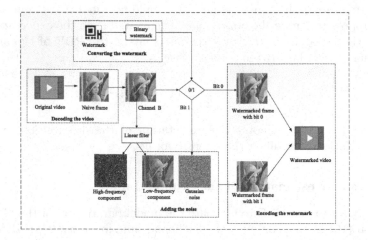

Fig. 1. Illustration of the proposed embedding algorithm.

The watermark is embedded by artificially adding noise or not, corresponding to *watermark bit* 1 or 0. Some measures are employed to strengthen our algorithm's robustness. Synchronization information added into the watermark bits and the repetitive insertion of the watermark information can together ensure the correct extraction of watermark even resisting against the frame insert and drop. As Fig. 1 illustrates, the general steps of our proposed watermark embedding algorithm are as follows:

1. *Decoding the video.* We first decode a clip of original video into naive frames.
2. *Converting the watermark.* The watermark image is binary image. It is proposed to convert the watermark image into binary sequence by row-scanning. Then, The watermark binary sequence can be obtained.
3. *Adding the noise.* We split the frame into three channels and embed the watermark into B channel (or green channel). If the watermark bit is 1, it is proposed to add the Gaussian-distributed noise into the noise-free naive frame (obtained by using a linear filter). In this context, the watermarked frame with bit 1 is defined as the noisy frame. It can be described as (7).
4. *Encoding the watermark.* Let us encode the watermarked frames into the video with copyright protection.

5   Proposed Watermark Extraction Scheme

In the scheme of watermark extraction, the watermarked video is first decomposed into frames. Then let us extract the B channel of each frame. Subsequently, we split out the high-frequency part of each frame using the linear filter. The watermark information can be discriminated based on the statistical distribution of the residual noise. Then it is assumed that if the statistical distribution follows the Gaussian distribution, the current watermark bit is 1, else is 0. Thus, it is proposed to establish the effective tests which are capable of distinguishing two different models followed by the extracted noise. To accomplish the task of effectively extracting the watermark from the video, we need test the distribution of the residual noise following the statistical model. In the following section, we mainly investigate the establishment of both LRT and GLRT, which have been studied to solve the problem of detection in the community of multimedia forensics (see [14–19] for details).

Besides, it is proposed to empirically verify the feasibility of the proposed scheme of watermark extraction. Let us denote "WM 0" as the frame with watermark bit 0 while "WM 1" represents the frame with watermark bit 1.

5.1   Design of LRT

With the help of hypothesis testing theory, let us establish our watermark extraction scheme based on the LRT and GLRT. Without loss of generality, the residual noise $\boldsymbol{\xi} = \{\xi_{i,j}\}, i = \{1, 2, \cdots, I\}, j = \{1, 2, \cdots, J\}$, follow a statistical model. We assume that the $\xi_{i,j}$ are independent and they all follow the same probability distribution, selecting from the Gaussian distribution or Laplace distribution, mapping to the watermark bit is 1 or 0 respectively. In order to detect the water-mark hidden with our embedding algorithm, the problem consists in choosing between the two following hypotheses $\mathcal{H}_0$: " $\xi_{i,j}$ *from the naive frame follows the Laplacian distribution* $\mathcal{P}_{\theta_0}$" and $\mathcal{H}_1$: " $\xi_{i,j}$ *from the noisy frame follows the Gaussian distribution* $\mathcal{Q}_{\theta_1}$" which can be formally written as:

$$
\begin{cases}
\mathcal{H}_0 : \{\xi_{i,j} \sim \mathcal{P}_{\theta_0}, \boldsymbol{\theta_0} = (e, b)\} \\
\mathcal{H}_1 : \{\xi_{i,j} \sim \mathcal{Q}_{\theta_1}, \boldsymbol{\theta_1} = (m, \sigma^2)\}
\end{cases}
\tag{13}
$$

The statistical test is a mapping $\theta : \mathbb{Z}^{i \cdot j} \mapsto \{\mathcal{H}_0, \mathcal{H}_1\}$ such that hypothesis $\mathcal{H}_i$ can be accepted if $\delta(\xi) = \mathcal{H}_i$ (see [25] for details on hypothesis testing). This paper follows the Neyman-Pearson bi-criteria approach: maximizing the true positive detection probability for a given false alarm rate α_0. Then Let:

$$
\mathcal{K}_{\alpha_0} = \left\{ \delta : \sup_{\theta} \mathbb{P}_{\mathcal{H}_0}[\delta(\boldsymbol{\xi}) = \mathcal{H}_1] \le \alpha_0 \right\},
\tag{14}
$$

be the class of tests with a false alarm rate upper-bounded by α_0. Here $\mathbb{P}_{\mathcal{H}_i}(A)$ denotes the probability of event A under hypothesis $\mathcal{H}_i, i = \{0, 1\}$, and let us understand the supremum over $\boldsymbol{\theta}$ as whatever the distribution parameters might be, in order to ensure that the false alarm rate α_0 can not be exceed. Among all the tests in $\mathcal{K}_{\alpha_0}$, it is aimed at finding a test δ which maximizes the power function, defined by the true positive detection probability:

$$
\beta_\delta = \mathbb{P}_{\mathcal{H}_1}[\delta(\boldsymbol{\xi}) = \mathcal{H}_1]
\tag{15}
$$

which is equivalent to minimize the missed detection probability $\alpha_1(\delta) = \mathbb{P}_{\mathcal{H}_1}[\delta(\boldsymbol{\xi}) = \mathcal{H}_0] = 1 - \beta_\delta$.

To solve the statistical detection problem such as Eq. (13), it follows from the Neyman-Pearson lemma that the most powerful test in the class $\mathcal{K}_{\alpha_0}$ (14) is the LRT defined, on the assumption that the the residual noise $\boldsymbol{\xi}$ are independent, as:

$$
\delta(\boldsymbol{\xi}) =
\begin{cases}
\mathcal{H}_0 \text{ if } \Lambda(\boldsymbol{\xi}) = \displaystyle\sum_{i=1}^{I} \sum_{j=1}^{J} \Lambda(\xi_{i,j}) < \tau \\
\mathcal{H}_1 \text{ if } \Lambda(\boldsymbol{\xi}) = \displaystyle\sum_{i=1}^{I} \sum_{j=1}^{J} \Lambda(\xi_{i,j}) \ge \tau
\end{cases}
\tag{16}
$$

where the decision threshold τ is the solution of the equation $\mathbb{P}_{\mathcal{H}_0}[(\xi) \ge \tau] = \alpha_0$, to ensure that the false alarm rate of the LRT equals α_0, and the log Likelihood Ratio (LR) for one observation is given, by definition, by:

$$
\Lambda(\xi_{i,j}) = \log \left(\frac{\mathcal{Q}_{\theta_1}[\xi_{i,j}]}{\mathcal{P}_{\theta_0}[\xi_{i,j}]} \right).
\tag{17}
$$

In fact, the LRT cannot help us solve the problem of extracting the embedded watermark since all the model parameters are assumed to be known. Therefore, it leads to design the GLRT with estimated parameters. In the practical procedure of extracting the watermark from each frame, under the proposed framework, it is proposed to compare the sum of GLR with the prescribed threshold $\hat{\tau}$, and decide the watermark bit.

6   Numerical Experiments

The main contribution of this paper is that we propose to design the scheme of our robust watermarking based on the statistical model. To verify the effectiveness of our presented framework, numerical experiments are illustrated on the benchmark set of testing videos. First, it is proposed to give the criterion for testing the integrity of the embedded watermark. In the community of robust watermarking, the integrity of the watermark is the first priority. When the extracted watermark from the copyright protected video is impaired, methodology of the proposed framework becomes invalid. Then, to verify the robustness of our proposed framework of robust watermarking, it is proposed to present the compared result with some prior arts, such as [3,4,6,10,22].

It is proposed to use the video *Foreman* with the dimension 287×350. Besides, the adopted digital watermark with the dimension 22×18 is demonstrated in Fig. 2. In our framework of embedding the digital watermark, we select the wavelet filter proposed in [12] as our linear denoising filter extracting the noise (see Sect. 3. It should be noted that the discussion of designing the linear filter is not the topic of this context we mainly focus on. In the future, we are planning to adopt the more effective filter to improve the performance of our proposed robust watermarking framework.

Fig. 2. Digital watermark used in our experiments

6.1   Watermark Integrity

To verify the integrity of the embedded watermark, we need compare the similarity between the original and extracted digital watermark, the normalized cross-correlation function is employed as Normalized Correlation (NC), which is formulated by:

$$NC(w, w') = \frac{\sum\limits_{i=1}^{N} \sum\limits_{j=1}^{M} w(i,j)w'(i,j)}{\sum\limits_{i=1}^{N} \sum\limits_{j=1}^{M} [w(i,j)^2]} \tag{18}$$

where w and w' are the original and extracted watermarks of size $N \times M$ respectively. The correlation coefficient $NC(w, w') = 1$ when extracted and original watermark is absolutely identical while the $NC(w, w')$ equal to zero means that they are completely uncorrelated.

In the following experiment of testing the robustness of the digital watermark, our proposed NC serves as the significant criterion to compare the robust performance of different algorithms.

6.2   Watermark Robustness

In the practical application of the robust watermarking technique, it is unavoidable that geometric transform can attack to the proposed methodology. After applying the geometric transform to the watermarked video, some watermarking detectors cannot be immune to the attacks due to the fact that the synchronization between the original watermark and extracted watermark cannot be guaranteed. The re-scaling operation is one of the common geometric attacks. To evaluate the performance of our proposed robust watermarking framework, re-scaling operations in spatial domain with different factors (for instance, 50%, 70%, 90%, and 130%) are performed on the video clip. By using the criterion NC, the robustness of our proposed framework and comparison with prior arts [4,6] are demonstrated in Table 1. It is can be clearly observed that our proposed method is capable of completely extracting the embedded watermark suffering from re-scaling (involving up-scaling and down-scaling) attacks with different factors. The robustness of our proposed algorithm resisting against the re-scaling attack remarkably performs better than some prior arts, such as algorithms proposed in [4,6].

Table 1. Performance comparison of the robust watermarking algorithms within re-scaling attacks; NC values are illustrated in the table.

Method	Re-scaling factor			
	50%	70%	90%	130%
The algorithm of [4]	0.706	0.736	0.852	0.790
The algorithm of [6]	0.818	0.941	1	1
Our proposed	1	1	1	1

In addition, it is proposed to test whether our proposed scheme has the capability of suffering from the attacks of cropping or rotation. First, it is proposed to crop the each watermarked video frame with factors such as 10%, 20%, and 30%. Then we still use the NC to measure the integrity of the embedded watermark. Similarly, let us rotate watermarked video frames from 15 to 120°. Then, the robustness of the proposed methodology is measured by NC. To this end, the experimental results are illustrated in Tables 2 and 3.

Table 2. Performance comparison of the robust watermarking algorithms within cropping attacks; NC values are illustrated in the table.

Method	Cropping factor		
	10%	20%	30%
The algorithm of [22]	0.995	0.994	0.989
The algorithm of [3]	0.940	0.862	0.858
The algorithm of [10]	0.947	0.927	0.924
Our proposed	1	1	1

Table 3. Performance comparison of the robust watermarking algorithms within rescaling attacks; NC values are illustrated in the table.

Method	Rotation factor			
	15°	45°	90°	120°
The algorithm of [3]	1	0.954	0942	0.940
The algorithm of [10]	0.989	0.973	0.972	0.969
Our proposed	1	1	1	1

Table 4. Robust performance of our proposed algorithm within M-JPEG compression attack

Quality factor	Extracted Watermark	NC value
80		1
70		1
60		0.998
50		0.907
40		0.747

With increasing the intensity of cropping, the performance of the algorithm proposed in [3] sharply degrades. Although the robustness of the watermarking schemes of [10,22] can be guaranteed, they hardly outperforms our proposed robust watermarking method at the given intensity of cropping. Furthermore, if we use the cropping factor equal to 40% or even 70%, the NC value still remains as 1. In fact, our embedded watermark is established under the framework of the statistical model with adding Gaussian-distributed noise, instead of directly embedding the watermark information into the spatial/frequency domain. Since it is hardly holds true that the tolerable cropping can easily change the entire distribution of each video frame, our proposed algorithm performs very strong robustness.

Finally, we are trying to test whether our proposed algorithm can resist against a typical compression attack, such as M-JPEG or H.264 video compression. In this context, let us define different quality factor = 100, 80, 70, 60, 50, and 40, describing the intensity of video compression. For instance, if the video is never compressed, its quality factor equals to 100. The Table 4 demonstrate the robustness of compression. Considering the attack from M-JPEG compression, our proposed algorithm performs well. Even if the quality factor equals 40, the digital watermark can still be extracted with the value of NC equal to 0.747.

7   Conclusions

In this practical context, a novel framework of robust video watermarking based on the statistical model is proposed. By investigating the distribution property of two statistical models, referring to the Laplacian and Gaussian model, we establish the new scheme of embedding the watermark with adding noise. When extracting the embedded watermark, both LRT and GLRT are proposed to deal with the problem of restoring the digital watermark. Finally, the numerical results verify that our proposed algorithm is capable of resisting against some attacks, such as re-scaling, cropping, rotation, and compression. In the future, we will enhance the robustness of the proposed algorithm considering H.264 compression attack.

Acknowledgments. This work was mainly supported by National Natural Science Foundation of China (No. 61370218, No. 61702150) and Public Welfare Technology Research Project Of Zhejiang Province(No. LGG18F020013)

References

1. Akhlaghian, F., Bahrami, Z.: A new robust video watermarking algorithm against cropping and rotating attacks. In: International Iranian Society of Cryptology Conference on Information Security and Cryptology, pp. 122–127 (2016)
2. Basu, A., Roy, S.S., Chattopadhyay, A.: Implementation of a spatial domain salient region based digital image watermarking scheme. In: Second International Conference on Research in Computational Intelligence and Communication Networks, pp. 269–270 (2017)
3. Bhatnagar, G., Wu, Q.M.J., Raman, B.: A new robust adjustable logo watermarking scheme. Comput. Secur. **31**(1), 40–58 (2012)
4. Biswas, S.N., et al.: Mpeg-2 digital video watermarking technique. In: Instrumentation and Measurement Technology Conference, pp. 225–229 (2012)

5. Cox, I.J., Kilian, J., Leighton, F.T., Shamoon, T.: Secure spread spectrum water-marking for multimedia. In: Proceedings of the IEEE International Conference on Image Processing 1996, vol. 3, no. 12, pp. 1673–1687 (1996)
6. Ding, H.Y., Zhou, Y.J., Yang, Y.X., Zhang, R.: Robust blind video watermark algorithm in transform domain combining with 3d video correlation. J. Multimed. 8(2) (2013)
7. Gupta, G., Gupta, V.K., Chandra, M.: Review on video watermarking techniques in spatial and transform domain. In: Satapathy, S.C., Mandal, J.K., Udgata, S.K., Bhateja, V. (eds.) Information Systems Design and Intelligent Applications. AISC, vol. 434, pp. 683–691. Springer, New Delhi (2016). https://doi.org/10.1007/978-81-322-2752-6_67
8. Kadu, S., Naveen, C., Satpute, V.R., Keskar, A.G.: Discrete wavelet transform based video watermarking technique. In: International Conference on Microelectronics, Computing and Communications, pp. 1–6 (2016)
9. Kumar, M., Hensman, A.: Robust digital video watermarking using reversible data hiding and visual cryptography. In: Signals and Systems Conference, pp. 1–6 (2013)
10. Lai, C.C., Tsai, C.C.: Digital image watermarking using discrete wavelet transform and singular value decomposition. IEEE Trans. Instrum. Meas. 59(11), 3060–3063 (2010)
11. Liu, S., Shi, F., Wang, J., Zhang, S.: An Improved Spatial Spread-Spectrum Video Watermarking. IEEE Computer Society (2010)
12. Lukas, J., Fridrich, J., Goljan, M.: Digital camera identification from sensor pattern noise. IEEE Trans. Inf. Forensics Secur. 1(2), 205–214 (2006)
13. Netravali, A.N., Haskell, B.G.: Digital Pictures. Plenum Press, New York (1988)
14. Qiao, T., Retraint, F., Cogranne, R., Thai, T.H.: Source camera device identification based on raw images. In: 2015 IEEE International Conference on Image Processing (ICIP), pp. 3812–3816. IEEE (2015)
15. Qiao, T., Retraint, F., Cogranne, R., Thai, T.H.: Individual camera device identification from JPEG images. Signal Process. Image Commun. 52, 74–86 (2017)
16. Qiao, T., Retraint, F., Cogranne, R., Zitzmann, C.: Steganalysis of JSteg algorithm using hypothesis testing theory. EURASIP J. Inf. Secur. 2015(1), 1–16 (2015)
17. Qiao, T., Zhu, A., Retraint, F.: Exposing image resampling forgery by using linear parametric model. Multimed. Tools Appl. 77, 1–23 (2017)
18. Qiao, T., Ziitmann, C., Cogranne, R., Retraint, F.: Detection of JSteg algorithm using hypothesis testing theory and a statistical model with nuisance parameters. In: Proceedings of the 2nd ACM Workshop on Information Hiding and Multimedia Security, pp. 3–13. ACM (2014)
19. Qiao, T., Zitzmann, C., Retraint, F., Cogranne, R.: Statistical detection of JSteg steganography using hypothesis testing theory. In: 2014 IEEE International Conference on Image Processing (ICIP), pp. 5517–5521. IEEE (2014)
20. Simoncelli, E.P., Adelson, E.H.: Noise removal via Bayesian wavelet coring. In: Proceedings of the International Conference on Image Processing, vol. 1, pp. 379–382 (1996)
21. Singh, D., Singh, S.K.: DWT-SVD and DCT based robust and blind watermarking scheme for copyright protection. Multimed. Tool Appl. 76, 1–24 (2016)
22. Tian, L., Zheng, N., Xue, J.: A blind and spatial-temporal based video watermarking for H.264/AVC. In: Pattern Recognition, pp. 598–602 (2012)

23. Trussell, H.J., Kruger, R.P.: Comments on "nonstationary assumptions for gaussian models in images". IEEE Trans. Syst. Man Cybern. **8**(7), 579–582 (1978)
24. Venugopala, P.S., Sarojadevi, H., Chiplunkar, N.N., Bhat, V.: Video watermarking by adjusting the pixel values and using scene change detection. In: Fifth International Conference on Signal and Image Processing, pp. 259–264 (2014)
25. Verlag, S.: Testing Statistical Hypotheses. Wiley, New York (1964)
26. Wei, Z., Wu, Y., Deng, R.H., Ding, X.: A hybrid scheme for authenticating scalable video codestreams. IEEE Trans. Inf. Forensics Secur. **9**(4), 543–553 (2014)
27. Zong, T., Xiang, Y., Natgunanathan, I., Guo, S., Zhou, W., Beliakov, G.: Robust histogram shape-based method for image watermarking. IEEE Trans. Circuits Syst. Video Technol. **25**(5), 717–729 (2015)

A Novel Nonlocal Low Rank Technique for Fabric Defect Detection

Jielin Jiang[1], Yan Cui[2(✉)], Yadang Chen[1], and Guangwei Gao[3]

[1] School of Computer and Software, Jiangsu Engineering Center of Network Monitoring, Nanjing University of Information Science and Technology, Nanjing, China
jiangjielin2008@163.com, cyd4511632@gmail.com
[2] College of Mathematics and Information Science, Nanjing Normal University of Special Education, Nanjing, China
cuiyan899@163.com
[3] Institute of Advanced Technology, Nanjing University of Posts and Telecommunications, Nanjing, China
tsyy_1314520@163.com

Abstract. In textile industry production, fabric defect inspection is a vital step to ensure the quality of fabric before spreading, cutting and so on. Recently, image characteristic of nonlocal self-similarity (NSS) is widely applied to image denoising due to its effectiveness. Actually, fabric defect detection can be considered as a problem that finds noises in an image. Based on the reason, we propose a simple yet effective method, namely nonlocal low rank approximation (NLRA), for fabric defect detection. In NLRA, an image to be processed is divided into many patches. For a given patch, we search its several similar patches and group them as a matrix. Then, the clean image patch can be reconstructed through solving the low rank approximation of the matrix. Finally, a new image will be synthesized from these estimated patches, the defects can be located by finding the difference between the original fabric image and the reconstructed image. Experimental results prove the validity and feasibility of the proposed NLRA algorithm.

Keywords: Fabric defect detection · Nonlocal self-similarity
Low rank approximate

1 Introduction

Fabric defect detection is an important link for textile factory to improve products quality and reduce products costs. The traditional inspection method mainly depends on human sight. This process is very dull and repetitive, the shortcoming of it is low speed, the high false detecting rate and so on. According to some studies, human visual inspection can only find around 70% of fabric defects by the most highly trained inspectors [1]. For this reason, in order to increase the competitive advantage of the products, visual inspection based fabric defects detection methods are developed to make up for the demerits of traditional method. A variety of fabric defects detection

© Springer Nature Switzerland AG 2018
X. Sun et al. (Eds.): ICCCS 2018, LNCS 11066, pp. 173–182, 2018.
https://doi.org/10.1007/978-3-030-00015-8_15

methods have been proposed to address this problem in past decades, which mainly include three classes: statistical approach, spectral approach, model-based approach.

Statistical approach is mainly applied for measuring the spatial distribution of pixel values, which can be classified into first order, second order and higher order statistics [2]. Statistical approach mainly includes co-occurrence matrix (CM), mathematical morphology and fractal dimension. Haralick et al. [3] originally proposed the CM and characterized texture features by measuring 2D spatial dependence of the gray values. Zhang and Bresee [4] applied morphological operations to fabric defect detection, which integrate histogram equalization, autocorrelation, thresholding, erosion, dilation and object classification for fabric defects detection. Bu et al. [5] jointly applied the multiple fractal features and support vector data description and achieved 98% detection rate.

In signal processing, the spectral approaches are popular in computer vision research work since frequency domain features are less sensitive to noise compared with spatial domain features. The most popular spectral approaches in fabric defect detection cover fourier transform, wavelet transform, Gabor transform and so on. The Fourier transform has the desirable properties of noise immunity, which is derived from the Fourier series. Various Fourier transform based methods are proposed for fabric defect detection such as Discrete Fourier Transform (DFT) [6, 7], Optical Fourier Transform (OFT) [8, 9] and windowed Fourier transform (WFT) [10, 11]. As one of the most popular of the time-frequency-transformations, wavelet transformation is commonly used for the feature extraction for plain and twill fabrics defect detection [12–14]. Han et al. [14] presented a wavelet transform based method to detect defects on images with high texture background, the fabric image is decomposed at several levels by wavelet transform, textures on the background are removed by selecting an appropriate level on the sub-image, which converted the texture defect detection problem to non-texture techniques. Gabor transform is a special case of the short-time Fourier transform, Zhang et al. [15] used a Gabor filter combine with Gaussian Mixture Models for fabric defect detection. Tong et al. [16] achieved the optimal feature extraction of fabric defects by utilizing composite differential evolution to optimize the parameters of Gabor filters. In [17], Gabor filter is combined with Principal Component Analysis is presented. Raheja et al. [18] proposed a gray level co-occurrence with Gabor filter based technique for fabric defect detection.

Image analysis methods can be classified as two categories: low-level algorithms and model-based approaches. Low-level algorithms can operate on the data directly, while model-based approaches focuses on the structure of the data. Fabric texture is very complex and can be modeled by a stochastic process. The advantage of this model is that it can produce textures to match the observed textures. Model-based approaches can be applied for fabric images with stochastic surface variations. Model-based approaches mainly include Autoregressive model, Markov Random Field model. An autoregressive model uses the linear dependence between different pixels of a texture and can be fully to describe the texture feature. Zhou et al. [19, 20] used dictionary learning framework to address textile fabric defects detection. This method involves learning a dictionary from defect-free samples, the dictionary is able to approximate training samples well through a linear summation of its elements. Experimental results show that it can achieve as high as 95% overall detection with 16% false alarm [19].

A Markov random field (MRF) is a set of random variables having a Markov property described by an undirected graph. Ozdemir and Ercil [21] combined Markov Random Fields and Karhunen-Loeve Transform for fabric defect detection.

At present, most of the methods mentioned above can well detect the defects when the defects are distinguishable, but they are not very efficient while the defects are small. As nonlocal self-similarity (NSS) has been successfully applied to image denoising and fabric defects can be regarded as noise. This paper we present a nonlocal low rank approximate based method for defects detection (NLRA). For the fabric image, we first divide it into many patches. Then for a given patch, we search several similar patches to it and group them as matrix. Finally, a new image will be synthesized from these estimated patches, and the defects are located by finding the difference between the original fabric image and the reconstructed image. Experimental results prove the effectiveness of the proposed NLRA algorithm.

The rest of the paper is organized as follows. In Sect. 2, we describe the proposed NLRA in detail. Section 3 gives experimental results. Conclusions are made in Sect. 4.

2   Nonlocal Low Rank Approximate (NLRA)

Currently, most of the methods can well detect the defects when the defects are obvious. As a matter of fact, fabrics often contain the defects in small size and low contrast, especially for solid color. Since small size defects can be regarded as random noise, a novel nonlocal low rank approximate (NLRA) algorithm will be developed for fabric defect detection.

The proposed method for fabric defect detection is a patch based method. For a fabric image y, it will be firstly divided into many patches. Following the notation in [22], let $y_i = R_i y$ be the stretched vector of an image patch of size n $\times$ n, where R_i is the matrix operator. The patch y_i can be set as a reference patch used for similarity searching. Temporarily, it is assumed that m-1 patches $\{y_{i,j}\}_{i=1}^{m-1}$ similar to y_i are found. If we represent y_i and its similar patch $y_{i,j}$ as vectors by concatenating all columns of each patch, a new $n^2 \times$ m matrix Y is formed as

$$Y = [y_i, y_{i,1}, \cdots y_{i,m-1}]. \tag{1}$$

Suppose that the defect-free image patch of Y is X. Clearly, we can assume that X is a low rank matrix because its columns are similar image patches. The defect detection problem turns to how to recover X from the matrix Y. Let

$$D = Y - X. \tag{2}$$

Since the column vector of Y are similar to each other, the recovered matrix X should be low rank. Then the problem of defect detection can be converted into searching a low rank approximate of X, and we have

$$\widehat{X} = \min_X \|Y - X\|_F^2 . \text{s.t.} rank(X) \leq r \tag{3}$$

Equation (3) is a low-rank approximation problem [23] and can be solved by the following singular value decomposition.

$$\begin{cases} (U, \delta, V) = svd(Y) \\ \widehat{\delta} = S_\beta(\delta) \end{cases} \tag{4}$$

where S_β denotes the soft thresholding operator with regularization parameter β and the image patch can be constructed as

$$\widehat{X} = U\widehat{\delta}V \tag{5}$$

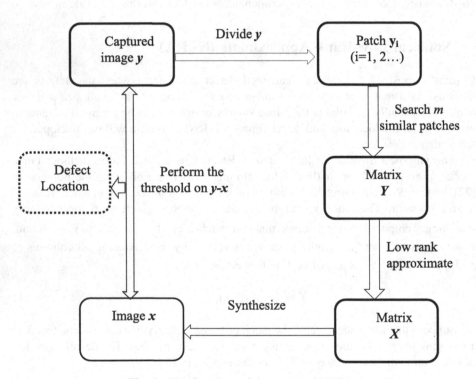

Fig. 1. The flowchart of the proposed NLRA

After each patch is handled by Eq. (3), then a new image x can be synthesized. In the new reconstructed image, the defect-free pixels are approximate to the pixels of original image, while the defect pixels are different from the pixels of original image. Thus defects can be detected by finding the difference between the original fabric image and the reconstructed image. NSS-based low rank approximate algorithm concatenates the similar image patches together to search its low rank approximate matrix, so the model of Eq. (3) can find the subtle variation of patterns and be good at detecting small defects. Because the proposed method mainly uses the idea of the nonlocal self-similarity of the fabric image and the low rank approximate strategy, so we call it defect detection based on nonlocal low rank approximate (NLRA). Figure 1 gives the flowchart of NLRA.

The advantage of the proposed NLRA algorithm:

(1) Robustness to illumination

The NLRA combined the image nonlocal self-similarity with low rank approximate to handle the detection problem. Since the intensity of local illumination is much smoother compared with the illumination on the whole. Therefore, NLRA is robust to illumination and able to find the defects precisely under uneven illumination distribution.

(2) The application of image nonlocal similarity

By adopting nonlocal low rank approximate model, nonlocal self-similarity of fabric structure is introduced into low rank approximate model, which is helpful to maintain the detail of the image features. Defect detection on patterned fabrics is a more challenging task compared with defect detection on solid color fabrics, but we can group texture part and non-texture part together, respectively. Therefore, NLRA can be applied on detecting patterned fabrics.

3   Experiments

In this section, experiments are carried out to demonstrate the performance of the proposed NLRA algorithm. There are several typical defects such as line defects, knot defects and spot defects. Where line defects are relatively big and easily to be detected, while knot defects and the spot defects are the most encountered defects in the factory and they are difficult to detect. This paper we mainly do experiments on these three kinds of defects.

3.1   Parameter Setting

There are several parameters to set in the proposed NLRA algorithm. Since the proposed method is a patch method for defect detection, the size of patch has straightforward effect on proposed algorithm performance. Considering the running time and defect detection effect, we set the size of patch as 7×7. The parameter β that balances the fidelity term and the regularization term for better defect detection performance, we set it 0.001 by experience.

3.2   Results

We conduct extensive experiments to demonstrate the performance of the proposed NLRA model. All detection models used in the experiments are realized under the image processing toolbox of MATLAB prototyping environment. Experiments are conducted on a personal computer under a Win8 operating system running on an Intelcore i7 processor. The performance of the defect detection model is visually assessed by the binary feature images. We did experiments on solid color woven fabrics. The NLRA model is applied on 100 fabric samples which are confirmed by the trained inspectors. In the experiments, we run the proposed NLRA algorithm on each test image separately. Some typical detection results are shown in Figs. 2, 3 and 4.

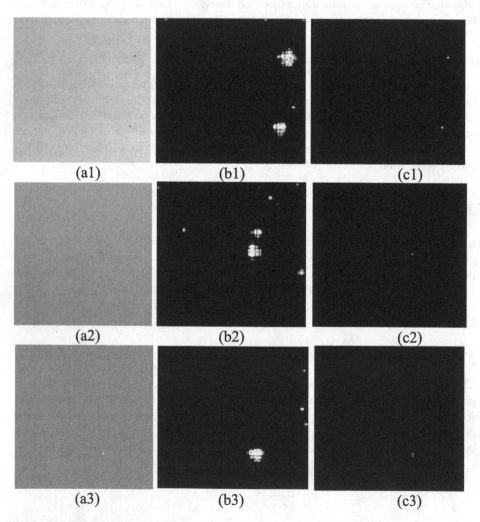

Fig. 2. Detection results of different methods. (a1)-(a3) are the original image. (b1)-(b3) are the results of [24]. (c1)-(c3) are the results of the NLRA algorithm.

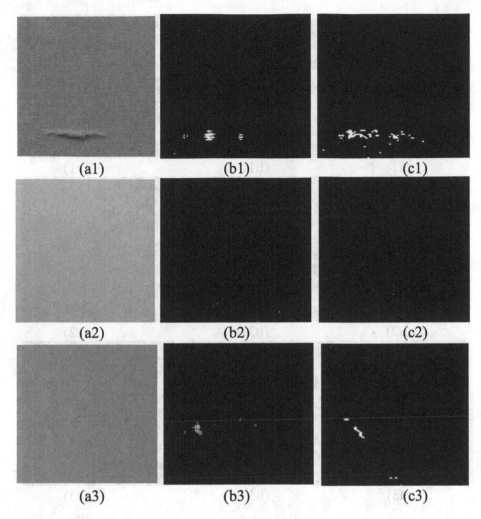

Fig. 3. Detection results of different methods. (a1)-(a3) are the original image. (b1)-(b3) are the results of [24]. (c1)-(c3) are the results of the NLRA algorithm.

In Figs. 2, 3 and 4, the first column is the original defective images, the second column is the detect results of [24], the third column shows the detection results of the proposed algorithm. In Figs. 2, 3 and 4, although some defects are very small, we can see that NLRA can still detect them accurately. The algorithm in [24] can well defect the small defects, but it has high false alarm. In all, all the experiments show that NLRA algorithm is effective for defects extraction in fabric image.

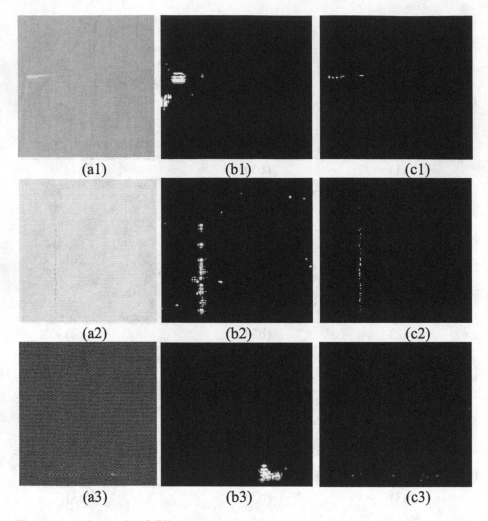

Fig. 4. Detection results of different methods. (a1)-(a3) are the original image. (b1)-(b3) are the results of [24]. (c1)-(c3) are the results of the NLRA algorithm.

4 Conclusion

In this paper, we presented a novel nonlocal low rank approximate model for fabric defect detection. By exploiting the image nonlocal similarity, we grouped similar patches as a matrix and sought for its low rank approximation. The defects were located by finding the difference between the original fabric image and the reconstructed image. The results on solid color fully show that NLRA achieves good defect detection performance.

Acknowledgments. This work was supported in part by the National Natural Science Foundation of China under Grants 61601235, 61502245, in part by the Natural Science Foundation of Jiangsu Province of China under Grants BK20160972, BK20170768, BK20160964, BK20150849, in part by the Natural Science Foundation of the Jiangsu Higher Education Institutions of China under Grants 16KJB520031, 17KJB520019, in part by the Startup Foundation for Introducing Talent of Nanjing University of Information Science and Technology (NUIST) under Grant 2243141601019.

References

1. Sari-Sarraf, H., Goddard, J.S.: Vision systems for on-loom fabric inspection. IEEE Trans. Ind. Appl. **35**(6), 1252–1259 (1999)
2. Mahajan, P.M., Kolhe, S.R., Pati, P.M.: A review of automatic fabric defect detection techniques. Adv. Comput. Res. **1**(2), 18–29 (2009)
3. Haralick, R.M., Shanmugam, K., Dinstein, I.: Textural features for image classification. IEEE Trans. Syst. Man Cybern. **3**(6), 610–621 (1973)
4. Zhang, Y.F., Bresee, R.R.: Fabric defect detection and classification using image analysis. Text. Res. J. **65**(1), 1–9 (1995)
5. Bu, H.-G., Wang, J., Huang, X.-B.: Fabric defect detection based on multiple fractal features and support vector data description. Eng. Appl. Artif. Intell. **22**(2), 224–235 (2009)
6. Chan, C.H., Pang, G.: Fabric defect detection by Fourier analysis. IEEE Trans. Ind. Appl. **36**(5), 1743–1750 (2000)
7. Tsai, D.-M., Heish, C.-Y.: Automated surface inspection for directional textures. Image Vis. Comput. **18**, 49–62 (1999)
8. Kim, S.W.: Rapid pattern inspection of shadow masks by machine vision integrated with Fourier optics. Opt. Eng. **36**(36), 3309–3311 (1997)
9. Hoffer, L.M., Francini, F., Tiribilli, B., Longobardi, G.: Neural network for the optical recognition of defects in cloth. Opt. Eng. **35**(11), 3183–3190 (1996)
10. Murtagh, F.D.: Automatic visual inspection of woven textiles using a two-stage defect detector. Opt. Eng. **37**(37), 2536–2542 (1998)
11. Campbell, J.G., Hasim, A.A., McGinnity, T.M., Lunney, T.F.: Flaw detection in woven textiles by neural network. In: Neural Computing: Research & Applications Iii, Proc Irish Neural Network Conference, St Patricks, vol. 1, pp. 208–214 (1997)
12. Yang, X.Z., Pang, G.K.H., Yung, N.H.C.: Discriminative fabric defect detection using adaptive wavelets. Opt. Eng. **41**(41), 3116–3126 (2002)
13. Tsai, D.M., Hsiao, B.: Automatic surface inspection using wavelet reconstruction. Pattern Recognit. **34**, 1285–1305 (2001)
14. Han, Y., Shi, P.: An adaptive level-selecting wavelet transform for texture defect detection. Image Vis. Comput. **25**(8), 1239–1248 (2007)
15. Zhang, Y., Lu, Z., Li, J.: Fabric defect detection and classification using Gabor filters and Gaussian mixture model. Asian Conf. Comput. Vis.-Accv **5995**, 635–644 (2009)
16. Tong, L., Wong, W.K., Kwong, C.K.: Differential evolution-based optimal Gabor filter model for fabric inspection. Neurocomputing **173**, 1386–1401(2016)
17. Srikaew, A., Attakitmongcol, K., Kumsawat, P., Kidsang, W.: Detection of defect in textile fabrics using optimal Gabor Wavelet Network and two-dimensional PCA. In: International Symposium on Visual Computing, pp. 436–445 (2011)
18. Rahejaa, J.L., Kumar, S., Chaudhary, A.: Fabric defect detection based on GLCM and gabor filter: a comparison. Optik **124**, 6469–6474 (2013)

19. Zhou, J., Semenovich, D., Sowmya, A., Wang, J.: Dictionary learning framework for fabric defect detection. J. Text. Inst. **105**(3), 223–234 (2014)
20. Zhou, J., Wang, J.: Fabric defect detection using adaptive dictionaries. Text. Res. J. **83**, 1846–1859 (2013)
21. Ozdemir, S., Ercil, A.: Markov random fields and Karhunen-Loeve transform for defect inspection of textile products. In: IEEE Conference on Emerging Technologies & Factory Automation, Efta, vol. 2, pp. 697–703 (1996)
22. Aharon, M., Elad, M., Bruckstein, A.M.: K-SVD: an algorithm for designing of overcomplete dictionaries for sparse representation. IEEE Trans. Signal Process. **54**, 4311–4322 (2006)
23. Cai, J.F., Candes, E.J., Shen, Z.: A singular value thresholding algorithm for matrix completion. SIAM J. Optim. **20**, 1956–1982 (2010)
24. Hu, G.H., Wang, Q.H., Zhang, G.H.: Unsupervised defect detection in textiles based on Fourier analysis and wavelet shrinkage. Appl. Opt. **54**, 2963–2980 (2015)

A Novel Steganography Scheme Based on Asymmetric Embedding Model

Xianglei Hu[1], Haishan Chen[2], Jiangqun Ni[1(✉)], and Wenkang Su[1]

[1] School of Data Science and Computer Technology, Sun Yat-sen University,
Guangzhou 510975, China
{huxiangl,suwenk}@mail2.sysu.edu.cn, issjqni@mail.sysu.edu.cn
[2] Nanfang College of Sun Yat-sen University, Guangzhou 510975, China
chenhsh3@mail3.sysu.edu.cn

Abstract. Recently, many high security steganographic schemes have been developed to approximate non-additive distortions with consideration of mutual adjacent modification influences. However, their security performance behaves volatilely and is very sensitive to the heuristically designed parameters and the initial additive distortion function. To make a stable security performance and to further improve the embedding security, a novel model-based steganographic scheme is proposed by incorporating the adjacent embedding information with no dependence on the heuristic parameters. We first divide the cover image into several interleaved sub-lattices, and then optimally embed message into each sub-lattice in sequence. In each sub-lattice, the embedding change rates for each pixel are optimized by utilizing the adjacent modifications as priori knowledge. During the optimization process, a novel asymmetric probability model is designed to simultaneously tackle with two inequivalent change rates for modifying the cover pixel by $+1$ and -1. Experimental results show that the proposed scheme can rival or outperform the prior arts, and moreover, can provide a stable security performance.

Keywords: Image steganography · Asymmetrical probability model
Mutually dependent embedding · Gaussian mixture model

1 Introduction

Image steganography is the science and art of embedding secret message into cover images by slightly modifying the pixel elements (in the spatial domain) or DCT coefficients (in JPEG domain). In the past two decades, image steganography has witnessed a rapid growth [5,7,10,11,14,16,18]. Recently, the most prevalent approach for image steganography is to form the problem of message embedding as source coding with a certain fidelity constraints, where the additive distortion function must be minimized for a given embedding rate. Let $\mathbf{x} = \{x_1, x_2, \ldots, x_N\}$ and $\mathbf{y} = \{y_1, y_2, \ldots, y_N\}$ represent the pixels of cover and

© Springer Nature Switzerland AG 2018
X. Sun et al. (Eds.): ICCCS 2018, LNCS 11066, pp. 183–194, 2018.
https://doi.org/10.1007/978-3-030-00015-8_16

the corresponding stego images, respectively. The additive distortion function can defined as:

$$D(\mathbf{x}, \mathbf{y}) = \sum_{i=1}^{N} \rho_i(\mathbf{x}, y_i), \tag{1}$$

where ρ_i is the embedding cost of changing the ith cover element from x_i to y_i. The minimization of Eq. (1) can be well accomplished using prevalent steganographic codes, e.g. syndrome-trellis codes (STCs), so as to approximate the rate-distortion bound [5].

Due to the near-bound performance, in the recent years, STCs has expedited an great amount of research on additive distortion functions for image steganography. Wavelet Obtained Weights (WOW) [10] realizes outstanding performance by deriving the embedding cost from several directional wavelet filters on spatial images. Spatial Universal Wavelet Relative Distortion (S-UNIWARD) [9] further improves the performance of WOW by slightly adjusting the cost function. HIgh-pass, Low-pass and Low-pass (HILL) [13] achieves better performance than WOW and S-UNIWARD by employing a composition of high-pass and two low-pass filters to obtain the embedding cost and to design a spreading rule to congregate the embedding into textured regions. Multivariate Gaussian (MG) model [7] introduces a multivariate Gaussian image model to minimize delectability by minimizing Kullback−Leibler divergence (KL divergence) between the cover and stego images. Later on, Multivariate Generalized Gaussian (MVG) [19] and Minimizing the Power of Optimal Detector (MiPOD) [18] further improves the performance of multivariate Gaussian model.

The above-mentioned additive distortion based steganographic schemes have made remarkable contribution to image steganography. However, adjacent modifications have mutual influence, these methods fail to synchronize the adjacent modifications towards the same direction, i.e., either $+1$ or -1, in elevating the security performance [2]. In this meaning, some attempts have been made on synchronizing the adjacent modifications in an additive form. Synchronized Selection Channel (Synch) [2] and Clustering Modification Directions (CMD) [15] tackle with the mutually dependent modifications by iteratively updating the additive costs, and hence we call them the distortion updating schemes. Synch [2] first divides the cover image into two interleaved sub-lattices for sub-lattice independent embedding, and then readjusts the additive cost for each pixel so as to synchronize with the adjacent modifications. CMD adopts a similar strategy, but makes more delicate design on the parameters for dividing sub-lattices and re-adjusting costs. Therefore, CMD presents improved performance than that of Synch. Compared to their previous additive schemes, both Synch and CMD greatly boost the security performance of steganography in spatial images.

Note that in both Synch and CMD, heuristically designed parameters are used in cost re-adjustment. As a result, it is difficult to maintain optimal performance when adopting other additive distortions or resisting different detectors. Therefore, in this paper, a novel Gaussian mixture model (GMM) based steganographic scheme is proposed to synchronize adjacent modifications using an asymmetric embedding model with no heuristically designed model parameters. In the proposed asymmetric embedding model, adjacent modifications, which are closely related to the weights of components in GMMs, play as the role of priori knowledge in obtaining the optimal embedding costs.

2   Related Works

This section briefs the common techniques of existing symmetric steganography methods, including the image models in MVG [19], the technique of of additive distortion minimization [5] and CMD [15].

2.1   Mutual Independent Based Image Models

One of the most successful cover image models in image steganography is MVG [19], where the pixels are modeled as the summation of noise-free contents and independent Gaussian noises. In MVG, the independent Gaussian noises can be denoted by $\mathbf{x} = (x_1, x_2, \ldots, x_N)$, and each noise x_i is modeled as a zero-mean Gaussian signal $x_i \sim N(0, \sigma_i^2)$ [18], where $1 \le i \le N$, N be the number of cover pixels, and σ_i^2 includes both the modeling error and the variance of acquisition noise. In MVG, σ_i^2 is obtained by firstly computing the noise residual using a simple denoising filter on the original image, and then the modeling the filtering residual with block-wise Least Square Estimation [19].

Let x_i and y_i denote the ith cover pixel ($1 \le i \le N$) and its counterpart stego pixel, β_i^+ and β_i^- be the change rates of modifying x_i by $+1$ and -1, respectively. The pixel x_i can be modified with probabilities of

$$\begin{aligned}
\mathbb{P}(y_i = x_i + 1) &= \beta_i^+, \\
\mathbb{P}(y_i = x_i - 1) &= \beta_i^-, \\
\mathbb{P}(y_i = x_i) &= 1 - \beta_i^+ - \beta_i^-.
\end{aligned} \tag{2}$$

Note that in Eq. (2), the embedding process can be regarded as adding random noises onto a cover image $\mathbf{x}$. Hence the embedding noise can be modeled as $\mathbf{e} = (e_1, e_2, \ldots, e_N)$ with probabilities of

$$\begin{aligned}
\mathbb{P}(e_i = +1) &= \beta_i^+, \\
\mathbb{P}(e_i = -1) &= \beta_i^-, \\
\mathbb{P}(e_i = 0) &= 1 - \beta_i^+ - \beta_i^-,
\end{aligned} \tag{3}$$

As a result, the embedding process can be simplified into a concise form as $\mathbf{y} = \mathbf{x} + \mathbf{e}$.

2.2 Minimization of Additive Distortion

Let $\mathbf{m}$ be the bit vector of payload. The syndrome-trellis codes STCs [5] can utilized to embed $\mathbf{m}$ into $\mathbf{x}$ with additive distortion minimization, as specified by

$$Emb(\mathbf{x}, \mathbf{m}) = \arg\min_{\mathbf{y} \in \mathbf{C}(\mathbf{m})} D(\mathbf{x}, \mathbf{y})$$

$$\text{and } \mathbf{H} \cdot \mathbf{y} = \mathbf{m}, \tag{4}$$

where $\mathbf{H}$ is the parity-check matrix, and $\mathbf{C}(\mathbf{m})$ is the coset corresponding to $\mathbf{m}$.

When assuming additive distortion in STC codes, the distortion function can be further written as

$$D(\mathbf{x}, \mathbf{y}) = \sum_{i=1}^{N} \rho_i(\mathbf{x}, y_i), \tag{5}$$

where $\rho_i(\mathbf{x}, y_i)$ is the embedding cost of modifying the cover pixel x_i to stego pixel y_i, which is asymmetric due to the change rates of β_i^+ and β_i^-. Following the work of Gibbs construction [4], the change rates can be further specified as

$$\beta_i^+ = \frac{\exp(-\lambda\rho_i^+)}{\exp(-\lambda\rho_i^+) + \exp(-\lambda\rho_i^-) + \exp(-\lambda\rho_i^{(0)})},$$

$$\beta_i^- = \frac{\exp(-\lambda\rho_i^-)}{\exp(-\lambda\rho_i^+) + \exp(-\lambda\rho_i^-) + \exp(-\lambda\rho_i^{(0)})}, \tag{6}$$

$$1 - \beta_i^+ - \beta_i^- = \frac{\exp(-\lambda\rho_i^{(0)})}{\exp(-\lambda\rho_i^+) + \exp(-\lambda\rho_i^-) + \exp(-\lambda\rho_i^{(0)})},$$

where λ is determined by the constraint of payload, ρ_i^+, ρ_i^-, $\rho_i^{(0)}$ denote the cost of modifying x_i by $+1$, -1 and 0, respectively.

2.3 The Symmetric Embedding Model of MVG

In the symmetric model of MVG [19], the steganographic scheme aims to minimize the Kullback-Leibler divergence between the probability distributions of the cover and stego (see Eq. (5)). In MVG, an independent cover image model is employed to define the KL divergence as the sum of KL divergence between each cover and stego pixels [19], as specified by

$$D_{\mathrm{KL}}(\mathbf{x}||\mathbf{y}) = \sum_{i=1}^{N} D_{\mathrm{KL}}(x_i||y_i) = \sum_{i=1}^{N} \frac{1}{2} I_i(0) \cdot \beta_i^2, \tag{7}$$

where $I_i(0)$ is the Fisher information of x_i, and β_i denotes the change rate of pixel x_i symmetrically by $+1$ or -1. Note that, the KL divergence, denoted by $D_{\mathrm{KL}}(\mathbf{x}||\mathbf{y})$, is a convex function of change rates $\boldsymbol{\beta}$, where $\boldsymbol{\beta} = \{\beta_1, \beta_2, \ldots, \beta_N\}$. Therefore, the KL divergence can be easily minimized at the constraint of payload, and the resulting change rates $\boldsymbol{\beta}$ are the optimal embedding change rates proposed by MVG [19].

3   The Proposed Method

In MVG [19], the KL divergence is simply optimized with symmetrical embedding rates, which may not be suitable enough for natural images. As a result, the embedding performance can still be improved. Therefore, in this paper, we propose a more generalized probability model to optimally handle asymmetric change rates. Specifically, we first illustrate on the probability model for optimizing the asymmetric change rates, then incorporate this model with the adjacent embedding modifications, at last, at the inspiration of MVG [19], we minimize the KL divergence between the distributions of $\mathbf{x}$ and $\mathbf{y}$ such that the delectability can be minimized.

For simplicity, the embedding procedure of the proposed work is illustrated in Fig. 1. Before embedding, the cover image is divided into four interleaved sub-lattices. Let L_k where $k \in \{1, 2, \ldots, 4\}$ denote a sub-lattice, and $\mathbf{x}_{L_k}$ be the corresponding pixel vector of L_k. L_k can be obtained using the equation

$$
\begin{aligned}
L_1 &= \{(r, c)|\ \mathrm{mod}\ (r, 2) = 1, \mathrm{mod}(c, 2) = 1\}, \\
L_2 &= \{(r, c)|\ \mathrm{mod}\ (r, 2) = 1, \mathrm{mod}(c, 2) = 0\}, \\
L_3 &= \{(r, c)|\ \mathrm{mod}\ (r, 2) = 0, \mathrm{mod}(c, 2) = 0\}, \\
L_4 &= \{(r, c)|\ \mathrm{mod}\ (r, 2) = 0, \mathrm{mod}(c, 2) = 1\},
\end{aligned}
\tag{8}
$$

where (r, c) denotes the 2-D pixel coordinates. With the obtained sub-lattices, embedding is performed iteratively into each sub-lattice L_k with payload $\mathbf{m}_k$. Note that, the implementation of the later three iterations (see Fig. 1) are the crucial part of the proposed work using information about adjacent modifications.

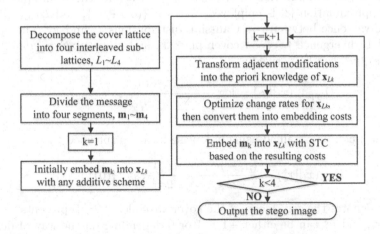

Fig. 1. Diagram of the proposed method.

3.1 Gaussian Mixture Model for Asymmetric Embedding

With the four interleaved image partition scheme, the adjacencies of pixel x_i in one sub-lattice L_k ($k \in \{1, 2, \ldots, 4\}$) will all come from the other three sub-lattices. Since the obtained sub-lattices are interleaved with each other, they can provide nearly the same embedding capacity, and thus the payload can be evenly allocated onto each sub-lattice.

Let α denote the required embedding rate for sub-lattice L_k, m be the number bits of payloads for L_k. The payload constraint on the change rates for an optimal scheme of embedding m bits into L_k can be written as

$$m = \alpha \cdot N/4 = \sum_{i \in L_k} h(\beta_i^+, \beta_i^-), \qquad (9)$$

where $h(\cdot)$ denotes the ternary entropy function of change rates as specified by

$$h(\beta^+, \beta^-) = -\beta^+ \log_2(\beta^+) - \beta^- \log_2(\beta^-) - (1 - \beta^+ - \beta^-) \log_2(1 - \beta^+ - \beta^-). \qquad (10)$$

When assuming x_i as a Gaussian signal, the stego image $\mathbf{y}$ is actually a Gaussian mixture model since each y_i is constituted of three components:

$$\begin{aligned} y_i &= x_i^{(0)} \beta_i^{(0)} + x_i^+ \beta_i^+ + x_i^- \beta_i^- \\ &= x_i^{(0)} (1 - \beta_i^+ - \beta_i^-) + x_i^+ \beta_i^+ + x_i^- \beta_i^-, \end{aligned} \qquad (11)$$

where $x_i^{(0)}$ denotes the original cover Gaussian variable, x_i^+ denotes a Gaussian variable which is derived from shifting $x_i^{(0)}$ by $+1$, and x_i^- is the one shifting by -1.

To make the computation of KL divergence feasible, the technique of variational approximation [8] is employed. Let $s \in \{(0), +, -\}$, and $D_{\mathrm{KL}}(x_i \| x_i^s)$ is the KL divergence between two Gaussian distributions x_i and x_i^s. The approximated KL divergence between cover pixel x_i and stego pixel y_i, denoted by $D_{\mathrm{approx}}(x_i \| y_i)$, can be derived as

$$D_{\mathrm{approx}}(x_i \| y_i) = \log \frac{1}{\sum_{s \in \{(0),+,-\}} \beta_i^s e^{-D_{\mathrm{KL}}(x_i \| x_i^s)}}. \qquad (12)$$

$D_{\mathrm{KL}}(x_i \| x_i^s)$ can be obtained using a concise form, as specified by

$$D_{\mathrm{KL}}(x_i \| x_i^s) = \frac{(\mu_i - \mu_i^s)^2}{2\sigma_i^2} = \frac{(\mu_i^s)^2}{2\sigma_i^2}, s \in \{(0), +, -\}, \qquad (13)$$

where μ_i denotes the zero-mean of the cover variable x_i, σ_i^2 represents the variance of x_i, and μ_i^s can be either $+1$, -1 or 0 depending on the way of deriving x_i^s from x_i.

It's obvious that, given the variance σ_i^2, the KL approximation $D_{\mathrm{approx}}(x_i \| y_i)$ is a function of change rates including β_i^+ and β_i^-, rather than one single variable β_i in the previous MVG model (see Eq. (7)). Therefore, the proposed method has to handle the problem of asymmetric embedding.

3.2   Incorporating Adjacent Embedding Modifications

It has been claimed that embedding modifications will be less detectable when executing the modification in a group of adjacent pixels [2,15]. Therefore, it would benefit when encouraging the adjacent modifications to **have the same sign, +1 or −1**. In this light, the proposed method takes into consideration the adjacent modifications of x_i when determining its change rates of β_i^+ and β_i^-. As a result, the embedding noise, denoted by $e_i \in \{-1, 0, 1\}$, is characterized by β_i^+ and β_i^- according to Eq. (3), and must be modeled to correlate with adjacencies, rather than assuming mutually independent (see Eq. (5)).

To model a correlational embedding noise $\mathbf{e} = \{\mathbf{e_1}, \mathbf{e_2}, ..., \mathbf{e_N}\}$, **we utilize the adjacencies of e_i as the priori knowledge** of its probability distribution. Furthermore, these adjacent modifications, denoted by $Adj(e_i)$, are treated as the samples of e_i, and their averaged modification can also be used to estimate the expectation of e_i, denoted by $\widehat{\mu}_{e_i}$, using the equation

$$\widehat{\mu}_{e_i} = \sum_{\dot{e}_j \in Adj(e_i)} \dot{e}_j / \#\{Adj(e_i)\}, \tag{14}$$

where $\#\{Adj(\cdot)\}$ denotes the number of the adjacent pixels, and $\dot{e}_j$ denotes the actual embedding modification previously made on the adjacent pixels of x_i. Acting as the priori knowledge of the probability distribution, the estimator $\widehat{\mu}_{e_i}$ synchronizes the adjacent modifications by encouraging e_i to be statistically consistent with its adjacencies.

On the other side, according to Eq. (3), the expectation of e_i can also be written in a closed form as specified by

$$\mu_{e_i} = \mathrm{E}[e_i] = 1 \cdot \beta_i^+ + (-1) \cdot \beta_i^- = \beta_i^+ - \beta_i^-. \tag{15}$$

Without loss of generality, we illustrate on the case when $\mu_{e_i} \geq 0$ (the other case when $\mu_{e_i} < 0$ can be analyzed in a similar way), we have $\beta_i^- \in [0, 1 - \mu_{e_i}]$ and $\beta_i^+ \in [\mu_{e_i}, 1]$. Therefore, with Eq. (15), the change rate β_i^+ in Eq. (12) can be replaced by $\widehat{\mu}_{e_i} + \beta_i^-$, and thus the optimization problem of minimizing KL divergence between $\mathbf{x}_{L_k}$ and $\mathbf{y}_{L_k}$ is simplified to

$$\begin{aligned} &\min_{\beta_{L_k}^-} \sum_{i \in L_k} D_{\text{variational}}(x_i \| y_i) \\ &s.t. \quad \sum_{i \in L_k} h(\widehat{\mu}_{e_i} + \beta_i^-, \beta_i^-) = \alpha \cdot N/4. \end{aligned} \tag{16}$$

It's obvious that such a convex optimization problem can be easily solved with an optimization toolbox, e.g., Interior Point OPTimizer (Ipopt) [20].

With the derived optimal β_i^+ and β_i^-, we can first obtain the corresponding embedding costs according to Eq. (6), and then send the embedding costs into STCs for embedding in sub-lattice L_k. The resultant modifications $\dot{\mathbf{e}}_{L_k}$ introduced by the STC embedder, will be incorporated for optimization in next sub-lattice L_{k+1}.

Note that, adjacent modifications usually introduce a non-zero expectation $\widehat{\mu}_{e_i}$, which, according to Eq. (15), usually brings about asymmetry to the embedding noise e_i, such that $\beta_i^+ \neq \beta_i^-$. Therefore, the previous model in MVG can only tackle with symmetric change rates with no consideration of synchronization between adjacent modifications.

Since the proposed work designs an **ASYM**metric **M**odel to synchronize adjacent modifications, we term the proposed model as ASYMM for convenience.

4 Experimental Results

In this section, quite a lot experiments are performed to verify the embedding performance with conventional experimental setups. We first introduce the parameters and steps of the performed experiments, and then compare the proposed method to the state-of-the-art works of CMD and Synch, for the security performance.

4.1 Experiment Setup

Source of Cover Images. All experiments are carried out on the image database BOSSbase ver. 1.01 [1], which contains 10,000 gray-scale images sized of 512×512. BOSSbase ver. 1.01 has been broadly used as the standard database in the community of steganography and steganalysis.

Embedding Parameters. The proposed method starts from embedding on the first sub-lattice L_1 with any additive distortion, and afterwards embeds asymmetrically on the remaining sub-lattices successively. HILL, S-UNIWARD and MiPOD are respectively selected for the initial additive distortion, and also used to serve CMD and Synch for comparisons.

Note that, in HILL, S-UNIWARD or MiPOD, their default parameters are employed. HILL applies a 3×3 KB filter and then a 3×3 averaging filter on the cover, and the resultant embedding costs are further smoothed by a quite large 15×15 filter [14]. S-UNIWARD employs the 8-tap Daubechies wavelet filter bank with $\sigma = 1$. In MiPOD, a 9×9 sliding window is firstly used to estimate the variance of each pixel (see Eq. (13)), and then a 7×7 averaging filter is employed for the Fisher information matrix [18].

In all the experiments, the STC simulator [5] is implemented for data embedding. Each steganographic algorithm are tested with 6 different embedding payload rates (0.05, 0.1, 0.2, 0.3, 0.4, 0.5 bits/pixel).

Feature Set and Classifier. There exist a variety of feature sets for spatial steganalysis, e.g., Subtractive Pixel Adjacency Matrix (SPAM) [17], Spatial Rich Model (SRM) [6] and recently emerged state-of-the-art maxSRMd2 (a selection-channel aware version of the SRM) [3]. In our experiments, both SRM and maxSRMd2 are employed in performance evaluation due to their superior performance in image steganalysis.

On the classifier side, ensemble with Fisher linear discriminant [12] is adopted to evaluate the security performance in terms of the minimal total probability error, denoted as $\overline{P}_E$, which is averaged performance over ten 5000/5000 database splits at equal priors P_E.

4.2 Security Performance

Figures 2, 3 and 4 illustrate the security performance when utilizing MiPOD, HILL and S-UNIWARD for initial additive distortion, respectively. The left-side sub-figures of Figs. 2–4 present the performance when detected with SRM, while the right-side sub-figures are obtained with maxSRMd2.

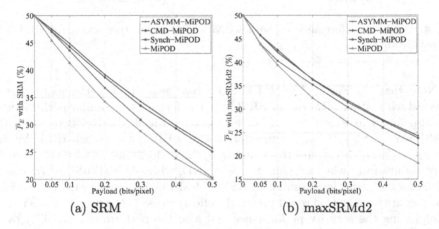

(a) SRM   (b) maxSRMd2

Fig. 2. Averaged performance $\overline{P}_E$ with MiPOD and feature sets of (a) SRM and (b) maxSRMd2.

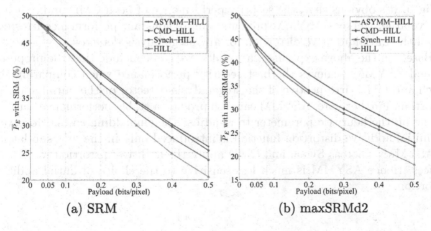

(a) SRM   (b) maxSRMd2

Fig. 3. Averaged performance $\overline{P}_E$ with HILL and feature sets of (a) SRM and (b) maxSRMd2.

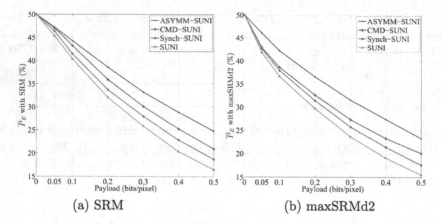

(a) SRM   (b) maxSRMd2

Fig. 4. Averaged performance $\overline{P}_E$ with S-UNIWARD and feature sets of (a) SRM and (b) maxSRMd2.

Note that, in Fig. 2, ASYMM-MiPOD represents best performance when detected with either SRM or maxSRMd2 as the feature set. Similar performance can also found in Figs. 3 and 4. For example, in Fig. 3(b) when detected with maxSRMd2, ASYMM-HILL outperforms CMD-HILL and Synch-HILL by an average of 2% and 3%, respectively; in Fig. 4, the performance of CMD and Synch drops significantly when utilizing S-UNIWARD, while ASYMM-SUNI retains a satisfactory security level similar to ASYMM-MiPOD and ASYMM-HILL. The above security evaluation result proves the effectiveness of the proposed ASYMM in improving the security performance and also the performance stability over different feature sets.

To further demonstrate on the performance stability, we compare the performance fluctuation induced by the type of initial additive distortion, as illustrated in Fig. 5. It's obvious that, the security performance of both CMD and Synch is very volatile, whereas ASYMM presents a more constant performance irrespective of the initial additive distortion for any steganalysis detector.

Based on the above experimental results, we can conclude that the proposed method ASYMM achieves the best security performance when comparing the Synch and CMD, irrespective of the steganalysis detector or the initial additive distortion. Furthermore, ASYMM can also provide a stable performance without relying on the heuristic parameter to re-adjust the embedding costs. Moreover, the initial additive distortion function is introduced only in the first sub-lattice by ASYMM, whereas Synch and CMD apply the additive distortion in all sub-lattices. Hence ASYMM is much less sensitive to the choice of initial additive distortion.

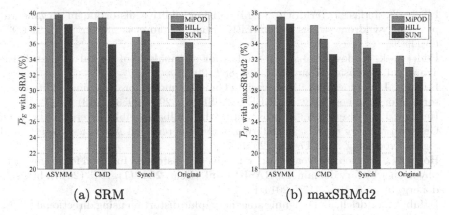

(a) SRM   (b) maxSRMd2

Fig. 5. Averaged performance $\overline{P}_E$ at $\alpha = 0.2$ bpp with different types additive distortions and feature sets of (a) SRM and (b) maxSRMd2. Each group of bars contain results when utilizing MiPOD, HILL and S-UNIWARD.

5   Conclusion

This paper proposes an asymmetric model-based steganographic scheme (ASYMM), which embeds on a cover image with consideration of adjacent modifications from the adjacent interleaved sub-lattices. The adjacent information is taken as the priori knowledge for the asymmetric change rates, which in turn are optimized with a Gaussian mixture model. Quite a lot experiments are performed and verified the superiority of ASYMM in improving the security performance and performance stability. Our future research will focus on looking for new statistical features of adjacent information to further improve the security.

Acknowledgments. This work was supported in part by the National Natural Science Foundation of China under Grant U1736215 and 61772573, and in part by the Science and Technology Program of Guangzhou under Grant 201707010029 and 201804010265.

References

1. Bas, P., Filler, T., Pevný, T.: "Break our steganographic system": the ins and outs of organizing BOSS. In: Filler, T., Pevný, T., Craver, S., Ker, A. (eds.) IH 2011. LNCS, vol. 6958, pp. 59–70. Springer, Heidelberg (2011). https://doi.org/10.1007/978-3-642-24178-9_5
2. Denemark, T., Fridrich, J.: Improving steganographic security by synchronizing the selection channel. In: 3rd ACM IH and MMS Workshop, pp. 5–14 (2015)
3. Denemark, T., Sedighi, V., Holub, V., Cogranne, R., Fridrich, J.: Selection-channel-aware rich model for steganalysis of digital images. In: IEEE International Workshop on Information Forensics and Security (2014)
4. Filler, T., Fridrich, J.: Gibbs construction in steganography. IEEE Trans. Inf. Forensics Secur. **5**(4), 705–720 (2010)

5. Filler, T., Judas, J., Fridrich, J.: Minimizing additive distortion in steganography using syndrome-trellis codes. IEEE Trans. Inf. Forensics Secur. **6**(3), 920–935 (2011)
6. Fridrich, J., Kodovský, J.: Rich models for steganalysis of digital images. IEEE Trans. Inf. Forensics Secur. **7**(3), 868–882 (2012)
7. Fridrich, J., Kodovsky, J.: Multivariate Gaussian model for designing additive distortion for steganography. In: IEEE ICASSP, pp. 2949–2953 (2013)
8. Hershey, J.R., Olsen, P.A.: Approximating the Kullback Leibler divergence between Gaussian mixture models. In: International Conference on Acoustics, Speech, and Signal Processing, pp. 317–320 (2007)
9. Holub, V., Fridrich, J., Denemark, T.: Universal distortion function for steganography in an arbitrary domain. EURASIP J. Inf. Secur. **2014**(1), 1–13 (2014). https://doi.org/10.1186/1687-417X-2014-1
10. Holub, V., Fridrich, J.: Designing steganographic distortion using directional filters. In: International Workshop on Information Forensics and Security, pp. 234–239 (2012)
11. Hu, X., Ni, J., Shi, Y.Q.: Efficient JPEG steganography using domain transformation of embedding entropy. IEEE Signal Process. Lett. **25**(6), 773–777 (2018)
12. Kodovský, J., Fridrich, J., Holub, V.: Ensemble classifiers for steganalysis of digital media. IEEE Trans. Inf. Forensics Secur. **7**(2), 432–444 (2012)
13. Li, B., Tan, S., Wang, M., Huang, J.: Investigation on cost assignment in spatial image steganography. IEEE Trans. Inf. Forensics Secur. **9**(8), 1264–1277 (2014)
14. Li, B., Wang, M., Huang, J., Li, X.: A new cost function for spatial image steganography. In: International Conference on Image Processing (ICIP), pp. 4206–4210 (2014)
15. Li, B., Wang, M., Li, X., Tan, S., Huang, J.: A strategy of clustering modification directions in spatial image steganography. IEEE Trans. Inf. Forensics Secur. **10**(9), 1905–1917 (2015)
16. Meng, R., Rice, S.G., Wang, J., Sun, X.: A fusion steganographic algorithm based on faster R-CNN. Comput. Mater. Continua **55**(1), 1–16 (2018)
17. Pevný, T., Bas, P., Fridrich, J.: Steganalysis by subtractive pixel adjacency matrix. IEEE Trans. Inf. Forensics Secur. **5**(2), 215–224 (2010)
18. Sedighi, V., Cogranne, R., Fridrich, J.: Content-adaptive steganography by minimizing statistical detectability. IEEE Trans. Inf. Forensics Secur. **11**(2), 221–234 (2016)
19. Sedighi, V., Fridrich, J.J., Cogranne, R.: Content-adaptive pentary steganography using the multivariate generalized Gaussian cover model. In: Proceedings of SPIE, Electronic Imaging, Media Watermarking, Security, and Forensics 2015, vol. 9409 (2015)
20. Wachter, A., Biegler, L.T.: On the implementation of an interior-point filter line-search algorithm for large-scale nonlinear programming. Math. Program. **106**(1), 25–57 (2006)

A Novel Watermarking Technology Based on Posterior Probability SVM and Improved GA

Shiqin Liu[1] , Minjun Zhao[1] , Jixin Ma[2] , Jiangyuan Yao[1],
Yucong Duan[1] , and Xiaoyi Zhou[1(✉)]

[1] School of Information Science and Technology,
Hainan University, Haikou 570208, China
xy.zhou.xy@gmail.com
[2] School of Computing and Mathematical,
University of Greenwich, SE10 9LS London, UK

Abstract. The widespread distribution of multimedia data cause copyright problems for digital content. This study makes use of digital image watermarking technology to protect copyright information, and proposes a scheme utilizes the support vector machine (SVM) based on posterior probability and the optimized genetic algorithm (GA). Firstly, each training image is divided into sub-blocks of 8 * 8 pixels, and they are trained and classified by the SVM to obtain the adaptive embedding strength. Secondly, after the operation of reproduction, crossover, mutation, the genetic algorithm generates new individuals in the search space by selection and recombination operators to optimize the objective function, and find out the best embedding position of the watermark. The 8 * 8 pixel sub-blocks were transformed by DCT when embedding. Finally, the watermark is extracted according to the embedding rules. Compared with the experimental results of other algorithms, the proposed scheme has better resistance against some common attacks, such as Histogram Equalization, Guassian Noise (0.04), Guassian Noise (0.05), JPEG (QF = 50), Salt-pepper Noise (0.01).

Keywords: Watermark · Support vector machine · Genetic algorithm
Posterior probability · Peak signal to noise ratio

1 Introduction

The progress of the digital age has led to the emergence of a large number of multi-media data, but the widespread distribution of multimedia data causes security problems, because digital content can be easily pirated or edited and modified by some software or tools. In order to overcome these problems with respect to images, the digital watermarking technique is introduced. Digital watermarking techniques are very effective in establishing copyright ownership, content authentication, broadcast monitoring, and device control. This technique embeds a small amount of copyright content (e.g., trademarks, unique watermarks) into the host image in a visible or invisible manner. Visible watermark technology is characterized by fast identification of image owners, but the main disadvantage is easy to be tampered with by attackers using

© Springer Nature Switzerland AG 2018
X. Sun et al. (Eds.): ICCCS 2018, LNCS 11066, pp. 195–207, 2018.
https://doi.org/10.1007/978-3-030-00015-8_17

image processing mechanism [1]. In invisible watermarks, watermarks are inserted into unknown locations in the image that are difficult to detect. The properties of the inserted watermark are similar to the original image, so it is difficult to recognize the watermark from the watermarked image. According to the watermark embedding domain, a digital watermark can be embedded into spatial domain or transform domain. The latter one provides higher embedding capacity, stronger robustness, and maintain imperceptibility. Therefore, transform domain watermark embedding algorithm is more popular.

There are three aspects to evaluate the performance of watermarking scheme: robustness, transparency, and capacity. Robustness ensures the watermarked image maintain its validity even after attacks. Transparency guarantees the quality of the watermarked image to be kept the same quality as the original one, thus the watermark is hard to be detected. Capacity is the number of watermark bits embedded into the image. There is always a trade-off among these three factors. Enhancing the robustness of the watermark will reduce its imperceptibility for the reason that high energy watermark is added to the host image [2]. In addition, increasing the capacity reduces the imperceptibility of the watermark because the embedding contents are larger, and more modifications are needed to be made to the host image. At present, digital watermarking techniques need to balance the requirements of robustness, imperceptibility and capacity. However, most of the watermarking techniques mainly consider robustness and imperceptibility [3, 4, 7–11, 15–20].

Robustness and imperceptibility can be optimized by software. Since 1990, machine learning and artificial intelligence have played a leading role in solving practical problems, because these techniques can be used for the training datasets into different sub-datasets for different problems. Training usually produces optimal or suboptimal solutions, and these solutions help to draw specific conclusions. Such techniques include neural network algorithm, ant colony algorithm (ACO), particle swarm optimization (PSO), fuzzy inference system (FIS), genetic algorithm (GA) and support vector machines (SVM). Neural network algorithms for optimizing watermark performance include single layer feedforward neural network (SLFNs), back propagation network (BPN) [5] and radial basis function neural network (RBF) [6], etc.

Huynh and Hua [7] proposed a novel robust blind watermarking method SMLE for color images. It allows gray-scale images to be embedded as watermarks into a color host images in the wavelet domain, and uses a two-dimensional Otsu algorithm in the extraction process. Compared with the one-dimensional Otsu algorithm, the two-dimensional algorithm has higher watermark detection accuracy. The experimental results show that the SMLE model not only ensures strong robustness against some common image attacks, but also effectively guarantees the imperceptibility of watermarks in host images. Nevertheless, this scheme performs poorly in the robustness test of lossy JPEG compression.

Arsalan and Qureshi [8] proposed a reversible watermarking technique that based on genetic programming (GP) which called IRW-Med. It uses companding function to reduce the embedding distortion, and integer wavelet transform (IWT) as the embedding domain to achieve watermark extraction. The experimental results show that this technique improves the imperceptibility compared with the existing reversible watermarking scheme, but the robustness still needs to be improved.

Maity and Sil [9] proposed an optimized multi-carrier (MC) spread spectrum (SS) image watermarking scheme using genetic algorithm (GA) and neural network (NN) hybridization. GA is used to determine a gradient threshold for pixel intensity to segment the host image into edge regions, smooth regions, and texture regions for watermark embedding intensity. A minimum mean square error (MMSE) decoder and neural network algorithm was used to train and learn to modify and optimize the weighting factors. The experimental results show that the watermarking scheme has better imperceptibility and robustness compared with existing biological excitation methods. Agarwal and Mishra [10] proposed a watermarking scheme using a hybrid intelligent network based on unidirectional propagation multilayer feedforward neural network algorithm (BPN) and genetic algorithm (GA) to embed binary watermarks into grayscale images. The scheme mainly utilizes the HVS's characteristics of images in DCT domain, and obtains the sequence of weighting factors by using the hybrid intelligent network, and then watermarks are embedded and extracted with weighting factors in DWT domain. Jawad and Khan [11] proposed a robust reversible watermarking algorithm to protect relational databases. It is based on the idea of differential expansion, and use genetic algorithm (GA) to improve the watermark capacity as well as to optimize the imperceptibility.

From the above research on watermarking techniques, it can be seen that the existing research works basically use nonlinear digital watermark technology such as neural network, chaos, etc., in which the optimization of the objective functions is based on empirical risk minimization, which cannot guarantee the generalization error. However, the SVM has strong ability of learning, generalization and nonlinear approximation, and it can solve the problem that the generalization error cannot be guaranteed less. Therefore, a digital image watermarking scheme in this study is improved based on adaptive SVM and optimized GA. SVM is used to determine the embedding strength of the watermark, and the embedding strength can be adaptive by the posterior probability. The improved GA is used to select the embedding position of watermark, and DCT transform is carried out during watermark embedding. The experimental results show that the watermark has good robustness to most common attacks while ensuring the watermark capacity and imperceptibility.

The rest of the paper is organized as follows: Sect. 2 introduces support vector machine (SVM), genetic algorithm (GA), and discrete cosine transform (DCT). Section 3 describes the experimental process. Section 4 describes the experimental results, and gives the analysis and evaluation of the experimental results. Section 5 summarizes the results of the study.

2 Preliminary Knowledge Introduction

2.1 Support Vector Machine (SVM)

Support vector machine (SVM) is a new pattern classification technique proposed by Vapnik and Guyon, it minimizes the error of sample size and reduces the upper limit of error involved in model generalization, thus solving the problems of over-learning, nonlinearity and dimension in modeling process [12, 13]. Unlike traditional methods of minimizing empirical training errors, SVM aims to minimize the upper bound of generalization errors by maximizing the separation of edges between hyperplanes and data, thus improving generalization accuracy, i.e. minimizing generalization loss by selecting the separator furthest from known samples, and this is also known as the maximum margin separator. A separator is defined as a collection of points, as shown in Eq. (1):

$$\{x : w * x + b\} \tag{1}$$

Parameter b is truncated and parameter w is vector. The maximum margin separator can be found by using gradient descent method to search the space formed by w and b. Under the condition that $m_i \geq 0$ and $\sum_i m_i y_i = 0$ are satisfied, the optimal solution can be found by solving Eq. (2).

$$argmax \sum_i m_i - \frac{1}{2} \sum_{i,j} m_i m_j y_i y_j (x_i x_j) \tag{2}$$

And then when figure out the optimal m_i, the maximum margin separator can be calculated by Eq. (3).

$$h(x) = sign\left(\sum_i m_i y_i (x * x_i) - b\right) \tag{3}$$

In order to overcome nonlinear and dimensional disasters, kernel function plays an important role in SVM. At present, the most commonly used kernel functions include polynomial kernel function, radial basis function, multilayer perceptron kernel function and so on. When SVM is used to classify images. Firstly, the image training set is selected to be trained by SVM, and then SVM can classify sub-blocks according to pre-set characteristic parameters. SVM based on posterior probability can calculate the probability of each sub-block in each class.

2.2 Genetic Algorithm (GA)

Genetic algorithm (GA) is a meta-heuristic algorithm which are inspired by evolutionary theory, which uses the concepts of natural selection, reproduction, crossover and mutation [14]. It is often used as a function optimizer, is a population-based model, using selection and reorganization operators in the search space to generate new individuals to optimize the objective function, usually composed of evaluation function and problem coding which rely on the problem. Here, a set of variables is optimized by maximizing some objectives or minimizing an error function, the objective function to be optimized being assumed to be a black box, and a series of control disks represent different parameters. And the black box's output represents the degree to which the evaluation function returns the optimization problem by combining the parameters. The GA is initialized by a set of random chromosomes, some functions determine the fitness of each chromosome, and another function selects a chromosome or individual from the population of $x_1, x_2, x_3, \ldots, x_n$, and replicates by applying the selection function given in Eq. (4).

$$S(x_i) = \frac{f(x_i)}{\sum_{k=1}^{n} f(x_i)} \tag{4}$$

Subsequently, the two selected chromosomes undergo a crossover process, that is, a process of exchanging genes between the two propagating chromosomes, and are split again. The next step is gene mutation. The above process is repeated a certain number of times, so that the chromosome has multiple breeding opportunities, the whole structure is evaluated, and the target problem is better solved.

2.3 Discrete Cosine Transform (DCT)

DCT is one of the methods to improve the robustness of watermarking technology. It decomposes a signal into three bands: low frequency band, intermediate frequency band and high frequency band. By using the attributes of the image, the band in which the watermark is embedded can be selected. DCT has a special attribute, called "energy compression characteristic", which indicates that most of the visually important information in an image is concentrated in only a few coefficients of DCT. The low-frequency part is a high-energy part that contains the most important visual part of the image, while the high-frequency part is usually more vulnerable to attack, so the intermediate-frequency part is usually chosen to embed the watermark.

3 Experimental Process

3.1 SVM to Train and Classify Sub-blocks

Each training image is divided into sub-blocks of 8 * 8 pixels, training them by using the svmtrain () function, and calculating the probabilities of 9 classes of each sub-block based on the posterior probabilities by using the svmpredict () function after the training is completed. Each class corresponds to a posterior probability, and the sum of the posterior probabilities of the 9 classes is equal to 1. The adaptive embedding strength can be obtained by multiplying the embedding strength corresponding to 9 classes of a sub-block with the corresponding posterior probability and then adding them together. Through a number of experiments and summary, the specified 1–9 categories corresponding to the experimental embedding strength is:

[21.1905, 15.4096, 17.6974, 18.1180, 25.1315, 18.4404, 18.4904, 19.8725, 18.6187].

Suppose that the embedding strength of a sub-block is D, the embedding strength of each class is $C_i (i = 1, 2, 3, \ldots, 9)$, and the corresponding posterior probability calculated for each class is $p_i (i = 1, 2, 3, \ldots, 9)$, so that the embedding strength D can be obtained from Eq. (5):

$$D = \sum_{i=1}^{9} C_i * p_i \tag{5}$$

3.2 GA to Select Watermark Embedding Location

After recording the fitness of each population of each generation, the best fitness point is found, and the best new population is selected. Then the crossover and mutation probability is corrected by using the crossover and mutation of GA, so as to obtain the best watermark embedding position.

Set the genetic iteration number $r = 1$, set the initial cross probability value PCInitial $= 0.7$, the final cross probability value PCFinal $= 0.3$, the initial mutation probability value PMInitial $= 0.01$, the final mutation probability value PMFinal $= 0.3$, cycle index $x \in (1, n)$.

The cross probability is defined as Pc and the variation probability is Pm, and the formula is as follows:

$$Pc = PCInitial - \left(\frac{PCInitial - PCFinal}{r} \right) * x \tag{6}$$

$$Pm = PMInitial + \left(\frac{PMInitial - PMFinal}{r} \right) * x \tag{7}$$

The crossover probability is modified by the crossover of GA, as shown in Eq. 8:

$$Pc = \begin{cases} k1 * \dfrac{\sin\left(\dfrac{\text{mean(Allfitvalue)}}{\text{max(Allfitvalue)}} \right)}{\frac{\pi}{2}}, & \sin\left(\dfrac{\text{mean(Allfitvalue)}}{\text{max(Allfitvalue)}} \right) < \frac{\pi}{6} \\ k1 * \left(1 - \dfrac{\sin\left(\dfrac{\text{mean(Allfitvalue)}}{\text{max(Allfitvalue)}} \right)}{\frac{\pi}{2}} \right), & \sin\left(\dfrac{\text{mean(Allfitvalue)}}{\text{max(Allfitvalue)}} \right) \geq \frac{\pi}{6} \end{cases} \tag{8}$$

k1 denotes the adjustment coefficient of adaptive Pc, and mean(Allfitvalue) denotes an average value of the fitness of each generation of population, and max(Allfitvalue) denotes a maximum value of the fitness of each generation of population. A new population is obtained by the current population crossing with the modified crossover probability.

The c mutation probability is modified by the mutation of GA, as shown in Eq. 9:

$$Pm= \begin{cases} k2 * \left(1 - \dfrac{\sin\left(\dfrac{\text{mean(Allfitvalue)}}{\text{max(Allfitvalue)}}\right)}{\frac{\pi}{2}}\right), & \sin\left(\dfrac{\text{mean(Allfitvalue)}}{\text{max(Allfitvalue)}}\right) < \frac{\pi}{6} \\[2em] k2 * \dfrac{\sin\left(\dfrac{\text{mean(Allfitvalue)}}{\text{max(Allfitvalue)}}\right)}{\frac{\pi}{2}}, & \sin\left(\dfrac{\text{mean(Allfitvalue)}}{\text{max(Allfitvalue)}}\right) \geq \frac{\pi}{6} \end{cases} \tag{9}$$

k2 denotes the adjustment coefficient of adaptive Pm, and mean(Allfitvalue) denotes an average value of the fitness of each generation of population, and max(Allfitvalue) denotes a maximum value of the fitness of each generation of population. Then using the current population after the previous crossing, the modified mutation probability is used to mutate it, and a new population can be obtained.

3.3 Embedding Watermark

The process of extracting watermark has three steps:

(1) Calculate that DCT coefficient $B(k)$ of the selected embed position;
(2) Calculating the product $C(k)$ of the correlation coefficient of the selected position in the sub-block and the first coefficient of the sub-block for judging whether a watermark is embedded or not;
(3) If $C(k) \leq B(k)$ and the watermark matrix value at k is 0, when the embedding coefficient matrix value $A(k)$ corresponding to the host image at k is less than 2.78 (After a lot of experiments, it is found that using 2.78 can make the performance of the watermark technology to achieve the best.), $B(k)$ is modified to $(C(k) - 20 * A(k))$, otherwise $B(k)$ is modified to $(C(k) - A(k))$. If $B(k) < C(k)$ and the watermark matrix value at k is 1, when the embedding coefficient matrix value $A(k)$ corresponding to the host image at k is less than 2.78, $B(k)$ is modified to $(C(k) + 20 * A(k))$, otherwise $B(k)$ is modified to $(C(k) + A(k))$, as shown in Eq. (8):

$$B(k) = \begin{cases} (C(k) - 20 * A(k)), & C(k) \leq B(k) \text{ and } w_k = 0 \text{ and } A(k) \leq 2.78 \\ (C(k) - A(k)), & C(k) \leq B(k) \text{ and } w_k = 0 \text{ and } A(k) > 2.78 \\ (C(k) + 20 * A(k)), & C(k) > B(k) \text{ and } w_k = 1 \text{ and } A(k) \leq 2.78 \\ (C(k) + A(k)), & C(k) > B(k) \text{ and } w_k = 1 \text{ and } A(k) > 2.78 \end{cases} \tag{10}$$

3.4 Extracting Watermark

The process of extracting watermark is the inverse process of embedding watermark. By comparing the relationship between $B(k)$ and $C(k)$, the corresponding value of the point watermark matrix is determined.

If $B(k) \geq C(k)$, the corresponding value of the watermark matrix is 1, otherwise, the corresponding value of the watermark matrix is 0.

4 Experimental Results and Analysis and Evaluation

The peak signal to noise ratio (PSNR) and normalization coefficient (NC) were used to evaluate the similarity between the original image and the watermarked image. The robustness of the watermark technique was tested by attack. The imperceptibility of the watermark technique was evaluated by PSNR value. The higher the PSNR value, the higher the imperceptibility and the better the watermarking technique is in terms of vision.

4.1 Experimental Results

Figure 1 is a comparison of the original image (256×256) with the watermarked image (32×32), and the original watermark with the extracted watermark. PSNR is 39.3273 and NC value is 1. According to the contrast between the original image and the watermarked image, and the PSNR value, the imperceptibility of the watermark embedding technology in this experiment is proved to be good.

(a) original image   (b) watermarked image

(c) original watermark   (d) extracted watermark

Fig. 1. Comparison before and after embedding watermark in image

Figure 1 shows the result of one cycle of GA. When the number of cycles is increased, PSNR and robustness will increase as the watermark embedding position is selected to be more optimized.

4.2 Experimental Analysis

In order to evaluate the imperceptibility of watermarks and prove the superiority of posterior probability SVM and improved GA, we compare ours results of PSNR with some papers, which have the same host image and without any attack. These documents include Liu and Zhou using wavelet transform domain of [15], Jiang et al. using logistic chaotic map and IWT - SVD of [16], Zhou et al. using DWT of [17]. The comparison results are shown in Table 1.

Table 1. Compares imperceptibility with [15–17]

Comparison type	[15]	[16]	[17]	Proposed
PSNR	28.7	34.9905	34.3243	39.3273
NC (No attack)	1	1	1	1

The comparison results show that our PSNR value is better under the condition that NC value is guaranteed to be 1, which proves that watermarking technology based on posterior probability SVM and improved GA are superior. It improves the imperceptibility, and makes the watermarked image more imperceptible in vision.

In order to evaluate the robustness of the watermark technique, 18 different attacks are performed on the embedded image. The NC values are calculated and the results are shown in Table 2. The results show that the proposed method is effective in resisting some attacks.

Table 2. NC values after 18 attacks on watermarked images

Index	1			2	3
Attack Type	JPEG (QF = 50)	JPEG (QF = 70)	JPEG (QF = 90)	Gaussian low-pass filtering (3,0.5)	Histogram Equalization
NC	0.80351	0.92327	0.9785	0.79595	0.96207
Index	4	5	6	7	8
Attack Type	Image Brightening	Image Dimming	Contrast Increasing (0.5,0.6)	Contrast Decreasing	Guassian Noise (0.003)
NC	0.62386	1	0.84379	0.64878	0.91121
Index	8		9		10
Attack Type	Guassian Noise (0.04)	Guassian Noise (0.05)	Salt-pepper Noise (0.005)	Salt-pepper Noise (0.01)	Product Noise (0.2)
NC	0.77081	0.74985	0.93826	0.8863	0.73999
Index	11	12		13	
Attack Type	Median filtering	Crop (1/4)	Crop (1/2)	Rotate (0.25)	Rotate (−0.25)
NC	0.11993	0.87742	0.68674	0.69104	0.67635
Index	14	15	16	17	18
Attack Type	Circular shift (100,100)	Average filtering (3*3)	Motion filter (9,0)	Image Resize (3)	Speckle Noise
NC	0.17282	0.25584	0.30632	0.83768	0.71952

As can be seen from Table 2, the attacks that can be well resisted are JPEG (QF = 70), JPEG (QF = 90), Gaussian low-pass filtering (3,0.5), Histogram Equalization, Image Dimming, Contrast Increasing (0.5,0.6), Guassian Noise (0.003), Salt-pepper Noise (0.005), Salt-pepper Noise (0.01), Image Resize (3), Crop (1/4). The attacked images and the extracted watermark extracted from the attacked images are listed, as shown in Table 3.

Table 3. Attacked image and extracted watermark

Attack Type	JPEG(QF=70)	JPEG(QF=80)	JPEG(QF=90)	Gaussian low-pass filtering (3,0.5)
Attacked Image				
Extracted Watermark				
Attack Type	Histogram Equalization	Image Dimming	Contrast Increasing (0.5,0.6)	Guassian Noise (0.003)
Attacked Image				
Extracted Watermark				
Attack Type	Salt-pepper Noise (0.005)	Salt-pepper Noise (0.01)	Image Resize (3)	Crop (1/4)
Attacked Image				
Extracted Watermark				

In this experiment, we compared with some papers, in the same case of host image, based on NC value, compared the NC value after attack. These papers include Huynh and Hua [18], Mishra and Rajpal [19], Cha and Kuo [20], the comparison results are shown in Tables 4, 5, and Fig. 4:

Table 4. Compares attack test results with [18]

Attack Type	Histogram Equalization	Guassian Noise(0.04)	Guassian Noise(0.05)	JPEG (QF=50)	JPEG (QF=70)	JPEG (QF=90)
NC of [18]	0.755	0.657	0.56	0.772	0.803	0.852
Proposed	0.96207	0.77081	0.74985	0.80351	0.92327	0.95347
Extracted Watermark						

Convert Table 4 to a line chart, as shown in Fig. 2.

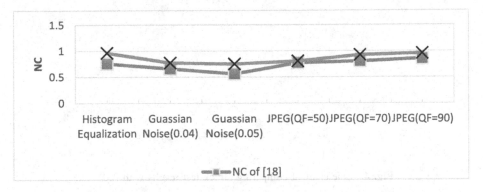

Fig. 2. Line chart of comparing attack test results with [18]

Table 5. Compares attack test results with [19]

Attack Type	Salt-pepper Noise (0.005)	Salt-pepper Noise (0.01)	Crop (1/4)	Crop (1/2)
NC of [19]	0.81	0.57	0.69	0.47
Extracted Watermark				
Proposed	0.95419	0.91348	0.99716	0.70309
Extracted Watermark				

Convert Table 5 to a line chart, as shown in Fig. 3.

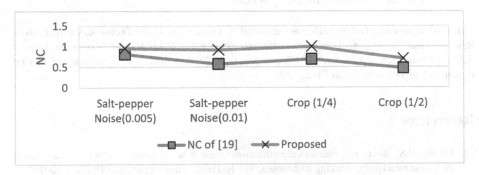

Fig. 3. Line chart of comparing attack test results with [19]

The comparison results show that our method significantly improves the robustness of the watermark, and the anti-attack ability of general attacks.

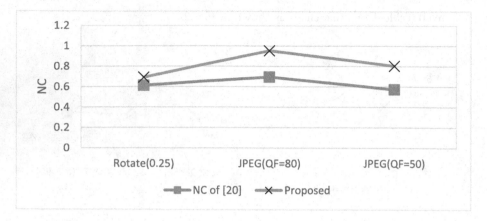

Fig. 4. Line chart of comparing attack test results with [20]

5   Conclusion

To consider the trade-off between invisibility and robustness of a watermarked image, a hybrid digital watermarking scheme SVM and GA was proposed in this study. The embedding intensity of the watermark was determined by the posterior probability of SVM, and the position of the watermark was embedded on the basis of the optimized GA with adaptive crossover probability and mutation probability. Compared with other algorithms, the comparison results show that our method significantly improves the robustness of the watermark, and the anti-attack ability of general attacks, such as Histogram Equalization, Guassian Noise, JPEG compression, Salt-pepper Noise is significantly better than some existing schemes. However, there is still a problem in extracting watermark. When adjusting the embedding and extracting rules to increase PSNR to 41.5, the NC value is less than 1 even the watermarked image is not attacked. Therefore, in the future research, we need to further optimize the watermark extraction to achieve better digital watermarking scheme.

Acknowledgement.   The research was supported by Hainan Provincial Technology Project (Key Research and Development Project, Grant No. ZDYF2017171), Hainan Provincial Natural Science Foundation (Grant No. 117063 and No. 617079) and State Key Laboratory of Marine Resource Utilization in South China Sea.

References

1. Chang, C.S., Shen, J.J.: Features classification forest: a novel development that is adaptable to robust blind watermarking techniques. IEEE Trans. Image Process. **PP**(99), 1 (2017)
2. Aslantas, V.: An optimal robust digital image watermarking based on SVD using differential evolution algorithm. Optics Commun. **282**(5), 769–777 (2009)
3. Bhatnagar, G.: A new facet in robust digital watermarking framework. AEUE – Int. J. Electron. Commun. **66**(4), 275–285 (2012)

4. Cox, I.J., Miller, M.L., Bloom, J.A., et al.: Index - digital watermarking and steganography. In: Digital Watermarking & Steganography, 2nd edn., pp. 183–212 (2007)
5. Yen, C.T., Huang, Y.J.: Frequency domain digital watermark recognition using image code sequences with a back-propagation neural network. Multimedia Tools Appl. **16**, 1–11 (2015)
6. Liu, Q., Jiang, X.: Design and realization of a meaningful digital watermarking algorithm based on RBF neural network. In: The Sixth World Congress on Intelligent Control and Automation, WCICA 2006, pp. 214–218. IEEE (2006)
7. Huynh-The, T., Hua, C.H., Tu, N.A., et al.: Selective bit embedding scheme for robust blind color image watermarking. Inf. Sci. **426**, 1–18 (2018)
8. Arsalan, M., Qureshi, A.S., Khan, A., et al.: Protection of medical images and patient related information in healthcare: Using an intelligent and reversible watermarking technique. Appl. Soft Comput. **51**, 168–179 (2017)
9. Maity, S.P., Maity, S., Sil, J., et al.: Perceptually adaptive MC-SS image watermarking using GA-NN hybridization in fading gain. Eng. Appl. Artif. Intell. **31**(5), 3–14 (2014)
10. Agarwal, C., Mishra, A., Sharma, A.: Gray-scale image watermarking using GA-BPN hybrid network. J. Vis. Commun. Image Representation **24**(7), 1135–1146 (2013)
11. Jawad, K., Khan, A.: Genetic algorithm and difference expansion based reversible watermarking for relational databases. J. Syst. Softw. **86**(11), 2742–2753 (2013)
12. Vapnik, V.: The Nature of Statistical Learning Theory. In: Conference on Artificial Intelligence, pp. 988–999. Springer, Heidelberg (1995). https://doi.org/10.1007/978-1-4757-3264-1
13. Boser, B.E., Guyon, I.M., Vapnik, V.N.: A training algorithm for optimal margin classifiers. In: The Workshop on Computational Learning Theory, pp. 144–152 (1992)
14. Holland, J.H.: Adaptation in natural and artificial systems: an introductory analysis with applications to biology, control, and artificial intelligence. Q. Rev. Biol. **6**(2), 126–137 (1992)
15. Liu, Y., Zhou, L.: Digital image embedding and extracting method based on wavelet transform domain. J. Shenyang Univ. Technol. **21**, 1–6 (2018)
16. Jiang, X.D., Fan, H.Y., Lu, Z.M.: Blind robust watermarking algorithm based on logistic chaotic mapping and IWT-SVD quantization. Transducer Microsyst. Technol. **37**(02), 131–135 (2018)
17. Zhou, Y., Jin, W.: A robust digital image multi-watermarking scheme in the DWT domain. In: International Conference on Systems and Informatics, Cairo, pp. 1851–1854 (2012)
18. Huynh-The, T., Hua, C.H., Tu, N.A., et al.: Selective bit embedding scheme for robust blind color image watermarking. Inf. Sci. **426**, 1–18 (2018)
19. Mishra, A., Rajpal, A., Bala, R.: Bi-directional extreme learning machine for semi-blind watermarking of compressed images. J. Inf. Secur. Appl. **38**, 71–84 (2018)
20. Cha, B.H., Kuo, C.C.J.: Robust MC-CDMA-based fingerprinting against time-varying collusion attacks. IEEE Trans. Inf. Forensics Secur. **4**(3), 302–317 (2009)

A Secure Blind Watermarking Scheme Based on Dual Frequency Domains and Ergodic Matrix

Minjun Zhao⬙, Shiqin Liu⬙, Chunjie Cao⬙, Jiangyuan Yao, and Xiaoyi Zhou⁽✉⁾⬙

School of Information Science and Technology, Hainan University, Haikou 570208, China
xy.zhou.xy@gmail.com

Abstract. Digital watermarking is considered to be a potential and effective solution to protect digital content. The key issue of a watermarking system is the trade-off between the robustness and transparency. Therefore, in order to improve these two characters, this paper proposes a digital image watermarking scheme based on discrete cosine transform (DCT) and discrete wavelet transform (DWT). After the host image was transformed by DWT, the low frequency band was selected and divided into 8×8 blocks. And then, each block was transformed by DCT. Meanwhile, the watermark was improved security by being encrypted using ergodic matrix, thus it cannot be recognized after the decryption. At the embedding process, the DCT coefficients at the five rows of the bottom of each block were exchanged by comparing the scrambled watermark information. At the extracting process, the watermark was recovered by comparing the value of two adjacent coefficients in the DCT block. Experimental results show that the proposed scheme has good imperceptibility as well as good robustness against common watermark attacks, such as Gaussian low-pass filtering, histogram equalization, image brighten/darken, contrast decreasing, salt-pepper noise, average filtering and cropping.

Keywords: Discrete cosine transform · Discrete wavelet transform
Ergodic matrix · Robustness · Blind watermarking

1 Introduction

With the advancement of computers and network technology, access, transmission, storage and distribution of digital images becomes much less complex. At the same time, copyright infringement is getting more and more serious, such phenomenon has drawn scholars' attention. It can be seen that digital images are easily captured, stored, forwarded and shared on common social networks such as Twitter, Facebook, Whatsapp and Instagram, and they may even be used for commercial or other purposes. Therefore, in order to prevent such risks, it is necessary to solve the problems related to copyright protection and authentication in image transmission, storage, and utilization. Digital image watermarking technology is used as an effective tool to prevent infringement and replication, in copy prevention, a watermark limits the copy, and in copyright protection, it authenticates the source [1].

© Springer Nature Switzerland AG 2018
X. Sun et al. (Eds.): ICCCS 2018, LNCS 11066, pp. 208–220, 2018.
https://doi.org/10.1007/978-3-030-00015-8_18

There are many kinds of classification methods for digital watermarking. According to whether the original data is used in the process of watermarking extracting and detecting, it can be divided into blind watermarking and non-blind watermarking. Non-blind watermarking means that the original data shall be used in the detection process, while blind watermarking only needs the secret keys. Non-blind watermarking is robust, but it is limited due to the cost of storage. Blind watermarking is more practical, but if the image is seriously attacked, the detection of watermark will be more difficult.

According to different embedding area, digital watermarking algorithm can be divided into spatial and transform domain watermarking. Due to the visualization and robustness limitations of watermarks in spatial domains, most image watermarking models are built on transform domains, such as cosine transform, Fourier transform and wavelet transform. DCT and DWT are two common transform domains frequently used in a digital watermarking algorithm. DCT is a kind of linear transform in digital signal processing [2], it has good decorrelation capability and energy compression ability. DWT is often used in singularity detection and image processing in practical engineering applications. It is also a block processing method used in JPEG2000. In image processing, since DWT is a local transform of an image, it can solve the problem of signal mutation.

DCT has the characteristics of simple calculation, compatibility with JPEG and MPEG, and better energy compression and so forth. The watermark can be embedded in the low frequency part of the image after DCT transform, and it has a good performance against JPEG compression. Most of the DCT based watermarking schemes use similar JPEG compression 8×8 block in DCT transform, such as the adaptive watermark scheme proposed by yang et al. [3] In their scheme, the host image, after DCT transform, is searched for finding the six consecutive DCT coefficients with the mean value close to zero. When the watermark is embedded, the variables of two levels are compared, and the DCT coefficients in the host image are modified, so that the embedded image resists compression attack. Soumitra Roy and Arup Kumar Pal proposed a blind DCT-based multi-watermark embedding algorithm [4]. The host image is a color image, and the chaotic watermark is inserted into the selected AC coefficient pairs of the DCT transform blocks of the image's green and blue components. This scheme has good imperceptibility and strong robustness, but it suffers from high computational complexity. Mohammad Moosazadeha and Gholamhossein Ekbatanifard [5] proposed a watermark algorithm based on YCoCg - R color space, which selects the appropriate block for embedding by the complexity of the host image block, and adaptively selects the embedding strength by the mean function. Because the components of YCoCg - R color space have good decorrelation characteristics, this scheme improves the robustness of the watermark. Chen et al. [6] proposed an improved genetic algorithm based on DCT transform domain and SVM image watermarking technology. The combination of SVM in DCT domain of the host image realized the variable embedding of watermark strength, so that the method has good anti-attack ability.

While DWT transform is used in digital watermarking, an image can be divided into four parts: one low frequency part and three high frequency parts. The low frequency part represents the contour part of the image, and the high frequency represents the detailed information. Embedding watermark in the low frequency subbands can make the watermark robust to attacks such as lossy compression and high frequency filtering. Embedding watermark in the high frequency part can make the watermark have better invisibility. Li et al. [7] embedded a watermark based on DWT and neural network, in which the scrambled host image is transformed by DWT, and the watermark is embedded in LH_1 and LL_1 bands, and extracted by back propagation (BP) neural network. The algorithm has good robustness and invisibility but consumes computational time. Ye et al. [8] proposed a blind watermarking algorithm based on DWT and SVD, which divides the low frequency subband of the host image into blocks and SVD on each sub-block, then embeds the feature watermark sequence into the maximum singular value of each sub-block by parity quantization rules, so that the algorithm has strong robustness and realizes full blind detection. Mishra et al. [9] proposed a watermarking scheme based on DWT and SVD. The singular value of the coefficients in LL_3 subband is modified by using the singular value of the watermark image through multiscale factors (MSFs), and a new Firefly Algorithm (FA) is used to optimize the MSFs to find a better multiscale factor. The scheme obtains higher PSNR value and robustness to some attacks except sharpening and clipping attacks compared with other schemes. Ren et al. [10] proposed a DWT domain robust watermarking algorithm based on SVD and HVS. Firstly, the low-frequency sub-band after two-level DWT is extracted and divided into blocks for SVD. Then the Arnold scrambled watermark is embedded into the optimal embedding position by using HVS. So that the watermark has good transparency and robustness. Zhang et al. [11] proposed an SVD - DWT watermarking algorithm based on chaos scrambling. After carrying out three-level DWT on the host image, the singular value of the watermark image is embedded in the low-frequency sub-band by modifying the singular value, and the watermark information is embedded in the intermediate-frequency sub - band. The watermark with good effect is selected for detection during extraction so as to obtain better robustness.

In general, DCT watermarking scheme still has some shortcomings, embedding in AC component of DCT domain is difficult to ensure the robustness of the watermark, while embedding in DC component is difficult to maintain the concealment of the watermark. Compared with DWT, DCT does not have good spatial direction selectivity and multi-resolution analysis ability. Nevertheless, DWT transform also has some disadvantages. Its inverse transform requires certain conditions, and the arrangement of the value at the image contour position is often out of order. At the same time, most watermarking algorithms have no preprocessing part, or only use Arnold scrambling algorithm or chaos algorithm to preprocess the watermark. Arnold scrambling algorithm has a short transformation period and can not provide sufficient security protection for watermark. Chaos algorithm also has some problems such as short period and has contradiction between accuracy and confidentiality. However, Ergodic matrix algorithm can distribute the original image uniformly and has a larger key space. Therefore, combining with ergodic matrix, this paper proposed a blind watermarking scheme for digital images based on DWT and DCT. In the proposed watermarking scheme, firstly, the host image is transformed by DWT, then the LL frequency band is selected and divided into 8×8 blocks, and then each block is transformed by DCT. Watermark information which was preprocessed by ergodic matrix was then embedded by comparing the DCT coefficients at a specific position. Afterwards, IDCT transformation and IDWT transformation were carried out after embedding to obtain a watermarked image similar to the original one. The experimental results show that the scheme not only has good robustness and invisibility, but realizes the blind extraction of watermark.

The remainder of this paper is organized as follows. Section two introduces the basic knowledge of watermark. Section three describes the proposed image digital watermarking model. Section four gives the experimental results and discussion. Section five summarizes the conclusions and the suggested future work is presented.

2   Basic Knowledge

2.1   Discrete Cosine Transform

Discrete Cosine Transform (DCT) is one of the most common conversion methods for converting from spatial domain to frequency domain. DCT is widely used in signal processing and image processing because of its energy compression characteristics. In image processing, two-dimensional discrete cosine transform is commonly used. The mathematical formula of two-dimensional discrete cosine transform and its inverse transform is:

$$U(x,y) = 2\frac{\alpha(x)\alpha(y)\sum_{m=0}^{p-1}\sum_{n=0}^{q-1} V(m,n) \times \cos\frac{(2m+1)x\pi}{2p} \times \cos\frac{(2n+1)y\pi}{2q}}{\sqrt{pq}} \tag{1}$$

$$V(m,n) = 2\frac{\sum_{x=0}^{p-1}\sum_{y=0}^{q-1} U(x,y)\alpha(x)\alpha(y) \times \cos\frac{(2m+1)x\pi}{2p} \times \cos\frac{(2n+1)y\pi}{2q}}{\sqrt{pq}} \tag{2}$$

$U(x,y)$ is DCT coefficient in formula (1), p and q represent the size of the block, and $V(m,n)$ is the pixel value of the original image. $\alpha(x)$ and $\alpha(y)$ are defined as:if $x,y = 0$, $\alpha(x),\alpha(y) = \frac{1}{\sqrt{2}}$; if $x,y \neq 0$, $\alpha(x),\alpha(y) = 1$.

As shown in Fig. 1, after the image has been DCT transformed, a single image block may be divided into a DC component in the upper left corner and an AC component occupying most of the image block. AC component coefficients can be divided into three parts, low frequency band, medium frequency band and high frequency band coefficients. Most of that energy of the image block is concentrate on the low band coefficients of the AC component, which have the low energy.

Fig. 1. DCT coefficient distribution diagram.

2.2 Discrete Wavelet Transform

The basic idea of wavelet transform is to represent the original signal as the superposition of wavelet by stretching and translating the original signal. Discrete wavelet transform (DWT) refers to the wavelet transform that samples the wavelet discretely. DWT provides a very good energy encapsulation effect, which is one of the main reasons why DWT is widely used in image processing applications such as image compression and image watermarking. When DWT is used in digital image watermarking scheme, the image transformed by DWT will be decomposed into four parts, one low frequency part, three high frequency parts, the low frequency part represents the outline part of the image, and the high frequency represents the detail part. The high frequency parts are HL, LH, HH. HL represents the image vertical direction detail information; LH section represents image horizontal direction detail information; HH section representing image diagonal direction detail information.

Figure 2 is a schematic diagram of the distribution of each region of the image after three-level wavelet transform. Broken lines with arrows indicate sorting by degree of energy concentration from large to small.

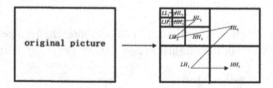

Fig. 2. Three-level DWT exploded diagram.

2.3 Ergodic Matrix

Ergodic matrix was proposed Zhao et al. in 2003 [12–15], its definition and theorem are as follows [13, 16]:

Definition 1: Given $Q \in \mathbb{F}_{n \times n}^q$, if $\forall v \in \mathbb{F}_{n \times 1}^q \setminus \{0\}$, $\{Qv, Q^2v, \dots, Q^{q^n-1}v\}$ just exhaust $\forall v \in \mathbb{F}_{n \times 1}^q \setminus \{0\}$, Q is called an ergodic matrix over finite field $\mathbb{F}^q$ (here $\mathbf{0} = [0 \ 0 \ \dots \ 0]^T$).

Theorem 1: $Q \in \mathbb{F}_{n \times n}^q$ is an ergodic matrix if and only if the multiplication period of Q on $\mathbb{F}^q$ is $(q^n - 1)$.

It can be seen from the definition and the theorem that all $n \times n$ ergodic matrices over the finite field $\mathbb{F}^q$. have the same number of elements and are larger than any $n \times n$ ergodic matrices. Taking a randomly selected ergodic matrix $Q \in \mathbb{F}^{q256}_{50 \times 50}$ as an example, the grayscale image and histogram of the ergodic matrix are shown in Fig. 3

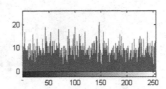

(a)Randomly selected
ergodic matrix gray scale graph   (b)Randomly selected matrix histogram

Fig. 3. Randomly selected ergodic matrix $Q \in \mathbb{F}^{256}_{50 \times 50}$ and its histogram.

Figure 3 shows that the values of the ergodic matrix diverge almost evenly and can therefore be used to encrypt the watermark as a preprocessing of the watermark.

2.4 Termark Preprocessing

To improve security, watermark was preprocessed with the ergodic matrix. Average divergence characteristics of the ergodic matrix scramble the watermark, change the location of the pixels from space, and achieve the effect of diffusion, so as to reduce the correlation between adjacent pixels of the image. Thus even if a watermark embezzler can recover the watermark, he cannot recover the original content because he has no secret keys. Transformation formula is shown in (3) [17]:

$$C(k) = M(k) \oplus \{[W(k) + M(k)] \bmod CLevel\} \oplus C(k-1) \qquad (3)$$

W(k) represents the current operating pixel of the watermark image, CLevel is the image color level, C(k−1) is the current last computed pixel of the encrypted image. The communication parties respectively select the first value as the initial value from the agreed key Qbkx and the original image. Qbkx is combined into a matrix M(k) consistent with the size of the original image, and pixels corresponding to the encrypted image are obtained according to formula (3). The receiver obtains that correspond pixel value of the original image by formula (4).

$$I(k) = \{M(k) \oplus C(k) \oplus C(k-1) + CLevel - W(k)\} \bmod CLevel \qquad (4)$$

In order to achieve a higher level of security, the communication parties can arbitrarily specify the round of diffusion. However, the experimental results show that the image is quite different from the original one even in one-round diffusion. The experimental results of one round of diffusion are shown in Fig. 4.

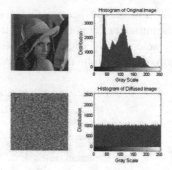

Fig. 4. Comparison of experimental results after one round of diffusion.

3 Watermarking Scheme

3.1 Watermark Embedding

I is an original grayscale image with a size of 512×512 and w is a binary watermark image with a size of 32×32. The watermark embedding process is as follows:

(1) Random scrambling of watermark image w. w' is the scrambled watermark image;
(2) DWT transform of original gray image I. After one-time DWT, I obtain the LL part with the size of 128×128;
(3) Part LL is transformed by DCT. Dividing the LL part with the size of 128×128 into 256 rectangular blocks with the size of 8×8, and performing DCT transformation on all sub-blocks;
(4) The lowest five lines of 8×8 DCT sub-blocks are taken as embedding positions. Scanning each DCT sub-block in the way shown in Fig. 5, the 64 coefficients are $B_{[(i,j),n]}(1 \le n \le 64)$. I is a row of the position of the DCT sub-block in the LL part, j is a column of the position, $B_{[(i,j),n]}(25 \le n \le 64)$ is taken as an embedding position;

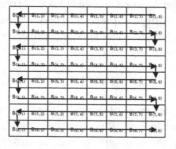

Fig. 5. 8×8 DCT sub-block.

(5) Embedding according to the scrambled watermark information. Scrambled water-mark is $W' = \{w_{(i,j)}|1 \leq i,j \leq 8\}$, I is the row at the location, j is the column where it is located. Group the coefficient $B_{[(i,j),n]}(25 \leq n \leq 64)$ in each DCT block. Two adjacent coefficients are divided into one group, which can be divided into a total of 20 groups. The embedding position is shown in formula (5).

$$G_{(i,j)} = \left\{ \left(B_{[(i,j),2m-1]}, B_{[(i,j),2m]} \right) | 13 \leq m \leq 32 \right\} \tag{5}$$

If $w_{(i,j)} = 1$, check the size of each set of coefficients $B_{[(i,j),2m-1]}$ and $B_{[(i,j),2m]}$ of the correspond DCT block $G_{(i,j)}$. If $B_{[(i,j),2m-1]} < B_{[(i,j),2m]}$, change the position of the two coefficients; if $B_{[(i,j),2m-1]} \geq B_{[(i,j),2m]}$, do nothing.

If $w_{(i,j)} = 0$, check the size of each set of coefficients $B_{[(i,j),2m-1]}$ and $B_{[(i,j),2m]}$ of the correspond DCT block $G_{(i,j)}$. If $B_{[(i,j),2m-1]} > B_{[(i,j),2m]}$, change the position of the two coefficients; if $B_{[(i,j),2m-1]} \leq B_{[(i,j),2m]}$, do nothing.

(6) Reconstructing image. After embedding all information of watermark, inverse DCT is carried out on all DCT sub-block coefficient, and all sub-blocks are combine to LL', and then inverse DWT is carried out on HL, LH and HH parts obtained in the step (2) to obtain the image I'.

3.2 Watermark Extracting

For watermark extraction, the specific method is as follows:

(1) Carry out a DWT transformation on the image I' containing the watermark to obtain the LL part;
(2) The LL part is divided into 256 rectangular blocks with 8×8 size, and perform DCT on all sub-blocks;
(3) Scanning each DCT sub-block in the way shown in Fig. 5, the 64 coefficients are $B_{[(i,j),n]}(1 \leq n \leq 64)$. i is a row of the position of the DCT sub-block in the LL part, j is a column of the position. Group the coefficient $B_{[(i,j),n]}(25 \leq n \leq 64)$ in each DCT block. Two adjacent coefficients are divided into one group, which can be divided into a total of 20 groups. The extracting position is shown in formula (5).
(4) Check the size of each set of coefficients $B_{[(i,j),2m-1]}$ and $B_{[(i,j),2m]}$ of the correspond DCT block $G_{(i,j)}$. If the number of groups that $B_{[(i,j),2m-1]} > B_{[(i,j),2m]}$ is bigger than 10, $w_{(i,j)} = 1$, Else, $w_{(i,j)} = 0$;
(5) Reversely scrambling the obtained watermark matrix to generate a corresponding binary image. Watermark extraction completes.

4   Experimental Results and Analysis

4.1   Experimental Results

In order to verify the effectiveness and feasibility of the proposed scheme, six grayscale images with a size of 512×512 pixels as shown in the "host image" row of Table 1 were selected as host images, and the binary image with a size of 32×32 pixels of Fig. 6 was selected as the original watermark image. As can be seen from the row "watermarked image" in Table 1, there is no significant difference between the watermarked image and the original image, which shows that the proposed algorithm has good concealment.

Fig. 6. Original watermark image.

Table 1. Experimental results on different host images.

Host images	Lena	Peppers	Couple	Boat	Barbara	Cameraman
Host image						
Water-marked image						
Extracted watermark	A	A	A	A	A	A
PSNR	37.6422	40.518	38.6251	38.1162	35.5293	39.9118
NC	0.99931	1	1	1	1	0.99656

4.2   Experimental Analysis

In the analysis, we select the Lena image embedded with watermark. Firstly, 18 kinds of attacks are carried out on the watermarked image, the NC values of the extracted watermark and the original watermark are shown in Table 2.

Table 2. NC values of 18 post-attack watermarks.

Attack type	NC	Attack type	NC	Attack type	NC
JPEG (QF = 10)	0.55937	Image Brighten	0.99862	Average filtering (3 × 3)	0.95148
JPEG (QF = 20)	0.65818	Image Darken	0.99862	Motion filter (9,0)	0.7444
JPEG (QF = 30)	0.7571	Contrast Increasing (0.5,0.6)	0.54081	Median filtering	0.77513
JPEG (QF = 50)	0.87341	Contrast Decreasing	0.99724	Gaussian low-pass filtering (3,0.5)	0.99038
JPEG (QF = 70)	0.92737	Product Noise (0.2)	0.77985	Rotate (0.25)	0.83748
Histogram Equalization	0.98701	Speckle Noise	0.82691	Rotate (−0.25)	0.83653
Salt-pepper Noise (0.01)	0.97655	Guassian Noise (0.003)	0.83598	Crop (192,320)	0.96486
Salt-pepper Noise (0.05)	0.82565	Guassian Noise (0.05)	0.75714	Circular shift (100,100)	0.73707
Salt-pepper Noise (0.2)	0.75451	Guassian Noise (0.2)	0.72449	Image Resize	0.99793

Attacks that can be well resisted are shown in Fig. 7:

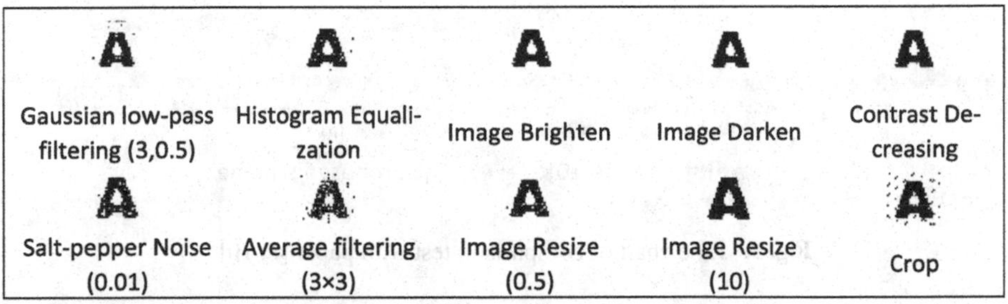

Fig. 7. Various watermarked images after attack and watermarks extracted after attack

As can be seen from Fig. 7, the method of the proposed scheme can effectively resist a variety of attacks. In order to further verify the feasibility of the proposed scheme, some anti-attack capabilities are compared with the data in other papers.

(1) Comparison test with paper [6]

The results of comparison with paper [6] are shown in Fig. 8.

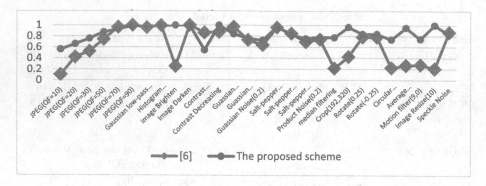

Fig. 8. Line chart of comparison test with paper [6]

Line chart Fig. 7 shows that the proposed algorithm is superior to the paper [6] in most attacks, especially image resize by 0.79141.

(2) Comparison test with paper [8, 10]

The results of comparison with paper [8, 10] are shown in Fig. 9.

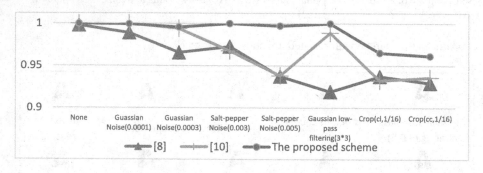

Fig. 9. Line chart of comparison test with paper [8, 10]

Line chart Fig. 9 shows that the proposed algorithm outperforms the paper [8, 10] in guassian noise, salt - pepper noise, Gaussian low - pass filtering, average filtering, and Crop, especially Salt-pepper Noise (0.005).

(3) Comparison test with paper [11]

The results of comparison with paper [11] are shown in Fig. 10.

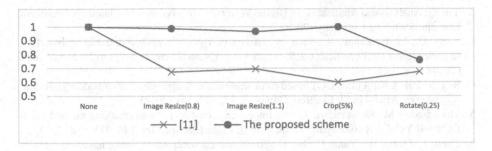

Fig. 10. Line chart of comparison test with paper [11]

Figure 10 shows that the proposed algorithm is superior to [11] in Image resize, Crop, and Rotate, especially Crop (5%).

By comparing with other papers, it is found that this paper has some advantages in watermark robustness.

5   Summary and Outlook

In this paper, the common DCT watermarking scheme was optimized with DWT and ergodic matrix. The scheme has good robustness to common watermark attacks, as well as ensure good invisibility. The host image is decomposed by wavelet and embedded in low frequency region, which makes the watermark scheme easier to recover from common geometric attacks and signal attacks. And the permutation technology based on ergodic matrix is used in embedding and extracting, which improves the security of watermark to some extent. However, there are still some limitations in this paper, for example,

(1) Robust watermark embedding with large capacity has not been realized.
(2) PSNR is lower than some other papers.

From the above point of view, there is still some room for improvement, and we need to do more work to achieve better digital image watermarking technology.

Acknowledgement. The research was supported by Hainan Provincial Natural Science Foundation (Grant No. 117063 and No. 617079), Hainan Provincial Technology Project (Key Research and Development Project, Grant No. ZDYF2017171) and State Key Laboratory of Marine Resource Utilization in South China Sea.

References

1. Parah, S.A., Sheikh, J.A., Loan, N.A., Bhat, G.M.: Robust and blind watermarking technique in DCT domain using inter-block coefficient differencing. Digit. Sig. Process. **53**(C), 11–24 (2016)

2. Yu, Y.: Analysis and Application of Digital Watermarking Technology Based on Transform Domain. Shandong University (2008)
3. Yang, Q., Li, F., Zhang, X., Shen, W.: Adaptive robust reversible data hiding based on modification of DCT coefficient. J. Shanghai Univ. (Natural Science Edition) **20**(5), 605–611 (2014)
4. Roy, S., Pal, A.K.: A blind DCT based color watermarking algorithm for embedding multiple watermarks. AEU – Int. J. Electron. Commun. **72**, 149–161 (2017)
5. Moosazadeh, M., Ekbatanifard, G.: An improved robust image watermarking method using DCT and YCoCg-R color space. Optik – Int. J. Light Electron Opt. **140**, 975–988 (2017)
6. Chen, J., Zhang, W., Yang, H., He, C.: Novel digital watermark scheme based on wavelet transform and neural network. Comput. Sci. **38**(6), 142–144 (2011)
7. Li, X., Zhou, X., Cao, C.: Image DCT domain watermarking technology based on improved genetic algorithm and SVM. Mod. Electron. Tech. **39**(20), 72–77 (2016)
8. Ye, T.: Perfectly blind self-embedding robust quantization-based watermarking scheme in DWT-SVD domain. J. Image Graph. **17**(6), 644–650 (2012)
9. Mishra, A., Agarwal, C., Sharma, A., Bedi, P.: Optimized gray-scale image watermarking using DWT–SVD and Firefly Algorithm. Expert Syst. Appl. Int. J. **41**(17), 7858–7867 (2014)
10. Ren, K., Liang, L., Yu, L.: Robust digital image watermarking in wavelet domain based on SVD and HVS. J. Electron. Measur. Instrum. **31**(6), 869–875 (2017)
11. Zhang, Q., Li, K., Yuan, Z.: Robust digital image watermarking algorithm based on chaos and SVD-DWT. Appl. Res. Comput. **27**(2), 718–720 (2010)
12. Jing, Z.J., Jiang, G.P., Gu, C.S.: A novel public key cryptosystem based on ergodic matrix over GF(2). In: International Conference on Computer Science & Service System, pp. 845–848. IEEE (2012)
13. Zhou, X., Ma, J., Du, W.: SoW: a hybrid DWT-SVD based secured image watermarking. In: International Conference on Sensor Network Security Technology and Privacy Communication System, pp. 197–200. IEEE (2013)
14. Zhou, X., Ma, J., Du, W., Zhao, B., Petridis, M., Zhao, Y.: BMQE system: a MQ equations system based on ergodic matrix, pp. 1–5. IEEE (2010)
15. Zhou, X., Ma, J., Du, W., Zhao, B., Chen, M., Zhao, Y.: Cryptanalysis of the bisectional MQ equations system. In: IEEE International Conference on Computer and Information Technology, pp. 1038–1043. IEEE Computer Society (2010)
16. Song, Y., Zhao, Y.Z.: Research on properties of I-H FEM public key cryptography scheme in the application of digital signature. J. Changchun Normal Univ. (2013)
17. Zhou, X., Ma, J., Du, W., Zhao, Y.: Ergodic matrix and hybrid-key based image cryptosystem. Int. J. Image Graph. Sig. Process. **3**(4) (2011)

Adaptive Robust Reversible Watermarking Scheme

Xiang Wang[✉], Tianze Shu, Min Xie, and Qingqi Pei

State Key Laboratory of Integrated Service Networks, Xidian University,
Xi'an 710071, Shaanxi, China
wangxiang@xidian.edu.cn

Abstract. Digital watermarking technology in the field of information hiding technology has become an important means to protect copyright in network transmission. Robust reversible digital watermarking has been studied for many years as a more adaptive technique for network lossy transmission environment. However, the algorithms proposed by the scholars have not done a good job in balancing the embedded distortion and robustness of the human eye. In this paper, an adaptive robust reversible digital watermarking technique is proposed, which distinguishes the texture complex region and the texture smoothing region by the method of complexity prediction, and selects different parameters to realize the function of embedding more bits in the complex texture region and embedding less bits in the smooth region. In this paper, the algorithm has a high robustness to better resist JPEG compression while there is less distortion of human eye observation. Experimental results show that the proposed scheme has better robustness and higher subjective quality than previous schemes.

Keywords: Robust reversible watermark · Human eye distortion
Complexity prediction · Subjective quality

1 Introduction

Digital watermarking is one of the most widely researched information hiding technologies, and robust reversible digital watermarking is an important part of digital watermarking because of its adaptability to network insecurity, which has been studied by scholars and has been put forward many related algorithms.

Robust reversible digital watermarking is used to embed watermark information in digital media, and to ensure high fidelity of host image. Robust reversible digital watermarking plays an important role in copyright protection and many other functions. Especially in the medical and military fields [1], data-hiding applications are broader.

The research of robust reversible digital watermarking can be divided into different types according to different evaluation criteria, which is usually divided into airspace and frequency domain according to the algorithm. About the spatial algorithm, De Vleeschouwer in [2] proposed a mapping transformation scheme against JPEG compression in 2003, but the salt-pepper noise produced by the mode 256 operation to deal with pixel overflow problem greatly reduces the quality of the watermark carrier.

© Springer Nature Switzerland AG 2018
X. Sun et al. (Eds.): ICCCS 2018, LNCS 11066, pp. 221–230, 2018.
https://doi.org/10.1007/978-3-030-00015-8_19

To resolve the overflow, in [3], Ni *et al.* in the image block in the two sets of pixel difference in the average value as a statistic, divided into different statistics to embed, to prevent overflow while avoiding the salt-pepper noise, but because the image block pixel overlap, error correction code must be used in this scheme. Gao *et al.* [4] and Zeng *et al.* [5] to improve the opinion. Gao *et al.* adopt a scheme to locate overlapping blocks, which are skipped when nested. Zeng *et al.* not only used preprocessing method to mark block type, but also adopted an improved strategy in embedding.

So far, although these schemes are dedicated to solving the robustness and solving the problem of overflow, but in the implementation of robustness and how to ensure that the small distortion, although there are some references to the relevant scheme, but are in the PSNR signal-to-noise ratio and other aspects of the improvement research, Better PSNR performance does not always mean better eye-view fidelity. Therefore, the previous research ignores the characteristics of human eye observation, if it can resist a certain degree of attack, often the image distortion degree is high, embedded image through the human eye can often observe the more obvious difference. If the distortion is small, it is difficult to resist JPEG attacks. While improving robustness, visual quality will also decrease [6], which may affect the continued use of the carrier image and is not conducive to privacy protection. The reason for this is that the watermark algorithm takes the same robust measure for all embedding. In view of the above problems, based on the prediction of the texture complexity of embedded blocks to adopt different parameters embedding, this paper proposes an adaptive robust reversible digital watermarking technology. The experimental results show that under the same robustness, the proposed scheme has lower human eye distortion than the previous scheme.

2 Related Work

In this section, we briefly introduce Zeng *et al.* algorithm, and illustrate some of the inspiration for our solutions. After this, we put forward our own plan based on Zeng *et al.*

2.1 Embedding Method of Zeng *et al*

Zeng *et al.* have proposed a robust reversible digital watermarking algorithm to combat certain degree of non-malicious attacks. This algorithm can still extract the embedded information after the image is compressed by JPEG.

The scheme divides the whole original image into non-overlapping blocks, each of which is composed of $m * n$ pixel values. Each block is divided into two parts, each with a $m * n/2$ number of pixels, called a A set and B set, $A (+)$ set and $B (-)$ sets of the pixel values alternating distribution. M, N is the width of each block. a_i and b_i are pixel values for A set and B set. For each block, the A set is the pixel value of the number of rows and columns that are equal, that is, the pixel of $mod (i, 2) = mod (j, 2)$ is a set. Similarly, the Pixel of $mod (i, 2) \neq mod (j, 2)$ is a set of B.

After the collection is divided in blocks and blocks, Zeng *et al.* algorithms need to compute the arithmetic difference of a block, which is used to distinguish whether the block is for embedding, and the algorithm is as follows:

$$\alpha^{(k)} = \sum_{i=1}^{m} \sum_{j=1}^{n} \left(C^{(k)}(i,j) * \mathrm{M}(i,j) \right) \tag{1}$$

$$M(i,j) = \begin{cases} 1 & \mathrm{mod}(i,2) = \mathrm{mod}(j,2) \\ -1 & \mathrm{mod}(i,2) \neq \mathrm{mod}(j,2) \end{cases} \tag{2}$$

Where, $C^{(k)}(i,j)$ is the value of the I row J column pixel of Block K, $M(i,j)$ is a mask to prevent overflow, make

$$M(i,j) = c * M(i,j). \tag{3}$$

Zeng *et al.* algorithm uses two threshold T and G, the two numbers are positive, all are designed for reasonable use of additional space for watermark embedding.

Next, in the Zeng *et al.* scheme, embedding, if the block α is in the $(-T, T)$ range, is used to embed, otherwise the displacement. And the scheme employs two parameters. b_1 for the translation of the α value of the interval beyond $(-T, T)$, b_2 is the displacement distance when embedding 1, the formula is as follows:

$$b_1 = \left\lceil \frac{(2 * G + T) * 2}{m * n} \right\rceil \tag{4}$$

$$b_2 = \left\lceil \frac{(G + T) * 2}{m * n} \right\rceil \tag{5}$$

The specific translation algorithm is as follows:

$$CB_1^k = \begin{cases} C^{(k)}(i,j) + c * b_1, & \alpha > T \text{ and } \mathrm{mod}\,(i,2) = \mathrm{mod}(j,2) \\ C^{(k)}(i,j) + c * b_1, & \alpha < -T \text{ and } \mathrm{mod}\,(i,2) \neq \mathrm{mod}(j,2) \\ C^{(k)}(i,j), & \text{otherwise} \end{cases} \tag{6}$$

The above operation allows the α to move out of $[T + G, 2T + G]$ and $[-(2T + G), -T-G]$, so that the operation can be embedded in this interval.

After the translation is done, the block for α in the $(-T, T)$ interval can be used for embedding. Embedding 0, the pixel value is unchanged, embedding 1, the pixel value moves b_2's distance, utilizes the space which is vacated after the translation to embed. The embedded formula used is as follows:

$$CB_2^k = \begin{cases} CB_1^k(i,j) + c * b_2, & \alpha \in [0,T] \text{ and } \mathrm{mod}\,(i,2) = \mathrm{mod}(j,2) \\ CB_1^k(i,j) + c * b_2, & \alpha \in [-T,0) \text{ and } \mathrm{mod}\,(i,2) \neq \mathrm{mod}(j,2) \\ CB_1^k(i,j), & \text{otherwise} \end{cases} \tag{7}$$

Because of the above algorithm and parameter setting, the regions embedded 0 and 1 and the 0 and translation regions are separated by interval G, so that the small changes to the host image caused by the non-malicious attack such as JPEG compression do not overlap the 0 regions and 1 regions, so that embedded information can be extracted correctly under such an attack.

3   Proposed Scheme

In this section, we present an adaptive robust reversible digital watermarking algorithm. The algorithm has been improved by the method of block complexity prediction and embedding with different parameters, which improves the robustness, improves the subjective quality and resists some non-malicious attacks such as JPEG.

3.1   Complexity Prediction

The complexity prediction is needed before the watermark is embedded and the embedded image is received, but the prediction method is slightly different. The image is divided into blocks, in this way the entire image is divided. The determination of complexity needs to be predicted by the complexity of the surrounding four blocks. If the predicted result is greater than the field value S, it is judged to be a complex region, or a smooth region if the predicted result is less than the field value S (Fig. 1).

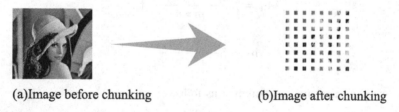

(a)Image before chunking   (b)Image after chunking

Fig. 1.   Image before and after chunking

The complexity prediction selection adopts the left, upper left, upper, upper right, the four blocks to predict. Before the watermark is embedded, all blocks other than the most outer block of the original image should be predicted, so that the predicted block can be predicted by the four blocks around it. After the receiver receives an image embedded in the watermark, the first block in the middle area is predicted, the watermark is extracted and the image is restored which will be a part of the four blocks to the second block, and so on (As shown in the following figure, the *A, B, C, F* block is used to predict *G*, and then the information in *G* is predicted and extracted, finally, *B, C, D, G* are used to predict *H*) (Fig. 2).

Because the extraction process is from scratch, followed from left to right, from top to bottom, each block restored to its original state becomes the next surrounding block to predict. In conjunction with the use of non-embedded blocks in the outer ring, the

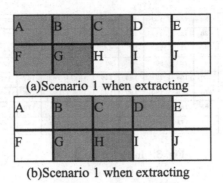

(a)Scenario 1 when extracting

(b)Scenario 1 when extracting

Fig. 2. Extraction steps

prediction of the complexity of each extraction is the same as the block used in the embedding, and the predicted results are consistent with the embedding.

To predict the complexity of each block, use:

$$0.25*\sqrt{\frac{1}{n*m-1}(\sum_{j=1}^{m}\sum_{i=1}^{n}(C\{a-1,b+1\}(i,j)-\overline{C\{a-1,b+1\}})^2+\sum_{j=1}^{m}\sum_{i=1}^{n}(C\{a-1,b\}(i,j)-\overline{C\{a-1,b\}})^2+\sum_{j=1}^{m}\sum_{i=1}^{n}(C\{a-1,b-1\}(i,j)-\overline{C\{a-1,b-1\}})^2+\sum_{j=1}^{m}\sum_{i=1}^{n}(C\{a,b-1\}(i,j)-\overline{C\{a,b-1\}})^2)} \quad (9)$$

to calculate. (where $C\{a, b\}$ is a block of column a and row b, $C\{a, b\}$ (i, j) is the pixel value of the i row j column in the Block, and m, n is the length and width of each block respectively. $\overline{C\{a,b\}}$ Is the average pixel value of the block.)

To illustrate, the calculation method for predicting complexity is to sum the variance of the four blocks around it and extract it then multiply it by 0.25 instead of the variance of the surrounding four blocks and multiply by 0.25. A more radical process is because that the image of the block variance is often very large, from 0 to hundreds of, thousands are possible, it is difficult to set thresholds to distinguish, the root is reduced complexity of the range of values so that set thresholds easy to distinguish texture complex and smooth area.

The method of complexity prediction of this scheme is as follows, taking 4 * 4 block as an example, the 8 * 12 region with the following image is divided into 6 blocks. Predicting E uses A, B, C, D four blocks (Figs. 3 and 4).

The variance of A is 1451.7, B variance is 950.93, C variance is 679.85, D variance is 727.73.

The complexity prediction result of E is $h = 0.25 *$ sqrt $(1451.7 + 950.93 + 679.85 + 727.73) = 15.43$. The field value S is set to 10 because $h > S$, the G of the block should be selected the larger $G_1(G_1 = 128$ and $G_2 = 96)$ as parameters. It means that the texture complexity of the block is higher, and it belongs to the more complex area, which can increase the robustness without causing the large distortion of the human eye, and use a larger embedding strength for the block, so that the spacing between 0 regions and 1 regions of the embedding process is G_1.

168	163	159	154	152	148	146	142	132	131	125	120
134	127	126	115	112	106	100	94	86	83	77	73
90	84	79	71	71	67	66	63	66	71	71	80
68	69	69	72	80	84	91	101	110	117	127	133
110	120	120	128	137	139	149	154	163	167	173	178
165	173	170	176	180	182	182	185	189	188	188	191
184	191	185	187	189	186	184	180	180	179	179	172
177	177	174	171	164	162	154	149	149	142	139	135

Fig. 3. Intercept pixel area

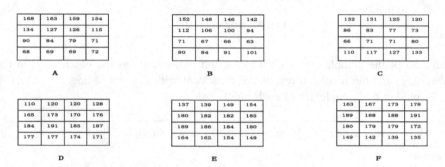

A

B

C

D

E

F

Fig. 4. Area chunking mode

This program fully utilizes the theory that human eye to the complex area of the change feeling is not obvious, but to the smooth region change feeling more obvious characteristics. According to the theory of JND [7], the parameters of embedding intensity are adaptively selected, so that the algorithm can correctly judge the parameters and extract the watermark according to the individual feature of the image to the maximum extent to a certain attack. The advantages of this scheme can be detected according to the SSIM of this kind of human eye observation features, after comparing with the previous scheme, it is proved that the scheme has better robustness under the same capacity and the same SSIM.

In particular, the complexity prediction provides the correct information of the effluent printing by drawing the α distribution of the entire graph from the embedded image, even without complexity prediction, in case of an attack (Fig. 5).

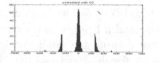   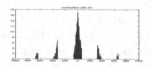

Fig. 5. Embedded with G_1 **Fig. 6.** Embedded with G_2

Take 8 * 8, $T = 64$, $G_1 = 256$, $G_2 = 192$ as an example. Figures 6 and 7 respectively draw the distribution of α of blocks embedded with G_1 and G_2 as parameters, Fig. 8 shows the embedded α distribution of all the blocks in an entire image (which is superimposed on Figs. 6 and 7). As you can see, because the parameters are selected properly, in the α distribution of all the blocks, 0 regions and 1 regions are significantly separated, and according to the judging α histogram, the corresponding block of α in the horizontal coordinate 0 is extracted 0, and the block corresponding to α of [64,384] and [−384, −64] is extracted 1. The α distribution of the block without embedding is also obvious, and the α distribution of the embedded 1 region is separated by a distance, so it can be clearly judged. In practice, it is not necessary to know the exact value of G_1 and G_2, according to the histogram of the horizontal axis of 0 and in the middle of the histogram distribution of the 1 region, you can correctly extract the effluent printing information. Because the selection of G_1 and G_2 makes the histogram of 0 regions, 1 regions, not embedded areas reasonable separation, even if the embedded image has been a certain degree of non-malicious attacks, such as JPEG compression, the region can remain separate state. Therefore, the correct extraction of water printing information.

3.2 Embedding Algorithm

The embedding process is in blocks. Before embedding, you have to compute the α of each block, and the formula is:

$$\alpha = 1/k \sum_{i=1}^{k} (a_i - b_i) \tag{10}$$

$K = m * n/2$, m,n is the width and length of each block. The a_i and b_i are pixel values for A set and B set. For each block, the definition of A set and B set are the same as Zeng et al. Also, calculate two parameters b_1 and b_2, $b_1 = \frac{(2 * G + T) * 2}{m * n} b_2 = \frac{(T + G) * 2}{m * n}$ where T is the threshold that can be used to control the embedded capacity, if T is greater than the α of all blocks, all blocks can be embedded. G is that we have to select one of the G_1 and G_2 according to the parameters of the complexity judgment. According to the above calculation formula, the α of each block in the middle region is calculated and recorded. Then according to the threshold T to determine whether these blocks are embedded. The blocks outside the $(-T, T)$ range are not embedded, should be moved, the move rule adopts (6).

Where c is the type tag of the k block, C (i, j) is the pixel of the block on I row and J column. As a result, there is no α between [T + G, 2 * T + G] and [−2 * T-G, −T-G], which is used to embed 1. After removing the blocks which are not embedded, embedding begins. The embedding rule is that for blocks which α is in $(-T, T)$, embedding bit 0. Embedding 1 is calculated according to the formula of (7).

Fig. 7. The α distribution of the block embedded in the whole picture

Thus, between $[T + G, 2 * T + G]$ and $[-2 * T\text{-}G, -T\text{-}G]$ are the areas that are used to embed bit 1. The extraction end can extract 0 in $(-T, T)$, extract 1 in $[T + G, 2 * T + G]$ and $[-2 * T\text{-}G, -T\text{-}G]$. The interval region between 0 regions and 1 regions is $G(G_1 \text{ or } G_2)$, which is used to increase image robustness. In the complex texture region, because of the low sensitivity of the human eye to the image change of the complex texture region, the larger G_1 is selected and has high robustness. In the texture smoothing area, because of the high sensitivity of the human eye to the region, the smaller G_2 is selected, and the embedding distortion of the image is small.

About the selection rules of T and G, it needs that T or G is integer times *of m*n/2*. If it is not guaranteed, bit 1 can't be embedded in the $[T + G, 2 * T + G]$ and $[-2 * T\text{-}G, -T\text{-}G]$ region, the extraction will produce errors. Because this plan takes the extraction completes to use the front block to continue to predict the following block, if the front block cannot restore the original image, will also appear the chain error, causes the rear to judge the G error, subsequent blocks also will be difficult to correctly extract and restores the original image. The embedding capacity becomes larger with T, the image robustness becomes stronger with G. When G is selected, this scheme will allow 1 regions of the smoothing region to fall between $[T, T + G_1]$ and $[-T\text{-}G_1, T]$, and the moved area of the smoothing region will be between $[2 * T + G, + \infty]$ and $[-\infty, -2 * T\text{-}G]$ so that will not coincide with the 1 region of the complex region.

The presence of G makes the 0 regions and 1 regions not overlap as a result of a malicious attack that undergoes a certain level of JPEG compression, thus causing no difficulty to the extraction end. Of course, JPEG compression cannot be too much. Because of the existence of G, the watermark information is robust.

4   Experimental Results

4.1   Assessment Criteria

We discussed the experimental results of our scheme and Zeng *et al.* scheme from two metrics, PSNR (Peak Signal to Noise Ratio) and SSIM (structural similarity index) [8–10]. The two criteria are used to measure the degree of image distortion. The difference is that the PSNR is based on the error of the corresponding pixel, i.e. the image quality evaluation based on the error sensitivity. Since the visual characteristics of the human eye are not taken into account, so the result of evaluation is inconsistent with the subjective feeling of person, SSIM, which measures the similarity of images from three aspects of brightness, contrast and structure, is a structural similarity index of images based on human eye observation rule.

4.2   Results and Experimental Analysis

In this paper, three-512 * 512 grayscale images are used to experiment. The experimental results were compared with two evaluation indexes of PSNR and SSIM.

The experimental environment selected in this scheme is 2000-bit embedded capacity and JPEG compression factor is 80. This is because if less than 80 of the compression factor, Zeng et al. scheme effect will be greatly reduced, if the compression factor is too high will be difficult to contrast robustness.

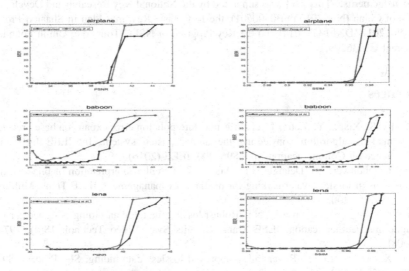

Fig. 8. Experiment contrast diagram (1)

The experimental results show that the algorithm is better than the Zeng *et al.* algorithm under the SSIM and PSNR evaluation criteria, the same embedding distortion, same capacity, same compression rate, especially under the high PSNR and high SSIM performance advantage. The performance of baboon is better, which shows that the algorithm is suitable for the application of complex texture images.

5   Conclusion

A robust reversible digital image watermarking algorithm which accords with human eye observation law is proposed in this paper.

Adaptive robust reversible watermarking scheme mainly by distinguishing the texture complexity of different regions and adopting different intensity embedding methods, so as to reduce the distortion by embedding the small intensity in the texture smoothing region, and to increase the robustness by embedding the large intensity in the complex texture region. Thus, the image has a good balance between robustness and distortion of human eye, which achieves the effect of improving the robustness and improving the subjective quality. Finally, the experimental results in the Zeng et al.

scheme and the comparison between this scheme, in PSNR and SSIM two kinds of measurement standards, the scheme is better than the Zeng et al. scheme. In the case of a non-malicious attack such as JPEG compression has a good robustness, at the same JPEG compression rate, the same capacity and the same distortion, the extraction end has a lower extraction error rate. And after embedding, there is a small distortion of the human eye. The kind of performance characteristic makes this scheme can be used in many areas of high image quality requirements.

Acknowledgements. This work was supported by the National Key Research and Development Program of China (No. 2016YFB0800601), the Key Basic Research Plan in Shaanxi Province (Grant No. 2017ZDXM-GY-014) and the Key Program of NSFC-Tongyong Union Foundation under Grant U1636209.

References

1. Elbadry, S., Xiang, Y., Zong, T., et al.: A new interpolation error expansion based reversible watermarking algorithm considering the human visual system. In: IEEE International Conference on Communications, pp. 896–900. IEEE (2016)
2. De Vleeschouwer, C., Delaigle, J.F., Macq, B.: Circular interpretation of bijective transformations in lossless watermarking for media asset management. IEEE Trans. Multimedia 5(1), 98–105 (2003)
3. Ni, Z., Shi, Y.Q., Ansari, N.: Robust lossless image data hiding designed for semi-fragile imageauthentication. IEEE Trans. Circuits Syst. Video Technol. 18(4), 497–509 (2008)
4. Gao, X., An, L., Li, X.: Reversibility improved lossless data hiding. Sig. Process. 89(10), 2053–2065 (2009)
5. Zeng, X.T., Ping, L.D., Pan, X.Z.: A lossless robust data hiding scheme. Pattern Recogn. 43(4), 1656–1667 (2010)
6. Sheikh, H.R., Bovik, A.C.: Image Information and Visual Quality. IEEE Press (2006)
7. Yang, H., Liu, L., Tang, H., et al.: Relationship of just noticeable difference (JND) in black level and white level with image content. J. Disp. Technol. 10(6), 470–477 (2017)
8. Oriani, E.: QPSNR: A quick PSNR/SSIM analyzer for Linux (2011)
9. Huynh-Thu, Q., Ghanbari, M.: Scope of validity of PSNR in image/video quality assessment. Electron. Lett. 44(13), 800 (2008)
10. Huynh-Thu, Q., Ghanbari, M.: The accuracy of PSNR in predicting video quality for different video scenes and frame rates. Telecommun. Syst. 49(1), 35–48 (2012)

An Improved Reversible Data Hiding Scheme with Large Payload Based on Image Local-Complexity

Fang Cao[1(⊠)], Yalei Zhang[2], Bowen An[1], Heng Yao[2], and Zhenjun Tang[3]

[1] College of Information Engineering, Shanghai Maritime University, Shanghai 200135, China
fangcao@shmtu.edu.cn
[2] School of Optical-Electrical and Computer Engineering, University of Shanghai for Science and Technology, Shanghai 200093, China
[3] Guangxi Key Lab of Multi-Source Information Mining & Security, Guangxi Normal University, Guilin 541004, China

Abstract. In this paper, a reversible data hiding scheme for digital images with high hiding capacity is proposed. Original image is segmented into smooth and rough regions based on local complexity. In order to achieve higher hiding capacity, we embed three bits into each pixel belonging to smooth region with lower local complexity and one bit is embedded into each pixel of rough region, which can effectively exploit more redundancy during data embedding compared with conventional methods of prediction error expansion (PEE). Additionally, the pixel selection mechanism is applied to reduce the number of shifted pixels, which leads to high visual quality of stego image. Experimental results show that, our scheme can achieve better rate-distortion performance than some of state-of-the-art schemes.

Keywords: Reversible data hiding · Prediction error expansion
Hiding capacity · Image quality

1 Introduction

In recent years, reversible data hiding (RDH) has become the research focus in the community of data hiding. RDH scheme in digital images can not only embed additional data into cover image, but also can fully recover the image to its original version after additional data are extracted, which can be widely applied in the fields of image labeling, authentication, and retrieval for the important images such as military and medical images [1].

Current RDH scheme in images can be categorized into three main types: RDH using lossless compression [2], RDH using difference expansion (DE) [3], and RDH using histogram shifting (HS) [4–7]. In the earlier work of RDH [2], the lossless compression technique was adopted to compress the LSB of cover image, and the vacated space can be utilized to embed additional data, which can also realize reversible image recovery by lossless decompression. However, the rate-distortion

© Springer Nature Switzerland AG 2018
X. Sun et al. (Eds.): ICCCS 2018, LNCS 11066, pp. 231–241, 2018.
https://doi.org/10.1007/978-3-030-00015-8_20

performance of this type of scheme was not satisfactory. In the DE-based RDH scheme [3], original image was segmented into a number of pixel pairs, and the difference of each pair was doubled and added with the additional bit to be embedded. Then, the modified difference was re-assigned to the two pixels of each pair. The receiver can easily retrieve additional bits according to the parity of the re-calculated differences of stego pixel pairs. Due to DE operation, some pixels may occur underflow and overflow problems, and location map was required to record the information of the non-used pixels for the reversibility. In the HS-based RDH scheme [4], the histogram bins of original image between the peak point and the zero point were shifted towards the direction of zero point by one, and one vacant histogram bin neighboring to the peak point was established. Then, in order to embed additional bits, the pixel values corresponding to the peak point were either kept unchanged or modified by one. However, the information of peak point and zero point should be transmitted to the receiver side. Additionally, the histograms of some images may not have zero points, thus, zero point should be created through the lowest bin in the histogram and extra information are also needed to be recorded. In order to further improve the performances of embedding rate and stego-image quality for DE-based and HS-based schemes, many studies investigated to introduce the prediction strategy into RDH [8–11]. Rather than directly utilizing original image as cover data, the relative data of original image, i.e., prediction error (PE), was constructed as cover data for embedding, and PE was acquired through the difference between original image and predicted image. Through the operations of DE or HS, PE was manipulated to carry secret bits and added back to predicted image to generate the final stego image.

Thodi and Rodriguez proposed an improvement of DE-based scheme in [9], which adopted prediction error expansion (PEE) for reversible data embedding. This scheme greatly increased the hiding capacity. After that, many researchers have investigated the PEE mechanism and a lot PEE-based schemes have been reported [10, 11]. The conventional PEE schemes can generally embed one secret bit in each available pixel. Obviously, different regions of cover image had different capabilities of data accommodation. Therefore, Li et al. proposed an adaptive PEE scheme based on the pixel selection strategy in [10], which can embed two secret bits per pixel in the smooth regions of cover image where the adjacent pixel values were similar with each other. This scheme can effectively improve the embedding rate. In this work, we claim that there is still improvement room for the embedding rate of Li et al. scheme [10]. In our scheme, we can embed three secret bits per pixel in smooth region, which can lead to greater embedding rate and also satisfactory stego-image quality.

2 Proposed Scheme

The complexity of original image is first calculated according to the relationship between the pixels, and the image is divided into smooth and rough region. Then, the optimal pixel-selection threshold can be acquired to select the embeddable pixels and the shiftable pixels, and the remaining pixels are not modified. The pixels in smooth and rough regions are embedded and shifted, respectively. Different with Li et al. [10], our scheme can adaptively embed three bits per pixel in the smooth region. In our scheme, the gradient-adjusted predictor (GAP) is used for pixel prediction [8], which calculated the changes in the horizontal, vertical, diagonal and anti-diagonal directions, respectively. Then, the current pixel $I_{i,j}$ can be predicted as $I'_{i,j}$ with a high accuracy, and the PE for the current pixel $I_{i,j}$ is: $P_{i,j} = I_{i,j} - I'_{i,j}$.

2.1 Adaptive Embedding Mechanism

Inspired by Li *et al.* scheme [10], we divide original image into smooth region and rough region according to the complexity. The scheme [10] adaptively embedded two bits in the smooth region, while embedded one bit in rough region. In our scheme, we manage to embed more bits in the smooth region compared with [10]. When the number of secret bits required for embedding is not too much, i.e., lower payload, the proposed scheme can achieve a greater embedding rate of each pixel and the number of pixels to be modified during the process of embedding is fewer, which leads to smaller distortion for stego image and a better performance of embedding efficiency.

In order to accurately determine the complexity of image pixels, the forward complexity C_f is calculated, which represents standard deviation of adjacent pixels:

$$C_f = \sqrt{\frac{\left[(I^e - I_f)^2 + (I^{sw} - I_f)^2 + (I^s - I_f)^2 + (I^{se} - I_f)^2\right]}{4}}, \tag{1}$$

where $I_f = (I^e + I^{sw} + I^s + I^{se})/4$. Since we extract the embedded bits and recover the stego image in the reverse order, hence, the value of C_f can be calculated with the pixels that have been recovered. Therefore, the value of C_f in both encoder and decoder are unchanged and used to determine the complexity.

At the beginning of adaptive embedding, the value C_f of each pixel is computed and an image-partition threshold τ_p is defined to divide all pixels into two parts. If C_f is smaller than τ_p, the pixel is classified into smooth region, otherwise rough region. Then, the pixels in both smooth and rough region are conducted with prediction. Finally, we embed three bits into each pixel belonging smooth region and shift its value:

$$I^*_{i,j} = \begin{cases} I_{i,j} + 7P_{i,j} + b, & P_{i,j} \in [-T_1, T_1) \\ I_{i,j} + 7T_1, & P_{i,j} \geq T_1, \\ I_{i,j} - 7T_1, & P_{i,j} < -T_1, \end{cases} \tag{2}$$

where $b \in \{0, 1, 2, 3, 4, 5, 6, 7\}$ denotes the three bits to be embedded currently. T is capacity-parameter, and $T_1 = \lfloor T/7 \rfloor$. In order to improve the visual quality of stego image, T should be taken the minimum within the desired range.

In rough region, we embed one bit into each pixel. If $P_{i,j}$ belongs to $[-T, T)$, the expanded prediction-error $P^k_{i,j}$ can be calculated by $P^k_{i,j} = 2P_{i,j} + b$, where $b \in \{0, 1\}$ denotes 1 bit to be embedded currently. Thus, the embedded pixel can be obtained:

$$I_{i,j}^* = I_{i,j}' + P_{i,j}^k = I_{i,j} - P_{i,j} + P_{i,j}^k = I_{i,j} + P_{i,j} + b. \tag{3}$$

If the prediction error $P_{i,j}$ belongs to the outer region $(-\infty, -T) \cup [T, \infty)$, $P_{i,j}$ is shifted to $P_{i,j}'$ by T. Consequently, the shifted pixel can be obtained:

$$I_{i,j}^* = \begin{cases} I_{i,j} + T, & \text{if } P_{i,j} \geq T, \\ I_{i,j} - T, & \text{if } P_{i,j} < -T. \end{cases} \tag{4}$$

There are two main parameters, i.e., image-partition threshold τ_p and capacity parameter T, in the proposed scheme. The selection of image-partition threshold τ_p is concerned with the selection of smooth region and the efficiency of the adaptive embedding. In the special case, when the threshold τ_p is set as 0, it means there is no smooth region in the whole image, and the adaptive embedding in this case is no different with the traditional PEE. Therefore, we should find the optimal threshold τ_p to achieve the satisfactory rate-distortion performance. On the other hand, the capacity parameter T determines the number of the embedded and shifted pixels.

The value of τ_p can be obtained through the iterations. Figure 1 shows the PSNR values of stego image with respect to different τ_p increasing from 1 to 8 for three standard images sized 512×512, including *Lena* and *Baboon*. Since hiding capacity affects the stego-image quality, thus, we also conducted experiments under different hiding capacities. The optimal threshold τ_p corresponding to the largest PSNR of stego image is marked with a red circle in Fig. 1. We can find that, the largest PSNR of stego image can be achieved when τ_p is set as 1 for most situations.

As for the capacity-parameter T, it can also be exploited through several iterations to seek out the optimal value. Denote the original image as $\mathbf{I} = \{(i, j): 1 \leq i \leq N_1, 1 \leq j \leq N_2\}$, and a sub-image $\mathbf{J} = \{(i, j): 1 \leq i \leq N_{1-2}, 1 \leq j \leq N_{2-2}\}$. Since the pixels at the image border need be used as reference pixels for prediction, thus, the sub-image $\mathbf{J}$ is utilized for data embedding. We predict $\mathbf{J}$ by GAP predictor and compute the prediction error $P_{i,j} = I_{i,j} - I_{i,j}'$ for each pixel with the coordinate $(i, j) \in \mathbf{J}$. Then, for $T \in \{1, ..., 255\}$, the following three sets are constructed:

- Expandable pixels: $E(T) = \{(i,j) \in \mathbf{J} : -T \leq \lfloor P_{i,j} \rfloor < T, \ 0 \leq I_{i,j} + \lfloor P_{i,j} \rfloor \leq 254\}$
- Shiftable pixels: $S(T) = \{(i,j) \in \mathbf{J} : P_{i,j} \geq T, I_{i,j} \leq 255 - T\} \cup \{(i,j) \in \mathbf{J} : P_{i,j} < -T, I_{i,j} \geq T\}$
- Overflow pixels: $O(T) = \mathbf{J} - E(T) - S(T)$

In our scheme, the shiftable pixels and the overflow pixels are not modified and all secret data are embedded into expandable pixels. Besides secret data, the auxiliary information and location map are also required for embedding. The bit numbers of pure secret data, auxiliary information and location map are N_i, N_{ai} and $\lceil \log_2(N_1 \times N_2) \times O(T) \rceil$, respectively. The hiding capacity is denoted as $|E(T)|$. Therefore, the optimal value T^* for the capacity-parameter can be obtained by:

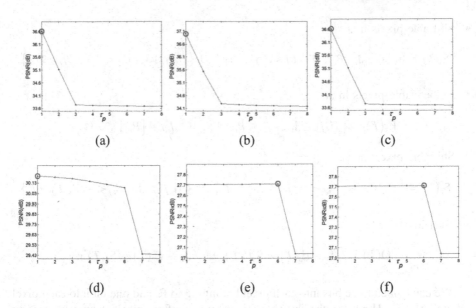

Fig. 1. PSNR of stego images v.s.τ_p under different hiding capacities. The first to the last row corresponds to *Lena* and *Baboon*, respectively. The first to the last column corresponds to hiding capacity of 20000, 40000 and 60000 bits, respectively.

$$T^* = \arg\min_{T}\{\,|E(T)| \geq N_i + N_{ai} + \lceil \log_2(N_1 \times N_2) \times O(T)\rceil\,\}. \tag{5}$$

2.2 Data Embedding

(1) *Image Partition*

The forward complexity C_f is first computed for each pixel by Eq. (1), and then the image **J** is partitioned into smooth region $\mathbf{J}_s$ and rough region $\mathbf{J}_r$ according to C_f of each pixel, where $\mathbf{J}_s = \{\,(i, j) \in \mathbf{J} : C_f < \tau_p\,\}$ and $\mathbf{J}_r = \{\,(i, j) \in \mathbf{J} : C_f \geq \tau_p\,\}$.

(2) *Capacity-Parameter Determination*

After computing the prediction error for each pixel $P_{i,j} = I_{i,j} - I'_{i,j}$, we select the pixels from **J** for embedding and shifting, respectively. Note that the capacity parameter $T \in \{1, 2, ..., 255\}$, and we set $T_1 = \lfloor T/7 \rfloor$ in our scheme.

- Embeddable pixels in $\mathbf{J}_s$:

$$E_s(T) = \{\,(i, j) \in \mathbf{J}_s : -T_1 \leq P_{i,j} < T_1,\ \ 0 \leq I_{i,j} + 7\lfloor P_{i,j}\rfloor \leq 248\,\}.$$

- Shiftable pixels in $\mathbf{J}_s$:

$$S_s(T) = \left\{ (i,j) \in \mathbf{J}_s : P_{i,j} \geq T_1,\ I_{i,j} \leq 255 - 7T_1 \right\} \cup \left\{ (i,j) \in \mathbf{J}_s : P_{i,j} < -T_1,\ I_{i,j} \geq 7T_1 \right\}.$$

- Embeddable pixels in $\mathbf{J}_r$:

$$E_r(T) = \left\{ (i,j) \in \mathbf{J}_r : -T \leq P_{i,j} < T,\ 0 \leq I_{i,j} + \lfloor P_{i,j} \rfloor \leq 254 \right\}.$$

- Shiftable pixels in $\mathbf{J}_r$:

$$S_r(T) = \left\{ (i,j) \in \mathbf{J}_r : P_{i,j} \geq T,\ I_{i,j} \leq 255 - T \right\} \cup \left\{ (i,j) \in \mathbf{J}_r : P_{i,j} < -T,\ I_{i,j} \geq T \right\}.$$

- Overflow pixels:

$$O(T) = \left(\mathbf{J}_s - E_s(T) - S_s(T) \right) \cup \left(\mathbf{J}_r - E_r(T) - S_r(T) \right).$$

We can embed three bits into each pixel belonging to E_s and one bit into each pixel belonging to E_r. However, the shiftable pixels and overflow pixels cannot be used to carry secret data, thus, the total number of the bits that can be embedded is $3|E_s| + |E_r|$, which should include pure secret bits as well as the auxiliary information and the location map. The number of pure secret bits is N_i and the auxiliary information occupies 60 bits. In addition, for the cover images sized 512×512, the location of each pixel requires $\log_2(512 \times 512) = 18$ bits to record, thus, the total number of bits used to record location map is $18|O(T)|$. As a result, the total number of the bits that should be embedded is $N_i + 60 + 18|O(T)|$. Therefore, corresponding to Eq. (5), we need to find an appropriate capacity-parameter threshold T to satisfy:

$$3|E_s| + |E_r| \geq N_i + 60 + 18|O(T)|. \tag{6}$$

For all possible values of T belonging to $\{1, 2, \ldots, 255\}$, we choose the minimum satisfying Eq. (6) as the optimal value of capacity-parameter threshold T^*.

(3) *Pixel-Selection Determination*

For each pixel in the sub-image $\mathbf{J}$, we calculate the forward complexity C_f by Eq. (1) and the backward-complexity C_b by Eq. (7), respectively:

$$C_b = \sqrt{\frac{(I^{nw} - I_b)^2 + (I^n - I_b)^2 + (I^{ne} - I_b)^2 + (I^w - I_b)^2}{4}}, \tag{7}$$

where $I_b = (I^{nw} + I^n + I^{ne} + I^w)/4$. Then, the maximum of C_f, C_b and $|I_f - I_b|$ is obtained:

$$M = \max(C_f,\ C_b,\ |I_f - I_b|). \tag{8}$$

Then, find the smallest pixel-selection threshold τ_m that satisfies the following relationship to set as the optimal pixel-selection threshold τ_m^*:

$$\tau_m^* = \arg\min_{\tau_m}\{\ 3|E_s(T^*,\ \tau_m)| + |E_r(T^*,\ \tau_m)| \geq N_i + 60 + 18|O(T)|\ \},\qquad(9)$$

where $E_s(T^*,\ \tau_m) = \{(i,\ j) \in E_s(T^*):\ M \leq \tau_m\}$ and $E_r(T^*,\ \tau_m) = \{(i,\ j) \in E_r(T^*): M \leq \tau_m\}$.

(4) *Embedding Process*

During the embedding process, the sub-image **J** is traversed in the raster-scanning and conducted with the following steps until all bits are embedded.

Step 1: Calculate backward-complexity C_b^* from each stego pixel and C_f of each original pixel.
Step 2: Select the pixels that satisfy the relationships: $C_f \leq \tau_m^*, C_b^* \leq \tau_m^* + T^*$, and $|I_f - I_f^*| \leq \tau_m^* + T^*$
Step 3: Record and denote the LSB of the first $60 + 18|O(T^*)|$ pixels in **J** as S.
Step 4: Replace the LSB of the first $60 + 18|O(T^*)|$ pixels in **J** with the binary bits for $T^*, \tau_m^*,\ \tau_p,\ |O(T^*)|$ and an end-location flag.
Step 5: In order to embed S and all secret bits, for all pixels satisfying Eq. (9), according to the locations of smooth region or rough region and the types of embeddable pixel or shiftable pixel, we embed one bit $b_1 \in \{0,\ 1\}$ or three bits $b_2 \in \{0, 1, ..., 7\}$ into each pixel, or conduct the shifting operation $(T_1^* = \lfloor T^*/7 \rfloor)$:

$$I_{i,j}^* = \begin{cases} I_{i,j} + \lfloor P_{i,j} \rfloor + b_1, & \text{if } (i,j) \in E_r(t) \cap P_{i,j} \in [-T^*,\ T^*), \\ I_{i,j} + T^*, & \text{if } (i,j) \in S_r(t) \cap P_{i,j} \geq T^*, \\ I_{i,j} - T^*, & \text{if } (i,j) \in S_r(t) \cap P_{i,j} < -T^*, \\ I_{i,j} + 7\lfloor P_{i,j} \rfloor + b_2, & \text{if } (i,j) \in E_s(t) \cap P_{i,j} \in [-T_1^*,\ T_1^*), \qquad(10) \\ I_{i,j} + 7T_1^*, & \text{if } (i,j) \in S_s(t) \cap P_{i,j} \geq T_1^*, \\ I_{i,j} - 7T_1^*, & \text{if } (i,j) \in S_s(t) \cap P_{i,j} < -T_1^*, \\ I_{i,j}, & \text{others.} \end{cases}$$

After finishing the above process, the final stego image can be produced.

2.3   Data Extraction and Image Recovery

On the receiver side, auxiliary information and location map are first retrieved by extracting the LSB of $60 + 18|O(T^*)|$ pixels in **J**. Then, the extracted $60 + 18|O(T^*)|$ bits can be transformed into $T^*, \tau_m^*, \tau_p, |O(T^*)|$ and the end-location flag, respectively. From the end-location flag, traverse the stego image in the reverse order of embedding process, and conduct the following steps until all embedded bits are extracted.

Step 1: Calculate the predicted result $I_{i,j}''$ for each pixel $I_{i,j}^*$ in the stego image and obtain the prediction error $P_{i,j}' = I_{i,j}^* - I_{i,j}''$.
Step 2: Calculate the values of C_f, C_b^* and $|I_f - I_b^*|$ for each stego pixel.

Step 3: For all pixels satisfying Eq. (6) and $(i,j) \notin O(T^*)$, all embedded bits can be extracted through:

$$b = \begin{cases} \left\lfloor P'_{i,j} \right\rfloor - 2 \left\lfloor \frac{P'_{i,j}}{2} \right\rfloor, & \text{if } C_f \geq \tau_p \cap P'_{i,j} \in [-2T^*, \, 2T^*), \\ \left\lfloor P'_{i,j} \right\rfloor - 8 \left\lfloor \frac{P'_{i,j}}{8} \right\rfloor, & \text{if } C_f < \tau_p \cap P'_{i,j} \in [-8T_1^*, \, 8T_1^*), \end{cases} \tag{11}$$

and all original pixel values in **J** can be recovered through:

$$I_{i,j} = \begin{cases} I_{i,j}^* - \left\lfloor P'_{i,j}/2 \right\rfloor - b, & \text{if } C_f \geq \tau_p \cap P'_{i,j} \in [-2T^*, \, 2T^*), \\ I_{i,j}^* - T^*, & \text{if } C_f \geq \tau_p \cap P'_{i,j} \geq 2T^*, \\ I_{i,j}^* + T^*, & \text{if } C_f \geq \tau_p \cap P'_{i,j} < -2T^*, \\ I_{i,j}^* - 7 \left\lfloor P'_{i,j}/8 \right\rfloor - b, & \text{if } C_f < \tau_p \cap P'_{i,j} \in [-8T_1^*, \, 8T_1^*), \\ I_{i,j}^* - 7T_1^*, & \text{if } C_f < \tau_p \cap P'_{i,j} \geq 8T_1^*, \\ I_{i,j}^* + 7T_1^*, & \text{if } C_f < \tau_p \cap P'_{i,j} < -8T_1^*, \\ I_{i,j}^*, & \text{others.} \end{cases} \tag{12}$$

After all embedded bits are extracted, the first extracted $60 + 18|O(T^*)|$ bits, i.e. S, are utilized to replace the LSB of the first $60 + 18|O(T^*)|$ pixels in **J** to produce the final recovered image, and the remaining bits are the secret data.

3 Experimental Results and Comparisons

In order to demonstrate the effectiveness and superiority of our scheme, experiments were carried out on a large number of standard images. Figures 2(a–b) illustrates four original test images, including *Lena* and *Baboon* sized 512×512 used in the following experiments. Figures 2(c–d) list two corresponding stego images that were both embedded with 1×10^5 secret bits. PSNR values of the stego images are 27.52 dB and 25.73 dB, respectively. It can be found that, the visual quality of stego images for the proposed scheme is satisfactory. Also, the stego images can be reversibly recovered as the same with original images.

(a)   (b)

Fig. 2. Original images and stego images.

Because the proposed scheme is an improvement of Li *et al.* scheme [10] for hiding capacity, therefore, we compared our scheme with [10] with respect to hiding capacity under the condition of the same number of the used, embedded pixels from the same smooth region, see Fig. 3. We can found that, the number of embedded secret bits for our scheme grows quickly with the increase of embedded pixels in the smooth region and is significantly greater than that of Li *et al.* scheme [10].

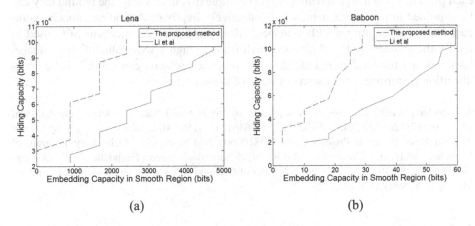

(a)   (b)

Fig. 3. Hiding capacity v.s. the number of embedded pixels in smooth region

In order to demonstrate the superiority of the proposed scheme, we compared our scheme with the two state-of-the-art RDH schemes based on PEE, i.e., Thodi and Rodriguez's scheme [9] and Li *et al.* scheme [10]. Figure 4 shows the ROC curves of PSNR values of stego images with respect to different embedding rates for *Lena*, and *Baboon*. It can be observed that, the proposed scheme can achieve better visual quality of stego image than [9, 10] under the same embedding rate. In other words, our scheme has superior rate-distortion performance compared with [9, 10].

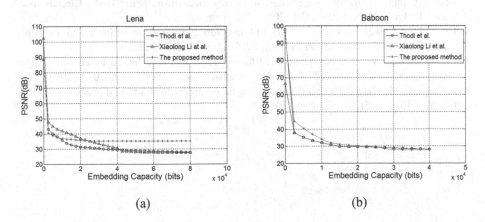

(a)   (b)

Fig. 4. Comparisons of ROC curves between the proposed method and [9, 10]

4 Conclusions

In this paper, we propose a novel, adaptive reversible data hiding scheme with high hiding capacity based on PEE. The original image is first segmented into smooth region and rough region according to local complexity, and one bit is embedded into each pixel of the rough region with high local complexity, and three bits are embedded into each pixel of smooth region with low local complexity. In this way, the redundancy can be exploited to a greater extent, which effectively improves the hiding capacity compared to the conventional PEE schemes. Also, pixel selection mechanism is used to reduce the number of shifted pixels, which leads to high PSNR value of stego image. Experimental results demonstrate that, the proposed scheme can achieve better rate-distortion performance than some of state-of-the-art schemes.

Acknowledgments. This work was supported by the National Natural Science Foundation of China (61171126, 61272452, 61702332, U1636101, 61562007), Ministry of Transport and Applied Basic Research Projects (2014329810060), and Science & Technology Program of Shanghai Maritime University (20130479), Natural Science Foundation of Guangxi (2017GXNSFAA198222), and Research Fund of Guangxi Key Lab of Multi-source Information Mining & Security (MIMS15-03).

References

1. Shi, Y.Q., Li, X., Zhang, X., Wu, H., Ma, B.: Reversible data hiding: advances in the past two decades. IEEE Access **4**, 3210–3237 (2016)
2. Celik, M.U., Sharma, G., Tekalp, A.M., Saber, E.: Lossless generalized-LSB data embedding. IEEE Trans. Image Process. **14**(2), 253–266 (2005)
3. Tian, J.: Reversible data embedding using a difference expansion. IEEE Trans. Circuits Syst. Video Technol. **13**(8), 890–896 (2003)
4. Ni, Z.C., Shi, Y.Q., Ansari, N., Su, W.: Reversible data hiding. IEEE Trans. Circuits Syst. Video Technol. **16**(3), 354–362 (2006)
5. Qin, C., Chang, C.C., Huang, Y.H., Liao, L.T.: An inpainting-assisted reversible steganographic scheme using a histogram shifting mechanism. IEEE Trans. Circuits Syst. Video Technol. **23**(7), 1109–1118 (2013)
6. Li, X., Li, B., Yang, B., Zeng, T.: General framework to histogram-shifting-based reversible data hiding. IEEE Trans. Image Process. **22**(6), 2181–2191 (2013)
7. Li, X., Zhang, W., Gui, X., Yang, B.: Efficient reversible data hiding based on multiple histograms modification. IEEE Trans. Inf. Forensics Secur. **10**(9), 2016–2027 (2015)
8. Fallahpour, M.: Reversible image data hiding based on gradient adjusted prediction. IEICE Electron. Express **5**(20), 870–876 (2008)

9. Thodi, D.M., Rodriguez, J.J.: Expansion embedding techniques for reversible watermarking. IEEE Trans. Image Process. **16**(3), 721–730 (2007)
10. Li, X., Yang, B., Zeng, T.: Efficient reversible watermarking based on adaptive prediction-error expansion and pixel selection. IEEE Trans. Image Process. **20**(12), 3524–3533 (2011)
11. Ou, B., Li, X., Zhao, Y., Ni, R., Shi, Y.Q.: Pairwise prediction-error expansion for efficient reversible data hiding. IEEE Trans. Image Process. **22**(12), 5010–5021 (2013)

An Improved Tamper Detection and Location Scheme for DOCX Format Documents

Guojiang Xin[1][(✉)], Xitong Qi[2], and Changsong Ding[1]

[1] School of Informatics, Hunan University of Chinese Medicine, Changsha 410208, Hunan, China
lovesin_guojiang@126.com
[2] College of Computer Science and Electronic Engineering, Hunan University, Changsha 410082, Hunan, China

Abstract. Content authentication of the text document has become a major concern in the current digital era. In this paper, a tamper locating algorithm for DOCX document content authentication is proposed. Firstly, according to the characteristics of DOCX format, the authentication information unrelated to the text content is embedded into the main setting file named document.xml by displaying characters segmentation. Then, identify the integrity of the text by confirming whether the embedded watermark is same to the authentication watermark. Experiments show that the algorithm is very fragile to any modification and can locate the tampered places very well.

Keywords: Text watermarking · Content authentication · Tamper located DOCX document

1 Introduction

Open Office XML(OOX) [1] is a new format of Office software series (Office2007-2016). DOCX is one of the suffix of the Word 2007 and the later version of the software. Many text documents such as government confidential files and economic contract texts use DOCX format to store and switch. Due to its transparency, operability, it may cause bad influence to the society and even serious political and economic losses, if the government confidential files and economic contract texts had been tampered. To avoid these cases, whether the integrity of the text content authentication is modified should be identified.

Many good approaches for content authentication are proposed, such as the fragile, semi-fragile watermarking and zero-watermarking. At present, the text authentication watermarking is divided into two categories. One is the text image authentication watermarking, which is mainly used in pixel variation method. The other is the normal text authentication watermarking, which mainly embeds watermarking through modifying text format, such as text font color [2], text font underline [3], RTF control field [4], and so on. Yang [5] proposed a text image authentication algorithm based on a large number of the adjacent pixels. For text image's uniform areas (all black or all white areas), Li [6] put forward a authentication method based on hierarchical structure, which embedded and extracted watermarking information through hierarchical. Jalil

X. Sun et al. (Eds.): ICCCS 2018, LNCS 11066, pp. 242–251, 2018.
https://doi.org/10.1007/978-3-030-00015-8_21

[7, 8] proposed two text zero-watermarking algorithms by partitioning text with preposition and extracting a feature in each partition. Karu [9] proposed a zero-watermarking method based on multiple occurrences of letters for text tampering detection. For Chinese text, many authentication watermarking methods based Chinese characteristics are proposed, such as Chinese characters' pinyin and tone [10], Chinese characters' radical [11] and Chinese characters' color [12].

The existing text fragile watermarking algorithms are mainly used in DOC and PDF format. The authentication methods for DOCX format are less. According to the characteristics of the DOCX format, a new watermarking method for the Chinese text content is proposed, which embeds the watermarking information to the text doing nothing with the text.

The remainder of this paper is organized as below: Sect. 2 introduces the related knowledge and technology. The proposed watermarking algorithm is described in Sect. 3. The experimental results are shown in Sect. 4. Section 5 presents the conclusion.

2   Related Work

2.1   The Basic Structure of DOCX Document

Word 2007 and the later versions are used the OOX file format, which is different from Word 2003. An OOX file is composed by many compression components, and these compression components are stored in a compressed package. The package is a normal ZIP file and it includes "pack content type", "relationship" and each "parts". Items and components can be seen as a ZIP file. Each package contains a "ZIP parts relationship", which contains all parts of the relationship among information inside the document. This structured information will be encoded as XML format and compressed. Therefore, compared with composite structure, OOX occupy less storage space.

2.2   Main Setting File

The file "document.xml" is the main setting file of Word 2007. Almost all of the displayed characters in the DOCX file are included in the main setting files. The complete code of the main setting file is as follow. "XML version" represents the XML version number, where "encoding" is the XML encoding and "standalone" means the XML is dependent or independent on external dtd file. w:document is the document element, which allows w:body to store the tag of the document text. Generally, the display character in a document is defined by three elements: the paragraph element (w: p), the run element (w:r) and the text element(w:t). The specification of OOX format stipulates that a w:p represents a paragraph, and a paragraph may contain a number of different w:r element. w:r element is able to define the format attribute of the lowest levels of elements. It also contains a number of w:t elements. w:t element is used to define the specific display character and store the print characters (such as a newline character or line breaks). As explained above, the string "this is a document of Word 2007" is the display character defined by w:t.

2.3 Text Segmentation

Text segmentation [13] is based on the properties that each paragraph elements (w:p) of the main setting file can contain multiple elements of the run (w:r). The original run element of a paragraph can be split into multiple run elements. The original text element (w:t) and a display character in the run element are also divided into many text elements and show characters. A new run element contains after segmentation a new text element and a new display character. After segmenting the master setting file "document.xml" in 2.2, the result is as follows:

```
<?xml version="1.0" encoding="utf-8" standalone="yes"?>
<w:documentxmlns:ve="http://schemas.openxmlformats.org/markup-compatibility/2006"
>
    <w:body>
    <w:p>

        <w:r>
                <w:t>这是一篇</w:t>
    </w:r>
    <w:r>
                <w:t> Word 2007</w:t>
    </w:r>
    <w:r>
                <w:t>文档</w:t>
        </w:r>
    </w:p>
    </w:body>
</w:document>
```

The format of the display character attribute information (font, color and size) are defined by the child nodes of w:p and w:r, which are defined by w:pPr and w:rPr. As long as the display character after segmentation is as same as before, the result of the text after segmentation is as same as before. In order to prevent two or more adjacent elements with the same properties being merged automatically by office programs, it needs to insert robust tag interval in the run element: <w:rPr> <w:rFontsw hint = "eastAsia"/> </w:rPr> .

3 Proposed Watermarking Algorithm

The algorithm idea: firstly, authentication watermark is embedded into the main document in the form of the space. Because Space tags are not added, thus these spaces will not be shown in the text. Then, display characters of the text can be divided into N pieces according to the length of the watermark information (fill the end of the paragraph with the space if the character is insufficient). In order to achieve the tamper localization of the text, each block is embedded with authentication watermark by the method of text segmentation. In order to make the adjacent elements with the same attributes not to be automatically merged, robust tag is inserted into the run element alternately. In the receiving side, whether the text was tampered is determined by matching the extracted watermark information from each block with the authentication watermark information.

3.1 Embedding Strategy

The number of display characters in each text element represents the embedded watermark. The difference of it represents different watermark information according to different requirements. If the embedded watermark information is "0101", "1" can be represented by choosing one display character and "0" can be represented by choosing two display characters, and "0101" can be completely embedded through four times segmentation; Also, "00" can be represented by choosing one display character and "01" can be represented by choosing two display characters, and "0101" can be completely embedded through only two times segmentation; Of course, "0000" can be represented by choosing one display character, and "1111" can be represented by choosing sixteen display characters, at this point, "0101" can be completely embedded through only one times segmentation. In order to achieve the precision tamper local-ization of the text, the embedding strategy adopted in this chapter is: "1" is represented by one display character, and "0" is represented by two display characters.

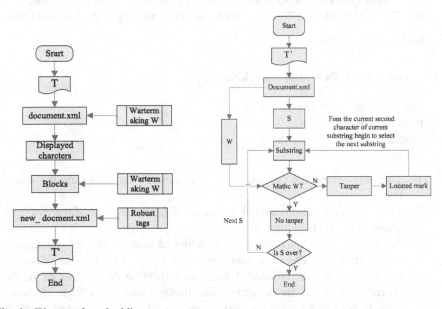

Fig. 1. Watermark embedding process   **Fig. 2.** Watermark detection process

3.2   Watermark Embedding Algorithm

The algorithm is shown in Fig. 1.
Input: the original text T, the watermark information W;
Output: the watermark text T'.
Begin:

(1) Unzip the original text T and get the main setting file document.xml;
(2) The watermark information W is embedded by adding spaces before the display character in the main setting file, if the watermark information is "0", two spaces are inserted; if the watermark bits is "1", one space is inserted; and robust tags are inserted alternately;
(3) The length of W is calculated according to the digits of W; because the embedding strategy adopted in this chapter is:"1" is represented by one display character, and "0" is represented by two display characters, if the number of "0" in W is a and the number of "1" is b, the length of W is $(2 * a + b)$; The display characters in the text can be divided into N small pieces according to the length of W, and the length of each small piece is equal to the length of W;
(4) W is embedded into each small piece by the text segmentation method and the new document new_document.xml is achieved;
(5) Robust tags are inserted into the run element of new_document.xml;
(6) The watermark text T' is achieved after compressing new_document.xml.

End

3.3   Watermark Detection Algorithm

The algorithm is shown in Fig. 2.
Input: the watermark text T';
Output: the detection result.
Begin

(1) The main setting file document.xml is achieved after unzipping the watermark text T'.
(2) The watermark information W is extracted from the front of the display characters in the main setting file;
(3) The number of display characters is achieved from all the text elements of the main setting file. The embedded watermark is "1" if the number of the display character is "1"; the embedded watermark is "0" if the number of the display character is "2"; if the number of the display character is other, it shows that there is not embedded watermark. Concatenate all the extracted characters to form a string S;
(4) Select the sub string "sub" sequentially from the string S equal to the length of W to match;
(5) If "sub" and W match exactly, it shows that the cascade in the full text has not been tampered and then choose the next substring until S is processed completely;

(6) If "sub" and W don't match exactly, it shows that this block of text is tampered, and the tampered place is tagged by adding color and the underline. Then select the next substring from the second character of this substring until S is processed completely.

End.

4   Experiment Result

The experiment is carried out with eclipse and XML parsing technology. 50 variable size text documents are used in our experiment. Generally, the performances of digital watermarking algorithm include imperceptibility, capacity, robustness and fragility. Here we analyze the imperceptibility and fragility to verify the effectiveness of the proposed algorithm.

Fig. 3. Watermarking imperceptibility

4.1 Imperceptibility

The proposed algorithm just embeds the run elements and the text elements into the main setting file, while not embeds any display characters into the original text. So, there is no influence on original text in visual and sense, and has good imperceptibility. As shown in the Fig. 3, the left is to embed watermarking to the main setting file while the right is the text shown on Word 2007. The text does not change in visual after embedding the watermarking "0100101".

The original text size is 20 kb. After embedding watermarking, the main setting file size will increase but the text size is reduced to 18 kb. The reason is that the DOCX format is made up of a series compressed parts and uses a zip compression technology. Text segmentation will produce much run elements which have a high degree of similarity so that the main setting file has great compression space, it will make watermarking text smaller than the original text after compression.

4.2 Fragility

The experiment is mainly compared with the methods in Refs [11, 12]. The method in [11] proposes a semi-fragile text watermarking scheme for content authentication of Chinese text documents, the watermarking bits are embedded by setting underlines to Chinese characters which are the embedding candidates and hiding the underlines simultaneously. The method in [12] is to embed watermarking into the fourth lowest bits of text's RGB color.

Table 1. Attack of Format

Algorithm	Attack mode				
	Font adjustment	Space addition or deletion	Punctuation changes	Paragraph adjustment	Format conversion
The proposed method	Y	Y	Y	Y	N
The method [11]	N	Y	Y	Y	N
The method [12]	N	N	N	Y	N

Format Attacks. When editing a text, format adjustments (such as space deletion, font color changing, and paragraph adjustment) are inevitable, and sometimes fully converting the text format is possible. Table 1 shows the experimental results of the format attacks, "Y" presents correct authentication while "N" means fault authentication.

As the proposed algorithm, the methods in [11, 12] are based on text format, so the watermark will lose if the format is fully converted. The two methods [11, 12] cannot detect and authentication text. Paragraph adjustment will break the watermark information, and all three algorithms can detect the tampered text. The watermark is embedded into the text's underline in the method [11], so the watermark will lose if the underline is cleared. The method [12] is to embed the watermark into the text's color, so the watermark will lose if the color is cleared. Thus, the two methods cannot identify whether the text is tampered. However, changing the font attributes has no effect on the proposed algorithm. The hash value of the text content will be changed with the pronunciations change, space inserting and space deletion. It will break the watermark of the method in [11] and can detect whether the text is tampered. The proposed algorithm can also detect whether the text is tampered because pronunciations and spaces are the display characters, which will decrease when insert or delete them. The results are shown in Table 1.

Content Attacks. The content attacks include synonym substitution and syntactic transformation. Random inserting and deleting attacks are one kind of common attacks. The main setting file which has been embedded watermark contains a property named <w:lang w:eastAsia = "zh-CN"/>. It's a property which proves the text is tampered. The methods in [11, 12] can also correctly detect whether the text is tampered because the hash value of the content has been changed with the synonym substitution and syntactic transformation. Random inserting and deleting attacks have influence on the length of the display character, even insert or delete one word can break the watermark. Thus, the algorithm is very fragile and sensitive to inserting and deleting attacks. Experiments show that the algorithm is very fragile to any modification and locate the tampered places.

4.3 Tamper Located and Extent of Tampered Calculation

Most text authentication watermarking has no standard measure, especially for a text deleted with a large number of sentences or paragraphs. In our algorithm, a calculation method for extent tampered is put forward. Let N be the total number of the embedded authentication watermark, Nr is the total number of extracted correct authentication watermark, then $N-Nr$ is the number of tampered or removed watermark, $(N-Nr)/N$ is the tamper rate.

Unlike the image which can locate the tampered places and recover them according to the prediction of surrounding pixels, text does not have the direct relation. Because the text is based on Unicode encoding, it is very hard to recover the deleted text.

(1) Punctuation changes. The comma in "后来大半忘却了,"is changed to semicolon;
(2) Synonym substitution. The "寂寞" in "有时也不免使人寂寞" is changed to "孤寂";
(3) Words deletion. The "曾经常常—" in "曾经常常,一几乎是每天"is deleted;
(4) Syntactic transformation. The "质铺的是比我高一倍"is changed to "铺的是矮一倍";
(5) Space addition or remove. A space is added before "因为开方的医生";
(6) Paragraph deletion. The penultimate paragraph is deleted;

In the experiment, the embedded watermark information is "0100101", and the embedded policy is that two characters represent "0", one character represents "1", and thus, the watermark information needs 11 display characters, which means 11 display characters is one block. When there is a tamper, each block will be marked. The embedded watermark information number is 123, that is, all the display characters of the text are divided into 123 blocks. After being tampered, the correct watermark information is extracted is 83, so the number of the tampered watermark is 40, the tamper rate is 32.5%. 7 blocks are marked (Punctuation change, Synonym substitution, Syntactic transformation, Space addition or remove only involve one block), which make the watermark information in the block to be changed. For example, when the comma is changed to semicolon, the extracted watermark is "11100101"; "寂寞" is substituted with "孤寂", the extracted watermark is "1000101"; if a space is added, the extracted watermark is "111100101". Since the extracted watermark does not match the embedded watermark, it can be judged that these blocks are tampered and can be marked; similarly, because the deleted words belong to two blocks, the watermarks in the two blocks are broken, the two blocks are tampered and be marked. Although it cannot mark the deleted paragraph, some display characters in the end of the paragraph before the deleted paragraph and some display characters in the beginning of the paragraph after the deleted paragraph will be marked. In other words, 33 blocks (363 characters) are deleted. From the mark of the end of penultimate paragraph and the start of last paragraph, we can conclude that some content between them are deleted.

5   Conclusion

In this paper, we propose a watermark scheme based on DOCX text document. The authentication information unrelated to the text content is embedded into the main setting file which is named document.xml by display characters segmentation. Identifying the integrity of the text content needs detect whether the embedded watermark is same to the authentication watermark. Besides, an extent of tampered calculation is proposed. Experiment results show that the algorithm can always detect tampered places when the text is modified and can locate the tampered places.

Acknowledgement. This paper is partially supported by Hunan Natural Science Foundation (2018JJ2301), the National Key Research and Development Program of China (2017YFC1703306), Doctoral Research Start-up Fund of Hunan University of Chinese Medicine (Human vision mechanism and its application in image fusion).

References

1. Frank, R.: Introducing the office (2007) open xml file formats. http://msdn2.microsoft.com/en-us/library/aa338205.aspx. Accessed 28 April 2018
2. Xiao, H.Q., Liu, G.S., Yin, M.L.: A new text content authentication technique based on CRC. J. Harbin Univ. Commer. (Natural Sciences Edition) (Chinese), **22**(4), 84–87 (2006)
3. Fang, W.Sh., Shu, M.L.: Fragile text watermarking based on changing the characters' underlining. Comput. Appl. Softw. (Chinese) **25**(11), 271–273 (2008)
4. Zou, X.G., Sun, Sh.H.: Fragile watermark algorithm in RTF format text. Comput. Eng. (Chinese) **33**(4), 131–133 (2007)
5. Yang, H.J., Kot, A.C.: Data hiding for binary images authentication by considering a larger neighborhood. In: Proceedings of IEEE International Conference on Circuits and Systems, pp. 1269–1272, New Orleans (2007)

6. Li, Zh.H., Hou, J.J., Song, W.: Binary document image authentication watermarking technique based on hierarchical structure. Acta Automatica Sinica (Chinese) **34**(8), 841–848 (2008)
7. Zunera, J., Anwar, M., Jabeen, H.: Word length based zero-watermarking algorithm for tamper detection in text documents. In: Proceedings of International Conference on Computer Engineering and Technology, pp. 378–382, Chengdu (2010)
8. Zunera, J., Anwar, M., Maria, S.: Content based zero-watermarking algorithm for authentication of text documents. Int. J. Comput. Sci. Inf. Secur. **7**(2), 212–217 (2010)
9. Kaur, S., Babbarr, G.: A zero-watermarking algorithm on multiple occurrences of letters for text tampering detection. Int. J. Comput. Sci. Eng. **5**(5), 294–301 (2013)
10. Zhao, L., Cui, D.W.: Text watermark algorithm based on tone of Chinese characters. Comput. Eng. **35**(10), 142–144 (2009)
11. Zhou, X.M., Wang, S.C., Zhao, W.D., et al.: A semi-fragile watermarking scheme for content authentication of Chinese text documents. In: Proceedings of 2nd IEEE International Conference on Computer Science and Information Technology, pp. 439–443, Beijing (2009)
12. Liang, H.Y., Cao, Y.: Text watermark algorithm based on color and font. Jo. South China Normal Univ. (Natural Science Edition), 87–90 (2011)
13. Fu, Z.J., Sun, X.M., Liu, Y.L.: Text split-based steganography in OOXML format documents for covert communication. Secur. Commun. Netw. **5**(9), 957–968 (2012)

An Information Hiding Algorithm for HEVC Videos Based on PU Partitioning Modes

Wen-chao Xie[1], Yi-yuan Yang[2], Zhao-hong Li[1(✉)], Jin-wei Wang[3], and Min Zhang[4]

[1] School of Electronic and Information Engineering,
Beijing Jiaotong University, Beijing 100044, China
zhhli2@bjtu.edu.cn
[2] School of Computer Science and Engineering, Beihang University,
Beijing 100083, China
[3] College of Computer and Software, Nanjing University of Information Science
and Technology, Nanjing 210044, China
[4] China Telecom, Beijing, China

Abstract. Video information hiding has attracted increasing attention in the field of information security. In the literature, great quantities of information hiding algorithms based on DCT and intra prediction mode have been proposed for the latest video coding standard - High Efficiency Video Coding (HEVC). However, few algorithms are reported to hide information in the inter prediction mode, one of the unique advantages of HEVC. This paper proposes an information hiding algorithm based on PU partitioning mode in P-frames, which realizes the embedding of hidden information without affecting the video quality. The PU partitioning mode selected by HEVC based on the optimum CU structure is recorded in the first round calculation and adopted as the reference for the modification process. PU partitioning modes are altered to embed hidden information. Since only the PU partitioning modes of P-frames is modified, the proposed algorithm can be combined with existing DCT-based or intra-prediction-based algorithms to greatly increase the embedding capacity while keeping the quality of the video sequence not being affected.

Keywords: Video data hiding · HEVC · PU partitioning modes

1 Introduction

Digital video, especially high-definition (HD) digital video, has gained a lot of applications in social life. However, coming with it, information security problems are popping up, such as the copyright protection, license authentication, and tamper-proof of HD video. To solve the problem, Information hiding, or data hiding are receiving more and more attention because they can achieve identity authentication, as well as copyright protection and piracy tracking of digital media. Therefore, it is of great importance to embed hidden information in digital videos.

HEVC is a new-generation encoding standard for HD video. Since its announcement, hiding information in HEVC video has attracted more and more attention in the

X. Sun et al. (Eds.): ICCCS 2018, LNCS 11066, pp. 252–264, 2018.
https://doi.org/10.1007/978-3-030-00015-8_22

field of information security. For the previous video coding standard, it is a common used method to embed hidden information by modifying the DCT coefficients. However, the modification of DCT coefficients would decrease the visual quality of the video and cause distortion. Because of the design of reference blocks, even tiny modification can be accumulated and cause serious reduction of the visual quality, which is called distortion drift. To solve the problem, Po-Chun Chang et al. firstly proposed a traditional DCT/DST-based information hiding algorithm for HEVC videos by selecting a specific embedded position [1, 2]. Although the modification of DCT coefficients can achieve large-capacity information embedding, the video quality still decreased even if the distortion was corrected or compensated. Therefore, an information embedding algorithm that does not destroy video visual quality needs to be put forward.

In addition to porting traditional information hiding algorithms to HEVC video, the unique features of HEVC video such as intra prediction have also received attention. In I-frames, HEVC reduces redundant information through 35 different intra prediction modes. Wang et al. proposed a series of information hiding algorithms for HEVC videos by modifying the intra prediction mode with different strategy [3–8]. Although the embedded capacity of these algorithms is not as good as the transform domain embedding algorithm, there is a great improvement in reducing the impact on the video quality. The information hiding algorithm based on the intra prediction mode has provided a new direction for the research of the new embedding algorithm.

Apart from intra prediction, the inter prediction of the HEVC is also very innovative, but attracted little attention. At present, only Li et al. proposed an information hiding algorithm based on motion vector space coding [9], which achieves the purpose of embedding hidden information by modifying inter prediction motion vectors in HEVC P-frames. In fact, similar to the design strategy of intra prediction mode, HEVC also sets different modes for inter prediction.

The information hiding algorithm proposed in this paper is to realize the embedding of hidden information by modifying the PU partition modes of HEVC video P-frames. Experimental results show that the algorithm proposed in this paper has very little impact on video quality when embedding hidden information. And unlike Chang's method at [2], the PSNR difference between the embedded video and the original video of the proposed algorithm remains small when the bitrate increase. Although compared with DCT and intra-frame-based information hiding algorithms, the embedded capacity is slightly insufficient, the algorithm in this paper only needs to control the PU partition mode of P-frames and does not depend on the intra prediction mode and the DCT coefficients. Therefore, the algorithm proposed in this paper can be used as a supplement to other embedding algorithms to greatly increase the embedded capacity without destroying the video quality.

The rest parts of this paper are organized in the following order. In the second section, we explain how to choose the best CU structure and PU partition mode in HEVC. And then the information hiding algorithm based on PU partitioning mode will be proposed in the third section, and the specific steps of the algorithm implementation is also introduced. The fourth section will show the experimental results. The fifth section is the summary.

2   PU Partitioning Modes in HEVC

2.1   Block Structures and Prediction Units in HEVC

In order to reduce the redundancy in the video to a greater extent, HEVC introduces a very flexible quadtree structure. When performing motion prediction on a moving object, the CTU needs to be divided into smaller blocks as much as possible according to the shape of the object. If a CTU is divided, it must be divided into 4 CUs which are half the size of the CTU at one time; if it is still necessary to continue splitting, then one CU can be divided into 4 smaller CUs. However, the smallest CU size is 8 × 8 pixels, the largest CU is with the same size of the CTU, which is 64 × 64 pixels by default (Fig. 1).

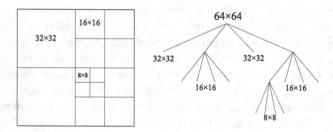

Fig. 1. Example for the partitioning of a 64 × 64 CTU into CUs of different sizes. The partitioning can be described by a quadtree, as shown on the *right*.

There are two kinds of prediction modes in HEVC, known as intra prediction and inter prediction. For intra prediction which mainly appeared in I-frames, there are only two kinds of PU partitioning modes. The entire CU will be coded as a single PU, referred to as $2N \times 2N$ mode, or split into four equal-sized square PUs, known as $N \times N$ mode. When it comes to inter prediction, there are eight different modes supported by HEVC for partitioning a CU into PUs. The first two modes are the same as $2N \times 2N$ and $N \times N$ mentioned above. Since the splitting of a CU into four PUs is conceptually equivalent to splitting the corresponding CU into four half-sized CUs and coding each of these CUs as a single PU, the $N \times N$ mode is only supported for the minimum CU size, which is 8 × 8 pixels by default. For splitting a CU into two PUs, there are another six partitioning modes in HEVC. A CU subdivided vertically or horizontally into two rectangular PUs of the same size is referred to $2N \times N$ mode or $N \times 2N$ mode. In additional to these symmetric partitioning modes, there are four asymmetric partitioning modes supported in HEVC, which subdivide the CU into two rectangular PUs of different sizes, as is illustrated in the bottom row of Fig. 2.

The smaller the PU was subdivided, the more accurate the prediction of the motion of the object in the image would be. But the cost of improving the visual quality is to sacrifice the transmission bandwidth and storage space. For a 16 × 16 or greater CU, the partitioning mode of PU can be selected from any of the eight modes. HEVC will select the most suitable one of subdivision for prediction based on the residuals and distortion costs generated by different types of division. For an 8 × 8 CU, to reduce the

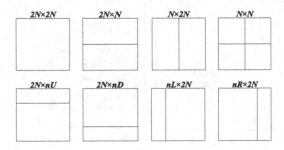

Fig. 2. Supported partitioning modes for splitting a CU into PUs.

complexity of the algorithm, it is only allowed to be divided into $2\,N \times 2\,N, N \times 2\,N$, $2\,N \times N$ and $N \times N$ modes. Employing different PU partitioning modes in P frame is an important innovation and pivotal technology of HEVC, and it also provides a new direction for the information hiding algorithm of this paper.

2.2 Best Mode Selection in HEVC

In order to hide binary bits through altering PU partition modes, it must be clear that how PU partitioning mode of HEVC is selected. Since the PU partitioning modes is based on the CU structure, it is necessary to show how the optimal structure of the CU is determined.

Through the study of the HEVC program, it can be certain that HEVC will encode one frame by cyclically calling the compression function of a single CTU. Repeat that process one frame by one frame, and finally the entire video will be compressed properly. In the CTU compression function, the most suitable quadtree partition structure is required first. For each CTU, HEVC will calculate the depth according to 4 layers. The largest 64×64 CU of which the division depth is 0 has a maximum of one CU. Followed by 32×32 CU, the division depth is 1, up to four CUs. Similarly, the 16×16 and 8×8 CUs are depth 2 and depth 3, and the maximum number of CUs is 16 and 64 respectively. HEVC will perform calculations on all 85 CUs with different PU partitioning modes of four depths. The optimal CTU quadtree structure is determined by the following procedure:

Step1. Divide the entire CTU into one CU and select the best PU partitioning mode. Mark this CU as CU NO.0, and the division depth is 0, as is shown on the *left* of Fig. 3

Step2. Split the CTU into four 32×32 CUs, with the Z-scan order, take the first CU which is marked as CU NO.1, and select the best PU partitioning mode. Since the CU was divided once, the division depth will be 1 (Fig. 4).

Step3. Split the CU selected in the previous step into four 16×16 CUs. According to Z-scan order, take the first CU marked as CU NO.2 with depth 2 to select a suitable PU partitioning mode.

Step4. The CU NO.2 is divided into four 8×8 CUs. These CUs will be marked as CU NO. 3, 4, 5 and 6 by Z-scan order. For each of the 8×8 CUs, the best PU partitioning mode is selected. Given that the smallest CU size is 8×8, the splitting won't continue. Since both CU NO.2 and CU NO.3 to 6 have selected the best mode,

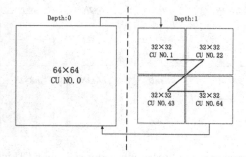

Fig. 3. Splitting depth and Z-scan order in HEVC. The number of CU indicate the coding order during the procedure.

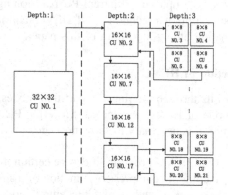

Fig. 4. The flow diagram to determine the best CU structure of a 32 × 32 CU. The example CU was selected in Step2.

HEVC will choose the best structure for this 16 × 16 CU. By comparing the *RDcost* of a single 16 × 16 CU with a combination of four 8 × 8 CUs, HEVC will decide whether compress a larger CU or compress four smaller CUs as the best CU structure.

Step5. For the rest three 16 × 16 CUs in Step3, the same process in Step4 will be performed. During the process, these CUs will be marked as CU NO.7, 12 and 17. After all four 16 × 16 CUs divided in Step3 were split properly, HEVC will compare CU NO. 1 with the combination of CU NO. 2, 7, 12 and 17, the better structure with lower *RDcost* will be selected as the structure of CU NO. 1.

Step6. Follow the same strategy to determine the best CU structure of the remaining three 32 × 32 CUs. Finally, compare the *RDcost* of CU NO.0 with the combination of four 32 × 32 CUs, the optimal CTU quadtree structure can be determined.

When determining the best CU structure, HEVC use a recursive function for 85 times to calculate all possible conditions in a single CTU, and the structure with lowest *RDcost* is ultimately reserved. In each calculation of CU, the best PU partitioning mode will be determined by the same approach. Starting from the $2N \times 2N$ mode, including intra prediction mode, merge and skip modes, then entering inter prediction mode. The cost of two symmetric partitioning modes is calculated separately at first, followed by four asymmetric partitioning modes for 16 × 16 and above CUs. By default, HEVC compares all possible PU partitioning modes, and select the optimal one for the corresponding CU. Nevertheless, in some occasions, it is necessary to accelerate the compression process, so it is optional to set the HEVC to use certain PU partitioning modes. The algorithm proposed in this paper requires all PU partitioning modes to be set by default setting of HEVC.

3   The Proposed Method

3.1   PU Partitioning Mode Analyze

The relationship between the determination of the CU structure and the PU partitioning modes in HEVC has been described above. The algorithm proposed in this paper only needs to modify the PU partitioning mode, but changing from the optimal mode to other modes may not only increase the cost, but also change the structure of the CU, and result in the invalidation of the modification. Therefore, different PU models need to be analyzed to minimize the increase in cost.

The establishment of multiple PU partition modes in HEVC aims to reduce the residual in inter prediction. For a stationary object in the video, the residual of the inter-frame prediction is approximately equal to zero. Both the CU structure and the PU partition will select a mode that is as simple as possible. For moving objects, there is often a large residual at the boundary. If a smaller CU is used, although the residual can be reduced, the penalty is to sacrifice more storage space and transmission bandwidth. In order to reduce the residual bandwidth while reducing the sacrifice, HEVC uses a quadtree CU partition structure to make the non-boundary CU as large as possible, and the boundary part of the CU as small as possible. On the other hand, in the boundary part, different PU modes are divided by HEVC to further fit the edges of the moving object.

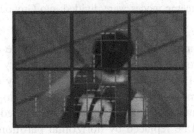

Fig. 5. Example of different CU structures and PU partitioning modes in HEVC video. The blue bold line in the figure represents the boundary of CTU, the red line is the boundary line of CU, and the green dotted line represents different PU partitioning modes. A CU without a green dotted line represents that the CU has a PU partition mode of 2 *N* × 2 *N*.

As can be seen from Fig. 5, the floor is a relatively stationary background in the video, its CU structure is simple. The CTU involving the player, which is regarding as the moving object, is divided by a complicated quadtree structure, and many CUs are divided into multiple PUs. By observing, the division of PU is usually divided according to the boundary of the moving object. Since the specific decision is based on the consideration of the prediction residual, the occupied bandwidth and the image quality after quantization, individual differences may also occur. Therefore, for the vertical PU partitioning mode, it is more reasonable to substitute another vertical partitioning mode, and the horizontal mode is similar.

3.2 The Proposed Method

Since HEVC has different PU partition modes, information can be hidden by changing the PU partition mode and using different modes to represent different information. In order to reduce the cost increase after replacing the best PU mode, we classify the other six modes except the $2 N \times 2 N$ and $N \times N$ modes into three groups. Each group contains a vertical partition type and a horizontal partition type (Fig. 6).

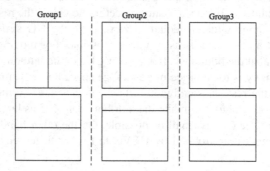

Fig. 6. Groups of different PU partitioning modes. Two symmetrical modes were divided into Group1, the other four asymmetric modes were divided into Group2 and Group3.

Taking embedded binary information as an example, we appoint that the Group1 represent binary bit 0, Group2 and Group3 represent binary bits 10 and 11, respectively. If a CU in size of 16×16 or 32×32 is divided by default into horizontally symmetrical partitioning mode in Group1 and the embedding bit is 0, the PU partitioning mode will be left unchanged. Otherwise, if the embedding bit is 10 or 11, the PU partitioning mode will be replaced by horizontal partitioning mode in Group2 or Group3. To reduce the impact on the video, no $2 N \times 2 N$ PU will be changed, since this partitioning mode occupies the main part. $N \times N$ mode only appear in 8×8 CUs, will be not modified either. The specific process of embedding information is given below.

Step1. Record the division depth and the selected PU partitioning mode of each CU in the process of determining the optimum CU structure for a CTU by HEVC. 85 sets of data will be recorded by default.

Step2. According to the division depth, determine whether the optimal CU structure contains 16×16 or 32×32 CUs. If not, follow the default process of HEVC to complete the compression, then return to Step1 to deal with the next CTU. If there is a suitable CU, go to Step3.

Step3. Perform a PU partitioning mode judgement for a CU that matches the specified size. If the PU partitioning mode of the CU does not belong to any of the three groups, no changes will be made to this CU. If the partitioning mode of PU belongs to one of the three groups, then it is determined according to the to-be-embedded binary information whether to modify the PU partitioning mode or not.

Step4. After completing the judgement of CUs, if there is no change in PU partitioning mode, the CTU will be compressed by default procedure of HEVC. If it is necessary to adjust the PU partitioning mode, the CU structure and the PU partitioning mode of the CTU need to be calculated again. And in the recalculation process, the PU partitioning mode of each CU is directly specified based on the data recorded during the first calculation and the modification result.

Step5. Once the second calculation finished, continuing the compression according to the default process of HEVC.

By accomplishing the process above, the CU structure of the CTU will be consistent with the best structure before embedding, and part of the PU mode will be adjusted according to the hidden binary bits. Thus, the hidden information is represented by these PU partitioning modes.

When extracting secret bits, it is only necessary to sequentially read the PU partitioning mode of the CU that meets the conditions according to Z-scan order. After corresponding to the represented binary bits according to different groups, the embedded information can be extract.

4 Experimental Results

4.1 Configurations

In this section, the experimental results of the proposed algorithm are given. Commonly used videos such as *BasketballDrill*, *BQMall*, *PartyScene* and *RaceHorses* were chosen to carry out the experiment. The video codec platform for HEVC is HM 16.15, 80 frames were encoded using frame rate 30fps, and the intra period is set as 16, the GOP size is 8.

In view of the fact that the proposed algorithm only selects CUs that perform detailed PU partitioning modes to modify, while most of the CUs in video are 2 N 2 N mode. Therefore, each qualified CU is embedded in the experiment in order to increase the embedding capacity. The embedded information is randomly generated, so the probability whether the PU partitioning mode needs to be modified is 50%. The embedding capacity is based on the binary bits that can be embedded in the entire sequence.

4.2 Subjective Visual Quality

The reconstructed images from the test sequences are shown in Fig. 7, if the PU partitioning mode of the frame is not given, it's difficult to visually find the difference between the video with or without hiding information.

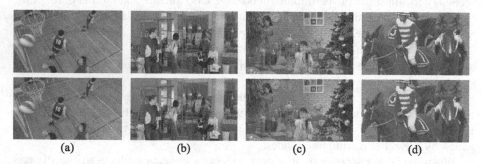

(a)   (b)   (c)   (d)

Fig. 7. Subjective performance evaluation of the second P-frames from: (a) *BasketballDrill*; (b) *BQMall*; (c) *PartyScene* and (d) *RaceHorses*. The frames with hidden information are placed in the first line, original frames are laid on the second line. These videos are compressed using the bitrate of 600 Kbps, and the resolution is 832 × 480.

The Fig. 8 shows partial PU partitioning mode of the second P-frame in *Basket-ballDrill*. By comparing the original video and the video with hidden information, the CU structure is almost the same, but part of PU partitioning modes changed. The change in PU mode is due to the embedding of hidden information, while the CU structure is expected to stay constant. Since the result of the first calculation is used completely during the recompression after the PU modification, the CU structure remains unchanged. However, before the current CTU calculation, its neighboring CTU or reference frame may have been modified, resulting in a corresponding has been changed in the default optimal CU structure of the current CTU. In other words, even if the current CTU is not modified, its best CU structure may be different from the video without hidden information. The process of determining the best CU structure has been introduced in the previous section. Although the CU structure has changed, it will not affect the embedding or extracting of the information hiding algorithm proposed in this paper.

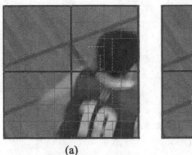 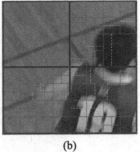

(a)   (b)

Fig. 8. The part of PU partitioning mode of the second P-frames of: (a) *BasketballDrill* with hiding information; (b) the same video without embedding. The bitrate is 600 Kbps.

4.3   Objective Performance Evaluation

Allocating higher bitrates for coding video often means higher PSNRs and embedding capacity. The performance of the proposed algorithm can be evaluated objectively by plots of bitrates vs distortion (RD) and bitrates vs. capacity (RC). The RD and RC plots of the proposed information hiding algorithm for four test videos have shown in Fig. 9.

As can be seen from the results, the proposed algorithm indeed has little impact on videos. In Fig. 9, the RD plots of the video with hidden information is almost identical to the curve of unembedded video, and the decrease of PSNR is less than 1% while the bitrate is around 15Mbps, unlike the RD plots of Chang's method at [2] which is given in Fig. 10. The PSNR of Chang's method decreases by 5%.

For the RC plots, the capacity of the proposed algorithm has an abnormal drop at the highest bitrate compared to lower bitrate. The reason for this phenomenon is related to the embedded strategy of this algorithm. As mentioned in Sect. 3, six different PU modes are classified into three groups that represent different information, and 8×8 CUs are not qualified to embed information. When the bitrate is high enough, such as 16Mbps for 480P videos in the experiment, HEVC will perform detailed division in P-frames. Therefore, a CU divided into 16×16 or 32×32 at lower bitrate will be divided into 8×8 CUs when at highest bitrate. According to the setting of this algorithm, the 8×8 CUs will not be embedded. So, in the RC chart, the curve shows a downward trend.

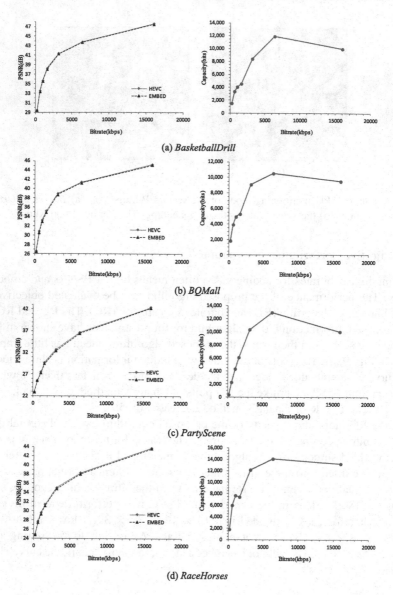

(a) *BasketballDrill*

(b) *BQMall*

(c) *PartyScene*

(d) *RaceHorses*

Fig. 9. PSNR vs. bitrate and capacity vs. bitrate plots of the proposed algorithm.

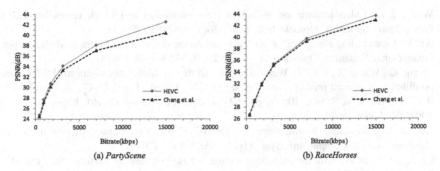

(a) *PartyScene*   (b) *RaceHorses*

Fig. 10. The PSNR vs. bitrate plots of Chang et al. at [2].

5   Conclusions

An information hiding algorithm for HEVC base on PU partitioning modes is proposed in this paper. According to the hidden information, the PU partitioning modes are modified during the inter prediction process. The quality of the video is undamaged since only partial PU partitioning mode needs to be modified. For each qualified CU, an average of 1.67 bits can be embedded. Although the capacity under the current strategy is slightly insufficient, the proposed information hiding algorithm has no conflict with existing embedding method neither in principle nor in implementation means. Therefore, it's convenient to embed hidden bits in I-frames by Chang and Wang's method, and combine with the algorithm proposed by this paper to greatly increase the capacity without further degradation in visual quality. Moreover, the storage space occupied by the inter prediction is much less than that of the intra prediction. To reduce the transmission bandwidth of the video, there surely will be more P- frames to replace I-frames in HD videos. Thus, the information hiding algorithm of HEVC P-frames will have a great application in the future.

Acknowledgement. This work is supported by the Project of National Science Foundation of China (No. 61702034) and Laboratory of Information Security Technology (Grant No. 2017B030314131).

References

1. Chang, P.-C., Chung, K.-L.: An error propagation free data hiding algorithm in HEVC intra-coded frames. In: 2013 Asia-Pacific Signal and Information Processing Association Annual Summit and Conference, APSIPA (2013)
2. Chang, P.-C.: A DCT/DST-based error propagation-free data hiding algorithm for HEVC intra-coded frames. J. Vis. Commun. Image Represent. **25**(2), 239–253 (2014)
3. Wang, J.-J.: An information hiding algorithm for HEVC based on intra prediction. Guangdianzi Jiguang/J. Optoelectron. Laser **25**(8), 1578–1585 (2014)
4. Wang, J.-J.: A high-capacity information hiding algorithm for HEVC based on intra prediction mode. J. Comput. Inf. Syst. **10**(20), 8933–8943 (2014)

5. Wang, J.-J.: Video information hiding in intra prediction and block codes for HEVC. Guangdianzi Jiguang/J. Optoelectron. Laser **26**(5), 942–950 (2015)
6. Xu, J.: A data hiding algorithm for HEVC based on the differences of intra prediction modes. Guangdianzi Jiguang/J. Optoelectron. Laser **26**(9), 1753–1760 (2015)
7. Sheng, Q., Wang, R., Pei, A., Wang, B.: An information hiding algorithm for HEVC based on differences of intra prediction modes. In: Sun, X., Liu, A., Chao, H.-C., Bertino, E. (eds.) ICCCS 2016. LNCS, vol. 10039, pp. 63–74. Springer, Cham (2016). https://doi.org/10.1007/978-3-319-48671-0_6
8. Xu, J.: An information hiding algorithm for HEVC based on intra-prediction modes and Hamming + 1. J. Comput. Inf. Syst. **11**(15), 5587–5598 (2015)
9. Li, S.-B.: A HEVC information hiding approach based on motion vection space encoding. Jisuanji Xuebao/Chin. J. Comput. **39**(7), 1450–1463 (2016)
10. Wang, J.-W.: Forensics feature analysis in quaternion wavelet domain for distinguishing photographic images and computer graphics. Multimedia Tools Appl. **76**(22), 23721–23737 (2017)
11. Ma, Y.-Y.: Selection of rich model steganalysis features based on decision rough set α-positive region reduction. IEEE Trans. Circ. Syst. Video Technol. (2018)
12. Zhang, Y.: On the fault-tolerant performance for a class of robust image steganography. Sig. Process. **146**, 99–111 (2018)

Attack on Deep Steganalysis Neural Networks

Shiyu Li[1], Dengpan Ye[1(✉)], Shunzhi Jiang[1], Changrui Liu[1], Xiaoguang Niu[2], and Xiangyang Luo[3]

[1] School of Cyber Science and Engineering, Wuhan University, Wuhan, China
yedp2001@163.com
[2] School of Computer Science, Wuhan University, Wuhan, China
[3] State Key Laboratory of Mathematical Engineering and Advanced Computing, Zhengzhou, China

Abstract. Deep neural networks (DNN) have achieved state-of-art performance on image classification and pattern recognition in recent years, and also show its power on steganalysis field. But research revealed that the DNN can be easily fooled by adversarial examples generated by adding perturbation to input. Deep steganalysis neural networks have the same potential threat as well. In this paper we discuss and analysis two different attack methods and apply the methods in attacking on deep steganalysis neural networks. We defined the model and propose the concrete attack steps, the result shows that the two methods have 96.02% and 90.25% success ratio separately on the target DNN. Thus, the adversarial example attack is valid for deep steganalysis neural networks.

Keywords: Adversarial example · DNN · Steganalysis

1 Introduction

It is about ten years since the BOSS competition [1], the first challenge on steganalysis in 2010, and many researchers conducted profound studies on steganalysis in this decade. Traditional steganalysis approaches mostly could be divided into two parts.

The first parts is the feature engineering. It is difficult to get sufficient information for learning without proper feature extract progress. In general there are two criterions of feature extraction, completeness [7] which demands that the features should have differences between a cover image and a stego one and diversity [4], which demands that those features should catch as many as stego information hidden in the image. In computer version field, there are many image feature extract methods such as HOG, LBP, Haar, QWT [22], etc.

Rich Models (RM) [3] is a powerful feature set proposed in 2012 and many other methods arose those years based on it. The second parts is the learning step to discriminate the exacted feature between a stego and a cover. The best

X. Sun et al. (Eds.): ICCCS 2018, LNCS 11066, pp. 265–276, 2018.
https://doi.org/10.1007/978-3-030-00015-8_23

and widely used classifier until 2015 was the EC, an ensemble classification for steganalysis. The RM+EC became the most powerful method when facing steganography problems shown in left part of Fig. 1. There are also some robust steganography [27] and some targeted steganalysis methods [11,12].

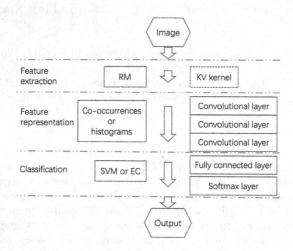

Fig. 1. A traditional steganalysis model and a deep steganalysis neural network. In DNN, we only apply a KV kernel, one of the filters in RM, however experiment [16] shows that it is comparable to RM, the high dimensional feature set.

But in the relative areas, such as computer version, the artificial neural networks and further the deep neural networks became the mainstream method those years. No longer the separated structure, feature extraction and learning step, a end-to-end architecture show its power on not only computer version and many other fields.

With the rapidly development of neural networks and deep learning recent years, the steganalysis field arose a batch of method based on it, the basic structure shown in right of Fig. 1. In 2015 a steganalysis CNN network proposed [16], the GNCNN reached a detect error 4% higher than SRM, the ensemble classifier with Spatial Rich Model, which show us the prospect applying the neural networks and the deep learning networks on steganalysis. After this, we can see if we add some domain knowledge such as KV linear filter kernel, adjust network structure carefully, use special components differ from empirical CV area (TLU [26]), or use paired training set aiming at a special Batch Normalization [24] in deep steganalysis network, we can reach or even better than the performance of RM+EC. The neural networks and the deep learning networks for steganalysis is a promising way for steganalysis.

Though deep neural networks are powerful and achieved surprising achievements not only in steganalysis field but also in other very extensive fields, as a result of the leak of great interpretability and some counter-intuitive properties, adversarial examples, by adding some perturbations to a test image, aiming to a particular neural networks structure could be produced easily [20]. We can get the perturbations by back propagation and it is not just caused by a overfitting model, it is a more general phenomenon in neural networks. So, steganalysis based on deep neural networks could also has same problems.

2   Adversarial Example

Since 2013, the deep neural networks has been widely used in many different filed and in some particular work in could reach or even better than the performance of human beings. But Szegedy [20] attend to that the whole function learned by neural networks are not continuous, which reveals a possibility that we may just add a very slight perturbation to the image then this image can be mis-classified, and even more this image can be classified to a specific label which we want. This attack method is called "Adversarial Example".

2.1   Fast Gradient Sign Method

One basic algorithm for generating adversarial sample is called "Fast Gradient Sign Method" proposed in 2015 [5] shown in Fig. 2.

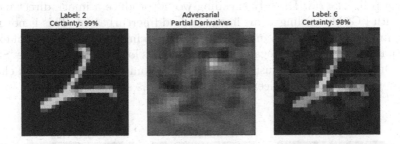

Fig. 2. A FGSM example on Mnist [10]. Here $\epsilon = 0.2$, and four step iterations.

For a linear model, we have a input $\mathbf{x}$ and an adversarial input $\widetilde{\mathbf{x}} = \mathbf{x} + \boldsymbol{\eta}$, $\boldsymbol{\eta}$ is a perturbation which is very small $\| \boldsymbol{\eta} \|_\infty < \epsilon$, where ϵ is small enough that will not change the classification of $\mathbf{x}$ normally if we do not select a particular $\boldsymbol{\eta}$ factitiously. For the adversarial example $\widetilde{\mathbf{x}}$:

$$\omega^{\mathrm{T}} \widetilde{\mathbf{x}} = \omega^{\mathrm{T}} \mathbf{x} + \omega^{\mathrm{T}} \boldsymbol{\eta} \tag{1}$$

Then the perturbation grows to $\omega^{\mathrm{T}} \boldsymbol{\eta}$. For creating a adversarial sample, we maximize this pertubration by assigning $\boldsymbol{\eta} = sign(\omega)$. A key point is the total perturbation will cumulate if ω have many dimensions. This show that the total perturbation could have a linear growth with the dimensions of ω at the same time $\| \boldsymbol{\eta} \|_\infty$ is independent of dimension, then even for a linear model we can also generate an adversarial sample.

Back to the neural networks, many of them are too 'linear' and can be easily attack [5]. Let θ be the weights of the neural network, x the raw image, y the right class of $\mathbf{x}$, and $J(\theta, x, y)$ the loss function for training the neural network. As the linear model, we have:

$$\eta = \epsilon sign(\nabla_x J(\theta, x, y)). \tag{2}$$

That is the "fast gradient sign method". And the gradient could be obtained efficiently using automatic differentiation provided by the deep-learning framework nowadays such as TensorFlow, and PyTorch.

In fact, the FGSM is somewhat in a white box scenario, where the attacker have all the control authority of both algorithm's details and execution environments. In FGSM we assume the attacker have all the details of the target neural network's information including the network's structure, the exact values of weights and biases, the adopted loss function, which demands much more information than usual black box attack. So for some limited scenarios, we next discuss another method One Pixel Attack [19].

2.2   One Pixel Attack

It is a EA (Evolution Algorithm)-based method got inspiration from Directly encoding [14]. The raw Directly encoding would produce a image directly compared with FGSM, needing a raw image and add perturbation. This is not meet our requirements which we want to convert a stego image to a adversarial example so that a deep-learning steganalysis network has low confidence on the 'Stego' class. "One pixel attack" is just like its name, in some scenario we could change only one pixel and fool the deep neural networks as shown in Fig. 3.

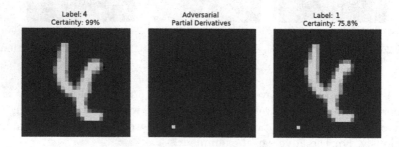

Fig. 3. A One Pixel Attack example on Mnist.

The Evolution Algorithm is a metaheuristic optimization algorithm. Let x be the input image, f is the function of classifier. $f_t(x)$ is the probability of the input x belonging to class t, then the optimize target is:

$$\arg\max_{\eta} f_{cover}(x_{stego} + \eta) \quad where \parallel \eta \parallel_0 \leq dim. \tag{3}$$

x_{stego} is a stego image as input. If we set $dim = 1$, it is a "One" pixel attack. And we use the "Differential evolution" (DE) to solve optimize problem. DE is a population based optimization algorithm for solving complex multi-modal optimization problems [2,18]. The basic Algorithm contain four parts: Initialization, Mutation, Recombination, and Selection.

3 Attack Steps

Generally, there are two different class of adversarial sample attack: targeted attack and non-targeted attack. Non-targeted attack means we just attempt to generate a adversarial sample classified to wrong class, and for targeted attack it should be classified to a particular class we set before. For steganalysis problem, a binary classification, we just regard it as a non-targeted attack target.

For a attack method we focus those metrics to evaluate it:

Success Ratio. In our problem, a non-targeted attack, it is the percentage of the generated adversarial images classified to wrong class, that classify the adversarial images created from stego image to 'Cover' class.

Confidence. The average of adversarial sample's label probability judged by the neural network.

PSNR [23] (Peak Signal-to-Noise Ratio). Here we use PSNR to evaluate the difference between the target image and the adversarial image. A bigger PSNR value means a smaller difference between two images.

3.1 The Steganographic Algorithm

For convenience, we take the LSB-based Jstego [21] steganographic algorithm. Jsteg encodes the serect information on the LSB (least significant bits) [8] of cover image's quantitatived DCT coefficients if it is not −1, 0 or +1. And during quantization progress, we use a non-standard quantization matrix to increase the available encode information length by setting mid-frequency quantization coefficients to 1, increasing the number of quantitatived DCT coefficients which is not −1, 0 or +1.

3.2 The Data Set

The BOSSBase [1] v1.0 have 10,000 512 * 512 grey-level images, for every image we divided it equally into four 256 * 256 images, then use LSB-Jsteg above encoded a 85 * 85 binary image with same key. So there are 80,000 images and we random select 64,000 images as training set and 16,000 images as testing set. For every set the cover image and the stego image are balanced and paired.

3.3 The Deep Steganalysis Neural Networks

Generally if neural networks without specific design considering the attack scenario when constructed, those neural networks will not show much difference when it facing adversarial images. So It is not very necessary for us to evaluate on the state-of-art steganalysis deep neural networks. Due to the key are same during the steganography progress, this data set is a little simple for neural networks in a certain sense [15]. Training on it even a simple FNN with a KV kernel can reach a great performance and here ours structure is as Fig. 4.

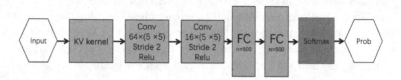

Fig. 4. The network architecture settings in our experiments.

3.4 Attack Step

FGSM. First we use I-FGM [9], the iteration form of FGSM, to generate adversarial images, which is very easy. But the key is if we do as the original procedure, the adversarial noise will most likely destroy the stego information due to the change appeared on every pixel of this image. Even we use a DCT-domain steganographic algorithm which has stronger robustness than on spatial domain, the adversarial noise will make the image hardly be decoded.

So to deal with this, our strategy contain two parts. First when we encode secret information to the cover image, we record the stego information's end point, and then when we add the adversarial noise to target image we do not change any pixels before this end point as shown in Fig. 5. This strategy is look like a 'crop' and 'splice' operation.

One Pixel Attack. The BP-based I-FGM is really powerful and easy to execution, but it do change a lot pixels in stego image. So we became interested in "One Pixel Attack" expecting a better performance.

To solve the same issue in I-FGM attack, we use the same strategy: we limit the position of perturbation so that it will not located in stego area. In Mutation step, we introduced randomness, so the "One Pixel Attack" may not produce a success adversarial result always.

4 Evaluation and Results

In this section, first we describe the architecture of our neural network. For detail training parameters, the batch size is 128, the learning rate 0.01, weight

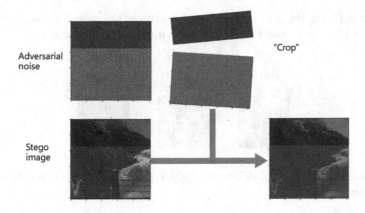

Fig. 5. The strategy we apply. The gray mask stands pixels under it contain stego information, and the red mask stands pixels under it contain adversarial noise.

initializer is truncated normal initializer, bias initialzation is constant 0.1, and no penalty term in loss function. All padding parameter are SAME, except the KV kernel layer using VALID. The data set contain 64000 training images and 16000 testing images. Our network was trained on a PC with Intel Core i7-7700 3.6GHz CPU and NVIDIA GTX 1080Ti 11G GPU. After training step, we got a neural network with 91% correct rate on testing set and saved for next step. Then focus on 8,000 images whose label is Stego in testing set to evaluate two attack methods. We define the success of a adversarial image is this image is classified to "Cover" class by more than 50% confidence.

4.1 FGSM

To start with, we display the classification results and label confidences of 3 adversarial images after cropping and splicing in Fig. 6. Due to the cropping and splicing strategy, even a single pixel containing stego information are not changed so that the extracted secret information from adversarial image and from raw stego image are completely identical.

As described before, we use I-FSM produce a set of adversarial images, and the success ratio, average label confidence, average PSNR shown in Table 1. For BOSSbase and LSB-based Jsteg steganography, our method achieves a good performance, for $\epsilon > 0.002$ our attack strategy has over 88% attack success ratio against a deep steganalysis neural network with 91% correct ratio.

In this subsection, for every target stego image we can always obtain a "adversarial image" no matter with the value of ϵ even this image may not be a success attack. So the Average confidence we caculate over the whole testing data.

With the step length ϵ range from 0.0005 to 0.01, the PSNR decrease slightly. The bigger ϵ, the stronger adversarial noise, and PSNR reduce naturely.

We also evaluate the attack performance against Xu's net [25] and in Table 2 we compare our net with Xu's net. As described before, DNNs show similar performance facing the adversarial samples attack. Because Xu's net have much more layers than ours, the FGSM attack is more significantly on it.

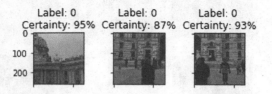

Fig. 6. 3 FGSM examples on BOSSbase. Here $\epsilon = 0.02$, and label 0 stands for Cover and 1 stands for Stego.

Table 1. The I-FGM result with two iteration steps.

ϵ	Success ratio	Average confidence	Average PSNR
0.0005	1.34%	0.0268	14.09669
0.001	47.66%	0.4662	14.09658
0.002	88.67%	0.8779	14.09602
0.003	96.02%	0.9577	14.09507
0.004	98.34%	0.9826	14.09371
0.005	99.00%	0.9901	14.09199
0.01	100.00%	1.0	14.07942

Table 2. Comparison of Xu's net and ours.

Atttack parameter	Success ratio of Xu's net	Success ratio of ours
$\epsilon = 0.0003$	12%	0.04 %
$\epsilon = 0.0005$	98.34%	1.34%
$\epsilon = 0.002$	100%	88.67%
$\epsilon = 0.003$	100%	96.02%

The FGSM is a powerful attack method and easily to executive, but a non-negligible disadvantage is the adversarial noise change the target stego image too much. As shown in Table 1, The average PSNR is around 14db and for human 38 dB or higher corresponds to an imperceptible signal.

4.2 One Pixel Attack

In Tables 3 and 4, for *Attack times* $T = 5$ and *Pixel count* > 60, it show a good attack success ratio, even for *Attack times* $T = 1$ the attack ratio is acceptable

Table 3. The one pixel attack on BOSSbase with *Attempt times* $T = 1$.

Pixel count P	Success ratio	Average confidence	Average PSNR
1	9.5%	0.5872	50.1752
10	12.26%	0.6082	42.8019
20	31.01%	0.6952	41.3967
40	69.17%	0.8019	39.7581
60	85.34%	0.9084	38.2834
80	90.25%	0.9521	37.1598

Table 4. The one pixel attack on BOSSbase with *Attempt times* $T = 5$.

Pixel count P	Success ratio	Average confidence	Average PSNR
1	11.02%	0.5721	50.0619
10	50.51%	0.7108	43.7798
20	60.17%	0.8148	41.3253
40	78.17%	0.9115	38.8201
60	83.33%	0.8937	38.24617
80	91.65%	0.9518	37.1923

when *Pixel count* > 40. Due to the limitation strategy, the pixel's perturbation have no influence on stego information and we can extract the secret information same with from target stego image. Here the average confidence is mean value of the success attack image's confidence, because for a target image and a not too small P we can obtain a success attack image by repeating several times so the failed attack is less meaningful (Fig. 7).

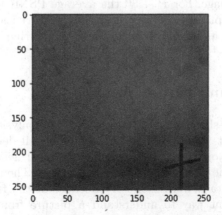

Fig. 7. A One Pixel Attack example on BOSSbase. The yellow pixel is the perturbation can fool our neural network.

Because during DE algorithm the randomness is introduced, One pixel attack method will not always generate a success attack sample from a stego image, different from the FGSM method. If we want to get adversarial image only one times attack seems to be not enough, so we define a parameter *Attack times T*. For a stego image, we use one pixel attack method to generate adversarial sample and if got a success adversarial image under T times, the method is success for this stego image. Another important parameter is *Pixel count P* stands for number of pixel we changed. Maybe this method should called "P pixel attack" here and the reason why one pixel is not enough will explain below.

We can see the exact 'One' Pixel Attack method's success ratio is very low and can not be treat as a feasible attack method. For a image having around 1000 pixels we may change only one pixel to fool neural network but for our stego image having over 60000 pixels, one pixel hardly have sufficient influence on the final classification result if the target stego image not very simple shown in Fig. 8.

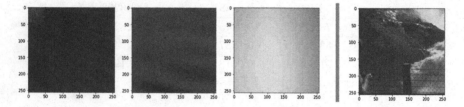

Fig. 8. Left part is a set of success images ($P = 1$). Those images are not complex comparing to image in right which we attacked more than 8,000 times and failed. In fact most of success images with $P = 1$ are very simple with lots of blooming and dark area.

The One Pixel Attack is a meaningful method for generating adversarial sample from stego image. For $P < 80$ the average PSNR is upper 37db which show a good imperceptible. The success attack perturbation is something like salt and pepper noise, and if add stronger limitation during DE the perturbation should be less obvious.

5   Conclusion and Future Works

Previous results have shown that we can fool a steganalysis DNN in two ways, FGSM is a somewhat white-box attack demanding all details of target DNN and one pixel attack only need the outputs of neural network but it have to attempt for a long time if the target image is complex. The reason why this type adversarial images attack work is mostly because of the fact that our human beings have a different way to understand a picture from a neural network. Where we see the whole picture, they see a combination of features to form an object [13]. Another noteworthy fact is that the adversarial images is high likely work on other neural networks, for example perturbations computed for VGG-19 [17] have 73.1% attack success ratio on VGG-16 [17], 45.5% on ResNet-152 [6]. For a same purpose, such as image classification, those neural networks do learn something in common so the adversarial perturbations can take effect on other neural networks. We expect in steganalysis there exist a similar phenomenon.

What can we do when facing this attack? A natural idea is we generate adversarial images and fine-tune the neural networks with those data. But it do not solve the problem entirely, the neural networks after fine-tuning has 80.0% attack success ratio [13] still. A simple way to prevent the neural networks from adversarial images is ensemble. The back propagation progress is much more difficult in a ensemble system and if you only generate aiming at one network, after voting the whole result may not as expected. But for steganalysis, due to the high similarity of target image, a adversarial perturbation may also fool other neural networks and it is left for future work.

Acknowledgments. This work was partially supported by the National Key Research Development Program of China (2016QY01W0200), the National Natural Science Foundation of China NSFC (U1636101, U1636219, U1736211).

References

1. Bas, P., Filler, T., Pevný, T.: "Break our steganographic system": the ins and outs of organizing BOSS. In: Filler, T., Pevný, T., Craver, S., Ker, A. (eds.) IH 2011. LNCS, vol. 6958, pp. 59–70. Springer, Heidelberg (2011). https://doi.org/10.1007/978-3-642-24178-9_5
2. Das, S., Suganthan, P.N.: Differential evolution: a survey of the state-of-the-art. IEEE Trans. Evol. Comput. **15**(1), 4–31 (2011)
3. Fridrich, J., Kodovsky, J.: Rich models for steganalysis of digital images. IEEE Trans. Inf. Forensics Secur. **7**(3), 868–882 (2012)
4. Fridrich, J., Kodovský, J., Holub, V., Goljan, M.: Breaking HUGO – the process discovery. In: Filler, T., Pevný, T., Craver, S., Ker, A. (eds.) IH 2011. LNCS, vol. 6958, pp. 85–101. Springer, Heidelberg (2011). https://doi.org/10.1007/978-3-642-24178-9_7
5. Goodfellow, I.J., Shlens, J., Szegedy, C.: Explaining and harnessing adversarial examples. arXiv preprint arXiv:1412.6572 (2014)
6. He, K., Zhang, X., Ren, S., Sun, J.: Deep residual learning for image recognition. In: Proceedings of the IEEE Conference on Computer Vision and Pattern Recognition, pp. 770–778 (2016)
7. Kodovský, J., Fridrich, J.: On completeness of feature spaces in blind steganalysis. In: Proceedings of the 10th ACM Workshop on Multimedia and Security, pp. 123–132. ACM (2008)
8. Kurak, C., McHugh, J.: A cautionary note on image downgrading. In: Eighth Annual Computer Security Applications Conference, Proceedings, pp. 153–159. IEEE (1992)
9. Kurakin, A., Goodfellow, I., Bengio, S.: Adversarial examples in the physical world. arXiv preprint arXiv:1607.02533 (2016)
10. LeCun, Y., Cortes, C.: MNIST handwritten digit database (2010). http://yann.lecun.com/exdb/mnist/

11. Luo, X., et al.: Steganalysis of HUGO steganography based on parameter recognition of syndrome-trellis-codes. Multimedia Tools Appl. **75**(21), 13557–13583 (2016)
12. Ma, Y., Luo, X., Li, X., Bao, Z., Zhang, Y.: Selection of rich model steganalysis features based on decision rough set α-positive region reduction. IEEE Trans. Circuits Syst. Video Technol. (2018)
13. Moosavi-Dezfooli, S.M., Fawzi, A., Fawzi, O., Frossard, P.: Universal adversarial perturbations. arXiv preprint (2017)
14. Nguyen, A., Yosinski, J., Clune, J.: Deep neural networks are easily fooled: high confidence predictions for unrecognizable images. In: Proceedings of the IEEE Conference on Computer Vision and Pattern Recognition, pp. 427–436 (2015)
15. Pibre, L., Pasquet, J., Ienco, D., Chaumont, M.: Deep learning is a good steganalysis tool when embedding key is reused for different images, even if there is a cover sourcemismatch. Electron. Imaging **2016**(8), 1–11 (2016)
16. Qian, Y., Dong, J., Wang, W., Tan, T.: Deep learning for steganalysis via convolutional neural networks. In: Media Watermarking, Security, and Forensics, vol. 9409, p. 94090J. International Society for Optics and Photonics (2015)
17. Simonyan, K., Zisserman, A.: Very deep convolutional networks for large-scale image recognition. arXiv preprint arXiv:1409.1556 (2014)
18. Storn, R., Price, K.: Differential evolution-a simple and efficient heuristic for global optimization over continuous spaces. J. Global Optim. **11**(4), 341–359 (1997)
19. Su, J., Vargas, D.V., Kouichi, S.: One pixel attack for fooling deep neural networks. arXiv preprint arXiv:1710.08864 (2017)
20. Szegedy, C., et al.: Intriguing properties of neural networks. arXiv preprint arXiv:1312.6199 (2013)
21. Upham, D.: Jsteg. Software available at ftp. funet.fi (1997)
22. Wang, J., Li, T., Shi, Y.Q., Lian, S., Ye, J.: Forensics feature analysis in quaternion wavelet domain for distinguishing photographic images and computer graphics. Multimedia Tools Appl. **76**(22), 23721–23737 (2017)
23. Winkler, S., Mohandas, P.: The evolution of video quality measurement: From psnr to hybrid metrics. IEEE Trans. Broadcast. **54**(3), 660–668 (2008)
24. Wu, S., Zhong, S.H., Liu, Y.: A novel convolutional neural network for image steganalysis with shared normalization. arXiv preprint arXiv:1711.07306 (2017)
25. Xu, G., Wu, H.Z., Shi, Y.Q.: Structural design of convolutional neural networks for steganalysis. IEEE Signal Process. Lett. **23**(5), 708–712 (2016)
26. Ye, J., Ni, J., Yi, Y.: Deep learning hierarchical representations for image steganalysis. IEEE Trans. Inf. Forensics Secur. **12**(11), 2545–2557 (2017)
27. Zhang, Y., Qin, C., Zhang, W., Liu, F., Luo, X.: On the fault-tolerant performance for a class of robust image steganography. Signal Process. (2018)

Attention-Based Chinese Word Embedding

Yiyuan Liang, Wei Zhang$^{(\boxtimes)}$, and Kehua Yang

College of Computer Science and Electronic Engineering, Hunan University,
Changsha 410082, China
zhangwei@hnu.edu.cn

Abstract. Recent studies have shown that the internal composition of the Chinese word provides rich semantic information for Chinese word representation. The Chinese word consists of one or more Chinese characters. Chinese characters have semantic information. And some Chinese characters have multiple meanings. Moreover, the composition of Chinese characters has different semantic contributions to word. In response to this phenomenon, this paper proposes a new attention-based model (ACWE) to learn Chinese word representation. At the same time, the "HIT IR-Lab Tongyici Cilin (Extended Version)" can calculate the semantic similarity between Chinese characters and words. And it can reduce the impact of data sparseness and improve the effectiveness of Chinese word representation. We evaluate the ACWE model from the similarity task and the analogical reasoning task, and the experimental results show that the ACWE model is superior to the existing baseline model.

Keywords: Chinese word embedding · Chinese character
Attention-based · Cilin · Semantic similarity

1 Introduction

Recently, deep learning technology has developed rapidly. It provides a powerful tool for speech recognition, images recognition and Natural Language Processing (NLP), and it also provides new opportunities for the rapid development of these fields. The most exciting breakthrough for deep learning and Natural Language Processing is the word embedding technology. Word embedding technology transforms words into dense vectors. At present, the popular word representation methods are: one-hot word representation and distributed word representation. The biggest problem of one-hot word representation is that it can't catch the similarity from words. Even synonyms can't see any relations from word vectors. In addition, this representation method is also prone to dimension disasters, especially in some applications related to Deep Learning. Distributed word representation was first proposed in 1986 [21]. The basic idea is to map each word into K dimensional real number vector (K is generally a super parameter in the

© Springer Nature Switzerland AG 2018
X. Sun et al. (Eds.): ICCCS 2018, LNCS 11066, pp. 277–287, 2018.
https://doi.org/10.1007/978-3-030-00015-8_24

model) through training, and to judge the semantic similarity between them by the distance between words (such as cosine similarity and Euclidean distance) [6].

Compared to Chinese, the English corpus doesn't require word segmentation. English words consist of letters. A single English letter doesn't have semantics. English is a morphological language. For example, run, running, and runs represent the different tenses of the same word. In the English word representation, they can share the same word vector. At present, the research of English word representation is relatively mature. Mikolov et al. (2016) proposed learning the affix vector to improve the word representation of low frequency words [16]. For example, "unofficial" is a low-frequency word and can't train a high-quality vector, but you can learn a good vector through the high-frequency affixes, such as "un" and "official". Because the Chinese word are composed by Chinese character, the Chinese character are semantic. Each Chinese character has a semantic contribution to a certain extent. Based on English word representation learning, Chen et al. (2015) proposed the Chinese word combined training model CWE [9]. Improvements have been made in the word vector generation section. Introduced the information of a single Chinese character of the word component, and improved the quality of word vector. But it doesn't consider the degree of semantic contribution of Chinese characters in the internal structure of Chinese word. Chen et al. proposed to introduce Cilin to improve word representation, especially for the low-frequency words, and to a certain extent, reduce the effect of data sparseness problems [14]. The main contribution is to integrate the distribution of Chinese characters into word embedding. Xu et al. proposed the Chinese word representation model SCWE based on semantic similarity, using the similarity between a word and its components as the semantic contribution of the internal composition of words [13]. A similarity-based method was proposed to learn word embedding and character embedding. This method can also identify non-composition words.

In this article, we mainly study Chinese word representation, inspired by the CWE model proposed by Chen et al. (2015) and the SCWE model proposed by Xu et al. (2016). Based on the CWE model. We have introduced an attention mechanism to learn Chinese word representation. By calculating the vector similarity of words in pre-trained Cilin, we express the degree of semantic contribution of Chinese characters within Chinese word, and at the same time represent the distribution of Chinese characters. Integrating into word embedding, only considering the internal composition of Chinese word that exist in the Cilin, reducing the influence brought by data sparseness, and reducing the influence of SCWE model due to inaccurate word translation.

Our main task is to calculate the semantic contribution of Chinese characters to the Chinese word. For example, the Chinese word "青蛙" (frog) is composed of the Chinese character "青" (blue or green) and "蛙" (frog). It is obvious that the "青蛙" (frog) is a kind of "蛙" (frog) and "青" (blue or green) is the color of the "蛙" (frog), the degree of semantic contribution of "青" (blue or green) and "蛙" (frog) to the word "青蛙" (frog) are different. In the CWE model, the difference in the degree of semantic contribution is not taken into account. SCWE is a model based on semantic similarity. It uses the method of translating Chinese "青蛙" into "frog", and also translating "青" and "蛙" into English. It calculates the *sim* values of English "青" and "蛙" with "青蛙" respectively, and takes its maximum value as its weight value, this method has the limitations of inaccurate translation, at the same time, which is easily affected by the English word vector effect. The main contributions of our model (ACWE) are:

1. The ACWE model introduces the attention mechanism, attention is attention, and the human brain has different attention to different parts. The reason for needing attention is very intuitive. For example, when we are taking the final exam, we need the teacher to draw the emphasis. The purpose of the key point is to try to put our attention on this part of the content. Hope to get the highest possible score with the least effort. The general model can be seen as the same in all parts of the attention, and the attention-based model here is different from different parts. We can use the attention-based model to learn Chinese word representation. Combine word2vec's CBOW model for Chinese word embedding training.
2. In this paper, the "HIT IR-Lab Tongyici Cilin (Extended Version)"—which we refer to as "Cilin" from now on—is introduced. The vocabulary contains 77,343 words. Some words are composed of Chinese characters, and some single Chinese characters represent a word. Cilin organizes all the entries in a hierarchical tree and has a five-tier structure. As the level increases, word definitions become finer and smaller. At the fifth level, the number of words in each category is not large. Many of them have only one word, which can be called an atomic group, atomic class, or atomic node. The classification results of different levels can provide different services for Natural Language Processing. In this article, we consider the fifth level of the dictionary. For the words that exist in Cilin, consider its internal composition. For example, the word "蓝瘦" (blue thin) doesn't exist in the dictionary, We don't need to consider the character-level embedding, because the relevance of "蓝" (blue) and "瘦" (thin) to the "蓝瘦" (blue thin) is very weak, it can reduce the reflect of data sparse. At the same time, we pre-train the word vector of Cilin, because if the words and the Chinese characters belong to the same semantic category, we can get a better weight value by calculating their cosine value.

In terms of word similarity tasks and word analogy tasks, our model (ACWE) is significantly better than the baseline models (CBOW, CWE, and SCWE).

2 Related Work

2.1 Cilin

HIT IR-Lab Tongyici Cilin (Extended version)contains 77,343 words. Cilin organizes all the entries in a hierarchical tree and has a five-tier structure. There are three categories: large, medium and small, there are 12 large categories, 97 middle classes, and 1,400 sub-categories [1]. There are many words in each sub-category. These words are divided into several word groups (paragraphs) based on the distance and relevance of word meanings. The words in each paragraph are further divided into several lines. The words in the same line either have the same meaning (some words are very similar) or have a strong correlation. For example, "蛙" (frog), "青蛙" (frog), "田鸡" (sora rail) on the same line, "牛蛙" (bullfrog), "树蛙" (tree frog), "雨蛙" (rain frog) are also on the same line. These words are not synonymous, but they are related. Cilin has a five-layer structure, as shown in Fig. 1. As the level increases, word definitions become finer and smaller. At the fifth level, the number of words in each category is small. Many words have only one word. They can be called atomic words, atomic classes, or atomic nodes. Different levels of classification results can provide different services for natural language processing. For example, the fourth level of classification and the fifth level of classification are applied in the fields of information retrieval, text classification, and automatic question and answer. Studies have shown that effectively expanding the meaning of the words or replacing synonyms with keywords can significantly improve the performance of information retrieval, text classification, and automated question answering systems.

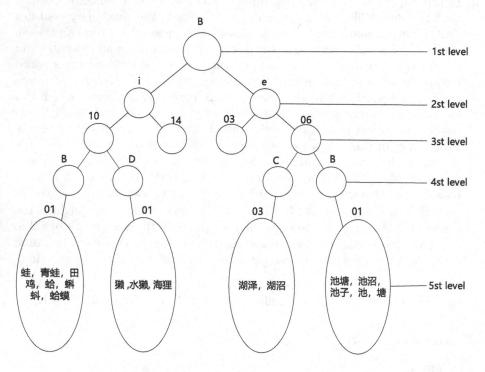

Fig. 1. The structure of the Cilin thesaurus.

In this article we have added the fifth layer of Cilin, as shown in Fig. 1. The words in each semantic category of the fifth level are semantically similar or related. We select Cilin as the auxiliary corpus to train. It is very advantageous to calculate the cosine values of the word and the components of the Chinese character vector by using the pre-trained word vectors. For example, "青蛙" (frog) and "蛙" (frog) are on the same line. They are not synonyms or related words. The cosine value of the their word vectors obtained from pre-training is obviously larger. Experiments have proved that using it as a weight value helps our model. We assume that the internal composition of the word not contained in Cilin is semantically irrelevant, so the introduction of Cilin can reduce the influences of data sparseness.

2.2 Word2vec

Word2vec is an effective tool released by Google in 2013, which represents the word as a real numerical vector. The model used are CBOW and Skip-gram. Word2vec can simplify the processing of text content into vector operations in K dimensional vector space through training. The CBOW model predicts the current word through the context. CBOW is a shallow neural network model. The hidden layer of the neural network is removed, the input layer directly uses the low-dimensional dense vector, and the projection layer is the average of the sum of the contextual word vectors. In contrast to the CBOW model, the Skip-gram model uses the current words to predict context. In this article we use the CBOW model. The goal of the CBOW model is to maximize the log-likelihood function:

$$L = \sum_{w \in C} \log p(w|context(w)) \tag{1}$$

C is the number of words in the corpus, w is any words in the corpus, and $context(w)$ is the context of word w.

As shown in Fig. 2, given a sentence "青蛙 (frog) 跳进 (jumps into) 池塘 (pond)", CBOW is predicted the word "跳进 (jump into)" by the word "青蛙 (frog)" and "池塘 (pond)".

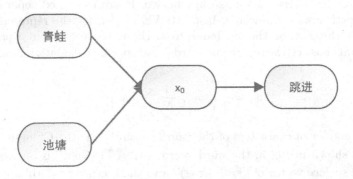

Fig. 2. Architecture of CBOW.

2.3   Attention-Based Model

Attention-based Model is actually a similarity measure. The more similar the current input and the target state, the greater the weight of the current input, which means that the current output is more dependent on the current input [15]. For example, the word "青蛙 (frog)" consists of the Chinese characters "青 (blue or green)" and "蛙 (frog)". Semantically, "青蛙 (frog)" is a kind of "蛙 (frog)", but it is not exactly a frog, it has its own characteristics. It is green. And the Chinese character "蛙 (frog)" contributes more power to the formation of the word "青蛙 (frog)" than the Chinese character "青 (blue or green)" to the word "青蛙 (frog)". We should learn a relative large weight for the Chinese character "蛙 (frog)".

Attention is actually a match between the current input and output. Attention-based is essentially to get the sum of the weighted vector:

$$C_i = \sum_{j=1}^{n} a_{ij} h_j. \tag{2}$$

n being the number of characters of the i-word, a_{ij} refers to the weight value of the j-th Chinese character that composes the i-th word. h_j refers to the semantic encoding of the j-th character (in this case, the vector). C_i is naturally the sum of weighted-vector of the internal components of the i-th word.

3   Our Model

Inspired by the CWE and SCME models, we propose a ACWE model based on the attention mechanism, which aims to get better word vectors through the training model. Inspired by the CWE and SCME models, we propose an ACWE model based on the mechanism of the intention, aiming to obtain a better word vector through the training model. When CWE conducts word vector training, the Chinese characters that make up the words are extracted separately and trained together with the words. In the CWE model, for the representation of the word in the text, on the one hand, from the word vector, and a part of the vectors from those characters in the words, the specific calculation method is as follows:

$$x_j = \frac{1}{2} \left(w_j + \frac{1}{N_j} \sum_{k=1}^{N_j} c_k \right). \tag{3}$$

N_j is the number of characters of the word, w_j and c_k is the Chinese character vector. As shown in Fig. 3, the word vector of "青蛙 (frog)" is one-half of the sum of the surface vector of "青蛙 (frog)" and the vector of "青 (blue)" and "蛙 (frog)", and one-half of the sum guarantees the word consistency of that have semantically compositional and the word doesn't have the semantic composition when calculating the distance.

SCWE takes into account the semantic contribution of Chinese characters to words, and relies on English word vectors. The semantic contribution is based on the calculation of English semantic similarity. It is also based on the joint training of Chinese characters and words, and the concrete methods are as follows:

$$x_j = \frac{1}{2} \left(w_j + \frac{1}{N_j} \sum_{k=1}^{N_j} sim(w_j, c_k) c_k \right). \tag{4}$$

As shown in Fig. 3, $sim(w_j, c_k)$ is calculated by the cosine value of the English vector of its corresponding Chinese characters and words, The maximum is taken when there are multiple sim values. The weight $sim(w_j, c_k)$ is a similarity measure that depends on the English word vector. There is a problem of inaccuracy in translation.

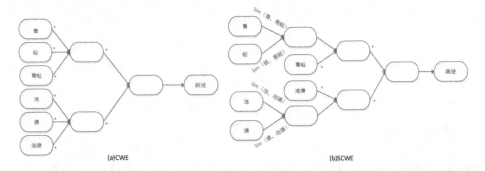

Fig. 3. The left is CWE and right is SCWE. "青蛙 (frog) 跳进 (jump into) 池塘 (pond)" is the word sequence. The word "青蛙" is composed of characters "青" (blue or green) and "蛙" (frog), and the word "池塘" (pond) is composed of characters "池" (pond, pool) and "塘" (pond).

The ACWE model we proposed is based on the Cilin word similarity computation, which is used as the semantic contribution degree between words and the internal Chinese characters. At the same time, the attention mechanism is added to get sum of the weighted Chinese character vectors inside the words. If the word doesn't in Cilin, we don't train Chinese character.

To a certain extent, the influences of data sparsity is reduced. The specific formula is as follows:

$$x_j = \frac{1}{2} \left(w_j + \frac{1}{N_j} \sum_{k=1}^{N_j} sim(w_j, c_k) c_k \right), \ w_j \in T, \ w_j, w_j \notin T. \tag{5}$$

The calculation of $sim(w_j, c_k)$ is based on the calculation of the similarity of word based on Cilin, combined with the above (2), there are

$$C_i = \sum_{k=1}^{N_j} sim(w_j, c_k)c_k. \tag{6}$$

The revised model is

$$x_j = \frac{1}{2}\left(w_j + \frac{1}{N_j}C_i\right), \ w_j \in T, \ w_j, w_j \notin T. \tag{7}$$

The ACWE model is shown in Fig. 4.

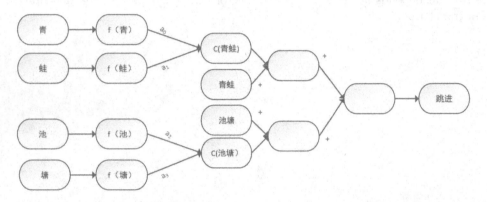

Fig. 4. Architecture of ACWE. Attention-based Model to calculate the C(青蛙) and the C(池塘), then trained with the surface word vector.

4   Experiment and Analysis

4.1   Experiments Settings

We pre-trained Cilin as an auxiliary word vector file for our model training. We chose the latest Chinese corpus of Wikipedia for our model to train Chinese word vectors, and introduced Cilin to determine whether word composition is semantically related. The training effect of the word vector is closely related to the size of the corpus. The size of the Wikipedia Chinese corpus we downloaded was 1. 44 G. Before training, corpus is extracted through text, font conversion, stop word, word segmentation and some other processing steps. Finally, we obtained the 727M training corpus. We loaded a custom dictionary when using the jieba word segmentation tool for Chinese word segmentation to achieve better word segmentation. The CBOW model, CWE model, and SCWE model are used as baseline models. The context window size is 5, the dimension of the word vector and the word vector are both set to 100, and the experimental parameters of each baseline model are the same.

4.2   Word Similarity

Word similarity computation is a standard to measure the effect of word vector. We use wordsim-240 and wordsim-297 two test sets as a measurement standard [17]. Wordsim-240 and wordsim-296 test set (similar to the English WordSimilarity-353 test set) contains 240 pairs and 297 pairs of Chinese vocabulary and artificially measured values of the semantic correlation between these word pairs. These test sets can be used for testing or training Chinese semantic correlation algorithm. The Spearman's rank correlation is applied to compute the correlation [12]. The experimental results are summarized in Table 1.

Table 1. Evaluation on wordsim-240 and wordsim-297.

Model	Wordsim-240	Wordsim-297
CBOW	52.78	61.96
CWE	56.83	62.47
SCWE	58.41	64.65
ACWE	59.49	68.37

We found that our method is superior to the baseline model on the wordsim-240 test set, but it is not very obvious, because the word pairs in wordsim-240 are mostly context-related, not semantic-related. But on the wordsim-297 test set, our method far outperforms the baseline model.

This is inseparable from the introduction of Cilin to calculate similarity. Because if Cilin is not synonymous, it is semantically related. Using it to calculate similarity is more conducive to the search for synonyms.

4.3   Analogical Reasoning

In addition to high efficiency, word2vec has been widely praised by its vector addition combination. For example, v ("King") + v ("Queen") = v ("Man") + v ("Woman"). One of the most popular internal task evaluations is the word vector analogy. In the word vector analogy, we first enter an incomplete analogy: a:b::c:?. The internal task evaluation system finds word vectors that maximize cosine similarity. This article uses the test set used by the CWE model for testing. Reasoning from three categories: (1) capitals of countries (687 groups); (2) states or provinces of cities (175 groups); and (3) family words (240 groups).

Our model introduces the attention mechanism to better learn word vectors from the context. Table 2 shows the results of word analogical reasoning assessments. Obviously, ACWE has improved a lot in the three categories of word analogical reasoning tasks. Especially in the first category, because Cilin was introduced, they are synonymous or semantically related words in Cilin, and they have been given higher similarity when learning word vectors, so it can play a positive role in word analogical reasoning tasks.

Table 2. Evaluation on analogical reasoning.

Method	Total	Capital	State	Family
CBOW	54.13	50.76	61.35	60.41
CWE	55.78	51.12	61.33	68.57
SCWE	56.32	52.38	62.07	67.66
ACWE	58.69	56.45	63.19	69.19

5   Conclusion and Future Work

In this article, we explored the inner structure of the Chinese word, and introduced the Cilin to calculate the semantic similarity between the Chinese word
and the Chinese character, which are used as the different semantic contribution degrees of the internal composition of the word. The attention mechanism is
added to the CBOW model of word2vec, which can better learn the Chinese word
embedding. The experimental results show that our model outperforms the existing baseline model in word similarity tasks and word analogical reasoning tasks.
It also proves that the internal structure of Chinese words, Chinese characters
plays a positive role in the task of learning Chinese word embedding. The Chinese
word is polysemous. When calculating the degree of semantic contribution, there
is no difference between them. Only one vector is used. Although polysemy is not
serious, we should consider polysemy into the future work. At present, learning
about Chinese word embedding is based on the radicals and pixels of Chinese
characters, and also based on pinyin pronunciation [18,19]. A new cooperation
result was released this year: cw2vec-Learning Chinese Word Embeddings with
Stroke n-grams [2]. Experiments show that cw2vec has achieved a consistent
improvement in the task of word similarity, word analogy, and text classification
and named entity recognition. This is also the direction we will study in the
future.

References

1. Mei, J., Zheng, Y., Gao, Y., Yin, H.: TongYiCiCiLin. The Commercial Press,
   Shanghai (1984)
2. Cao, S., Lu, W., Zhou, J., Li, X.: cw2vec: Learning Chinese word embeddings
   with stroke n-gram information. Association for the Advancement of Artificial
   Intelligence, pp. 158–160 (2018)
3. Li, Z.: Parsing the internal structure of words: a new paradigm for chinese word
   segmentation. In: Proceedings of the 49th Annual Meeting of the Association for
   Computational Linguistics, pp. 1405–1414 (2011)
4. Li, M., Zong, C., Ng, H.T.: Automatic evaluation of Chinese translation output:
   word-level or character-level. In: Proceedings of ACL, pp. 159–164 (2011)
5. Mikolov, T., Sutskever, I., Chen, K., Corrado, G.S., Dean, J.: Distributed representations of words and phrases and their compositionality. In: Proceedings of NIPS,
   pp. 3111–3119 (2013)

6. Mikolov, T., Chen, K., Corrado, G., Dean, J.: Efficient estimation of word representations in vector space. arXiv preprint arXiv, pp. 131–145 (2013)
7. Botha, J.A., Blunsom, P.: Compositional morphology for word representations and language modelling. In: Proceedings of ICML, pp. 1899–1907 (2014)
8. Hermann, K.M., Blunsom, P.: Multilingual models for compositional distributed semantics. arXiv preprint arXiv, pp. 4–14 (2014)
9. Chen, X., Xu, L., Liu, Z., Sun, M., Luan, H.: Joint learning of character and word embeddings. In: Proceedings of the 25th International Joint Conference on Artificial Intelligence (IJCAI), pp. 101–115 (2015)
10. Li, Y., Li, W., Sun, F., Li, S.: Component-enhanced Chinese character embeddings. arXiv preprint arXiv, pp. 8–15 (2015)
11. Lai, S., Liu, K., Xu, L., Zhao, J.: How to Generate a Good Word Embedding. arXiv, pp. 7–18 (2015)
12. Myers, J.L., Well, A., Lorch, R.F.: Research design and statistical analysis. pp. 29–41 (2010)
13. Xu, J., Liu, J., Zhang, L., Chen, H.: Improve Chinese word embeddings by exploiting internal structure. In: Proceedings of NAACL-HLT 2016, pp. 1041–1050 (2016)
14. Chen, X., Jin, P., McCarthy, D., Carroll, J.: Integrating character representations into chinese word embedding. Chinese Lexical Semantics. LNCS (LNAI), vol. 10085, pp. 335–349. Springer, Cham (2016). https://doi.org/10.1007/978-3-319-49508-8_32
15. Cao, K., Rei, M.: A joint model for word embedding and word morphology. In: Proceedings of the 1st Workshop on Representation Learning for NLP, pp. 18–26 (2016)
16. Bojanowski, P., Grave, E., Joulin, A., Mikolov, T.: Enriching Word Vectors with Subword Information. arXiv, pp. 7–16 (2016)
17. Jin, P., Wu, Y.: Semeval-2012 task 4: evaluating Chinese word similarity. In: Proceedings of the Sixth International Workshop on Semantic Evaluation, pp. 374–377 (2012)
18. Su, T.-R., Lee, H.-Y.: Learning Chinese Word Representations From Glyphs Of Characters. arXiv, pp. 17–28 (2017)
19. Zamani, H., Crof, W.B.: Relevance-based Word Embedding. arXiv, pp. 5–17 (2017)
20. Yu, J., Jian, X., Xin, H., Song, Y.: Joint embeddings of Chinese words, characters, and fine-grained subcharacter components. In: Proceedings of the 2017 Conference on Empirical Methods in Natural Language Processing, pp. 286–291 (2017)
21. Rumelhart, D.E., Hinton, G.E., Williams, R.J.: Learning representations by back-propagating errors. Cogn. Model. 3–5 (1988)

Covert Communication by Exploring Statistical and Linguistical Distortion in Text

Huanhuan Hu, Xin Zuo, Weiming Zhang$^{(\boxtimes)}$, and Nenghai Yu

University of Science and Technology of China, Hefei, China
zhangwm@ustc.edu.cn

Abstract. Most state-of-the-art text steganography algorithms are designed based on synonym substitution with the concern of simplicity and robustness. However, synonym substitution will cause some detectable impact on cover texts. In this paper, we propose an content-adaptive text steganography to minimize the impact caused by embedding process. We believe that synonym substitution will cause a hybird distortion consists of statistical distortion and linguistical distortion. We design a double-layered STC embedding algorithm (HSL) to minimize the distortion. Experiments results indicate that the security performance of HSL is better compared with traditional methods based on synonym substitution.

Keywords: Steganography · Synonym substitution
Statistical distortion · Linguistical distortion

1 Introduction

Encryption is a technique of protecting communications and its application can be found in all aspects of life. However, the garbled encrypted data will attract the attention from attackers which is not expected. The pursuit of steganography is behavioral safety. The existence of secret communication is hidden to avoid attackers attention. This does not mean that steganography is superior to encryption. The combination of these two methods can protect the secret information better [1].

There are many types of cover used in steganography such as text [2], image [3], audio [4] and video [5]. Because images, videos, etc. have redundant content and are not sensitive to modification, steganography developed for these cover has rich achievement. However, steganography that uses texts as cover develop slow as a result of the small content redundancy. However, the use of text data is increasing day by day with the rapid development of internet technology. This provides a natural environment for text steganography. The application prospect

---

An earlier version of this paper was presented at the 2nd IEEE International Conference on Data Science in Cyberspace.

© Springer Nature Switzerland AG 2018
X. Sun et al. (Eds.): ICCCS 2018, LNCS 11066, pp. 288–301, 2018.
https://doi.org/10.1007/978-3-030-00015-8_25

of text steganography is positive. Therefore, it is significant to design a secure steganography algorithm that is suitable for text cover.

Because of the high robustness and simplicity of the text steganography based on synonym substitution, this method is widely used [6–8]. However, the frequency distribution of synonyms in the cover text will change during the process of synonym substitution and causes statistical distortion. On the other hand, the meaning of a word is related to the content of the context. So the meanings of two synonyms in a particular context may not necessarily be the same and synonym substitution can cause linguistical distortion.

We will develop the rest of this paper as follows. In Sect. 2 we analyze the statistical distortion caused by synonym substitution. In Sect. 3 we introduce the method to estimate the linguistical distortion. The scheme for minimizing distortion of synonym substitution are elaborated in Sect. 4. Experimental results on resisting steganalyzers are shown for comparing with previous methods in Sect. 5. Section 6 gives the conclusion of this paper.

2 Statistical Distortion

2.1 Notation

To describe the proposed method more clearly, we give some notations as follows.

Definition 1. Embedding rate in steganography based on synonym substitution refers to the value of the number of bits embedded divided by the number of bits encoded by all synonyms in a text. The embedding capacity in synonym substitution steganography is decided by how many synonyms appear in a text file.

Definition 2. A synonym set is a word set which includes more than one words having similar meaning. The synonyms in the synonym set are order by the descending order of their frequencies which are derived from N-gram corpus. It's a open source corpus that can be downloaded from the Internet.

For example, (*Cow, Cattle*) is a synonym set that contains two synonyms and the frequency of Cow is bigger than Cattle.

To make the description in the rest of the paper simpler, we use a letter in lower case with a subscript and a superscript, take s_i^j for example, to represent a synonym. The corresponding synonym set is denoted as S_i, i.e., $s_i^j \in S_i$. $\|S_i\|$ denotes the number of synonyms in S_i. Herein, the subscript i is used to represent the position of the synonym appears in the text. The superscript j represents the order of the synonym in the corresponding synonym set. In this paper, if the logical expression I is true, we define the value of Iverson bracket $[I]$ to be 1. Otherwise, the value of Iverson bracket $[I]$ is defined to be 0.

Definition 3. A synonym sequence is defined as a sequence of synonyms. The synonyms are sorted in the increasing order of positions where they appear in the text. For example, if there are n synonyms in a text, the synonym sequence can be denoted as $(s_1^{j_1}, s_2^{j_2}, ..., s_n^{j_n})$.

2.2   Estimation of Statistical Distortion

Text steganography based on synonym substitution is widely used because it's simple and robust. In this kind of steganography, the sender and the receiver have the same synset. Different synonyms are encoded as different message bits. After we substitute some synonyms in cover text, the synonym sequence can represent the secret message. The semantics of the text remain almost unchanged. It's hard to distinguish if the text is modified. From this perspective, synonym substitution steganography is practical. However, experiments show that some statistical features of cover text will change during the process of synonym substitution.

As is known to all, synonyms appear at different frequencies in corpus. Rare synonyms refers to synonyms that hardly appear in corpus, while some synonyms appear frequently in corpus. We think that the message bits is random, **0** and **1** appear at the same probability in message. The number of **0** and the number of **1** in message are almost the same. As a result, rare synonyms appear at higher frequencies in stego texts than in cover texts. It can be utilized by attackers.

In this paper, we denote the synonym which has the highest frequency in a synonym set as MFS (Most Frequent Synonym). And the proportion of MFSs to all synonyms in a text is called Ratio of MFSs, denoted as R_M. We select 100 cover texts from wiki corpus. The size of these texts are 100 kB. We use Bsyn [9] to generate stego texts. The embedding rate is 0.5. We get R_M from these cover texts and stego texts and the results are shown at Fig. 1.

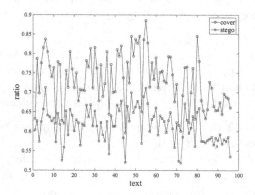

Fig. 1. Ratios of MFSs on the method Bsyn [9].

We can see from Fig. 1 that synonym frequencies will change if we embed message in the text by synonym substitution. It is regarded as statistical distortion which is not expected. As synonym substitution steganography is widely used, some researchers start research on text steganalysis. Text steganalysis can be used to detect the existence of secret messages in text files. Attackers may utilize text steganalysis tools to prevent covert communication. It's not we want if there is a need to transfer secret messages. However, most state-of-the-art synonym substitution steganography algorithms can not resist this kind of attack. In the perspective of statistical discrepancy, traditional synonym substitution steganography has room for improvement. The security performance of synonym substitution steganography need to be promoted and this is what we will do in this paper.

In this paper, the statistical distortion is estimated with the help of relative word frequency. If we substitute s_i^j with s_i^k, the statistical distortion is

$$SD(s_i^j, s_i^k) = \begin{cases} (log\frac{f(s_i^j)}{f(s_i^k)})^\alpha, \ if \ f(s_i^j) > f(s_i^k) \\ -(log\frac{f(s_i^k)}{f(s_i^j)})^\alpha, \ if \ f(s_i^j) <= f(s_i^k) \end{cases} \tag{1}$$

where the constant α is a parameter used to tune the sensitivity of the distortion to the frequency. $f(s_i^j)$ and $f(s_i^k)$ denote the frequencies of synonym s_i^j and s_i^k respectively, which are derived from the N-gram corpus.

3   Linguistical Distortion

3.1   Word to Vector

The research on how to represent words in the form of vectors has attracted much attention in recent years [10–12]. In [13], Bengio proposed a widely used model which could be used to estimate neural network language model. In Bengio's model, a feedforward neural network structure was adopted. With the help of a non-linear hidden layer and a liner projection layer, the performance of Bengio's model is somewhat satisfying. Many other later works learned how to build the neural network structure from Bengio's model. Another common structure of neural network language model was proposed in [14,15]. In this model, the word vectors were firstly learned using neural network with a single hidden layer. Then the word vectors were utilized to train the neural network language model. So the word vectors could be learned without constructing a complete neural network language model.

In [16], Tomas et al. proposed two new models for learning word vectors: Continuous Bag-of-Words (CBOW) and ssSkip-gram. CBOW model use the future and history words as input to predict the current word. Continuous Skip-gram model use the current word as input to predict words within a certain distance to the current word. In this paper, we use CBOW model to train word vectors. The architecture of CBOW is shown at Fig. 2.

It is noticed that the application of word vectors is not limited to simple linguistic regularities. Through applying simple addition and substraction operations on the word vectors, we can get the word vector of another word. For example, the result of word vector(King) - word vector(Man) + word vector(Woman) has a closest distance with the vector of the word "Queen" in vector space.

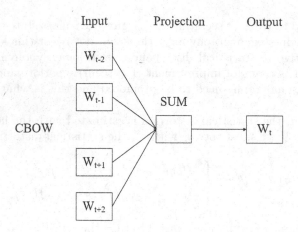

Fig. 2. The architecture of CBOW.

3.2 Estimation of Linguistical Distortion

A word can express different meanings in different contexts. Although the synonyms in a synset have the similar meaning, the substitution of synonyms will still cause a semantic mismatch in a specific context. It's necessary to quantify the linguistical distortion. In this paper, we utilize the word vectors to calculate the linguistical distortion caused by synonym substitution. Given a specific context, we can predict the current word with the help of word vectors. The prediction is realized by applying algebraic operation on the context word vectors and the result is in the form of a word vector. The weighted average of the context word vectors is the prediction result. And if the context is extracted from a text, we know the original word at this position in the text. We can calculate the distances between vector of the predicted word and vector of the original word. The distances is a measurement of how a word fits the specific context. In the remainder of this subsection, the calculation of linguistical distortion is given in detail.

For every synonym s_i^j, we can extract the N words before and after it as its context, denoted by $C_i = (c_{i,0}, c_{i,1}, ..., c_{i,2N-2}, c_{i,2N-1})$. The size N is called context window size. The vector representation of the context is $V_i = (v_{i,0}, v_{i,1}, ..., v_{i,2N-2}, v_{i,2N-1})$. Since context words are often not of the same importance, we give different weights to the context words. $W_i = (w_{i,0}, w_{i,1}, ..., w_{i,2N-2}, w_{i,2N-1})$ is the weights of C_i. Given the context and the weights, we can predict the current word which may be not the same as the word appears in the text. The vector representation of the predicted word can be gotten by Eq. (2).

$$V_{ip} = \sum_{k=0}^{2N-1} v_{i,k} \times w_{i,k} \qquad (2)$$

The vector representation of synonym s_i^j is denoted as v_i^j. It is considered that the closer between V_{ip} and v_i^j, the better s_i^j fits the context. In this paper, we choose cosine distance to measure the distance between two vectors. The reason of choosing cosine distance is given in Sect. 5. The cosine distance between V_{ip} and v_i^j is denoted as Cd_i^j.

$$cd_i^j = 1 - \frac{v_i^j \cdot V_{ip}}{|v_i^j| \times |V_{ip}|} \tag{3}$$

If we substitute s_i^j with s_i^k, the linguistical distortion is

$$LD(s_i^j, s_i^k) = \begin{cases} (log \frac{cd_i^k}{cd_i^j})^\beta, \ if \ cd_i^k > cd_i^j \\ -(log \frac{cd_i^j}{cd_i^k})^\beta, \ if \ cd_i^k <= cd_i^j \end{cases} \tag{4}$$

The parameter β is used to tune the proportion of linguistical distortion in total distortion.

4   The Proposed Scheme HSL

4.1   Preprocess the Synonym Sets

Considering the following two points, we firstly preprocess the synonym sets to guarantee that each synonym set contains 2 or 4 words to reduce the complexity of embedding algorithm.

(1) Little synonym set contains more than four synonyms;
(2) If $\|S_i\|$ =3 and synonyms in S_i are encoded into two bits, there will be wet elements in multi-layer STC [17].

The preprocess of synonym sets is conducted in the following ways: If a synonym set has three synonyms, remove the synonym with the lowest frequency. If a synonym set has more than four synonyms, remove the synonym with the lowest frequency until the synonym set contains only four synonyms.

We embed message by modifying the order j of the word s_i^j and substituting it with the corresponding synonym. To reduce embedding distortion with binary stego coding technology, we construct two binary cover sequences with the LSB (Least Significant Bit) and MSB (Most Significant Bit) of the order j of the synonym s_i^j. And if the synonym set includes only two words, the corresponding MSB will be empty.

For example, there is a synonym sequence $(s_0^0, s_1^0, s_2^1, s_3^2)$ and $\|S_0\| = 2, \|S_1\| = 2, \|S_2\| = 4, \|S_3\| = 4$. The two binary cover sequences are shown in Fig. 3.

4.2   Defining Distortion Function

In this paper, the distortion caused by substituting s_i^j with s_i^k is defined as

$$D(s_i^j, s_i^k) = SD(s_i^j, s_i^k) + LD(s_i^j, s_i^k) \tag{5}$$

Synonym	s_0^0	s_1^0	s_2^1	s_3^2
LSB	0	0	1	0
MSB	–	–	0	1

Fig. 3. Example of constructing cover sequences from synonym sequence.

We assume that the distortion of substitution of different synonyms is independent and the total embedding impact on cover text is the sum of distortion caused by every synonym substitution.

In the next subsection, we apply "minimizing distortion model for steganography" with Eq. (5) as the distortion metric. The distortion function $SD(s_i^j, s_i^k)$ means that replacing a word having higher frequency with one having lower frequency will introduce large costs, so such substitution will be limited, which can preserve the statistical character of texts. On the other hand, distortion function $LD(s_i^j, s_i^k)$ means substituting a synonym which fit the context better with another one will cause linguistical distortion. Therefore, by distortion metric (5), we take into account statistical distortion and linguistical distortion at the same time.

4.3 Applying Double-Layered STC

When the payload and distortion function are given, matrix embedding is a tool that can be employed to reduce the distortion during the process of embedding. Syndrome-trellis code (STC), a practical optimal code, can be utilized to hide message near the rate-distortion bound [18]. STC adopt convolutional code together with a Viterbi algorithm-based encoder for the purpose of minimizing the additive distortion. Previous works which use the framework of STC achieved satisfying performances [19–21]. Motivated by this, we developed a double-layered STC algorithm to implement the text steganography method proposed in this paper.

Suppose there is a synonym sequence $(s_1^{j_1}, s_2^{j_2}, ..., s_n^{j_n})$ in a cover text which is denoted as $\boldsymbol{x}$. $s_i^{j_i}$ belongs to synonym set $S_i = \{s_i^0, s_i^1, ...s_i^{n_i-1}\}$. It's possible that $S_i = S_k(i \neq k)$. We want to embed m bits of message into the text. After the message is embedded, the synonym sequence changes to $(s_1^{k_1}, s_2^{k_2}, ..., s_n^{k_n})$ which is denoted as $\boldsymbol{y}$. All possible value of $\boldsymbol{y}$ constitute a set which is denoted as $\boldsymbol{y}$. During the embedding process, the total distortion is formed as the sum of distortion caused by every synonym substitution.

$$D(\boldsymbol{x}, \boldsymbol{y}) = \sum_{i=1}^{n} D(s_i^{j_i}, s_i^{k_i}) \qquad (6)$$

The probability of changing the synonym sequence from $\boldsymbol{x}$ to $\boldsymbol{y}$ is denoted as $\pi(\boldsymbol{y}) = p(\boldsymbol{y}|\boldsymbol{x})$. The amount of bits can be sent is calculated by

$$H(\pi) = -\sum_{y \in \boldsymbol{y}} \pi(\boldsymbol{y}) log \pi(\boldsymbol{y}). \qquad (7)$$

Average distortion is calculated by

$$E_\pi(D) = \sum_{y \in y} \pi(y)D(x,y). \tag{8}$$

The task of embedding while trying to reduce the embedding impact is in the following form:

$$minimize\ E_\pi(D)\ \ subject\ to\ H(\pi) = m \tag{9}$$

According to the maximum entropy principle, the solution to Eq. (9) has a form of Gibbs distribution [22]

$$\pi(y) = \frac{exp(-\lambda D(x,y))}{\sum_{z \in y} exp(-\lambda D(x,z))} \tag{10}$$

the parameter λ can be obtained by the constraint Eq. (9).

$$\pi(s_i^{k_i}) = p(s_i^{k_i}|s_i^{j_i}) = \frac{exp(-\lambda D(s_i^{j_i}, s_i^{k_i}))}{\sum_{z=0}^{n_i-1} exp(-\lambda D(s_i^{j_i}, s_i^z))} \tag{11}$$

If $\|S_i\| = 2$, the possibility that the LSB of k_i is 0 is

$$p_{1i} = \pi(s_i^0) \tag{12}$$

If $\|S_i\| = 4$, the possibility that the LSB of k_i is 0 is

$$p_{1i} = \pi(s_i^0) + \pi(s_i^2) \tag{13}$$

According to [17], to reduce the embedding impact caused by embedding process, the payload of the first layer in double-layer STC is

$$m_1 = \sum_{i=1}^{n} -p_{1i}log p_{1i} - (1 - p_{1i})log(1 - p_{1i}) \tag{14}$$

In the first layered embedding, the equivalent cover sequence is denoted as x_{1i} and

$$x_{1i} = [p_{1i} < 0.5], 1 \le i \le n \tag{15}$$

And the corresponding distortion metric of the element in the first layer cover sequence is

$$\rho_{1i} = |ln(\frac{p_{1i}}{1 - p_{1i}})| \tag{16}$$

The first layer stego sequence is denoted as y_{1i} $(1 \le i \le n)$, which is obtained by applying the STC to embed m_1 bits of message into the sequence x_{1i} $(1 \le i \le n)$.

The payload of the second layer binary sequence is

$$m_2 = m - m_1 \tag{17}$$

If $\|S_i\| = 4$, we can embed message into the MSB of the synonym. The possibility that the MSB of k_i is 0 is

$$p_{2i} = \begin{cases} \frac{\pi(s_i^0)}{\pi(s_i^0)+\pi(s_i^2)}, \ if \ y_{1i} = 0 \\ \frac{\pi(s_i^1)}{\pi(s_i^1)+\pi(s_i^3)}, \ if \ y_{1i} = 1 \end{cases} \tag{18}$$

where $i \in \{i|\ \|S_i\| = 4, i = 1, 2, ..., n\}$. In the second layered embedding, the equivalent binary cover sequence is denoted as x_{2i} and

$$x_{2i} = [p_{2i} < 0.5] \tag{19}$$

The corresponding distortion metric of the element in the second layer cover sequence is

$$\rho_{2i} = |ln(\frac{p_{2i}}{1 - p_{2i}})| \tag{20}$$

The second layer stego binary sequence is denoted as y_{2i}. When $i \in \{i|\ \|S_i\| = 4, si = 1, 2, ..., n\}$, y_{2i} is gotten by applying the STC to embed messages into x_{2i}. If $\|S_i\| = 2$, we set $y_{2i} = 0$. Finally, we set

$$k_i = 2y_{2i} + y_{1i} \tag{21}$$

Through comparing the difference between j_i and k_i, we know how to substitute the synonyms to get stego texts.

Note that the above double layered STC is different with that used for ± 1 embedding in images [17]. In image steganography, the embedding distortion is greatly influenced by the modification's amplitude and large modification amplitude means large distortion. Therefore ± 1 embedding overmatch two-layer LSB replacement for image steganography. When decomposing ± 1 embedding, some wet elements (disable elements) will appear in the second layer which may lead embedding failure, and thus we have to repeat the embedding process. However, in the proposed scheme, the cover element j is the order of a word in the synonym set. Large modification amplitude on j does not always mean large distortion. In fact, negative distortion may arise when a word with lower frequency is changed to one with high frequency. That's why we use two-layer LSB replacement instead of ± 1 embedding. For such cover on synonym substitution, we design a special double-layered STC to assign the payload to two layers of LSBs according to the distortion metric and the modification manner, which can achieve larger capacity than ± 1 embedding and will not yield wet elements. The details of the embedding and extraction procedures of the proposed method are described in Algorithm 1 and Algorithm 2 respectively.

5   Experiment Results

In this section, we first introduce the training process of the word to vector model. We adopt the CBOW model to train word vectors. The texts used as

Algorithm 1. Embedding Procedure

1: Get the synonym sequence x of cover text.
2: Calculate the distortion metric of x by using Eq. (5).
3: Determinate the value of λ by constraint Eq. (9).
4: Get the x_{1i} and the distortion metric of x_{1i}. Apply STC encoder to get y_{1i}.
5: Get the x_{2i} and the distortion metric of x_{2i}. Apply STC encoder to get y_{2i}.
6: Calculate k_i with Eq. (21) and generate y.
7: Compare x and y, replace the corresponding synonyms.

Algorithm 2. Extracting Procedure

1: Get the synonym sequence y of stego text.
2: Apply STC decoder to the LSB sequence of y get a part of message.
3: Apply STC decoder to the MSB sequence of y get the rest of message.

input are segmented from WIKI corpus. The size of input text ranges from 5 kB to 200 kB. The dimension of every word vector is 400-D. We set the context window size (parameter N) to 5 and abandon the words appeared less than 5 times during the training process. The synsets is extracted from Wordnet [23]. The synonyms in the synset are sorted in the descending order of their frequencies which are derived from N-gram corpus. In anti-detection experiments to evaluate the performance of different embedding methods, 5,000 texts are used as cover texts. The size of the text varies from 10 kB to 3000 kB. We try to guarantee these text files have a wide range of embedding capacities which is an effort to make the evaluation of the proposed method objective.

In Sects. 2 and 3, we give the calculation of statistical distortion and linguistical distortion in detail. The quantification of linguistical distortion is completed with the help of word vector. The distance between word vectors can be a measurement of linguistical distortion. Common vector distances include cosine distance and Euclidean distance. To determine the value of parameter α, β and find out which kind of vector distance can estimate linguistical distortion better, 1,000 texts was selected randomly from the WIKI corpus which are different from the 5,000 texts mentioned above. The stego texts are generated by HSL when α, β take different values and using different kind of vector distance. The embedding rate is 50%. The steganalysis tool is WFST. The detection result of steganalysis tool is displayed in Tables 1 and 2.

Table 1. Detection rate when α and β have different values (cosine distance)

Parameter	$\beta = 0$	$\beta = 0.5$	$\beta = 1.0$	$\beta = 1.5$
$\alpha = 0.0$	0.8319	0.8125	0.8286	0.8451
$\alpha = 0.5$	0.7958	0.7412	0.7882	0.8046
$\alpha = 1.0$	0.8033	**0.6769**	0.7426	0.7726
$\alpha = 1.5$	0.8154	0.7518	0.7274	0.7529

298   H. Hu et al.

Table 2. Detection rate when α and β have different values (Euclidean distance)

Parameter	$\beta = 0$	$\beta = 0.5$	$\beta = 1.0$	$\beta = 1.5$
$\alpha = 0.0$	0.8319	0.8347	0.8551	0.8879
$\alpha = 0.5$	**0.7958**	0.8124	0.8485	0.8677
$\alpha = 1.0$	0.8033	0.8204	0.8467	0.8754
$\alpha = 1.5$	0.8154	0.8136	0.8652	0.8839

Compare Tables 1 and 2, we can know that the linguistical distortion can be better estimated by cosine distance. And HSL achieves optimal anti-detection when $\alpha = 1.0$ and $\beta = 0.5$. In the experiments later, we set $\alpha = 1.0$ and $\beta = 0.5$.

In Sect. 2, the ratios of MFSs are given to explain the statistical distortion caused by synonym substitution. In this section, the same experiment is implemented. The cover texts are identical with cover texts used in Sect. 2. The stego texts are generated by HSL (embedding rate = 0.5). Results are displayed in Fig. 4. Compare Figs. 1 and 4, we can see that the frequency distribution of synonyms in stego texts generated by HSL is closer to cover texts compared with stego texts generated by traditional method.

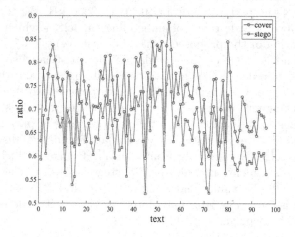

Fig. 4. Ratios of MFSs on the proposed method.

To further evaluate the security of HSL, two different steganalysis tools are used to detect stego text files produced by four methods: Bsyn, Tlex and Ctsyn [9] and HSL. Bsyn, Tlex and Ctsyn are all synonym substitution steganography. In Bsyn, the codewords of every synonym have the same length. Message are divided into many pieces of equal length. T-lex and Ctsyn don't limit the number of synonyms in synonym sets. T-lex uses WordNet to select synonyms with correct senses. Only the words appeared in the identical synonym set in WordNet database are grouped in a synonym set. Messages can be embedded into cover text as follow. First, encode the message letters with Huffman coding. Then, represent the encoded binary string in multi-base form. Finally, choose which synonym to appear in the text according to the multi-base form. Ctsyn constructs a binary tree for each synonym set with the synonyms as the leaves. Different synonyms represent message pieces of different lengths. For each steganographic method, two groups of stego texts are generated with two embedding rates 25% and 50%.

The first steganalysis tool is WFST. The detection results is displayed in Table 3. The second steganalysis tool is based on the context [24]. It's denoted as CST. The detection results is displayed in Table 4.

Table 3. Detection results of WFST

Embedding rate	Bsyn	Tlex	Ctsyn	HSL
25%	0.6907	0.6877	0.6802	**0.6131**
50%	0.8473	0.8359	0.8124	**0.7185**

Table 4. Detection results of CST

Embedding rate	Bsyn	Tlex	Ctsyn	HSL
25%	0.8995	0.8747	0.8864	**0.6639**
50%	0.9360	0.9214	0.9011	**0.7742**

From experiments results displayed above we can know that the security performance of HSL is better compared with other methods. HSL can resist steganalysis tools better by minimizing the designed distortion. It indicates the distortion quantification is reasonable.

6   Conclusions

In this paper, we analyze the distortion caused by synonym substitution from both the statistical and semantic perspectives. We apply minimal distortion model to synonym substitution steganography and design a double-layered embedding algorithm HSL to impact on cover texts during embedding process. Experiments show that HSL is more secure when attacked by different steganalysis tools compared with traditional synonym substitution steganography algorithms.

References

1. Shivani, Kumar, V., Batham, S.: A novel approach of bulk data hiding using text steganography. Procedia Comput. Sci. **57**, 1401–1410 (2015)
2. Huanhuan, H., Xin, Z., Weiming, Z., Nenghai, Y.: Adaptive text steganography by exploring statistical and linguistical distortion. In: 2017 IEEE Second International Conference on Data Science in Cyberspace (DSC), pp. 145–150. IEEE (2017)
3. Denemark, T., Bas, P., Fridrich, J.: Natural steganography in JPEG compressed images. In: Electronic Imaging (2018)
4. Tayel, M., Gamal, A., Shawky, H.: A proposed implementation method of an audio steganography technique. In: 2016 18th International Conference on Advanced Communication Technology (ICACT), pp. 180–184. IEEE (2016)
5. Sadek, M.M., Khalifa, A.S., Mostafa, M.G.: Robust video steganography algorithm using adaptive skin-tone detection. Multimedia Tools Appl. **76**(2), 3065–3085 (2017)
6. Shirali-Shahreza, M.H., Shirali-Shahreza, M.: A new synonym text steganography. In: International Conference on Intelligent Information Hiding and Multimedia Signal Processing, IIHMSP 2008, pp. 1524–1526. IEEE (2008)
7. Yuling, L., Xingming, S., Can, G., Hong, W.: An efficient linguistic steganography for chinese text. In: IEEE International Conference on Multimedia and Expo, pp. 2094–2097. IEEE (2007)
8. Muhammad, H.Z., Rahman, S.M.S.A.A., Shakil, A.: Synonym based malay linguistic text steganography. In: Innovative Technologies in Intelligent Systems and Industrial Applications, CITISIA 2009, pp. 423–427. IEEE (2009)
9. Xiang, L., Sun, X., Luo, G., Xia, B.: Linguistic steganalysis using the features derived from synonym frequency. Multimedia Tools Appl. **71**(3), 1893–1911 (2014)
10. Hinton, G.E.: Distributed representations (1984)
11. Hinton, G., Rumelhart, D., Williams, R.: Learning internal representations by back-propagating errors. In: Parallel Distributed Processing: Explorations in the Microstructure of Cognition 1 (1985)
12. Elman, J.L.: Finding structure in time. Cogn. Sci. **14**(2), 179–211 (1990)
13. Bengio, Y., Ducharme, R., Vincent, P., Jauvin, C.: A neural probabilistic language model. J. Mach. Learn. Res. **3**, 1137–1155 (2003)
14. Mikolov, T.: Language Modeling for Speech Recognition in Czech. Ph.D. thesis, Masters thesis, Brno University of Technology (2007)
15. Mikolov, T., Kopecky, J., Burget, L., Glembek, O., et al.: Neural network based language models for highly inflective languages. In: IEEE International Conference on Acoustics, Speech and Signal Processing, ICASSP 2009, pp. 4725–4728. IEEE (2009)
16. Mikolov, T., Chen, K., Corrado, G., Dean, J.: Efficient estimation of word representations in vector space. arXiv preprint arXiv:1301.3781 (2013)
17. Filler, T., Fridrich, J.: Minimizing additive distortion functions with non-binary embedding operation in steganography. In: 2010 IEEE International Workshop on Information Forensics and Security, pp. 1–6, December 2010
18. Filler, T., Judas, J., Fridrich, J.: Minimizing additive distortion in steganography using syndrome-trellis codes. IEEE Trans. Inf. Forensics Secur. **6**(3), 920–935 (2011)
19. Huang, F., Luo, W., Huang, J., Shi, Y.Q.: Distortion function designing for JPEG steganography with uncompressed side-image. In: Proceedings of the First ACM Workshop on Information Hiding and Multimedia Security. IH & MMSec 2013, pp. 69–76. ACM, New York (2013)

20. Li, B., Wang, M., Huang, J., Li, X.: A new cost function for spatial image steganography. In: 2014 IEEE International Conference on Image Processing (ICIP), pp. 4206–4210, October 2014
21. Zhao, Z., Guan, Q., Zhao, X.: Constructing near-optimal double-layered syndrome-trellis codes for spatial steganography. In: Proceedings of the 4th ACM Workshop on Information Hiding and Multimedia Security, pp. 139–148. ACM, New York (2016)
22. Fridrich, J., Filler, T.: Practical methods for minimizing embedding impact in steganography (2007)
23. Miller, G.A.: WordNet: a lexical database for English. Commun. ACM **38**(11), 39–41 (1995)
24. Chen, Z., Huang, L., Miao, H., Yang, W., Meng, P.: Steganalysis against substitution-based linguistic steganography based on context clusters. Comput. Electr. Eng. **37**(6), 1071–1081 (2011)

Fast Three-Phase Fabric Defect Detection

Jielin Jiang[1], Yan Cui[2(✉)], Zilong Jin[1], and Chunnian Fan[1]

[1] School of Computer and Software, Jiangsu Engineering Center of Network
Monitoring, Nanjing University of Information Science and Technology,
Nanjing, China
jiangjielin2008@163.com, zljin85@163.com,
yuuqingnuist@163.com
[2] College of Mathematics and Information Science, Nanjing Normal University
of Special Education, Nanjing, China
cuiyan899@163.com

Abstract. In textile industry production, fabric defect inspection is a very important step to ensure the quality of fabric. At present, most of the methods can detect the defects for solid color with the distinguishable defects, but they are not very efficient for small defects, especially for the defects which has small difference with the background. In this paper, we propose a three-phase method, mean filter, convolution operator combined with variance (MCV), for fabric defect detection. For a fabric image, we first use mean filter to suppress noise, then convolution operator is applied to enhance image. Based on enhanced image, we divide it into many patches. For a given patch, we calculate its variance and then use the threshoding to decide whether the patch is free defect or not. Finally, a defect image will be synthesized from these processed patches. Experimental results prove the effectiveness of the proposed MCV algorithm.

Keywords: Fabric defect detection · Variance · Convolution operator

1 Introduction

Fabric defect detection is now integral for textile factory to improve products quality. Currently, the fabric inspection for most weaving industry is based on production machine which is operated by a skilled staff. When a defect is found on the moving fabric, the machine will be stopped, and the defect can be located. Although humans can do the job effective in many case. There has many drawbacks for the visual inspection. For example, visual inspection is a very tedious task even for the best trained staff. Research shows that human visual inspection can only find around 70% of fabric defects even for the most highly trained inspectors [1]. For this reason, human try to use automated fabric inspection system to replace manual visual inspection. The core of automated fabric inspection system lies in efficient algorithms. A variety of fabric defect detection methods have been proposed in past decades, which mainly include three classes: statistical approach, spectral approach, model-based approach.

Statistical approach is applied for the analysis and interpretation of data, which mainly includes co-occurrence matrix (CM) [2–4], mathematical morphology [5] and fractal dimension [6]. Spectral approaches are a class of techniques designed to solve

© Springer Nature Switzerland AG 2018
X. Sun et al. (Eds.): ICCCS 2018, LNCS 11066, pp. 302–312, 2018.
https://doi.org/10.1007/978-3-030-00015-8_26

certain differential equations. The idea is to write the solution of the differential equation as a sum of certain basis functions. The most popular spectral approaches in fabric defect detection include fourier transform [7–10], wavelet transform [11–14], Gabor transform [15–17] and so on. Model-based approaches mainly include Autoregressive model [18, 19], Markov Random Field model [20].

At present, most of the methods mentioned above can well detect the defects for solid color with the distinguishable defects, but they are not very efficient for small defects or blurry defects. In this paper, we propose a three-phase method, mean filter, convolution operator combined with variance (MCV), for fabric defect detection. For a fabric image, we first use mean filter and convolution operator to enhance image. Then based on enhanced image, we divide it into many patches. For a given patch, we calculate its variance and use the threshoding to decide whether the patch is free defect or not. Finally, a new image will be synthesized from these processed patches, and the defects are located by finding the difference between the original fabric image and the reconstructed image. Experimental results prove the effectiveness of the proposed MCV algorithm.

The rest of the paper is organized as follows. The defect detection model is given in Sect. 2. In Sect. 3, we describe the proposed MCV in detail. Section 4 gives experimental results. Conclusions are made in Sect. 5.

2 The Defect Detection Model

Denote by x a defect-free image. Let y be the defect observation of x. Similar to the image noise model, the defect detection model can be described as

$$y = x + n, \tag{1}$$

where n is the defect that we want to find.

3 Fast Three-Phase Fabric Defect Detection

3.1 Mean Filter

During a fabric image acquisition and transmission processes, noise will be more or less introduced. Noise will not only affect the defect detection rate, but also increase the false alarm. Therefore, we should do some pretreatment before implementing defect detection. In this paper, mean filter is applied to smooth images and suppress noise. The idea of mean filtering is to replace each pixel value in an image with the mean value of its neighbors. A $n \times n$ averaging kernel is used in mean filtering, a kernel of 3×3 can be written as Table 1.

Figure 1 gives a detect result by a 3×3 mean filter combined with variance. Figure (1) (b) is the mean filter result of Fig. (1) (a), Although Fig. (1) (b) looks the same as Fig. (1) (a), they are different essentially. To make a clearer explanation of their differences, Fig. (1) (c) and (d) give their defect detection results with variance based method. From Fig. (1) (c) and (d), we can see that the variance combined with mean filter can suppress the noise effectively.

304   J. Jiang et al.

Table 1. A 3 × 3 kernel

1/9	1/9	1/9
1/9	1/9	1/9
1/9	1/9	1/9

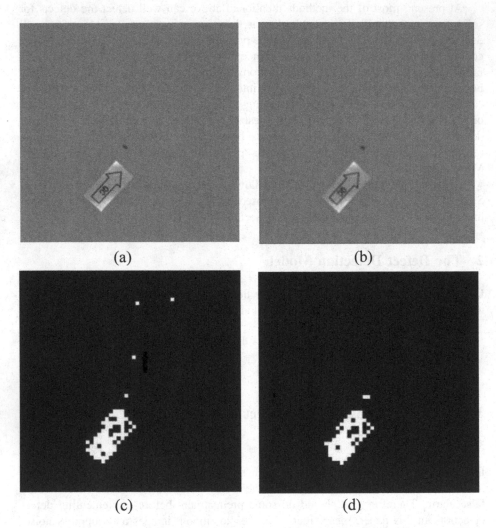

Fig. 1. (a) Original image (b) mean filter image (c) variance based method without mean filter (d) variance based method with mean filter

3.2 Enhance Convolution Operator

Currently, most of the methods mentioned above can well detect the defects when the defects are obvious. As a matter of fact, fabrics often contain the defects in small size and low contrast, especially for solid color which has small difference with the background. In order to highlight the defects is different from the background of an image, we first convolves each column of y with the filter operator u, and then it convolues each row of the result with the filter operator v. The enhanced image y_e can be written as

$$y_e = u * v * y \qquad (2)$$

Where $*$ denotes the convolution.

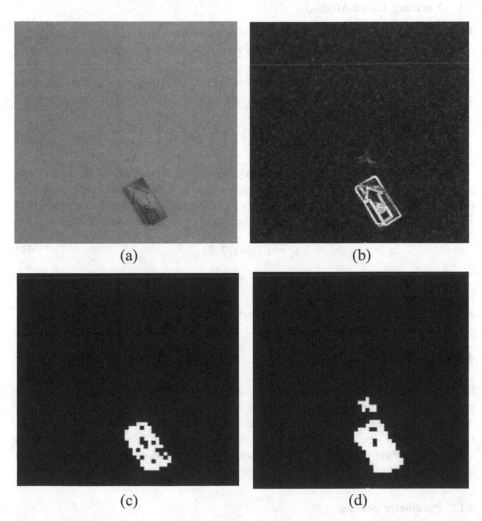

Fig. 2. (a) Original image (b) enhanced image (c) variance based method without convolution operator (d) variance based method with convolution operator

Let's use an example to investigate the effect of convolution operator. We did experiment on a defect image in which the gray value between the defect and the background is small. After the defect image is processed by mean filter, the defect is located by variance based method without convolution operator and with convolution operator, respectively. From Fig. (2), we can see that the variance based method can not detect defects (Fig. (2) (c)), while variance based method combined with convolution operator can well detect defects (Fig. (2) (d)).

3.3 Variance Based Method

After the acquired image are handled by the mean filter and enhanced convolution operator, we adopt a patch based method for fabric defect detection. Denote by $x \in R^N$ a fabric image, let $x_i = R_i x \in R^n$ be the stretched vector of an image patch extracted at location i [21], where R_i is the patch extraction operator and the size of x_i is $n \times n$. After all image patches are obtained, the least square solution of x can be reconstructed by

$$x = \left(\sum_i R_i^T R \right)^{-1} \left(\sum_i R_i^T x_i \right) \tag{3}$$

For an enhanced fabric image y_e contains defects, it will be firstly divided into many patches y_i, i = 1,2...m−1. In this step, variance is used as a measure. For the plain weave fabric, irregulars areas will have a relatively big variance value then the regular defect areas. This step is to locate the defects in the image, which can be written as

$$y_i > \tau, i = 1, 2, 3 \ldots \tag{4}$$

After each patch is handled by Eq. (4), then a defect image x can be synthesized by Eq. (3). Defect position can be located by the original fabric image and the reconstructed image. Figure 3 gives the flowchart of MCV.

4 Experiments

In this section, experiments are carried out to demonstrate the performance of the proposed MCV algorithm. Where line defects are relatively big and easily to be detected, while knot defects and the spot defects are the most encountered defects in the factory and they are difficult to detect, especially for the defects which has small difference with the background. The performance of the proposed model is compared with the model in [22].

4.1 Parameter Setting

There are several parameters to set in the proposed MCV algorithm. Since the proposed method is a patch based method for defect detection, the size of patch can affect the algorithm performance directly. Considering the running time and defect detection rate, we set the size of patch as 7×7. The mean kernel n is set as 3 or 5 by experience. The column operator u and the row operator v are set as [1 0 0] and [0.1 0.1], respectively.

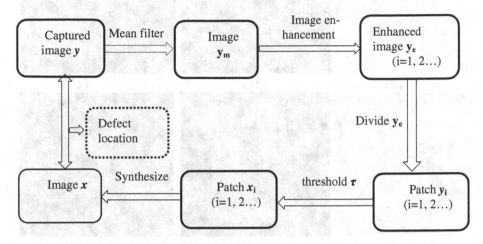

Fig. 3. The flowchart of the proposed MCV

4.2 Results

The experiments were tested in MATLAB language. Experiments are conducted on a personal computer under a Win8 operation system running on an Intelcore i7 processor. Some typical detection results are shown in Figs. 4, 5 and 6. In Figs. 4, 5 and 6, the first column are the original defective images, the second column are the detect results of [22], the third column shows the detection results of the proposed MCV algorithm. In Fig. 4, although the defects are very small and the diameter of each defect is less than 1 mm, we can see that MCV algorithm can still detect them accurately. The algorithm in [22] can well defect the small defects, but it has high false alarm. Figures 5 and 6 have the similar conclusion. In all, all the experiments show that MCV algorithm is effective for fabric defect detection. If MCV is rewritten in C++ language. The time needed for detecting each image is about 0.6 s. Therefore, the time consumption of the MCV algorithm can meet the real-time detection requirements.

308   J. Jiang et al.

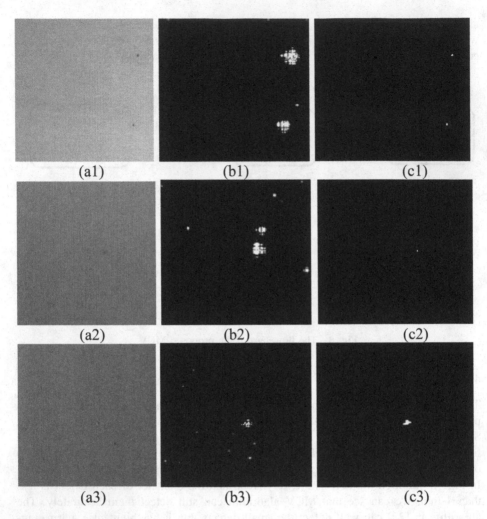

Fig. 4. Detection results of different methods. (a1)–(a3) are the original image. (b1)–(b3) are the results of [22]. (c1)–(c3) are the results of the MCV algorithm.

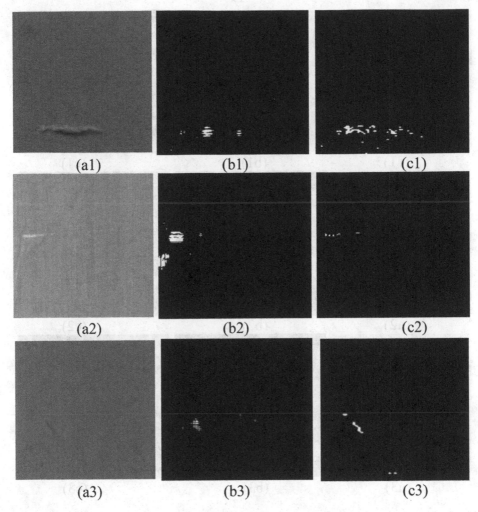

Fig. 5. Detection results of different methods. (a1)–(a3) are the original image. (b1)–(b3) are the results of [22]. (c1)–(c3) are the results of the MCV algorithm.

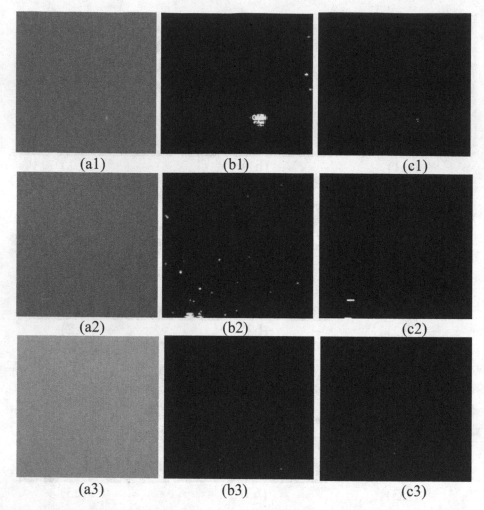

Fig. 6. Detection results of different methods. (a1)–(a3) are the original image. (b1)–(b3) are the results of [22]. (c1)–(c3) are the results of the MCV algorithm.

5   Conclusion

This paper proposed a new method, mean filter, convolution operator combined with variance (MCV), for fabric defect detection. By exploiting the mean filter, noise can be suppressed effectively. Convolution operator is applied to enhance image in low contrast. After the image is handled by the mean filter and convolution operator, variance based method is adopted for defect detection. The performance of the proposed MCV model is evaluated on the several typical defect images. Experimental results showed the MCV model achieves good defect performance.

Acknowledgments. This work was supported in part by the National Natural Science Foundation of China under Grants 61601235, 61602252, in part by the Natural Science Foundation of Jiangsu Province of China under Grants BK20160972, BK20170768, BK20160967, in part by the Natural Science Foundation of the Jiangsu Higher Education Institutions of China under Grants 16 KJB520031, 17KJB520019, 16KJB510024, 17KJB520021, in part by the Startup Foundation for Introducing Talent of Nanjing University of Information Science and Technology (NUIST) under Grant 2243141601019.

References

1. Sari-Sarraf, H., Goddard, J.S.: Vision systems for on-loom fabric inspection. IEEE Trans. Ind. Appl. **35**(6), 1252–1259 (1999)
2. Haralick, R.M., Shanmugam, K., Dinstein, I.: Textural features for image classification. IEEE Trans Syst. Man Cybern. **3**(6), 610–621 (1973)
3. Tsai, I.S., Lin, C.H., Lin, J.J.: Applying an artificial neural network to pattern recognition in fabric defects. Text. Res. J. **65**(3), 123–130 (1995)
4. Latif-Amet, A., Ertuzun, A., Ercil, A.: An efficient method for texture defect detection: subband domain co-occurrence matrices. Image Vis. Comput. **18**, 543–555 (2000)
5. Zhang, Y.F., Bresee, R.R.: Fabric defect detection and classification using image analysis. Text. Res. J. **65**(1), 1–9 (1995)
6. Bu, H.-G., Wang, J., Huang, X.-B.: Fabric defect detection based on multiple fractal features and support vector data description. Eng. Appl. Artif. Intell. **22**(2), 224–235 (2009)
7. Chan, C.H., Pang, G.: Fabric defect detection by Fourier analysis. IEEE Trans. Ind. Appl. **36**(5), 1743–1750 (2000)
8. Murtagh, F.D.: Automatic visual inspection of woven textiles using a two-stage defect detector. Opt. Eng. **37**(37), 2536–2542 (1998)
9. Tsai, I.S., Hu, M.C.: Automated inspection of fabric defects using an artificial neural networks. Text. Res. J. **66**, 474–482 (1996)
10. Tsai, D.-M., Heish, C.-Y.: Automated surface inspection for directional textures. Image Vis. Comput. **18**, 49–62 (1999)
11. Yang, X.Z., Pang, G.K.H., Yung, N.H.C.: Discriminative fabric defect detection using adaptive wavelets. Opt. Eng. **41**(41), 3116–3126 (2002)
12. Han, Y., Shi, P.: An adaptive level-selecting wavelet transform for texture defect detection. Image Vis. Comput. **25**(8), 1239–1248 (2007)
13. Tsai, D.M., Hsiao, B.: Automatic surface inspection using wavelet reconstruction. Pattern Recogn. **34**, 1285–1305 (2001)
14. Tsai, D.M., Chiang, C.H.: Automatic band selection for wavelet reconstruction in the application of defect detection. Image Vis. Comput. **21**, 413–431 (2003)
15. Kumar, A., Pang, G.K.H.: Defect detection in textured materials using Gabor filters. IEEE Trans. Ind. Appl. **38**(2), 425–440 (2002)
16. Zhang, Yu., Lu, Z., Li, J.: Fabric defect detection and classification using Gabor filters and gaussian mixture model. In: Zha, H., Taniguchi, R.-i., Maybank, S. (eds.) ACCV 2009. LNCS, vol. 5995, pp. 635–644. Springer, Heidelberg (2010). https://doi.org/10.1007/978-3-642-12304-7_60
17. Tong, L., Wong, W.K., Kwong, C.K.: Differential evolution-based optimal Gabor filter model for fabric inspection. Neurocomputing **173**, 1386–1401 (2016)
18. Zhou, J., Semenovich, D., Sowmya, A., Wang, J.: Dictionary learning framework for fabric defect detection. J. Text. Inst. **105**(3), 223–234 (2014)

19. Alata, O., Ramananjarasoa, C.: Unsupervised textured image segmentation using 2-D quarter plan autoregressive model with four prediction supports. Pat. Rec. Lett. **26**(8), 1069–1081 (2005)
20. Ozdemir, S., Ercil, A.: Markov random fields and Karhunen-Loeve transform for defect inspection of textile products. In: IEEE Conference on Emerging Technologies & Factory Automation, pp. 697–703 (1996)
21. Aharon, M., Elad, M., Bruckstein, A.M.: K-SVD: An algorithm for designing of overcomplete dictionaries for sparse representation. IEEE Trans. Signal Process. **54**, 4311–4322 (2006)
22. Hu, G.H., Wang, Q.H., Zhang, G.H.: Unsupervised defect detection in textiles based on Fourier analysis and wavelet shrinkage. Appl. Opt. **54**, 2963–2980 (2015)

Improving Testing Accuracy of Convolutional Neural Network for Steganalysis Using Segmented Subimages

Yifeng Sun[✉], Xiaoyu Xu, Haitao Song, Guangming Tang, and Shunxiang Yang

Zhengzhou Information Science and Technology Institute, Zhengzhou, Henan, China
yfsun001@163.com

Abstract. Recent studies have proved a well-designed convolutional neural network (CNN) is a good steganalytic tool. In this paper, based on the previous work, we report a method using segmented subimages to improve the testing accuracy of CNN for steganalysis. In training phase, a CNN is trained on training set of whole image. In testing phase, for a given testing image, a sliding window is employed to segment the whole testing image into subimages. Each subimage is feed into the trained CNN respectively to obtain a subdecision. The final decision is obtained through majority vote. Experiments show that the proposed method achieves significant improvement on testing accuracy when detecting S-UNIWARD and HILL under payload of 0.4 bpp, whereas the time efficiency is only slightly worse compared with previous work.

Keywords: Convolutional neural networks · Deep learning
Steganalysis

1 Introduction

Steganography is to conceal information communication by means of hiding secret messages in public media covers, such as images. Steganalysis is the counter-technology of steganography, which aims at detecting the very presence of secret message in cover medium. Current steganalysis methods can be divided into two categories: The first one is the traditional steganalysis method, which is mainly based on hand-extracted features and machine learning classifier [1–5]. The second one is steganalysis based on deep learning technology. With the

Supported by 1. National Natural Science Foundation of China, NO. 61601517. 2. Foundation of Science and Technology on Information Assurance Laboratory, NO. KJ-15-106.

X. Sun et al. (Eds.): ICCCS 2018, LNCS 11066, pp. 313–323, 2018.
https://doi.org/10.1007/978-3-030-00015-8_27

development of big data and computing performance, deep learning technology has been applied to steganalysis. Convolutional neural network (CNN) is one of the typical deep learning models. It is able to learn representation of image with multiple levels of abstraction and it has been proved to be an effective tool for steganalysis [6,8,9,12–19].

In their pioneering work, Tan and Li [6] firstly proposed a CNN for steganalysis which comprises three stages of alternating convolutional and max pooling layers, and sigmoid nonlinear activations. They involved a high-pass kernel [2,7] into parameter initialization of the first convolutional layer, and pre-training all of the parameters with unsupervised learning. Qian et al. [8] presented a CNN equipped with a high-pass filtering (HPF) layer, Gaussian non-linear activations, and average pooling for steganalysis. The reported detection error rates of CNNs proposed by Tan and Qian are still inferior to that of SRM with ensemble classifiers. However, along this direction, Xu et al. [9] proposed a CNN that tries to incorporate the knowledge of steganalysis. The reported detection error rates are 1%–4% lower than those achieved by the SRM with ensemble classifiers on the BOSSbase when detecting S-UNIWARD [10] and HILL [11]. This network in [9] now becomes a base model for several more complex CNN models [12–14]. Wu et al. [15,16] employed residual learning in steganalysis and achieved low detection error rates when cover images and stego images are paired. Ye et al. in [17] incorporated the truncation technique into the design of steganalytic CNN models and obtained significant performance on resampled and cropped images. Xu et al. [18] also proposed a network based on residual learning and achieved better detection accuracy than traditional methods in compressed domain. Wu et al. [19] proposed a neural network with Shared Normalization for steganalysis and achieved better performance than previous methods.

Although using CNN models has achieved remarkable progress in steganalysis, improving the testing accuracy of detector is still an aspiration of researchers. We have noticed that the global pooling layer in the architecture of CNN in [9] enables it to process input images with arbitrary sizes. Moreover, one of the differences between steganalysis task and computer vision task is that, in steganalysis, any subregions of an image are able to be samples for detection. Based on the previous works, in this paper, we propose a method to improve testing performance of CNN for Steganalysis. In testing phase, a fixed sliding window is employed to segment the whole image into a number of subimages. Then each subimage is put forward through the trained CNN to form a subdecision. The final decision is made via majority vote. The reported testing accuracy are 0.09–0.11 higher than that achieved by method in [9], and 0.05–0.08 higher than that achieved by method in [19].

2   Related Works

In this section, we review the architecture and some details of the designed CNN stated in [9]. Figure 1 illustrates the overall architecture of used CNN. An HPF layer whose parameters are not optimized during training is placed at the very beginning to transform original images to noise residuals to enhance the signal-to-noise/interference ratio. The CNN structure consists of two modules: one is a convolutional module which transforms the images to feature vectors, and the other is a linear classification module which transforms feature vectors to output probabilities for each class. Convolutional layers, pooling layers, Batch Normalization (BN) layers, TanH layers, ReLU layers, and an Absolute Activation (ABS) layer are placed in the convolutional module, whereas a full-connected layer and a softmax layer are placed in the linear classification module. The network configuration is illustrated in Table 1. For more details about the CNN structure, refer to [9].

A global pooling layer is placed in L6. The global pooling layer processes feature maps with arbitrary size into a single unit. Different from that in conventional pooling, the sliding window in global pooling layer adapts its size to that of input feature map as shown in Fig. 2. This flexibility enables the CNN to process input images with arbitrary sizes.

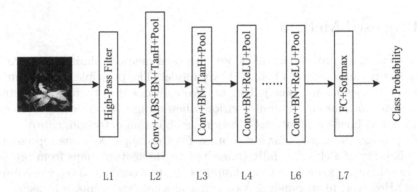

Fig. 1. Overall Architecture of CNN in [9]. Conv means convolution; ABS means absolute activation; BN means batch normalization; FC means fully connection. L5 which is the same as L3 and L4 is not shown.

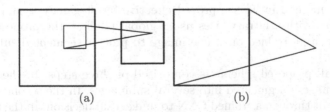

Fig. 2. Conventional pooling and global pooling. (a) Conventional pooling. (b) Global pooling.

Table 1. Network configuration

	Layer	Filter size	#Filters	Stride	#Output maps
L1	HPF	$5 \times 5 \times 1$	1	1	1
L2	Conv	$5 \times 5 \times 1$	8	1	8
	Pool	5×5	\	2	8
L3	Conv	$5 \times 5 \times 8$	16	1	16
	Pool	5×5	\	2	16
L4	Conv	$1 \times 1 \times 16$	32	1	32
	Pool	5×5	\	2	32
L5	Conv	$1 \times 1 \times 32$	64	1	64
	Pool	5×5	\	2	64
L6	Conv	$1 \times 1 \times 64$	128	1	128
	Pool	Global	\	\	128

3 Proposed Method

In this section, we provide details of our proposed method, aiming at improving the testing performance of a trained CNN model. The principle is to use multiple image subregions for joint judgment. We consider that there is a difference between steganalysis and computer vision when using CNN. In computer vision tasks, such as image content classification or objection detection, convolutional kernels process the whole image to obtain feature maps. Neurons representing the probability of a class are fully connected by the feature maps from previous layer. In other words, final decision should be made according to the whole image content. However, in steganalysis tasks, if the whole stego image is segmented into subimages, modification on pixels will exist in each subimage. Figure 3 shows an example. Figure 3(a) is the original image whereas the Fig. 3(b) is its modification map. Although some regions in the image are modified more seriously than others, the modification is almost across the whole image. Any subimage is a sample which can be used to determine whether it is stego or not. Therefore, any subimage can make a decision based on trained CNN.

Since the method in [9] has proved effective for steganalysis and is able to process images with arbitrary sizes using global pooling, the proposed scheme use the CNN in [9] trained on whole image to process segmented subimages in testing phase.

The overall proposed scheme is comprised of three steps. In the first step, the testing image is segmented into several subimages. In the second step, each subimage is put through a trained CNN to make a subdecision. In the third step, obtained subdecisions are jointed to make the final decision via majority vote. The key points of the proposed method in testing phase are stated in detail as follows:

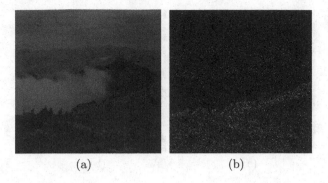

(a)   (b)

Fig. 3. Original image and modification map. (a) Original image. (b) modification map. The modification map is obtained via embedding with S-UNIWARD of 0.4 bpp.

3.1   Image Segmentation

The testing image is segmented into several subimages. For a given testing image in size of $M \times N$, a sliding window in size of $a \times a$ $(a < M, a < N)$ on the whole testing image is used to produce the subimages with stride of d in both horizontal and vertical directions. (1) computes the amount of subimages segmented from one image. The function $floor(.)$ denotes rounding down.

$$num = floor\left(\frac{M-a}{d}\right) \times floor\left(\frac{N-a}{d}\right) \tag{1}$$

Although adjacent subimages may share some same image content with each other, they are distinct samples in steganalysis. The reasons are as follows. Firstly, the same image content locates in different positions in different subimages. In Fig. 4, the circled regions share the same image content, but they locate in different positions in respective subimages. Secondly, more important is that the different image contents in adjacent subimages make spatial changing trend of complexity of texture different in subimages. In Fig. 4, the boxed regions are different image contents. The boxed region in the left subimage is very different with that in the right subimage, which makes spatially changing trend of complexity of texture different in the two subimages. Since steganalysis pays more attention to spatially changing trend of complexity of texture than to image content, adjacent subimages are very different samples in steganalysis. The diversity of samples will enable the majority vote to improve the testing accuracy significantly.

3.2   Subdecisions and Majority Vote

Each segmented subimage is put forward through the trained CNN model. The CNN adopts the structure of [9], and is trained on whole images (not segmented) before testing phase. One subdecision can be formed by one subimage. P_1 denotes

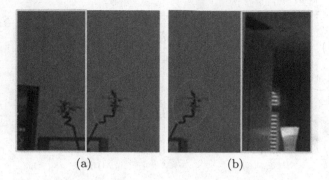

(a)   (b)

Fig. 4. Comparison between adjacent subimages. Size of sliding window is 128×128. Both vertical and horizontal stride are 64.

the probability output by the neural presenting stego, and P_0 denotes the probability output by the neural presenting cover. D_l denotes the subdecision formed with lth subimage. Decision 1 means stego, and decision 0 means cover.

$$D_l = \begin{cases} 1 & when \ P_1 > P_0 \\ 0 & otherwise \end{cases} \qquad (2)$$

Then subdecisions are formed. The process is illustrated in Fig. 5.

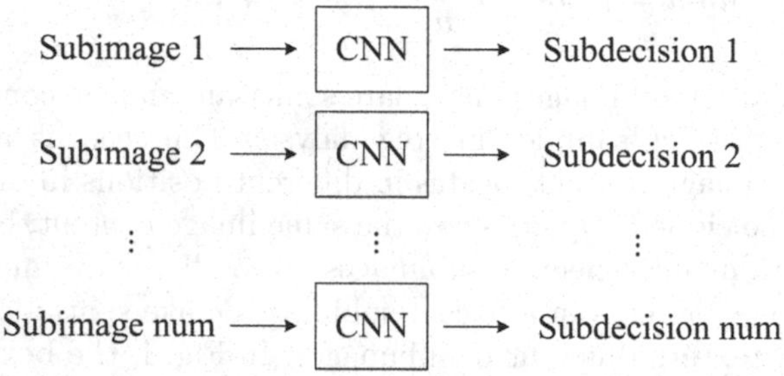

Subimage 1 $\longrightarrow$ CNN $\longrightarrow$ Subdecision 1

Subimage 2 $\longrightarrow$ CNN $\longrightarrow$ Subdecision 2

$\vdots$ CNN $\vdots$ $\vdots$

Subimage num $\longrightarrow$ CNN $\longrightarrow$ Subdecision num

Fig. 5. Each subimage is put through the trained CNN respectively and forms a subdecision.

The final decision is formed through majority vote. D denotes the final decision. Decision 1 means stego, and decision 0 means cover.

$$D = \begin{cases} 1 & when \ \sum_{l=1}^{num} D_l > num/2 \\ 0 & when \ \sum_{l=1}^{num} D_l < num/2 \\ random & otherwise \end{cases} \qquad (3)$$

3.3 Parallel Processing Strategy

One of the advantages of the proposed method is that it can be easily employed in parallel computing environment to improve the time efficiency. In spite of a high computational complexity, device of GPU can accelerate the process to a large extent. Firstly, sub-images can be produced simultaneously. Each sub-image can be segmented directly rather than being segmented in order, since the coordinates of each sub-image can be computed using its index. Denote w_s, h_s, w_e and h_e as coordinates of four vertexes of the ith sub-image. Function $rem(.)$ means remainder operator. Function $ceil(.)$ means rounding up.

$$w\_s = (rem(\frac{i}{floor((M-a)/d)}) - 1) \times d + 1 \tag{4}$$

$$h\_s = (ceil(\frac{i}{floor((N-a)/d)}) - 1) \times d + 1 \tag{5}$$

$$w\_e = w\_s + d - 1 \tag{6}$$

$$h\_e = h\_s + d - 1 \tag{7}$$

Secondly, the processes of CNN model on each sub-image are uncorrelated. These processes can be simultaneous but separate.

4 Experiment

4.1 Dataset and Platforms

We performed experiments using our proposed method to detect two spatial domain content-adaptive steganographic algorithms: S-UNIWARD and HILL, with embedding rates of 0.4 bpp. The corresponding performances achieved by methods in [9, 19] are used as references. All of the experiments using the CNN are performed on a modified version of Caffe toolbox [21] with GPU Nvidia tesla K40c. The dataset used is BOSSbase v1.01 [22] containing 10 000 cover images of size 512 × 512. Image data of the other class (stego) are generated through data embedding into the cover images.

4.2 Training Deep CNN

The deep CNN is trained on 5000 cover images and their corresponding stegos. The CNN is validated on other 2000 images and their corresponding stegos during training phase. The remaining 3000 images are left for test. The order of samples is disrupted in both training phase and testing phase (cover and stego are not coupled). The deep CNN is trained on whole image in training set, not segmented subimages.

Mini-batch GD is used in the training phase, and the batch size of training is fixed to 32. Notice that the batch size used in [9] is 64, and has been reduced to 32 due to hardware limitation. The momentum is fixed to 0.9. The learning rate is initialized to 0.001 and scheduled to decrease 0.1 every 5000 iterations. Parameters in convolution kernels and full-connected layer are initialized by random numbers generated from zero-mean Gaussian distribution with standard deviation of 0.01. We choose the CNN models that achieve best validation accuracy, as shown in Table 2. These CNN models are used in testing phase.

Table 2. Iterations, Val-accuracy and Val-loss of CNN models used in testing phase

	Iterations	Val-accuracy	Val-loss
S-UNIWARD	365000	0.8160	0.37336
HILL	295000	0.7710	0.47733

Table 3. Best testing accuracy of proposed method and that of other methods against S-UNIWARD and HILL

	Method in [9]	Method in [19]	Proposed method
S-UNIWARD	0.7903	0.8347	**0.8913**
HILL	0.7758	0.8013	**0.9008**

4.3 Testing Results

The comparison of testing accuracy among method in [9], method in [19], and the proposed method is shown in Table 3. Our proposed method has competitive performance compared to method in [9] and method in [19]. The reported testing accuracies are 0.09–0.11 higher than that achieved by method in [9], and 0.05–0.08 higher than that achieved by method in [19].

Table 4 illustrates the testing accuracy of proposed method under different hyper parameters of stride d and size of sliding window $a \times a$. Testing accuracy of proposed method is insensitive to these two hyper parameters.

Table 5 records the comparison of testing time efficiency between method in paper [9] and the proposed method. The unit of time efficiency is seconds per image (spi). Although the computational complexity of proposed method is obviously higher than that of method in [9], the average testing time efficiency of proposed method is 0.005933 higher than that of method in [9], which is only slightly worse.

Table 4. Testing accuracy of proposed method under different hyper-parameters—stride and size of sliding window. '\' denotes that the result is not reported in the paper.

	Stride	Size					
		96 × 96	128 × 128	156 × 156	172 × 172	192 × 192	216 × 216
S-UNIWARD	32	0.8827	0.8772	0.8673	0.8593	0.8566	0.8589
	40	0.8702	0.8700	0.8730	0.8600	0.8635	0.8662
	48	0.8683	0.8710	0.8678	0.8717	0.8688	0.8754
	56	0.8768	0.8610	0.8662	0.8672	0.8659	0.8603
	64	0.8652	0.8762	0.8717	0.8770	0.8744	0.8744
	72	0.8767	0.8754	0.8865	0.8618	0.8820	0.8696
	80	0.8785	0.8595	0.8693	0.8610	0.8617	0.8688
	96	0.8522	0.8747	0.8813	0.8825	0.8883	**0.8913**
	120	\	0.8893	0.8620	0.8605	0.8643	0.8665
	144	\	\	0.8725	0.8772	0.8800	0.8828
HILL	32	0.9005	0.8787	0.8712	0.8612	0.8608	0.8662
	40	0.9005	0.8803	0.8712	0.8668	0.8615	0.8683
	48	0.8892	0.8756	0.8767	0.8697	0.8623	0.8653
	56	**0.9008**	0.8817	0.8774	0.8710	0.8752	0.8788
	64	0.8848	0.8850	0.8751	0.8787	0.8787	0.8657
	72	0.8940	0.8887	0.8734	0.8670	0.8730	0.8738
	80	0.8968	0.8757	0.8699	0.8776	0.8780	0.8847
	96	0.8730	0.8815	0.8980	0.8970	0.8888	0.8945
	120	\	0.8997	0.8792	0.8820	0.8815	0.8818
	144	\	\	0.8862	0.8892	0.8883	0.8915

Table 5. Average testing time efficiency (spi) of proposed method and method in [9]

Method in [9]	Proposed method
0.019377	0.025310

5 Conclusion

In this paper, it is shown that the testing accuracy of CNN for steganalysis can be further improved using segmented subimages. However, we acknowledge that if a steganographier deliberately hide secret information in a small subregion of the whole image, our proposed method will be in a dilemma. It would be interesting future works to solve this problem by means of, for example, giving each subdecision a weight before vote. Besides, exploring what kind of sub-region can be beneficial for detection would be another important future work.

References

1. Pevný, T., Bas, P., Fridrich, J.: Steganalysis by subtractive pixel adjacency matrix. IEEE Trans. Inf. Forensics Secur. **5**(2), 215–224 (2010)
2. Fridrich, J., Kodovský, J.: Rich models for steganalysis of digital images. IEEE Trans. Inf. Forensics Secur. **7**(3), 868–882 (2012)
3. Holub, V., Fridrich, J.: Random projections of residuals for digital image steganalysis. IEEE Trans. Inf. Forensics Secur. **8**(12), 1996–2006 (2013)
4. Denemark, T., Sedighi, V., Holub, V., Cogranne, R., Fridrich, J.: Selection-channel-aware rich model for steganalysis of digital images. In: IEEE International Workshop on Information Forensics and Security, pp. 48–53. IEEE (2014)
5. Kodovský, J., Fridrich, J., Holub, V.: Ensemble classifiers for steganalysis of digital media. IEEE Trans. Inf. Forensics Secur. **7**(2), 432–444 (2012)
6. Tan, S., Li, B.: Stacked convolutional auto-encoders for steganalysis of digital images. In: Signal and Information Processing Association Annual Summit and Conference, pp. 1–4. IEEE, Chiang Mai (2014)
7. Ker, A.D., Böhme, R.: Revisiting weighted stego-image steganalysis. In: Security, Forensics, Steganography, and Watermarking of Multimedia Contents X, vol. 6819, p. 681905. International Society for Optics and Photonics (2008)
8. Qian, Y., Dong, J., Wang, W., Tan, T.: Deep learning for steganalysis via convolutional neural networks. In: Media Watermarking, Security, and Forensics, vol. 9409, p. 94090J. International Society for Optics and Photonics (2015)
9. Xu, G., Wu, H.Z., Shi, Y.Q.: Structural design of convolutional neural networks for steganalysis. IEEE Signal Process. Lett. **23**(5), 708–712 (2016)
10. Holub, V., Fridrich, J., Denemark, T.: Universal distortion function for steganography in an arbitrary domain. EURASIP J. Inf. Secur. **2014**(1), 1–13 (2014)
11. Li, B., Wang, M., Huang, J., Li, X.: A new cost function for spatial image steganography. In: IEEE International Conference on Image Processing, pp. 4206–4210. IEEE (2014)
12. Zeng, J., Tan, S., Li, B., Huang, J.: Large-scale JPEG image steganalysis using hybrid deep-learning framework. IEEE Trans. Inf. Forensics Secur. **13**(5), 1200–1214 (2018)
13. Tang, W., Tan, S., Li, B., Huang, J.: Automatic steganographic distortion learning using a generative adversarial network. IEEE Signal Process. Lett. **24**(10), 1547–1551 (2017)
14. Chen, M., Sedighi, V., Boroumand, M., Fridrich, J.: JPEG-phase-aware convolutional neural network for steganalysis of JPEG images. In: Proceedings of the 5th ACM Workshop on Information Hiding and Multimedia Security, pp. 75–84. ACM (2017)
15. Wu, S., Zhong, S., Liu, Y.: Deep residual learning for image steganalysis. Multimedia Tools Appl., 1–17 (2017)
16. Wu, S., Zhong, S.H., Liu, Y.: Residual convolution network based steganalysis with adaptive content suppression. In: IEEE International Conference on Multimedia and Expo, pp. 241–246. IEEE (2017)
17. Ye, J., Ni, J., Yi, Y.: Deep learning hierarchical representations for image steganalysis. IEEE Trans. Inf. Forensics Secur. **12**(11), 2545–2557 (2017)
18. Xu, G.: Deep convolutional neural network to detect J-UNIWARD. In: Proceedings of the 5th ACM Workshop on Information Hiding and Multimedia Security, pp. 67–73. ACM (2017)

19. Wu, S., Zhong, S.H., Liu, Y.: A Novel Convolutional Neural Network for Image Steganalysis with Shared Normalization. arXiv preprint arXiv:1711.07306 (2017)
20. Yang, J., Shi, Y.Q., Wong, E.K., Kang, X.: JPEG Steganalysis Based on DenseNet. arXiv preprint arXiv:1711.09335 (2017)
21. Jia, Y., Shelhamer, E., Donahue, J., et al.: Caffe: Convolutional architecture for fast feature embedding. In: Proceedings of the 22nd ACM international conference on Multimedia, pp. 675–678. ACM (2014)
22. Bas, P., Filler, T., Pevný, T.: "Break our steganographic system": the ins and outs of organizing BOSS. In: Filler, T., Pevný, T., Craver, S., Ker, A. (eds.) IH 2011. LNCS, vol. 6958, pp. 59–70. Springer, Heidelberg (2011). https://doi.org/10.1007/978-3-642-24178-9_5

IPFRA: An Online Protocol Reverse Analysis Mechanism

Zhang Xiaoming[1], Qiang Qian[1(✉)], Wang Weisheng[1],
Wang Zhanfeng[2], and Wei Xianglin[3]

[1] National Computer Network Emergency Response Technical
Team/Coordination Center of China, Beijing 100000, China
qq@cert.org.cn
[2] School of Computer Science and Engineering, Southeast University,
Nanjing 211189, China
[3] Nanjing Telecommunication Technology Research Institute,
Nanjing 210007, China

Abstract. Protocol reverse engineering is of great significance for discovering protocol vulnerabilities, improving protocol security and reusing protocol. The existing protocol reverse analysis methods usually need a great deal of computation and often takes a long time, which seriously affects the effect of real-time analysis. This paper proposes an incremental protocol format extraction algorithm, which divides the network traffic into different substreams, and introduces error decision mechanism to avoid local errors caused by partition, so as to ensure the correctness. By dynamic evaluation of the complexity of the protocol analysis, the incremental protocol analysis method can effectively improve the efficiency of the protocol reverse engineering.

Keywords: Industrial control protocol · Reverse analysis · Online analysis
Incremental learning

1 Introduction

Protocol reverse engineering is the process of extracting protocol format and protocol state machine information by monitoring and analyzing network input/output packets, system behaviors and instruction execution processes without protocol description. Since the network security has attracted the attention, protocol security analysis is increasingly subject to attention to the relevant departments, has become the focus of academic research, the protocol is widely used in reverse engineering such as intrusion detection, vulnerability mining and reuse of protocol [1–4].

Protocol reverse analysis technology mainly includes two stages: protocol format analysis and protocol state machine inference. For unknown protocols, protocol format is an indispensable basis for state annotation, so protocol format analysis is the precondition for inference of protocol state machines. According to the different analysis objects, protocol format analysis technologies can be divided into two categories, which are network traffic based analyzing technologies and execution trace based analysis technologies, respectively. Compared to execution trace based analysis

X. Sun et al. (Eds.): ICCCS 2018, LNCS 11066, pp. 324–333, 2018.
https://doi.org/10.1007/978-3-030-00015-8_28

technologies, network traffic based analyzing technologies are easier to be implemented. Because of the great gaps between the structure and characteristics of the values of different protocol packets, the correctness of the reverse results are not guaranteed. At the same time, the high time consuming heavily affect the widespread usage of protocol reverse analysis when analyzing large number of samples. At present, the research of protocol format analysis and protocol state machine inference has made some progress 45, but there are still many problems in efficiency, accuracy and implementation complexity, which deserve further study.

This paper proposes an incremental protocol format analysis algorithm, which divides the network traffic into different substreams, and introduces error decision mechanism to avoid local errors caused by partitioning so as to ensure the correctness. By verifying on the known protocols, the proposed method performs a higher accuracy and can greatly provide the real-time and response efficiency of protocol analysis.

2 Related Work

In protocol reverse engineering by the research objects, protocol format analysis technology can be divided into network traffic based analyzing technologies and execution trace based analysis technologies [1]. Based on the execution trace, protocol format analysis technology uses dynamic Taint Analysis Technology to track the parsing process of the program to the message data, and realizes the protocol format extraction [9] according to the protocol entity to parse the message field. However, this method depends on application program, so the network traffic based methods are more universal, which is the focus of this article.

Protocol format analysis technology based on network traffic can be divided into two categories sequence alignment based algorithms and non-sequence alignment based algorithms. Marshall Beddoe et al. launched PI project [5] (Protocol Information Project) in 2004, by introducing the sequence alignment algorithm of bioinformatics, to infer the structure of target protocol. The PI project has 3 steps: first, the distance matrix between the message byte sequences is calculated through the local sequence alignment algorithm; secondly, phylogenetic trees is constructed by UPGMA algorithm; finally, progressive alignment algorithm is used to perform multiple sequence alignment. Unlike the PI project, RolePlayer [10] and ScriptGen [4] didn't aim to analyze the complete agreement, their key contributions are the recognition of the user parameter, state identification message structure and length of dynamic field. Besides, they can identify the protocol categories of the received packets, and update the dynamic field of the packets and replay communications. Cui et al. put forward a protocol reverse scheme Discoverer [6], which is based on recursive clustering. It implements initial field partition by segmentation, and compares sequences based on field. Moreover, Discoverer can also recognize the semantics of format, length, offset and cookie with heuristic methods.

Non-sequence alignment based algorithms also introduce speech recognition model n-gram language model or hidden Markov model to infer the protocol format, but these methods can barely derive a complete protocol format, and ignore the value constrained of fields [2, 11, 12]. In comparison, the multiple sequence alignment algorithm can be used to divide the whole packet and extract the features, which is more practical. Therefore, this paper is based on the progressive multi sequence alignment algorithm to improve the time efficiency of the protocol analysis and ensure the accuracy of the analysis.

3 Modeling of Protocol Format Analysis

Sequence alignment is an important step to implement protocol format analysis. This section mainly describes how to implement protocol format analysis by sequence alignment.

3.1 Pairwise Sequence Alignment

The task of double sequence alignment is to find out the similarity between the testing sequence and the target sequence, including dot matrix method, dynamic programming algorithm, FASTA algorithm and BLAST algorithm [12]. Among them, the dynamic programming algorithm has high sensitivity when identifying the similarity, and it is the most commonly used sequence alignment algorithm. In the following section, this paper introduces the most commonly used Needleman-Wunsch algorithm and Smith-Waterman algorithm [2, 12].

The Needleman-Wunsch algorithm is a global optimal double sequence alignment algorithm, which includes 3 steps: similarity scoring, score calculation and optimal backtracking.

1. Similarity scoring. For two different sequences with the length of m and n respectively, a $(n + 1) \times (m + 1)$ similarity matrix S is constructed. For matching symbol pairs, the similarity score is marked as 1; otherwise, the similarity score is 0.
2. Summing of similarity score. The similarity matrix is iteratively calculated and the new matrix M is obtained. The sum formula is shown as follows, in which the penalty score w is set to 0.

$$M_{ij} = \max \begin{cases} M_{i-1,j-1} + S_{ij} \\ M_{i,j-1} + w \\ M_{i-1,j} + w \end{cases} \qquad (1)$$

where M_{ij} and S_{ij} are the similarity score between the i-th and j-th sequences in the matrix and sequences themselves respectively.

3. Optimal back-trace. The backtracking of similarity matrix start in cell with the highest value and traverse matrix to the beginning. The rule of backtracking is to assess the left, upper and diagonal cell and move to the one with the maximum score. If all cells are equal, we move to the diagonal cell. If moving diagonally, nothing should be done. Otherwise, we insert gap into the sequence.

The idea of Smith-Waterman algorithm is one of Needleman-Wunsch algorithm, and the differences are: (1) the mismatch score and the vacancy penalty are negative, and once the sum of the sum matrix is less than 0, the comparison is restarted; (2) the comparison of the sequences is not necessarily terminated in the lower right corner, but can end with any position of the matrix. The Smith-Waterman algorithm has higher sensitivity than the two sequences with local similarity, but cannot obtain the overall sequence comparison. Both the Smith-Waterman algorithm and the Needleman-Wunsch algorithm need to calculate all the matrix elements, so the time complexity of the two is O(mn).

3.2 Multiple Sequence Alignment

The multiple sequence alignment is essentially a generalization of the double sequence alignment. The common multiple sequence alignment algorithms are mainly divided into 3 categories: the exact alignment algorithm, the iterative comparison algorithm (Interactive Alignment) and the progressive alignment algorithm (noted as PA). If the precise alignment algorithms of dynamic programming extend to multi sequence alignment, they can obtain the optimal results. However the complexity of the algorithms are $2^n \times L^n$, their complexity increases exponentially with the sequence, will produce enormous amount of computer in practical application, where n denotes the number of packets, L denotes packet length.

Iterative alignment algorithm is based on a preliminary sequence alignment result, and improves multiple sequence alignment through a series of iterations until the result cannot be improved. Although the iterative algorithm has the advantages of good robustness and insensitivity on sequence numbers, the iterative calculation process still requires considerable computational resources. The progressive alignment algorithm adopts the idea of greedy algorithm, starting with the comparison of two sequences, and gradually adding new sequences until all sequences are added. Compared with the previous two kinds of algorithms, the asymptotic alignment algorithm has an obvious advantage in efficiency. Although the optimal comparison results cannot be guaranteed, the asymptotic alignment can still obtain satisfactory results when the similarity of the sample is higher. Therefore, the existing protocol analysis methods based on network traffic mostly adopt progressive multiple sequence alignment algorithm.

Progressive multiple sequence alignment generally consists of 3 steps:

1. Calculating the distance matrix. The most commonly used Smith-Waterman algorithm is used to find the best local alignment between every two sequences, and the similarity between sequences is calculated, and the distance matrix D of the two sequences is constructed, denoted as D_{pq}, where p and q denote the two compared sequence.
2. Constructing and partitioning guide tree. Unweighted pair-group method with arithmetic means 15 is used to calculate the distance between subclasses, and the subclass with the minimum distance is gradually merged. The distance between the subclass C_i and C_j can be calculated by Formula (2).

$$d_{ij} = \frac{1}{|C_i||C_j|} \sum_{p \in C_i, q \in C_j} D_{pq} \qquad (2)$$

Since there may be a variety of protocol format types, a large number of invalid filling bits may be added to the sequence if the asymptotically multiple sequence alignment is used. In order to improve the accuracy of sequence alignment, a distance threshold d_{ij} is set as stop merging condition and finally multiple boot trees are obtained. In the tree, the leaf nodes represent the original sample sequences, intermediate nodes represent the child nodes are aligned sequences of pairwise sequence alignment.

3. Performing the asymptotically multiple sequence alignment. After traversing the boot tree, the Needleman-Wunsch algorithm is used to compare the dynamic programming of the double sequence, and the unaligned bytes are filled. When multiple boot trees are constructed, the progressive multiple sequence alignment will get multiple sample subsets.

Progressive multiple sequence alignment algorithms can effectively reduce the complexity of multiple sequence alignment in the analysis of complex protocols, but there are the following defects:

1. Some alignments between samples with great gap are useless, Pre-clustering can separate them roughly so as to decrease time consuming. As the format type of the packets is not considered when the comparison is performed, it will reduce the accuracy of the protocol analysis by forcibly aligning the different format of the message sample. The accuracy of the double sequence alignment is based on the higher sequence similarity, and if the sequence difference is big, the comparison effect will be seriously affected.
2. The comparison result is a flat alignment byte sequence, which ignores the field hierarchy in the packets. Compared to the protocol specification model, the results of the algorithm lack the analysis of the packet structure, and do not include the structure attribute rules.
3. The time complexity increase a lot when analysis long packet bytes sequence. At the same time, the overhead of sequence alignment is further increased because of the more type of format, which is larger than the increase of the sample set.

4   Incremental Protocol Format Analysis Algorithm

4.1   The Main Idea of the IPFRA

When dealing with a large number of data, especially the online flows, it may result in overflow of program memory. However, the incremental protocol format analysis can obtain real-time incremental analysis results to achieve a better user response. This paper designs an incremental protocol format reverse analysis algorithm (An Incremental Protocol Format Reverse Analysis Algorithm, IPFRA).

For the sake of simplicity, a formal description is given. Let F denotes the network traffic data. In the incremental protocol analysis, the flow F is divided into several stages, which are denoted as $Flow = <flow_0, flow_1, flow_2,..., flow_n>$. The process time of the each ubstream can be represented as $T = <t_0, t_1, t_2,..., t_n>$, where n is a positive integer. Let δ_t denote the maximum toleration time, which is the time from the beginning of extraction on the network traffic to the generation of the initial analysis result. In other words, t_0 must be smaller than δ_t.

Generally, incremental protocol analysis can be divided into two stages: the initial stage and the incremental analysis stage. The initial stage refers to the process of importing packet data or capturing traffic to the generation of the initial result. Incremental analysis is the process of gradual analysis on the remaining packets or coming packets. After initial stage, we compare new packets with initial inferred format, gather messages failed to be parsed by existing format, divide the later packets into different groups, and then analyze the substreams and merge the format results. In this process, when there exists a difference between the former result and the latter result, there are two ways to deal the with the analysis results: one is to compare the analysis results of the later arriving packets with the result of the initial stage, find the differences and update the result, and the other is to divide the later packets into different groups for analysis, then merge the ubstreams to re-perform the analysis to generate a new result. Generally speaking, the first method is simpler, but it will increase the risk of local optimum. Therefore, our proposed algorithm used the second one.

In fact, IPFRA is a variation of the gradual progressive multiple sequence alignment algorithm, and its basic idea of the algorithm is as follows: Firstly, Clustering with length of packets is carried out, because the length of messages in different format do not vary too much. Then, analyze the - packets in the same cluster and combined the results incrementally to get the final results.

The IPFRA algorithm is illustrated as Fig. 1.

The pseudo codes of the IPFRA algorithm are as follows (Fig. 2):

In order to reduce the response time of users, the processing time of each substream is less than δ_t when the substream is partitioned. In the experiment, δ_t is set to be 1 min, and the length of the sub stream is 500. In the process of protocol format analysis, the speed of the algorithm is mainly affected by the two factors the number and the length of the packets.

4.2   Complexity Analysis

The packet number of substream is n, the average character number of the packets is m, and the average tree number of asymptotically multiple sequence alignment is r. The IPFRA algorithm is actually the improvement of progressive sequence. Progressive multiple sequence alignment is composed of 3 parts: distance matrix calculated by Smith-Waterman algorithm, UPGMA algorithm and Needleman-Wunsch algorithm.

1. The complexity of Smith-Waterman algorithm which is used to calculate the distance matrix is $O(m^2n^2)$, and it is assumed that the time frequency of the algorithm is Am^2n^2, where A is a constant.
2. The complexity of the UPGMA algorithm which is used to construct the boot tree is $O(n^2)$, and it is assumed that the time frequency of the algorithm is Bn^2, where B is constant.
3. The complexity of the Needleman-Wunsch algorithm is $O(m^2n)$, and it is assumed that the time frequency of the algorithm is Cm^2n, where C is constant.

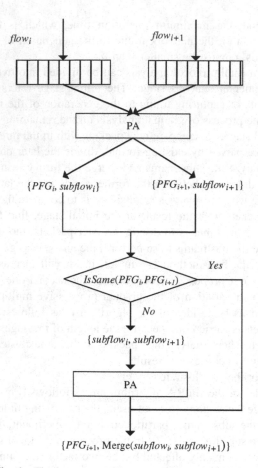

Fig. 1. The key steps of incremental protocol analysis

As a result, the complexity of the analysis of a substream protocol format is $Am^2n^2 + Bn^2 + Cm^2n$.

5 Experiments and Verification

5.1 The Complexity of Original PA Algorithm

The proposed method bases on the observation that as the increase of the packet length and packet number, the time consuming shows a nonlinear growth. In order to verify this observation, the FTP protocol is chosen as an example to perform protocol reversal analysis. Firstly, a long FTP traffic flow is captured by Wireshark, then the running time of the original PI were recorded by dividing the flow into four groups, which is composed of the first 1000, 2000, 3000 and 4000 packets. Figure 3 gives the experiment results, in which the horizontal axis represents the number of packets, the vertical axis represents the time (in seconds). It can be found the consuming time is nonlinear

Input: *Flow*=<*flow*$_0$, *flow*$_1$, *flow*$_2$,...,*flow*$_n$>
Output: *PFG*

Begin
1: *flow*$_i$=*recievePacket*(); *Flow*← *flow*$_i$
2: (*PFG*$_i$, *substream*$_i$)=*PA*(*flow*$_i$)
3: *flow*$_{i+1}$=*recievePacket*(); *Flow*← *flow*$_{i+1}$
4: (*PFG*$_{i+1}$, *substream*$_{i+1}$)=*PA*(*flow*$_i$)
5: if (!*IsSame*(*PFG*$_i$, *PFG*$_{i+1}$))
6:      (*PFG*$_{i+1}$, *substream*$_{i+1}$)=*PA*(*substream*$_i$, *substream*$_{i+1}$)
7: else
8:      *substream*$_{i+1}$=*Merge*(*substream*$_i$, *substream*$_{i+1}$)
9: *skip to step* 3
10: No incoming packets
11: }
12: return *PFG*
End

Fig. 2. The pseudo codes of the IPFRA algorithm

growth. Therefore, with the increase in the number of packets, it will take a long time for the user to get the results. The nonlinear increase will heavily affect user experience, for a long flow will run out of memory.

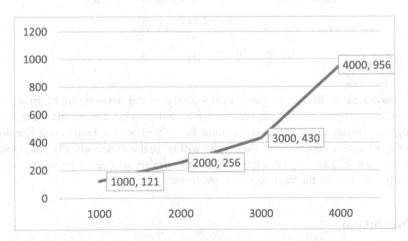

Fig. 3. The time efficiency of PA algorithm (The x-axis denotes the packet number to be processing and the y-axis denotes the processing time)

5.2   The Verification of IPFRA

In order to verify the effectiveness of our proposed algorithm IPFRA, 5000 packets of two most common protocols, i.e. FTP and HTTP, are captured. In incremental analysis, the length of the substream is set to be 500. To make a comparison, two efficient protocol analysis methods, i.e. Discoverer and the original PA, are run on the same dataset. Table 1 shows the accuracy of field recognized by IPFRA, Discoverer, and original PI. We can find that for the FTP protocol, the three methods can identify the packet structure more accurately, and the accuracy of the Discoverer algorithm is 99%. This is because the method can accurately identify the space symbols to divide the field boundaries in FTP packets by predefined special characters, while IPFRA and PI are based on multiple sequence alignment and Abnormal data lead to error recognition. In the more complex HTTP protocol, the effect of IPFRA is obviously better than that of Discoverer, almost as well as original PI.

Table 1. Comparison of accuracy of field boundary division

Protocol	IPFRA	Discoverer	PA
FTP	0.97	0.97	0.99
HTTP	0.83	0.74	0.85

Table 2 gives the time spent on the analysis procedure of the 3 algorithms. Because IPFRA algorithm adopts incremental analysis, the protocol format analysis time is relatively fixed, thus its sequence alignment data scale is far less than the total quantity analysis time.

Table 2. Algorithm time analysis efficiency (second)

Protocol	IPFRA	Discoverer	PA
FTP	80	386	402
HTTP	100	456	540

As illustrated in the former part, IPFRA analyzes the network traffic in an incremental manner, it avoids the long waiting time, and provide a better user experience. Although the result the initial result cannot be treated as the final result due to the processing of subsequent packets, the results will be updated periodically and approach the optimal result. Just like the other algorithms, the recall rate of protocol format is apparently affected by the captured network traffic.

6 Conclusion

This paper proposes an incremental protocol format analysis algorithm, which divides the network traffic into different substreams, and introduces error decision mechanism to avoid local errors caused by partitioning, so as to ensure the correctness of the protocol format inference. Compared with Discoverer and PA algorithm on real FTP and HTTP dataset, IPFRA has high accuracy and response time is significantly shorter than Discover and PA algorithm. Because the algorithm uses incremental design, it can interact with users quickly, so it has a good promotion effect for the application of protocol reverse analysis. Next, we will further study the incremental protocol format analysis algorithm and improve the accuracy of protocol recognition.

Acknowledgment. This work was supported by the National Key R&D Program of China Grant No. 2017YFC1201204, the National Natural Science Foundation of China under Grant No. 61402521, and Youth Foundation OF under Grant No. 2016QN-004.

References

1. Pan, F., Hong, Z., Du, Y.X., et al.: Recursive clustering based method for message structure extraction. J. Sichuan Univ. **44**(6), 137–142 (2012)
2. Leita, C., Dacier, M., Massicotte, F.: Automatic handling of protocol dependencies and reaction to 0-day attacks with scriptgen based honeypots. In: Zamboni, D., Kruegel, C. (eds.) RAID 2006. LNCS, vol. 4219, pp. 185–205. Springer, Heidelberg (2006). https://doi.org/10.1007/11856214_10
3. Comparetti, P.M., Wondracek, G., Kruegel, C., et al.: Prospex: protocol specification extraction. In: Proceedings of the 30th IEEE Symposium on Security and Privacy. IEEE Press, Oakland (2009)
4. Wei-Ming, L.I.: An automatic network protocol fuzz testing and vulnerability discovering method. Chin. J. Comput. **34**(2), 242–255 (2011)
5. Marshall Beddoe. Protocol Information Project. [EB/OL], 5 October 2004. http://www.4tphi.net/~awalters/PI/PI.html. Accessed 20 Mar 2011
6. Cui, W., Kannan, J., Wang, H.J.: Discoverer: automatic protocol reverse engineering from network traces. In: 16th USENIX Security Symposium, pp. 199–212 (2007)
7. Vogt, H.H., Swierstra, S.D., Kuiper, M.F.: Higher order attribute grammars. In: Conference on Program Language Design and Implementation, pp. 131–145 (1989)
8. Caballero, J., Yin, H., Liang, Z., et al.: Polyglot: automatic extraction of protocol format using dynamic binary analysis. In: 14th ACM Conference on Computer and Communications Security (CCS), pp. 317–329 (2007)
9. Cui, W., Paxson, V., Weaver, N., Katz, R.H.: Protocol-independent adaptive replay of application dialog. In: Proceedings of the 13th Network and Distributed System Security Symposium (2006)
10. Whalen, S., Bishop, M., Crutchfield, J.P.: Hidden Markov models for automated protocol learning. In: Jajodia, S., Zhou, J. (eds.) SecureComm 2010. LNICST, vol. 50, pp. 415–428. Springer, Heidelberg (2010). https://doi.org/10.1007/978-3-642-16161-2_24
11. Krueger, T., Krämer, N., Rieck, K.: ASAP: automatic semantics-aware analysis of network payloads. In: Dimitrakakis, C., Gkoulalas-Divanis, A., Mitrokotsa, A., Verykios, V.S., Saygin, Y. (eds.) PSDML 2010. LNCS (LNAI), vol. 6549, pp. 50–63. Springer, Heidelberg (2011). https://doi.org/10.1007/978-3-642-19896-0_5
12. Yipeng, W., Xiaochun, X., Zubair M., et al.: A semantics aware approach to automated reverse engineering unknown protocols. In: ICNP (2012)
13. Jain, K., Murty, M., Flynn, P.: Data clustering: a review. ACM Computing Surveys (CSUR) **31**(3), 264–323 (1999)

Medical Image Watermarking Based on SIFT-DCT Perceptual Hashing

Jialing Liu[1], Jingbing Li[1,3(✉)], Jing Chen[2(✉)], Xiangxi Zou[1],
Jieren Cheng[1], and Jing Liu[1]

[1] College of Information Science and Technology, Hainan University, Haikou 570228, China
jialing_hainu@163.com, Jingbingli2008@hotmail.com,
zouxxhainu@163.com, cjr22@163.com, jingliuhnu2016@hotmail.com
[2] Department of Radiology, HaiKou People's Hospital, The Affiliated Hospital of Xiangya
Medical School of Central South University, Haikou 570228, Hainan, China
jingchen_haiko@163.com
[3] State Key Laboratory of Marine Resource Utilization in the South China Sea, Hainan University,
Haikou 570228, China

Abstract. Medical image containing patient information is often faced with various attacks in the transmission process. In order to enhance the medical information system security, and effectively solve the problem of medical data protection, a new algorithm of medical image watermarking based on SIFT-DCT perceptual hashing (scale invariant feature transform and discrete cosine transform) is proposed. Firstly, use SIFT-DCT perceptual hashing to extract features for the original medical images and quantize to generate hashing sequences. Then, use chaotic maps to encrypt the watermarking and embed it in the medical image. Finally, calculate the correlation coefficients of the embedded and extracted watermarking sequences to reflect the robustness of the algorithm. The results of experiment show that the proposed algorithm has good robustness against conventional attacks and geometric attacks, especially in terms of rotation, translation and clipping.

Keywords: Medical image · Zero watermarking · SIFT-DCT
Perceptual hashing · Robustness

1 Introduction

In recent years, with the rapid development of big data technologies and cloud platforms, medical methods have gradually shifted from traditional medicine to telemedicine, resulting in more and more medical images being transmitted and shared in the network [1]. Due to the particularity of medical images, the protection of their private information becomes particularly important. The digital watermarking technology of medical images is to solve the problem that it may be subject to tampering, misappropriation, distortion, unrecognizable and other issues in the process of transmission sharing [2, 3]. Combining zero watermarking technology with perceptual hashing technology as a security technology of information security, through the unique invisibility, robustness and other

© Springer Nature Switzerland AG 2018
X. Sun et al. (Eds.): ICCCS 2018, LNCS 11066, pp. 334–345, 2018.
https://doi.org/10.1007/978-3-030-00015-8_29

characteristics, to protect the privacy of the patient. And zero watermarking can avoid the medical data that has been tampered, so as to achieve related patient information needed for remote medical diagnosis and remote surgery is transmitted and shared on the Internet.

Image-perceptual hashing is one of the important branches of perceptual hashing, and it is a kind of image-based content hashing algorithm. Usually, the image hashing should satisfy the requirements of perceptual robustness, uniqueness and security. The core of image-perceptual hashing algorithm is feature selection and coding. There are many algorithms for feature extraction. Finding an algorithm which is robust and resistant to various attacks is crucial. According to these key data, choosing the appropriate coding method can achieve the effect of security and tamper-proof. In addition, the characteristics of image hashing technology security make the copyright protection of image become possible. The main image hashing methods now mainly focus on the characteristics of robustness study [4, 5]. And these features can be divided into two categories: global features and local features. Global features include grayscale features, frequency characteristics, color features, and texture features. For example, the discrete cosine transform to extract the feature is considered to be an ideal method. The most common local feature is scale-invariant feature transform (SIFT) [6]. The algorithm is a local feature descriptor in the field of image processing. Key points can be detected in the image, include the position, scale, and rotation invariant of extreme points in the spatial scale. The extracted sift features have good robustness to rotation, scaling, and brightness changes [7, 8].

In order to study the influence of geometric attacks on medical images, this paper proposes a medical image watermarking based on SIFT-DCT perceptual hashing algorithm that combines global features with local features. The algorithm uses the robust hashing sequence in medical image transform domain to construct the zero watermarking, instead of modifying the features of medical image. It can adapt to the characteristics of medical data, can resist strong attack, and has very strong robustness.

2   Basic Theory

2.1   Scale Invariant Feature Transform

SIFT is a local feature extraction method that researchers are more interested in in recent years. The uniqueness of SIFT lies in the use of image pyramids, which are located at different levels of the pyramid depending on the size of the pyramid. Its role is to find some "robust points" similar to image fingerprints from the pixels of the image. The essence of these key points is the maximum value of the image grayscale image, and contains information such as its position, size, and direction. In addition, they also have good robustness, uniqueness, versatility, high speed and so on.

The SIFT algorithm extracts features from the image generally includes the following steps.

(1) Extreme values detection in scale space: Using different scales of Gaussian differential kernels and image convolutions, as shown in Eq. 2. Figure 1 shows a schematic diagram of an image pyramid.

$$D(x, y, \sigma) = (G(x, y, k\sigma) - G(x, y, \sigma)) * I(x, y)$$
$$= L(x, y, k\sigma) - L(x, y, \sigma) \tag{1}$$

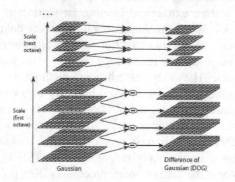

Fig. 1. Gaussian pyramid and DOG pyramid.

Where $G(x, y, \sigma)$ is a scale-variable Gaussian function and (x, y) is a spatial scale coordinate.

To find extreme points, each sample point must be compared with all its neighbors. As shown in Fig. 2, the middle detection point and its 8 points adjacent to the same scale and the 9×2 points corresponding to the upper and lower adjacent scales are compared for a total of 26 points to ensure the space in the scale and 2D Extreme points are detected in the space.

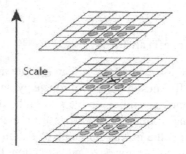

Fig. 2. Comparison of SIFT extreme points.

(2) Key point location: At each candidate location, the location and scale are determined by a fine-fitting model. At the same time, the edge effect will be removed to enhance the matching stability and improve the anti-noise ability.

(3) Direction determination: Sampling in the neighborhood centered on the key point and use the histogram to count the gradient directions of neighboring pixels. All subsequent manipulations of the image data are transformed with respect to the orientation, scale and position of the key points, providing invariance to these transformations.

(4) Key point descriptor: In the neighborhood around each key point, a local coordinate system is established with the main direction of the key point at 0 degrees to ensure rotation invariance (Fig. 3).

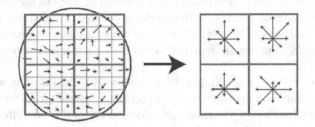

Fig. 3. SIFT feature vector generation.

2.2 Discrete Cosine Transform

The DCT is a transform associated with the Fourier transform that is similar to the Discrete Fourier Transform but it uses only real numbers. When DCT transform is used in digital watermarking, the image is often processed in blocks, and 2×2 blocks are set by default in the experiment.

The DCT transform formula for $N \times N$ images is as follows:

$$F(u, v) = C(u) \bullet C(v) \sum_{x=0}^{N-1} \sum_{y=0}^{N-1} f(x, y) \bullet \cos\left[\frac{(x+0.5)\pi}{N} \bullet u\right] \bullet \cos\left[\frac{(y+0.5)\pi}{N} \bullet v\right] \quad (2)$$

$$\text{Where } C(v) = \begin{cases} \sqrt{\frac{1}{N}}, & u = 0 \\ \sqrt{\frac{2}{N}}, & u \neq 0 \end{cases}$$

, f (x, y) is the pixel value at the point (x, y), F (u, v) is the 2D-DCT transform coefficients for f (x, y).

2.3 Logistic Mapping

Logistic mapping is one of the most famous chaotic maps. It is a simple dynamic nonlinear regression with chaotic behavior. Its mathematical definition can be expressed as follows:

$$x_{k+1} = \mu \cdot x_k \cdot (1 - x_k) \tag{3}$$

Where x_k belongs to (0,1), $0 < u <= 4$; Experiments show that when $3.5699456 < u <= 4$, the logistic map enters a chaotic state and the Logistic chaotic sequence can be used as an ideal key sequence.

3   Perceptual Hashing

Perceptual hashing is an algorithm based on the visual features of the image. It uses a hash function to generate a series of "fingerprints" of fixed or indefinite length images for comparing similarities. The core of image-perceptual hashing algorithm is feature selection and coding. Finding an algorithm that is robust and resistant to various attacks is crucial.

To perceptual hashing, a novel algorithm based on SIFT-DCT is presents for medical image watermarking. The algorithm is used to extract features of medical image, which can increase the robustness of watermarking algorithm and achieve the effect of security. At the same time, the binarization rules are as follows:

$$h(n) = \begin{cases} 1, & if \ s(i,j) \geq m \\ 0, & if \ s(i,j) < m \end{cases}, \quad i \in [M_1, M_2] \ j \in [N_1, N_2] \tag{4}$$

Where S (i, j) represents the corresponding cell value in the 4×8 sub-module. The m is the mean of the 4×8 sub-module. Figure 4 depicts the algorithm flow. The specific steps are as follows:

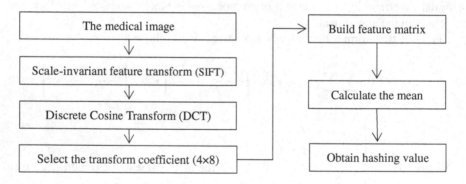

Fig. 4. Perceptual Hashing algorithm flow.

Step 1.   Extract key points.
Step 2.   Discrete Cosine Transform.
Step 3.   Select the transform coefficient (4×8).
Step 4.   Build feature matrix.
Step 5.   Calculate the mean.
Step 6.   Obtain hashing sequence.

4   Zero Watermarking Algorithm

Zero watermarking is beneficial to improve the robustness of the algorithm. It mainly includes the embedding and extraction of watermarking.

4.1   Watermarking Embedding

The watermarking embedding process is shown in Fig. 5. The specific steps are as follows:

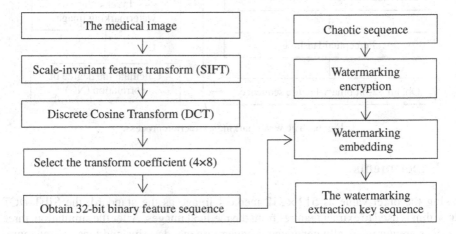

Fig. 5. The watermarking embedding process.

Step 1.   The medical image could be processed by SIFT-DCT.
Step 2.   Select the transform coefficient (4×8).
Step 3.   Obtain 32-bit binary feature sequence of medical image.
Step 4.   Generates appropriate length of the chaotic sequence for scrambling the original watermarking image.
Step 5.   Generates the watermarking extraction key sequence though XOR operation.

4.2   Watermarking Extraction

The watermarking extraction process is shown in Fig. 6. The specific steps are as follows:

Step 1.   The attacked medical image could be processed by SIFT-DCT.
Step 2.   Using the same method to obtain 32-bit binary feature sequence of attacked medical image.
Step 3.   Let the binary feature sequence of attacked medical image XOR the watermarking extraction key sequence.
Step 4.   Inverse the scramble watermarking image.
Step 5.   Calculate the degree of correlation judging the watermarking embedding.

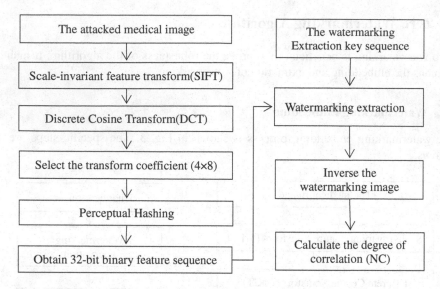

Fig. 6. The watermarking extraction process.

5 Experiments

Taking the pixel value as 512×512 medical image as the standard, the SIFT-DCT algorithm is used to extract features from the medical images. After the simulation, three matrices are automatically generated. They are image, descrips and locs. Image represents the input image matrix. Descrips represents the normalized feature descriptor (n $\times$ 128 dimensions, and the sum of squares of elements in each row is 1). Locs represent key points (n $\times$ 4, the first two elements of each row are key coordinates, the third element is the key dimension, and the fourth element is the key point angle). Select the 4×8 sub-matrix in the DCT matrix of descrips and obtain 32-bit binary feature sequence. The value of NC is between 0 and 1, and 1 represents the most similar. Besides, less than 0.5 will be treated as different image experimental processes. There are four medical images of difference parts in Fig. 7. Table 1 shows that the feature sequences are not the same for different parts of the medical image. And the first abdominal image

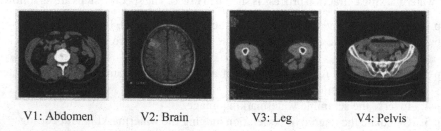

V1: Abdomen   V2: Brain   V3: Leg   V4: Pelvis

Fig. 7. Medical slice images at different locations.

is selected as the original medical image to test conventional attacks and geometric attacks are performed. The medical image without attack is shown in Fig. 8.

Table 1. Hashing sequences of medical images at different locations.

Slices in different positions	Feature sequence
V1: Abdomen	0010 1000 1000 0000 1000 1000 1000 1000
V2: Brain	1100 1000 0010 0010 0111 0000 1000 1101
V3: Leg	0000 1000 1001 0000 0010 1001 0010 1000
V4: Pelvis	1000 1000 0000 1000 0000 0000 1000 0000

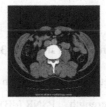

PSNR= 102.3162dB   NC=1

Fig. 8. Medical image and Extracted watermarking without attack.

5.1 Conventional Attacks

Multiple conventional attacks are performed on the medical image, and the value of NC are recorded in the Table 2.

Table 2. PSNR and NC under conventional attacks based on SIFT-DCT.

Conventional attack	Gaussian noise			JPEG compression			Median filter (ten times)		
	2%	4%	15%	5%	20%	50%	3×3	5×5	7×7
PSNR (dB)	19.00	16.10	10.97	26.65	32.91	36.67	28.41	24.92	23.13
NC	0.67	0.62	0.67	0.61	0.80	0.89	0.62	0.62	0.68

It can be found that there is a steady state for conventional attacks. The value of NC is near 0.6 in Gaussian noise attack. When JPEG attacked is 5%, its value of NC can get 0.61. So, the proposed watermarking algorithm is practical.

Gaussian Noise. When the medical image is under Gaussian noise (15%) attacks, the value of NC is 0.6737. The data proved that the algorithm has robustness against Gaussian noise attacks. As is shown in Fig. 9.

Fig. 9. Medical image and Extracted watermarking under Gaussian noise attack 15%.

5.2 Geometric Attacks

The robustness of geometric attacks has always been a problem. This algorithm tests a series of Geometric attacks. And the results are shown in Table 3.

Table 3. PSNR and NC under Geometric Attacks based on SIFT-DCT.

Geometric attacks	Attack strength	PSNR (dB)	NC
Rotation (clockwise)	10°	16.23	0.80
	30°	14.05	0.81
	40°	13.72	0.73
Rotation (Anticlockwise)	10°	16.23	0.79
	30°	14.71	0.79
	40°	13.72	0.79
Translation (left)	8%	16.71	0.90
	30%	13.57	0.90
Translation (up)	20%	14.46	0.89
	45%	12.46	0.89
Clipping (Y direction)	8%	–	0.81
	15%	–	0.74
Clipping (X direction)	8%	–	0.90
	40%	–	0.81

Rotation Clockwise Attack. When the medical image is rotated 30° (clockwise), the extracted watermarking is shown in Fig. 10. In this case, the degree of correlation is 0.807. So, the proposed algorithm has a good robustness against the rotation attacks.

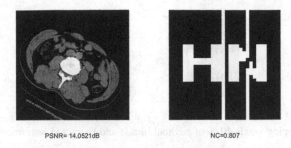

PSNR= 14.0521dB   NC=0.807

Fig. 10. Medical image and Extracted watermarking under rotation attack 30°.

Translation Attacks. Medical image is translated attack. When left translated 30%, the value of NC is 0.8954. And the watermarking is close to the original watermarking. When up translated 45%, the value of NC is 0.89. As is can be seen in Fig. 11. This show that the algorithm has a fine robustness resist translation attacks.

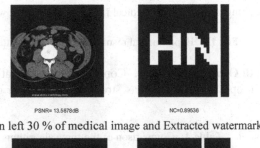

PSNR= 13.5678dB   NC=0.89536

(a) Translation left 30 % of medical image and Extracted watermarking.

PSNR= 12.4556dB   NC=0.89201

(b) Translation up 45 % of medical image and Extracted watermarking.

Fig. 11. Experimental results under translation attack.

Clipping Attacks. Medical image is clipped about 40% in the x-axis direction. The cropped medical image is given in Fig. 12(a). The degree of correlation is 0.8088. When it is clipped about 15% in the y-axis direction, the clipped medical image is shown in Fig. 12(b). The degree of correlation is 0.7445. Therefore, the watermarking algorithm has strong robustness against clipping attacks.

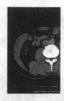

(a) Clipping x-axis 40 % of medical image and Extracted watermarking.

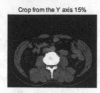

(b) Clipping y-axis 15 % of medical image and Extracted watermarking.

Fig. 12. Experimental results under cropping attack.

Comparison with Other Algorithms. Comparing the simulation results of the three algorithms, the proposed algorithm has strong robustness to geometric attacks (see Table 4).

Table 4. Comparison of the three algorithms.

Attacks strength	PSNR (dB)			NC		
	DCT	SIFT	SIFT-DCT	DCT	SIFT	SIFT-DCT
Rotation 40° (clockwise)	13.72	13.71	13.72	0.60	0.59	0.73
Rotation 40° (Anticlockwise)	13.72	13.72	13.72	0.60	0.78	0.79
Translation 30%(left)	13.56	13.57	13.57	0.59	0.81	0.90
Translation 45% (up)	12.95	12.45	12.46	0.62	0.59	0.89
Cropping 40% (X axis)	–	–	–	0.42	0.45	0.81

6   Conclusion

This paper combining two algorithms proposes the medical image watermarking based on the SIFT-DCT perceptual hashing. And it uses zero watermarking to improve the robustness. The algorithms can not only extract local features and obtain key points, but also reduce the complexity. From the simulation results, it can be known that the proposed algorithm has good robustness, especially in the face of rotation, translation, and shear attacks. In addition, the algorithm is flexible and it is suitable for applications in the field of identification. It can play a prominent role in the medical image processing to ensure the security of image transmission. In the next study, we plan to find more representative parts in many key points to deal with the attacks that are not yet ideal in this study.

Acknowledgment. This work is supported by the Key Reach Project of Hainan Province (ZDYF2018129), the National Natural Science Foundation of China (61762033), and the National Natural Science Foundation of Hainan (617048, 2018CXTD333).

References

1. Giakoumaki, A., Pavlopoulos, S., Koutsouris, D.: Multiple image watermarking applied to health information management. IEEE Trans. Inf Technol. Biomed. **10**(4), 722–732 (2006)
2. Wu, J.H.K., Chang, R.F., Chen, C.J.: Tamper detection and recovery for medical images using near-lossless information hiding technique. J. Digital Imaging **21**(1), 59–76 (2008)
3. Tan, C.K., Ng, J.C., Xu, X.: Security protection of DICOM medical images using dual-Layer reversible watermarking with tamper detection capability. J. Digital Imaging **24**(3), 528–540 (2011)
4. Li, Q.L., Wang, G.Y., Liu, J.G.: Robust scale-invariant feature matching for remote sensing image registration. IEEE Geosci. Remote Sens. **6**(2), 287–291 (2012)
5. Lei, Y., Wang, Y., Huang, J.: Robust image hash in radon transform domain for authentication. Signal Process.: Image Comm. **26**(6), 280–288 (2011)
6. Lowe, D.G.: Distinctive image features from scale-invariant keypoints. Int. J. Comput. Vis. **60**(2), 91–110 (2004)
7. Kim, H.-D., Lee, J.-W., Oh, T.-W.: Robust dt-cwt watermarking for dibr 3D images. IEEE Trans. **58**(4), 533–543 (2012)
8. Sun, J.G., Lan, S.S.: Geometrical attack robust spatial digital watermarking based on improved SIFT. In: IEEE International Computer Society, pp. 98–101 (2010)
9. Priyatham, B., Nilkanta, S., Arijit, S.: SIFT based robust image watermarking resistant to resolution scaling. In: IEEE International Conference Image Processing (ICIP), pp. 5507–5510 (2014)
10. Han, L., Zhou, G.Y., Xu, L., Fang, L.: Beyond SIFT using binary features in loop closure detection. In: IEEE International Conference on Intelligent Robots and Systems, pp. 4057–4063 (2017)
11. Zhao, M., Jiang, J.G., Hong, R.C.: SIFT matching optimization based on RANSAC. In: Optoelectronic Engineering, pp. 62–69 (2014)
12. Vishal, M., Brian, L.E.: Perceptual image hashing via feature points performance evaluation and trade-offs. IEEE Trans. Image Process. **15**(11), 3452–3455 (2006)
13. Lv, X.D., Wang, J.: Perceptual image hashing based on shape contexts and local feature points. IEEE Trans. Inf. Forensics Secur. **7**(3), 1081–1093 (2012)
14. Liu, Z.Q., Li, Q., Liu, J.R.: SIFT based image hashing algorithm. Chin. J. Sci. Instrum. **32**(9), 2024–2028 (2011)
15. Dai, S.S., Tian, Y.L.: Research on SIFT algorithm based on image texture features. In: Semiconductor Optoelectronics, pp. 107–110 (2014)
16. Monga, V., Mhcak, M.K.: Robust and secure image hashing via non-negative matrix factorizations. Proc. IEEE Trans. Inf. Forensics Secur. **2**(3), 376–390 (2007)
17. Kozat, S., Venkatesan, R., Mihcak, M.: Robust perceptual image hashing via matrix invariants. In: IEEE International Conference on Image Processing (ICIP), pp. 3443–3446 (2004)
18. Chen, Y., Li, B., Dong, R.: Contourlet-SIFT feature matching algorithm. J. Electron. Inf. Technol. 203–209 (2013)

Network Storage Covert Channel Detection
Based on Data Joint Analysis

Guangxin Fu[1](✉), Qingbao Li[1], Zhifeng Chen[1], Guangyu Zeng[1],
and Juanjuan Gu[2]

[1] State Key Laboratory of MEAC,
No. 62 Science RD, Zhengzhou 450001, China
1716773926@qq.com
[2] Dongguan Xinda Fusion Innovation Institute,
No. 62 Science RD, Zhengzhou 450001, China

Abstract. Aiming at the problem that the existing network storage covert channel detection algorithm can not take into account both the detection rate and the computational complexity, a network storage covert channel detection method based on data joint analysis is proposed. This method studies the information hiding mechanism of the network storage covert channel according to related documents. Based on this, the regularity characteristics of the packets in each field of the network data packet and the correlation characteristics between the packets are analyzed. The above characteristics are further transformed into eigenvector matrices through kernel density estimation, variation coefficient, fragility entropy, and autocorrelation coefficient. And SVM classifier is trained using eigenvector matrices. The experimental test shows that this method has a high detection rate and its computational complexity is small.

Keywords: Network storage covert channel · Regularity · Association
Support vector machine

1 Introduction

In recent years, with the rapid development of intrusion detection technology, traditional Trojan horse technology has been difficult to penetrate into network systems or private terminal equipment. Therefore, the network covert channel technology emerges [1]. It can bypass the detection of defense mechanisms and reside on the network system or the user's computer for a long time. It can use this to send sensitive data to the outside world and achieve the purpose of network stealing.

In the detection of network storage covert channels, the typical method is the detection method based on the fixed field features in network protocols proposed by Coma et al. [2–4]. It detects redundant fields or fixed fields in the data packet. If the value of this field does not conform to the standard of the normal channel, it is considered to be threatened by the network to store the hidden channel. This method can effectively detect the value of the fixed field, but cannot detect a network storage covert channel where the value of the fixed field is a random variable. Yao [5–7] et al. proposed a network storage covert channel detection method based on statistical

© Springer Nature Switzerland AG 2018
X. Sun et al. (Eds.): ICCCS 2018, LNCS 11066, pp. 346–357, 2018.
https://doi.org/10.1007/978-3-030-00015-8_30

analysis. It considers that the statistics of the values of the fields in the network packets of the normal channel will obey the Poisson distribution or normal distribution. This method can detect most network storage covert channels, but it cannot detect the network storage covert channels that the attacker carefully laid out by using replay attacks. In order to make the detection method more versatile, Sohn et al. [8] proposed a detection method based on the support vector machine, which trains the CNN classifier by collecting normal channel traffic and covert channel traffic to determine whether the channel to be detected is network storage covert channel. This method can effectively detect the specified type of network storage covert channel, but its computational complexity will increase exponentially with the detection of feature vectors, leading to excessive time overhead, not suitable for real-time detection. The network storage covert channel detection method based on cluster analysis is proposed by Filex et al. [9]. This method can detect only the known network storage covert channels. Because the unknown type of network storage covert channels cannot with obvious clustering features, the detection method is easy to fail. It can be seen that the existing methods have largely achieved detection of covert channels in network storage, but there are still problems in which the computational complexity and detection rate cannot be taken into account.

In view of the above problems, this paper researches and proposes a TCP/IP protocol network storage covert channel detection method based on data joint analysis. Firstly, according to the related documents, the information hiding mechanism of the network storage covert channel is studied. Based on the analysis, the regularity characteristics and the inter-packet correlation characteristics of the packets in each field of the network data packet are analyzed. The above characteristics are further transformed into eigenvector matrices through kernel density estimation, variation coefficient, fragility entropy, and autocorrelation coefficient. Then, SVM classifiers are trained according to eigenvector matrices and classified and detected. Finally, the methods proposed in this paper are tested through the constructed experiments to verify whether the method can fully and accurately detect the network storage covert channel, and the time cost can meet the actual work requirements.

2 Analysis of Storage Covert Channel Hiding Mechanism

In order to fully and accurately detect the network storage covert channel implemented using the TCP/IP protocol, various fields of the header field of the data packet need to be analyzed in depth. And the system description of TCP/IP in the RFC 791 and RFC 793 documents is studied [10]. The carrier fields that can be used to embed hidden information in the headers, then analyze their definitions in detail and classify them.

2.1 Definition of Carrier Field in TCP/IP Protocol

A TCP/IP-based network storage covert channel requires the selection of part of the header field as a carrier for information hiding. To achieve the detection of covert channels for such network storage, it is necessary to analyze the offset and significance of the head structure. Through in-depth analysis, the fields that may have embedded information in their heads are summed up as follows. These fields are hidden carrier fields often used by attackers.

TOS: Use to set the necessary parameters for the service. Identification: Use to identify the IP packets sent by the host. Each time the terminal sends a packet, the value is automatically incremented by one. If the length of the transmitted packet exceeds the maximum packet length, the fragmented transmission mechanism is used. This field of all fragmented network packets has the same value and is mainly used in the reorganization of subsequent fragments. Flags: Use to identify whether the IP packet is fragmented. Offset: Use to recognize the order of fragments when reassembling IP packets. TTL: The number of times the packet is routed in the network. The value of the packet is automatically decremented by one every hop. ISN: In the case where the terminal newly establishes a TCP connection, the terminal is the serial number randomly generated by the first TCP packet. Seq: Use to indicate the sequence number of the first byte of the data packet in the transmitted data byte stream. Ack: Use to represent the sequence number of the data packet that the receiver needs to receive. If it succeeds, its value will be automatically increased by one. TCP Control Bit: Use to state machine for controlling TCP.

2.2 Classification of Carrier Fields in TCP/IP Protocol

Based on the above analysis of the header fields, the network storage covert channel constructed by the attacker not only can bypass the operating system's defense mechanism, but also can effectively avoid the intrusion detection system's review and realize the purposes of covert communication and network stealing. Further, this chapter divides the scope of hidden data into three categories: constant domain, variable domain, and idle domain.

Constant field: The value of the field in the classification is a fixed value or the value of the field is related to the status of other fields. For example, the network header length (IHL) field, Checksums field, etc. If the field in the domain is selected as the embedded covert information carrier, the concealment is poor and it is easily detected.

Variable field: The value of the field in the classification can be changed within a certain range. Such as the initial sequence number (ISN) field and identification (IP ID) field. The value of this type of field can change according to the change of the behavior pattern and has certain randomness. If the field in the domain is selected as the embedded covert information carrier, the concealment is strong and it is difficult to be detected.

Idle domain: indicates that the value of the field in the classification does not have a fixed value range and is highly random. For example, the network packet IP source port (Source Port) field and the IP destination port (Destination Port) field. Using the fields in this domain as the network storage covert channel embedded in the covert information carrier has the strongest concealment and can hardly be detected by the existing methods.

The classified fields are shown in Fig. 1. Through the classification and analysis of the fields, a corresponding method can be taken to examine the distribution of field values in the suspicious domain. Since the network storage covert channel needs to embed covert information into the normal channel, it will inevitably cause the regularity in the normal channel network packet or the correlation between the data packets to change. Therefore, it can be determined whether there is a network storage covert channel by comparing the regularity in the packets of the normal channel and the channel to be detected or the correlation between the data packets.

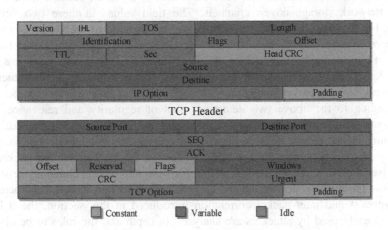

Fig. 1. Classification of carrier fields in TCP/IP protocol

3 Data Joint Analysis

3.1 Characteristic Analysis of Packet Header Fields

Through the above analysis of the TCP/IP protocol header fields, summed up the three scopes of the hidden data, according to the three scopes it is not difficult to find that all vector fields can pass the regularity of the packet within the network packet or The correlation between data packages is shown. The regularity in the data packet and the association between data packets are the behavior characteristics of the header field itself. Therefore, both characteristics of the network storage covert channel and the normal channel exist, but the characteristics of the two network communication channels are bound to have great difference. Detecting the network storage covert channel can be based on the fact that since the network stores the covert channel, it needs to embed covert information in the normal network communication channel, which will inevitably cause the regularity in the original channel network packet or the correlation between the data packets. Therefore, the constant domain type network storage covert channel can be detected using the regularity within the packet, and the idle domain and variable domain type network storage covert channel can be detected using the association between packets. By comparing the regularity in the network data packet of the normal network communication channel and the to-be-detected channel or the correlation characteristic between the data packets, it is determined whether there is a network storage covert channel.

The regularity of the packet is mainly aimed at the constant domain type network storage covert channel. The value of the field in this field is relatively fixed and can be described by the inherent statistical characteristics of the header field, such as entropy, coefficient of variation, etc. If the behavior of a field in the TCP/IP protocol header conforms to the above rule, then it can be determined according to the rule degree characteristic whether there is a network storage covert channel.

The inter-packet correlation characteristics mainly focus on variable-domain, idle-domain network storage covert channels. The field values in these two fields are variable, but they can be described by the trend relationship of the values of the head field between adjacent data packets, such as kernel density estimation, autocorrelation coefficient and so on. If the behavior of a field in the TCP/IP header conforms to the above rules, it can be determined based on the association characteristics whether there is a network storage covert channel.

According to the above two detection rules of regularity and relevance, if the network storage covert channel implemented using the TCP/IP protocol embeds covert information in the header field of the normal channel, it will inevitably change the regularity characteristics or the correlation between the packets in the packet. The feature, based on this, can be used as a basis for detecting hidden channels for storage. Combining the three scopes introduced in the previous section with the characteristics of intra-packet and inter-packet correlation introduced in this section, the 9 header fields frequently used by attackers are analyzed in depth and the rules to be observed are studied. Based on the three scopes introduced and the characteristics of the regularity within the package and the association between packages, the rules of the behavior of the protocol field are summarized in Table 1.

Table 1. Protocol field behavior rule characteristics

Protocol field	Behavior rule
TOS	Regularity characteristics
Identification	Correlation characteristics
Flags	Regularity characteristics
Offset	Correlation characteristics
TTL	Correlation characteristics
ISN	Correlation characteristics
SEQ	Correlation characteristics
ACK	Correlation characteristics
TCP control	Regularity characteristics

3.2   Selection of Feature Vectors Based on Regularity and Relevance

The header field, which is often used as a covert information carrier, is analyzed through two different rules of packet internal regularity and correlation between packets. After qualitative analysis, the two rules need to be described in a specific mathematical language. The characteristics of the regularity in the packet and the correlation among the packets can be described by the four metrics: nuclear density estimation, coefficient of variation, fragility entropy, and autocorrelation coefficient:

Kernel Density Estimation ($\hat{f}(P)$): Kernel Density Estimation is a non-parametric method for estimating the probability density function. It can measure the frequency of the appearance of the header field values and can reflect the discreteness of the inter-packet fields.

Coefficient of variation (C_v): The coefficient of variation can reflect the absolute value of the degree of discretization of the data. It can not only reflect the statistical law of the field within the packet itself, but also reflect the degree of discrepancies between the fields of the packet.

Entropy (*Ent*): Entropy can reflect uncertainty in a process. The higher the entropy value, the more information the packet header field contains.

Autocorrelation coefficient ($R(\tau)$): The degree of similarity of the data at different times can be described. The larger the autocorrelation coefficient, the more similar the header fields are.

Assume that a window size contains network data streams of n data packets. After preprocessing, the network data packets are converted into a sequence of header fields. Kernel density estimation, coefficient of variation, entropy, and autocorrelation coefficient are calculated as follows:

$$\hat{f}(P) = \frac{1}{nh} \sum_{i=1}^{n} K\left(\frac{P_i - P}{h}\right) \tag{1}$$

$$C_v = \frac{\sigma}{\mu} \tag{2}$$

$$Ent(P_1, P_2, \ldots P_n) = -\sum_{i=1}^{n} p_i \cdot \log p_i, i = 1, 2, \ldots, n \tag{3}$$

$$R(\tau) = \frac{E[(P_i - \mu)(P_{i+\tau} - \mu)]}{\sigma^2}, i = 1, 2, \ldots, n \tag{4}$$

According to the above formula, the four metrics describe the head field information of the network data flow from the regularity within the data and the correlation between the data, and describe its behavior characteristics in a comprehensive manner. Then you can get the four-dimensional feature vector used to train the SVM classifier as shown in Eq. 5:

$$V = (\hat{f}(P), C_v, Ent, R(\tau)) \tag{5}$$

According to the eigenvectors obtained in equation, the intra-packet regularity characteristics and inter-packet correlation characteristics of all training data sets can be described by a four-dimensional eigenvector matrix, as shown in Eq. 6.

$$
\begin{pmatrix} V_1 \\ V_2 \\ \vdots \\ V_m \end{pmatrix} = \begin{pmatrix} \hat{f}(P)_1 & C_{v1} & Ent_1 & R(\tau)_1 \\ \hat{f}(P)_2 & C_{v2} & Ent_2 & R(\tau)_2 \\ \vdots & \vdots & \vdots & \vdots \\ \hat{f}(P)_m & C_{vm} & Ent_m & R(\tau)_m \end{pmatrix} \tag{6}
$$

3.3   Detection Model

In order to detect the network storage covert channel based on the TCP/IP protocol, this chapter proposes a detection model based on data joint analysis. The detection model is shown in Fig. 2.

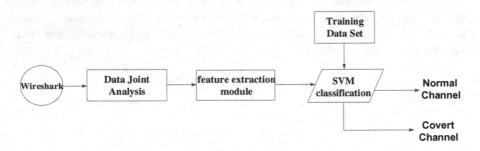

Fig. 2. Detection system model

First, according to the different ways of information hiding, the test data set and training data set header fields are divided into three categories: constant domain, variable domain and free domain. Then, these three types of header fields are converted according to the regularity of the packets of the network data packet or the correlation between the data packets, and an intermediate data set containing the characteristics of the packets or the characteristics of the packets is generated. According to the four metrics of nuclear density estimation, variation coefficient, fragility entropy and autocorrelation coefficient, the intermediate data set is transformed into four-dimensional feature vector to train the support vector machine classifier. Finally, a classifier is used for detection, and its classification result is the detection result of the network storage covert channel.

4   Detection Method

The simulation experiment test environment is shown in Fig. 3. Among them, the IP addresses 172.16.1.2-172.16.1.4 are the senders of three different network storage covert channels, 172.16.1.5 is the sender of the normal channel, 172.16.1.6 is the detector, and 172.16.6.2 is the receiver.

4.1   Data Set

In order to train the classifier, an experimental training set needs to be collected. For the sample of the normal network communication channel, it is possible to use the HTTP session for file transfer by two hosts in the LAN, and use Wireshark to capture the relevant data packets to obtain samples [11]. For network storage covert channel samples, different types of tools are used to construct different types of network storage covert channels, such as Covert_Tcp, Steg_Tunnel, and NUSHU [12]. Among them, Covert_Tcp can implement two kinds of network storage covert channels: IP identification field and initial sequence number field. Steg_Tunnel builds a network storage covert channel based on the sending sequence number field. NUSHU is a network storage covert channel with extended interface, and can implement the remaining header fields. The training set consists of 200,000 samples, of which 100,000 originates from the normal channel and 100,000 originates from three network storage covert channels. Similarly, the test set consists of 40,000 samples, of which 20,000 originates from the normal channel and 20,000 from the three network storage covert channels.

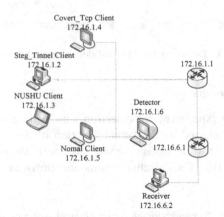

Fig. 3. Experiment environment

4.2   Detection Window Parameter Determination

When the network storage covert channel is detected, the value of the detection window size is taken as 100, 200, 400, 600, 800, 1000, 1500, 2000, 2500 in order. The test results are shown in Fig. 4. It can be seen from Fig. 4 that the detection performance is related to the value of the detection window. When the detection window value is greater than 1,000, the detection rate can reach 96%, false alarm rate and false negative rate are below 5%, and the detection performance tends to be stable. When the detection window value is less than 1,000, the detection rate is significantly reduced, false alarm rate and false negative rate are significantly increased, and the trend of change is faster and faster as the detection window value decreases. When the detection window value is 100, the detection rate is only 53% and the false alarm rate is 33%. This situation occurs because when the detection window becomes smaller, the amount of data contained in it is too small to extract enough regularity and correlation characteristics, leading to the inability to rely on nuclear density estimation, coefficient of variation, fragility entropy, and autocorrelation. The coefficients effectively distinguish between normal channels and network storage covert channels. Therefore, based on the above experimental results, in order to achieve better detection performance, the size of the detection window selected in this chapter is 1,000.

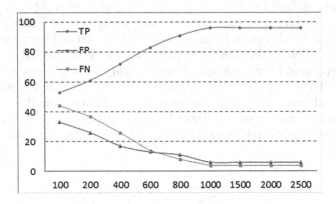

Fig. 4. Detection window and detection performance

4.3   Experimental Results

According to the above experiment, the detection window size is chosen as 1000, and the Sigmoid kernel is selected by the kernel function of the SVM classifier. In this paper, three different network storage covert channels are detected: Covert_Tcp, Steg_Tunnel, and NUSHU. The detection results are shown in Table 2.

Table 2. Network storage covert channel detection results

Channel name	Carrier	TP (%)	FP (%)	FN (%)
Covert_Tcp	Identification	95.2	2.6	4.3
	ISN	93.5	3.7	4.2
Steg_Tunnel	SEQ	92.8	3.1	5.7
	TOS	98.7	2.3	0.9
NUSHU	TTL	96.1	3.9	5.1
	ISN	91.4	5.8	7.0

From the test results, it can be seen that the method proposed in this chapter can effectively detect the network storage covert channel implemented using the TCP/IP protocol. The detection rate of the network storage covert channel using the service type field, the IP identification field, and the time-to-live field type is all above 95%; the detection rate of the network storage covert channel using the initial sequence number field and the transmission sequence number field type is Above 90%. Among them, the detection rate of NUSHU using the initial sequence number field is lower than that of Covert_Tcp using the same field. This is because NUSHU first encrypts the message, and then embeds the encrypted information in the initial sequence number field to send. As a result, its anti-detection performance has been further enhanced.

4.4 Performance Comparison and Analysis

The detection rate, false alarm rate and time complexity are three key indicators to measure the performance of network storage covert channel detection. The following three key indicators of the detection method proposed in this chapter are compared with the typical detection methods in related literature [13, 14]. The algorithms involved in the comparative analysis include the detection algorithms proposed in this paper. For method 1, and the detection algorithm proposed in [15], they are called method 2, method 3, and method 4, respectively.

Method 2: The detection method firstly performs density cluster analysis on the head field to obtain the clustering characteristics of normal channels and NUSHU. Then, whether the channel to be detected is a normal channel is determined by comparing the feature differences between them.

Method 3: The detection method adopts a heuristic neural network to learn the initial sequence number field in the network storage covert channel. After self-learning, the model can obtain the behavior characteristics of the field, and then use a classifier to determine whether the to-be-detected channel is a normal channel.

Method 4: The detection method uses two simple statistical features of mean and variance as the feature vector to train the SVM classifier, and then uses the classifier to determine whether the channel to be detected, is a normal channel.

In terms of the detection rate, it can be seen from Fig. 12 that the detection rates of Method 2 and Method 4 are not ideal, and the detection rates are 73% and 82% respectively. The reason for the poor detection rate of Method 2 is due to the use of transmission. The sequence number field is used as a carrier of covert information. The distribution of the transmission sequence number field has a strong randomness and cannot be effectively clustered, and therefore an effective clustering feature cannot be obtained, so the detection rate is low. The reason for the poor detection rate of Method 4 is that it uses only simple statistical features to train SVM classifiers, and does not consider the regularity characteristics of data packets and the correlation characteristics between data packets, resulting in The network storage covert channel detection rate is low. The low detection rates of Method One and Method Three were 91% and 94%, respectively. This is due to the fact that method one analyzes the internal regularity and external correlation of the header field of the data packet, and introduces complex statistical features as a classifier for feature vector training support vector machine to combat the covert channel with strong randomness of embedded information field distribution. The third method is to use heuristic neural networks to learn the behavior characteristics of network packets. The model has a high degree of self-learning ability, and it can have a good detection effect without the introduction of features or laws, so the detection of method 3 The highest rate.

In terms of false alarm rate, the false alarm rates for Methods 1, 2 and 4 are basically the same, while the false alarm rate for Method 3 is significantly higher. This is due to the fact that the neural network model is prone to over-learning and results in the determination of normal traffic as traffic in the network-stored covert channel, and as a result false positive rates are high.

In terms of time complexity, the time overhead performance of method two is the smallest, the time overhead of method one and method four is the next, and the time expenditure of method three is the largest. The second method uses the cluster analysis method to detect the covert channel, and the time complexity of the clustering algorithm increases linearly. The time complexity is $O(N \times logN)$, so the time overhead is very small. The time complexity of method 1 is related to the total number of samples N, the size of the detection window W, and the running time $C(\cdot)$ of the support vector machine. Each time it passes through a window, it is detected once. Then its time complexity is $O((N/W)C(W)))$. Method 3 requires a large amount of experimental data for self-learning, and the convergence time of the model increases exponentially with the number of experimental data sets. The time complexity is $O(N^3)$, so the time overhead is maximum.

In summary, Method 1 has the best overall performance in the four network storage covert channel detection methods, with higher detection rate, lower false alarm rate, and less time overhead. The second method has the lowest time overhead. However, the detection rate is the lowest; the detection rate of Method 3 is higher, but it is not dominant in other aspects.

5 Conclusion

This paper proposes a network storage covert channel detection method based on feature rules of TCP/IP protocol. Firstly, according to the related documents, the information hiding mechanism of the network storage covert channel is studied. Based on the analysis, the regularity characteristics and the inter-packet correlation characteristics of the packets in each field of the network data packet are analyzed, and the core density estimation, the variation coefficient, and the richness are analyzed. The entropy and autocorrelation coefficients further transform the above features into feature vector matrices. Then, the SVM classifier is trained according to the eigenvector matrix, and then the classifier is used to determine whether the channel to be detected is a normal channel. Finally, the proposed method is experimentally verified and the performance analysis is performed. The method proposed in this chapter can completely and accurately detect the network storage covert channel using TCP/IP protocol, and the time overhead is relatively small, which solves the problem that the existing detection method can not take into account both the detection rate and the computational complexity.

References

1. Archibald, R., Ghosal, D.: A comparative analysis of detection metrics for covert timing channels. Comput. Secur. **45**(8), 284–292 (2014)
2. Zseby, T., Vázquez, F.I., Bernhardt, V., et al.: A network steganography lab on detecting TCP/IP covert channels. IEEE Trans. Educ. **59**(3), 224–232 (2016)
3. Shrestha, P.L, Hempel, M., Rezaei, F., et al.: Leveraging statistical feature points for generalized detection of covert timing channels. In: IEEE Military Communications Conference, pp. 7–11. IEEE Computer Society (2014)
4. Hélouët, L., Jard, C., Zeitoun, M.: Covert channels detection in protocols using scenarios. In: Proceedings of Spv' Workshop on Security Protocols Verification (2003)
5. Rezaei, F., Hempel, M., Shrestha, P.L., et al.: Detecting covert timing channels using nonparametric statistical approaches. In: Wireless Communications and Mobile Computing Conference, pp. 102–107. IEEE (2015)
6. Zhang, L., Liu, G., Dai, Y.: Network packet length covert channel based on empirical distribution function. J. Netw. **9**(6) (2014)
7. Cao, P., Liu, W., Liu, G., et al.: A wireless covert channel based on constellation shaping modulation. Secur. Commun. Netw. 1–15 (2018)
8. Cabuk, S., Brodley, C.E., Shields, C.: IP covert timing channels: design and detection. In: ACM Conference on Computer and Communications Security, CCS 2004, Washington, DC, USA, October, pp. 178–187. DBLP (2004)
9. Berk, V., Giani, A., Cybenko, G.: Detection of covert channel encoding in network packet delays. Rapport Technique Tr (2009)
10. Pang, P., Zhao, H., Bao, Z.: A probability-model-based approach to detect covert timing channel. In: IEEE International Conference on Information and Automation, pp. 1043–1047. IEEE (2015)
11. Shrestha, P.L., Hempel, M., Rezaei, F., et al.: A support vector machine-based framework for detection of covert timing channels. IEEE Trans. Dependable Secur. Comput. **13**(2), 274–283 (2016)
12. Gianvecchio, S., Wang, H.: An entropy-based approach to detecting covert timing channels. In: ACM Conference on Computer and Communications Security, Alexandria, Virginia, USA, pp. 307–316. DBLP, October 2011
13. Shah, G., Molina, A., Blaze, M.: Keyboards and covert channels. In: Conference on Usenix Security Symposium. USENIX Association (2009)
14. Lin, Y., Malik, S.U.R., et al.: Designing and modeling of covert channels in operating systems. IEEE Trans. Comput. **69**(5), 224–232 (2015)
15. Bloch, M.R.: Covert communication over noisy channels: a resolvability perspective. IEEE Trans. Inf. Theor. **62**(5), 2334–2354 (2016)

Optimal Resource Allocation for Underlay Cognitive Radio Networks

Xiaoli He[1,2($\boxtimes$)], Hong Jiang[1($\boxtimes$)], Yu Song[3], and He Xiao[1]

[1] School of Information Engineering, South West University of Science
and Technology, Mianyang 621010, Sichuan, China
hexiaoli_suse@hotmail.com,
jianghong_swust@hotmail.com
[2] School of Computer Science, Sichuan University of Science and Engineering,
Zigong 643000, China
[3] Department of Network Information Management Center, Sichuan University
of Science and Engineering, Zigong 643000, China

Abstract. In order to improve the effective utilization of available resources in the traditional wireless network, this paper studies the optimization of resource allocation (RA) in the underlay cognitive radio network (CRN). Our goal is to maximize the sum rate of the whole system (e.i., primary users (PUs) and secondary users (SUs)), taking into account the constraints of interference temperature (IT) and minimum rate, and the Quality of Service (QoS) guarantees. A heuristic algorithm is proposed to solve the non-convex non-linear programming optimization problem. Theoretical analysis and simulation results show that this algorithm can effectively reduce the power interference to the PUs, maximize the transmission rate of PUs and SUs, and improve resource utilization of the CRN.

Keywords: Cognitive radio networks · Resource allocation
Interference temperature · Convex

1 Introduction

In recent years, with the breakthrough of wireless network technology and the rapid development of Internet services, the communication business has transformed from a simple voice call into a network capable of carrying complex mixed services (e.g., audio, video, and data). On the one hand, the user's Quality of Service (QoS) is not an easy task due to delay and bit error rate. On the other hand, due to serious users' interference, channel fading and noise, network resource utilization is low. Therefore, how to improve resource utilization while ensuring that the user's QoS is a problem to be solved.

In Cognitive Radio Networks (CRN), Secondary Users(SUs) achieve spectrum sharing by dynamically accessing the licensed spectrum of the Primary Users(PUs). At present, there are three ways to share spectrum, which are interweave, overlay and underlay. Among them, the underlay cognitive radio mode increases spectrum utilization through frequency reuse, and requires that the SUs transmit power cannot

X. Sun et al. (Eds.): ICCCS 2018, LNCS 11066, pp. 358–371, 2018.
https://doi.org/10.1007/978-3-030-00015-8_31

exceed the maximum tolerable noise of the PUs [1]. The Federal Communications Commission (FCC) defines the tolerable interference of PUs as a measurable Interference Temperature (IT) [2]. Therefore, as long as the interference generated by the SUs does not exceed the IT threshold of the PUs receiver, the PUs and SUs can coexist.

1.1 Related Work

At present, the research on the CRN resources allocation (RA) mainly centers on two directions, that is, the primary network (licensed users) protection and secondary network (unlicensed users) performance (e.g., QoS, throughput, fairness, and energy efficiency, etc.). However, RA optimization is a key function for CRN. Therefore the literature [3] has studied the RA optimization problem of CRN very well.

In order to solve the problem of power and admission control, which was NP-hard, the literature [4] considered imperfect channel state information. A distributed algorithm has proposed. Hence, the goal of joint optimization ensured a certain QoS for each connection. But, it needed relatively high communication and computation, meanwhile required for distributed implementation. Literature [5] used game theory, duality in convex optimization and the decomposition method to maximization of the sum-rate of SUs for spectrum sharing. A low complexity semi-distributed algorithm was proposed for multi-input-multi-output antenna multi-band cognitive radio networks. However, suboptimal performance did not guarantee the QoS of SUs.

Literature [6] presented a resource allocation framework for spectrum underlay in CRNs. Both interference constraints for PUs and QoS constraints for SUs were considered. Joint power/rate allocation with proportional and max-min fairness criteria as optimization problem was formulated. Globally optimal solutions can be obtained by convex optimization. However, the maximum network performance was not achieved. Literature [7] introduced stochastic resource allocation algorithms for both interweave (also known as overlay) and underlay cognitive radio paradigms. The algorithms were designed to maximize the weighted sum-rate of orthogonally transmitting SUs under average-power and probabilistic interference constraints. However, it was not considered that when the rate of one SU was small but the sum rate was the largest, and not proved the convergence of the algorithm at the same time. And a multiuser CRN transmission was studied in literature [8]. The joint solution was proposed to enhance the secondary system's throughput in literature [8]. They faced many problems, such as high complexity, suboptimal performance, no guarantee of QoS, and possibly increased delay yet.

The above RA schemes mainly considered establishing optimization objective function subject to IT or QOS of the SUs, but ignored the QOS of the PUs and the complexity of the algorithm. Thus, how to design an effective RA scheme with joint consideration of the PUs protection and the SUs performance improvement for the underlying CRN is a significant research work. As far as we know this work is still an open research issue in the CRN.

1.2 Contribution

In this study, unlike previous works, we aim to optimize the RA of the PUs and SUs for maximizing the sum-rate in the underlay CRN. Hence, we evaluate the optimal RA under IT, maximum power budget, minimum primary and secondary QoS constraints, and minimum the rate of PUs and SUs. More specifically, our main contributions of this work are summarized as follows:

- Firstly, this paper considers the RA of both PUs and SUs. Therefore, a sum transmission rate maximization problem in terms of the IT and the QoS requirements is formulated. Moreover, multiple SUs are permitted to reuse the same spectrum resource in this optimization problem;
- Subsequently, a heuristic alternative algorithm with low computational complexity is proposed to solve the RA optimization problem, which is a non-convex nonlinear programming optimization problem.
- As a consequence, we provide numerical results to evaluate the effectiveness of our proposed RA algorithm. Numerical simulation results show that the algorithm is more effective than the strategy of average power allocation algorithm. In addition, the algorithm can obtain better theoretical optimal performance in the scenarios with higher signal to interference plus noise ratio (SINR). Furthermore, these work also provide some insights for the research of CRN.

1.3 Organization

The remainder of this paper is organized as follows. Section 2 presents the system model and problem statement. Section 3 establishes optimization problems and uses algorithms to convert non-convex to convex optimization to solve problems. Numerical results are presented in Sect. 4. Finally, Sect. 5 concludes this paper.

2 Network Model and Problem Statement

2.1 System Model

We consider a underlay CRN scenario that is illustrated in Fig. 1. One Base Station (BS) is located in the centre of the CRN while N_{PU} PUs and N_{SU} pairs (i.e., secondary transmitter and receiver) are distributed. Let us assume that the total bandwidth is W which is divided into K sub-channels, and K/W is much smaller than the correlation bandwidth of the wireless channel. Hence, each sub-channel is approximately flat fading. Suppose that the $PU_i(i \in \Phi_{PU} = \{1, 2, \ldots, N_{PU}\})$ denotes the i th PUs, and $SU_j(j \in \Phi_{SU} = \{1, 2, \ldots, N_{SU}\})$ denotes the j th SUs. Meanwhile we assume that the SUs links can only reuse the uplink spectrum resources of the PUs to complete local data transmission, and there are a total of N_{SU} cognitive links in the network, and each link will interfere with PUs. Different from the general OFDMA system, we not only consider the interference to the PUs, but also consider the interference between SUs.

2.2 Problem Statement

According to the system hypothesis, the primary signal y_{PU} at the receiver of PUs which is denoted as PU_Rx_i can be written:

$$y_{PU} = \sqrt{p_i g_{iB}} x_i + \sum_{j=1}^{N_{SU}} \sqrt{p_j g_{jB}} x_j + n_0 \tag{1}$$

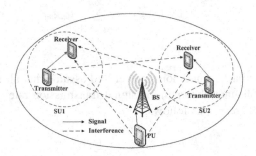

Fig. 1. System model of the underlay CRN

Where p_i and p_j are the transmission power of the i th PUs and the j th SUs. x_i and x_j are the signals of the PUs and SUs transmitters, where $\mathrm{E}\left[|x_i|^2\right] = 1$ and $\mathrm{E}\left[|x_j|^2\right] = 1$. n_0 is the additive white Gaussian noise power with mean value of 0 and variance of σ^2. g_{iB} is the channel power gain for the data link from PU_i to BS, and g_{jB} is the channel power gain for the interference link from SU_j to BS.

In the same way, we can get the secondary signal y_{SU} at SU_Rx_j as follows:

$$y_{SU} = \sqrt{p_j g_{jj}} x_j + \sqrt{p_i g_{ij}} x_i + \sum_{\substack{m=1 \\ m \neq i}}^{N_{SU}} \sqrt{p_m g_{mj}} x_m + n_0 \tag{2}$$

Where p_m is the transmission power of the m th SUs, and x_m is the signals of the SUs transmitters with $\mathrm{E}\left[|x_m|^2\right] = 1$. g_{jj} is the channel power gain for the data link of $SU_j . g_{ij}$ and g_{mj} are the channel power gain for the interference link from PU_i to SU_j and SU_m to SU_j, respectively.

Considering the effect of large-scale path loss and small-scale channel fading, we denote the channel power gain coefficient as

$$g_{X,Y} = |h_{X,Y}|^2 D_{X,Y}^{-\alpha} \quad (X, Y \in \{\Phi_{PU}, \Phi_{SU}, B\}) \tag{3}$$

Where $h_{X,Y}$ is the corresponding channel gain, $D_{X,Y}$ is the distance between X and Y, α is the path loss exponent between X and Y. Based on the previous analysis, the SINR of the PU_i and SU_j can be expressed as

$$\gamma_{PU_i} = \frac{p_i g_{iB}}{\sigma^2 + \sum_{j=1}^{N_{SU}} p_j g_{jB}} \tag{4}$$

$$\gamma_{SU_j} = \frac{p_j g_{jj}}{\sigma^2 + p_i g_{ij} + \sum_{\substack{m=1 \\ m \neq j}}^{N_{SU}} p_m g_{mj}} \tag{5}$$

Let σ^2 denote the background noise power and assume that all users are the same. Thus, according to Shannon theorem, the signal transmission rate of the PU_i and SU_j on the channel are expressed as follows:

$$R_{PU_i} = W \log_2 \left(1 + \gamma_{PU_i}\right) \tag{6}$$

$$R_{SU_j} = W \log_2 \left(1 + \gamma_{SU_j}\right) \tag{7}$$

Where γ_{PU_i} and γ_{SU_j} can be obtained from Eqs. (4) and (5).

2.3 Optimization Problem Establishment

This paper investigates the optimal resource allocation (i.e., power allocation) problems between PUs and SUs by studying the sum rate maximization problem which is denoted as **P1**:

$$\mathbf{P1} : \max_{\{p_i, p_j\}} R_{sum}(\{p_i, p_j\}) \tag{8a}$$

$$s.t. \ R_{PU_i} \geq R_{PU}^{\min}, (\forall i \in \Phi_{PU}) \tag{8b}$$

$$R_{SU_j} \geq R_{SU}^{\min}, (\forall j \in \Phi_{SU}) \tag{8c}$$

$$p_i \leq p_{PU}^{\max}, (\forall i \in \Phi_{PU}) \tag{8d}$$

$$p_j \leq p_{SU}^{\max}, (j \in \Phi_{SU}) \tag{8e}$$

$$\sum_{j=1}^{N_{SU}} p_j g_{jB} \leq I_{th}, (j \in \Phi_{SU}) \tag{8f}$$

Where R_{sum} is the sum Shannon capacity of all the users including PUs and SUs. It can be written as

$$R_{sum}(\{p_i, p_j\}) = \sum_{i=1}^{N_{PU}} R_{PU_i} + \sum_{j=1}^{N_{SU}} R_{SU_j} \tag{9}$$

R_{PU_i} and R_{SU_j} are the rate of the i th PU and j th SU, which can be obtained by Eqs. (6) and (7). In Eqs. (8b) and (8c), R_{PU}^{min} and R_{su}^{min} denote the minimum transmission rate for the PUs and SUs. Hence, the actual transmission rate must higher than this value. Meanwhile, the (8d) and (8e) represent the maximal transmit power of the PUs and SUs must lower than the available power. Equation (8f) means the constrain on the interference from SUs to PUs, which can ensure the QoS of PUs subject to unacceptable impacts.

3 Algorithms Analysis

Specifically, in order to solve the above optimization problem, we can divide **P1** into two sub-optimization problems, namely, **P2** optimized for PUs and **P3** for SUs.

The **P2** optimization target expression is as follows:

$$\mathbf{P2} : \max_{\{P_i\}} \sum_{i=1}^{N_{PU}} R_{PU_i} \tag{10a}$$

$$s.t. \ 8(b), 8(d) \tag{10b}$$

The **P3** optimization target expression is as follows:

$$\mathbf{P3} : \max_{\{p_j\}} \sum_{j=1}^{N_{SU}} R_{SU_j} \tag{11a}$$

$$s.t. \ 8(c), 8(e), 8(f) \tag{11b}$$

Obviously, in terms of power level, **P2** and **P3** are non-convex optimization problems for all users due to the constraints (i.e., (10b), (11b))and the objective function are not convex. However, through some methods, we can convert the non-convex optimization problem into a convex one to obtain the global optimal solution. The first method is that the concave problem can be transformed into a convex problem by a logarithmic transformation. The second method is that the maximization concave function can also be equivalently converted to the minimization convex function [9]. In addition, geometric planning is also an effective method to solve this problem. However, this method has high algorithm complexity due to the change of variables, so it is not suitable for large-scale networks. Hence, we use the second method to solve the above problem.

3.1   Power Allocation Algorithm for the PUs

Through the analysis of the previous algorithm, we write the convex optimization form of **P2** as follows:

$$\mathbf{P2}: -\min_{\{P_i\}} \sum_{i=1}^{N_{PU}} W \log_2 \left(1 + \frac{p_i g_{iB}}{\sigma^2 + \sum_{j=1}^{N_{SU}} p_j g_{jB}} \right) \tag{12a}$$

$$s.t. \ R_{PU}^{\min} - R_{PU_i} \leq 0, (\forall i \in \Phi_{PU}) \tag{12b}$$

$$p_i - p_{PU}^{\max} \leq 0, (\forall i \in \Phi_{PU}) \tag{12c}$$

Where the Eq. (12c) is a linear constraint, the convexity of the objective function and the constraint (12b) can be proved by the Hessian matrix and the second-order partial derivative with respect to the variable p_i, respectively [10]. Hence the **P2** can be solved by convex.

Firstly, according to the theory of Lagrangian dual decomposition, we relax the constraints and construct the Lagrange function

$$L(p_i, \lambda_1, \lambda_2) = \sum_{i=1}^{N_{PU}} W \log_2 \left(1 + \frac{p_i g_{iB}}{\sigma^2 + \sum_{j=1}^{N_{SU}} p_j g_{jB}} \right) - \lambda_1 \left(R_{PU_i} - R_{PU}^{\min} \right) - \lambda_2 \left(p_i - p_{PU}^{\max} \right)$$

$$\tag{13}$$

Where λ_1 and λ_2 are Lagrange factors, satisfying $\lambda_1 \geq 0$ and $\lambda_2 \geq 0$ at the same time.

Secondly, by using Lagrange dual constraint decomposition method, a sub-gradient iterative algorithm is constructed to solve the dual problem. The dual function of Eq. (13) is

$$D(p_i, \lambda_1, \lambda_2) = \min L(p_i, \lambda_1, \lambda_2) \tag{14}$$

The dual problem of Eq. (14) can be written as follows

$$\max D(p_i, \lambda_1, \lambda_2)$$

$$s.t. \ \lambda_1 \geq 0, \lambda_2 \geq 0 \tag{15}$$

In order to obtain the optimal power for each PU_i, the power p_i can be derived according to the Karush Kuhn Tucker (KKT) condition with a value of zero:

$$\frac{\partial L(p_i, \lambda_1, \lambda_2)}{\partial p_i} = 0 \tag{16}$$

We can get the PUs optimal transmission power P_i^* as follows

$$p_i^* = \left[\frac{1}{W\lambda_1 + \lambda_2 \ln 2} - \frac{\sigma^2 + \sum_{j=1}^{N_{SU}} p_j g_{jB}}{g_{iB}} \right]^+ \tag{17}$$

The Lagrange multiplier is updated by sub gradient iterative algorithm:

$$\lambda_1(t+1) = \left[\lambda_1(t) + \alpha_1(t)\left(R_{PU_i} - R_{PU}^{\min} \right) \right]^+ \tag{18}$$

$$\lambda_2(t+1) = \left[\lambda_2(t) + \alpha_2(t)\left(p_i - p_{PU}^{\max} \right) \right]^+ \tag{19}$$

Where α_1 and α_2 are iterative steps, which are positive numbers, t is the number of iterations, and the maximum transmission rate of the PUs is $[R_{PU}]^+ = \max\{R_{PU}, 0\}$.

Power allocation algorithm for the PUs steps are as follows:

Algorithm 1. CRN Resource Allocation Optimization Algorithm for the PUs

---

1) Initialization: $t = 0, p_i \leq p_{PU}^{\max}, \lambda_1(0) > 0, \lambda_2(0) > 0, \forall i$;

2) Measurements: PU_Rx_i and SU_Tx_j to BS channel gains g_{iB} and g_{jB} , noise power σ ;

   3) Calculate the power: $p_i^*(t+1)$

   4) Multiplier update: the Lagrange multiplier is updated using formula (18) - (19).

   5) Current iteration number increases by 1.

   6) Return: step 2);

   7) Output: optimal solution p_i .

3.2 Power Allocation Algorithm for the SUs

Similarly, we can write the convex optimization form of **P3** as follows

$$\mathbf{P3}: -\min_{\{p_j\}} \sum_{j=1}^{N_{SU}} W \log_2 \left(1 + \frac{p_j g_{jj}}{\sigma^2 + p_i g_{ij} + \sum_{\substack{m=1 \\ m \neq j}}^{N_{SU}} p_m g_{mj}} \right) \tag{20a}$$

$$s.t. \ R_{SU}^{\min} - R_{SU_j} \leq 0, (\forall j \in \Phi_{SU}) \tag{20b}$$

$$p_j - p_{SU}^{\max} \leq 0, (j \in \Phi_{SU}) \tag{20e}$$

$$\sum_{j=1}^{N_{SU}} p_j g_{jB} - I_{th} \leq 0, (j \in \Phi_{SU}) \tag{20f}$$

For the above optimization problem **P3**, the objective function is proved to be a convex function in the literature [11]. The feasible domain of the optimization goal here is also a convex set. Therefore, a convex optimization n method can be used to analyze the power allocation scheme for the SUs subject to the total power and IT limit constraints.

First, we construct the Lagrangian function as follows

$$L\big(p_j, \lambda_3, \lambda_4\big) = \sum_{j=1}^{N_{SU}} W \log_2 \left(1 + \frac{p_j g_{jj}}{\sigma^2 + p_i g_{ij} + \sum_{\substack{m=1 \\ m \neq j}}^{N_{SU}} p_m g_{mj}} \right) - \lambda_3 \big(R_{SU_j} - R_{SU}^{\min} \big)$$

$$- \lambda_4 \big(p_j - p_{SU}^{\max} \big) - \lambda_5 \left(\sum_{j=1}^{N_{SU}} p_j g_{jB} - I_{th} \right)$$

$$\tag{21}$$

Where λ_3, λ_4 and λ_5 are Lagrange factors with $\lambda_3 \geq 0$, $\lambda_4 \geq 0$ and $\lambda_5 \geq 0$. According to the KKT theorem, we can get

$$\frac{\partial L\big(p_j, \lambda_3, \lambda_4, \lambda_5\big)}{\partial p_j} = 0 \tag{22}$$

Therefore, the power allocation for each SU_j is

$$p_j^* = \left[\frac{1}{W\lambda_3 + \lambda_4 \ln 2 + \lambda_5} - \frac{\sigma^2 + p_i g_{ij} + \displaystyle\sum_{\substack{m=1 \\ m \neq j}}^{N_{SU}} p_m g_{mj}}{g_{jj}} \right]^+ \tag{23}$$

The Lagrange multiplier is also updated by sub gradient iterative algorithm as follows:

$$\lambda_3(t+1) = \left[\lambda_3(t) + \alpha_3(t)\left(R_{SU_j} - R_{SU}^{\min}\right)\right]^+ \tag{24}$$

$$\lambda_4(t+1) = \left[\lambda_4(t) + \alpha_4(t)\left(p_j - p_{SU}^{\max}\right)\right]^+ \tag{25}$$

$$\lambda_5(t+1) = \left[\lambda_5(t) + \alpha_5(t)\left(\sum_{j=1}^{N_{SU}} p_j g_{jB} - I_{th}\right)\right]^+ \tag{26}$$

Where α_3, α_4 and α_5 also are iterative steps, which are positive numbers, and the maximum transmission rate of the SUs is $[R_{SU}]^+ = \max\{R_{SU}, 0\}$.
Power allocation algorithm for the PUs steps are as follows:

Algorithm 2. CRN Resource Allocation Optimization Algorithm for the SUs

1) Initialization: $t = 0, p_j \leq p_{SU}^{\max}, \lambda_3(0) > 0, \lambda_4(0) > 0, \lambda_5(0) > 0, \forall j$;

2) Measurements: PU_Rx_i and SU_Tx_j to BS channel gains g_{iB} and g_{jB} , noise power σ ;

   3) Calculate the power: $p_j^*(t+1)$

   4) Multiplier update: the Lagrange multiplier is updated using formula (24) -(26).

   5) Current iteration number increases by 1.

   6) Return: step 2);

   7) Output: optimal solution p_j .

Through the analysis of problems **P2** and **P3**, the problem **P1**, (i.e., maximizing the sum rate of all users of the system) has also been solved. We can prove that the two numbers are the maximum and the sum is also the maximum. Therefore, according to the problems **P2** and **P3**, we can get the optimal power of PUs and SUs, which makes the problem **P1** reach the maximum value.

4 Simulation and Result Analysis

In this section, the numerical simulations are used to evaluate the performance of proposed algorithm. The simulation assumes that the network coverage is 150 m × 150 m, where the BS, two PUs, and four pairs of SUs (e.i., receiver and the transmitter) distribute randomly in the network. The SU receiver is uniformly distributed on a circle centered on the SU transmitter with a radius of 10 m. The fading obeys Rayleigh distribution, and the system simulation parameters are set as shown in Table 1. Besides, all of the simulation model and algorithms are coded in the MATLAB 2015b and optimized using the convex optimization toolbox.

Table 1. Comparison table of system parameters

Parameters	Value	Parameters	Value
Spectrum bandwidth W	10 kHz	Path-loss exponent α	3
Number of PUs N_{PU}	5	PUs maximum power p_{PU}^{max}	7 dBm
Number of SUs N_{SU}	5	SUs maximum power p_{SU}^{max}	3 dBm
Noise power σ^2	−174 dBm/Hz	PUs minimum rate R_{PU}^{min}	1 bps/Hz
Interference temperature I_{th}	3 dBm	SUs minimum rate R_{SU}^{min}	1 bps/Hz

We solve the RA problem in CRN communication systems by the convex optimization algorithm, where we want to maximize the transmission rate of multiple users, subject to minimum rate level, lower and upper bounds on powers, and the IT of PUs. The numerical data for the specific experiment is composed as follows.

According to the convex optimization algorithm, we can obtain the optimal power allocation scheme for the PUs and SUs, as shown in Fig. 2. Therefore, from the Fig. 2, we can see that in order to protect the PUs, the power of the PUs is greater than that of the SUs. In experiments, the number of PUs and SUs is taken as five. Among them, the power of PU_4 is the largest and the power of SU_4 is the smallest. At the same time, all the PUs powers do not exceed the value of the $p_{PU}^{max} = 7dBm$, and the powers of the SUs do not exceed the value of the $p_{SU}^{max} = 3dBm$.

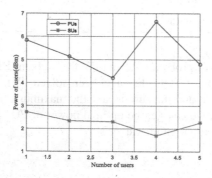

Fig. 2. Power allocation for PUs and SUs

Figure 3 shows that the power of SUs varies with the number of iterations. It can be seen that the transmit powers of all five SUs do not exceed the value of the IT, that is, the green dotted line in the Fig. 3. The transmission power of SU_1 is the largest, followed by SU_2, SU_3 and SU_5, and SU_4 is the smallest. We use SU_3 as an example to analyze the specific process. The interferences of SU_3 mainly come from the PUs, the neighbor nodes SU_1, SU_2 and the background noise. To improve the system capacity and reduce the interruption, we need to control the power of neighbor SUs. Through the proposed optimization algorithm, the transmission power of SU_3 is improved and the optimal transmission power is achieved. After 6 iterations, each cognitive user can quickly converge to its optimal power solution, and it is more stable. The convergence in the iteration process is shown in Fig. 3.

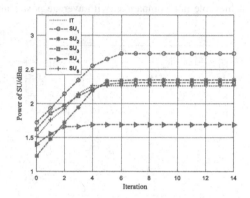

Fig. 3. Power variation of SUs with iteration

In the following, in order to evaluate the effectiveness of the proposed algorithm, we will compare the proposed algorithm with the average power allocation algorithm. Legends "Proposed" and "APAA" represent the resource allocation scheme proposed in this paper, and the resource allocation scheme only under equal power control, respectively.

Figure 4 illustrates the comparison of the different users and the PUs rate, SUs rate and sum rate of the two algorithms. The results show that the proposed scheme can significantly improve the average achievable rate. For example, when the number of user is four, the PUs rate is about 22.3 bit/s/Hz according to the proposed algorithm, however, the APAA is about 20.2 bit/s/Hz, i.e., around a 10% improvement. The SUs rate and sum rate improve by about 3% and 15%, respectively. Therefore, regardless of the different user, the proposed scheme is superior to the APAA schemes.

In the Fig. 5, the proposed optimization algorithm obtains the higher system capacity, compared with the APAA. When the SNR is low, the system capacities corresponding to the two algorithms do not differ greatly. However, as the SNR increases, the gap will increase, where the APAA is the lowest. Then, it can be seen that the proposed optimization algorithm is superior to the APAA, regardless of the high or low SNR.

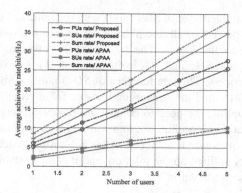

Fig. 4. The average achievable rate comparison with average power allocation algorithm

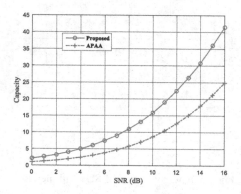

Fig. 5. The capacity comparison with average power allocation algorithm

5 Conclusions

To sum up the above, in the process of studying the optimization of CRN resource allocation, we propose to use convex optimization to solve the two sub-optimization problems, respectively. The goal of the optimization is to maximize the system's sum rate, subject to the QOS, power control, and interference constrains of the PUs and SUs. This problem is solved by using the Lagrangian dual method to convert non-convex optimization to convex optimization. Finally, an optimal heuristic algorithm is used to obtain the optimal solution. The algorithm proposed in this paper helps reduce power consumption and energy consumption, and is conducive to the rational allocation of resources. Through experimental simulation, the effect is better than the average power allocation algorithm.

Acknowledgments. This work is supported in part by National Natural Science Foundation of China (No. 61379005) and (No. 61771410), 2016 Key base of tourism and scientific research of Sichuan Provincial Tourism Administration (No. ZHZ16-02), and 2017, 2018 Artificial Intelligence Key Laboratory of Sichuan Province (No. 2017RYY05, No. 2018RYJ03), and 2017

Horizontal Project (No. HX2017134), and 2015 Teaching Reform Project (No. B11605035), and 2018 Postgraduate Innovation Fund Project by Southwest University of Science and Technology (No. 18ycx115).

References

1. Benaya, A.M., Rosas, A.A., Shokair, M.: Proposed scheme for maximization of minimal throughput in MIMO underlay cognitive radio networks. Wirel. Pers. Commun. **96**(4), 5947–5958 (2017)
2. FCC. Notice of proposed rule making and order. ET Docket No03-322 (2003)
3. Xiong, W., Mukherjee, A., Kwon, H.M.: MIMO cognitive radio user selection with and without primary channel state information. IEEE Trans. Veh. Technol. **65**(2), 985–991 (2016)
4. Adian, M.G., Aghaeinia, H., Norouzi, Y.: Spectrum sharing and power allocation in multi-input–multi-output multi-band underlay cognitive radio networks. IET Commun. **7**(11), 1140–1150 (2013)
5. Le, L.B., Hossain, E.: Resource allocation for spectrum underlay in cognitive radio networks. IEEE Trans. Wirel. Commun. **7**(12), 5306–5315 (2008)
6. Marques, A.G., Lopez-Ramos, L.M., Giannakis, G.B., Ramos, J.: Resource allocation for interweave and underlay CRs under probability-of-interference constraints. IEEE J. Sel. Areas Commun. **30**(10), 1922–1933 (2012)
7. Lopez-Ramos, L.M., Marques, A.G., Ramos, J.: Joint sensing and resource allocation for underlay cognitive radios. In: IEEE International Conference on Acoustics, Speech and Signal Processing (ICASSP), Florence, Italy, pp. 7283–7287, May 2014
8. Sidhu, G.A.S., Shah, S., Gao, F.: User assignment, power allocation, and mode selection schemes in cognitive radio networks. In: IEEE 80th Vehicular Technology Conference (VTC Fall), Vancouver, BC, Canada, pp. 1–5, September 2014
9. Zhang, L., Sun, J.: Channel allocation and power control scheme over interference channels with QoS constraints. In: IEEE International Conference on Control & Automation. IEEE (2017)
10. Zhou, F., Beaulieu, N.C., Li, Z., et al.: Energy-efficient optimal power allocation for fading cognitive radio channels: ergodic capacity, outage capacity, and minimum-rate capacity. IEEE Trans. Wirel. Commun. **15**(4), 2741–2755 (2016)
11. Xu, Y., Zhao, X.: Distributed power control for multiuser cognitive radio networks with quality of service and interference temperature constraints. Wirel. Commun. Mob. Comput. **15**(14), 1773–1783 (2015)

Reversible Data Embedding and Scrambling Method Based on JPEG Images

Yi Puyang[1,3], Zhaoxia Yin[1,2(✉)], and Xinpeng Zhang[3]

[1] Key Laboratory of Intelligent Computing and Signal Processing, Ministry of Education, Anhui University, Hefei 230601, People's Republic of China
[2] Department of Computer Science, Purdue University, West Lafayette 47906, USA
yinzhaoxia@ahu.edu.cn
[3] Shanghai Institute for Advanced Communication and Data Science, School of Communication and Information Engineering, Shanghai University, Shanghai 200072, People's Republic of China
xzhang@shu.edu.cn

Abstract. With the continuous development of Internet technology, a joint method of data embedding and scrambling has become a new research trend. As the most frequently used image in our daily life, JPEG is applied in many ways. In this paper, we present a new reversible data embedding and scrambling scheme based on JPEG images. We use the histogram shifting method to embed the secret data for the AC coefficients after decoding the JPEG image. And for the DC coefficients, we apply the re-encoding method to embed the data, and then scramble the DCT blocks of the JPEG image. The experimental results show that we can easily achieve high embedding capacity and scrambling effect by using the proposed scheme. At the same time, the original image can be perfectly reconstructed after the secret data extraction.

Keywords: Data embedding · Scrambling · JPEG · Histogram shifting

1 Introduction

In recent years, data hiding technique for digital content has become a hotspot as an important research field of information security, which can be classified two disciplines, namely: data embedding, and perceptual encryption. Data embedding consists of two branches, which are irreversible and reversible [1]. Compared with the irreversible data embedding, reversible data embedding has excellent characteristics and has a wide range of applications (such as military, medical, etc.), so it encourages the research community to study reversible data embedding techniques. At present, reversible data embedding technology is mainly based on the following three principles, lossless compression [2, 10], difference expansion (DE) [3, 4], and histogram shifting (HS) [5]. In addition, the perception encryption (hereinafter refer to scrambling) [9] is another important research topic in data hiding. Traditionally, data embedding and perception encryption are studied independently, but with the changing of people's needs, a joint method is evolving [6]. Unlike traditional data embedding

X. Sun et al. (Eds.): ICCCS 2018, LNCS 11066, pp. 372–381, 2018.
https://doi.org/10.1007/978-3-030-00015-8_32

method, in the joint scheme, there's no concern about the visual quality, we need to embed the secret data to seriously degrade the image quality on the contrary. However, due to a large number of modifications to the original image, the image reconstruction is more technically challenging than the traditional data embedding scheme.

Most of the data embedding and scrambling schemes are based on uncompressed images [7, 8], and the study of JPEG compressed images is more technically challenging. One of the main reasons is that the JPEG image is less redundant than the uncompressed image, so the payload of the compressed image will be lower. Another reason is that the modification to the DCT domain will make it much more hard to reconstruct the image. Although the joint scheme based on JPEG image is more difficult, JPEG image is widely used in our daily life as a common image format, so it is more practical to adopt the method of reversible data embedding and scrambling on JPEG image. For the first time, an embedded and scrambling scheme based on the compressed domain is proposed by Kundur et al. [13], but this method is irreversible. Then, a novel JPEG-based embedding and scrambling scheme is proposed in 2015 by Ong et al. [14], but the data payload of the scheme is not ideal, and the scrambling effect of the JPEG image has further improved space. In this paper, we propose a new joint scheme of reversible data embedding and scrambling based on JPEG image. First, After decoding the JPEG image, the secret data is embedded on the AC coefficients using the histogram shifting method. In addition, for the DC coefficients, the re-encoding method is used to embed the secret data, then scramble the DCT blocks of the JPEG image. There are two main advances in this scheme compared with the existing scheme: (1) The embedding capacity of this scheme is larger due to the introduction of the histogram shifting method. (2) The scrambling effect of the proposed scheme is obvious because of the re-encoding of the DC coefficients and the scrambling of the DCT blocks.

The rest of this paper is arranged as follows. In Sect. 2, the proposed reversible data embedding and scrambling method for JPEG is introduced. Experimental results and the comparison study are given in Sect. 3. Finally, we conclude in Sect. 4.

2 Proposed Method

In our method, firstly, the JPEG image is decoded to obtain AC and DC coefficients respectively. Then, we need to count the AC coefficient histogram and embed the data by histogram shifting. For DC coefficients, since the correlation of DC coefficient between adjacent DCT blocks is quite close, they are predicted by the median edge detection predictor (MED), and the prediction error of each DC coefficient is calculated. Then, the original DC coefficients are replaced by the mixed coding of the prediction error and the secret data to achieve data embedding and scrambling. The detailed procedure is described in the following subsection.

2.1 The Processing of AC Coefficients

The processing of AC coefficient includes data embedding, extraction and restoration. Before that, the peak point selection is the key.

(A) Peak point selection

Figure 2 shows the histogram of all the AC coefficients of the Lena image with QF = 60 and 90, respectively. We can easily get from the Fig. 2 that most of the AC coefficients are 0, and the histogram of the AC coefficients are rather sharp. Therefore, it is very suitable to embed data by using histogram shifting. However, when embedding data on JPEG compressed images, it is necessary to consider not only the embedding capacity but also the file size. In the JPEG encoding process, the value of 0 is not encoded for the AC coefficients, and only the non-zero AC coefficients are encoded. Therefore, when the histogram is used to embed the data in the AC coefficient, the 0-value AC coefficient is taken as the peak value, and the 0-value AC coefficient becomes a nonzero value, which results in a sharp increase in the size of the JPEG file (Fig. 1).

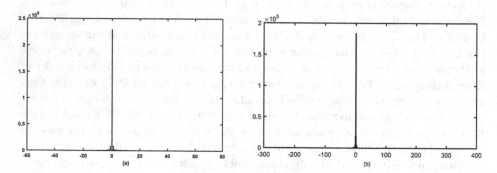

Fig. 1. Histograms of all AC coefficients of the Lena image: (a) QF = 60 (b) QF = 90.

As shown in Fig. 3, considering the increase of JPEG file size mentioned above, we count the histogram of all nonzero AC coefficients of the Lena image when QF = 60 and 90. We can get from the Fig. 3 that the histogram is still very sharp, so the histogram shifting is suitable for data embedding, and we can also see from the Fig. 3 that the two peak points are −1 and 1. The proposed scheme selects −1 and 1 as the peak points, the coefficients on the left side of −1 and the coefficients on the right side of 1 are shifted outward respectively to free up space for the embedded data.

(B) Embedding, Extraction, and Restoration Algorithm.

All nonzero AC coefficients are denoted as $X = \{X_1, X_2, X_3, \dots, X_N\}$, where N is the number of all nonzero AC coefficients in the JPEG image. According to the above analysis, we select -1 and 1 as the peak points. Therefore, the data embedding algorithm can be described as Eq. (1), where $\widetilde{X}_i$ represents the nonzero AC coefficient in the marked JPEG image, and $m \in \{0, 1\}$ represents the embedded secret data.

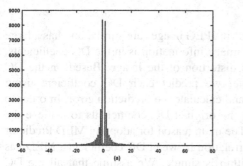 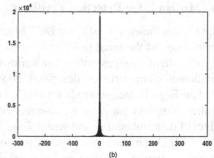

Fig. 2. Histograms of all nonzero AC coefficients of the Lena image: (a) QF = 60 (b) QF = 90.

$Y_{i,3}$	$Y_{i,2}$	
$Y_{i,1}$	Y_i	

Fig. 3. The neighbors of Y_i

$$\widetilde{X}_i = \begin{cases} X_i + 1 & \text{if } X_i > 1 \\ X_i - 1 & \text{if } X_i < -1 \\ X_i + m & \text{if } X_i = 1 \\ X_i - m & \text{if } X_i = -1 \end{cases} \tag{1}$$

The data extraction algorithm and the nonzero AC coefficient reconstruction algorithm can be represented by the following equation. Where m' and X' represent the extracted secret data and the recovered AC coefficients, respectively.

$$m' = \begin{cases} 0 & \text{if } |\widetilde{X}_i| = 1 \\ 1 & \text{if } |\widetilde{X}_i| = 2 \end{cases} \tag{2}$$

$$X' = \begin{cases} \widetilde{X}_i - 1 & \text{if } \widetilde{X}_i \geq 2 \\ \widetilde{X}_i + 1 & \text{if } \widetilde{X}_i \leq -2 \end{cases} \tag{3}$$

2.2 The Processing of DC Coefficients

For DC coefficients, the median edge detection predictor (MED) is first used to predict it. Then we introduce the embedding, extraction, and restoration algorithm of DC coefficients in detail.

(A) Median Edge Detection Predictor

The DC coefficients of adjacent DCT blocks in JPEG images are similar and has a large correlation. At the same time, most of the image information is in the DC coefficients, so very slight changes will cause serious distortion of the image. Based on the DC coefficient characteristics described above, we predict each DC coefficient using Median Edge Detection Predictor (MED) and calculate the prediction error. In order to further compress the data, we re-encoded the original DC coefficients to achieve the effect of data embedding and scrambling. The main reason for adopting MED Predictor is that MED can make good use of the correlation between DC coefficients, MED has higher prediction accuracy and the algorithm is simple. We assume that all the DC coefficients are denoted as $= \{Y_1, Y_2, Y_3, \ldots, Y_M\}$, where M is the number of all DC coefficients in the JPEG image. We make all the DC coefficients into a matrix, and keep the first row and first column of the DC coefficients as the reference values without making predictions. As shown in Fig. 4, Y_i represents the DC coefficient to be predicted, $Y_{i,1}$, $Y_{i,2}$, $Y_{i,3}$ represents the three adjacent DC coefficients of Y_i, and the predicted value of Y_i can be calculated by Eq. (4).

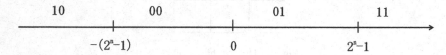

Fig. 4. Assignment of division information

$$\widetilde{Y}_i = \begin{cases} max\left(Y_{i,1}, \ Y_{i,2}\right) & if \ Y_{i,3} \leq min\left(Y_{i,1}, Y_{i,2}\right) \\ min\left(Y_{i,1}, \ Y_{i,2}\right) & if \ Y_{i,3} \geq max\left(Y_{i,1}, Y_{i,2}\right) \\ Y_{i,1} + Y_{i,2} - Y_{i,3} & otherwise \end{cases} \quad (4)$$

(B) Embedding, Extraction, and Restoration Algorithm

First, the prediction error of each DC coefficient is calculated according to $e_i = Y_i - \widetilde{Y}_i$. Then, all the prediction errors are divided into four parts by using the parameter n. In Fig. 5, each part is marked with $d_1 d_2 \in \{00, 01, 10, 11\}_2$ to distinguish the positive and negative of the prediction error. When the prediction error e_i is between $-(2^n - 1)$ and $2^n - 1$, which is encoded with n bits and denoted as $(e_i, n)_2$, then the secret message msg is embedded. As shown in Eq. (5), the remaining two parts are encoded with 8 bits, and no data is embedded. Where $\left(Y_i'\right)_2$ represents the DC coefficient binary of the marked JPEG image, msg is the embedded secret message, $|e_i|$ is the absolute value of the prediction error e_i, and $||$ represents the connection operator. Finally, we replace the original DC coefficients with the re-encoded DC coefficients. Further, in order to enhance the effect of scrambling, it is necessary to use the key K to perform shuffle operations on DCT blocks of the JPEG image.

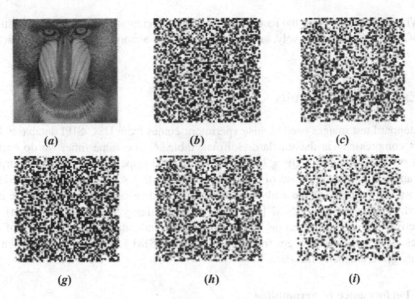

(a)   (b)   (c)

(g)   (h)   (i)

Fig. 5. Embedded-scrambled Baboon image using the proposed method. (a) The original image. (b) QF = 20, SSIM = 0.0051. (c) QF = 40, SSIM = 0.0083. (d) QF = 60, SSIM = 0.0094. (e) QF = 70, SSIM = 0.0109. (f) QF = 80, SSIM = 0.0251.

$$\left(Y_i'\right)_2 = \begin{cases} d_1 d_1 \|msg\|(|e_i|, n)_2 & \text{if } d_1 d_2 = 00_2 \\ d_1 d_1 \|msg\|(e_i, n)_2 & \text{if } d_1 d_2 = 01_2 \\ d_1 d_1 \|(|e_i|, 8)_2 & \text{if } d_1 d_2 = 10_2 \\ d_1 d_1 \|(e_i, 8)_2 & \text{if } d_1 d_2 = 11_2 \end{cases} \tag{5}$$

Data extraction is an inverse operation. First, we still restore the out-of-order DCT blocks in the JPEG image according to the key K, and then sequentially read the DC coefficients in each block to form a matrix. We convert each DC coefficient into 2 binary form and read the first 2-bits $d_1 d_1$. If $d_1 d_2 \in \{00, 01\}_2$, then we can extract the secret data msg, the last n-bits is the absolute value of the prediction error of the DC coefficient, and the positive and negative conditions of the prediction error are determined according to $d_1 d_1$. We process each DC coefficient with the same method to extract all the secret data and the absolute value of each DC coefficient prediction error can also be reconstructed. After obtaining the absolute value of the prediction error of each DC coefficient, the predicted value of the DC coefficient is calculated again according to the MED prediction algorithm using the reference value of the first row and the first column of the DC coefficient. Finally, the original DC coefficients can be reconstructed by Eq. (6).

$$\widehat{Y}_i = \begin{cases} \widetilde{Y}_i + |e_i| & \text{if } d_1 d_2 \in \{01, 11\}_2 \\ \widetilde{Y}_i - |e_i| & \text{if } d_1 d_2 \in \{00, 10\}_2 \end{cases} \tag{6}$$

Where $\widehat{Y}_i$, $\widetilde{Y}_i$ represent the reconstructed DC coefficient and the prediction value of the DC coefficient, respectively, and $|e_i|$ represents the absolute value of the prediction error.

3 Experimental Results

The standard test images used in this experiment comes from USC-SIPI databases [12] and is compressed via the standard Huffman table. At the same time, we do experiments on JPEG images in QF = 20, 40, 60, 70 and 80 respectively. The main purpose is to analyze the performance of the proposed scheme's scrambling and embedding capacity. The quality of the embedded-scrambled and reconstructed images are considered objectively using SSIM [11] (Structural Similarity Index Measurement) and subjectively by visual inspection, where SSIM is an indicator of the similarity of two images. The SSIM value ranges from 0 to 1, and the SSIM value is equal to 1 when the two images are exactly the same.

3.1 Performance of Scrambling

In this subsection, the scrambling performance of the proposed scheme is analyzed. As the Fig. 6 shows, a more representative image (Baboon) with more complex texture features is as an example. It can be observed from the subjective vision that the proposed scheme has a good scrambling effect on JPEG images with different QF values, and the information of the original image (Baboon) is completely imperceptible. We use the SSIM value to evaluate the similarity between the embedded-scrambled image and the original image of the same QF value objectively. And the SSIM values of JPEG images with different QF values are very small after processed by the proposed scheme. We can see that when QF = 20, the SSIM value of embedded-scrambled Baboon image is 0.0051, and when QF = 80, the SSIM value of embedded-scrambled Baboon image is still 0.0251. Thus, it is objectively proven that the scrambling of the proposed scheme is very effective.

At the same time, the reconstruction performance of the proposed scheme is also analyzed. We perform the embedding and scrambling operations on the Baboon compressed images with QF = 20, 40, 60, 70, 80 respectively by the same way as mentioned above, and finally, original image is reconstructed. As shown in Fig. 7, the SSIM values of the reconstructed images of JPEG compressed images with different QF values are equal to 1. It proves that for embedded-scrambled image with different QF values, the proposed scheme can reconstruct the original image perfectly and achieve a reversible effect.

3.2 Performance of Data Payload

In this subsection, we still use the standard test image to experiment and count the payload of six standard test images with different QF values. As shown in Table 1, we can see that the proposed scheme has a high data embedding payload for JPEG images with different QF values. When QF = 10, the average data embedded payload is 23,201

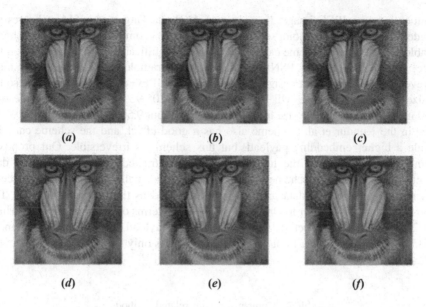

Fig. 6. Reconstructed Baboon image using the proposed method. (a) The original image. (b) QF = 20, SSIM = 1. (c) QF = 40, SSIM = 1. (d) QF = 60, SSIM = 1. (e) QF = 70, SSIM = 1. (f) QF = 80, SSIM = 1.

bits, when QF = 80, the average data payload reaches 42,636 bits. The experimental data shows that the proposed reversible data hiding and scrambling method has a high data embedding payload for JPEG compressed images.

Table 1. The data payload of standard test images with QF = 10, 20, 30, 40, 50, 60, 70, 80 respectively.

Payload [Bits]	QF = 10	QF = 20	QF = 30	QF = 40	QF = 50	QF = 60	QF = 70	QF = 80
Lena	21,019	24,067	26,218	27,783	29,254	31,012	33,876	38,262
Jet	21,831	25,100	26,982	28,309	29,570	31,081	33,198	36,344
Peppers	21,003	23,735	25,671	27,398	29,411	31,661	35,196	40,087
Baboon	31,112	39,608	44,479	47,889	50,582	53,343	56,740	61,313
Tiffany	20,188	23,542	25,876	27,886	29,774	31,971	35,701	40,457
House	24,057	28,687	31,177	32,911	34,152	35,269	36,930	39,351
Avg	23,201	27,456	30,067	32,029	33,790	35,722	38,606	42,635

3.3 Comparison with Related Works

We compare the proposed scheme with the existing schemes using the standard test images (i.e., Baboon, Jet, Lena, and Peppers), each compressed at the quality factor of 80. Rad et al.'s [8] method was originally implemented in the spatial domain, where we introduce it to the JPEG image. Kundur et al. [13] and Ong et al.'s [14] schemes are embedding and scrambling joint scheme based on JPEG compression image. As shown in Table 2, Rad et al.'s scheme can produce a very significant scrambling effect on the image, and the SSIM and PSNR of the output scrambled image are very small. However, this method is not designed specifically for JPEG compressed images, so the file size of the JPEG image will increase too high (205.96%), comparing to the proposed method where the file size increased by only about 9.50%. The scrambling of the image in the Kundur et al.'s scheme also has a good effect, and the scheme can also provide a higher embedding payload, but this scheme is irreversible. Our proposed scheme is reversible, and the image can be reconstructed perfectly after the data extraction. In Ong et al.'s scheme, the JPEG file size is smaller, but its performance in the scrambling effect and data payload is not as good as the proposed scheme. The proposed scheme is superior to Ong et al.'s scheme in terms of SSIM and PSNR, which is 0.0261 and 6.8709, respectively. The average data payload of the proposed scheme is 42,635 bits, while the upper limit of the data payload is only 14,861 bits in Ong et al.'s scheme.

Table 2. Comparison with related methods.

Method	SSIM	PSNR	Payload [Bits]	Increased file size [%]	Reversibility
Rad et al. [8]	0.0192	7.85	32,768	205.96	Reversible
Kundur et al. [13]	0.4155	18.79	63,698	-0.01	Irreversible
Ong et al. [14]	$0.0638 \sim 0.9152$	$10.05 \sim 36.47$	$669 \sim 14,861$	– $0.48 \sim 3.19$	Reversible/Irreversible
Proposed	*0.0261*	*6.8709*	*42,635*	*9.50*	*Reversible*

4   Conclusions

In this paper, a new reversible data hiding and scrambling method for JPEG images is proposed. Using the proposed scheme, we can easily achieve a high payload and good scrambling effect on JPEG images. In the proposed method, we use SSIM to measure image quality. We embed the secret data on the AC coefficients using the histogram shifting method, which can achieve a very high embedding capacity. In addition, for the DC coefficients, we apply the coding method to embed the secret data, and then scramble the DCT blocks in the JPEG image, which can achieve a good scrambling effect. The experimental results show that the proposed scheme can provide a high payload and good scrambling effect for compressed images with different QF values, and the SSIM value of the embedded-scrambled image is less than 0.03. And using our scheme, the original image can be perfectly reconstructed after the secret data extraction.

Acknowledgements. This research work is partly supported by National Natural Science Foundation of China (61502009, U1536109), Foundation of China Scholarship Council (201706505004), Anhui Provincial Natural Science Foundation (1508085SQF216) and Key Program for Excellent Young Talents in Colleges and Universities of Anhui Province (gxyqZD2016011).

References

1. Shi, Y.Q., Li, X., Zhang, X., et al.: Reversible data hiding: advances in the past two decades. IEEE Access **4**, 3210–3237 (2016)
2. Celik, M.U., Sharma, G., Tekalp, A.M., et al.: Lossless generalized-LSB data embedding. IEEE Trans. Image Process. **14**(2), 253 (2005)
3. Li, J., Li, X., Yang, B.: Reversible data hiding scheme for color image based on prediction-error expansion and cross-channel correlation. Signal Process. **93**(9), 2748–2758 (2013)
4. Ou, B., Li, X., Zhao, Y., et al.: Reversible data hiding based on PDE predictor. J. Syst. Softw. **86**(10), 2700–2709 (2013)
5. Ni, Z., Shi, Y.Q., Ansari, N., et al.: Reversible data hiding. IEEE Trans. Circuits Syst. Video Technol. **16**(3), 354–362 (2013)
6. Ong, S.Y., Wong, K.S., Tanaka, K.: A scalable reversible data embedding method with progressive quality degradation functionality. Signal Process. Image Commun. **29**(1), 135–149 (2013)
7. Zhang, X.: Separable reversible data hiding in encrypted image. IEEE Trans. Inf. Forensics Secur. **7**(2), 826–832 (2012)
8. Rad, R.M., Wong, K.S., Guo, J.M.: A unified data embedding and scrambling method. IEEE Trans. Image Process. **23**(4), 1463–1475 (2012). A Publication of the IEEE Signal Processing Society
9. Qian, Z., Zhang, X., Ren, Y.: JPEG encryption for image rescaling in the encrypted domain. J. Vis. Commun. Image Represent. **26**(C), 9–13 (2012)
10. Fridrich, A.J., Goljan, M., Du, R.: Lossless data embedding for all image formats. Proc. SPIE-Int. Soc. Opt. Eng. **4675**, 572–583 (2002)
11. Wang, Z., Bovik, A.C., Sheikh, H.R., et al.: Image quality assessment: from error visibility to structural similarity. IEEE Trans. Image Process. **13**(4), 600–612 (2004). A Publication of the IEEE Signal Processing Society
12. Schaefer, G., Stich, M.: UCID: an uncompressed color image database **5307**, 472–480 (2004)
13. Kundur, D., Karthik, K.: Video fingerprinting and encryption principles for digital rights management. Proc. IEEE **92**(6), 918–932 (2004)
14. Ong, S.Y., Wong, K.S., Tanaka, K.: Scrambling–embedding for JPEG compressed image. Signal Process. **109**, 38–53 (2004)

Reversible Data Hiding for Video

Dong Li, YingNan Zhan, Ke Niu$^{(\boxtimes)}$, and XiaoYuan Yang

Key Laboratory of Network and Information Security Under the People's Armed
Police, Electronic Department, Engineering University of People's Armed
Police, Xi'an 710086, China
18792733969@163.com

Abstract. Difference expansion (DE) and histogram modification (HM) are efficient ways for reversible data hiding (RDH) into digital video. In most occasions, the reversibility of an algorithm cannot be confirmed until the data extracting experiments have been carried out, it means the design of a reversible data hiding algorithm lacks theoretical guidance. In this paper, by studying some typical algorithms, we presented a method called shifting mode diagram. From the shifting mode diagram, we can judge the reversibility of an algorithm by three rules, and more importantly, one can design a reversible data hiding algorithm or optimize the existing methods by using the rules. According to the characters of shifting mode diagram, we summarized a number of formulas, with the formulas, we can estimate the embedding capacity with a high accuracy, experiments have proven that, and the factors that influence the accuracy are also studied.

Keywords: Reversible data hiding · Video · Histogram modification
Difference expansion

1 Introduction

Data hiding means to embed secret information into the cover media [1]. In most circumstances, the media will suffer some irreversible distortions after data embedded, it means the anamorphic media will not be recovered even after the data is extracted. However, in some conditions the irreversible distortions are unacceptable [2], and we need the data-embedded media to be recovered completely. Reversible data hiding (RDH) means the cover media could be recovered thoroughly after the information is extracted [3].

In 1997, the first RDH algorithm was presented for image authentication [4], since then many RDH techniques have been reported, some of the methods are used for authentication [4, 5], some for medical image handling [6] and some for trusted cloud computing [7]. Honsinger et al. [5] realized RDH by employing modulo-256 operation. Tian [8] presented a RDH algorithm based on DE, which enjoys a high embedding capacity. Compared with images, digital video possesses lots of advantages, which means video is suitable for data hiding, and digital video is more convenient to get than before [9], the protection of copyright for video is worth researching. Alattar [3] developed the DE method from two pixels to three or four pixels. Peng et al. [10] presented a reversible watermarking scheme by using improved DE. Coltuc [11] presented a low distortion for reversible watermarking based on prediction error expansion, which employed a linear predictor and the expanded prediction error is embedded into the current pixel and its prediction context. Chun et al. [12] proposed an intra-frame error concealment algorithm based on RDH. Vleeschouwer [13] presented an algorithm that satisfies different quality and functionality requirements of intact watermarking by using circular interpretation of bijective transformations. An et al. [14] proposed a new practical framework used to construct watermark hiding process by employing histogram shifting.

Among all the methods, DE and HM are two mainly methods used for video RDH. Zhao et al. [15] proposed a two dimensional histogram modification (2DHM) based RDH for H.264 video, the algorithm is implemented based on the quantized discrete cosine transform (QDCT) coefficients. Niu et al. [16] presented a RDH method based on HM by using motion vector. In this paper, we proposed a method called shifting mode diagram based on the HM algorithms, with the method, we can not only judge the reversibility of an algorithm theoretically, but also estimate the embedding capacity of an algorithm with a high accuracy.

2 Shifting Mode Diagram

2.1 2DHM

Zhao et al. [15] proposed a RDH algorithm by using two dimensional histogram modification, the algorithm takes full advantage of the relation between two QDCT coefficients and increases the embedding capacity greatly compared with the conventional HM algorithm. The algorithm can be described as follows:

(1) Randomly select 4×4 luminance blocks, the blocks will be used to embed data.
(2) Randomly select two alternating coefficients from each 4×4 block, the two coefficients will make up an embedding pair. Before the data embedding, the value of embedding pair can be divided into 19 nonoverlapping sets.
(3) According to the set that the selected pair belongs to, we can embed data into the coefficients by modifying the value of the embedding pair and every set has a corresponding embedding algorithm.

The Shifting mode diagram of embedding process is shown in Fig. 1.

384	D. Li et al.

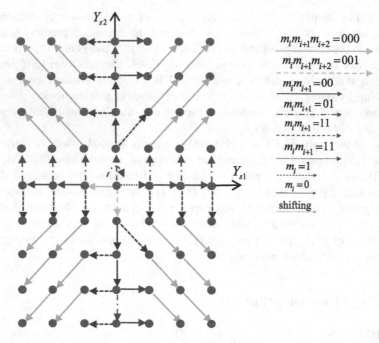

Fig. 1. Embedding process of 2DHM

2.2 MVHM

The 2DHM algorithm is implementing on the compress field, Niu et al. [16] presented a method using motion vector. The embedding method employed RDH from Ni et al. [17], and the process can be expounded as follows:

(1) Decode the H.264 video to get the motion vectors.
(2) In the coding process, denote mv_{ij} as the j-th motion vector of the i-th frame, mvx_{ij} is the horizontal component of mv_{ij} and mvy_{ij} the vertical component, $b \in \{0,1\}$ is the to-be embedded data bit. Then the data embedding can be achieved by the following equations:

$$mvx'_{ij} = \begin{cases} mvx_{ij} & if\,(mvx_{ij} = 0\,or\,\mathrm{mod}\,(i,K) = 0) \\ \frac{4mvx_{ij} + sign(mvx_{ij})}{4} & if\,(|4mvx_{ij}| > 1\,and\,Key(i) = 1) \\ \frac{4mvx_{ij} + sign(mvx_{ij})b}{4} & if\,(|4mvx_{ij}| = 1\,and\,Key(i) = 1) \end{cases} \quad (1)$$

$$mvy'_{ij} = \begin{cases} mvy_{ij} & if\,(mvy_{ij} = 0\,or\,\mathrm{mod}\,(i,K) = 0) \\ \frac{4mvy_{ij} + sign(mvy_{ij})}{4} & if\,(|4mvy_{ij}| > 1\,and\,Key(i) = 1) \\ \frac{4mvy_{ij} + sign(mvy_{ij})b}{4} & if\,(|4mvy_{ij}| = 1\,and\,Key(i) = 1) \end{cases} \quad (2)$$

K is the interval of reference frame, by adjusting K, the message can be embedded into all the frames evenly.

(3) Encode the data-embedded motion vectors into H.264 streams.

The shifting mode diagram of MVHM is shown in Fig. 2.

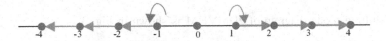

Fig. 2. Shifting mode diagram of MVHM

2.3 2DMVHM

In our early work, we found that for the MVHM algorithm, only one component of motion vector is modified at one time, it limits the embedding efficiency, so we proposed an improved algorithm called 2DMVHM. In the 2DMVHM method, the horizontal and vertical components are modified at the same time, experiments proved that the embedding capacity has improved greatly and the distortion performance decreases slightly. The algorithm can be described as follows:

(1) Encode the video sequence by H.264 standard, in the process of coding, select the motion vectors used for data embedding.

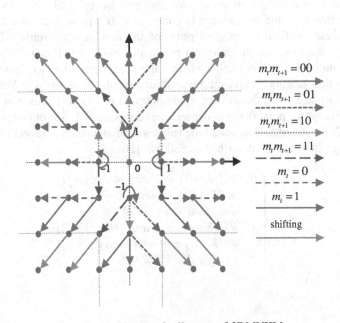

Fig. 3. Shifting mode diagram of 2DMVHM

(2) For every selected motion vector, get the horizontal and vertical component, denoted as (mvx, mvy), which makes up an embedding pair, before embedding, all the pairs would be divided into 17 nonintersecting sets, and each set has an embedding algorithm.

(3) According to which set the embedding pair belongs to, use the corresponding embedding algorithm to modify the value of the pair, and data would be embedded at the same time.

The shifting mode diagram of 2DMVHM is shown in Fig. 3.

2.4   Judgement of Reversibility

As the message embedded into the cover media, the original media must be changed, then the process of change can be described by a shifting mode diagram, which can be used to judge the reversibility of an algorithm. The judgement can be proceeded from the point of in-degrees and out-degrees. By researching the shifting mode diagram, we find that:

(1) In-degree of all the points is 0 or 1.
(2) Out-degree of all the points must be 0 (if the in-degree of the point is 0) or N (if the in-degree of the point is 1).
(3) Where there is an in-degree, there is an out-degree.

When the shifting mode diagram satisfies all the conditions above, the algorithm must be reversible. The in-degree is 1 ensures that even after modified, the origin of marked point is still unique, it means we can get the original point by a reverse operation, in this way, the reversibility is guaranteed. If a point is modified and it has shifted to a new position, the original point of the new position must shift to other positions to make room for the modified point, otherwise it will cause a problem of overlapping, then we would not know whether the point is modified to the position or it is in the position originally, and the reversibility would be destroyed. We will take MVHM for instance, from the shifting mode diagram of MVHM shown in Fig. 2, we can see that except for point 0, the in-degree of every point is 1, and out-degree of point 1 and −1 is 2, the diagram satisfies all the rules, so the algorithm is reversible, the data extracting algorithm can be described as follows [16]:

$$
b' = \begin{cases}
0 & if\,(((Key(i) = 1\ and\ |4mvx'| = 1) \\
 & or\,(Key(i) = 0\ and\ |4mvy'| = 1)) \\
 & and\,(mod(i,K) \neq 0)) \\
1 & if\,(((Key(i) = 1\ and\ |4mvx'| = 2) \\
 & or\,(Key(i) = 0\ and\ |4mvy'| = 2)) \\
 & and\,(mod(i,K) \neq 0))
\end{cases}
\tag{3}
$$

b' is the extracted data bit, after data has been extracted, the video can be recovered, as we have analyzed the reversibility of the algorithm, the recovering algorithm [16] is the reverse process that shown in Fig. 2:

$$
mvx''_{ij} = \begin{cases} mvx'_{ij} & if\,(mvx'_{ij} = 0\,or\,Key(i) = 0 \\ & or\,\mathrm{mod}(i, K) = 0\,or\,\left|4mvx'_{ij}\right| = 1) \\ \frac{4mvx'_{ij} - sign(mvx'_{ij})}{4} & if\,(\left|4mvx'_{ij}\right| \geq 2 \\ & and\,Key(i) = 1) \end{cases} \tag{4}
$$

$$
mvy''_{ij} = \begin{cases} mvy'_{ij} & if\,(mvy'_{ij} = 0\,or\,Key(i) = 1 \\ & or\,\mathrm{mod}(i, K) = 0\,or\,\left|4mvy'_{ij}\right| = 1) \\ \frac{4mvy'_{ij} - sign(mvy'_{ij})}{4} & if\,(\left|4mvy'_{ij}\right| \geq 2 \\ & and\,Key(i) = 0) \end{cases} \tag{5}
$$

mvx''_{ij}, mvx''_{ij} are the recovered components of a motion vector, when the data has been extracted, the recover process is finished too.

2.5   Characters of Shifting Mode Diagram

We have mentioned that from the shifting mode diagram, we can estimate the capacity. As a point is modified, there will be several directions for the point to shift, the directions, or out-degrees, is related to capacity directly.

For the single point, denote D as the number of out-degrees, then the number of data bit that can be embedded in this point is $\log_2 D$, let $d_1 = \lfloor \log_2 D \rfloor$, $d_2 = \lceil \log_2 D \rceil$. Then we can know that $d_1 \leq \log_2 D \leq d_2$, it means this point can embed d_1 bits at least and d_2 bits at most at one time.

For the point, all the out-degrees can be formed by $\left(2^{d_1 + 1} - D\right)$ d_1-bit codes and $\left(2D - 2^{d_1 + 1}\right)$ d_2-bit codes. Specially, if $d_1 = d_2$, D d_1-bit codes will make up all the out-degrees. The capacity of the single point can be expressed as:

$$
EC_i = \frac{1}{2^{d_1}} \cdot d_1 \cdot \left(2^{d_1 + 1} - D\right) + \frac{1}{2^{d_2}} \cdot d_2 \cdot \left(2D - 2^{d_1 + 1}\right) \tag{6}
$$

then the total embedding capacity can be expressed as:

$$
EC = \sum_{i=1}^{n} EC_i \tag{7}
$$

We will take the point (0,0) of Fig. 2 for instance. From Fig. 2, we can find that the out-degree of point (0,0) is 5 and in-degree is 1, then $d_1 = 2$ and $d_2 = 3$, and we can also know that for point (0,0), the out-degrees can be formed by 3 two-bit codes and 2 three-bit codes. In reference [15], when the selected embedding pair is (0,0), the corresponding embedding algorithm is:

$$
(Y'_{s1}, Y'_{s2}) = \begin{cases} (Y_{s1}, Y_{s2}) & \text{if } m_i m_{i+1} = 01 \\ (Y_{s1} + 1, Y_{s2}) & \text{if } m_i m_{i+1} = 10 \\ (Y_{s1}, Y_{s2} + 1) & \text{if } m_i m_{i+1} = 11 \\ (Y_{s1} - 1, Y_{s2}) & \text{if } m_i m_{i+1} m_{i+2} = 000 \\ (Y_{s1}, Y_{s2} - 1) & \text{if } m_i m_{i+1} m_{i+2} = 001 \end{cases} \tag{8}
$$

In the equation, (Y_{s1}, Y_{s2}) are the selected coefficients, (Y'_{s1}, Y'_{s2}) are the marked coefficients or the data-embedded coefficients, m_i is the to-be embedded data bit. It is obviously that the 5 out-degrees contains 3 two-bit codes (01, 10, 11) and 2 three-bit codes (000, 001). It proves the theoretical analysis above is correct.

3   Experimental Results

We employed 2DMVHM method for experiments, in the experiments, we would take 8 video sequences: foreman, coastguard, mobile, news, city, carphone, salesman and container, they are all QCIF (176×144) video. For every video, we would select 20 frames to embed message to compare the embedding capacity with the theoretical capacity. Experimental results are shown in Fig. 4.

From the comparison, we can see that by using shifting mode diagram, the embedding capacity of an algorithm can be estimated with a high accuracy. As shown in Fig. 3, we divide the payload into 3 types, the type like point (1,0) can embed 2 bit at one time, the type like point (0,2) can embed 1.5 bit at one time, and the type like point (1,1) can embed 1 bit at one time, the rest points are shifting but without embedding data, from Fig. 4, we can find that for the video foreman, news, city and carphone, the theoretical results are quite similar to the experimental results, but for other videos, the similarity is relatively lower. During the experiments, we find that's because distribution of motion vector is more concentrated, we will take the video sequence carphone and mobile for instance. For the two video, we take the 19-th frame, and only investigate the case of payloads, as we mentioned, the payload can be classified to 3 types, they are 2-bit type, 1.5-type and 1-bit type, respectively. We will calculate the ratio of different payload type. The results are shown in Table 1.

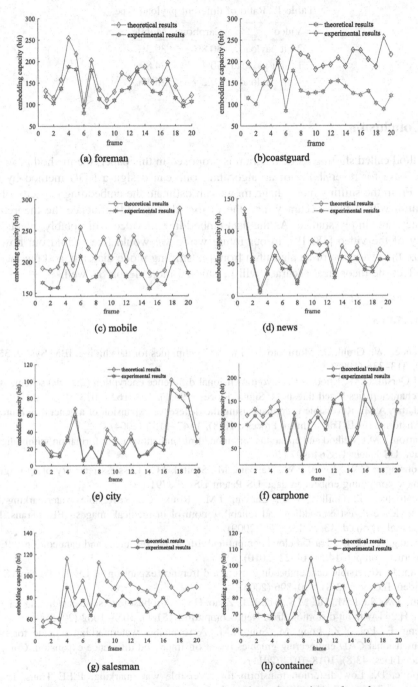

Fig. 4. Contrast between theoretical results and experimental results

390 D. Li et al.

Table 1. Ratio of different payload type

Video	Carphone	Mobile
2-bit payload	30.8%	39.3%
1.5-bit payload	50%	34.8%
1-bit payload	19.2%	26.1%

4 Conclusion

A method called shifting mode diagram is proposed in this paper, the method provides theory base for reversibility of an algorithm, one can design a RDH method by the rules. From the shifting mode diagram, we can estimate the embedding capacity of an algorithm with a high accuracy, and the factors that would influence the theoretical accuracy are simply studied. As the data embedding in video will notably affects the quality of the video [18, 19], in our future work, we would like to find out how to analyze the distorsion of an algorithm from the shifting mode diagram, and the factors that affect the theoretical accuracy will be studied more deeply as well.

References

1. Bender, W., Gruhl, D., Morimoto, N., Lu, A.: Techniques for data hiding. IBM Syst. J. **35**(3, 4), 313–336 (1996)
2. Al-Qershi, O.M., Khoo, B.E.: Two-dimensional difference encryption (2D-DE) scheme with a characteristics-based threshold. Signal Process. **93**(1), 154–162 (2013)
3. Alattar, A.M.: Reversible watermark using the difference expansion of a generalized integer transform. IEEE Trans. Image Process. **13**(8), 1147–1156 (2004)
4. Barton, J.M.: Method and apparatus for embedding authentication information within digital data. US Patent US5646997 (1997)
5. Honsinger, C.W., Jones, P.W., Rabbani, M., Stoffel, J.C.: Lossless recovery of an original image containing embedded data. US Patent US6278791 (2001)
6. Coatrieux, G., Guillou, C.L., Cauvin, J.M., Roux, C.: Reversible watermarking for knowledge digest embedding and reliability control in medical images. IEEE Trans. Inf. Technol. Biomed. **13**(2), 158–165 (2009)
7. Hwang, K., Li, D.: Trusted cloud computing with secure resources and data coloring. IEEE Internet Comput. **14**(5), 14–22 (2010)
8. Tian, J.: Reversible data embedding using a difference expansion. IEEE Trans. Circ. Syst. Video Technol. **13**(8), 890–896 (2003)
9. Liu, Y.X., Ju, L.M., Hu, M.S., Ma, X.J., Zhao, H.G.: A robust reversible data hiding scheme for H.264 without distortion drift. Neurocomputing **151**(1), 1053–1062 (2015)
10. Peng, F., Lei, Y.Z., Long, M., Sun, X.M.: A reversible watermarking scheme for two-dimensional CAD engineering graphics based on improved difference expansion. Comput. Aided Des. **43**(8), 1018–1024 (2011)
11. Coltuc, D.: Low distortion transform for reversible watermarking. IEEE Trans. Image Process. **21**(1), 412–417 (2012)

12. Chung, K.L., Huang, Y.H., Chang, P.C., Liao, H.Y.M.: Reversible data hiding-based approach for intra-frame error concealment in H.264/AVC. IEEE Trans. Circ. Syst. Video Technol. **20**(11), 1643–1647 (2010)
13. Vleeschouwer, D.C., Delaigle, J.F., Macq, B.: Circular interpretation of bijective transformations in lossless watermarking for media asset management. IEEE Trans. Multimedia **5**(1), 97–105 (2003)
14. An, L.L., Gao, X.B., Li, X.L., Tao, D.C., Deng, C., Li, J.: Robust reversible watermarking via clustering and enhanced pixel-wise masking. IEEE Trans. Image Process. **21**(8), 3598–3611 (2012)
15. Zhao, J., Li, Z.T., Feng, B.: A novel two-dimensional histogram modification for reversible data embedding into stereo H.264 video. Multimedia Tools Appl. **75**, 5959–5980 (2016). https://doi.org/10.1007/s11042-015-2558-9
16. Niu, K., Yang, X.Y., Zhang, Y.N.: A novel video reversible data hiding algorithm using motion vector for H.264/AVC. Tsinghua Sci. Technol. **22**(5), 489–498 (2017). ISSN 1007-0214 05/10
17. Ni, Z.C., Shi, Y.Q., Ansari, N., Su, W.F.: Reversible data hiding. IEEE Trans. Circ. Syst. Video Technol. **16**(3), 354–362 (2006)
18. Zeng, X.A., Chen, Z.Y., Chen, M., Xong, Z.: Reversible video watermarking using motion estimation and prediction error expansion. J. Inf. Sci. Eng. **27**(2), 465–479 (2011)
19. Zeng, X., Chen, Z., Xiong, Z.: Issues and solution on distortion drift in reversible video data hiding. Multimedia Tools Appl. **52**(2–3), 465–484 (2011)

Reversible Data Hiding in JPEG Images Based on Two-Dimensional Histogram Modification

Sijin Cheng[1] and Fangjun Huang[1,2]([✉])

[1] Guangdong Key Laboratory of Information Security Technology, School of
Data and Computer Science, Sun Yat-sen University, Guangzhou 510006,
Guangdong, People's Republic of China
huangfj@mail.sysu.edu.cn
[2] State Key Laboratory of Information Security, Institute of Information
Engineering, Chinese Academy of Sciences,
Beijing 100093, People's Republic of China

Abstract. The joint photographic experts group (JPEG) is the most popular
image format in our daily life, and it is widely used by digital cameras and other
photographic capture devices. Recently, reversible data hiding (RDH) for JPEG
images has become an active research area in the field of data hiding. In this
paper, a new two-dimensional coefficient-histogram based RDH scheme for
JPEG image is proposed. First, a two-dimensional quantized discrete cosine
transform (DCT) coefficient-histogram is generated. Then, data are embedded
according to a specifically designed coefficient-pair-mapping (CPM). Here, by
the proposed approach, compared with the one-dimensional histogram-based
RDH for JPEG images, the increased file size is minimized. Moreover, the
selection strategy based on the optimal frequency band of the DCT coefficient-
pairs is proposed, by which the distortion of the marked JPEG image is minimized. Compared to some state-of-the-art RDH methods for JPEG images,
experimental results show the superiority of our methods both in image quality
and increased file size.

Keywords: Reversible data hiding · JPEG · Two-dimensional histogram
Coefficient-pair-mapping (CPM)

1 Introduction

In the past two decades, reversible data hiding (RDH) is one of the hottest topics in the
field of data hiding. For most data hiding methods, the cover medium will be distorted
during the data embedding process and hence the original medium cannot be restored
any more. To solve this issue, reversible data hiding, also called lossless or invertible
data hiding, is proposed.

In general, the existing reversible data hiding schemes in spatial domain are mainly
classified into three categories: lossless compression [1, 2], difference expansion
(DE) [3–5] and histogram shifting (HS) [6–9]. The idea behind the lossless compression schemes is to release some space by losslessly compressing a subset of the cover
image, and utilize the saved space to embed data. In 2003, Tian [3] first proposed

DE-based RDH that makes use of the difference between two adjacent pixels to embed messages. Later, several improved techniques for DE-based embedding were put forward, such as location map reduction [4] and sorting [5]. In 2006, Ni et al. [6] proposed the histogram shifting (HS) technique, which selected a pair of peak and zero bins in the histogram and then shifted the bins between the two bins by 1 toward zero bin for embedding. In 2007, Thodi and Rodriguez [10] proposed a method that exploited the prediction error (PE) of pixel around it to expand and the derived prediction-error histogram (PEH) is more sharply distributed, which has a superior performance compared with DE methods. In 2016, Ou et al. [11] develop the pixel-value-ordering (PVO) embedding in two-dimensional space and utilizes the prediction-error expansion (PEE) for data embedding.

Compared to an uncompressed image, it is more difficult to hide secret messages into a JPEG image because of its less redundancy. Here, some RDH schemes in JPEG images which are based on the manipulation of quantized discrete cosine transform (DCT) coefficients will be introduced.

In 2016, Huang et al. [12] proposed an HS-based RDH method for JPEG images. In their scheme, zero coefficients remain unchanged and the coefficients with values 1 and -1 are employed for data embedding, thus the storage size of the marked JPEG image is well preserved. As all of the non-zero coefficients in the DCT domain could be modified by one at most, the quality of the marked-image is maintained. Moreover, a block selection strategy according to the number of zero coefficients in each 8×8 block is designed and so the distortion of the marked JPEG image is minimized. Later on, based on [12], Yin et al. [13] proposed an algorithm to adaptively select the optimal expandable bins-pair at image level by adopting k-nearest neighbors (KNN) algorithm.

In this paper, we first propose a new reversible data hiding scheme for JPEG images based on two-dimensional coefficient histogram modification. By dividing the quantized DCT coefficients into pairs, a two-dimensional coefficient-histogram is constructed first. Then a specific coefficient-pair-mapping (CPM) for RDH is designed. In order to further reduce the distortion, some new insights on how to choose the optimal region of the DCT coefficient-pairs are also depicted. Experimental results demonstrate that the proposed method can achieve better performance compared to the state-of-the-art method [12, 13].

The rest of the paper is organized as follows. In Sect. 2, the details of the proposed RDH scheme for JPEG images is introduced. The comparison results with the prior arts are shown in Sect. 3. Finally, a conclusion is drawn in Sect. 4.

2 Proposed Scheme

In this section, a brief introduction of JPEG compression is given first. After that, the two-dimensional coefficient-histogram is constructed and a specifically designed coefficient-pair-mapping (CPM) is presented. Then, how to select the optimal frequency band of the DCT coefficient-pairs is analyzed. Finally, the detailed embedding and extraction procedures of our scheme are summarized.

2.1   JPEG Compression

The process of JPEG compression coding is shown in Fig. 1. The original image is first divided into the non-overlapped 8×8 blocks, and then DCT is applied to each block. The DCT coefficients obtained by the DCT transform will be sent to the quantizer, and they are quantized by using a pre-programmed quantization table which corresponds to different quality factor (QF). After quantization, the quantized coefficients are scanned in the zigzag manner as shown in Fig. 2. The direct current (DC) coefficients are encoded by the differential pulse code modulation (DPCM), and run length encoding (RLE) is applied to the alternating current (AC) coefficients. Finally, the symbol string is converted to a data stream by Huffman coding, and we can obtain the final JPEG file after pre-pending the header.

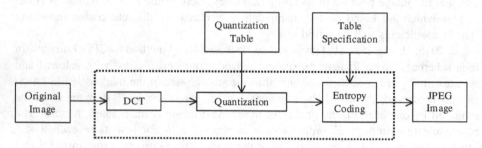

Fig. 1. JPEG compression process

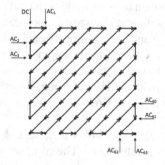

Fig. 2. Zigzag sequence.

Specifically, the RLE for AC coefficients can be described as (Runlength/Size, Amplitude). Here, Runlength denotes the number of zero AC coefficients before the next nonzero AC coefficients, and Size denotes the number of bits needed to represent the next nonzero AC coefficient. Amplitude denotes the value of the nonzero AC coefficient. Each Amplitude is encoded with a variable-length integer (VLI) code, whose length in bits and code word are given in the Table 1. There are 160 combinations of Runlength and Size. Each Runlength/Size is encoded with a variable-length code (VLC) from the Huffman table. The code word of Runlength/Size is combined with the code word of Amplitude to form the final JPEG bit stream.

Table 1. The description of AC coefficients.

AC coeffcients (Amplitude)	Size	Code word
0	N/A	–
−1, 1	1	0,1
−3, −2, 2, 3	2	00, 01, 10, 11
−7... −4, 4...7	3	000...011, 100...111
−15... −8, 8, 15	4	0000...0111, 1000...1111
−31... −16, 16...31	5	00000...01111, 10000...11111
−63... −32, 32...63	6	000000...011111, 100000...111111
−127... −64, 64...127	7	00000000...0111111, 1000000...1111111
−255... −128, 128...255	8	00000000...01111111, 10000000...11111111
−511... −256, 256...511	9	...
−1023... −512, 512...1023	10	...
−2047... −1024, 1024...2047	11	...
−4095... −2048, 2048...4095	12	...
−8191... −4096, 4096...8191	13	...
−16383... −8192, 8192...16383	14	...
−32767... −16384, 16384...32767	N/A	...

2.2 CPM for RDH in JPEG Images

In light of the characteristics of the DCT coefficients, we propose a new framework which is suitable for JPEG images. For each 8×8 block, the quantized DCT coefficients are divided into 32 pairs (according to the zig-zag scanning order as shown in Fig. 2), and the two-dimensional coefficient-histogram is constructed by the DCT coefficient-pairs. Then we define the coefficient-pair-mapping (CPM) on the coefficient-pairs as shown in Fig. 3. The points with different colors represent the different types of coefficient-pairs.

For ease of explanation, all the coefficient-pairs are classified as six different types, i.e., Type A-F. The coefficient-pairs of Type A-C, Type D-E, and Type F are expandable, shiftable, and unchangeable pairs, respectively. Note that those pairs to be

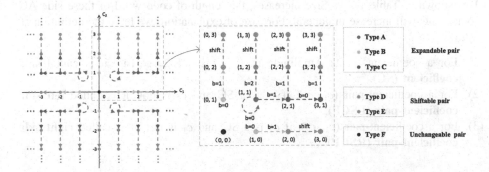

Fig. 3. CPM for illustrating the proposed data embedding procedure. (Color figure online)

expanded to carry the message bits are defined as expandable pairs, the pairs to be shifted to ensure the reversibility of RDH are defined as shiftable pairs, and those to be kept unchanged in the embedding process are defined as unchangeable pairs.

(1) Type A: $(c_1, c_2) = \{(-1, 1), (1, 1), (1, -1), (-1, -1)\}$. The coefficient-pairs of this type are represented with red points, and the modification directions are indicated by red arrows. Note that each point in type A has three directions to expand. Thus the message bits to be embedded is converted into a ternary stream first, and each point of Type A can be embedded with $\log_2 3$ bits [11].

(2) Type B: $(c_1, c_2) = \{(0, 1), (1, 0), (0, -1), (-1, 0)\}$. The coefficient-pairs of this type are represented with yellow points. The point of this type keeps unchanged if the to-be-embedded data bit b = 0. And when b = 1, the modification direction is indicated by a yellow arrow.

(3) Type C: $(c_1, c_2) = \{c_1 > 1 \text{ or } c_1 < -1, c_2 = \pm 1\}$. The coefficient-pairs of this type are represented with purple points. And the modification directions are indicated by purple arrows. If b = 0, the modification direction is "horizontal". If b = 1, the modification direction is "vertical".

(4) Type D: $(c_1, c_2) = \{c_1 > 1 \text{ or } c_1 < -1, c_2 = 0\}$. The coefficient-pairs of this type are represented with green points. Each point of this type is shifted to the horizontally adjacent point, which is indicated by a green arrow.

(5) Type E: $(c_1, c_2) = \{c_2 > 1 \text{ or } c_2 < -1\}$. The coefficient-pairs of this type are represented with blue points. Each point of this type is shifted to the vertically adjacent point, which is indicated by a blue arrow.

(6) Type F: $(c_1, c_2) = (0, 0)$. The coefficient-pairs of this type are represented with black points. These coefficient-pairs are kept unchanged. In view of that modifying zero coefficients may increase the image file size significantly [12], $c_1 = 0$ or $c_2 = 0$ won't be changed in our designed CPM mechanism.

2.3   Evaluation for CPM

It should be mentioned that there are many ways to design CPM. Next, the superiority of our designed CPM is experimentally demonstrated.

As shown in Table 1, if the Amplitude $2^k - 1 (k = 1, 2, \ldots, 14)$ is modified by 1, there will be one more bit needed to represent the Amplitude (i.e., Size will increase by 1 as shown in Table 1). As Size increases, the length of code word of these side AC coefficients will increase in general. For ease of explanation, we have the definition as follows:

(1) For a coefficient, if its Amplitude is $2^k - 1 (k = 1, 2, \ldots, 14)$, it is called **side coefficient (SC)**.

(2) For a coefficient-pair (c_1, c_2), if c_1 is a SC and c_2 is not, it is called **left side coefficient-pair (LSCP)**.

(3) For a coefficient-pair (c_1, c_2), if c_2 is a SC and c_1 is not, it is called **right side coefficient-pair (RSCP)**.

After performing the expanding or shifting, the length of JPEG bit stream will increase due to the modification to SCs. Generally speaking, this may result in the increment of the JPEG file size. For simplicity, we only take the increased bit of Size into consideration.

For the one-dimensional histogram-based RDH for JPEG images [12], its capacity can be denoted as EC_{hs} and the ratio of the increased bit of Size is

$$R_{hs} = \frac{\frac{1}{2} \times N_{exp} + N_{shift}}{EC_{hs}} \quad (1)$$

Where N_{exp} represents the number of SCs in expandable coefficients. With the assumption that the "0" and "1" in the secret message are equally distributed, (1/2) in (1) denotes that only half of the histogram bins 1 and -1 are modified by 1. N_{shift} denotes the number of SCs in shiftable coefficients.

According to Fig. 3, for the proposed CPM-based scheme, its capacity can be denoted as EC_{pro} and the ratio of the increased bit of Size can be clearly formulated as

$$R_{pro} = \frac{\frac{1}{3} \times (N_{A1} + N_{A2}) + \frac{1}{2} \times (N_{B1} + N_{B2}) + \frac{1}{2}(N_{C1} + N_{C2}) + N_{D1} + N_{E2}}{EC_{pro}} \quad (2)$$

where N_{A1} and N_{A2} represent the number of LSCPs and RSCPs in Type A. Since a pair (c_1, c_2) in Type A have three modification directions, the probability that c_1 may be modified horizontally by 1 is one-third. And the probability that c_2 may be modified vertically by 1 is one-third. N_{B1} and N_{B2} represents the number of LSCPs and RSCPs in Type B. And pairs in Type B, the probability for them to be modified by 1 is one-half. As shown in Fig. 3, pairs in Type C have the same possibility of expanding vertically and horizontally. N_{C1} and N_{C2} represent the number of LSCPs and RSCPs in Type C, respectively. N_{D1} represents the number of LSCPs in Type D. In our mapping mechanism, the proposed method only modifies the c_2 in Type E. Here, N_{E2} represents the number RSCPs in Type E.

The ratio is a measurement of performance for preserving the file size. As shown in Table 2, the comparisons are conducted on the six images with QF = 70. Referring to this table, our method always has a smaller ratio, the superiority of the two-dimensional histogram for JPEG images is thus verified.

Table 2. Comparisons for the ration of increased bits between the proposed scheme and the methods of Huang *et al.* [12].

JPEG image (QF = 70)	Proposed scheme (CPM)	[12] (HS)
Lena	0.6245	0.6726
Peppers	0.5962	0.6486
Boat	0.6753	0.7091
Baboon	0.7105	0.7360
Splash	0.5551	0.5998
Tank	0.6046	0.6493

2.4   Optimum Frequency Band of the DCT Coefficient-Pair

In the aforementioned algorithm, the quantized DCT coefficients are divided into 32 pairs in the zig-zag sequence. As shown in Fig. 4, the first pair (DC and AC_1) in black region is not utilized for data hiding, but some auxiliary information can be embedded in this pair (some explanations will be given next). As we have known that the DCT coefficients belonging to low frequency have less influence on the image quality [14], we propose to prioritize the coefficient-pairs belonging to low frequency band for data embedding. Then we set a cutoff value $C_v(2 \leq C_v \leq 32)$ to record which coefficient-pairs are selected for reversible data hiding. For example, when $C_v = 5$, the coefficient-pairs selected for data hiding (with red color) are shown in Fig. 4.

	1	2	3	4	5	...	4096
	DC AC_1	DC AC_1	DC AC_1	DC AC_1	DC AC_1	:	DC AC_1
	AC_2 AC_3	AC_2 AC_3	AC_2 AC_3	AC_2 AC_3	AC_2 AC_3	:	AC_2 AC_3
	AC_4 AC_5	AC_4 AC_5	AC_4 AC_5	AC_4 AC_5	AC_4 AC_5	:	AC_4 AC_5
	AC_6 AC_7	AC_6 AC_7	AC_6 AC_7	AC_6 AC_7	AC_6 AC_7	:	AC_6 AC_7
	AC_8 AC_9	AC_8 AC_9	AC_8 AC_9	AC_8 AC_9	AC_8 AC_9	:	AC_8 AC_9
	:	:	:	:	:	:	:
	AC_{62} AC_{63}	AC_{62} AC_{63}	AC_{62} AC_{63}	AC_{62} AC_{63}	AC_{62} AC_{63}	AC_{62} AC_{63}	AC_{62} AC_{63}

Fig. 4. The description of coefficient-pairs in each 8×8 block. ($C_v = 5$) (Color figure online)

Considerable experiments have demonstrated that for a specific image, if the length of secret messages is different, the optimal cutoff pair C_v will be different. For example, when embedding secret messages into 512×512 Lena with QF = 70, the relation between peak signal to noise ratio (PSNR) and C_v is displayed in Fig. 5. When the payload is 5000 bits and 10000 bits, it is observed that the optimum C_v values for Lena (QF = 70) are 6 and 9, respectively.

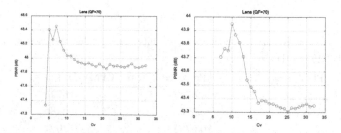

Fig. 5. Selecting of C_v values for Lena (QF = 70) with different embedding payloads: (a) 5000 bits, (b) 10000 bits.

How to find the best cutoff value C_v? A minimum value C_v is determined according to the payload first. Then the zero coefficients (not including the first pair) in each 8×8 block are calculated. The blocks which contain more zero coefficients are utilized to embed secret messages. And we set a threshold $T_h(0 \leq T_h \leq 62)$ to record which blocks are selected. If the zero coefficients in the block are more than or equal to threshold T_h, this block will be utilized; else skip this block. The coefficient-pairs satisfying the conditions are processed to embed the payload according to the CPM shown in Fig. 3. After that, the performance of the marked image is measured and recorded. The same process is repeated via increasing C_v one by one. The C_v associated with the largest PSNR is selected as the optimum value.

2.5 Embedding and Extraction Algorithm

The proposed data embedding procedure can be summarized as follows.

Step (1) For each 8×8 block, the quantized DCT coefficients are divided into 32 pairs in a zig-zag scanning order. Empty the LSBs (least-significant-bits) of the AC_1 coefficients in the first pair of each block to prepare for auxiliary information. Append the replaced LSBs as a part of payload.
Step (2) Find the optimum C_v and corresponding T_h according to the method detailed in the Sect. 2-D. After this step, the payload embedding is completed.
Step (3) Embed two threshold $\{C_v, T_h\}$ along with the message length L into the LSBs of the AC_1 coefficients in the first pair.
Step (4) After all message bits are embedded, encode the coefficients and we get the marked JPEG image.

The corresponding data extraction and image restoration process is quite simple which is described as follows.

Step (1) Divide the quantized DCT coefficients into 32 pairs. Extract the message length L and the thresholds $\{C_v, T_h\}$ from the host image according to the extracted LSBs of AC_1 coefficients in the first pair.
Step (2) In this step, according to the thresholds $\{C_v, T_h\}$, restore the marked DCT coefficient-pairs by the reverse of CPM. And the embedded payload is extracted. Then, restore the LSBs of AC_1 coefficients.
Step (3) After all the changed coefficient-pairs are restored, the original JPEG image is recovered.

3 Experimental Results

In this section, several experiments are conducted on six grayscale images as shown in Fig. 6. Three image quality factors, i.e., QF = 70, 80 and 90 are tested. We evaluate our proposed scheme by comparing the visual quality and the file size preservation, and two current state-of-the-art RDH methods designed for JPEG images are selected for comparison. These two schemes were proposed in [12, 13]. In addition, in order to demonstrate the effectiveness of the proposed frequency selection strategy, the proposed algorithm without using this strategy (labeled as "Non-adaptive") are also used to compare. The experimental results are shown in Figs. 7 and 8.

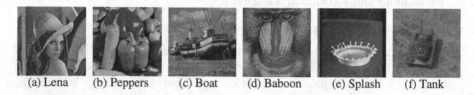

(a) Lena   (b) Peppers   (c) Boat   (d) Baboon   (e) Splash   (f) Tank

Fig. 6. Test images

For image quality comparisons, it can be observed that our method can achieve better visual quality than that obtained by [12], the underlying reason behind the results is that the proposed method utilize optimal frequency band of the DCT coefficient-pairs to be embedded. Moreover, in addition to coefficients with values 1 and −1, other DCT coefficients can also be used. However, for some specific images, the PSNR values of the proposed method is a little bit smaller than [13], the reason for this phenomenon is that the bins-pair (1, −1) for some images are not the best to embed the data bits, and we mainly utilize these coefficients to form a coefficient pair to expand. However, without using the frequency selection (labeled as "Non-adaptive"), the PSNR values are less than the proposed method, and the superiority of the frequency selection for JPEG images is shown in the comparison.

For file size preservation comparisons, increased file size between the original image and the embedded image file are shown in Fig. 8(a)–(d), it is demonstrated that our proposed method can always preserve the file size better than [12, 13]. And the file size of the marked image obtained by the proposed method without using frequency selection is less than that of the previous methods.

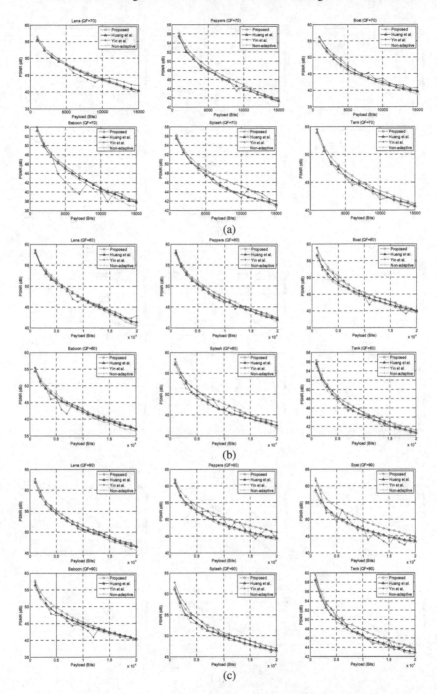

Fig. 7. Visual qualities for six test images: (a) QF = 70 (b) QF = 80 (c) QF = 90.

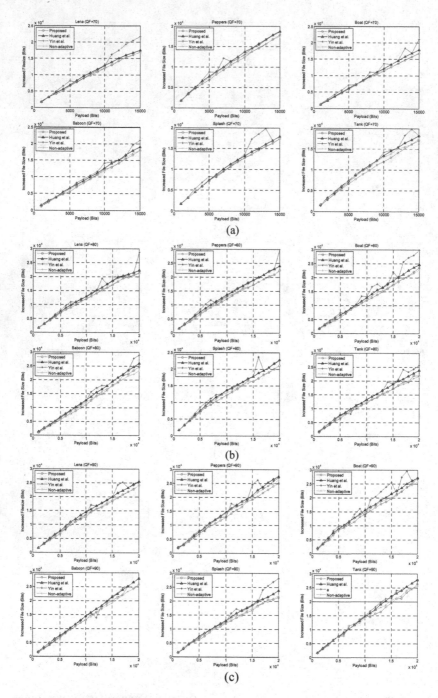

Fig. 8. Increased file sizes for six test images: (a) QF = 70 (b) QF = 80 (c) QF = 90.

4 Conclusion

In this paper, we presented a new RDH scheme for JPEG images based on the two-dimensional coefficient-histogram. Nowadays, apart from the embedding capacity and fidelity that need to be taken into consideration, the storage size of the marked-image is seen as a crucial issue, which is of great concern. Observed form the experimental results, the proposed scheme gains significant results in term of file size preservation. In the meanwhile, good visual quality can be obtained.

Acknowledgments. This work is partially supported by the National Natural Science Foundation of China (61772572), The NSFC-NRF Scientific Cooperation Program (61811540409), the Natural Science Foundation of Guangdong Province of China (2017A030313366), and the Fundamental Research Funds for Central Universities (17lgjc45).

References

1. Fridrich, J., Goljan, M.: Lossless data embedding for all image formats. In: SPIE Proceedings of Photonics West, Electronic Imaging, Security and Watermarking of Multimedia Contents, vol. 4675, pp. 572–583 (2002)
2. Celik, M.U., Sharma, G., Tekalp, A.M.: Lossless watermarking for image authentication: a new framework and an implementation. IEEE Trans. Image Process. 12(4), 1042–1049 (2006)
3. Tian, J.: Reversible data embedding using a difference expansion. IEEE Trans. Circ. Syst. Video Technol. 13(8), 890–896 (2003)
4. Hu, Y., Lee, H.K., Li, J.: DE-based reversible data hiding with improved overflow location map. EEE Trans. Circuits Syst. Video Technol 19(2), 250–260 (2009)
5. Kamstra, L., Heijmans, H.J.A.M.: Reversible data embedding into images using wavelet techniques and sorting. IEEE Trans. Image Process. 14(12), 2082–2090 (2005)
6. Ni, Z., Shi, Y., Annsari, N., Wei, S.: Reversible data hiding. IEEE Trans. Circ. Syst. Video Technol. 16(3), 354–362 (2006)
7. Lee, S.-K., Suh, Y.-H., Ho, Y.-S.: Reversible image authentication based on watermarking. In: Proceedings of IEEE International Conference Multimedia Expo, pp. 1321–1324 (2006)
8. Li, X., Li, B., Yang, B., Zeng, T.: General framework to histogram shifting-based reversible data hiding. IEEE Trans. Image Process. 22(6), 2181–2191 (2013)
9. Li, X., Zhang, W., Gui, X., Yang, B.: Efficient reversible data hiding based on multiple histograms modification. IEEE Trans. Inf. Forensics Secur. 10(9), 2016–2027 (2015)
10. Thodi, D.M., Rodriguez, J.J.: Expansion embedding techniques for reversible watermarking. IEEE Trans. Image Process. 16(3), 721–730 (2007)
11. Ou, B., Li, X., Wang, J.: High-fidelity reversible data hiding based on pixel-value-ordering and pairwise prediction-error expansion, Signal Processing. J. Vis. Commun. Image Represent. 39, 12–23 (2016)
12. Huang, F., Qu, X., Kim, H.J., Huang, J.: Reversible data hiding in JPEG images. IEEE Trans. Circ. Syst. Video Technol. 26(9), 1610–1621 (2016)
13. Yin, J., Wang, R., Guo, Y., Liu, F.: An adaptive reversible data hiding scheme for JPEG images. In: Shi, Y.Q., Kim, H.J., Perez-Gonzalez, F., Liu, F. (eds.) IWDW 2016. LNCS, vol. 10082, pp. 456–469. Springer, Cham (2017). https://doi.org/10.1007/978-3-319-53465-7_34
14. Xuan, G., Shi, Y.Q., Ni, Z., Chai, P., Cui, X., Tong, X.: Reversible data hiding for JPEG images based on histogram pairs. In: Kamel, M., Campilho, A. (eds.) ICIAR 2007. LNCS, vol. 4633, pp. 715–727. Springer, Heidelberg (2007). https://doi.org/10.1007/978-3-540-74260-9_64

Reversible Embedding to Covers Full of Boundaries

Hanzhou Wu[1]([✉]), Wei Wang[1], Jing Dong[1], Yanli Chen[2], Hongxia Wang[2], and Songyang Wu[3]

[1] Institute of Automation, Chinese Academy of Sciences, Beijing 100190, China
h.wu.phd@ieee.org
[2] School of Information Science and Technology, Southwest Jiaotong University, Chengdu 611756, China
[3] Key Laboratory of Information Network Security, Ministry of Public Security, Shanghai, China

Abstract. In reversible data embedding, to avoid overflow and underflow problem, before data embedding, boundary pixels are recorded as side information, which may be losslessly compressed. The existing algorithms often assume that a natural image has few boundary pixels so that the size of side information could be rather small. Accordingly, a relatively high pure payload could be achieved. However, there actually may exist a lot of boundary pixels in a natural image, implying that, the size of side information could be very large. Thus, when to directly use the existing algorithms, the pure embedding capacity may be not sufficient. In order to address this important problem, in this paper, we present a new and efficient framework to reversible data embedding in images that have lots of boundary pixels. The core idea is to losslessly preprocess boundary pixels so that it can significantly reduce the side information. We conduct extensive experiments to show the superiority and applicability of our work.

Keywords: Reversible data hiding · Watermarking · Location map
Side information · Prediction · Histogram shifting

1 Introduction

Reversible data embedding [1,2] also called reversible data hiding, reversible watermarking, lossless embedding, is a special *fragile* technique that could benefit sensitive applications that require no distortion of the cover. It works by hiding a message such as authentication data within a cover by slightly altering the cover. At the decoder side, one can extract the hidden data from the marked content. And, the original content can be perfectly reconstructed. One will find the marked content is not authentic if it was tampered or lossy processed.

Reversible data embedding can be modeled as a rate-distortion optimization problem. We hope to embed as many message bits as possible while the

© Springer Nature Switzerland AG 2018
X. Sun et al. (Eds.): ICCCS 2018, LNCS 11066, pp. 404–415, 2018.
https://doi.org/10.1007/978-3-030-00015-8_35

introduced distortion is kept low. A number of algorithms have been proposed in the past years. Early algorithms use lossless compression to vacate room for data embedding. More efficient approaches are introduced to increase the data embedding capacity or reduce the distortion such as difference expansion [1], histogram shifting [3] and other methods [4,5]. Nowadays, advanced algorithms [6–11] use prediction-errors (PEs) of the cover to hide secret data since PEs could provide superior rate-distortion performance.

For an image, to avoid underflow and overflow problem during data embedding, the boundary pixels should be adjusted into the reliable range and recorded as side information, which will be embedded into the cover image together with the secret data. The existing algorithms often assume that, the used cover image is natural and thus the size of side information could be small, which has ignorable impact on the pure embedding capacity. However, even for natural images, there may exist a lot of boundary pixels. This implies that, the side information may have significant impact on the pure embedding capacity.

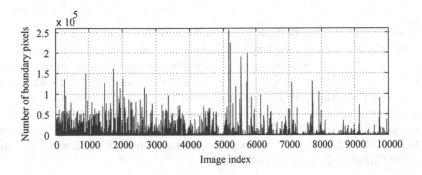

Fig. 1. The number of boundary pixels in each image.

We use the image database BOSSBase[1] [12] for explanation. There are a total of 10,000 images in BOSSBase and all images are 8-bit grayscale with a size of 512×512. We assume that the pixels with a value of 0 or 255 are boundary pixels. Figure 1 shows the number of boundary pixels in each image. It is observed that, there are many images that have lots of boundary pixels, implying that the corresponding side information may require a lot of bits. In reversible data embedding, a commonly used operation to construct the side information is first to assign one bit to each pixel representing whether the present pixel is a boundary or not. Then, the resulting binary matrix also called the location map is losslessly compressed. This operation is effective when the number of boundary pixels is small. However, it may have poor performance in images containing a lot of boundary pixels, especially for the case that boundary pixels are widely distributed within the cover. Figure 2 shows an example. Regardless of the lossless compression algorithm to be used, the compression ratio for the location map would be intuitively very low.

---

[1] Online available: http://agents.fel.cvut.cz/stegodata/.

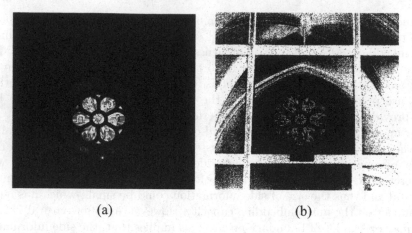

<table>
<tr><td>(a)</td><td>(b)</td></tr>
</table>

Fig. 2. An image full of boundary pixels selected from BOSSBase. (a) 5727.pgm, (b) the location map where the boundary pixels are in white area.

We sort all images in BOSSBase according to the number of the boundary pixels. We choose the top-200 largest number of boundary pixels of images out and construct the losslessly compressed location maps by arithmetic coding. Figure 3 shows the size of the losslessly compressed location map for each image. It is observed that, the sizes of the compressed location maps are all very large, indicating that, many existing algorithms may carry a very low pure payload and even cannot carry extra bits for those natural images full of boundary pixels. This has motivated the authors in this paper to propose an efficient algorithm to address this very important problem.

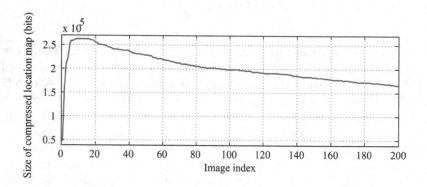

Fig. 3. The size of losslessly compressed location map for each of the selected images. Index 1 means the image has the largest number of boundary pixels.

The rest are organized as follows. In Sect. 2, we introduce the proposed reversible data embedding framework for images that have lots of boundary pixels. Then, we conduct experiments to show the performance in Sect. 3. Finally, we conclude this paper in Sect. 4.

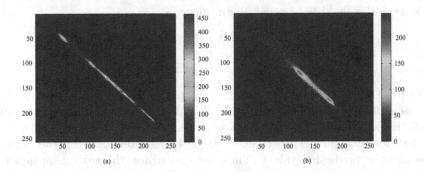

Fig. 4. The statistical distribution between the pixel values and their prediction values. (a) Lena, (b) Baboon. Both are 8-bit grayscale and sized 512×512.

2 Proposed Framework

The proposed work involves three steps. First, all pixels are preprocessed by prediction, for which the number of boundary pixels will be significantly reduced, resulting in a small size of the compressed location map. Then, any suitable reversible embedding operation can be applied to the preprocessed image to carry a payload. Finally, the data extraction and image recovery can be performed in a similar way.

2.1 Prediction-Based Preprocessing

Let $\mathbf{X} = \mathcal{I}^{n \times m}$ denote the original image sized $n \times m$ with the pixel range $\mathcal{I} = \{0, 1, ..., 2^d - 1\}$, where $d > 0$, e.g., $d = 8$. For compactness, we sometimes consider $\mathbf{X}$ as the set including all pixels and say "pixel $x_{i,j}$" meaning a pixel located at position (i, j) whose value is $x_{i,j}$. $x_{i,j} \in \mathbf{X}$ is a boundary pixel if

$$x_{i,j} \in [0, T) \cup (2^d - 1 - T, 2^d - 1], \tag{1}$$

where $T > 0$ is a predetermined parameter relying on the data embedding operation. It is always assumed that $T \ll 255 - T$.

We are to preprocess $\mathbf{X}$ to generate a new image $\mathbf{Y}$ and a location map $\mathbf{L}$. First, we divide $\mathbf{X}$ into two subsets, i.e.,

$$\mathbf{X}_b = \{x_{i,j} \in \mathbf{X} \mid (i + j) \bmod 2 = b\}, b \in \{0, 1\}. \tag{2}$$

Then, we use $\mathbf{X}_1$ to predict $\mathbf{X}_0$. In detail, for each $x_{i,j} \in \mathbf{X}_0$, we determine its prediction value by:

$$\hat{x}_{i,j} = \left\lceil \frac{x_{i-1,j} + x_{i+1,j} + x_{i,j-1} + x_{i,j+1}}{4} \right\rceil. \tag{3}$$

where $[\cdot]$ returns a nearest integer. It is easy to modify Eq. (3) slightly in case that a pixel position is out of the image. Notice that, one may use other efficient predictor to predict a pixel.

We use a threshold t_0 to generate an image $\mathbf{X}^{(0)}$, i.e.,

$$x_{i,j}^{(0)} = \begin{cases} x_{i,j} + T, & \text{if } \hat{x}_{i,j} < t_0 \text{ and } x_{i,j} \in \mathbf{X}_0, \\ x_{i,j} - T, & \text{if } \hat{x}_{i,j} > 2^d - 1 - t_0 \text{ and } x_{i,j} \in \mathbf{X}_0, \\ x_{i,j}, & \text{otherwise.} \end{cases} \quad (4)$$

The principle behind Eq. (4) is that, if the prediction value of a pixel is close to the boundary value, its original value should be close to the boundary value as well. Figure 1 shows two examples by using the predictor in Eq. (3). It is seen that, for both images, there exist strong correlations between the original values and the prediction values. Thus, we can adjust the raw value into the reliable range according to its prediction value. For each $x_{i,j} \in \mathbf{X}_1$, we continue to compute its prediction value in $\mathbf{X}^{(0)}$ by:

$$\hat{x}_{i,j}^{(0)} = \left[\frac{x_{i-1,j}^{(0)} + x_{i+1,j}^{(0)} + x_{i,j-1}^{(0)} + x_{i,j+1}^{(0)}}{4} \right]. \quad (5)$$

We use a threshold t_1 to generate another image $\mathbf{X}^{(1)}$ from $\mathbf{X}^{(0)}$ by:

$$x_{i,j}^{(1)} = \begin{cases} x_{i,j}^{(0)} + T, & \text{if } \hat{x}_{i,j}^{(0)} < t_1 \text{ and } x_{i,j} \in \mathbf{X}_1, \\ x_{i,j}^{(0)} - T, & \text{if } \hat{x}_{i,j}^{(0)} > 2^d - 1 - t_1 \text{ and } x_{i,j} \in \mathbf{X}_1, \\ x_{i,j}^{(0)}, & \text{otherwise.} \end{cases} \quad (6)$$

The pixel values of $\mathbf{X}^{(1)}$ must be in range $[-T, 2^d - 1 + T]$. We will adjust the pixels in $\mathbf{X}^{(1)}$ into the range $[T, 2^d - 1 - T]$ to generate the final image $\mathbf{Y}$. In detail, for all possible $y_{i,j} \in \mathbf{Y}$, we compute it as follows:

$$y_{i,j} = \begin{cases} T, & \text{if } x_{i,j}^{(1)} < T, \\ 2^d - 1 - T, & \text{if } x_{i,j}^{(1)} > 2^d - 1 - T, \\ x_{i,j}^{(1)}, & \text{otherwise.} \end{cases} \quad (7)$$

$\mathbf{Y}$ will not contain boundary pixels. We record such pixel positions (i, j) that $x_{i,j}^{(1)} \in [-T, T) \cup (2^d - 1 - T, 2^d - 1 + T]$. We construct a $(2T + 1)$-ary location map $\mathbf{L} = \{0, 1, ..., 2T\}^{n \times m}$ to address this issue, i.e.,

$$l_{i,j} = \begin{cases} x_{i,j}^{(1)} + T, & \text{if } x_{i,j}^{(1)} < T, \\ 2^d - 1 + T - x_{i,j}^{(1)}, & \text{if } x_{i,j}^{(1)} > 2^d - 1 - T, \\ 2T, & \text{otherwise.} \end{cases} \quad (8)$$

2.2 Reversible Data Embedding

We embed the required payload $\mathcal{P}$ and the losslessly compressed $\mathbf{L}$ into $\mathbf{Y}$, rather than $\mathbf{X}$. It is seen that, there has no need to construct a new location map since $\mathbf{Y}$ does not contain boundary pixels. It is inferred that, one can use many existing state-of-the-art algorithms for reversible data embedding since the data embedding operation here is open to design. We will not focus on the detailed reversible embedding operation.

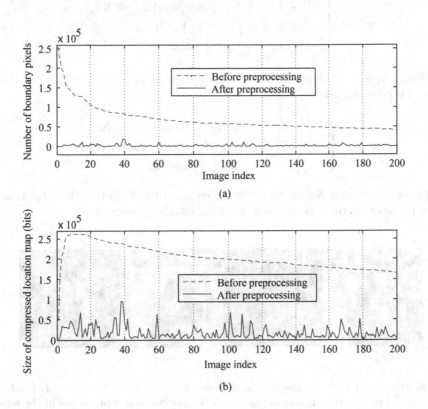

Fig. 5. Comparison for the number of boundary pixels as well as the size of compressed location map before/after preprocessing: $t_0 = 1$ and $t_1 = 4$.

2.3 Data Extraction and Image Recovery

Suppose that, we have embedded $\mathcal{P}$, $\mathbf{L}$ and data embedding parameters into $\mathbf{Y}$, resulting in a marked image $\mathbf{Z}$. Notice that, $\mathbf{L}$ has been compressed in advance. For a receiver, he needs to extract the embedded data and reconstruct $\mathbf{Y}$ from $\mathbf{Z}$. It is straightforward to reconstruct $\mathcal{P}$, $\mathbf{L}$ and $\mathbf{Y}$ from $\mathbf{Z}$. Our goal is to reconstruct $\mathbf{X}$. With Eqs. (7 and 8), it is straightforward to reconstruct $\mathbf{X}^{(1)}$ according to $\mathbf{Y}$ and $\mathbf{L}$ by:

$$x_{i,j}^{(1)} = \begin{cases} y_{i,j}, & \text{if } l_{i,j} = 2T, \\ l_{i,j} - T, & \text{if } l_{i,j} \neq 2T \text{ and } y_{i,j} = T, \\ 2^d - 1 + T - l_{i,j}, & \text{otherwise.} \end{cases} \tag{9}$$

Thereafter, we reconstruct $\mathbf{X}^{(0)}$ from $\mathbf{X}^{(1)}$. First, we initialize $\mathbf{X}^{(0)} = \mathbf{X}^{(1)}$. Then, we predict all $x_{i,j}^{(0)}$ corresponding to $\mathbf{X}_1$ by Eq. (5). According to t_1, $\mathbf{X}^{(0)}$ is finally determined as:

$$x_{i,j}^{(0)} = \begin{cases} x_{i,j}^{(1)} - T, & \text{if } \hat{x}_{i,j}^{(0)} < t_1 \text{ and } x_{i,j} \in \mathbf{X}_1, \\ x_{i,j}^{(1)} + T, & \text{if } \hat{x}_{i,j}^{(0)} > 2^d - 1 - t_1 \text{ and } x_{i,j} \in \mathbf{X}_1, \\ x_{i,j}^{(1)}, & \text{otherwise.} \end{cases} \quad (10)$$

Similarly, we initialize $\mathbf{X} = \mathbf{X}^{(0)}$. We predict all $x_{i,j} \in \mathbf{X}_0$ by Eq. (3). With t_0, $\mathbf{X}$ can be reconstructed as:

$$x_{i,j} = \begin{cases} x_{i,j}^{(0)} - T, & \text{if } \hat{x}_{i,j} < t_0 \text{ and } x_{i,j} \in \mathbf{X}_0, \\ x_{i,j}^{(0)} + T, & \text{if } \hat{x}_{i,j} > 2^d - 1 - t_0 \text{ and } x_{i,j} \in \mathbf{X}_0, \\ x_{i,j}^{(0)}, & \text{otherwise.} \end{cases} \quad (11)$$

Therefore, $\mathcal{P}$ and $\mathbf{X}$ can be perfectly reconstructed. Notice that, t_0, t_1 and T are parameters that should be embedded into $\mathbf{Y}$ previously.

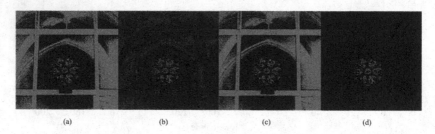

Fig. 6. Different location maps due to different t_0 and t_1: (a) $t_0 = t_1 = 1$, (b) $t_0 = 1, t_1 = 4$, (c) $t_0 = 4, t_1 = 1$, and (d) $t_0 = t_1 = 4$. The boundary pixels are in the white area.

3   Performance Evaluation and Analysis

The core contribution of our work is that, we introduce an efficient losslessly processing technique to significantly reduce the sizes of location maps for images containing lots of boundary pixels. To verify the performance, we choose the 200 images mentioned in Fig. 3 for experiments. For an original image $\mathbf{X}$, we set $T = 1$ and use arithmetic coding to losslessly compress the corresponding location map. For the corresponding $\mathbf{Y}$, we define $y_{i,j} \in \mathbf{Y}$ as a boundary pixel if $l_{i,j} \neq 2T$. We first use $t_0 = 1$ and $t_1 = 4$ to compare the compression performance for the location maps.

As shown in Fig. 5(a), the number of boundaries is significantly reduced. In Fig. 5, "before preprocessing" corresponds to $\mathbf{X}$ and the other one corresponds to $\mathbf{Y}$. As shown in Fig. 5(b), the size of location map is significantly reduced as well, meaning that, a sufficient pure payload could be carried. We define two ratios as follows:

$$r_0 = \frac{\text{Number of boundaries in } \mathbf{Y}}{\text{Number of boundaries in } \mathbf{X}} \times 100\%, \qquad (12)$$

and

$$r_1 = \frac{\text{Size of compressed } \mathbf{L}}{\text{Size of compressed location map for } \mathbf{X}} \times 100\%. \qquad (13)$$

We compute the mean value of r_0 and r_1 for the 200 images. They are 3.40% and 8.21%, respectively. It has shown that our work can significantly reduce side information, which would be quite helpful for subsequent data embedding operation.

Table 1. The mean values of r_0 (%) due to different t_0 and t_1.

	$t_1 = 1$	$t_1 = 2$	$t_1 = 4$	$t_1 = 8$	$t_1 = 16$
$t_0 = 1$	52.83	4.26	3.40	2.84	2.30
$t_0 = 2$	52.17	3.79	2.47	1.91	1.37
$t_0 = 4$	52.05	3.65	2.29	1.72	1.18
$t_0 = 8$	51.90	3.50	2.13	1.55	1.00
$t_0 = 16$	51.73	3.34	1.96	1.38	0.83

Table 2. The mean values of r_1 (%) due to different t_0 and t_1.

	$t_1 = 1$	$t_1 = 2$	$t_1 = 4$	$t_1 = 8$	$t_1 = 16$
$t_0 = 1$	73.08	9.89	8.21	7.10	5.98
$t_0 = 2$	72.58	8.93	6.14	4.95	3.75
$t_0 = 4$	72.48	8.68	5.75	4.51	3.27
$t_0 = 8$	72.36	8.40	5.41	4.12	2.83
$t_0 = 16$	72.22	8.08	5.07	3.74	2.39

Table 3. The test image indexes.

5162	5215	5726	5543	1732	5542	922	5723
2025	269	7718	1851	5718	5716	7082	1465
5370	2668	1933	5727	7912	2724	5722	6147
5717	318	3382	2066	5859	9740	1890	5493
5371	5729	5724	1	7091	2202	2547	5541

Table 4. The number of embeddable images among 40 test images.

Method in [6]		Method in [8]		Method in [10]	
Before	After	Before	After	Before	After
5	40	5	40	5	40

Table 5. r_{emb} (bpp) for the embeddable images.

Image	Method in [6]		Method in [8]		Method in [10]	
	Before	After	Before	After	Before	After
5162.pgm	0.79	0.98	0.79	0.97	0.78	0.96
5215.pgm	0.38	0.97	0.37	0.97	0.36	0.95
5726.pgm	0.15	0.86	0.14	0.88	0.13	0.85
5543.pgm	0.04	0.84	0.06	0.88	0.04	0.84
5541.pgm	0.02	0.87	0.04	0.90	0.02	0.87

Actually, different t_0 and t_1 will result in different performance. Figure 6 shows the different location maps for the image shown in Fig. 2 due to different t_0 and t_1. It is observed that $t_0 < t_1$ results in a smaller number of boundary pixels. The reason is that, when to predict the pixels corresponding to $\mathbf{X}_1$, the contexts are prediction values, which will result in degradation of the prediction accuracy. To further evaluate the impact due to different t_0 and t_1, we perform experiments on the 200 images. Tables 1 and 2 shows the mean values of r_0 and r_1. It has verified our perspective. And, it is suggested to use $t_1 \geq 2$ since it is expected to use $t_0 < t_1$ (as mentioned above) and $t_0 \geq 1$.

With a preprocessed image $\mathbf{Y}$, we need to embed $\mathcal{P}$ together with the compressed $\mathcal{L}$ and other parameters. We focus on the data embedding capacity (bits per pixel, bpp):

$$r_{emb} = |\mathcal{P}_{max}|/|\mathbf{Y}|, \tag{14}$$

where $|\mathcal{P}_{max}|$ represents the size of the maximum embeddable payload $\mathcal{P}_{max}$ and $|\mathbf{Y}|$ shows the total number of pixels.

One can apply any efficient data embedding algorithms. We use the methods presented in [6,8,10] for experiments to evaluate rate-distortion performance. The PSNR is considered as the distortion measure, and is determined between $\mathbf{X}$ and $\mathbf{Z}$. We choose the top-40 largest number of boundary pixels of images for experiments. The image indexes in BOSSBase have been given in Table 3. We compare r_{emb} and the corresponding distortion for both the original image and the corresponding preprocessed image. We vary t_0 and t_1 from 1 to 16 by a step of 1 for optimization. The one resulting in the maximum r_{emb} will be selected as the result since a data hider always has the freedom to choose t_0 and t_1. During the data embedding, for the original image, the boundary pixels are recorded by a location map losslessly compressed by arithmetic coding. For fair comparison, the corresponding location maps for the preprocessed images are compressed by arithmetic coding as well. Thereafter, both the original image and the preprocessed image are embedded.

Experimental results show that, there has a large ratio of images that the existing algorithms cannot be applied to them directly, namely, $r_{emb} = 0$ for the original images since the size of compressed location maps are too large to embed extra bits. As shown in Table 4, we count the number of embeddable images (i.e., $r_{emb} > 0$). In Table 4, "before" corresponds to the original image, and "after" corresponds to the preprocessed image. It can be observed that, the proposed work significantly improves the ability of carrying additional data for the existing works. We compare r_{emb} and PSNR for those embeddable images. Tables 5 and 6 show the results. It can be seen that, the proposed work significantly increases the capacity, and provides a high image quality. We further determine the mean value of r_{emb} and PSNR for the 40 test images using the three data embedding algorithms equipped with the preprocessing technique. Table 7 provides the results, which has implied that, the proposed work has good ability to improve the rate-distortion performance of many existing algorithms on images containing lots of boundary pixels.

Table 6. The PSNRs (dB) for the marked images.

Image	Method in [6]		Method in [8]		Method in [10]	
	Before	After	Before	After	Before	After
5162.pgm	44.23	44.23	44.35	46.61	45.61	45.60
5215.pgm	44.68	44.25	47.00	46.58	46.00	45.58
5726.pgm	45.05	44.41	47.27	46.69	46.31	45.56
5543.pgm	45.17	44.52	47.30	46.73	46.38	45.60
5541.pgm	47.49	44.49	49.07	46.63	48.35	45.44

Table 7. The mean value of r_{emb} (bpp) and PSNR (dB) for the 40 test images using the proposed preprocessing technique.

Method in [6]		Method in [8]		Method in [10]	
r_{emb}	PSNR	r_{emb}	PSNR	r_{emb}	PSNR
0.63	46.69	0.67	47.16	0.63	46.75

4 Conclusion and Discussion

In practice, it is quite easy to acquire images full of boundary pixels such as medical images, remote sensing images and natural sceneries, e.g., white cloud and dark night. The existing works often focus on images having little boundary pixels and provide superior rate-distortion performance on them. However, they may not work very well for images full of boundaries. In this paper, we present an efficient losslessly preprocessing algorithm to reversible data embedding in images that contain lots of boundary pixels. The reversible embedding operation for the proposed work is open to design. Experimental results have shown that our work could significantly reduce the size of the side information, which can benefit reversible data embedding performance a lot.

We point out that, the prediction based preprocessing perspective is simple, effective, and quite suitable for real-world applications. One may design other prediction based methods as long as the prediction procedure is invertible to a receiver. From the viewpoint of rate-distortion optimization, there has room for improvement, e.g., a future work is to design data embedding algorithms that can well exploit the statistical characteristics of the preprocessed image. In addition to prediction based preprocessing, there may be other more efficient and novel methods for reducing boundary pixels, which is the next work.

Acknowledgement. This work was supported by the National Natural Science Foundation of China under Grant Nos. 61502496, U1536120, and U1636201, and the National Key Research and Development Program of China under Grant No. 2016YFB1001003, Key Lab of Information Network Security, Ministry of Public Security.

References

1. Tian, J.: Reversible data embedding using a difference expansion. IEEE Trans. Circ. Syst. Video Technol. **13**(8), 890–896 (2003)
2. Wu, H., Shi, Y., Wang, H., Zhou, L.: Separable reversible data hiding for encrypted palette images with color partitioning and flipping verification. IEEE Trans. Circ. Syst. Video Technol. **27**(8), 1620–1631 (2017)
3. Ni, Z., Shi, Y., Ansari, N., Su, W.: Reversible data hiding. IEEE Trans. Circ. Syst. Video Technol. **16**(3), 354–362 (2006)
4. Ma, B., Shi, Y.: A reversible data hiding scheme based on code division multiplexing. IEEE Trans. Inf. Forensics Secur. **11**(9), 1914–1927 (2016)
5. Wu, H., Wang, H., Hu, Y., Zhou, L.: Efficient reversible data hiding based on prefix matching and directed LSB embedding. In: Shi, Y.-Q., Kim, H.J., Pérez-González, F., Yang, C.-N. (eds.) IWDW 2014. LNCS, vol. 9023, pp. 455–469. Springer, Cham (2015). https://doi.org/10.1007/978-3-319-19321-2_35
6. Hsu, F., Wu, M., Wang, S.: Reversible data hiding using side-match prediction on steganographic images. Multimedia Tools Appl. **67**(3), 571–591 (2013)
7. Ou, B., Li, X., Zhao, Y., Ni, R., Shi, Y.: Pairwise prediction-error expansion for efficient reversible data hiding. IEEE Trans. Image Process. **22**(12), 5010–5021 (2013)
8. Li, X., Zhang, W., Gui, X., Yang, B.: Efficient reversible data hiding based on multiple histogram modification. IEEE Trans. Inf. Forensics Secur. **10**(9), 2016–2027 (2015)
9. Wu, H., Wang, H., Shi, Y.: Dynamic content selection-and-prediction framework applied to reversible data hiding. In: Proceedings of IEEE International Workshop Information Forensics, Security, pp. 1–6 (2016)

10. Wu, H., Wang, H., Shi, Y.: PPE-based reversible data hiding. In: Proceedings of ACM International Workshop Information Hiding Multimedia Security, pp. 187–188 (2016)
11. Wu, H., Wang, W., Dong, J., Chen, Y., Wang, H.: Ensemble reversible data hiding. arXiv:1801.04747 (2018)
12. Bas, P., Filler, T., Pevný, T.: "Break our steganographic system": the ins and outs of organizing BOSS. In: Filler, T., Pevný, T., Craver, S., Ker, A. (eds.) IH 2011. LNCS, vol. 6958, pp. 59–70. Springer, Heidelberg (2011). https://doi.org/10.1007/978-3-642-24178-9_5

Robust H.264/AVC Video Watermarking Without Intra Distortion Drift

Yue Li and Hong-Xia Wang[✉]

School of Information Science and Technology, Southwest Jiaotong University,
Chengdu 611756, China
liyue859000040@my.swjtu.edu.cn, hxwang@swjtu.edu.cn

Abstract. A robust H.264/AVC video watermarking algorithm without intra distortion drift is proposed in this paper for the copyright protection of digital videos. The classic distortion drift-free method limits the size of watermark image because of limited capacity. The improved intra distortion drift free method proposed in this paper enlarges the capacity and promote the visual quality with a reasonable classification according to intra prediction modes of H.264. Embedding pretreated watermarks into middle-frequency coefficient-pairs of 4 × 4 luminance blocks, which makes the scheme achieve robustness. Experimental results show that our algorithm achieve high robustness and good visual quality without huge bit-rate increasing. The capacity of proposed scheme is doubled than the classic scheme as well.

Keywords: Digital watermarking · High capacity · Distortion drift
H.264/AVC

1 Introduction

Nowadays, the problem about the copyright of digital videos becomes more and more urgent when videos are being shared. H.264/advanced video coding (AVC) [1] depends on its high compression efficiency and the well adapted for network transmission, quickly becomes a widespread video compression standard in our daily internet life.

Thus, watermarking for videos as an effective way to solve problems above has emerged. Clarifying concretely, the inserted watermark information is retrieved from the content to prove ownership during a dispute [2]. Just as algorithms described in [3,4], they can authenticate the existence of embedded content. In [3] the authors employ a human visual model based on 4 × 4 block discrete cosine transform (DCT) coefficients to embed the watermark into quantized alternating current (AC) DCT coefficients of the luminance residual blocks. In [4], a gray-scale image as the watermark is embedded into H.264 compression videos

---

Supported by the National Natural Science Foundation of China (NSFC) under the grant No. U1536110.

for copyright protection. A novel method which watermark bits are embedded into the middle-frequency coefficients in the diagonal position of 4×4 blocks are proposed in this paper. These are very basic work, but as the foundation of watermarking, these schemes have a deep influence on the development of future works. Because of the limited visual quality and capacity in these works, researchers start to think about how to promote the performance of watermarking. In 2010, Ma etc. proposed an important algorithm about preventing distortion drift in [5]. By using the intra prediction mode depending on different reference pixels, they classified four categories for watermarking and prevented distortion drift effectively. Unfortunately, they neglected the fifth category, which related to all the reference pixels of 4×4 intra prediction mode. Besides, the capacity is still a big problem. Later, in paper [6], Lin etc. improved the capacity of the algorithm in [5], but again, they failed to make full use of each category.

In recent years, the method of preventing distortion drift has been applied in many occasions, such as reversible data hiding [7], robust watermarking [8]. They all meet the same questions about the classification of category and the capacity. Thus, the goal of our paper is to present an algorithm that has reasonable robustness, high capacity and distortion drift-free. A high capacity means each category of 4×4 intra prediction mode need to be well classified. On the other hand, the way to keep balance between visual quality and capacity is that one modified pixel can embed information at least one bit. Robustness means the watermark still can be extracted after tampered of video sequences. If using spread-spectrum technology to improve the robustness in our paper, the proposed algorithm need to have high capacity and well visual quality as support.

The structure of this paper is organized as follows. Section 2 introduces the method of how to prevent distortion drift. Section 3 presents the proposed watermarking algorithm in detail. Then, the experimental results are shown in Sect. 4, which followed by conclusion in Sect. 5.

2 The Method of Preventing Distortion Drift

2.1 The Different Categories of Blocks Based on Intra Prediction Mode

Intra prediction as a unique and indispensable part is adopted on H.264/AVC coding standard for the first time [1]. There are nine intra prediction modes for luminance 4×4 blocks. The 16 pixels of luminance block $B_{i,j}^r$ are labeled from $\bar{a}$ to $\bar{p}$ as shown in Fig. 1. Four adjacent luminance blocks of $B_{i,j}$ are named as $B_{i+1,j+1}$, $B_{i,j+1}$, $B_{i+1,j-1}$ and $B_{i+1,j}$ respectively. And the reference pixels $\bar{d}, \bar{h}, \bar{l}, \bar{m}, \bar{n}, \bar{o}$ and $\bar{p}$ are used to predict the pixels of four adjacent blocks by intra prediction modes.

The embedding process introduces deviation in blocks $B_{i+1,j+1}$, $B_{i,j+1}$, $B_{i+1,j-1}$ and $B_{i+1,j}$ when hidden bits are embedded in $B_{i,j}$. This phenomenon which is defined as intra distortion drift. To prevent distortion drift, a classification about 4×4 luminance blocks of different cases are given as Table 1 [5].

Where $M_{i,j+1}$, $M_{i+1,j-1}$, $M_{i+1,j}$ and $M_{i+1,j+1}$ represent the selected prediction modes for $B_{i,j+1}$, $B_{i+1,j-1}$, $B_{i+1,j}$ and $B_{i+1,j+1}$, respectively. If the condition meets Case 1, $\bar{d}, \bar{h}, \bar{l}, \bar{p}$ are the reference pixels for predicting $B_{i,j+1}$. Case 2 occurs when $\bar{m}, \bar{n}, \bar{o}, \bar{p}$ are reference pixels for predicting $B_{i+1,j}$, $B_{i+1,j-1}$. If $\bar{p}$ is the only reference pixel for predicting, the prediction modes meet the condition of Case 3.

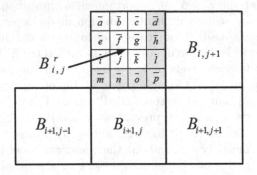

Fig. 1. The encoded luminance block and its four-affected adjacent luminance blocks in encoding procedure.

Table 1. The prediction modes of the adjacent blocks to prevent distortion drift.

No.	The prediction modes of adjacent blocks
Case 1	$M_{i,j+1} \in \{1,2,4,5,6,8\}_{4\times4}$
Case 2	$M_{i+1,j} \in \{0,2,3,4,5,6,7\}_{4\times4} \&\& M_{i+1,j-1} \in \{3,7\}_{4\times4}$
Case 3	$M_{i+1,j+1} \in \{4,5,6\}_{4\times4}$

According to the relationship between reference pixels and prediction modes, five categories are divided in Table 2. Where X means that the case is not considered, NIL represents there is no reference pixels, and ALL represents all seven pixels are used for predicting.

Actually, in [5], they solve the distortion drift of the first four categories in Table 2. Without considering the existence of Cat 5, they failed to present a scheme to avoid distortion drift of Cat 5, even if Cat 5 takes a huge percent of luminance blocks. Based on six different quantization parameters (QP), we take video sequence Foreman as an example, the percentage of each category has been shown in Table 3. It's easy to know that more than 50% of 4×4 luminance blocks fail to fix the problem about distortion drift in [5]. With the using of Cat 5, the capacity can be enlarged as well. So, preventing all intra 4×4 blocks from distortion drift when embedded and enlarging the capacity for embedding the spread-spectrum watermark are our purpose.

Table 2. Five categories of optimally selected modes of adjacent luminance blocks and the related reference pixels

	Case 1	Case 2	Case 3	Reference pixels
Cat 1	TRUE	FALSE	X	$\bar{d}, \bar{h}, \bar{l}, \bar{p}$
Cat 2	FALSE	TRUE	X	$\bar{m}, \bar{n}, \bar{o}, \bar{p}$
Cat 3	FALSE	FALSE	FALSE	NIL
Cat 4	FALSE	FALSE	TRUE	$\bar{p}$
Cat 5	TRUE	TRUE	X	ALL

Table 3. The percentage of each category in 4×4 luminance block

QP	Cat 1	Cat 2	Cat 3	Cat 4	Cat 5
18	17%	21%	1%	4%	57%
23	18%	21%	1%	4%	56%
28	17%	23%	1%	4%	55%
33	18%	24%	1%	4%	53%
38	18%	23%	1%	4%	54%
43	15%	18%	1%	4%	62%
Average	17%	22%	1%	4%	56%

2.2 The Analysis of Embedding Scheme Without Distortion Drift

In this section, the analysis of how to watermark without distortion drift is introduced. The residual $R_{i,j}^p$ is calculated by $R_{i,j}^p = B_{i,j} - B_{i,j}^p$, where $B_{i,j}$ is the original block, $B_{i,j}^p$ is the predicted block. The progress of integer DCT transform and quantization is shown in Eq. 1.

$$R_{i,j}^{QDCT} = (C_f R_{i,j}^p C_f^r) \otimes (\frac{E_f}{Q}) = \begin{bmatrix} Y_{00} & Y_{01} & Y_{02} & Y_{03} \\ Y_{10} & Y_{11} & Y_{12} & Y_{13} \\ Y_{20} & Y_{21} & Y_{22} & Y_{23} \\ Y_{30} & Y_{31} & Y_{32} & Y_{33} \end{bmatrix} \tag{1}$$

where $C_f = \begin{bmatrix} 1 & 1 & 1 & 1 \\ 2 & 1 & -1 & -2 \\ 1 & -1 & -1 & 1 \\ 1 & -2 & 2 & -1 \end{bmatrix}$, $E_f = \begin{bmatrix} a^2 & \frac{ab}{2} & a^2 & \frac{ab}{2} \\ \frac{ab}{2} & \frac{b^2}{4} & \frac{ab}{2} & \frac{b^2}{4} \\ a^2 & \frac{ab}{2} & a^2 & \frac{ab}{2} \\ \frac{ab}{2} & \frac{b^2}{4} & \frac{ab}{2} & \frac{b^2}{4} \end{bmatrix}$, $a = \frac{1}{2}$ and $b = \sqrt{\frac{2}{5}}$; the

operator "$\otimes$" means an element-by-element multiplication of two matrices, Q is the step size parameter determined by QP. In the decoding part, to reconstruct the residual block $R_{i,j}^r$, the dequantization and the inverse DCT procedure are implemented to $R_{i,j}^{QDCT}$ as follows:

$$R_{i,j}^r = C_r^T (R_{i,j}^{QDCT} \times Q \otimes E_r) C_r \tag{2}$$

where $C_f = \begin{bmatrix} 1 & 1 & 1 & 1 \\ 1 & \frac{1}{2} & -\frac{1}{2} & -1 \\ 1 & -1 & -1 & 1 \\ \frac{1}{2} & -1 & 1 & -\frac{1}{2} \end{bmatrix}$ and $E_r = \begin{bmatrix} a^2 & ab & a^2 & ab \\ ab & b^2 & ab & b^2 \\ a^2 & ab & a^2 & ab \\ ab & b^2 & ab & b^2 \end{bmatrix}$

Taking Cat 1 as the example to analysis the distortion, we choose four vertical $QDCT$ coefficient-pairs $S_v = \{(Y_{00}, Y_{02}), (Y_{10}, Y_{12}), (Y_{20}, Y_{22}), (Y_{30}, Y_{32})\}$. The watermark bits are embedded by modifying the values of $R_{i,j}^{QDCT}$, so the pair (Y_{00}, Y_{02}) can be modified by $(Y_{00}+1, Y_{02}-1)$ for embedding one bit information. The difference after embedded is calculated as follows:

$$\Delta R_{i,j}^{QDCT} = R_{i,j}^{QDCT'} - R_{i,j}^{QDCT} = \begin{bmatrix} 1 & 0 & -1 & 0 \\ 0 & 0 & 0 & 0 \\ 0 & 0 & 0 & 0 \\ 0 & 0 & 0 & 0 \end{bmatrix} \qquad (3)$$

where $R_{i,j}^{QDCT'}$ represents the block after embedded. And $R_{i,j}^{r'}$ can be calculated by Eq. 2. Therefore, the difference between $R_{i,j}^{r'}$ and $R_{i,j}^{r}$ is performed as Eq. 4:

$$\Delta R_{i,j}^r = R_{i,j}^{r'} - R_{i,j}^r = C_r^T(\Delta R_{i,j}^{QDCT} \times Q \otimes E_r)C_r = Q \times \begin{bmatrix} 0 & 2a^2 & 2a^2 & 0 \\ 0 & 2a^2 & 2a^2 & 0 \\ 0 & 2a^2 & 2a^2 & 0 \\ 0 & 2a^2 & 2a^2 & 0 \end{bmatrix} \qquad (4)$$

Because $B_{i,j}^{r'} = B_{i,j}^p + R_{i,j}^r + \Delta R_{i,j}^r$ and $B_{i,j}^r = B_{i,j}^p + R_{i,j}^r$, the rightmost column elements of $\Delta R_{i,j}^r$ are zeroes, which means the rightmost column of $B_{i,j}^{r'}$ is the same as that of $B_{i,j}^r$. The reference pixels of Cat 1 are the elements of rightmost column, there is no modification implies there is no distortion drifting to other blocks. The other three pairs $(Y_{10}, Y_{12}), (Y_{20}, Y_{22})$, and (Y_{30}, Y_{32}) of S_v has the same principle.

For other categories, they are the same theory except selecting coefficient-pairs. For Cat 2 $S_H = \{(Y_{00}, Y_{20}), (Y_{01}, Y_{21}), (Y_{20}, Y_{22}), (Y_{30}, Y_{32})\}$ are chosen. For Cat 5, four elements $(Y_{00}, Y_{02}, Y_{20}, Y_{22})$ are chosen. As for Cat 4, strategy of either Cat 1 or Cat 2 can be used on it.

3   The Proposed Scheme

This section consists of four subsections. The pre-processing of watermark reduces the bits have to embed and improves its robustness. The improved method of preventing distortion drift enlarges the capacity and keeps the high visual quality of videos. And the last two subsections introduce every step of watermarking and extracting in detail.

3.1   Watermark Pre-processing

Because the capacity of the method without distortion drift is limited even if the method has been improved. And the spread-spectrum scheme enlarges the quantity of embedding bits for robustness. So, the watermark pre-processing method put forward here to reduce the embedded bits of watermark images and improve the robustness as well. In our experiments, the size of the watermarks are $M \times M$.

(1) Integer DCT transform and quantization: Decomposing the watermark image into nonoverlapping 4×4 block which denoted as $p(i,j)(0 \leq i,j \leq M/4)$. Then, each block need to be transformed and quantized by

$$P(u,v) = IntQDCT\{p(i,j)\} \qquad 0 \leq u,v \leq M/4 \qquad (5)$$

where $IntQDCT\{\cdot\}$ represents the process of the 4×4 integer DCT transform with quantization, which contributes to a better performance for digital watermarking compared to traditional DCT.

(2) Zigzag-scan and coefficients choice: The 2-D coefficients $P(u,v)$ are zigzag scanned into a 1-D sequence of coefficients $P(k)$, where $k \in [0,15]$ indicates the zigzag position. Not every coefficient is irreplaceable in 16-integer DCT coefficients of each block, most of them become constant zero after quantization. So, nonzero coefficients are selected with the zero coefficients are discarded.

(3) Transformation: After coefficients choice, there is a significant difference between the dynamic range of every two coefficients. In order to narrow down these dynamic ranges for better distortion control, the selected coefficients $P(k)$ can be transformed as follows:

$$m(k) = 15 \times \frac{p(k) - min_{value}}{max_{value} - min_{value}} \qquad 0 \leq k \leq 15 \qquad (6)$$

where max_{value} is the maximum of all chosen coefficients, min_{value} represents the minimum of all chosen coefficients. k is a dynamic number for each block, its value depends on the number of nonzero coefficients in each block. In the experiments, k is kept as a key sequence along with the max_{value} and min_{value}. Keys are stored in a key parameter file for future reconstruction.

(4) Watermark spread-spectrum: The coefficients $m(k)$ are round numbers after transformation. For the convenience of embedding, these coefficients are converted to Binary-Coded Decimal (BCD) format. Each coefficient of $m(t)$ is binary, where $0 \leq t \leq 4k$. $m(t)$ is spread by Eq. 7:

$$b(n) = m(t) \qquad tS \leq n \leq (t+1)S \qquad (7)$$

S is the spreading factor, determined experimentally according to the video frame size and the watermark size.

3.2   The Watermarking and Extracting Rules of Each Category

The purpose of this section is to improve the method in [5]. With the enlarged capacity, the proposed scheme has a high capacity while maintain the visual quality.

For Cat 1, it is available to watermark by changing coefficient-pairs according to Sect. 2.2, but just one-bit is embedded for each pair. So, we introduce novenary EMD embedding algorithm [9] here. Transform three continuous hidden bits from binary to novenary, denoted as w. Define a set of coefficients $Q = \{Y_{00}, Y_{10}, Y_{20}, Y_{30}\}$ as a vector of EMD embedding algorithm. Then, the f value of N-dimensional space of the vector is calculated as Eq. 8

$$f(Y_{00}, Y_{10}, Y_{20}, Y_{30}) = (Y_{00} \times 1 + Y_{10} \times 2 + Y_{20} \times 3 + Y_{30} \times 4) mod9 \qquad (8)$$

If $w = f(Y_{00}, Y_{10}, Y_{20}, Y_{30})$, keep w unchanged. Otherwise, calculate the f value (as Eq. 8) of Y'_{i0} circularly until find a Y'_{i0} meets the condition $f(Y_{00}, \ldots, Y'_{i0}, \ldots) = w$, where $Y'_{i0} = Y_{i0} + 1$ or $Y'_{i0} = Y_{i0} - 1$. The final watermarking step as Eq. 9.

$$(Y'_{i0}, Y'_{i2}) = \begin{cases} (Y_{i0} + 1, Y_{i2} - 1) & if\ Y'_{i0} = Y_{i0} + 1 \\ (Y_{i0} - 1, Y_{i2} + 1) & if\ Y'_{i0} = Y_{i0} - 1 \\ (Y_{i0}, Y_{i2}) & else \end{cases} \qquad (9)$$

The extraction rule is easier than embedding, as shown in Eq. 10.

$$w' = (Y'_{00} + Y'_{10} \times 2 + Y'_{20} \times 3 + Y'_{30} \times 4) mod9 \qquad (10)$$

For Cat 2, the embedding and extraction rules are the same as Cat 1. The difference need to pay more attention is the vector of EMD embedding algorithm changed to $Q = (Y_{00}, Y_{01}, Y_{02}, Y_{03})$. Corresponding, the final embedding step of Cat 2 need to adapt for the vector, as shown in Eq. 11. Equation 12 presents the extraction process.

$$(Y'_{0i}, Y'_{2i}) = \begin{cases} (Y_{0i} + 1, Y_{2i} - 1) & if\ Y'_{0i} = Y_{0i} + 1 \\ (Y_{0i} - 1, Y_{2i} + 1) & if\ Y'_{0i} = Y_{0i} - 1 \\ (Y_{0i}, Y_{2i}) & else \end{cases} \qquad (11)$$

$$h' = (Y'_{00} + Y'_{01} \times 2 + Y'_{02} \times 3 + Y'_{03} \times 4) mod9 \qquad (12)$$

For Cat 3, if the value of a $QDCT$ coefficient Y_{ij} is zero, its unnecessary to embed any hidden bits, otherwise, the embedding procedure is Eq. 13.

$$Y'_{ij} = \begin{cases} Y_{ij} + 1 & if(Y_{ij}\%2 = 1, p = 1, Y_{ij} \geq 0) or(Y_{ij}\%2 = 0, p = 0, Y_{ij} \geq 0) \\ Y_{ij} - 1 & if(Y_{ij}\%2 = 1, p = 1, Y_{ij} \leq 0) or(Y_{ij}\%2 = 0, p = 0, Y_{ij} < 0) \\ (Y_{ij}) & others \end{cases}$$
$$(13)$$

where p represents one-bit watermark message. And the extraction method is to judge the parity of Y'_{ij} :

$$p' = \begin{cases} 1 & if\ Y'_{ij}\%2 = 0 \\ 0 & else \end{cases} \qquad (14)$$

For Cat 5, the watermarking has been given in Eq. 15.

$$
(Y'_{00}, Y'_{02}, Y'_{20}, Y'_{22}) = \begin{cases} (Y_{00} + 1, Y_{02} - 1, Y_{20} - 1, Y_{22} + 1) & if\,(Y_{00}\%2 = 0, p = 1, Y_{00} \geq 0) \\ & or\,(Y_{00}\%2 = 1, p = 0, Y_{00} \geq 0) \\ (Y_{00} - 1, Y_{02} + 1, Y_{20} + 1, Y_{22} - 1) & if\,(Y_{00}\%2 = 1, p = 0, Y_{00} < 0) \\ & or\,(Y_{00}\%2 = 0, p = 1, Y_{00} < 0) \\ (Y_{00}, Y_{02}, Y_{20}, Y_{22}) & others \end{cases}
$$

(15)

where p represents one-bit embedded watermark message. Then, extraction only need to judge the parity of Y'_{00}:

$$
p' = \begin{cases} 0 & if \;\; Y'_{ij}\%2 = 0 \\ 1 & else \end{cases}
$$

(16)

As for Cat 4, strategy of either Cat 1 or Cat 2 can be used on it.

3.3   The Watermarking Algorithm

The details of watermarking process as follows:
step1: Pretreat the chosen watermark image as Sect. 3.1. At the same time, get the intra prediction mode of sixteen 4×4 blocks in each macroblock.
step2: Classify luminance blocks into different categories, from Cat 1 to Cat 5, as introduced in Sect. 2.1. Furthermore, the blocks of each category that meet the condition given in Eq. 17 are chosen for watermarking.

$$
\begin{cases} |Y_{00}| > T & InCat3 \\ \left| \sum_{i=0}^{3} \sum_{j=0}^{3} Y_{ij} \right| & others \end{cases}
$$

(17)

step3: Modify the $QDCT$ coefficients of the selected blocks according to Sect. 3.2.
step4: Repeat steps 2–3 until all the watermark information bits are watermarked.

3.4   The Extracting Algorithm

To extract the watermark information just need to know the prediction modes of 4×4 blocks and their $QDCT$ coefficients, the entirely decoding of video sequences is not necessary.
step1: Decode the I frames of the embedded video sequence to acquire the blocks' prediction modes of each macroblock, along with the $QDCT$ coefficients.
step2: Only if the block satisfies the condition in Eq. (17), will this block be selected for the extracting algorithm. After that, classify the selected blocks into different categories (Cat 1–Cat 5).

424   Y. Li and H.-X. Wang

step3: Following the extracting rules in Sect. 3.2 to extract the bitstream of watermark message.
step4: Repeat steps 1–3 until all hidden bits are extracted.
step5: Because the bitstream we get here is the message after spread-spectrum, the extracted watermark bits are calculated as follows:

$$w_j = \sum_{i=0}^{S} \oplus b_i' \quad (j = 0, 1, 2, \dots) \tag{18}$$

where b_i' is the bitstream that extracted from the video sequence, S represents the spread factor which defined in formula (7).
step6: The reverse of watermark pre-processing is the way to reconstruct the watermark image. Noticed that, the key to reconstruct the watermark image is the key kept in Sect. 3.1.

4 Experimental Results

The proposed algorithm has been implemented in the H.264/AVC reference software version JM19.0. Seven standard video sequences (QCIF, 176 × 144) Foreman, Bridge-close, Carphone, News, Coastguard, Container, Mobile are used for experiments. All the video sequences are encoded into 300 frames at 30 frame/s with an intra-period of 30 (group of picture IBPBPBP). The original H.264 encoder used the fixed quantization step parameter 28 for all frames. The threshold T is 1 and the spread factor S equals 7 in our experiments. The watermark patterns for experiments are grayscale patterns of the same size 32 × 32.

4.1 The Comparison of Visual Quality

Table 4 shows the difference values of PSNR between original sequences and watermarked sequences. The average decrease between watermarked and original is 0.2 dB, which clearly shows this method without distortion drift applied in our paper maintain the imperceptibility of watermarking well.

Figure 2 is the comparison of visual effect between original I frames and water-marked I frames. Subjectively, the watermarked frames reveal the same visual effect as original frames.

Table 4. Comparison of PSNR(dB) between original and watermarked video sequences

Sequence	Forman	Bridge-close	Carphone	Coastguard	News	Container	Mobile
Original	36.19	35.35	36.84	34.38	37.25	36.60	33.20
Watermarked	36.01	35.10	36.69	34.24	36.92	36.35	33.06
DPSNR	−0.18	−0.25	−0.15	−0.14	−0.33	−0.25	−0.14

(a)Original frames

(b)watermarked frames

Fig. 2. Comparison of visual effect between original and watermarked frames

4.2 Capacity and Bitrate

Table 5 illustrates the comparison of experiment results between references and proposed. The huge increasement of capacity is taking a risk with the increase of bitrate. The higher capacity of proposed algorithm is the reason why the bitrate increases faster than reference papers. However, the values of BRI for different video sequences are still reasonable in proposed method. Our algorithm has better PSNR values when the capacity is double even triple larger than the reference papers, besides, with the controllable bitrate growth, the maximum only increase 3.52%. In order to show the excellent performances of our algorithm, in Table 6, only Cat 2 is chosen for watermarking. Because the data of Ref. [8] and Ref. [10] is same as Table 5, only data of proposed algorithm is shown in Table 6.

It's not hard to find from Table 6, with a lower capacity, the PSNR values become better, and the average of BRI change from 3.11% to 1.08%. In this condition, the capacity is still better than Ref. [8], as well as the PSNR value and BRI.

Table 5. The comparison of experiment results between references and proposed algorithm

Sequence	Ref. [8]			Ref. [10]			Proposed		
	PSNR (dB)	Capacity (bits)	BRI (%)	PSNR (dB)	Capacity (bits)	BRI (%)	PSNR (dB)	Capacity (bits)	BRI (%)
Foreman	35.73	1960	1.15	35.92	1564	2.78	36.01	7996	3.52
Bridge-close	34.01	2827	1.33	33.55	3427	2.27	35.10	9291	3.14
Carphone	36.05	2420	1.01	35.57	2202	1.74	36.69	7837	2.88
Coastguard	33.45	2352	2.72	34.21	5680	1.53	34.24	13708	3.21
News	35.74	2547	2.42	35.12	2185	2.71	36.92	7978	3.63
Container	35.25	2345	2.42	34.72	1876	1.96	36.35	6689	2.85
Mobile	32.35	3541	1.21	32.84	5782	1.43	33.06	13611	2.57

Table 6. The experiment results of only one category (Cat 2) is chosen for watermarking

Sequence	PSNR (dB)	Capacity (bits)	BRI (%)
Foreman	36.13	3270	1.40
Bridge-close	35.29	2862	0.68
Carphone	36.78	3513	1.17
Coastguard	34.36	2169	0.35
News	37.07	4413	1.65
Container	36.54	1527	1.67
Mobile	33.16	4425	0.67

In our analysis, although the method of preventing distortion drift has been used in Ref. [8], they failed to classify the fifth category (Cat 5). The distortion drift of Cat 5 influences the visual quality badly. Without the right classification of categories, its also impossible for them to make full use of each pixel to embed information. As for Ref. [10], JND model is a nice try to enhance imperceptibility of watermarking, however, it's also the weakness of capacity. The pixels can meet the conditions of JND model are limited.

4.3 Robustness

Table 7 compares the robustness with different attacks by bit-error rate (BER). In Ref. [10], they embedded watermarks in high and middle-frequency components with spread-spectrum method, which leads to higher robustness than Ref. [8]. And the BER of Ref. [10] are approximate to the proposed. Only re-encoding attack is implemented in Ref. [8], thus, the BER of Ref. [8] under Gaussian low-pass filter attack are the simulation results by ourselves. As shown in Table 7, our algorithm shows stronger robustness than Ref. [8]. The reason of the proposed scheme has stronger robustness is the setting of spread factor S. The higher value of S is, the stronger robustness achieves. In Ref. [8], the corrected bits for robustness are limited with error correcting code.

Table 7. Comparison of robustness with different attacks

Sequence	Re-encoding QP = 28			Gaussian low-pass filter (5 × 5)		
	Ref. [8]	Ref. [10]	Proposed	Ref. [8]	Ref. [10]	Proposed
Foreman	3.63%	2.98%	1.33%	8.33%	2.42%	3.54%
Bridge-close	5.23%	4.04%	3.75%	10.67%	4.21%	5.57%
Carphone	0.19%	2.02%	3.76%	3.61%	3.28%	4.17%
Coastguard	11.54%	3.71%	4.35%	7.95%	3.80%	2.29%
News	2.58%	3.50%	2.15%	9.06%	5.98%	6.75%
Container	2.50%	2.35%	1.23%	7.00%	3.42%	5.39%
Mobile	1.97%	4.12%	3.50%	9.41%	4.89%	3.20%

5 Conclusion

We have presented a new watermarking algorithm to solve the capacity limitation and robustness without distortion drift at the same time. With the improved distortion drift free method, the capacity is enlarged and the visual quality is promoted by a reasonable classification of luminance blocks. The robustness of watermarking is guaranteed by the pre-processing method of watermarks. As shown in experiment results, the watermarking scheme can achieve high robustness and good visual quality with a high capacity. How to improve the robustness and do more tests on robustness are our future work.

Acknowledgment. This work was supported by the National Natural Science Foundation of China (NSFC) under the grant No. U1536110.

References

1. Wiegand, T., Sullivan, G.J., Bjontegaard, G., Luthra, A.: Overview of the H.264/AVC video coding standard. IEEE Trans. Circ. Syst. Video Technol. **13**(7), 560–576 (2003)
2. Yiqi, T., KokSheik, W.: An overview of information hiding in H.264/AVC compressed video. IEEE Trans. Circ. Syst. Video Technol. **24**(2), 305–319 (2014)
3. Noorkami, M., Mersereau, R.M.: A framework for robust watermarking of H.264 encoded video with controllable detection performance. IEEE Trans. Inform. Forensics Secur. **2**(1), 14–23 (2007)
4. Zhang, J., Ho, A.T.S., Qiu, G.: Robust video watermarking of H.264/AVC. IEEE Trans. Circ. Syst. II: Express Briefs **54**(2), 205–209 (2007)
5. Ma, X.J., Li, Z.T., Tu, H., Zhang, B.C.: A data hiding algorithm for H.264/AVC video streams without intra frame distortion drift. IEEE Trans. Circ. Syst. Video Technol. **20**(10), 1320–1330 (2010)
6. Lin, T.J., Chung, K.L., Chang, P.C., Huang, Y.H.: An improved DCT-based perturbation scheme for high capacity data hiding in H.264/AVC intra frames. J. Syst. Softw. **86**(3), 604–614 (2013)
7. Liu, Y.X., Chen, L., Hu, M.S., Jia, Z.J., Jia, S.M.: A reversible data hiding method for H.264 with Shamirs (t, n)-threshold secret sharing. Neurocomputing **188**(2), 63–70 (2016)
8. Liu, Y.X., Ju, L., Hu, M.: A robust reversible data hiding scheme for H.264 without distortion drift. Neurocomputing **151**(1), 1053–1062 (2015)
9. Zhang, X., Wang, S.: Efficient steganographic embedding by exploiting modification direction. IEEE Commun. Lett. **10**(11), 781–783 (2006)
10. Zhang, W.W., Li, X., Zhang, Y.Z., Zhang, R., Zheng, L.X.: Robust video watermarking algorithm for H.264/AVC based on JND model. KSII Trans. Internet Inf. Syst. **11**(5), 2741–2761 (2017)

Steganography by Constructing Marbling Texture

Zhenxing Qian[1], Lin Pan[1], Sheng Li[2], and Xinpeng Zhang[2(✉)]

[1] School of Communication and Information Engineering, Shanghai University, Shanghai 200444, China
[2] School of Computer Science, Fudan University, Shanghai 200433, China
zhangxinpeng@fudan.edu.cn

Abstract. This paper proposes a novel steganographic method to hide secret data during the generation of marbling patterns. We select some points on white paper to represent secret information. These points are connected with lines to construct an original pattern. With a series of deformation operations, the original pattern is transformed to generate a marbling pattern. During the process of data hiding, we construct a unit library containing different deforming operations. The library records the parameters of each deformation, and defines the mapping between the binary data and the deformation type. The unit library is shared with the recipient so that the deformation parameters can be recovered correctly. After using reverse deformations, the recipient identifies the location of the inflection points and extracts the secret data. Experimental results show that the proposed method performs high security and flexible embedding capacity. Meanwhile, the marbling images have a good visual effect. Furthermore, the proposed steganography provides a capability of countering JPEG compression.

Keywords: Steganography · Data hiding · Marbling

1 Introduction

Steganography is a science about information hiding, between a data-hider and a recipient. The technique prevents the third-party from knowing the fact of secret transmission. In recent years, steganography has become the focus of information security. There are many traditional steganographic algorithms that have been studied, such as LSB, JSteg [1–3]. In the LSB steganography, the secret information is directly replaced with the low bit of the multimedia data. LSB is a common algorithm in the airspace method, suitable for digital still bitmap images. Jsteg steganography embeds information by continuously performing LSB substitution in the carrier image DCT domain. Their common drawback is that the modified steganography carrier has considerable vulnerability. Then there are many other more secure steganography methods, such as steganography based on WPC [4], divide the carrier image into several image blocks, embed the secret information in the dry area of each small block, the method is embedded in a large amount and the extraction is simple. Another example is the F5 algorithm [5], using matrix coding to embedded information in the

X. Sun et al. (Eds.): ICCCS 2018, LNCS 11066, pp. 428–439, 2018.
https://doi.org/10.1007/978-3-030-00015-8_37

non-zero AC coefficient. This method can reduce the number of LSBs that are changed when embedding information, thus effectively improving the security of steganography. In addition, there are some algorithms that can reduce the modification of the carrier through improving the embedding rate. Representative algorithms are ZZW [6] and STC [7]. However, a large amount of steganalysis methods has also been proposed. It is easy to detect these steganography, so some more aggressive steganographic algorithms need to be proposed.

At present there has been a constructive steganography method. Instead of embedding secret information by modifying the digital carrier, the core idea of this method is driven by secret information to generate a dense digital carrier. The representative scheme is based on texture synthesis, firstly proposed by Otrori and Kuriyama [8, 9]. Since this scheme has a problem of low capacity and error extraction, a new solution was proposed in [10], which can achieve large-capacity information hiding through the index selection. In addition, a reversible texture synthesis method [10] employs a rule of generating an index table and pasting source patches to construct a composition image. But this steganography method has been pointed out that it has serious security problems. Zhou et al. proposed an attacking method [11], which can not only detect the stego-images but can also extract the hidden messages. Qian et al. [12] proposes a robust steganography which hides secret messages during the process of synthesizing a texture image. The proposed method provides an approach robustness and large payloads.

Among the various types of textures, marbling texture is a type of decorative patterning. It spread to Europe in the 16th century where its primary application was producing covers for books. Marling gradually developed into an art. The rich patterns can bring people a wonderful artistic experience and visual enjoyment. Traditionally, marbling texture is produced by these steps: firstly drop colorful ink on the water, and then use tools (such as a stick or comb) to mix the colors on the surface, finally form various patters. There have been some mathematical methods to simulate the deformation process of marbling texture [13, 14], Fig. 1 shows an example of marbling.

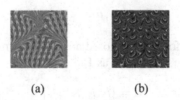

(a)   (b)

Fig. 1. An example of marbling texture

This paper proposes a new constructive steganographic algorithm by constructing marbling textures. We hide information by the mapping between the points and the binary data. Some mathematical methods of marbling are applied to form the secret image with a good visual effect. The secret message can be extracted correctly from the marbling image. Furthermore, the generated marbling texture image is robust to JPEG compression.

2   Proposed System

We represent a method to hide information while generating marbling image. The recipient can extract the hidden message from the image. The proposed system of data hiding is illustrated in Fig. 2. The data-hider needs to design a unit library and share it with the data recipient. The data-hider firstly selects some points on white paper to represent secret information according to the data to be hidden. Connect these points to construct a lot of graphs. These graphs are filled with rich colors. Adjacent graphs are filled with different colors, so that the points on the outline of the graphs can be successfully extracted. If there are some blank areas in the image, the hider can continue to add some background colors. A series of deformations which are selected from the unit library are employed to generate marbling patterns. And all the parameters of deforming operations will be embedded in the marbling image to obtain the stego image.

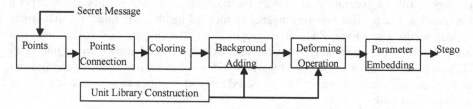

Fig. 2. Framework of the proposed method

2.1   Secret Mapping and Graphs Construction

Suppose that the length of the data **S** to be hidden is N. By using of the parity of the coordinates, odd number represents binary 1, even represents 0, each point can represent 2-bits data. There need to be $N/2$ points to represent N-bits data. These points can be represented by set **P**.

$$\mathbf{P} = \{p_1, p_2, \ldots, p_{N/2}\} \tag{1}$$

We use these points to form some closed areas to construct patterns. Suppose there are k closed curves that can be marked as **L**.

$$\mathbf{L} = \{l_1, l_2, \ldots, l_k\} \tag{2}$$

Each closed curve should have an average of d points to represent data, where $d=$ $N/2\ k$. A closed curve l_i $(i \le k)$ can be constructed by $\mathbf{P}_j$, $\mathbf{P}_j$ is a subset of **P**. The set **P** can also be expressed as:

$$\mathbf{P} = \{\mathbf{P}_j\}_{j=1}^{k} = \{p_1, p_2, \ldots, p_{N/2}\} \tag{3}$$

In order to ensure that each point can be identified in the process of extracting information, we must ensure no three or more points are connected by a same straight line. Thus we select points one by one, but not completely random. For example, we have defined p_1 and p_2, and we are looking for p_3. If there are a point can be select but it will be on the same line with p_1 and p_2, we must discard this point and look for another point as p_3.

In order to get a more beautiful pattern, we can choose inflection points of regular polygons (such as the five-pointed star) as points of information hiding. A five-pointed star has 10 inflection points that can be marked as $\mathbf{R} = \{r_1, r_2, \ldots, r_{10}\}$. These points can represent 20-bits secret data, and the parity of the coordinates needs to be adjusted according to the secret data. For example, the coordinate of r_1 is (30, 40), the data that are represented by r_1 is 01. According to odd number representing binary 1, even number representing 0, we can adjust the ordinate of r_1 to 39 or 41.

In each collection $\mathbf{P}_j$, we connect points with lines to form closed curve l_i according to the order in which they are selected. Then we fill the closed areas with colors, adjacent areas are filled with different colors. Such as Fig. 6a, there are five polygons, each polygon has 10 inflection points to represent the secret data. Each of the two adjacent polygons are filled with different colors. When the recipient obtains the image, he can extract the outlines of each closed area and identify each inflection point. Of course, we can also use other connection modes to construct different pattern effects, Fig. 3(b–d) show more examples.

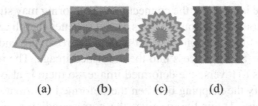

(a)   (b)   (c)   (d)

Fig. 3. Examples of the secret pattern

The deformation operations are used to simulate the texture of the marbling pattern, and the deformation function is used for the whole image. There are many kinds of functions such as tooth deformation, stroke deformation, sinusoidal deformation, circular deformation, power deformation, etc. [13, 14]. In the realization of the process we can be combine a variety of deformations to get more complex pattern texture. Some effects of these deformation operations are shown in Fig. 7. The following content describes two basic deformation functions that are commonly used.

The tooth deformation is a commonly used deformation function. If the pixel in the original image is $P(x, y)$, the mapping point after tooth deformation is $P_1(x_1, y_1)$. The deformation process is:

$$\begin{cases} x_1 = x \\ y_1 = y - \frac{\alpha y}{d+\gamma} \\ d = s/2 - |\text{fmod}(x, s) - s/2| \end{cases} \tag{4}$$

Where α is the maximum displacement, γ is used to control the sharpness of the tooth, s control the size of the tooth profile, fmod (·) for the residual function.

For a stroke deformation, each $P\ (x,\ y)$ coordinate is mapped to $P_2\ (\ x_2,y_2)$:

$$\begin{cases} x_2 = x \\ y_2 = y + z \times u^{|x - x_L|} \\ u = 1/2^{1/c} \end{cases} \tag{5}$$

The parameter z and u control the maximum displacement and sharpness of the bends, and x_L controls the horizontal distance of the position to be stroked (Fig. 4).

(a) tooth deformation   (b) stroke deformation

Fig. 4. Patterns of two basic deformations

Consider that the image after the connection and coloring may still have many blank areas, we can add some background colors to get a better marbling effect. In order to facilitate the successful extraction of secret data at the receiving end, the hider embeds the parameters in the above process into the deformed image. The receiver can use the extracted parameters to reverse the deformed image, so there is also a need for a secret unit library to specify the mapping between the deformed information and binary data.

As shown in Table 1, this library gives the corresponding rules between data and deformed information. The first is the background colors that can be filled in the image before deformation. The library also gives the correspondence between the deformed species and the binary data. Considering that each deformation can have a certain direction angle, we define the four directions and each direction is represented by two bits of data. In addition, in order to let the receiver accurately know the information of deformation, the type and order of parameters of each deformation are also given in the unit library. We assign 8 bits of data to each parameter value. Such as the tooth deformation, since the deformation type and direction each occupy 2-bits data, 3 parameters are required to implement this deformation operation, so the tooth deformation operation is composed of 28-bits data.

For a more intuitive illustration, here is a specific example. For example, employ the tooth deformation to an image, the deforming direction is 90 degrees, and the parameters of the value are: the maximum displacement α is 20, the sharpness γ is 8, the size of the tooth profile s is 16. The flag data of the deformation is 00, the direction is 01, the 8-bits binary data of the parameter α is 00010100, the binary data of the parameter γ is 00001000, the binary data of the parameter s is 00010000, thus the whole binary data stream of the tooth deformation is 0001000101000000100000010000. The data stream will be embedded in the marbling image after deformations.

Table 1. Example of the secret unit library

Color	[255, 0,0]	[255, 255, 0]	[0, 0, 255]	[0, 255, 255]
Data	00	01	10	11
Deformation	Tooth	Stroke	Tangent	Power
Data	00	01	10	11
Direction	0	90	180	270
Deformation	Tooth	Stroke	Tangent	Power
Parameters	α	z	α	α
	γ	c	β	β
	s	l	t	w

2.2 Parameter Embedding and Extraction

We apply an algorithm which utilizes the relationship between coefficients of some adjacent DCT blocks in [15]. The embedding process includes the following parts:

(a) Selecting the embedding domain

Take the marbling image and perform entropy decoding to get the 8×8 quantized DCT coefficients blocks: $\mathbf{B}_z = \{B_z(i)\}_{i=0}^{63}$, where $z = 0, 1, 2, ..., Z - 1$, Z is the number of the blocks, $\mathbf{B}_z$ is the zth DCT block, and $B_z(i)$ is the ith DCT coefficient in the block $\mathbf{B}_z$.

We divide four adjacent DCT blocks into a group, each group embeds 1 bit message s. Take a group $\mathbf{G}_1$ of four adjacent DCT blocks $\mathbf{B}_{z1}, \mathbf{B}_{z2}, \mathbf{B}_{z3}, \mathbf{B}_{z4}$ as example. We embed 1 bit data in block $\mathbf{B}_{z1}$ by utilizing its relationship with $\mathbf{B}_{z2}, \mathbf{B}_{z3}, \mathbf{B}_{z4}$. The rules are as follows:

$$\text{If } s = 1, B_{z_1}^s(i_0) = \begin{cases} \overline{M} + D, \text{ if } B_{z_1}(i_0) < \overline{M} + D \\ B_{z_1}(i_0), otherwise \end{cases} \tag{6}$$

$$\text{If } s = 0, B_{z_1}^s(i_0) = \begin{cases} \overline{M} - D, \text{ if } B_{z_1}(i_0) > \overline{M} - D \\ B_{z_1}(i_0), otherwise \end{cases} \tag{7}$$

Where $B_{z_1}^s(i_0)$ is the changed DCT coefficient at the i_0th position of DCT coefficients block $\mathbf{B}_{z_1}$ when embedding 1 bit message s. $\overline{M} = (B_{z_2}(i_0) + B_{z_3}(i_0) + B_{z_4}(i_0))/3$, $0 \le i_0 \le 63$. The parameter D is a variable parameter.

(b) Adjust the parameter

The parameter D determines the change magnitude of the DCT coefficients. In order to improve the correction rates of extracted messages under JPEG compression, we can adjust the parameter D according to following steps.

Step 1: Set the initial value D of each group as 1, and the iteration step $T=1$;

Step 2: Using the value of D, embed 1 bit message s at location i_0 in block $\mathbf{B}_{z_1}$ according to the algorithm in (a);

Step 3: Compress the stego image under quality factor Q, calculate the change amounts Δ_1 and Δ_2 of $B_{z_1}(i_0)$ and $\overline{M}$ before and after JPEG compression. Take group G_1 for example, $\Delta_1 = B_{z_1}(i_0) - \widehat{B}_{z_1}(i_0)$, $\Delta_2 = \overline{M} - \widehat{\overline{M}}$. Then adjust the parameter D using the following formula:

$$\text{If } s = 0, D = \begin{cases} D+1, \Delta_2 - \Delta_1 > D \\ D, otherwise \end{cases} \tag{8}$$

$$\text{If } s = 1, D = \begin{cases} D+1, \Delta_1 - \Delta_2 > D \\ D, otherwise \end{cases} \tag{9}$$

Step 4: If the parameter D corresponding to the coefficient $B_{z_1}(i_0)$ satisfies the requirement, or T achieves the specified iteration steps T_{max}, save the value of D and exit, otherwise $T = T+1$ and go to Step 2.

The extraction process corresponding to the embedding process can be described as follows. We get the DCT coefficients blocks of marbling image after data embedded. The DCT blocks can be marked as: $\widehat{\mathbf{B}}_z = \left\{\widehat{B}_z(i)\right\}_{i=0}^{63}$, where $z = 0,1,2,..., Z-1$, Z is the number of the blocks, $\widehat{\mathbf{B}}_z$ is the zth DCT block, and $\widehat{B}_z(i)$ is the ith DCT coefficient in the block $\widehat{\mathbf{B}}_z$. We divide four adjacent DCT blocks into a group, each group extracts 1 bit message $\widehat{s}$. Take a group $\mathbf{G}_1 = \{\widehat{\mathbf{B}}_{z1}, \widehat{\mathbf{B}}_{z2}, \widehat{\mathbf{B}}_{z3}, \widehat{\mathbf{B}}_{z4}\}$ as example. The extraction rules are as follows:

$$\widehat{s} = \begin{cases} 1, \widehat{B}_{z_1}(i_0) > \widehat{\overline{M}} \\ 0, otherwise \end{cases} \tag{10}$$

Where $\widehat{B}_{z_1}(i_0)$ is the DCT coefficient at the i_0th position of DCT coefficients block $\mathbf{B}_{z_1}$. $\widehat{\overline{M}} = (\widehat{B}_{z_2}(i_0) + \widehat{B}_{z_3}(i_0) + \widehat{B}_{z_4}(i_0))/3$, $0 \le i_0 \le 63$, i_0 is the message embedding position in the DCT coefficients blocks.

2.3 Data Extraction

After the information recipient extracts the data of deformation from the stego image, according to the unit library, he can obtain the type and specific parameter values of each deformation. Thus the marbling image can be operated by reverse deformation through functions of reverse deformations. For example, for the reverse tooth deformation, if the pixel in the secret image is $Q(x, y)$, the mapping point after reverse tooth deformation is $Q_1 (x_1, y_1)$.

$$\begin{cases} x_1 = x \\ y_1 = y + \frac{\alpha\gamma}{d+\gamma} \\ d = s/2 - |\text{fmod}(x, s) - s/2| \end{cases} \tag{11}$$

The parameter α is the maximum displacement, γ is used to control the sharpness of the tooth, s control the size of the tooth profile, fmod ($\cdot$) for the residual function.

After the process of reverse deformations, the background colors can be removed according to the unit library. The recipient extracts all the outlines of the graphs in the image and identifies all the connection points of the outlines. Finally, as the parity of the coordinates of the points can be mapped to 0 or 1, the secret data can be recovered successfully. The extraction of the secret data from the marbling image can be realized with the following steps.

(1) Extract the parameters of deformations from the stego image.
(2) Convert the data to specific parameter information of deformations according to the unit library. Obtain the type and specific parameter values of each deformation.
(3) Do the reverse deformation to the image according to the extracted deformation parameters.
(4) Remove the background according to the background color in the unit library. Then extract outlines and identify all the connection points of the outlines in the image, finally extract the secret message which is represented by the parity of the coordinates.

3   Experimental Results

In our experiment, we first establish a unit library (Table 2). There are many background colors can be used to fill the blank area in the image. There are four types of deformations, the unit library defines the binary data which represent the specific type. And each deformation have four directions, each direction also can be represented by 2-bits data.

Table 2. The secret unit library of experiment

Color	[100, 250, 200]	[100, 200, 250]	[180, 160, 200]	[245, 210, 210]
Data	00	01	10	11
Deformation	Tooth	Stroke	Sinusoidal	Circular
Data	00	01	10	11
Direction	0	90	180	270
Deformation	Tooth	Stroke	Sinusoidal	Circular
Parameters	α	z	w	r
	γ	c	A	a
	s	l	θ	t
	l	l	t	e

3.1   Various Marbling Effects

There are 1600 bits secret data, since the two-dimensional coordinates have parity, each coordinate point can represent 2 bits of secret data. We select 800 points to represent the secret message in a blank image (512 × 512 pixels), even number represents 0, odd number represents 1. We connect these points and fill colors to form a pattern (Fig. 5a). Since there are many blank areas in the image, we fill the blank area with the color given in the unit library (Fig. 5b). In this experiment, multiple stroke deformations in two different directions (180 and 270 degree) are used to form the marbling image as shown in Fig. 5c. In the deformation process, the various types of deformation, directions and parameter values are recorded. Since a stroke deformation has three parameters and each parameter has 8-btis data, including the data of type and direction, the whole data stream of a stroke operation is 28 bits. In every direction, five times of stroke are applied, thus we can get a binary data stream of 280 bits. The iteration steps are set to $T_{max} = 3$, the data stream of deformations are embedded in the marbling image (Fig. 5c) to form a stego image(Fig. 5d).

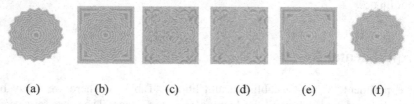

(a)   (b)   (c)   (d)   (e)   (f)

Fig. 5. An experimental example of hiding information with the algorithm in this article.

During the information recovery process, the binary data stream should been extracted from the stego image. According to the data stream and unit library, we can know the type, direction and parameter values of deformation. Then the image can be subjected to reverse deformation operations (Fig. 5e). The embedding of parameters causes the change of some pixel values, the values of colors in the unit library need to be modified with a value 10 in this experiment. For example, the value of the red channel of an original background color is G, then the modified value is in the range of $[G - 10, G + 10]$. We remove the background pattern according to the modified colors values. Finally identify the inflection points of the graphical edge lines in Fig. 8f, and recover the secret information according to their coordinate parity. The experimental results show that the information can be extracted without error.

Through different connection method and deformations, we can obtain marbling pattern with different visual effects, Fig. 6 is another set of experiments. In a blank image (512 × 512 pixels) we select 500 locations to represent 1000 bits data, and connect them with tooth lines to form an initial pattern as shown in Fig. 6a. Using the same unit library as Table 2, fill the background with the color that has been given in the unit library (Fig. 6b). Multiple stroke deformations are performed in different directions, the final formation of the secret marbling image is shown in Fig. 6c. There are many other different ways of deformation to get rich marbling effects. As shown in

Fig. 6d, it's the effect of combining stroke deformations and circular deformation. Similarly, we can get the stego image by embedding parameters of deformations in the marbling image, and correctly extract the message through our extraction algorithm.

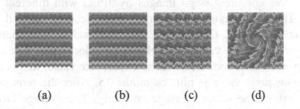

(a)   (b)   (c)   (d)

Fig. 6. Another experimental examples of different marbling effects.

3.2 Marbling Effect of Different Data Embedded

The method proposed in the paper has a flexible steganographic capability. With the different amount of data embedding, we also can get different visual effects of the marbling images. We have done some experiments to show that. As show in Fig. 7, We apply stroke deformation and tooth deformation to obtain a marbling image. 500 bit messages are hidden in the image (512 × 512). Another experiment as show in Fig. 8, we embed 2000-bits data.

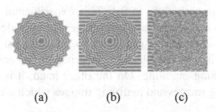

(a)   (b)   (c)

Fig. 7. Experimental examples of 500-bits data hiding.

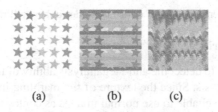

(a)   (b)   (c)

Fig. 8. Experimental examples of 2000-bits data hiding.

3.3 Analysis of Countering JPEG Compression

When the image is compressed as a JPEG image in the transmission, we still can extract the secret information through our extraction algorithm. A group of results are shown in Fig. 9. We compress stego images by JPEG with different quality factors from 10 to 90. The information extraction algorithm can be applied to these JPEG images to extract secret data. Considering that pixel values will change after JPEG compression, so we adjust the values of background colors again. The values of colors in the unit library need to be modified with an experience value. In this experiment, the change of the color pixel value is plus or minus 15. After the removal of the background we can extract the secret message correctly. The average error rates of the extracted bits in these images are calculated. The results of four groups of experiments are shown in Fig. 9. The red and green curves respectively represent the experiment with 400-bits and 500-bits data embedding. The yellow and blue curves show the results of 1000-bits and 2000-bits data embedding.

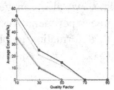

Fig. 9. Experimental results of error rate under different JPEG compression

3.4 Analysis of Security

We also do experiments to detect the anti-steganalysis ability of this algorithm, we used the Rich-Model for analysis. Since the texture of the marbling images is different from normal images, it is not suitable to use normal images as contrast. We use some normal marbling images to do comparative experiments. Firstly we take 50 natural images as training images of Rich-Model, separately detect the normal tangle images and secret tangle images, and obtain the error rate r_1 and r_2. After a lot of experiments, we find that the rate r_1 and r_2 are both close to 0.1. This experimental result means that both normal marbling images and secret marbling images are considered as stego images by steganalysis of Rich-Model. So we can get two conclusions: on the one hand, the traditional steganalysis is not suitable for analyzing the steganography which hides information by constructing marbling. On the other hand, it is difficult to distinguish between normal marbling images and marbling images which are embedded with secret messages by our scheme.

4   Conclusion

This paper proposes a reversible steganography algorithm. Take a blank image, we can select a number of points to represent the secret messages. These points are connected by lines to form some closed areas, and the closed areas are filled with different colors.

Combined with the deformation operations, we can obtain a secret marbling image. Diverse marbling effects can be formed through using different deforming methods. The secret image has a good art effect and ornamental value. In addition to that, we can extract the secret data from JPEG compressed images. Due to the particularity of image texture, the images generated by our algorithm are difficult to detect by general steganalysis.

Acknowledgement. This work was supported by Natural Science Foundation of China (Grant U1536108, Grant 61572308).

References

1. Wang, H., Wang, S.: Cyber warfare: steganography vs steganalysis. Commun. ACM **47**(10), 76–82 (2004)
2. Chan, C., Cheng, L.: Hiding data in images by simple LSB substitution. Pattern Recogn. **37**, 469–474 (2004)
3. Fridrich, J., Goljan, M.: Practical steganalysis of digital images - state of the art. In: Proceedings of SPIE Security and Watermarking of Multimedia Contents IV, vol. 4675, pp. 1–13 (2002)
4. Fridrich, J., Goljan, M., Lisoněk, P., Soukal, D.: Writing on wet paper. IEEE Trans. Signal Process. **53**(10), 3923–3935 (2005)
5. Westfeld, A.: F5—a steganographic algorithm high capacity despite better steganalysis. In: Proceedings of the Second International Workshop on Digital-Forensics and Watermarking, Seoul, Korea, pp. 154–167 (2003)
6. Zhang, W., Zhang, X., Wang, S.: Maximizing steganographic embedding efficiency by combining hamming codes and wet paper codes. In: Solanki, K., Sullivan, K., Madhow, U. (eds.) IH 2008. LNCS, vol. 5284, pp. 60–71. Springer, Heidelberg (2008). https://doi.org/10.1007/978-3-540-88961-8_5
7. Filler, T., Judas, J., Fridrich, J.: Minimizing additive distortion in steganography using syndrome-trellis codes. IEEE Trans. Inf. Forensics Secur. **6**(3), 920–935 (2011)
8. Otori, H., and Kuriyama, S.: Data-embeddable texture synthesis. In: Proceedings of the 8th International Symposium on Smart Graphics, Kyoto, Japan, pp. 146–157 (2007).
9. Otori, H., Kuriyama, S.: Texture synthesis for mobile data communications. IEEE Comput. Graph. Appl. **29**(6), 74–81 (2009)
10. Wu, K., Wang, C.: Steganography using reversible texture synthesis. IEEE Trans. Image Process. **24**(1), 130–139 (2015)
11. Zhou, H., Chen, K., Zhang, W., Yu, N.: Comments on steganography using reversible texture synthesis. IEEE Trans. Image Process. **26**(4) (2017)
12. Qian, Z., Zhou, H., Zhang, W., Zhang, X.: Robust Steganography Using Texture Synthesis. Advances in Intelligent Information Hiding and Multimedia Signal Processing. SIST, vol. 63, pp. 25–33. Springer, Cham (2017). https://doi.org/10.1007/978-3-319-50209-0_4
13. Jaffer, A. Inkmarbling, http://people.csail.mit.edu/jaffer/Marbling (2011)
14. Lu, S., Jaffer, A., Jin, X., Zhao, H., Mao, X.: Mathematical marbling. IEEE Comput. Graph. Appl. **32**(6), 26–35 (2012)
15. Xu, J., et al.: Hidden message in a deformation-based texture. Vis Comput. **31**, 1653–1669 (2015)

Style Transferring Based Data Hiding for Color Images

Yi Puyang[1,2], Zhenxing Qian[2], Zhaoxia Yin[1,3(✉)], and Xinpeng Zhang[2]

[1] Key Laboratory of Intelligent Computing and Signal Processing, Ministry of Education,
Anhui University, Hefei 230601, People's Republic of China
yinzhaoxia@ahu.edu.cn
[2] Shanghai Institute for Advanced Communication and Data Science,
School of Communication and Information Engineering, Shanghai University,
Shanghai 200072, People's Republic of China
zxqian@shu.edu.cn
[3] Department of Computer Science, Purdue University, West Lafayette, Indiana 47906, USA

Abstract. This paper proposes a joint scheme of data hiding and style transfer, which embeds secret data during the procedure of transferring natural images into comic styles. While most data hiding algorithms employ clean images as covers, we employ the processed images that are popular on social networks. The style transfer based data hiding includes two phases. In the first phase, we brighten the image and remove the details by enhancing the saturation and smoothing the content. In the second phase, we propose an edge marker embedding based algorithm to enhance the contours and generate comic-style stego images. Experimental results show that the proposed approach provides a large embedding capacity and a good capability of resisting steganalysis.

Keywords: Data hiding · Color image · Style transferring · Edge

1 Introduction

As an important research area of information security, data hiding embeds secret data into digital media with a small distortion via the encoding redundancy of carrier signals. Not only of great significance in military, intelligence, and medicine [8, 9], data hiding is also closely related to personal privacy protection. With the rapid development of Internet, digital medias are widely spread, such as image, audio, and video. Image is often used as carrier signals due to their high structure and encoding redundancy. Therefore, data hiding technology that take image as communication carrier has important research value and wide application prospects.

At present, common data hiding technology is mainly based on the following three principles. The first one is lossless compression-based approach [1, 10]. This method utilizes image redundancy to make room for embedded data by lossless compression. But the data embedding capacity of this method is very low and the image quality can not be kept well. The second approach is based on difference expansion (DE) [3, 4], which embed the secret data using the difference between pixels or the difference

© Springer Nature Switzerland AG 2018
X. Sun et al. (Eds.): ICCCS 2018, LNCS 11066, pp. 440–449, 2018.
https://doi.org/10.1007/978-3-030-00015-8_38

between the original and predicted pixel. Last but not least, the other data hiding technology is based on histogram-shifting [11, 12], it embeds secret data into high-frequency values by statistical analysis of pixels or prediction errors. Since Ni et al. [5] first proposed a histogram-based embedding method, the scheme was extended quickly.

It's a pity that most of current data hiding research is based on unprocessed image. But actually sharing of processed images on social platforms has become the norm. On the Internet platform, with the rapid development and widespread use of a large number of images processing software, such as Photoshop, faceu, etc., people are increasingly inclined to share processed images on a social platform after contrast enhancement, brightness improvement, saturation adjustment, and style transfer. Compares to natural images spreading processed images on social networks is more likely to be regarded as a normal behavior, which providing a vast space for data secretive transmission on social platforms. This paper proposes a joint scheme of data embedding and style transferring based on color images. The proposed scheme embeds secret data during the procedure of transferring natural images into comic styles. First, according to comic image features, such as bright colors, fewer image details and prominent outlines, we conduct saturation enhancement and smoothing to original images. Our proposed edge marker embedding (EME) scheme not only enables data embedding, but also highlights the image edge contour to make the image has comic-style features. Combining data hiding with image style transferring is a major contribution to the proposed scheme, providing a more secure and reliable way for secret data to be transmitted on social platforms.

The rest of the paper is structured as follows: Sect. 2 presents the proposed method in detail. Experimental results and analysis are presented in Sect. 3. Finally, we conclude in Sect. 4.

2 Proposed Method

Through the analysis of comic-style images, we can conclude that such images have the following characteristics: (1) bright color; (2) fewer image details; (3) prominent edge outline. According to three characteristics of the comic-style images, we deal with them respectively. First, we use image interpolation to make the image brighter. Then, for the second feature, we use a bilateral filter to smooth the image and remove certain image detail, while retaining a clear edge. Finally, we use the EME scheme to embed the secret data and achieve the effect of highlighting the edge contour of the image.

2.1 Improve the Saturation of Image

The higher saturation is, the more bright color image will appear. Otherwise the image will look gloomy. Therefore, we use image extrapolation to increase the image color saturation. Assuming original color image is $X = \{ r_Y, g_Y, b_Y \}$, where r_X, g_X, b_X denote three color channel of original image respectively. The grayscale image h_X of the original image is from the function $rgb2gray()$ calculation, as shown in Eq. (1). As shown in Eq. (2), this grayscale image is used as a template to perform image interpolation processing on each channel respectively, thereby improving the image saturation. The symbol '∗' represents the value multiplication corresponding to the same position, and α represents the adjust intensity parameter of image saturation. Finally, the saturation-improved image can be represented as $Y = \{r_Y, g_Y, b_Y\}$.

$$h_X = rgb2gray(X) \tag{1}$$

$$\begin{cases} r_Y = & r_X * \alpha + h_X * (1 - \alpha), \\ g_Y = g_X * \alpha + h_X * (1 - \alpha), \\ b_Y = & b_X * \alpha + h_X * (1 - \alpha). \end{cases} \tag{2}$$

2.2 Remove the Area Details of Image

From the perspective of image processing, the so-called 'detail' refers to high-frequency components in the image. Therefore in this section, we use bilateral filtering to smooth the image and remove the image details. The major reason for choosing bilateral filtering is that the bilateral filter can remove the internal information of the area while retaining clear edge information at the same time. The specific filter calculation is shown in Eq. (3), and the filtered image can be expressed as $\hat{Y} = \{\hat{r}_Y, \hat{g}_Y, \hat{b}_Y\}$.

$$\hat{Y}(x, y) = \frac{\sum\limits_{(i,j)\in Sxy} w(i,j) \cdot Y(i,j)}{\sum\limits_{(i,j)\in Sxy} w(i,j)} \tag{3}$$

$\hat{Y}(x, y)$ denotes the pixel after filtering at the position (x, y), Sxy denotes a $(2r + 1) \times (2r + 1)$-size region centered on (x, y), and r is a intensity parameter that adjusting smoothing effect. The essence of this formula is to calculate the weighted average of the pixel values in the neighborhood of the center pixel. The weight w is composed of two parts: $w(i,j) = w_s(i,j) \times w_r(i,j)$, the weights are defined respectively from the relationship between the pixel position and the relationship between the pixel values. The specific calculations are shown in Eqs. (4) and (5). The parameters δ_s and δ_r correspond to the adjustments w_s and w_r, respectively.

$$w_s(i,j) = \exp(-\frac{|i - x|^2 + |j - y|^2}{2\delta_s^2}) \tag{4}$$

$$w_r(i,j) = \exp(-\frac{|Y(i,j) - Y(x,y)|^2}{2\delta_r^2}) \tag{5}$$

2.3 The Process of Data Embedding

In this section, we first adopt the Sobel edge detection algorithm to obtain the edge position marker information of the image. Then, based on this edge position marker information, we embed the data in three different channels of the image. We call this method the edge marker embedding method (EME). The specific steps are as follows:

(1) As shown in Fig. 1, set Sobel edge detection convolution factor then use it to do horizontal and vertical plane convolution operation with image respectively $G_x = Q_x \otimes \hat{Y}, G_y = Q_y \otimes \hat{Y}$, where $\otimes$ is a convolution operation;

-1	0	+1
-2	0	+2
-1	0	+1

Q_x

+1	+2	+1
0	0	0
-1	-2	-1

Q_y

Fig. 1. Sobel edge detection convolution factor

(2) Calculate the convolution result for each pixel, as shown in Eq. (6);

$$G(x, y) = \sqrt{G_x^2 + G_y^2} \qquad (6)$$

(3) Set threshold T and use matrix E to record the edge position marker information. If it is bigger than or equal to the threshold, mark it as 1, otherwise mark it as 0.

$$E(x, y) = \begin{cases} 0 & if \ G(x, y) < T, \\ 1 & if \ G(x, y) \geq T. \end{cases} \qquad (7)$$

(4) Divide each channel of the image into two areas, painted and blank $\hat{r}_Y^i, \hat{r}_Y^o, \hat{g}_Y^i, \hat{g}_Y^o$ and $\hat{b}_Y^i, \hat{b}_Y^o$, as shown in Fig. 2.

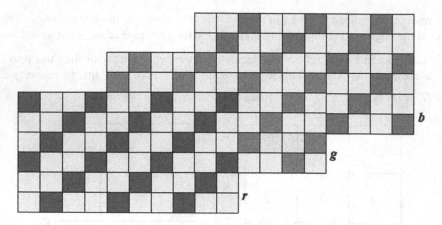

Fig. 2. Division of three channels

(5) Taking the image channel R as an example, embed a secret data at an edge position that belonging to a blank area and enhance the image edge contour at the same time, as shown in Eq. (8).

$$r_z(x, y) = \begin{cases} \hat{r}_Y(x, y) - \hat{r}_Y(x, y) \cdot E(x, y) + m & \text{if } E(x, y) = 1 \text{ and } \hat{r}_Y(x, y) \in \hat{r}_Y^o \\ \hat{r}_Y(x, y) - \hat{r}_Y(x, y) \cdot E(x, y) & \text{otherwise} \end{cases} \quad (8)$$

(6) Perform the same embedding on the remaining two channels, and finally get a stylized stego image that can be represented as: $Z = \{r_Z, g_Z, b_Z\}$.

2.4 The Process of Data Extraction

(1) As the embedding step (4), Divide each channel of the image into two areas, painted and blank $\hat{r}_Y^i, \hat{r}_Y^o, \hat{g}_Y^i, \hat{g}_Y^o$ and $\hat{b}_Y^i, \hat{b}_Y^o$, as shown in Fig. 2.
(2) According to the pixel information of the painted area of a certain channel, if the value is 0, 2 bits secret data is extracted in the remaining channels, as shown in Eq. (9).

$$[m_1, m_2] = \begin{cases} [g_Z(x, y), b_Z(x, y)], & \text{if } r_Z(x, y) = 0 \text{ and } r_Z(x, y) \in r_Z^i, \\ [r_Z(x, y), b_Z(x, y)], & \text{if } g_Z(x, y) = 0 \text{ and } g_Z(x, y) \in g_Z^i, \\ [r_Z(x, y), g_Z(x, y)], & \text{if } b_Z(x, y) = 0 \text{ and } b_Z(x, y) \in b_Z^i. \end{cases} \quad (9)$$

3   Experimental Results and Analysis

In this experiment, we choose image sets misc [2] and cambridge [6], saturation parameters $\alpha = 2$, bilateral filtering parameters $r = 5$, $\delta_s = 3$, $\delta_r = 0.1$. Section 3.1 discusses the effect of thresholds T on embedded capacity and image stylization. In addition, in Sect. 3.2, RS method is used to steganalysis for the stylized stego image and detect the security performance of stego image.

3.1 The Performance of the Proposed Scheme

In our proposed scheme, the threshold T is used to control the image edge detection intensity, and our proposed edge marker embedding scheme (EME) embeds the data at the border position of an image. Therefore, the threshold selection plays a crucial role in the embedded capacity of the proposed scheme. As shown in Table 1, we use standard test image Lena, Jet, Peppers, House, and Baboon to conduct experiments. We tested the total embedded capacity of the proposed scheme under different thresholds. From Table 1, we can clearly see that as the threshold T increases, the secret data that the image can embed decreases. In addition, as shown in Fig. 3, we use a color image House as an example to detect the stylized effect of the proposed scheme when the threshold T takes different values. It is obvious from the figure that after the original image being processed by the proposed scheme, its style changes significantly, and when the threshold T at a smaller value, the edge contour of the stylized stego image becomes more apparent. As the threshold T gradually increases, the image becomes smoother and the stylized effect gradually decreases. To sum up, the selection of threshold in the proposed scheme should not be too large. What threshold selection range we recommend is $T \in [0.1, 0.3]$.

Table 1. Payload with different threshold T

Payload [bits]	$T = 0.01$	$T = 0.02$	$T = 0.03$	$T = 0.04$	$T = 0.05$
Lena	49422	34232	26644	21890	18502
Jet	46912	37228	32100	28854	26312
Peppers	53498	33692	25826	21264	18364
House	79170	65498	55914	48452	41756
Baboon	151538	130988	116228	104022	92924
Sailboat	70748	56970	49470	43648	38836

As mentioned previously, the edge marker embedding scheme (EME) proposed in this paper is embedding data at the image edge. Therefore, the embedded capacity of this scheme is not only related to threshold selection, but also to the texture complexity of image itself. For standard test images, the texture of Baboon is much more complicated than the texture of Lena, as shown in Fig. 4. From Fig. 4, it can be clearly observed that, regardless of the threshold selection, Baboon has much higher embedding capacity than other test images. This is because Baboon has more complex texture complexity.

Original image $T = 0.01$ $T = 0.02$

$T = 0.03$ $T = 0.04$ $T = 0.05$

Fig. 3. Effect of style transfer with different threshold T

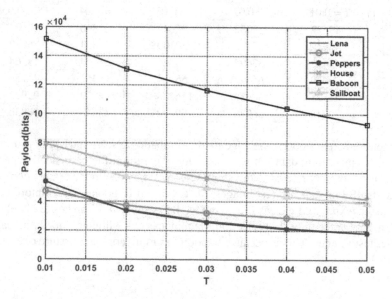

Fig. 4. Payload of different texture images

3.2 Steganalysis Using RS Scheme

In this section, we use RS detection scheme [7] to carry out steganalysis on the stego image to detect the safety performance of the proposed scheme. RS scheme is an effective scheme that can detect whether the low bit plane of an image is embedding data, such as LSB algorithm. We first define a decision function that measures the image smoothness. Normal data embed will add noise to the image, and the function value changes accordingly. RS scheme divides pixels into regular groups, singular groups, and unusable groups based on this decision function and a pre-defined mask. M. (R_M, R_{-M}) and (S_M, S_{-M}) represent the ratio of the regular group and the singular group respectively. If the image to be detected has no embedded data, R_M will be approximately equal to R_{-M}, S_M will also be approximately equal to S_{-M}, and $R_M > S_M, R_{-M} > S_{-M}$. RSv is applied to measure the security performance of the proposed scheme. The closer the value of RSv is to 0, the better resistance detection ability the stego image will have. RSv is defined as shown in Eq. (10).

$$RSv = \frac{|R_M - R_{-M}| + |S_M - S_{-M}|}{R_M + S_M} \tag{10}$$

We randomly select 100 images from the image set cambridge [6] to experiment and obtain 100 full-embedded stylized stego images. In this experiment, the mask $M = [-1, 0, 1, -1, 0, 0, -1, 1, 0, -1, 1, 0, -1, 0, 1, 1]$, threshold $T = 0.02$, the experimental results are shown in Fig. 5. The experimental results show that RSv of the three channels of the stylized stego image are close to 0, which proves that the stego image has good anti-detection capability and the proposed scheme has great security performance.

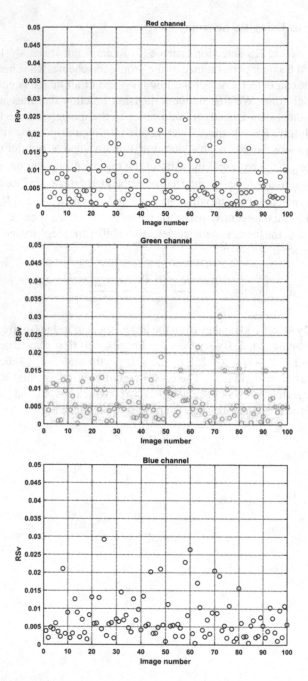

Fig. 5. RS detection values of 100 fully embedded images

4 Conclusions

This paper proposes a joint scheme based on color image data hiding and style transferring. According to the comic-style image features, we perform operations such as increasing image saturation and removing image internal details respectively. At the same time, our proposed edge marker embedding (EME) scheme embeds the secret data while highlighting the image edge contour, making the image obtain comic style features. The main contribution of this paper lies in the combination of information hiding and image stylization. Experimental results shows that the proposed scheme has high embedding capacity and good security performance.

Acknowledgements. This work was supported by Natural Science Foundation of China (Grant 61502009, Grant U1536109, Grant 61572308, Grant U1536108, Grant U1736213, Grant U1636206, Grant 61525203, Grant 61472235), Foundation of China Scholarship Council (Grant 201706505004), the Shanghai Dawn Scholar Plan (Grant 14SG36), and the Shanghai Excellent Academic Leader Plan (Grant 16XD1401200).

References

1. Celik, M.U., Sharma, G., Tekalp, A.M., et al.: Lossless generalized-LSB data embedding. IEEE Trans. Image Process. **14**(2), 253 (2005)
2. http://sipi.usc.edu/database/database.php?volume=misc
3. Li, J., Li, X., Yang, B.: Reversible data hiding scheme for color image based on prediction-error expansion and cross-channel correlation. Sig. Process. **93**(9), 2748–2758 (2013)
4. Qiu, Y., Qian, Z., Yu, L.: Adaptive reversible data hiding by extending the generalized integer transformation. IEEE Signal Process. Lett. **23**(1), 130–134 (2015)
5. Ni, Z., Shi, Y.Q., Ansari, N., et al.: Reversible data hiding. IEEE Trans. Circuits Syst. Video Technol. **16**(3), 354–362 (2004)
6. http://imagedatabase.cs.washington.edu/groundtruth/cambridge/
7. Fridrich, J., Goljan, M., Du, R.: Reliable detection of LSB steganography in color and grayscale images. In: Mm & Sec Proceedings of the Workshop on Multimedia & Security New Challenges, vol. 8, pp. 22–28 (2002)
8. Pandey, R., Singh, A.K., Kumar, B., et al.: Iris based secure NROI multiple eye image watermarking for teleophthalmology. Multimedia Tools Appl. **75**(22), 1–17 (2016)
9. Parah, S.A., Sheikh, J.A., Ahad, F., et al.: Information hiding in medical images: a robust medical image watermarking system for E-healthcare. Multimedia Tools Appl. **76**(8), 10599–10633 (2017)
10. Fridrich, A.J., Goljan, M., Du, R.: Lossless data embedding for all image formats. Proc. SPIE - Int. Soc. Opt. Eng. **4675**, 572–583 (2002)
11. Hou, D., Wang, H., Zhang, W., et al.: Reversible data hiding in JPEG image based on DCT frequency and block selection. Signal Processing (2018)
12. Wedaj, F.T., Kim, S., Kim, H.J., et al.: Improved reversible data hiding in JPEG images based on new coefficient selection strategy. Eurasip J. Image Video Process. **2017**(1), 63 (2017)

Synthesis of Quantum Barrel Shifters

Zhiqiang Li[1(✉)], Gaoman Zhang[1], Wei Zhang[1],
Hanwu Chen[2], and Marek Perkowski[3]

[1] College of Information Engineering, Yangzhou University, Yangzhou, China
yzqqlzq@163.com
[2] College of Software Engineering, Southeast University, Nanjing, China
101010297@seu.edu.cn
[3] Department of ECE, Portland State University, Oregon, USA

Abstract. A barrel shifter is a common component of high-speed processor, which can realize the displacement operation of the specified number of data word in a single cycle. On the basis of the inverse logic circuit, a displacement device with n inputs and m control bits is proposed, which is denoted as (n, m) shifter, and a set of control inputs that specify how to shift in data between input and output. On the basis of the quantum reversible logic circuits, for synthesizing the barrel shifter, we present the novel method based on the decomposition of the permutation group and some Construction Rules. It only uses (3, 1) shifter and controlled swap gate to quickly synthesize any controlled shifter with low quantum cost, and any (n, k) barrel shifter can be got by cascading the least of k corresponding $(n, 1)$ shifters. The quantum circuit shifters generated by this method can reduce the number of quantum gates, reduce the quantum cost and improve the efficiency of the algorithm, so that all kinds of reversible barrel shifter can be rapidly designed. In this article, we mainly give the ways on qubit left circular shifts, bit permutation and line permutations, and other types of basic shift circuits are also designed.

Keywords: Barrel shifter · Decomposition of permutation group
Quantum gate · Quantum cost · Circuit synthesis

1 Introduction

Quantum computer can be equivalent to a quantum Turing machine, and the quantum Turing machine can also be equivalent to a quantum logic circuit. The combination and cascade of the quantum logic gates are the basic elements for composing a quantum computer. In recent 30 years, various quantum gates have been proposed, such as controlled not (CNOT) [1], Toffoli, controlled swap (Fredkin) [2] gates and so on, and the input and output values of each quantum ware are all binary ground state. The quantum circuit is reversible, and reversible logic had been widely applied in many emerging technologies, such as low-power CMOS circuit, optical calculations, etc. [3]. Obviously the reversible logic is mainly applied in quantum computing, and the essence of constructing the quantum circuit automatically is the reversible logic synthesis. So lots of research have been done to present many quantum circuit synthesis

© Springer Nature Switzerland AG 2018
X. Sun et al. (Eds.): ICCCS 2018, LNCS 11066, pp. 450–462, 2018.
https://doi.org/10.1007/978-3-030-00015-8_39

algorithms, such as the 3-bit [4–7] and 4-bit [8–12] quantum circuit synthesis algorithms. Otherwise, some special methods based on the existing methods can be introduced to synthesize some special reversible logic circuits for improving the efficiency of the algorithm [13].

A barrel shifter is a common component of high-speed processor, which can realize the displacement operation of the specified number of data word in a single cycle. A barrel shifter is a combinational logic circuit with n data inputs, n data outputs, and a set of control inputs that specify how to shift in data between input and output. On the basis of the quantum reversible logic circuits, we present a new method based on the decomposition of permutation group, and any sizes of reversible barrel shifter without using any ancilla inputs, can be synthesized rapidly, so various reversible barrel shifters can also be synthesized quickly. However, there are many kinds of displacement types, such as rotation left shift, rotation right shift, rotate left through carry, rotate right through carry, arithmetic left shift, arithmetic right shift, logical left shift and logical right shift. This article takes the left circular shift as a major example, and other kinds of shifts are similar. [9] puts forward the concept of controlled reversible barrel shifter, but does not give the detailed construction, so this article solves this design problem efficiently.

2   The Basic Concept

2.1   XOR Quantum Gate

The XOR quantum gate, namely controlled-NOT gate (CNOT gate), is very similar to the classical XOR gate. In Fig. 1, it has two input bits: a is the control qubit, and b is the target qubit. If the control qubit is in the 1 state, that is, at the upper level, the target qubit will be reversed, otherwise it will be unchanged.

Note: The name of each line in this circuit is represented by the input value. As shown in Fig. 1, line b refers to the line below since the input value of the line is b.

2.2   Toffoli Quantum Gate

The Toffoli quantum gate is denoted as T(C; T), and it is the promotion of the controlled behavior of the CNOT gate. The Toffoli gate is a common quantum gate with two controlled qubits and one target qubit. Unlike the CNOT gate, the qubit of the Toffoli gate is reversed only when the two controlled qubits are set to 1, then $|A,B;C\rangle \rightarrow |A,B;AB \oplus C\rangle$, as shown in Fig. 2.

2.3   Fredkin Quantum Gate

Fredkin gate is also called controlled swap gate, and is noted for F(C; T). Figure 3 is the symbol of Fredkin gate. Its behavior can be described as follows: if the control qubit C is set to 1, $(a\overline{C} + bC)|_{C=1} = b$, $(b\overline{C} + aC)|_{C=1} = a$, the outputs of line a and line b are swapped, otherwise $(a\overline{C} + bC)|_{C=0} = a$, $(b\overline{C} + aC)|_{C=0} = b$, they remain unchanged.

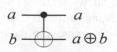

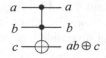

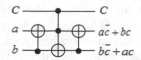

Fig. 1. XOR quantum gate

Fig. 2. Toffoli gate

Fig. 3. Controlled swap gate

2.4   Permutation Group

Let M be a nonempty finite set. A bijection $\sigma : M \to M$ is called a permutation of M. If $|M| = n$, σ is a $n-$ permutation. Let $M = \{0, 1, \cdots, n-1\}$, and $i \in \{0, 1, \ldots, n-1\}$, any permutation of n integers from 0 to n-1 can be written as: $\sigma = \begin{pmatrix} 0 & 1 & \cdots & n-1 \\ \sigma(0) & \sigma(1) & \cdots & \sigma(n-1) \end{pmatrix}$, where $\sigma(i) \in \{0, 1, \ldots, n-1\}$, then its inverse is the permutation $\sigma^{-1} = \begin{pmatrix} \sigma(0) & \sigma(1) & \cdots & \sigma(n-1) \\ 0 & 1 & \cdots & n-1 \end{pmatrix}$, $\sigma^{-1}(\sigma(i)) = i$, a function $\sigma = \begin{pmatrix} 0 & 1 & \cdots & n-1 \\ 0 & 1 & \cdots & n-1 \end{pmatrix}$ on M is an identical permutation, denoted as e. For any permutation σ on M, there is a property: $\sigma \circ e = e \circ \sigma = \sigma$ and $e(i) = i$.

Permutation σ can be represented by a more compact way, which is expressed as a product of disjoint cycles. For example, $\begin{pmatrix} 0 & 1 & 2 & 3 & 4 & 5 \\ 3 & 2 & 5 & 0 & 4 & 1 \end{pmatrix} = (0\ 3)\ (1\ 2\ 5)\ (4)$, where (4) is called a single cycle, and it represents that 4 is changed into 4, that is, 4 is not changed, so the 1-cycle can be ignored. (0 3) is a 2-cycle, which represents the exchange between 0 and 3. The shifter (1 2 5) is called a 3-cycle, then 1 is sent to 2, 2 is sent to 5, and 5 is sent to 1.

Generally, $(p_1 p_2 \ldots p_k)$ is a k-cycle, and k is the length of the cycle. The cycle of two numbers is called swap. Clearly, two disjoint cycles can be exchanged equivalently. For example:
$\begin{pmatrix} 0 & 3 & 1 & 2 & 5 \\ 3 & 0 & 2 & 5 & 1 \end{pmatrix} = (0\ 3)(1\ 2\ 5) = (1\ 2\ 5)(0\ 3) = \begin{pmatrix} 1 & 2 & 5 & 0 & 3 \\ 2 & 5 & 1 & 3 & 0 \end{pmatrix}$. The digitals in the same cycle can be recycled while their results are not changed, such as $(1\ 2\ 5) = (2\ 5\ 1) = (5\ 1\ 2)$.

Any recycle can be separated into several swap products including the same digitals. Nevertheless, there are two kinds of the operation order of the permutation group:

From right to left: $\begin{pmatrix} 0 & 2 \\ 2 & 0 \end{pmatrix} \begin{pmatrix} 0 & 1 \\ 1 & 0 \end{pmatrix} = \begin{pmatrix} 0 & 1 & 2 \\ 1 & 2 & 0 \end{pmatrix} = (0\ 1\ 2)$, then $(0\ 1\ 2) = (0\ 2)(0\ 1)$.

From left to right: $\begin{pmatrix} 0 & 1 \\ 1 & 0 \end{pmatrix} \begin{pmatrix} 0 & 2 \\ 2 & 0 \end{pmatrix} = \begin{pmatrix} 0 & 1 & 2 \\ 1 & 2 & 0 \end{pmatrix} = (0\ 1\ 2)$, then $(0\ 1\ 2) = (0\ 1)(0\ 2)$.

Let $P(G)$ be the permutation of the quantum circuit G, and $P(g)$ be the permutation of the quantum gate g.

While quantum circuits usually work with left input and right output, we assume that the quantum circuit G has two quantum gates, $g1$ and $g2$, from left to right. Their corresponding permutations are $P(g1) = (0\,1)$ and $P(g2) = (0\,2)$, respectively, then the permutation of circuit G is $P(G) = P(g1\ g2) = P(g1)P(g2) = (0\,1)(0\,2) = (0\,1\,2)$. The advantage of this rule is that the order of multiply product of permutations is the same as the sequence order of quantum gates, so the permutation product in this article adopts the way of operation from left to right.

3 Synthesis Method of Barrel Shifters

3.1 Synthesis of the (3, 1) Shifter

We assume that the controlled shifter has one controlled value and three input values, that is (3, 1) shifter, then we can build the truth table of the circuit as shown in Table 1, the permutation is (9 10 12) (11 14 13). Then using our [10] literature method, the optimal 4-qubit circuit has been synthesized as shown in Fig. 4.

Table 1. Truth Table for (3, 1) Shifter

In					Out				
C	a	b	c	$(Cabc)_2$	C	b	c	a	$(Cbca)_2$
0	0	0	0	0	0	0	0	0	0
0	0	0	1	1	0	0	0	1	1
0	0	1	0	2	0	0	1	0	2
0	0	1	1	3	0	0	1	1	3
0	1	0	0	4	0	1	0	0	4
0	1	0	1	5	0	1	0	1	5
0	1	1	0	6	0	1	1	0	6
0	1	1	1	7	0	1	1	1	7
1	0	0	0	8	1	0	0	0	8
1	0	0	1	9	1	0	1	0	10
1	0	1	0	10	1	1	0	0	12
1	0	1	1	11	1	1	1	0	14
1	1	0	0	12	1	0	0	1	9
1	1	0	1	13	1	0	1	1	11
1	1	1	0	14	1	1	0	1	13
1	1	1	1	15	1	1	1	1	15

In Fig. 4, when $C = 0$, the output values are the same as the input values. But in Fig. 5, when $C = 1$, the input values are abc as well as the output values are bca, so the function of moving a bit left is realized, that is to say, b moves to a, c moves to b, and *a* moves to *c*, and we call this the line permutation of quantum circuit. It can be expressed as the permutation $\begin{pmatrix} a & b & c \\ b & c & a \end{pmatrix}$, or $(a\,b\,c)$. Based on the property of special quantum circuits with the line permutation, we present the novel efficient synthesis algorithm for these circuits.

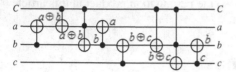

Fig. 4. Line permutation of (3, 1) shifter is *I* when *C* = 0.

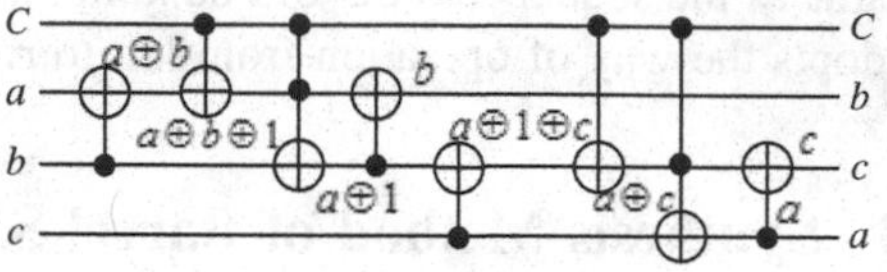

Fig. 5. Line permutation of (3, 1) shifter is $(a\,b\,c)$ when *C* = 1.

3.2 Synthesis of (*N*, 1) Shifter

If $n \geq 4$, the optimal $(n, 1)$ shifter was still difficult to be synthesized directly by the program, so we used the special rules of shifter and decomposition of permutation group to rapidly synthesize the shifter circuit.

If $n = 4$, that is the shifter performed a one-qubit left circular shifts on four input values. When the control qubit is set to 1, the shifter performs line permutation $(a\,b\,c\,d)$. Using the decomposition of group permutation, we will get $(a\,b\,c\,d) = (a\,b\,c)(a\,d)$, and we can achieve the permutation $(a\,b\,c)$ using the circuit in Fig. 5, and the permutation $(a\,d)$ could be realized by controlled swap gate. It is important to note that the value of line *a* is not *a* when swapping *a* and *d*, but the output value of line *c* is *a* after the permutation of $(a\,b\,c)$. After performing permutation $(a\,b\,c)$, permutation $(b\,c\,a)$ will be got, and the output value of line *c* is value *a*, which is as the * in the Fig. 6. Because if we swap line *d* and line *a*, but now the output value of line *a* is changed to value *b* as shown ^ in Fig. 6, if line *a* is used, then value *b* and value *d* will be exchanged, it cannot meet the requirements obviously. Therefore, the location of the input line at the current gate is determined by the input value of current gate, not necessarily by the name of the line.

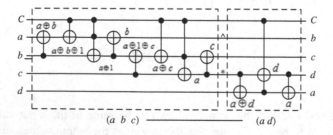

Fig. 6. Line permutation of (4, 1) shifter is $(a\,b\,c\,d)$ when *C* = 1.

In Fig. 6, the permutation of the front circuit is $(a\ b\ c)$, in which a corresponds to line a, b corresponds to line b, and c corresponds to line c, and it can be implemented using the circuit of Fig. 5. The permutation of the rear circuit is $(a\ d)$, namely swapping a and d, and it can be implemented using controlled swap gate.

The several of shifts should be implemented in the shifter. For example, when the inputs are $a\ b\ c\ d$, and their 2-qubit left circular shift is $\begin{pmatrix} a & b & c & d \\ c & d & a & b \end{pmatrix}$, their 3-qubit left circular shift is $\begin{pmatrix} a & b & c & d \\ d & a & b & c \end{pmatrix}$. Let the permutation be $\begin{pmatrix} a & b & c & d \\ a & d & b & c \end{pmatrix}$, whose circuit is seemingly different from other circuits, but it can be got using the line permutation of the circuit in Fig. 6 to reduce the complexity of the circuit synthesis greatly.

Example 1 , $\begin{pmatrix} a & b & c & d \\ c & d & a & b \end{pmatrix} = (a\quad c)(b\quad d)$ can be cascaded using two controlled swap gates. As shown in Fig. 7, since $(a\ c)$ and $(b\ d)$ have no the same elements, the front gate can't affect the rear gate.

Example 2 , $\begin{pmatrix} a & b & c & d \\ d & a & b & c \end{pmatrix} = (a\quad d\quad c\quad b) = (a\quad d\quad c)(a\quad b)$, it can be cascaded using the circuit in Fig. 5 and one controlled swap gate. As shown in Fig. 8, since $(a\ d\ c)$ and $(a\ b)$ have the same element a, the front circuit must affect the rear circuit. The circuit in Fig. 5 performs line permutation $(a\ b\ c)$, but we want to get line permutation $(a\ d\ c)$. This circuit can be got using the topological change of Fig. 5. That is, in Fig. 5, line b should be replaced by line d as well as line a and line c are not changed, the original d line can only be replaced by b line, finally the lines of the circuit are from top to bottom ordered as $abcd$, so line a and c, are kept in their original positions and line b is moved to the position of line d to obtain the desired circuit.

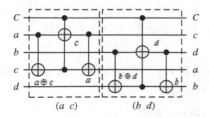
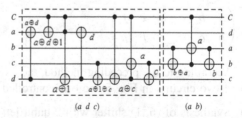

Fig. 7. Line permutation of Circuit is $(a\ c)$ $(b\ d)$ circuit when $C = 1$.

Fig. 8. Line permutation of Circuit is $(a\ d\ c)$ $(a\ b)$ circuit when $C = 1$

Example 3 , $\begin{pmatrix} a & b & c & d \\ a & d & b & c \end{pmatrix} = (a)(b \quad d \quad c) = (b \quad d \quad c)$, in the same way, in

Fig. 5, line a is moved to the position of line b, the original line b is moved to the position of line d, and line c remains the original position, then we get the circuit of $(b \; d \; c)$ as shown in Fig. 9.

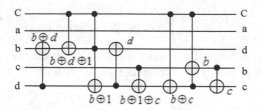

Fig. 9. Circuit of line permutation $(b \; d \; c)$ circuit when $C = 1$.

3.3 Synthesis of (N, K) Shifter

[9] gives that the minimum value of k in (n, k) barrel shifter is $\lceil \log(n) \rceil$. The design example of barrel shifter is given below that if $n = 6$ in (n, k) barrel shifter, then $\min(k) = \lceil \log(n) \rceil|_{n=6} = 3$.

Example 4 , synthesis of (6, 3) barrel shifter.

The barrel shifter has 6 inputs and outputs, and the minimum value of the control bits is 3, therefore it has at least 3 layers of (6, 1) shifters which implement 1-qubit, 2-qubit and 4-qubit left circular shift respectively, thus we can achieve all left circular shifts of six inputs using six kinds of combinations by three controlled qubits.

(1) Synthesis of (6, 1) shifter with 1-qubit left circular shift.

Let the input binary values be $(abcdef)_2$, which will be $(bcdefa)_2$ after performing 1-qubit left circular shift. The permutation is

$$\begin{pmatrix} a & b & c & d & e & f \\ b & c & d & e & f & a \end{pmatrix} = (a \quad b \quad c \quad d \quad e \quad f) = (a \quad b \quad c)(a \quad d \quad e)(a \quad f).$$

According to the preceding method, the circuit in Fig. 10 can be rapidly generated using two circuits in Fig. 5 and one controlled swap gate.

(2) Synthesis of (6, 1) shifter with 2-qubit left circular shift.

Let the input binary values be $(abcdef)_2$, which will be $(cdefab)_2$ after performing 2-qubit left circular shift. Let the input binary values be $(abcdef)_2$, which will be $(efabcd)_2$ after performing 4-qubit left circular shift. The permutation is

$$\begin{pmatrix} a & b & c & d & e & f \\ c & d & e & f & a & b \end{pmatrix} = (a \ c \ e)(b \ d \ f).$$ According to the preceding

method, the circuit in Fig. 11 can be rapidly generated using two circuits in Fig. 5.

(3) Synthesis of (6, 1) shifter with 4-qubit left circular shift. Let the input binary values be $(abcdef)_2$, which will be $(efabcd)_2$ after performing 4-qubit left circular shift.

The permutation is $\begin{pmatrix} a & b & c & d & e & f \\ e & f & a & b & c & d \end{pmatrix} = (a \ e \ c)(b \ f \ d)$, According to

the preceding method, the circuit in Fig. 12 can be rapidly generated using two circuits in Fig. 5.

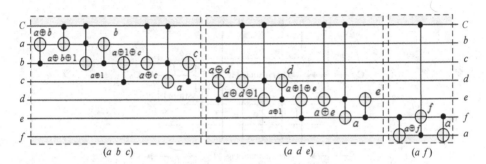

Fig. 10. (6, 1) shifter with 1-qubit left circular shift when $C = 1$.

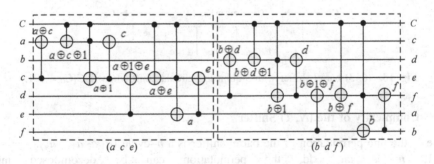

Fig. 11. (6, 1) shifter with 2-qubit left circular shift when $C = 1$.

The barrel shifter (6, 3) can be synthesized by cascading the circuits in Figs. 10, 11 and 12. In Fig. 13, the barrel shifter performs 5-qubit left circular shifter when the control value is $(C_2C_1C_0)_2 = (101)_2 = 5$. Thus the input binary values be $(abcdef)_2$, which will be $(efabcd)_2$ after performing 5-qubit left circular shift and the outputs binary values of the circuit.

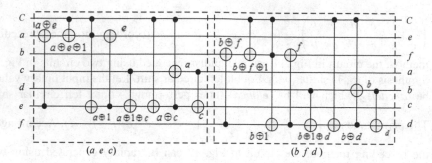

Fig. 12. (6, 1) shifter with 4-qubit left circular shift when $C = 1$.

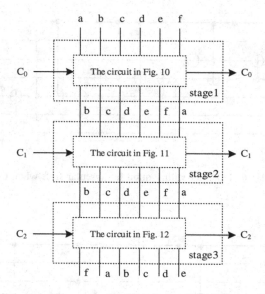

Fig. 13. (6, 3) barrel shifter with 5-qubit left circular shift when $C_2C_1C_0 = 101$.

3.4　Complexity of the $(N, 1)$ Shifter

Case 1: the line permutation of the barrel shifter is a n–cycle $(a_1 \, a_2 \, a_3 \dots a_n)$.

If n is an odd, the permutation can be decomposed into $(a_1 \, a_2 \, a_3)(a_1 \, a_4 \, a_5) \dots (a_1 \, a_{n-1} \, a_n)$. There is a repeating element a_1, and the permutation of every 3 elements can correspond to the circuit in Fig. 5, so the circuit can be synthesized by using $(n - 1)/2$ circuits in Fig. 5. The count of basic gates is

$$8 * (n - 1) / 2 = 4n - 4, \tag{1}$$

and the total of quantum cost is

$$(6 + 2^*5)\,(n - 1)\,/2 = 8n - 8. \tag{2}$$

If n is an even the permutation can be decomposed into $(a_1\,a_2\,a_3)(a_1\,a_4\,a_5)\ldots(a_1\,a_n)$. There is a repeating elements a_1, and the permutation of every 3 elements can correspond to the circuit in Fig. 5, so the circuit can be synthesized by using one controlled swap gate and $(n - 2)/2$ circuits in Fig. 5. The count of basic gates is

$$3 + 8^*(n - 2)/2 = 4n - 5, \tag{3}$$

and the total quantum cost is

$$(1 + 5 + 1) + (6 + 2^*5)\,(n - 2)/2 = 8n - 9. \tag{4}$$

Therefore, the worst case is the first. That is, the total number of basic gates is $4n$-4, and the total quantum cost is $8n - 8$.

Case 2: the line permutation of the barrel shifter is the product of m-cylcle $(a_1\,a_2\,a_3\ldots a_m)$ and $(n-m)$–cycle $(b_1\,b_2\,b_3\ldots a_{n-m})$. From the worst case of (1) and (3), the maximum amount of basic gates is

$$(4m - 4) + (4\,(n - m) - 4) = 4n - 8, \tag{5}$$

and from the worst case of (2) and (4), the maximum of the total quantum cost is

$$(8m - 8) + (8\,(n - m) - 8) = 8n - 16. \tag{6}$$

Comparing (3) with (5), and (4) with (6), we get that the more the line permutation is decomposed into cycles, the more the count of basic gates and total quantum cost can be reduced, so the maximum of the count of basic gates in the $(n, 1)$ shifter is

$$4n - 4, \tag{7}$$

and the maximum of the total quantum cost is

$$8n - 8. \tag{8}$$

3.5   Complexity of the (N, K) Barrel Shifter

As we know that $\min(k) = \lceil \log(n) \rceil$, and from (7), the maximum of the count of basic gates in the (n, k) barrel shifter is $\lceil \log(n) \rceil (4n - 4)$, And from (8), the maximum of the total quantum cost is $\lceil \log(n) \rceil (8n - 8)$.

3.6   Design of the (3, 1) Barrel Shifter for Other Displacement Types

Rotate left through carry is equivalent to using carry CF as the highest bit of Operand (that is, merge together), then rotation left shift. And this function can be realized in Fig. 6.

Rotation right shift is the right loop to move the specified number of figures. Arithmetic left shift or logic left shift is to move the assigned number to the left in turn, and then add 0 to the right. The arithmetic right shift is to move the assigned number to the right in turn, and then make up with the original symbol on the left side. The logical right shift is to move the assigned number to the right in turn, and then add 0 on the left.

In Figs. 14, 16, 18 and 20 when $C' = 0$, the output values are the same as the input values.

But in Fig. 15, when $C' = 1$, the input values are abc as well as the output values are cab, so the function of moving a bit rotation right is realized.

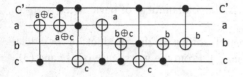

Fig. 14. Line permutation of (3, 1) rotation right shifter is I when $C' = 0$.

Fig. 15. Line permutation of (3, 1) rotation right shifter is $(a\ b\ c)$ when $C' = 1$.

Note that In Figs. 16, 17, 18, 19, 20 and 21, line 0 is an ancillary line.

In Fig. 17, when $C' = 1$, the input values are abc as well as the output values are $bc0$, so the function of moving a bit arithmetic left, as well as logical left is realized.

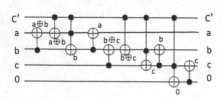

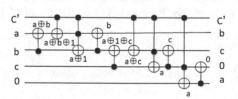

Fig. 16. Line permutation of (3, 1) arithmetic left, logical left shifter is I when $C' = 0$.

Fig. 17. Line permutation of (3, 1) arithmetic left, logical left shifter is $(a\ b\ c)$ when $C' = 1$.

In Fig. 19, when $C' = 1$, the input values are abc as well as the output values are aab, so the function of moving a bit arithmetic right is realized.

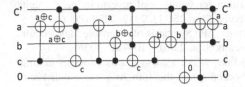

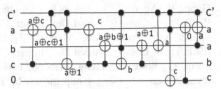

Fig. 18. Line permutation of (3, 1) arithmetic right shifter is I when $C' = 0$.

Fig. 19. Line permutation of (3, 1) arithmetic right shifter is $(a\ b\ c)$ when $C' = 1$.

In Fig. 21, when $C' = 1$, the input values are abc as well as the output values are $0ab$, so the function of moving a bit logical right is realized.

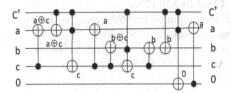

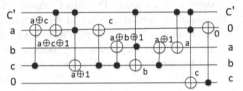

Fig. 20. Line permutation of (3, 1) logical right shifter is I when $C' = 0$.

Fig. 21. Line permutation of (3, 1) logical right shifter is $(a\ b\ c)$ when $C' = 1$.

4 Conclusion

In this article, we mainly give the ways on qubit left circular shifts, bit permutation and line permutations, and other types of basic shift circuits are also designed. In reversible shifter, we build large shifter circuits using small shifter circuits based on the decomposition of permutation group. This method can reduce the quantum gates count and the quantum cost, and it also can improve efficiency of the algorithm. We can set the control lines to 0 or 1 based on request in the barrel shifter, that is, it can output the desired shift result.

Acknowledgment. This work is supported by the Natural Science Foundation of Jiangsu Province (Grant No. BK20171458).

References

1. Feynman, R.P.: Quantum mechanical computers. Found. Phys. **16**(6), 507–531 (1986)
2. Fredkin, E., Toffoli, T.: Conservative logic. Int. J. Theor. Phys. **21**(3–4), 219–253 (1982)
3. Vedral, V.V., Barenco, A., Ekert, A.: Quantum networks for elementary arithmetic operations. Phys. Rev. Atom. Mol. Opt. Phys. **54**(1), 147 (1996)
4. Maslov, D., Dueck, G.W., Miller, D.M.: Toffoli network synthesis with templates. IEEE Trans. Comput. Aided Des. Integr. Circuits Syst. **24**(6), 807–817 (2005)

5. Gupta, P., Agrawal, A., Jha, N.K.: An algorithm for synthesis of reversible logic circuits. IEEE Trans. Comput. Aided Des. Integr. Circuits Syst. **25**(11), 2317–2330 (2006)
6. Shende, V.V., Prasad, A.K., Markov, I.L., Hayes, J.P.: Synthesis of reversible logic circuits. IEEE Trans. Comput. Aided Des. Integr. Circuits Syst. **22**(6), 710–722 (2006)
7. Yang, G., Song, X., Hung, W.N.N., Perkowski, M.A.: Fast synthesis of exact minimal reversible circuits using group theory. In: Proceedings of the 10th Asia and South Pacific Design Automation Conference, vol. 2, pp. 18–21 (2005)
8. Li, Z., Chen, H., Xu, B., Liu, W.: Fast algorithm for 4-qubit reversible logic circuits synthesis. In: Evolutionary Computation, vol. 36, pp. 2202–2207. IEEE (2008)
9. Thapliyal, H., Bhatt, A., Ranganathan, N.: A new CRL gate as super class of fredkin gate to design reversible quantum circuits. In: Midwest Symposium on Circuits & Systems, pp. 1067–1070 (2013)
10. Li, Z., Chen, H., Yang, G., Liu, W.: Efficient algorithms for optimal 4-bit reversible logic system synthesis. J. Appl. Math. **2013**, 289–325 (2013)
11. Gaur, H.M., Singh, A.K., Ghanekar, U.: In-depth comparative analysis of reversible gates for designing logic circuits. Procedia Comput. Sci. **125**, 810–817 (2018)
12. Handique, M., Sonkar, A.: An extended approach for mapping reversible circuits to quantum circuits using ncv-$|v1\rangle$ library. Procedia Comput. Sci. **125**, 832–839 (2018)
13. Wang, Y., Shen, X., Zhou, Y.: Design method for reversible shift register based on reversible flip flop. J. Nanjing Univ. Aeronaut. Astronaut. **46**(4), 537–555 (2014)

Text Coverless Information Hiding Based on Word2vec

Yi Long and Yuling Liu[✉]

College of Computer Science and Electronic Engineering, Hunan University,
Changsha 410082, Hunan Province, China
longyi_@hnu.edu.cn , yuling_liu@126.com

Abstract. Coverless information hiding does not make any modifications to the carrier, so it can effectively resist the various steganalysis and detection algorithms. However, the existing methods still have some problems that include low hiding capacity and unsatisfactory hiding success rate. To address these problems, this paper proposes a method of text coverless information hiding based on word2vec. The method uses distance algorithm provided by word2vec to obtain similar keywords, then utilize similar keywords to enlarge the set of keywords, finally retrieve the stego-texts that contains the combination of the location tags and the keywords. The experimental results and analysis show that the method can ensure the hiding success rate of 100%, and the hiding capacity is 2.87.

Keywords: Text coverless information hiding · Word2vec
Text big data · Similar keywords · Location tag

1 Introduction

As a branch of the security field, information hiding plays a crucial role in data communication. It mainly uses the redundancy of covers such as texts, images, videos and audios to execute hiding [1]. Texts are the important media of communication for human beings, so many information hiding methods are based on text hide information. The early hiding methods based on text format mainly hide information by changing the character space, inserting invisible characters, and modifying the format of documents [2–4]. Some methods are proposed by modifying text content [5,6]. Some hiding methods hide information by modifying the text image [7–9]. Because these hiding methods modify the carrier, they are hard to resist the detection of steganalysis tools [10–12]. In theory, as long as the covers are modified, the secret information will certainly be detected. To avoid modifying the covers, a novel method called coverless information hiding is proposed. The main idea of the method is that it can directly retrieve the covers containing the secret message. Different from the traditional hiding schemes, the proposed method can hide without the modifying the covers. It can effectively protect the security of the information, so it has been developed rapidly.

© Springer Nature Switzerland AG 2018
X. Sun et al. (Eds.): ICCCS 2018, LNCS 11066, pp. 463–472, 2018.
https://doi.org/10.1007/978-3-030-00015-8_40

Based on Chinese mathematical expression, the coverless information hiding method is proposed [13]. It directly generate the stego-vector, then retrieve the covers that contain secret message in the text big data. A method based on the rank map of the words is proposed [14], but only the single word in each stego-text can be sent to the receiver without any modification. By using the frequent words distance, a method of based on hash and word rank map is proposed [15]. In this method, an stego-text can hide only one secret keyword. To solve this problem, a hiding method based on multi-keywords is proposed [16]. The main idea of the method is that the number of keywords will be hidden in the texts with the keywords. However, its hiding success rate is very low. A natural language coverless information hiding scheme is proposed by introducing the active learning based on named entity recognition [17]. The method uses entity recognition system to mark the location of the keywords, then retrieves the secret message by rank algorithm. A coverless information hiding method by the Chinese Character encoding is proposed [18]. In this method, the Chinese characters are transformed into a binary number to locate. Reference [19] proposes a way to retrieve the Web Text Big Data, the undetectability of the method is greatly improved. Moreover, many coverless information methods for image are presented. For instance, reference [20] divides image into several nonoverlapping blocks, then mapped image blocks to secret information by image hashing. Reference [21] introduces a hiding framework based on scale invariant feature transform (SIFT) and bag of feature (BOF) model. Reference [22] constructs a robust image hash with SIFT algorithm to hide the secret data.

From above, we can see that the coverless information hiding methods have made a lot of achievements. However, there are still some problems such as low hiding capacity, unsatisfying success rate. In order to overcome these flaws while ensuring the security and anti-steganalysis, a coverless information hiding method based on word2vec is proposed [23,24]. In this paper, the original keyword is replaced by similar keyword when cannot retrieve stego-texts in text big data. This method improves the capacity, and the meaning of secret information without changing anything. The success rate is 100%, and the mismatch rate is low in texts. Experimental results show that the method will not leave any modification trace in texts, and it is robust for current steganalysis tools. It improves the hiding capacity and hiding success rate.

The rest of this paper is organized as follows. Section 2 performs the framework of text coverless information hiding. Section 3 describes information hiding and extract algorithms. Section 4 shows performance analysis and experimental results, and the conclusions are presented in Sect. 5.

2   Text Coverless Information Hiding

The method dose not any modify natural texts, and does not need additional covers. It divides the secret messages into several keywords, and converts them, then generates the combinations of converted keywords and location tags, finally retrieves the texts that contains the combinations in text big data. Figure 1 shows the hiding process.

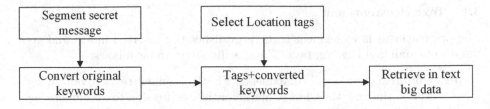

Fig. 1. The hiding process

In the hiding process, word conversion is used to convert keywords. This step is to protect the security of information, but the extracting is very difficult. The location tags is used to mark the location of the keywords. In terms of location tags, it should satisfy randomness, universality, and distinguishability [13]. The existing methods mainly have the word rank map [14], the entity recognition system [17] and the Chinese character encoding [18]. Furthermore, a method called Chinese mathematical expression is applied to describe the Chinese character. Every character can be processed as combination of components according to six spatial relations [13]. By decomposing Chinese characters into some components, the position of the Chinese keyword behind the component is determined.

3   Proposed Method

Coverless information hiding use the location tags and text big data to hide information. Different from the method by Chen [13], we remove the step of word conversion and use word2vec to enlarge the keywords. The framework of the method is shown in Fig. 2, and the details are introduced as follow:

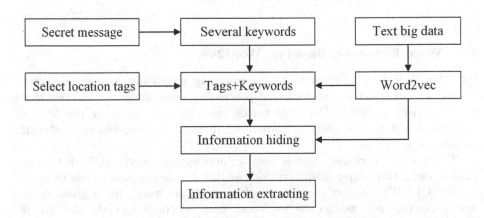

Fig. 2. The framework of our method

3.1 Text Pretreatment

The pretreatment is to segment texts, establishes the inverted index, and gets the set of candidate location tags. The specific steps are as follows:

Step 1. Obtain keywords and components. Firstly, segment texts to obtain keywords, then use the Chinese mathematical expression to decompose keywords to get components. Supposed that the combination of location tag l and keyword w is denoted as $C = \{c_i | i = 1, 2, \cdots\}$, where $c_i = l_i + w_i$.

Step 2. Eliminate redundancy. Except the first keyword, all components of the previous keyword w_{i-1} are the location tags of keyword w_i ,which are denoted as $L_{w_i} = \{l_1, l_2, \cdots\}$.

    (a) Check each tag l_i, $l_i \in L_{w_i}$. If l_i is not occupied by another keyword, let it be the located tag of keyword w_i. Otherwise, if the corresponding keyword w' has additional tag, delete l_i from $L_{w'}$, and l_i is the tag of the keyword w_i, if not, delete l_i from L_{w_i}.

    (b) If several tags are not used, assign these tags to keywords in order.

Step 3. Build inverted index. The index structure is shown as Table 1.

Step 4. For each component, count the number of keywords that can be located in text big data, and rank the statistical results in descending order. Select top N components as the candidate tags and rearrange them by the receiver's key.

Table 1. The index structure

Index entry	Path of texts
tag+keyword	text1, text2, text3, ...

3.2 Word Expansion Based on Word2vec

Word2vec is a very efficient tool for converting words into real-value vectors [23,24]. It can transform text content processing into simple vector operations by using deep learning. The word vector can represent words in the form of vectors, and it has excellent performances in machine translation, clustering, recommendation system.

There are two training models and two accelerating methods, both training models use a three-layer neural network model. In the continuous bag of words model (CBOW), context is represented by multiple words for a given target words. For instance, we can use "cat" and "tree" as context words, and "climb" is regarded as the target word. It removes the most time-consuming nonlinear hidden layer, so it's relatively fast. On the contrary, Skip-Gram model reverses the use of target and context words. It reflects the true meaning of the sentence, improves the accuracy of training, also has better support for rare words. For both models, word2vec has two frameworks: hierarchical softmax and negative sampling. Negative sampling method is sampling randomly, its training is more efficient. Another way do convert words with Huffman coding is relatively slow, but the word vector is more accurate. In order to ensure the accuracy of secret message, we use Skip-Gram model and training methods with higher level of acceleration. The steps of expansion as follow:

Step 1. Train all texts, and obtain a file that stores the word vector information for each word in the dictionary.

Step 2. Calculate the similarity of words by using the distance algorithm provided by word2vec, and obtain the similar keywords for each word.

3.3   Information Hiding

The key of coverless information hiding is to retrieve a suitable cover which contains secret message. Firstly, we segment the secret message into a sequence of keywords. Secondly, we obtain the candidate location tags according to the key of receiver, and assign the location tags for keywords. Then, we search the natural texts in the text big data. Finally, we send stego-texts to the recipient in order. Figure 3 shows the specified process.

Step 1. Secret message is segmented into keyword sequences, denoted as $K = \{k_i | i = 1, 2, \cdots, l\}$, l is the amount of keywords.

Step 2. Select location tags based on the recipient's key, the location tags denoted as $L = \{l_i | i = 1, 2, \cdots, n\}$. Then assign tags to keywords in order, $H = \{h_i | i = 1, 2, \cdots, l\}$, denoted these combinations, where $h_i = l_i + k_i$, if $l > n$, the tag collection will be used continuously.

Step 3. Apply word2vec to obtain the set of similar keywords SK of k_i, $SK = \{sk_j | j = 1, 2, \cdots, m\}$, where m is the amount of the similar keywords.

Step 4. Retrieve the set of texts that contain h_i in text big data, denoted as T_i . If T_i is null, get the similar keywords for k_i, then retrieve the text collection that contains $l_i + sk_j$, if the retrieve is failed, the keyword will be split into k_1 and k_2, then retrieve the corresponding tags, if it still fails means that the keyword will is mismatched. If the text collection can be found, execute Step 5.

Step 5. Retrieve the next combination in texts T_i, get the text set T_i', if T_i' is null, the keyword is replaced by sk_j, then search for replacement combinations. Otherwise, search for the next combination and record the successful times until failed.

Step 6. Repeat Step 4 and Step 5 until all the keywords are hidden. In order to extract accurately, select the stego-texts by making a pre-extraction.

Step 7. Send the stego-texts in order.

3.4   Information Extraction

The recipient receives the stego-texts and extracts the information according to the key. The specific step is shown as follows, Fig. 4 shows the process of the extraction algorithm.

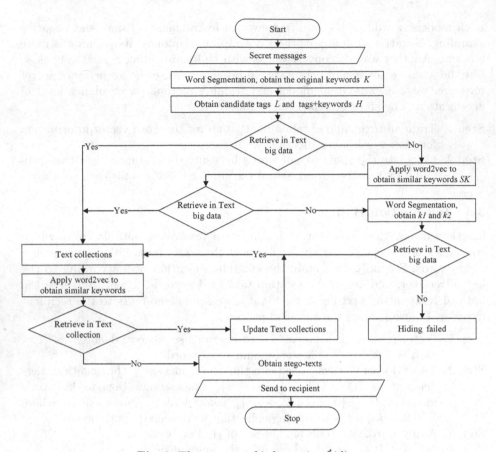

Fig. 3. The process of information hiding

Step 1. Preprocess the stego-texts by the same steps as Sect. 3.1, and obtain the set of combination $H = \{h_i | i = 1, 2, \cdots \}$.

Step 2. Use the key to confirm the candidate tags $L_c = \{l_i | i = 1, 2, \cdots, N_1\}$.

Step 3. Retrieve the hidden keywords according to the corresponding combinations, execute semantic analysis of two adjacent keywords. If not idiomatic, save the extracted keywords.

Step 4. Generate the candidate secret information by Step 3. Combine the language analysis with Chinese grammar, obtain the secret messages.

4   Experiment and Analysis

In this section, all experiments have been done in Eclipse and Pycharm. The secret messages are adopted mainly from the Chinese corpus of Sogou Lab [25], their size is 1~6 KB. The size of large-scale text big data is 10.2 GB, and texts are mainly derived from crawling and downloading on the web. In order to make

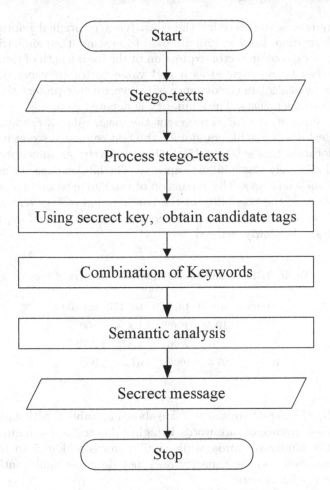

Fig. 4. The process of information extraction

the experiment more convincing, we tested the results under different parameters that include the number of candidate tags and the size of text. We have used the following evaluation indicators to measure the performance, which are hiding success rate, hiding capacity and accuracy rate. Assume the amount of secret keyword is l, and the number of hidden Chinese characters in each text is m. The capacity ϵ is denoted by formula (1):

$$\epsilon = \frac{l}{m} \tag{1}$$

Supposed that c is the amount of failed keyword, the success rate σ is represented by formula (2):

$$\sigma = 1 - \frac{c}{l} \tag{2}$$

The accuracy rate is to determine the consistency of original information and extracted information. Doc2vec [26] are used to measure their similarity. Similar to Word2vec, it can obtain vector expression of the fixed length of the document. A document can be represented as a real value vector by using this scheme. Therefore, we can calculate the distance of the vector to represent the similarity between the two documents. The similarity is denoted as α.

In our experiment, the $\bar{\epsilon}, \bar{\sigma}, \bar{\alpha}$ represent the mean value of ϵ, σ and α respectively. We select a set of 20 files randomly, the text context is secret information. The size of location tags is 50,100,150,200 respectively. As shown in Table 2. It has high and relatively stable hiding capacity. The hidden capacity decreases as the range of labels increases. The expansion of random location tags makes some of the tags rare, so the possibility of the combination of tags and keywords is reduced. It is more difficult to retrieve the combination. Therefore, the hidden capacity will also be slowly reduced.

Table 2. The result of the different numbers of tags

Number	top50	top100	top150	top200
$\bar{\sigma}$	100%	100%	100%	100%
$\bar{\epsilon}$	2.97	2.96	2.87	2.79
$\bar{\alpha}$	97%	98%	97%	98%

The results of different sizes of text are shown in Table 3. Although the probability of the occurrence of rare words is higher due to the increasing text size, we can retrieve similar keywords, while similar words seldom exist in the same text with rare words, so the capacity does not decrease significantly, but the accuracy rate is slightly lower.

Table 3. The result of the different size of hidden texts

KB	1	2	3	4	5	6
$\bar{\sigma}$	100%	100%	100%	100%	100%	100%
$\bar{\epsilon}$	2.81	2.71	3.11	2.25	2.44	2.93
$\bar{\alpha}$	98%	98%	98%	99%	99%	97%

As shown in the tables above, the hiding success rate is 100% due to we made a similar treatment to individual keywords. This result is basically in line with the theoretical analysis. Certainly, the method will fail when the specific keyword is not existed in the text big data. But if not, we can always find similar word to replace the keyword. Therefore, the keyword will be hidden successfully and the hiding success rate is 100%.

According to the results of experiment, the mean capacity are calculated. The hiding capacity and the hiding success rate are compared with [13]. Table 4 shows the result. That shows that our method can enhance the capacity and improve the hiding success rate to some extent.

Table 4. The result of comparing the two methods

Methods	Mean capacity	Hiding success rate
Literature [13]	2.11	97%
Our Method	2.87	100%

5   Conclusion

This paper proposed a novel method of coverless information hiding based on word2vec. The method makes use of Chinese character components as the location tags, and retrieve stego-texts that contains keywords in text big data. Furthermore, The method obtains similar keywords by using word2vec, the keyword can be used to replace the similar words when the texts retrieval fails. The method not only ensured the 100% hiding success rate, but also improved the hiding capacity. Compared with the existing coverless information hiding methods, the results of extraction have advantages in performance. However, the hidden capacity is still difficult to meet the actual demand, which needs to be further studied in the future.

References

1. Cox, I., Miller, M.: The first 50 years of electronic watermarking. J. Appl. Signal Proc. **2**, 126–132 (2002)
2. Brassil, J., Low, S., Maxemchuk, N., Gorman, L.: Electronic marking and identification techniques to discourage document copying. J. IEEE J. Sel. Areas Commun. **13**, 1495–1504 (1994)
3. Low, S., Maxemchuk, N.: Performance comparison of two text marking methods. J. Sel. Areas Commun. **16**, 561–572 (1998)
4. Brassil, J., Low, S., Maxemchuk, N.: Copyright protection for the electronic distribution of text documents. Proc. IEEE **87**, 1181–1196 (1999)
5. Nematollahi, M.A., Al-Haddad, S.A.R.: An overview of digital speech watermarking. Int. J. Speech Technol. **16**, 471–488 (2013)
6. Mali M.L., Patil N.N., Patil J.B.: Implementation of text watermarking technique using natural language. In: IEEE International Conference on Communication Systems and Network Technologies, pp. 482–486 (2013)
7. Satir, E., Isik, H.: A compression-based text steganography method. J. Syst. Softw. **85**, 2385–2394 (2012)

8. Xia, Z.H., Wang, S.H., Sun, X.M., Wang, J.: Print-scan resilient watermarking for the chinese text image. Int. J. Grid Distrib. Comput. **6**, 51–62 (2013)
9. Daraee, F., Mozaffari, S.: Watermarking in binary document images using fractal codes. Pattern Recogn. Lett. **35**, 120–129 (2014)
10. Sui XG, Luo H.: A steganalysis method based on the distribution of space characters. In: Proceedings of IEEE International Conference on Communications, Circuits and Systems, pp. 54–56 (2006)
11. Meng, P., Huang, L.S., Yang, W.: Attacks on translation based steganography. In: IEEE Youth Conference on Information, Computing and Telecommunication, Beijing, China, pp. 227–230 (2009)
12. Goyal, L., Raman, M., Diwan, P.: A robust method for integrity protection of digital data in text document watermarking. Int. J. Innovative Res. Sci. Technol. **1**, 14–18 (2014)
13. Chen, X., Sun, H., Tobe, Y., Zhou, Z., Sun, X.: Coverless information hiding method based on the Chinese mathematical expression. In: 1st International Conference on Cloud Computing and Security, Nanjing China (2015)
14. Zhang, J., Shen, J., Wang, L., et al.: Coverless text information hiding method based on the word rank map. In: International Conference on Cloud Computing and Security. Nanjing China, pp. 145–155 (2016)
15. Zhang, J., Xie, Y., Wang, L., Lin, H.: Coverless text information hiding method using the frequent words distance. In: 3rd International Conference on Cloud Computing and Security, pp. 121–132 (2017)
16. Zhou, Z., Mu, Y., Zhao, N., et al.: Coverless information hiding method based on multi-keywords. In: International Conference on Cloud Computing and Security. Nanjing, China, pp. 39–47 (2016)
17. Grishman, S.H.R., Wang, Y.: Active learning based named entity recognition and its application in natural language coverless information hiding. the. J. Internet Technol. **18**, 443–451 (2017)
18. Xia, Z.H., Xuan, L.: Coverless information hiding method based on LSB of the character's unicode. J. Internet Technol. **18**, 1353–1360 (2017)
19. Shi, S.W., Qi, Y.N., Huang, Y.F.: An approach to text steganography based on search in internet. In: International Computer Symposium (ICS), pp. 227–232 (2016)
20. Zhou, Z., Sun, H., Harit, R., Chen, X., Sun, X.: Coverless image steganography without embedding. In: Huang, Z., Sun, X., Luo, J., Wang, J. (eds.) ICCCS 2015. LNCS, vol. 9483, pp. 123–132. Springer, Cham (2015). https://doi.org/10.1007/978-3-319-27051-7_11
21. Yuan, C.S., Xia, Z.H., Sun, X.M.: Coverless image steganography based on SIFT and BOF. J. Internet Technol. **18**, 435–442 (2017)
22. Zheng, S., Wang, L., Ling, B., Hu, D.: Coverless information hiding based on robust image hashing. In: Huang, D.-S., Hussain, A., Han, K., Gromiha, M.M. (eds.) ICIC 2017. LNCS (LNAI), vol. 10363, pp. 536–547. Springer, Cham (2017). https://doi.org/10.1007/978-3-319-63315-2_47
23. Mikolov, T., Chen, K., Corrado, G., et al.: Efficient Estimation of Word Representations in Vector Space. arXiv:1301.3781.(2013)
24. Mikolov, T., Sutskever, I., Chen, K., Corrado, G., Dean, J.: Distributed Representations of Words and Phrases and their Compositionality. arXiv.1301.4546 (2013)
25. http://download.labs.sogou.com (2016)
26. Le, Q.V., Mikolov, T.: Distributed Representations of Sentences and Documents. arXiv:1405.4053 (2014)

Text Information Hiding Method
Using the Custom Components

Jianjun Zhang[1,2(✉)], Yicheng Xie[2], Jun Shen[1], Lucai Wang[2], and Haijun Lin[2]

[1] College of Computer Science and Electronic Engineering, Hunan University,
Changsha 410080, China
jianjun998@163.com, 842166947@qq.com
[2] College of Engineering and Design, Hunan Normal University, Changsha 410081, China
1431330481@qq.com, wlucai9776@vip.sina.com,
linhaijun801028@126.com

Abstract. Open Office Xml (OOX) is the Microsoft Office document format type, which has been widely used in the world. It is of great significance to research the OOX document information hiding technology. In this paper, a text information hiding algorithm was proposed. The proposed method used OOX document custom components to hide secret information. Because the custom component was not referenced by the main document, the content and format of the main document have not been modified. In addition, since the information hiding process does not cause any change in the content and semantics of the displayed text in the document, it can resist content-based attacks, semantics-based attacks, and format-based attacks.

Keywords: Text information hiding · Custom components · OOX

1 Introduction

Information Hiding, also known as Steganography, can be informally defined as an application that is not detectably passing secret information in a carrier object [1]. This technology mainly uses the redundancy of the digital signal such as texts [2], images [3, 4], and videos [5] to achieve information hiding. Steganography can be used for intellectual property protection [6]. For example, reference [7, 8] introduced two methods of detecting illegal copies of copyrighted images. Since the text is frequently used in people's daily lives, text information hiding has attracted many researchers' interest [9]. Classified by the covers, text steganography could be put into main three types: text format-based [10–12], generating-based and embedding-based natural language information hiding.

Today, Microsoft's office document is one of the most widely used types of text documents in the world [13]. It is of great significance to research the OOX document information hiding technology. Microsoft's previous office documents used a composite document structure [14], such as office97, offcie2003, and so on. This form of composite documents uses binary forms for document storage and does not meet market demands such as "swiftly extracting relevant business information from text and data exchange

X. Sun et al. (Eds.): ICCCS 2018, LNCS 11066, pp. 473–484, 2018.
https://doi.org/10.1007/978-3-030-00015-8_41

between heterogeneous applications". As a result, Microsoft released Office Open XML (OOX), a new document format based on eXtensible Markup Language (XML), which solves the above problems. XML is a simple, flexible text format that is commonly used for extensive data exchange on the Internet. Therefore, this new document format enhances file and data management capabilities, data recovery capabilities, and interoperability with line-of-business systems, among others [15]. The OOX document format is compatible with the Open Document Format (ODF) and the Unified Office Document Format (UOF), and became the European Organization of Computer Manufacturers (ECMA) standard in December 2006 and the International Organization for Standardization (ISO) standard in 2008.

In this paper, a text information hiding algorithm was proposed. The proposed method used OOX document custom components for information hiding. By adding a custom component in the OOX document and then writing the encrypted secret information to the XmlTextWriter object tag in the custom component, the secret information is hidden in the OOX document. Because the custom component is not referenced in the main document component of the OOX document, the information hiding process does not produce visual differences or changes, and the secret information has better concealment. At the same time, because the custom component is not referenced by the main document, the content and format of the main document have not been modified. In addition, since the information hiding process does not cause any change in the content and semantics of the displayed text in the document, it can resist content-based attacks, semantics-based attacks, and format-based attacks.

2 Proposed Method

2.1 OOX Documents

OOX documents use ZIP compression technology to store documents, and all the contents of the documents are stored in a ZIP container, which follows the XML reference architecture. The OOX document structure is shown in Fig. 1. It can be seen from Fig. 1 that the OOX file container contains custom defined XML, embedded code or macros, charts, audio and video, and file contents. These file contents are stored separately as a single ZIP component in the entire file. The specific structure of an OOX document file is shown in Fig. 2. It can be seen from Fig. 2 that the OOX document file is composed of a series of collections called "parts", such as docProps, media, theme, etc., which describe the attributes of documents, multimedia and theme, etc. Most of them are XML data used to describe application data, metadata, and custom data. There are also some components used to describe the relationship between components and components, such as _rels components. The relationship specifies how the collection of parts is bound together in a document, and this method specifies how the source and destination parts are connected. In this way, a series of components compose the content of the OOX document, and the relationship describes how the document content is organized together [15].

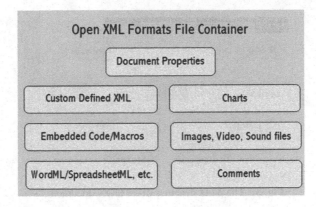

Fig. 1. The open XML formats file container.

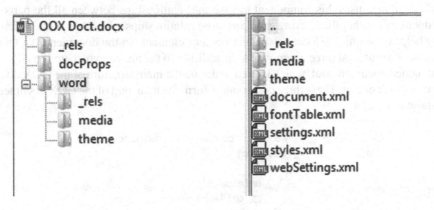

Fig. 2. The directory structure of an OOX document.

2.2 The Design of the Information Hiding Method

An OOX document is stored as a container (compressed package) that contains all the components used in the document. This container is a ZIP archive that can be opened with a ZIP program to access each component. The OOX document's component structure is shown in Fig. 3. It can be seen from Fig. 3 that the components in the OOX document have font tables, styles, footers, and headers, and can also include custom components of the type "Custom XML." The internal structure of the OOXML document is composed of many components. Each component has its own function. It also provides an interface for adding custom components and can add arbitrary data information. The information hiding method based on the custom component is to hide the secret information by adding a custom component to the OOX document. The added CustomXML component only plays the function of hiding the information. It does not play an actual role in the document and has a good concealment and reliability.

In the root directory of the ZIP archive, there is a component (file) named [Content_Types].xml. This file stores the file content types in other parts of the entire

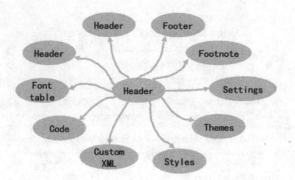

Fig. 3. The parts structure of an OOX document.

archive, such as pictures, sounds, videos, etc. Another very important part is _rels. The OOX document uses this component to save the relationships between all the parts of the document, rather than having each part store relationships with other parts, which is very helpful for quickly locating specific content elements in the document. An OOX document has at least three components. In addition to the above two, there is a component named document.xml, which is used to define the main structure of the OOX document display content. These three components form the main part of the OOX document, as shown in Fig. 4.

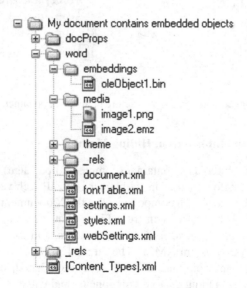

Fig. 4. The important parts structure of an OOX document.

The document.xml component defines the type, target storage location, font, and other styles of the document display content. An example is shown in Fig. 5. This document.xml file contains a picture, and it defines the type, ID, storage location, and the name of the picture. When the application opens the OOX document, it first reads the document.xml component and uses the _rels component to find the association between the displayed content based on the type of the [Content_Types].xml component definition, so that the display content is normally presented to the user. The information hiding method based on the custom component adds a custom component to the OOX document, but does not associate the added custom component in the _rels component, so the custom component is not displayed when the document content is finally presented to the user. The purpose of information hiding is achieved.

```
xmlns:wpc="http://schemas.microsoft.com/office/word/2010/wordprocessingCanvas">
- <w:body>
  - <w:p w:rsidRDefault="004F54DC" w:rsidR="00476A68">
    - <w:r>
        <w:t>T</w:t>
      </w:r>
    - <w:r>
      - <w:rPr>
          <w:rFonts w:hint="eastAsia"/>
        </w:rPr>
        <w:t xml:space="preserve">his </w:t>
      </w:r>
    - <w:r>
        <w:t>is an example.</w:t>
      </w:r>
  </w:p>
  - <w:p w:rsidRDefault="00A221AB" w:rsidR="00A221AB">
      <w:bookmarkStart w:name="_GoBack" w:id="0"/>
    - <w:r>
      - <w:rPr>
          <w:noProof/>
        </w:rPr>
      - <w:drawing>
        - <wp:inline distR="0" distL="0" distB="0" distT="0">
            <wp:extent cy="5600700" cx="5274310"/>
            <wp:effectExtent r="2540" b="0" t="0" l="0"/>
            <wp:docPr name="picture 1" id="1"/>
          - <wp:cNvGraphicFramePr>
              <a:graphicFrameLocks noChangeAspect="1" xmlns:a="http://schemas.openxmlformats.org/drawingml/2006/main"/>
            </wp:cNvGraphicFramePr>
          - <a:graphic xmlns:a="http://schemas.openxmlformats.org/drawingml/2006/main">
```

Fig. 5. The document.xml file of an OOX document.

2.3 The Algorithms of Information Hiding and Extracting

2.3.1 Information Hiding Algorithm

>   **Input:** An OOX document--- C, Secret Information--- M,
>   Encryption Algorithm--- E, Key--- k.
>   **Output:** Stego-text--- S.

>   STEP 1:
>   Encrypt the secret information M by using E and k, and let $M' = E(M,k)$.
>   STEP 2:
>   Convert M' to the hexadecimal format and let it is H. $H = H_1 H_2 \cdots H_i \cdots$, in which H_i is a hexadecimal number.
>   STEP 3:
>   Open the compressed package of C, and locate to the MainDocument component.
>   STEP 4:
>   Create a new CustomXML part for the MainDocument component, and create a new XmlTextWriter object.
>   STEP 5:
>   Write H to the new XmlTextWriter object.
>   STEP 6:
>   Recompress each component to form a new compressed package, and let it be S and store it.
>   STEP 7:
>   Output S.

2.3.2   Information Extracting Algorithm

Input: Stego-text (OOX document) ---S, Decryption Algorithm--- D, Key--- k.
Output: Secret Information--- M.

STEP 1:
Open the compressed package of S, and locate to the MainDocument component.
STEP 2:
Locate to the XmlTextWriter object of the CustomXML part in the MainDocument component.
STEP 3:
Get the label value of the XmlTextWriter object, and let it be H.
STEP 4:
Convert H to the bit string, and let it be M' .
STEP 5:
Decrypt M' by using D and k, and let the plain test be M. $M = D(M', k)$.
STEP 6:
Recompress each component to form a compressed package, and store it.
STEP 7:
Output M.

3   Discussion

In order to test the proposed information hiding method using the custom components, we downloaded more than 5,000 OOX documents from the Internet. The contents include science and technology, medical and health, history and culture, sports and entertainment, and commercial economy. We designed and developed an information hiding and forensic prototype system based on OOX documents. With the downloaded OOX documents and the prototype system, the proposed OOX information hiding method was tested, and the test effect was good.

3.1   The Design of the Prototype System

In order to test the OOX document information hiding method based on custom components, we designed and developed the OOX document information hiding and extraction prototype system. The operating system used for prototype system development is Microsoft Windows 7, the development software platform is Visual Studio 2010, and the OOX document format uses the Microsoft Office 2007 format. To make it easier to manipulate OOX documents, we used the Microsoft Office Open XML SDK 2.5 (Open XML SDK 2.5 Community Technical Preview (CTP) for Office) toolkit. At the same time, we use the C# language for programming and use the .NET Framework 4.0 framework class library for development. The class used by the prototype system is shown in Fig. 6.

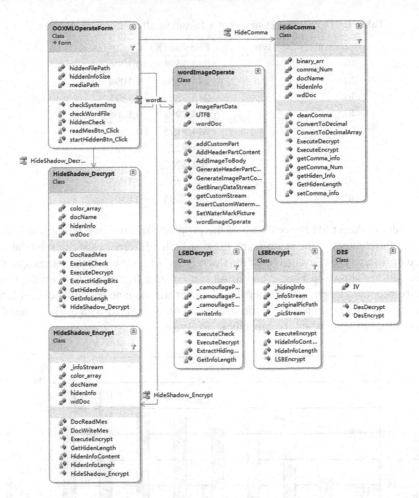

Fig. 6. The classes in the prototype system.

3.2 The Concealment Analysis

In the information hiding process, since the added custom component is not referenced in the main document component documents.xml, there is no any modification to the content and format of the original document. Because the added custom component is "independent" from the main document component, the document will not have any change in the display content and the display format after hiding the information, and the hidden information has good concealment.

At the same time, the document size has not changed significantly after information hiding. Table 1 shows the file size changing after hiding information. It can be seen from Table 1 that the document size changes are relatively small after hiding the information.

Table 1. The file size changing of a document after information hiding

Secret message (Byte)	File size (K)	Changing (K)
10	244.7598	0.1006
20	244.7686	0.1094
30	244.7803	0.1211
40	244.7998	0.1406
50	244.8125	0.1533
60	244.8223	0.1631
70	244.8262	0.167
80	244.8457	0.1865
90	245.4893	0.8301

In order to detect the concealment of the proposed information hiding method, we analyzed the changes of the stego-texts' file size under different capacities. At the same time, we also analyzed the changes of the stego-texts' file size under the same capacities. The results are shown in Figs. 7 and 8. As can be seen from Fig. 7, when the hidden capacity becomes larger, the size of the file after the steganography becomes larger. From Fig. 8, it can be seen that the file size changing is reduced with the increase of the file size of stego-texts when the capacity is 50 Bytes.

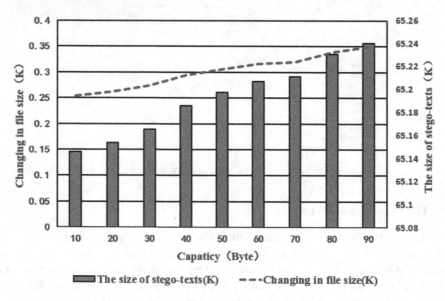

Fig. 7. The file size changing of a stego-text after information hiding.

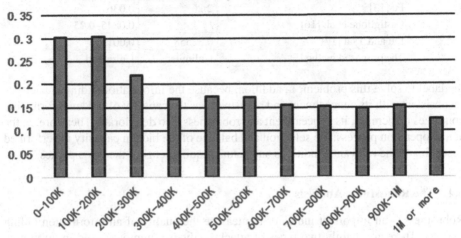

Fig. 8. The file size changing of some stego-texts after information hiding.

3.3 The Capacity Analysis

The capacity is generally examined by two indicators [13]. One indicator is the number of bits that can be embedded in each word in the stego-texts, and the other is the number of bytes that can be embedded in each byte of the stego-text files. They are expressed with the bit rate 1, and bit rate 2 respectively. They are calculated as follows:

$$\text{Bit rate } 1 = \frac{Average\ Capacity\ (bits)}{Average\ Number\ of\ Words\ in\ the\ Stego-texts}$$

$$\text{Bit rate } 2 = \frac{Average\ Capacity\ (Bytes)}{Average\ File\ Size\ of\ the\ Stego-texts}$$

The proposed method complements the information hiding process by adding a custom component in the OOX document. In theory, the capacity of information hiding is limited only by the length of the tag content in the XML language. Because the XML language does not limit the length of the label content, the information hiding capacity of this method is theoretically unlimited. Table 2 gives a comparison of the capacity of the proposed method with another information hiding methods.

However, due to the different limitations of different OOX document parsing development packages, the capacity is still limited during actual operation. For example, there are many ways for Java to parse XML. After Scala 2.11.x, there are some separate jar packages. The parsing is very convenient and simple. However, there is a limit to the length of the content of the XML tag—the length is no more than 6K characters, and it cannot be parsed normally after exceeding 6K characters [18]. However, for labels with more than 6K characters, regular expressions can also be used to obtain the contents of

Table 2. The comparison of capacity between different methods

Information hiding method	Bit rate 1	Bit rate 2
Fu [13]	2.26	0.036
Castiglione et al. [16]	/	0.0845–0.25
Liu and Tsai [17]	0.32558	0.00133
The proposed method	Unlimited	Unlimited

the label to solve this problem. In addition, because the information hiding capacity is inconsistent with its concealment and robustness, as the capacity of hidden information continues to increase, its concealment and robustness also deteriorate. Therefore, in the actual operation process, the selection and balance of the hidden capacity is performed according to the relevant conditions and actual requirements of the three parties.

3.4 The Robustness Analysis

Robustness is an important indicator to measure the quality of an information hiding method. There are mainly two types of attack methods commonly used in text information hiding: content-based attacks and format-based attacks. Content-based attack methods mainly include text modification methods such as replacing texts, inserting texts, and deleting texts. Format-based attack methods mainly include changing fonts, fonts, font sizes, and font modifications (special styles such as shadow and Word Art). The proposed method hides the secret information by adding a custom component in the document, and the added custom component is not referenced by the main document. So, there are any modification to the original content and format of the stego-texts, and it can resist steganalysis based on text content and text format. Table 3 gives a comparison of the resistance to attack between the proposed method and another methods.

Table 3. The comparison of the resistance to attack between different methods

Information hiding method	Attack based on content			Attack based on format	
	Insert	Replace	Delete	Font	Adorn
Fu [13]	√	√	×	√	√
Castiglione et al. [16].	√	√	√	√	√
Liu and Tsai [17]	×	×	×	√	√
The proposed method	√	√	√	√	√

4 Conclusions

In this paper, we proposed an OOX text information hiding method based on custom components. This method hides information by adding a custom component to the OOX document and writing secret information to the custom component's XmlTextWriter tag. The added custom component is not referenced in the main document. Therefore, no modification has been made to the original document content and format. Since the hidden information is stored in the XmlTextWriter tag content, and the custom component is not referenced in the document.xml of the OOX document, the hidden information will not appear when the carrier document is displayed. In addition, in the process of information hiding, this method does not make any changes to the display content and display format of the stego-text. This method can resist attacks based on text content and text format. In addition, because the XML language does not limit the length of the label content, the capacity of the proposed method is unlimited. However, in the actual operation process, it is also necessary to comprehensively consider the concealment, robustness and capacity in order to achieve the best information hiding effect.

Acknowledgments. This work is supported by National Natural Science Foundation of China (61304208), Open Fund of Demonstration Base of Internet Application Innovative Open Platform of Department of Education (KJRP1402), Open Fund of China-USA Computer Science Research Center (KJR16239), Hunan Province Science And Technology Plan Project Fund (2012GK3120), Scientific Research Fund of Hunan Province Education Department (13CY003, 14B106), Changsha City Science and Technology Plan Program (K1501013-11), Hunan Normal University University-Industry Cooperation.

References

1. Fridrich, J.: Steganography in Digital Media – Principle, Algorithms, and Application. National Defense Industry Press, Beijing (2014)
2. Por, L.Y., Ang, T.F., Delina, B.: WhiteSteg: a new scheme in information hiding using text steganography. WSEAS Trans. Comput. **7**(6), 735–745 (2008)
3. Xia, Z., Lv, R., Zhu, Y., Ji, P., Sun, H., Shi, Y.: Fingerprint liveness detection using gradient-based texture features. Sig. Image Video Process. **11**(2), 381–388 (2017)
4. Huang, L., Tseng, L., Hwang, M.: The study on data hiding in medical images. Int. J. Netw. Secur. **14**(6), 301–309 (2012)
5. Wang, S., Xiao, C., Lin, Y.: A high bitrate information hiding algorithm for video in video. J. Comput. Electr. Autom. Control Inf. Eng. **3**(11), 2572–2577 (2009)
6. Liu, T.Y., Tsai, W.H.: A new steganographic method for data hiding in microsoft word documents by a change tracking technique. IEEE Trans. Inf. Forensics Secur. **2**(1), 24–30 (2007)
7. Zhou, Z., Wang, Y., Wu, Q.M.J., Yang, C., Sun, X.: Effective and efficient global context verification for image copy etection. IEEE Trans. Inf. Forensics Secur. (2016). https://doi.org/10.1109/TIFS.2016.2601065
8. Xia, Z., Wang, X., Zhang, L., Qin, Z., Sun, X., Ren, K.: A privacy-preserving and copy-deterrence content-based image retrieval scheme in cloud computing. IEEE Trans. Inf. Forensics Secur. **11**(11), 2594–2608 (2016)
9. Zhang, J., Shen, J., Wang, L., Lin, H.: Coverless text information hiding method based on the word rank map. In: Sun, X., Liu, A., Chao, H.-C., Bertino, E. (eds.) ICCCS 2016. LNCS, vol. 10039, pp. 145–155. Springer, Cham (2016). https://doi.org/10.1007/978-3-319-48671-0_14
10. Low, S.H., Maxemchuk, N.F., Brassil, J.T.: Document marking and identification using both line and word shifting. In: Proceedings of INFOCOM 1995, vol. 2007, pp. 853–860. IEEE (1995)
11. Low, S.H., Maxemchuk, N.F., Lapone, A.M.: Document identification for copyright protection using centroid detection. IEEE Trans. Commun. **46**(3), 372–383 (1998)

12. Brassil, J.T., Low, S.H., Maxemchuk, N.F.: Copyright protection for the electronic distribution of text documents. Proc. IEEE **87**, 1181–1196 (1999)
13. Fu, Z.J.: The research of OOX security protect technology (Doctor Thesis). Hunan University, Changsha, Hunan, China (2012)
14. Microsoft Compound Document File Format. http://www.openoffice.org/sc/compdocfileformat.pdf
15. OfficeOpenXMLFormats.   http://www.microsoft.com/china/msdn/library/office/office/OfficeOpenXMLFormats.mspx?mfr=true
16. Castiglione, A., De Santis, A., Soriente, C.: Taking advantages of a disadvantage: digital forensics and steganography using document metadata. J. Syst. Softw. **80**(5), 750–764 (2007)
17. Liu, T., Tsai, W.: A new steganographic method for data hiding in microsoft word documents by a change tracking technique. IEEE Trans. Inf. Forensics Secur. **2**(1), 24–30 (2007)
18. XML File Parsing-the Limit of Length of Tag Content. https://my.oschina.net/devjing/blog/335521

Text Semantic Steganalysis Based on Word Embedding

Xin Zuo, Huanhuan Hu, Weiming Zhang[✉], and Nenghai Yu

CAS Key Laboratory of Electromagnetic Space Information,
University of Science and Technology of China, Hefei, China
zhangwm@ustc.edu.cn

Abstract. Most state-of-the-art detection methods against synonym substitution based steganography extract features based on statistical distortion. However, synonym substitution will cause not only statistical distortion but also semantic distortion. In this paper, we propose word embedding feature (WEF) to detect the semantic distortion. Furthermore, a fused feature called word embedding and statistical feature set (WESF) which consists of WEF and statistical feature based on word frequency is designed to improve detection performance. Experiments show that WESF can achieve lower detection error rates compared with prmethods.

Keywords: Text steganalysis · Semantic distortion
Word embedding

1 Introduction

Linguistic steganography is the art of hiding messages in digital text without drawing suspicion from steganalysis [1,2]. Linguistic steganography can be broadly divided into two main categories. One is text generation based steganography [3,4]. The generated text can be easily distinguished from natural texts by steganalysis [5]. The other is cover modification based steganography [6–10]. In this category, synonym substitution (SS) based steganography is widely used as it is robust and effective. And the meaning of the text remains almost unchanged during the embedding process, such as T-lex [11] and CoverTweet [12].

In recent years, a few of linguistic steganalysis paradigms have been developed to detect SS steganography. The very first attack of SS steganography was described by Taskiran *et al.* [13]. In this work, 3-g language model was used to distinguish cover and stego text by Support Vector Machine (SVM). With the help of Google, Yu *et al.* [14] constructed a detector to evaluate suitability of synonyms for their context in text. Although it can achieve reliable results when the embedding rates were very high, it had to access Google frequently, which led to a very low running speed. Chen *et al.* [15] proposed the concept of context cluster score (CCS) to evaluate the fitness of the substitution of SS steganography. Xiang *et al.* [16] extracted a statistical feature from synonym appeared in text based on word frequency.

© Springer Nature Switzerland AG 2018
X. Sun et al. (Eds.): ICCCS 2018, LNCS 11066, pp. 485–495, 2018.
https://doi.org/10.1007/978-3-030-00015-8_42

All the methods mentioned above treat words as atomic units. It is difficult to find the relationship between each synonym and its context, just like one-hot representation. Recently, numerous effective word embedding methods have been developed, such as word2vec [17], fasttext [18], and wordRank [19], to describe the semantic relations among words in vector space. For example, *vector("King")* − *vector("Man")* + *vector("Woman")* results in a vector that is closest to the vector representation of the word *Queen* [17]. What's more, those methods are all based on statistical distortion such as: the offsets of word frequency or N-gram. However, synonym substitution will cause not only statistical distortion but also semantic distortion: the offsets of synonym in semantic space.

In this paper, we propose a new steganalysis scheme to analyze SS steganography. Since SS steganography would cause statistical and semantic distortion, we extracted statistical feature based on word frequency and semantic feature based on word2vec [17]. Experiments results verify the effectiveness of the proposed steganalysis method for different embedding rates compared with previous methods.

In the next section, we briefly introduce the previous work. The new scheme is explained in Sect. 3. All experimental results are listed and interpreted in Sect. 4. Future directions and a summary appear in Sect. 5.

2   Previous Work

2.1   Xiang et al.'s Features

To describe Xiang et al.'s feature [16], we first define some notations as follow.

Definition 0. A synset is a set of words with the similar meaning, and the dimension of a synset is the number of synonyms it contains. For example, [Cow, Cattle] is a synset that contains two synonyms, and the dimension of this synset is 2.

Definition 1. Attribute pair of a synonym is defined as its position in a synset and the dimension of the synset, denoted by an ordered pair $< pos, dim >$, where $pos \in \{0, 1, ..., dim - 1\}$.

Definition 2. Relative frequency $p(j, k)$ of attribute pair $< j, k >$ in a text is given by

$$p(j, k) = \frac{f(j, k)}{\sum_{i=0}^{k-1} f(i, k)}, \tag{1}$$

where $f(j, k)$ is the number of total occurrences of $< j, k >$ in the text, and $\sum_{i=0}^{k-1} f(i, k)$ represents the total number of attribute pairs that appear in the text.

The synonyms in the synset are sorted in the descending order of their frequencies. When $j < h$, $h \in \{1, .., k - 1\}$, the cover text would contain more synonyms with attribute pair $< j, k >$ than the ones with attribute pair $< h, k >$.

$$f_c(j,k) > f_c(h,k), j < h, \tag{2}$$

$$p_c(j,k) - p_c(h,k) > 0, j < h, \tag{3}$$

where the subscript c represents the cover text.

Due to the randomness of the message, if a synonym w contains a secret message and its attribute pair is $< pos, k >$, pos may be a random value varying from 0 to $k - 1$ in a stego text. Therefore, the proportion of synonyms with attribute pair $< j, k >$ is $1/k$. The relationship of cover and stego can be deduced as following equations:

$$f_s(j,k) = (1-r)f_c(j,k) + \frac{1}{k}r\sum_{i=0}^{k-1}f_c(i,k), \tag{4}$$

$$p_s(j,k) - p_s(h,k) = \frac{f_s(j,k) - f_s(h,k)}{\sum_{i=0}^{k-1}f_s(i,k)} = (1-r)(p_c(j,k) - p_c(h,k)), \tag{5}$$

where the subscript s represents the stego text, r is the embedding rate. As $0 < r < 1$, thus

$$p_s(j,k) - p_s(h,k) < p_c(j,k) - p_c(h,k), j < h. \tag{6}$$

The final feature vector proposed in [16] includes six elements such as $p(0,2) - p(1,2)$, $p(0,3) - p(1,3)$, $p(0,3) - p(2,3)$, $p(0,4) - p(1,4)$, $p(0,4) - p(2,4)$, and $p(0,4) - p(3,4)$.

2.2   Chen et al.'s Features

Considering the fitness of synonym and its context, Chen et al. [15] proposes the concept of context cluster score (CCS). For a synonym S_i and its context $C_i = \{c_{i,0}, c_{i,1}, ..., c_{i,2W-1}\}$, the number of element compositions for a S_i is not more than $2^{2W} - 1$. Each element composition is a context cluster, and the CCS of context cluster ς is denoted by V_ς:

$$V_\varsigma = \frac{f_\varsigma K^\alpha}{\sum_{i=0}^{K-1} lg(1+f_i)}, \tag{7}$$

where K represents the number of the elements in ς, $f_\varsigma, f_0, ..., f_{K-1}$ represent the frequency of ς and the frequencies of the elements in ς respectively, and α is accelerating exponent.

The context fitness of the ith synonym denoted by γ_i is defined as follows:

$$\gamma_i = \frac{1}{2^{2W}-1}\sum_{\varsigma\in\Phi}V_\varsigma, \tag{8}$$

where Φ is the context cluster set.

On the basis of context fitness, two classification features: Context Maximum Rate (CMR) and Context Maximum Deviation (CMD) of a text are denoted by λ and θ, respectively:

$$\lambda = \frac{1}{n} \sum_{i=0}^{n-1} [\gamma_i = \gamma_{i,max}], \tag{9}$$

$$\theta = \frac{1}{n} \sum_{i=0}^{n-1} (\gamma_i - \gamma_{i,max})^2, \tag{10}$$

where $[\gamma_i = \gamma_{i,max}] = \begin{cases} 1 & \gamma_i = \gamma_{i,max} \\ 0 & \gamma_i \neq \gamma_{i,max} \end{cases}$ and $\gamma_{i,max}$ is the maximum context fitness of the synset.

2.3   Word2Vec Model

Word2vec [17] model was proposed by Mikolov *et al.* to learn distributed representations of words. It has two mirror frame named CBOW(continuous bag-of-words) and Skip-gram. The frameworks are displayed in Fig. 1. There are both three layers in these two frames: input layer, projection layer, output layer. In CBOW model, it uses several history words and future words to estimate current word. In order to achieve this goal, CBOW builds a log-linear classifier with future and history words at the input to classify the current word. The Skip-gram is similar to CBOW, it also builds a log-linear classifier but the input of this classifier is each current word. And the aim of this classifier is to predict words within a certain range before and after the current word.

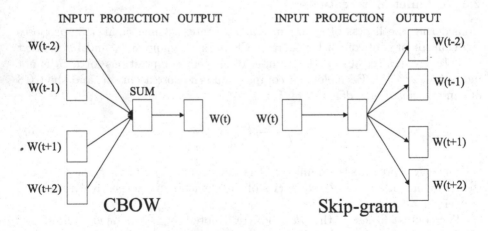

Fig. 1. Word2Vec model framwork.

3   The Proposed Scheme

Although the synonyms in a synset have the similar meaning, the substitution of synonyms would still cause a semantic mismatch in the context. After we are aware of this, the process of steganalysis seems like playing a *banked close game*. For a text, all synonyms are replaced by blanks. For each blank, there is a synset. And we need to choose the one that best fits the context from this synset. We confidently think our choice is the right answer. So if the synonym appears in the text and our choice are not the same, this synonym is mismatched with its context. The number of mismatch can be used to distinguish cover from stego.

In a text, we can extract a sequence of synonyms $S = \{S_1, ..., S_i, ..., S_n\}$ with the help of thesaurus. S_i represents the ith synonym that appears in the text, and $\hat{S}_i$ denotes the synset of S_i. For any synonym S_i, we can also extract the N words before and after it as its context, denoted by $C_i = \{c_{i,0}, c_{i,1}, ..., c_{i,2N-2}, c_{i,2N-1}\}$. And the size of N is called context window size. $\overrightarrow{S}_i$ and $\overrightarrow{C}_i$ represent the vector space representation of $\hat{S}_i$ and C_i respectively.

Since context words are often not of the same importance, we give different weights to the context words. $W = \{w_0, w_1, ..., w_{2N-2}, w_{2N-1}\}$ is the weights of $\overrightarrow{C}_i$, called context weights. And the value of context weights W will be discussed in Sect. 4. We calculate the vector representation of the weighted context, denoted as WC_i.

$$WC_i = \sum_{j=0}^{2N-1} w_j \overrightarrow{c}_{i,j}. \tag{11}$$

The energy function is defined as the inner product of two vectors, denoted by $E(\overrightarrow{A}, \overrightarrow{B})$.

$$E(\overrightarrow{A}, \overrightarrow{B}) = \overrightarrow{A} \cdot \overrightarrow{B}, \tag{12}$$

where $\overrightarrow{A}$ and $\overrightarrow{B}$ represent two word vectors. For example, the energy of synonym $\overrightarrow{S}_i$ and its weighted context WC_i can be calculated by $E(\overrightarrow{S}_i, WC_i) = \overrightarrow{S}_i \cdot WC_i$.

Using the energy function, we can calculate the conditional probability of $\overrightarrow{S}_i$ with weighted context WC_i, denoted by $P(\overrightarrow{S}_i | WC_i)$.

$$P(\overrightarrow{S}_i | WC_i) = \frac{e^{E(\overrightarrow{S}_i, WC_i)}}{\sum_{v \in \hat{S}_i} e^{E(v, WC_i)}}. \tag{13}$$

For any synonym v in the synset $\hat{S}_i$, we can calculate $P(v|WC_i)$. We think v with maximum conditional probability is the one that best fits the context, so if $v \neq \overrightarrow{S}_i$, the synonym $\overrightarrow{S}_i$ that appears in the text is not fit with the context. In other words, S_i and $\overrightarrow{C}_i$ are mismatched, denoted by $M(\overrightarrow{S}_i, WC_i)$, as follows:

$$M(\overrightarrow{S}_i, WC_i) = \begin{cases} 0 & P(\overrightarrow{S}_i | WC_i) > P(v|WC_i), v \in \hat{S}_i, v \neq \overrightarrow{S}_i \\ 1 & else \end{cases}. \tag{14}$$

We calculate the cosine distance between $\vec{S}_i$ and WC_i as another measure of mismatch. Denote by $MC(\vec{S}_i, WC_i)$ as follows:

$$MC(\vec{S}_i, WC_i) = \begin{cases} 0 & \cos(\vec{S}_i, WC_i) > \cos(v, WC_i), v\epsilon \vec{S}_i, v \neq \vec{S}_i \\ 1 & else \end{cases}. \quad (15)$$

The reason we choose the cosine distance is that it can better characterize the similarity between words. Word2vec [17], fasttext [18] and wordRank [19] are all use cosine distance to calculate similarity of words.

We calculate the two mismatches for each of the synonyms appearing in the text, and get two binary sequences with the same length. The sum of the two binary sequences yields a new sequence L. The value of L ranges from 0 to 2. The elements of L are divided into $\lceil n/M \rceil$ groups. And the parameter M is called cluster size. After summarizing each group, we get sequence L'. The features are composed of mean, variance, third order central moments, kurtosis, and skewness of L'.

For example, in Fig. 2, there are two binary sequences: $seq1$ and $seq2$ that calculated by Eqs. (14) and (15), where $n = 15$ and $M = 5$. The WEF is [5 1 0 1.5 0] calculated from L'.

seq1	0	1	0	1	1	0	0	1	0	1	1	1	0	1	0
seq2	0	1	1	0	1	0	0	1	1	1	0	0	0	1	0
L	0	2	1	1	1	0	0	2	1	2	1	1	0	2	0
L'			6					5					4		

Fig. 2. Example of extracting WEF from text.

The details of the extraction procedure of the WEF are described in Algorithm 1.

The proposed text semantic steganalysis process is shown in Fig. 3. The dashed box represents steganalysis with the fused feature WESF.

4   Experiments

4.1   Experimental Setup

The thesaurus is extracted from Wordnet [20], the mean of synset size is 2.26 words. The synonyms in the synset are sorted in the descending order of their frequencies which are derived from a huge corpus.

Algorithm 1. Extraction procedure of the WEF:

1: Get the synonym sequence and its contexts of text.
2: Calculate two binary sequences $seq1$ and $seq2$ by using Eq. (14) and Eq. (15).
3: Calculate L by summing $seq1$ and $seq2$.
4: Divide L into $\lceil n/M \rceil$ groups.
5: Calculate L' by summing each group.
6: Calculate mean, variance, third order central moments, kurtosis, and skewness of L'.

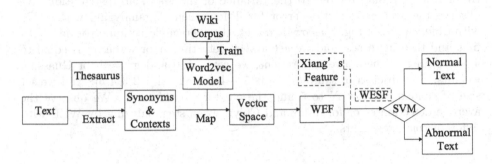

Fig. 3. Proposed text semantic steganalysis process.

All our experiments are carried out on Wiki corpus. The texts are all segmented from this corpus, and the size of text ranges from 5k Bytes to 200k Bytes. The detectors are trained as binary classifiers implemented using SVM [21] with linear kernel.

The Wiki corpus is divided into three parts, training set, validation set and test set, where proportions are 0.7, 0.1 and 0.2. The training set is used to train the word2vec using skip-gram model [17]. The dimension of every word vector is 400-D. We set the window size of word2vec to 5 and abandon the words appeared less than 5 times in training set. We use gensim which is a package for Python to bulit our word2vec model. The validation set is used for model selection. Here, it is used to select cluster size M (see Sect. 3) and determine context weights W. The test set is used to generate the cover text and stego text for evaluating the performance of steganalysis.

We selected two SS steganography techniques: T-lex [11] and its variant Ctsyn [16]. Since CoverTweet needs to be manually selected when multiple candidate results appeared, we do not discuss here. T-lex uses WordNet to select synonyms with correct senses. Only the words appeared in the identical synset in WordNet [20] database are grouped in a synonym set. Messages can be embedded into cover text as follow. First, encode the message letters with Huffman coding. Then represent the encoded binary string in multi-base form. Finally, choose which synonym appears in the text according to the multi-base form. The only difference between T-lex and Ctsyn is the coding strategy. Ctsyn [16] constructs a binary tree for each synset with the synonyms as the leaves while T-lex [11] sets the synsets $sn_0, sn_1, ..., sn_n$ with sizes $k_0, k_1, ..., k_n$.

4.2 Experimental Results

The first part of experiments is to find the effect of context weights W on the detection performance. We consider two cases: one is that all words in context have same weights, the other is that the word which is closer to current synonyms has larger weight. In this case, the context weights are sampled from the Gaussian distribution $N(\mu, \sigma^2)$. We suppose that the context words before and after the synonyms have the same weights, so we set μ to 0. Under this assumption, the weights are only related to the variance of the Gaussian distribution. We observe the average detection error for T-lex when steganalyzing with WEF with different σ^2. In Fig. 4, as σ^2 increases, the average detection error decreases first and then increases, and we get lowest detection error when σ^2 is equal to 4. According to the above experiment, we set $\mu = 0$ and $\sigma^2 = 4$ for Guassian weights. The abscissa of samples are $[-5\ -4\ -3\ -2\ -1\ 1\ 2\ 3\ 4\ 5]$. And we set size of context window N to 5 and the cluster size M to 40. We observe the average detection error for T-lex and Ctsyn when steganalyzing by WEF with different context weights.

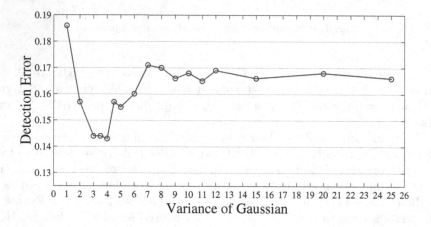

Fig. 4. Average detection error for T-lex [11] with different Gaussian weights.

Our next experiment is aimed at finding the effect of cluster size M on the detection effect. The WEF is extracted with Gaussian weights as described in previous experiment. We observe the average detection error for T-lex when steganalyzing with WEF with different cluster size M. In Fig. 5, as M increases, the average detection error decreases first and then increases in each embedding rate. Also we found out that the average detection error is minimum when M is 40 or 50 in each embedding rate, and 40 is more stable in each embedding rate.

The next part of experiments is to compare the detection performances of Xiang et al.'s features [16], Chen et al.'s features [15] and WEF. As described in the above two experiments, we use Gaussian weights and set cluster size to 40. The context window size $N = 5$. The results are listed in Table 1 and Fig. 6.

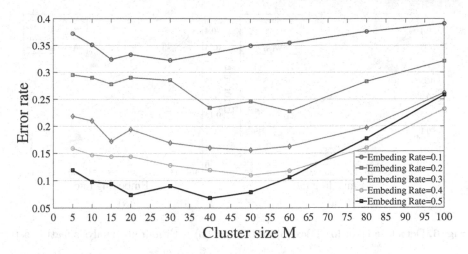

Fig. 5. Average detection error for T-lex [11] when steganalyzing with WEF with different cluster size M.

Firstly, the results indicate that WEF performs better at each embedding rate although WEF and Chen et al.'s features are both considering the fitness of synonyms. This is mostly because the performance of word2vec in semantics is better than statistic natural language processing. Secondly, although the Xiang et al.'s feature set can achieve reliable results when the embedding rate is high, the detection performance of WEF is still better than it. This proves that both the statistical distortion features and the semantic distortion features can distinguish cover and stego text, and it seems that semantic distortion features are more effective. We also notice that Ctsyn appears more secure than T-lex [11].

As synonym substitution will cause not only statistical distortion but also semantic distortion, we propose a fused feature called word embedding and statistical feature set (WESF) which consists of Xiang et al.'s features and WEF.

Table 1. Average detection error $\overline{P}_E$ for two embedding algorithms and four steganalysis feature sets at various kinds of embedding rates.

Stego algorithm	Features	0.1	0.15	0.2	0.25	0.3	0.4	0.5
T-lex	Xiang6	0.395	0.337	0.287	0.248	0.198	0.141	0.09
	Chen	0.396	0.352	0.32	0.277	0.257	0.209	0.171
	WEF	0.334	0.253	0.210	0.186	0.143	0.085	0.064
	WESF	**0.313**	**0.226**	**0.172**	**0.146**	**0.110**	**0.056**	**0.042**
Ctsyn	Xiang6	0.396	0.343	0.293	0.252	0.204	0.144	0.092
	Chen	0.401	0.355	0.321	0.281	0.26	0.211	0.175
	WEF	0.341	0.263	0.218	0.191	0.139	0.116	0.076
	WESF	**0.322**	**0.236**	**0.177**	**0.152**	**0.097**	**0.071**	**0.046**

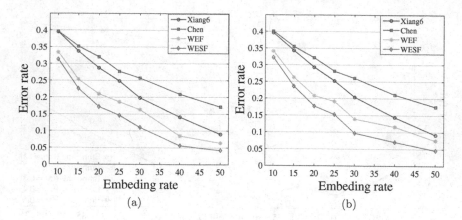

Fig. 6. Detection error for T-lex (a) and Ctsyn (b) with four steganalysis feature sets.

The detection errors of WESF is smaller than both WEF and Xiang et al.'s features, as shown in Fig. 6.

5   Conclusion

In this paper, we propose a novel steganalysis method named WESF to detect synonym substitution based steganography by making use of semantic and statistical distortion. For semantic distortion, we apply word2vec to quantify the distortion magnitude caused by synonym substitution with its context in vector space. We extracted 5-D features, whose detection effect is better than statistical distortion based steganalysis. For statistical distortion, we adopt the 6-D feature set proposed by Xiang et al. By combining the above semantic distortion features and statistical distortion features, we get an 11-D feature set whose detection performance is better than any other feature sets. Our future work includes applying improved semantic distortion to other linguistic steganography such as CoverTweet.

Acknowledgements. This work was supported in part by the Natural Science Foundation of China under Grant U1636201, 61572452.

References

1. Pevný, T., Fridrich, J.: Benchmarking for steganography. In: Solanki, K., Sullivan, K., Madhow, U. (eds.) IH 2008. LNCS, vol. 5284, pp. 251–267. Springer, Heidelberg (2008). https://doi.org/10.1007/978-3-540-88961-8_18
2. Fridrich, J.: Steganography in Digital Media: Principles, Algorithms, and Applications. Cambridge University Press, New York (2009)
3. Chapman, M., Davida, G.: Hiding the hidden: a software system for concealing ciphertext as innocuous text. In: Han, Y., Okamoto, T., Qing, S. (eds.) ICICS 1997. LNCS, vol. 1334, pp. 335–345. Springer, Heidelberg (1997). https://doi.org/10.1007/BFb0028489

4. Liu, Y., Sun, X., Liu, Y., Li, C.T.: MIMIC-PPT: Mimicking-based steganography for microsoft power point document. Inf. Technol. J. **7**(4), 654–660 (2008)
5. Chen, Z., et al.: Linguistic steganography detection using statistical characteristics of correlations between words. In: Solanki, K., Sullivan, K., Madhow, U. (eds.) IH 2008. LNCS, vol. 5284, pp. 224–235. Springer, Heidelberg (2008). https://doi.org/10.1007/978-3-540-88961-8_16
6. Bolshakov, I.A.: A method of linguistic steganography based on collocationally-verified synonymy. In: Fridrich, J. (ed.) IH 2004. LNCS, vol. 3200, pp. 180–191. Springer, Heidelberg (2004). https://doi.org/10.1007/978-3-540-30114-1_13
7. Yuling, L., Xingming, S., Can, G., Hong, W.: An efficient linguistic steganography for Chinese text. In: 2007 IEEE International Conference on Multimedia and Expo, pp. 2094–2097. IEEE (2007)
8. Muhammad, H.Z., Rahman, S.M.S.A.A., Shakil, A.: Synonym based Malay linguistic text steganography. In: Innovative Technologies in Intelligent Systems and Industrial Applications, CITISIA 2009, pp. 423–427. IEEE (2009)
9. Shirali-Shahreza, M.H., Shirali-Shahreza, M.: A new synonym text steganography. In: International Conference on Intelligent Information Hiding and Multimedia Signal Processing, IIHMSP 2008, pp. 1524–1526. IEEE (2008)
10. Wilson, A., Ker, A.D.: Avoiding detection on twitter: embedding strategies for linguistic steganography. Electron. Imaging **2016**(8), 1–9 (2016)
11. Winstein, K.: Lexical steganography Through Adaptive Modulation of the Word Choice Hash (1998, unpublished). http://www.imsa.edu/~keithw/tlex
12. Wilson, A., Blunsom, P., Ker, A.D.: Linguistic steganography on twitter: hierarchical language modeling with manual interaction. In: IS&T/SPIE Electronic Imaging, p. 902803. International Society for Optics and Photonics (2014)
13. Taskiran, C.M., Topkara, U., Topkara, M., Delp, E.J.: Attacks on lexical natural language steganography systems. In: Electronic Imaging 2006, p. 607209. International Society for Optics and Photonics (2006)
14. Yu, Z., Huang, L., Chen, Z., Li, L., Zhao, X., Zhu, Y.: Detection of synonym-substitution modified articles using context information. In: Second International Conference on Future Generation Communication and Networking, FGCN 2008, vol. 1, pp. 134–139. IEEE (2008)
15. Chen, Z., Huang, L., Miao, H., Yang, W., Meng, P.: Steganalysis against substitution-based linguistic steganography based on context clusters. Comput. Electr. Eng. **37**(6), 1071–1081 (2011)
16. Xiang, L., Sun, X., Luo, G., Xia, B.: Linguistic steganalysis using the features derived from synonym frequency. Multimed. Tools Appl. **71**(3), 1893–1911 (2014)
17. Mikolov, T., Chen, K., Corrado, G., Dean, J.: Efficient estimation of word representations in vector space. arXiv preprint arXiv:1301.3781 (2013)
18. Joulin, A., Grave, E., Bojanowski, P., Mikolov, T.: Bag of tricks for efficient text classification. arXiv preprint arXiv:1607.01759 (2016)
19. Ji, S., Yun, H., Yanardag, P., Matsushima, S., Vishwanathan, S.: WordRank: Learning word embeddings via robust ranking. arXiv preprint arXiv:1506.02761 (2015)
20. Miller, G.A.: Wordnet: a lexical database for English. Commun. ACM **38**(11), 39–41 (1995)
21. Cortes, C., Vapnik, V.: Support-vector networks. Mach. Learn. **20**(3), 273–297 (1995)

The Assessment Research of Communication Jamming Effect Based on Grey Relational Analysis

Ruowu Wu[1], Sen Wang[2], Hui Han[1], Xiang Chen[1], Xuhong Yin[2], and Yun Lin[2(✉)]

[1] State Key Laboratory of Complex Electromagnetic Environment Effects on Electronics and Information System (CEMEE), Luoyang 471003, Henan, China
[2] College of Information and Communication Engineering, Harbin Engineering University, Harbin, China
linyun_phd@hrbeu.edu.cn

Abstract. At present, the research on the evaluation methods of communication jamming effectiveness is in its infancy, a comprehensive evaluation method based on Grey relational analysis method is proposed in this paper. Firstly, signal characteristics of the jamming signals are analyzed and evaluation indexes are proposed. Then, this paper introduces the Grey relational analysis and the data processing method. In the end, evaluation process of jamming schemes is proposed and the simulation verifies the rationality and feasibility of this evaluation method.

Keywords: Characteristics of jamming signals · Grey relational analysis Jamming effectiveness evaluation

1 Introduction

The jamming effectiveness of jamming technology can reflect the research progress of electronic countermeasure technology and the result of electronic countermeasure experiment. Therefore, how to evaluate the jamming effectiveness has been the research object of experts. The mainly methods are divided into two categories: the evaluation methods based on single index and comprehensive evaluation methods. The former method idea is to select one of the signal characteristics as an evaluation index and set a threshold value [1–3], when the jamming effectiveness of the jamming scheme reaches the threshold, the jamming scheme is judged to be valid. The evaluation methods based on the comprehensive evaluation methods actually contains two aspects: the selection of the evaluation index and the selection of the evaluation model. The comprehensive evaluation method chooses multiple indicators as the evaluation index of the jamming scheme, and at the same time adopts the traditional evaluation model. This method makes up for the one-sidedness of the single index evaluation method and does not require too much data. The research on the method of radar electronic jamming effect evaluation is adequate. Reference [4] selected the general mean square error of image quality, the peak offset of the image and the degree of

© Springer Nature Switzerland AG 2018
X. Sun et al. (Eds.): ICCCS 2018, LNCS 11066, pp. 496–505, 2018.
https://doi.org/10.1007/978-3-030-00015-8_43

correspondence index of the image as the evaluation index of the ISAR signal jamming effectiveness. Reference [5] selected the probability of detection, the effectiveness of hiding jamming, the loss of radar detection range and the degree of loss of radar observation sector as the evaluation indexes and used the weighted summation to evaluate the radar jamming scheme. Reference [6] used a multi-level fuzzy comprehensive evaluation method to establish a multi-index evaluation model for ISAR system. At present, the research on the communication jamming effectiveness evaluation is still in its infancy.

In this paper, a comprehensive evaluation method of the communication jamming system is studied. Firstly, this paper analyzes the characteristics of jamming signal and proposes an evaluation index system of the communication system. Secondly, a method of evaluating the jamming scheme based on grey relational analysis is proposed. In the end, the simulation results and the conclusion are given.

2 Characteristics of Modulated Signal

This section will analyze the characteristics of several modulated signals, including AM, FM, PM, BPSK, 4QAM.

The AM signal is also called amplitude modulation. The modulation signal $m(t)$ controls the instantaneous amplitude of its carrier signal $s(t)$, and the instantaneous amplitude of the carrier signal $s(t)$ changes linearly with the modulation signal $m(t)$. Let the carrier be a sinusoidal signal of frequency f_c. The general expressions of the time and frequency domain of the amplitude modulation signal are:

$$s_{AM}(t) = Am(t)\cos(\omega_c t + \varphi_0) \tag{1}$$

$$s_{AM}(t) = F[s_{AM}(t)] = \frac{A}{2}[M(\omega - \omega_c) + M(\omega + \omega_c)] \tag{2}$$

where A is the carrier amplitude, $m(t)$ is the modulation signal, ω_c is the carrier angular frequency, and φ_0 is the carrier initial phase.

Frequency modulation (FM) is a kind of nonlinear modulation with more applications. The carrier amplitude is constant and the instantaneous angular frequency changes linearly with the modulation signal.

$$\Delta\omega(t) = \frac{d\varphi(t)}{dt} = K_f \cdot m(t) \tag{3}$$

In this case $\omega(t) = \omega_c + K_f \cdot m(t)$, the time domain expression of the FM signal is:

$$s_{FM}(t) = A\,\cos(\omega_c t + K_f \int m(t)dt) \tag{4}$$

where K_f is the frequency offset constant that characterizes the sensitivity of the tuner, in $\mathrm{rad}/\mathrm{V}\cdot\mathrm{s}$.

Phase modulation (FM) means that the instantaneous phase offset changes linearly with the modulation signal $m(t)$.

$$s_{PM}(t) = A \cos[\omega_c t + K_p m(t)] \qquad (5)$$

where K_p is the phase modulation sensitivity (rad/V), which means the phase shift of the PM signal caused by the amplitude of the unit modulation signal.

Let the modulation signal be a sine wave of a single frequency. When it modulates the carrier phase, the PM signal is:

$$\begin{aligned} s_{PM}(t) &= A \cos[\omega_c t + K_p A_m \cos \omega_m t] \\ &= A \cos[\omega_c t + m_p \cos \omega_m t] \end{aligned} \qquad (6)$$

The binary phase-shifted keying (BPSK) signal has only two phase values. The two 0 and π of the carrier are respectively controlled by 0 and 1 of the binary sequence of the baseband signal, and the time domain expression of the BPSK signal is:

$$s_{BPSK}(t) = \left[\sum_n a_n g(t - nT_s) \right] \cdot \cos(\omega_c t + \varphi_n) \qquad (7)$$

where a is different from the ASK signal. The ASK signal is a unipolar digital signal, and the PSK is a bipolar digital signal.

$$a_n = \begin{cases} +1, & \text{probability is } P \\ -1, & \text{probability is } 1 - P \end{cases} \qquad (8)$$

The time domain expression of the 4-ary quadrature amplitude modulation (4QAM) signal is:

$$s_{4QAM}(t) = m_I(t) \cos \omega_c t + m_Q(t) \sin \omega_c t \qquad (9)$$

where $\cos \omega_c t$ is the in-phase signal (I signal) and $\sin \omega_c t$ is the quadrature signal (Q signal).

Orthogonal amplitude modulation uses two independent baseband waveforms to perform double-sideband modulation of carrier suppression on two mutually orthogonal carrier waves of the same frequency, enabling two parallel digital information transmissions.

3 Characteristics of Jamming Signal

Because signals have many kinds of processing ways, the jamming signal needs to be represented by some characteristics together, and its evaluation result should be determined by the multi-characteristics of signals. The jamming signal should have the following characteristics:

3.1   Frequency Domain Characteristics

The frequency domain characteristic of the jamming signal contains two aspects: First, the frequency of the jamming signal should fall within the acceptable range of the receiver. Usually, the receiver bandwidth is much larger than the bandwidth of the communication signal. If the center frequency of the jamming signal is not much different from the center frequency of the communication signal, the jamming signal will be received by the receiver. Second, the frequency domain of the jamming signal partially overlaps with the frequency domain of the communication signal, and the frequency domain of the jamming signal preferably has a bandwidth (Fig. 1).

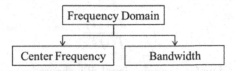

Fig. 1. The evaluation indexes of frequency domain. The two indexes are center frequency and bandwidth.

3.2   Energy Domain Characteristics

The energy of the interfering signal transmitted to the receiver is affected by many factors, including the transmitting antenna performance and erection height, propagation path, receiving antenna performance and erection height. The jamming signal needs to have enough energy to achieve effective jamming effect. If the jamming signal energy is large enough, the poor jamming pattern can also have a good jamming effect. Otherwise, if the energy of jamming signal is much less than the energy of the communication signal, neither of the jamming patterns will cause effective jamming. The jamming effectiveness is closely related to the jamming energy. The ratio of the jamming signal energy to the signal energy is an important indicator for evaluating the energy domain of the jamming signal, which is usually expressed by the jamming-to-signal ratio (JSR). JSR is shown in formula (10), where P_J is the jamming signal power, P_S is communication signal power.

$$JSR = 10 \times \lg(\frac{P_J}{P_S}) \tag{10}$$

3.3   Time Domain Characteristics

If the time domain characteristics are not the same, the jamming effect is different even if the spectrum and energy of the two interfering signals are the same. The time domain characteristics of the interfering signal include not only the starting time of the signal, but also the amplitude and period of the signal (Fig. 2).

The jamming time should partially overlaps with the communication time. If the times of signals are different, the jamming signal is not only meaningless but also

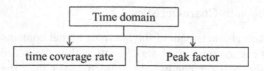

Fig. 2. The evaluation indexes of time domain. The two indexes are time coverage rate and Peak factor.

exposes itself to the receiver. The degree of overlap in time can be represented by the time domain coverage rate E_T. It can be written as the formula (11). T_J is the jamming time of the jamming signal. T_S is the communication time of the communication signal.

$$E_T = \frac{T_S \cap T_J}{T_S \cup T_J} \tag{11}$$

When the jamming signal is a certain signal, it is theoretically easy to be suppressed by the receiver. The interfering signal is preferably a random signal in the time domain. In the time domain, the peak factor (PF) α_f is usually used to represent the statistical structural characteristics of a signal. U_f Is the signal peak, U_j is the mean square value, the peak factor as shown in Eq. (12).

$$\alpha_f = \frac{U_f}{U_j} \tag{12}$$

3.4 Information Spectrum Characteristics

In digital communication system, whether the code element is correct, it will affect the transmission of information. The bit error rate (BER) can directly reflect the degree of damage to the information caused by the jamming scheme. If the entropy of the signal received by the receiver is H_{s+j} and the entropy of the jamming signal is H_j, the information entropy value of the message part of the signal sent by the communicating party can be written as:

$$H_{(s+j,j)} = H_{s+j} - H_j \tag{13}$$

if $H_{(s+j,j)}$ is larger than the entropy of the communication signal, the receiver may recover the transmitted information of the intercommunication signal. Therefore, it is necessary to reduce $H_{(s+j,j)}$, that is, increase the entropy of the jamming signal H_j. When the signal instantaneous value obeys the normal probability distribution, the entropy value is the largest. Therefore, in the aspect of the information field of the jamming signal, it is better to select Gaussian white noise as the jamming signal.

3.5   Modulation Domain Characteristics

To make the baseband signal easier to spread in space, the signal usually needs to be modulated. Similarly, different jamming modulation modes (MM) require different modulation parameters. If the jamming modulation modes are different, jamming effects may be different even though other characteristics are the same (Fig. 3).

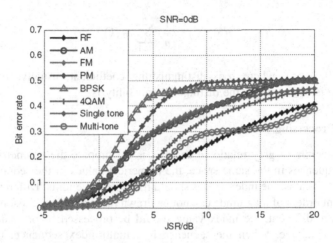

Fig. 3. The error rate curves of jamming signal for BPSK signal with different modulation modes. When the bit error rate is greater than 0.2 for effective interference, it can be seen that the jamming method with the same communication modulation mode requires the minimum interference power. The evaluation indexes of time domain. The two indexes are time coverage rate and Peak factor.

4   Grey Relational Analysis Algorithm

4.1   Classical Grey Relational Analysis

In Grey Relational Analysis theory, there is not have two extremes situations: the "white" with complete information and complete information and the "black" with no knowledge of information in real life. In communication jamming system, "Grey" represents the extent to which the jamming scheme is held by the evaluator. This theory can transform incomplete and explicit information into "white" information, which has no requirement on the number of samples. It is easy to calculate, and the evaluation result is consistent with the qualitative analysis of the evaluator.

The fundamental theory is to calculate the relational grade between the jamming schemes by comparing the degree of similarity between the geometry of the statistical series curves. If the reference sequence is $X_0 = (x_0(1), x_0(2), \cdots, x_0(n))$, the objective sequence is $X_i = (x_i(1), x_0(2), \cdots, x_i(n))$, $(i = 1, 2, \cdots, m)$. The grey relational coefficient (GRC) is given by $\varepsilon_{0i}(k)$ and the grey relational grade (GRG) of X_i and X_0 is $\gamma(X_0, X_i)$.

$$mm = \min_i \min_i |x_0(t) - x_i(t)|, \ (t = 1, 2, \cdots, n) \tag{14}$$

$$MM = \max_i \max_i |x_0(t) - x_i(t)|, \ (t = 1, 2, \cdots, n) \tag{15}$$

$$\varepsilon_{0i}(k) = \frac{mm + \rho \cdot MM}{|x_0(k) - x_i(k)| + \rho \cdot MM} \tag{16}$$

$$\gamma(X_0, X_i) = \frac{1}{n} \cdot \sum_{i=1}^{n} \varepsilon_{0i}(k) \tag{17}$$

where $\rho \in (0, +\infty)$, where ρ is distinguishing coefficient, usually, $\rho = 0.5$. The smaller the ρ is, the stronger the distinguish capability is.

4.2   Data Processing

The basic principle of grey relational analysis is to compare the geometric shapes of numerical sequences in the same space, the numerical values in the sequences should be comparable, that is, the index values should have the same units. Different indicators units, different orders of magnitude can not be drawn reasonable conclusions. When the index units are different, the index value should be processed before calculating the grey relational degree. When the sequence is a multi-index sequence, the types of indicators can be divided into three categories:

(1) Benefit indexes: the scheme with the largest index value is the best;
(2) Cost indexes: the scheme with the smaller index value is the best;
(3) Fixed indexes: the scheme which has a certain value is the best scheme.

If $X_i = (x_i(1), x_i(1), \cdots, x_i(n))$, $(i = 1, 2, \cdots, m)$ is the i-th comparison sequence, the $x_i(k)$, $(k = 1, 2, \cdots, n)$ represents the k-th index value, the following is the data processing method:

(1) Transformation of benefit indexes:

$$XD_1 = (x_1(1)d_1, x_2(1)d_1, \cdots, x_m(1)d_1) \tag{18}$$

$$X(k)d_1 = \frac{x_i(k) - \min_i x_i(k)}{\max_i x_i(k) - \min_i x_i(k)} \tag{19}$$

(2) Transformation of cost indexes:

$$XD_2 = (x_1(1)d_2, x_2(1)d_2, \cdots, x_m(1)d_2) \tag{20}$$

$$X(k)d_2 = \frac{\max_i x_i(k) - x_i(k)}{\max_i x_i(k) - \min_i x_i(k)} \tag{21}$$

(3) Transformation of fixed indexes:

$$XD_3 = (x_1(1)d_3, x_2(1)d_3, \cdots, x_m(1)d_3) \tag{22}$$

$$X(k)d_3 = 1 - \left| \frac{x_i(k) - \gamma(k)}{\max_i |x_i(k) - \gamma(k)|} \right| \tag{23}$$

5 Experiments and Results

The basic experimental steps are as follows: Firstly, establishing evaluation index system; Secondly, index weighting; Thirdly, establishing ideal jamming scheme and then calculating GRA; Finally, ranking schemes based on the GRA (Fig. 4).

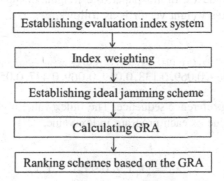

Fig. 4. The evaluation process of jamming schemes based on the grey relational analysis.

Table 1 shows the jamming schemes with different jamming patterns. When the levels of jamming effectiveness are the same, this experiment evaluated and sorted the jamming schemes based on the GRA. The communication signal is BPSK modulated signal, the center frequency (CF) is 50 kHz, the signal bandwidth (SB) is 20 kHz, the signal power is 100 w and the communication time is 10 s.

Step 1: Processing the program data. Evaluation indexes are jamming signal center frequency x_1, bandwidth x_2, jamming signal power x_3, peak factor x_4, time coverage x_5, bit error rate x_6, information entropy x_7 and jamming patterns x_8. x_3 is the cost index. x_1. x_4 are fixed indexes. The others are benefit indexes. Table 2 shows the data after the processing.

Table 1. The jamming schemes

	CF	SB	JSR	PF	Time	BER	MM
1	50	10	3.5	1.99	10	0.246	FM
2	52	12	10	5.3	10	0.240	AM
3	54	6	9	35	10	0.222	RF
4	49	12	5	1.5	10	0.252	PM
5	49	10	6	1.99	10	0.228	QAM
6	51	5	4.5	1.99	10	0.249	BPSK

Table 2. The processing data

	x_1	x_2	x_3	x_4	x_5	x_6	x_7	x_8
1	1	0.71	1	0.99	1	0.8	1	0.6
2	0.5	1	0	0.9	1	0.6	1	0.6
3	0	0.14	0.15	0	1	0	1	0.6
4	0.75	1		0.77	0.98	1	1	1	0.6
5	0.75	0.71	0.62	0.99	1	0.2	1	0.6
6	0.75	0	0.85	0.99	1	0.9	1	1

Step 2: Weighting indexes. In this paper, the weights of indicators are given based on AHP. The indexes weight vector is as follows.

$$W = (\omega_1, \omega_2, \omega_3, \omega_4, \omega_5, \omega_6, \omega_7, \omega_8)$$
$$= (0.069, 0.069, 0.138, 0.069, 0.069, 0.477, 0.0545, 0.0545)$$

Step 3: Establishing reference sequence. The index value in the reference sequence is the maximum value of each program index value.

$$X_0 = (1, 1, 1, 0.99, 1, 1, 1, 1)$$

Step 4: Calculating the grey relational degree of the jamming scheme. The grey relational degree of each scheme is shown in Table 3.

Table 3. The grey relational grade

Scheme	1	2	3	4	5	6
GRG	0.81	0.62	0.43	0.90	0.57	0.82

The priority of the program is in the following order: $X_4 \succ X_6 X_1 \succ X_2 \succ X_5 \succ X_3$. The simulation results not only reflect the preference of the assessors on the importance of the evaluation indexes, but also make a comprehensive ranking of the jamming schemes based on the many evaluation indexes. The highest priority is given to scheme 4, which has the highest bit error rate and a wide bandwidth. In Scheme 6, Bit error rate have the biggest the weight value, so it is better than the program one. The center frequency of the Scheme 3 has the largest deviation from the center frequency of the communication signal and its peak factor is larger, which is more easily suppressed by the receiver, so the priority of Scheme 3 is the smallest.

6 Conclusion

In this paper, a comprehensive evaluation method of communication jamming effectiveness is proposed. The signal characteristics that the jamming signal should have are analyzed. An effective jamming scheme should have the 5 kinds of signal characteristics, jamming signal center frequency, bandwidth, jamming signal power, peak factor, time coverage, bit error rate, information entropy and jamming patterns of the corresponding signal characteristics is selected as the evaluation indexes. This paper establishes an evaluation process of communication jamming scheme based on grey relational analysis and the simulation proves this method is reasonable and scientific.

Acknowledgement. This work is supported by the National Natural Science Foundation of China (61771154).

This paper is funded by the International Exchange Program of Harbin Engineering University for Innovation-oriented Talents Cultivation.

Meantime, all the authors declare that there is no conflict of interests regarding the publication of this article.

We gratefully thank of very useful discussions of reviewers.

References

1. McGuffin, B.F.: Jammed FH-FSK performance in Rayleigh and Nakagam in fading. In: IEEE Military Communications Conference, pp. 1077–1082 (2003)
2. Che, J., Li, Z., Gao, B.: Evaluation method based on the image correlation for laser jamming image. In: International Symposium on Photoelectronic Detection & Imaging (2013)
3. Zhao, L.W., Zhang, L.: Study on voice jamming effect evaluation based on Mel scale. Radio Eng. 2(32–35), 40 (2017)
4. Peng, S.R., Li, X., Pan, Y.C., et al.: Study on quantitative efficiency evaluation for deception jamming to ISAR. In: Asian-Pacific Conference, pp. 544–547. IEEE (2009)
5. Huang, G.M., Liu, L.: Research on radar masking jamming effectiveness evaluation measure method. Modern Radar. 8, 10–13 (2005)
6. Wang, Z., Xin, J., Yin, C.B.: The multi-layer fuzzy comprehensive judgment model for ISAR jamming effectiveness evaluation. In: International Symposium on Antennas, Propagation and Em Theory, pp. 1326–1329. IEEE (2008)

The Phase and Amplitude Errors Frequency Dependence in L-Band Aperture Synthesis Radiometer Using External Noise Sources

Shilin Li, Jing Wu, Taoyun Zhou[(✉)], Dengzhun Wang,
and Zhuolin Gao

Hunan University of Humanities, Science and Technology, Loudi, China
lishilin09@163.com, taoyun_2000@mail.nwpu.edu.cn

Abstract. The frequency dependence of the antenna voltage patterns and the amplitude and phase errors calibrated by external noise sources is analyzed and verified by simulations and experiments, an improved calibrated method using external single signal is proposed to be an alternative to the external noise sources, and the simulations and experiments show that the improved method can mitigate the effect of the frequency dependence of that can be as an alternative in the calibration of aperture synthesis radiometer.

Keywords: Aperture synthesis radiometer · Frequency dependence
Calibration · Amplitude and phase errors

1 Introduction

Since Aperture synthesis radiometers are of increasing interest in earth observation applications due to reduced mass and volume of instruments compared to the traditional real-aperture radiometers in the past decades. In recent decades several aperture synthesis radiometers have been study in spaceborne applications of earth observation, such as ESTAR [1], MIRAS [2], and GeoSTAR [3].

In aperture synthesis radiometers, the amplitude and phase calibration of the measured visibility samples are a key problem. The customary method is correlated noise injection using a calibration subsystem, such as in MIRAS, HUT-2D [4] and the prototype of GeoSTAR. However, correlated noise injection method [5] needs a added power distributed network [6], which is difficult from the viewpoint of mass, volume, power and phase equalization of the noise injected in each channel, and unlikely feasible for aperture synthesis radiometers with large arrays for higher frequencies. Moreover, it cannot correct the imperfections of the antenna array, for example, antenna pattern amplitude and phase errors, antenna pointing errors, position errors [7, 8], which are significant for aperture synthesis radiometers with high frequencies. But using external calibrated (calibration) methods, they can overcome the above problems.

One of external calibrated methods is carried out using single external noise source in a known location, this approach can calibrate the amplitude and phase errors of aperture synthesis radiometers without extra calibration hardware [9]. Moreover, the external source method can calibrate some errors that can't be taken into account by the

X. Sun et al. (Eds.): ICCCS 2018, LNCS 11066, pp. 506–517, 2018.
https://doi.org/10.1007/978-3-030-00015-8_44

correlated noise injection method. But the power of external noise source is not strong enough and constant within the bandwidth of aperture synthesis radiometers, and the power of external noise source presents a small variation within the receivers' bandwidth. In the classical equation and the Corbella equation, they don't take into account the antenna voltage pattern frequency dependence, the antenna voltage patterns do also present a small variation within the receivers' bandwidth, so the antenna voltage pattern frequency dependence has some impact in the calibration using external noise sources, and the amplitude and phase errors have frequency dependence calibrated by external noise sources.

In this paper, the amplitude and phase errors frequency dependence in aperture synthesis radiometers using external noise sources have been analyzed, and the relationship of using external noise source and single frequency signal source as an external calibrated source is studied. A novel external calibration method based on three external single frequency signals is proposed for the calibration of amplitude and phase. Basic equations and the formulation of calibration using external noise sources have been presented. Simulations and experiments are also conduced to demonstrate the validity of the proposed method and the amplitude and phase frequency dependence. The method can be used as an alternative in the calibration of an aperture synthesis radiometer.

2 Basic Function

2.1 The Visibility Function

In aperture synthesis radiometers, the correlation of signals collected by two antennas are called the samples of the visibility function V (in units of kelvin) when observe a scene with the brightness temperature $T_B(\xi, \eta)$. Without considering system imperfections, the equation that relates the samples of visibility function, which are measured by two antenna elements k and j, to the brightness temperature is given by [1, 10]

$$
V_{kj}^{id}(u_{kj}, v_{kj}) = \frac{1}{\sqrt{\Omega_k \Omega_j}} \iint_{\xi^2 + \eta^2 \leq 1} \frac{T_B(\xi, \eta) - T_{rec}}{\sqrt{1 - \xi^2 - \eta^2}} \cdot F_{nk}(\xi, \eta) F_{nj}^*(\xi, \eta)
$$
$$
\cdot \tilde{r}_{kj}\left(-\frac{u_{kj}\xi + v_{kj}\eta}{f_o}\right) \cdot e^{-j2\pi(u_{kj}\xi + v_{kj}\eta)} d\xi d\eta \tag{1}
$$

Where $T_B(\xi, \eta)$ is the brightness temperature, T_{rec} is the receiver's physical temperature (assumed equal in all elements) [10], $\Omega_{k,j}$ is the antenna solid angle, F_{nk} and F_{nj} are the normalized antenna copolar voltage patterns, $f_0 = c/\lambda$ is the center frequency, and (u_{kj}, v_{kj}) is called the "baseline" and equal to the difference between the antenna k and j positions over XY plane normalized to the wavelength at the central frequency f_0, $(\xi, \eta) = (\sin \theta \cos \varphi, \sin \theta \sin \varphi)$ are the direction cosines with respect to the X and Y axis. $\tilde{r}_{kj}$ is the so-called fringe-washing function that accounts for spatial decorrelation effects [11]

$$\tilde{r}_{kj}(\tau) = \frac{1}{\sqrt{B_k B_j}} \int_{-f_0}^{\infty} H_{nk}(f + f_0) \cdot H_{nj}^*(f + f_0) e^{j2\pi f\tau} df$$
$$= \frac{e^{-j2\pi f_0 \tau}}{\sqrt{B_k B_j}} \int_0^{\infty} H_{nk}(f) \cdot H_{nj}^*(f) e^{j2\pi f\tau} df \tag{2}$$

Which depends on the normalized receivers' frequency response $H_{nk,\,j}(f)$; the transit time τ form a given direction (ξ, η) to the pair of elements involved, its defined as $\tau = -(u_{kj}\xi + v_{kj}\eta)/f_0$, and the noise equivalent bandwidth $B_{k,j}$ are defined as $B_{k,j} = \int_0^{\infty} |H_{nk,j}(f)|^2 df$.

The so-called modified brightness temperature is defined as [12]

$$T_M(\xi, \eta) = \frac{T_B(\xi, \eta) - T_{rec}}{\sqrt{1 - \xi^2 - \eta^2}} \cdot F_{nk}(\xi, \eta) \cdot F_{nj}^*(\xi, \eta) \tag{3}$$

In the ideal case, (antenna patterns $F_{nk}(\xi, \eta) = F_{nj}(\xi, \eta) = F_n(\xi, \eta)$), the modified brightness temperature can be recovered by means of a discrete Fourier transform of the visibilities as

$$T_M(\xi, \eta) = F^{-1}[V^{id}(u, v)] \tag{4}$$

The above Eq. (1) can be rewritten in its discrete as follow

$$V_{kj}^{id}(u_{kj}, v_{kj}) = \Delta S \cdot \sum_{m=0}^{M} \sum_{n=0}^{N} \frac{T_B(\xi_{mn}, \eta_{mn}) - T_{rec}}{\sqrt{1 - \xi_{mn}^2 - \eta_{mn}^2}} F_{nk}(\xi_{mn}, \eta_{mn}) F_{nj}^*(\xi_{mn}, \eta_{mn})$$
$$\cdot \tilde{r}_{kj}(-\frac{u_{kj}\xi_{mn} + v_{kj}\eta_{mn}}{f_0}) \cdot e^{-j2\pi(u_{kj}\xi_{mn} + v_{kj}\eta_{mn})} \tag{5}$$

Where ΔS is the pixel area in the (ξ, η) domain. (For example, $\Delta S = \sqrt{3}d^2/2$ when the distribution of the antennas is "Y"-shaped with the distance of adjacent antennas is d.)

2.2 The Frequency Dependence in Visibility Function

In (1) and (2), they always assume the system is perfection and the only frequency-dependent magnitudes are normalized receivers' frequency responses $H_{nk,j}(f)$. However, the system is imperfection and exists many errors, such as antenna errors, channel errors and baseline errors. And the antenna voltage patterns $(F_{nk,j}(\xi, \eta; f))$ do present a small variation with the receivers' bandwidth B and actually this term in (1) should appear inside the integral of the fringe-washing function (2). To simplify the notation, only the frequency dependence will be made explicit in each product of antenna patterns. In this case, the Corbella function can be written as [13]

$$V_{kj} = \frac{1}{\sqrt{\Omega_k \Omega_j}} \int_{\xi^2 + \eta^2 \le 1} \frac{1}{\sqrt{1 - \xi^2 - \eta^2}} \cdot \frac{e^{-j2\pi f_0 \tau}}{\sqrt{B_k B_j}} \{\int_0^{\infty} [(T_B(\xi, \eta) - T_{rec}) \cdot F_{nk}(\xi, \eta; f) \cdot$$
$$F_{nj}^*(\xi, \eta; f) \cdot H_{nk}(f) \cdot H_{nj}^*(f)] e^{j2\pi f\tau} df\} d\xi d\eta \tag{6}$$

Now, following the procedure as (1) to (5), (6) also can be discretized as

$$V_{kj}^{id}(u_{kj}, v_{kj}) = \Delta S \cdot \sum_{m=0}^{M} \sum_{n=0}^{N} \frac{1}{\sqrt{1 - \xi_{mn}^2 - \eta_{mn}^2}} \frac{e^{-j2\pi f_0 \tau}}{\sqrt{B_k B_j}} \{ \int_0^{\infty} [T_B(\xi_{mn}, \eta_{mn}) - T_{rec}] \cdot F_{nk}(\xi_{mn}, \eta_{mn}; f)$$
$$\cdot F_{nj}^*(\xi_{mn}, \eta_{mn}; f) \cdot H_{nk}(f) \cdot H_{nj}^*(f) \cdot e^{j2\pi f \tau} df \} \cdot e^{-j2\pi(u_{kj}\xi_{mn} + v_{kj}\eta_{mn})}$$

$$(7)$$

Since the antenna voltage pattern frequency dependence is small at each (ξ, η), each of the integrals versus frequency can be evaluated using a Taylor series of the product of the antenna voltage patterns around $f \approx f_0$ $(f = f_0 + f'. f' \approx 0)$[13], so

$$\frac{e^{-j2\pi f_0 \tau}}{\sqrt{B_k B_j}} \int_0^{\infty} [\cdot F_{nk}(\xi, \eta; f) \cdot F_{nj}^*(\xi, \eta; f) \cdot H_{nk}(f) \cdot H_{nj}^*(f)] e^{j2\pi f \tau} df$$
$$= \tilde{r}_{kj}(\tau) \cdot [\tfrac{1}{4} F_{nk}(\xi, \eta; f_0 - B/2) \cdot F_{nj}^*(\xi, \eta; f_0 - B/2) + \tfrac{1}{2} F_{nk}(\xi, \eta; f_0) \cdot F_{nj}^*(\xi, \eta; f_0)$$
$$+ \tfrac{1}{4} F_{nk}(\xi, \eta; f_0 + B/2) \cdot F_{nj}^*(\xi, \eta; f_0 + B/2)]$$

$$(8)$$

2.3 The Errors Model

In the ideal case that all antennas have the same radiation pattern, but this is impossible due to mechanical tolerances. The model of amplitude and phase errors of the antenna voltage patterns can described as follow

$$F_{nk}(\xi, \eta) = F_n(\xi, \eta)[1 + \Delta F_{nk}(\xi, \eta)] e^{j\Delta \varphi_{ak}(\xi, \eta)} \tag{9}$$

Where $F_{nk}(\xi, \eta)$ is the radiation voltages of antenna element K, $F_n(\xi, \eta)$ is the average radiation voltages of all the antenna elements, $\Delta F_{nk}(\xi, \eta)$ and $\Delta \varphi_{ak}(\xi, \eta)$ are the voltage amplitude and phase errors (at each (ξ, η)), respectively.

So the measured visibility and the ideal visibility samples can be further models as.

$$V_{kj}^{mea} = g_k g_j V_{kj}^{id} \cdot e^{j(a_k - a_j + a_{kj} + \varphi_n)} \tag{10}$$

Where g_k and g_j are the relative amplitude errors of element k and j (antenna plus receiver), $g_k = (1 + \Delta F_{nk}(\xi, \eta)) \cdot g_{rk}$, in which $g_{rk} = \sqrt{T_{ak}/(T_{ak} + T_{rk})}$ is the amplitude errors of receiver k, with T_{ak} and T_{rk} are the antenna temperature and the equivalent noise temperature of receiver k, respectively. a_k and a_j are the phase errors of element k and j, $a_k = \Delta \varphi_{ak} + \Delta \varphi_{rk}$ is the sum of antenna phase errors and receiver phase errors of element k. a_{kj} is the phase of the fringe-washing function, which depends on the discrepancies in filter frequency responses receiver k and j, and the last phase term φ_n is a random phase caused by the thermal noise of receiver, which can be negligible when the correlation value is large (large signal-to-noise ratio) and the integration time is long enough.

So when the amplitude and phase errors are estimated, the measured visibility can be corrected as

$$V_{kj}^C = g_k^{-1} g_j^{-1} V_{kj}^{mea} \cdot e^{-j(a_k - a_j + a_{kj} + \varphi_n)} \tag{11}$$

In the following sections, an external calibration method (noise source and single frequency signal source) for calibrating instrumental amplitude and phase errors will be introduced, the frequency dependence of the phase and amplitude errors of receiver will be analyzed, and a an improved calibration method base on three single frequency signals will be proposed.

3 Noise Modeling Correction of Instrumental Phase and Amplitude Errors Using External Point Sources

This section introduces a method to calibrate the measured visibility by a external noise source, and analyzes the amplitude and phase errors frequency independence by external single frequency signals, the relationship of using external noise source and single frequency signal source as an external calibrated source is investigated, finally presents an improved calibrated method for the amplitude and phase errors of instrument.

3.1 Calibrated by an External Noise Source

Assume that an external noise source with apparent brightness temperature T_{ps} placed at pixel (ξ_{ps}, η_{ps}) is given by

$$T_{B\_P}(\xi_{mn}, \eta_{mn}) = T_{ps} \cdot \delta(\xi_{mn} - \xi_{ps}, \eta_{mn} - \eta_{ps}) \tag{12}$$

Where δ is the 2-D Dirac delta, and (ξ_{ps}, η_{ps}) is precisely known. The external noise source visibility measured by antennas k and j is given by introducing (12) and (10) into (5) as

$$V_{kj}^{PS}(u_{kj}, v_{kj}) = g_k g_j \Delta S \cdot \frac{T_{B\_P}(\xi_{ps}, \eta_{ps}) - T_{rec}}{\sqrt{1 - \xi_{ps}^2 - \eta_{ps}^2}} \left| F_n(\xi_{ps}, \eta_{ps}) \right|^2$$
$$\cdot \tilde{r}_{kj}\left(-\frac{u_{kj}\xi_{ps} + v_{kj}\eta_{ps}}{f_o}\right) \cdot e^{-j2\pi(u_{kj}\xi_{ps} + v_{kj}\eta_{ps})} \cdot e^{j(\varphi_{ak} - \varphi_{aj} + \varphi_{kj} + \varphi_n)} \tag{13}$$

Where it has taken into account the amplitude and phase errors of instruments (antennas plus receivers), and the fringe-washing function is known. In ideal case, the measured visibility of the same noise source is

$$V_{kj}^{PS\_ideal}(u_{kj}, v_{kj}) = \Delta S \cdot \frac{T_{B\_P}(\xi_{ps}, \eta_{ps}) - T_{rec}}{\sqrt{1 - \xi_{ps}^2 - \eta_{ps}^2}} \left| F_n(\xi_{ps}, \eta_{ps}) \right|^2$$
$$\cdot \tilde{r}_{kj}\left(-\frac{u_{kj}\xi_{ps} + v_{kj}\eta_{ps}}{f_o}\right) \cdot e^{-j2\pi(u_{kj}\xi_{ps} + v_{kj}\eta_{ps})} \tag{14}$$

Therefore, the relationship of (13) and (14) can be rewritten as (9)

$$V_{kj}^{PS} = g_k g_j V_{kj}^{PS\_ideal} \cdot e^{j(a_k - a_j + a_{kj} + \varphi_n)} \tag{15}$$

Considering the first receiver as a reference, and assign its amplitude and phase be 1 and 0°, respectively, so the other receiver's amplitude errors related with the first receiver is

$$[|g_1|^2 \quad |g_2|^2 \quad \cdots \quad |g_M|^2] = |g_1|^2 [1 \quad |g_2/g_1|^2 \quad \cdots \quad |g_M/g_1|^2] \tag{16}$$

And the relative amplitude errors is defined as

$$\Gamma = [1 \quad |g_2/g_1| \quad \cdots \quad |g_M/g_1|] \tag{17}$$

In (14), the self-correlations of all elements are the same

$$V_{kk}^{PS\_ideal} = V_{jj}^{PS\_ideal} \ (k \neq j) \tag{18}$$

So, we can get the relative amplitude errors as

$$|\Gamma_i| = \sqrt{V_{kk}^{PS}/V_{11}^{PS}} \tag{19}$$

While, the phase of measured visibility can be written as

$$\varphi_{kj}^{PS}(u_{kj}, v_{kj}) = angle(V_{kj}^{ps}) \tag{20}$$

So

$$\varphi_{kj}^{PS}(u_{kj}, v_{kj}) = -2\pi(u_{kj}\xi_{ps} + v_{kj}\eta_{ps}) + a_k - a_j + a_{kj} + \varphi_n \tag{21}$$

The location of external calibrated noise is precisely known, the phase of fringe-washing function term a_{kj} must be known or negligible, and the last term φ_n can be negligible due to large signal-to-noise radio, so we can get

$$a_{kj}^{cal} = a_k - a_j \tag{22}$$

By all the measured visibility, we can get the phase errors matrix H

$$H = angle(W) = \begin{bmatrix} 0 & a_2 - a_1 & a_3 - a_1 & a_4 - a_1 & \cdots & a_M - a_1 \\ & 0 & a_3 - a_2 & a_4 - a_2 & \cdots & a_M - a_2 \\ & & 0 & a_4 - a_3 & \cdots & a_M - a_3 \\ & & & 0 & \ddots & \vdots \\ & & & & 0 & a_M - a_{M-1} \\ & & & & & 0 \end{bmatrix} \tag{23}$$

The phase errors a_k are now retrieved by solving the above equation in a least-squares sense even in the case that only the equations related to visibility samples with large signal-to-noise ratio are used. Once the individual phase errors related to each antenna are obtained, all the visibility samples measured when imaging a target scene can be corrected as

$$V_{kj}^{cal} = V_{kj}^{taerget} \cdot e^{-j(a_k - a_j)} / g_k g_j \qquad (24)$$

Using the above method, the amplitude and phase errors of instruments can be calibrated as long as the visibility samples with higher signal-to-noise ratio.

3.2   The Phase and Amplitude Errors Frequency Dependence

In the above, we assume the apparent brightness temperature of the external noise source is constant. In fact, its apparent brightness temperature also presents a small frequency dependence within the bandwidth of the system. Each of the integrals versus frequency can be evaluated using a Taylor series of the product of the antenna voltage patterns and the external noise source's apparent brightness temperature (derived in detail in appendix) around $f \approx f_0$ $(f = f_0 + f'. f' \approx 0)$ [14], so

$$\frac{e^{-j2\pi f_0 \tau}}{\sqrt{B_k B_j}} \int_0^\infty [(T_B(\xi, \eta; f) - T_{rec}) \cdot F_{nk}(\xi, \eta; f) \cdot F_{nj}^*(\xi, \eta; f) \cdot H_{nk}(f) \cdot H_{nj}^*(f)] e^{j2\pi f \tau} df$$
$$\approx \tilde{r}_{kj}(\tau) \cdot [\tfrac{1}{4}(T_B(\xi, \eta; f_0 - B/2) - T_{rec})F_{nk}(\xi, \eta; f_0 - B/2) \cdot F_{nj}^*(\xi, \eta; f_0 - B/2)$$
$$+ \tfrac{1}{2}(T_B(\xi, \eta; f_0) - T_{rec})F_{nk}(\xi, \eta; f_0) \cdot F_{nj}^*(\xi, \eta; f_0) \qquad (25)$$
$$+ \tfrac{1}{4}(T_B(\xi, \eta; f_0 + B/2) - T_{rec})F_{nk}(\xi, \eta; f_0 + B/2) \cdot F_{nj}^*(\xi, \eta; f_0 + B/2)]$$

It is note that the frequency dependence of the antenna voltage patterns and the brightness temperature of the external calibrated source within the bandwidth of receivers can be related to the product of them at three single frequency $f_0 - B/2$, f_0, $f_0 + B/2$, if the amplitude and phase errors at the three frequency can be calibrated by the same method with single frequency signal as an external calibrated source, and assume the amplitude and phases errors calibrated by external single frequency signal source are $g_{f_0 - B/2}$, g_{f_0}, $g_{f_0 + B/2}$ and $a_{f_0 - B/2}$, a_{f_0}, $a_{f_0 + B/2}$, respectively. Finally the amplitude and phase errors can be calculated as

$$g = \frac{1}{4} g_{f_0 - B/2} + \frac{1}{2} g_{f_0} + \frac{1}{4} g_{f_0 + B/2} \qquad (26)$$

$$a = \frac{1}{4} a_{f_0 - B/2} + \frac{1}{2} a_{f_0} + \frac{1}{4} a_{f_0 + B/2} \qquad (27)$$

After that, g and a can be used to calibrate the measured visibility as (11) and (24). It must be point that the phase of fringe washing function a_{kj} and random phase φ_n due to thermal noise have been negligible in (24). In order to reduce the residual errors, we can get the more accuracy phase a_{kj}, the single frequency signal has a large SNR and extend the integrate time to negligible random phase φ_n, that can be easily meet using a single frequency signal as an external calibration source. It must be point that an artificial point with single frequency placed on appropriate on the Earth, which could be switched on and off as sequence, would be a good alternative method to calibrate the radiometer in orbit.

4   Simulation

In this section, numerical simulations are conducted to validity the performance of the proposed method. Because the proposed calibrated method is not independent of the antenna array of aperture synthesis radiometers, any kind antenna array can be chosen to test the method and only to known the displacement of antenna array. In simulation, the number of antennas is 50, the minimum separation is about 10.6 cm (0.5λ), center frequency is 1413.5 MHz, bandwidth is 20 MHz, integral time is 0.03 s. The receiver noise temperature is 300 K, the excess noise ratio (ENR) of the external noise source is about 13.15 dB within the bandwidth, the power of external single frequency signals is about -80 dBm, both are kept in the dynamic range of receivers.

In order to consideration about the impact of thermal noise and non-separable phase term, the amplitude and phase errors are added to a random amplitude term with 0.005 standard deviation and a random phase errors with $1°$ deviation.

The results calibrated by the external noise source and the proposed compared to the raw amplitude and phase errors are shown in Fig. (1). This demonstrates that the proposed method can calibrate the amplitude and phase errors as well as the external noise source. In Fig. (2) shows that the residual errors calibrated by the both methods. The standard deviations of amplitude and phase errors calibrated by the external noise source are 0.26% and $0.5344°$, respectively, and that calibrated by the proposed method are 0.26% and $0.7055°$, respectively. Although, the results show that the residual errors calibrated by the external noise source are better than that calibrated by the proposed method, the results calibrated by the proposed method are acceptable. So the proposed method can be as an alternative method in the calibration of in-orbit synthesis aperture radiometers.

5   Experiment

The amplitude and phase errors frequency dependence and the proposed calibrated method are validated by L-band 5-channel aperture synthesis radiometer developed by China Academy of Space Technology (Xi'an). The arrangement of the antenna array is linear minimum redundancy, their position are [0 2 3 6 7] (unit space is half-wavelength). In order to verify the errors frequency dependence and the proposed method, the external calibrated sources are noise source and signal source with variable frequency, respectively.

The results of the experiment are shown in the following figures. Because of the 1th channel as a reference one, the amplitude errors are always 1 and the phase errors are zero in Fig. 3. In this figure, we can known that the change of the amplitude errors frequency dependence in the 1401 Mhz−1425 MHz are with in 0.05, the minimum

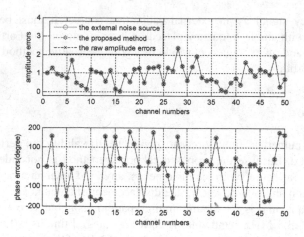

Fig. 1. The amplitude (top) and phase (bottom) errors calibrated by the external noise source and the proposed method.

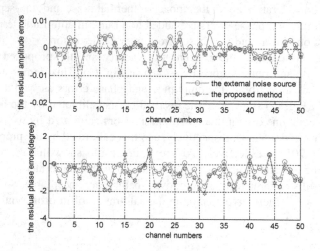

Fig. 2. The residual amplitude (top) and phase (bottom) calibrated by the external noise source and the proposed method.

change is the 5th channel, that is about 0.01, this indicates the frequency response of 5th channel is good and its performances are stable and reliable. The change of the 4th is also about 0.01 if do not consider the frequency of 1401 MHz. The change of the other two channels (2th and 3th) is not good. In fact, the performance of the aperture synthesis radiometers is more stable and reliable, the performance of the proposed method is better.

Figure 4 shows a comparison of the amplitude (up) and phase (bottom) errors obtained by the external noise and the proposed method, the results are consistent with previous derived results and simulations. So the proposed method can be as an alternative in the calibration of aperture synthesis radiometers.

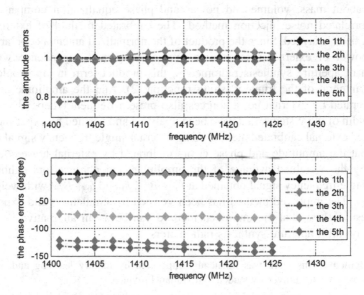

Fig. 3. The frequency dependence of the amplitude (top) and phase (bottom) errors calibrated by the proposed method (analyze the phase errors propagation in details).

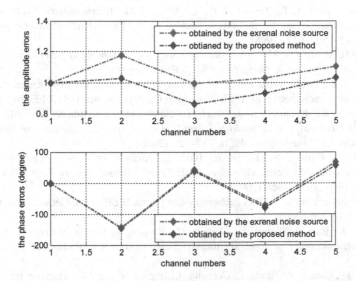

Fig. 4. The amplitude (top) and phase (bottom) errors calibrated by the external noise source and the proposed method (analyze the phase errors propagation in details).

6 Conclusion

The calibrated method that (using) the external noise source can overcome some problems about mass, volume and power and phase equalization compared to the internal correlated noise injection method. The calibrated method of external noise source has been analyzed. Since the product of the normalized antenna copolar patterns and the power of external noise source present frequency dependence within the bandwidth of aperture synthesis radiometers, this product term in (1) should appear inside the integral of the fringe-washing function (2). And the amplitude and phase errors calibrated by external noise sources also present frequency dependence within the bandwidth of the systems, that have been analyzed and verified by experiments, and an improved external calibrated method using external single frequency signal has been present, that the amplitude and phase errors calibrated by external noise sources are replaced by the weighted average of the amplitude and phase errors calibrated by external single frequency signal obtained at $f_0 - B/2, f_0$ and $f_0 + B/2$ with weights 1/4, 1/2 and 1/4. The improved method has been verified by simulations and experiments, and the results show that the improved method can be as an alternative in the calibration of on-orbit aperture synthesis radiometers.

Acknowledgment. This work was financially supported by inquiry learning and innovation experiment program for university students in Hunan Province.

References

1. Ruf, C.S., Swift, C.T., Tanner, A.B., Le Vine, D.M.: Interferometric synthetic aperture microwave radiometry for the remote sensing of the Earth. IEEE Trans. Geosci. Remote Sens. **26**(5), 597–611 (1998)
2. Kerr, Y.H., et al.: The SMOS mission: new tool for monitoring key elements of the global water cycle. Proc. IEEE **98**(5), 666–687 (2010)
3. Tanner, A.B., et al.: Initial results of the GeoSTAR prototype (geosynchronous synthetic thinned array radiometer). In: IEEE Aerospace Conference, pp. 1–9. IEEE, Big Sky (2006)
4. Rautiainen, K., Kainulainen, J., Auer, T., Pihlflyckt, J., Kettunen, J., Hallikainen, M.: Helsinki University of Technology L-band airborne synthetic aperture radiometer. IEEE Trans. Geosci. Remote Sens. **46**(3), 717–726 (2008)
5. Corbella, I., Camps, A., Torres, F., Bará, J.: Analysis of noise-injection networks for interferometric radiometer calibration. IEEE Trans. Microw. Theory Tech. **48**(4), 545–552 (2000). **45**(7), 1958–1966 (2007)
6. Lemmetyinen, J., et al.: SMOS calibration subsystem. IEEE Trans. Geosci. Remote Sens. **45** (11), 3691–3700 (2007)
7. Camps, A., Bara, J., Torres, F., Corbella, I., Romeu, J.: Impact of antenna errors on the radiometric accuracy of large aperture synthesis radiometers. Radio Sci. **32**(2), 657–668 (1997)
8. Torres, F., Camps, A., Bara, J., Corbella, I.: Impact of receiver errors on the radiometric resolution of large two-dimensional aperture synthesis radiometers. Radio Sci. **32**(2), 629–641 (1997)

9. Ke, C., Wei, G., Qingxia, L., Fangmin, H., Rong, J.: Phase and amplitude calibration of HUST Ku-band aperture synthesis radiometer using external source. In: IEEE International Symposium on MAPE, pp. 356–359. IEEE, Beijing (2009)
10. Corbella, I., Duffo, N., Vall-llossera, M., Camps, A., Torres, F.: The visibility function in interferometric aperture synthesis radiometry. IEEE Trans. Geosci. Remote Sens. **42**(8), 1677–1682 (2004)
11. Butora, R., Martin-Neira, M., Rivada, A.: Fringe-washing function calibration in aperture synthesis microwave radiometry. Radio Sci. **38**(2), 15-1–15-5 (2003)
12. Camps, A.: Application of interferometric radiometry to earth observation. Ph.D. dissertation, Department Telecommunication Engineering, niv. Politècnica deCatalunya, Barcelona, Spain (1996)
13. Camps, A., et al.: The impact of antenna pattern frequency dependence in aperture synthesis microwave radiometers. IEEE Trans. Geosci. Remote Sens. **43**(10), 2218–2224 (2005)
14. Torres, F., Tanner, A.B., Brown, S.T., Lambrigsten, B.H.: Analysis of array distortion in a microwave interferometric radiometer: Application to the GeoSTAR project. IEEE Trans. Geosci. Remote Sens. **45**(7), 1958–1966 (2007)

Tracing System of Meat Supply Based on RFID and Two-Dimensional Code Technology

Xu Yang[1], Yongbin Zhao[1], Ranran Li[1(✉)], Fengfeng Li[2], and Xiaolin Qi[3]

[1] School of Information Science and Technology, Shijiazhuang Tiedao University, Shijiazhuang, Hebei 050043, China
13259823032@163.com, zhaoyungbin@163.com,
liranranhl@163.com
[2] Shijiazhuang City Hydropower and Rural Electrification Development, Shijiazhuang, Hebei 050051, China
1059903655@qq.com
[3] Beijing Railway and Track Maintenance Department, China Railway Beijing Group Co, Ltd., Beijing 100077, China
592377732@qq.com

Abstract. In recent years, with the rapid development of agricultural Internet of things, many different agricultural and sideline products can be bought easily which from different regions, but it also brings about more problems of foods safety (production and sale of fake eggs, water injection Pork, etc.). These issues affect social development and people's health seriously. According these issues, all stages of agricultural products should be monitor and control. This paper introduces the traceability system which integrates RFID and EPC technologies, and uses ONS database to store key information. The tracing information can be queried that user login in traceability system and identify the two-dimensional code. People use the mobile scan to encrypted the QR code to get the information of agriculture and food products they need. The traceability system guarantees the safety of meat in all aspects of the supply chain. The system should be developed and promoted in society.

Keywords: Internet of Thing · Traceability system · Agricultural safety

1 Introduction

1.1 Background

The development of agriculture is a premise for the country's harmony and stability. As the country develops rapidly, the problem of food safety is increasing. For example: various meat which many people eat is also at the center of the whirlpool of the problem. In recent years, there have been many security incidents, such as injections of meat growth and other security incidents, which impact the meat market. Although the relevant government departments have already issued corresponding policies to

© Springer Nature Switzerland AG 2018
X. Sun et al. (Eds.): ICCCS 2018, LNCS 11066, pp. 518–527, 2018.
https://doi.org/10.1007/978-3-030-00015-8_45

supervise and manage these issues, but the effect is small. So ensuring the safety of meat foods has become an important task at present. For the traceability systems, foreign countries have already established a sound mechanism to monitor and manage food safety. Our country should also follow the wave of Internet of Things technology closely to provide a powerful means for domestic food safety supervision and tracing.

1.2 Development Status

Supply chain of meat had many problems: unqualified meat breeding and processing, lacking of supervision during transportation and so on. Foreign scientists had already put forward corresponding solutions at the end of the 20th century, and then they had improved the theory and achieve it. In 1997, the European Union established a complete traceability system for cattle, beef and beef products after suffering from mad cow disease. The EU is considered a pioneer of the food traceability system, because it has been concentrate on developing and improving of the food information traceability system for many years. At present, the traceability system for agricultural products that the EU has established includes livestock animals and animal products, genetically modified organisms, and foods and feeds containing genetically modified organisms. In 2001, Japan also began promoted traceability systems for agricultural and food products, and implemented a traceability system for beef in 2003. At present, Japan also has a relatively complete traceability system for agricultural and food products. After the "9.11" incident, the United States also urged various filed to establish traceability systems, and there is currently a mature system. However, our country's traceability system has evolved later than other Western countries, Jufang Xie and others did a research on pork traceability system in 2003, in the next year, Shandong Province explored the traceability system of vegetable quality and safety. In 2007, our country achieved a traceability system for beef firstly. The project of quality of beef traceability system was launched in Xinjiang which ensure the supply chain security and provide safety meat for consumers. Not only that, our traceability system platform is not uniform. At present, there are five influential agricultural products traceability system platforms in China. However, they are not completely unified in all aspects, storing and sharing information cannot be achieved, which making users to query information inconvenient. The inconvenience has limited the promotion of domestic traceability systems. In many respects, there is still a big gap with foreign countries.

1.3 Internet of Things Concepts and Architecture

The concept of the Internet of Things was introduced in 1999. It was also known as Web of Things and was regarded as an extension of the Internet. Application innovation is the core and Innovation based on user experience is the soul of the Internet of Things develop. At the World Summit on the Information Society held in Tunis in 2005, the International Telecommunication Union released the "ITU Internet Report 2005: Internet of Things," which officially put forward the concept of "Internet of Things." Some people have also defined the Internet of Things: Real-time acquisition of any monitoring and connection through a variety of information sensing devices, such as sensors, radio frequency identification (RFID) technology, global positioning systems, infrared sensors, laser scanners and other devices and technologies, an interactive object or process that collects information about its sound, light, heat, electricity, mechanics, location, etc. and forms a huge network with the Internet. It purpose is to achieve the connection between things and things, things and people, all the items and the network facilitate identification, management and control.

The Internet of Things architecture is divided into three layers: the sensor layer, the network layer, and the application layer, as shown in Fig. 1:

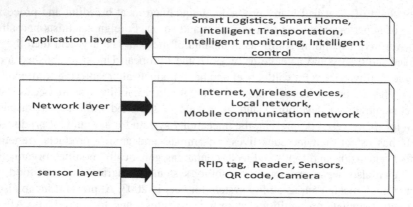

Fig. 1. The Internet of Things architecture is divided into three layers

(1) The sensory layer is located at the bottom of the Internet of Things. It mainly solves the problem of object recognition and object information acquisition. It is divided into two steps. The first step is to complete the data acquisition through the sensing device. The second step is to transmit the data to the corresponding component through the transmission device.

(2) The network layer is located between the sensory layer and the application layer. It is based on the existing network that passes the information obtained by the sensory layer to the upper layer users. It involves many protocol and is a more difficult part to understand.

(3) The application layer is the top layer of the Internet of Things. It is mainly through the information obtained to achieve the correct control.

1.4 RFID Technology

Radio Frequency Identification (RFID) is a wireless communication technology that can identify specific targets and read and write related data through radio signals without identifying the mechanical or optical contact between the system and a specific target. It is similar to bar code scanning, which similar with bar code. For bar code technology, it attaches a bar code that is encoded in advance to a target object and scans it with a dedicated scanner. The scanner uses an optical signal to transmit bar magnetic signals to a scanning reader/writer. RFID, on the other hand, uses a dedicated RFID reader and a dedicated RFID tag that can be attached to the target, and uses frequency signals to transmit information from the RFID tag to the RFID reader.

The RFID tag is composed a coil and a tag core. The core can store a specified format and a certain amount of electronic data. It is divided into two kinds of active and passive tags. After receiving the signal from the reader, the tag is sent the stored information at the core, which known as passive tags. RFID tags can be made in different sizes and shapes, and they are extremely portable and have excellent adhesive properties.

For the disadvantages of low efficiency and labor intensity of barcode scanning technology, RFID technology undoubtedly changed the status. The readers do not need light source, superior penetrating ability, and can read multiple labels at the same time, and also reduce the labor intensity, and less affected by environmental factorsso I chose RFID technology.

Although RFID has many advantages, there are also many problems:

(1) Expensive prices: At present, the price of RFID electronic tags is still very high, and companies need a lot of funds to invest in this area. If the classification of electronic tags is required, I am afraid that the prices are even more expensive.
(2) There is no harmonization of international standards: The practical standards for RFID electronic tags are different, and their operating frequencies are not the same, which affects general promotion.
(3) Breakthrough in technology: Nowadays, RFID technology can easily affect communication signals and affect normal use.

But the development prospect of RFID technology is very broad. In the future, more fields will surely be applied. It deserves more in-depth research and promotion.

A typical RFID system consists of three parts: RFID tags, readers and back-end servers. As shown in Fig. 2.

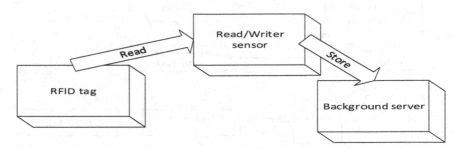

Fig. 2. A typical RFID system consists of three parts

(1) RFID Tag: It consists of a coupling element and a chip. Each tag has a unique electronic code and is attached to the object to identify the target object.
(2) Reader: A device that reads tag information and can be designed to be handheld or stationary.
(3) Background database: It used to store background data.

1.5   EPC Internet of Things Technology

EPC Technology Introduction (Third Level)
EPC (Electronic Product Code) Internet of Things technology is a typical Internet of Things technology and finally goal is to establish a worldwide, open identification standard for each single commodity. It consists of global product electronic code system, radio frequency identification system, and information network system.

Global product electronic code EPC coding system is a new generation of GTIN-compatible coding standard. It is the extension and extension of the global unified identity system and is an important part of the global unified identity system, which is the core part and key part of the EPC system. The EPC code is a segment number composed of data fields such as a version number, a domain name manager, an object classification number, a serial number. In the past, EPC uses a 64-bit encoding structure due to cost work and now the most commonly EPC encoding standard uses a 96-bit data junction.

EPC Internet of Things Workflow (Third Level)
The data is only the EPC which read from RFID by the reader and the product information according to the EPC is stored in the EPCIS server. The address of the EPCIS server is stored in the ONS. As shown in Fig. 3. This picture is shows EPC Internet of Things workflow.

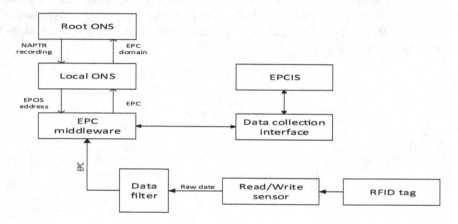

Fig. 3. The EPC Internet of Things workflow

(1) The reader can quickly read information of tag and filter data and the transmit the information to the EPC internet of things When the RFID tag passes from the inspection point. The EPC middleware is a device for controlling and managing FRID tags and readers. The collected EPC information is stored in EPCIS.
(2) The user needs to store the EPC information on his own EPCIS server and register it on the ONS server.

(3) The local ONS is firstly queried When user want to query data. When there is record, the local ONS returns the EPCIS address and query information by this address; when there is no record, the local ONS inquires the root ONS and the root ONS returns the remote ONS and query information by this address.

Combining RFID technology and EPC technology. The supply chain of pork can be linked effectively by RFID tag so that each piece of meat corresponds to the pig one by one. Through the EPC code, each piece of pork can be provided with a unique identification. For example: 53,13234346,1004,111002314. 53 is the version number, which represents the selected EPC-96 encoding; 13234346 is the domain name manager, 13 represents the farm, 23 represents the slaughterhouse, 43 represents the split packaging plant, 45 represents transport company and 46 represents the sales shop; 1004 is the object classification number, representing the hind leg meat from the left dichotomous body; 111002314 is the serial number, 111002 represents October sales time, and 314 is the serial number. Finally convert the code to hexadecimal. The information stored in the ONS database which is the EPC code that is easy to read.

1.6   Two-Dimensional Code Technology

Technology Introduction

Matrix two-dimensional code has a great influence in the current society, such as social services, payment services or security checks and so on. However, it also brings certain risks, QR code will be injected virus. So in this section we will focus on enhancing the security of QR codes.

Western countries began to study two-dimensional code technology in 1980s and now they have a mature code system. PDF417 QR Code, QR Code, etc. compared with other countries, QR code technology started late in my country, but we also made corresponding progress in the security of QR codes.

In this paper, we combine the QR code and the DES encryption and use DES to encrypt QR codes during the transmission process which can improve safety of system.

Image Encryption

Main steps for encrypting and decrypting a QR code

(1) Select any encryption key;
(2) Encrypt the QR code which was converted to the type of string;
(3) Observe the changes;
(4) Select a random number for second encryption;
(5) Decryption and encryption are opposite.

The core of encryption algorithm code is following.

Algorithm 1: DES encryption

Input: A byte array arrBTmp
Output: Ciphertext

    arrB ← byte [], i ← 0

    while i < arrBTmp.Length and arrB.Length do

        arrB[i] ← arrBTmp[i]

    end while

    Key ← DES encryption

    Return Key

---

2 Traceability System

2.1 Traceability System Introduction

The traceability system of meat refers to the tracking of information from the breeding to the purchase of entire supply and saves the collected information in supply chain. The stored information includes farming, processing, transportation and sales, which can be queried by users. Consumers can login system and find information they need by scanned QR code and regulators can also use system to investigate the problem of meat and handle it quickly and accurately.

2.2 System Structure

For the meat supply chain, we designed this system structure. As shown in Fig. 4.

(1) Business layer: This layer includes various subsystems: breeding, slaughtering, transportation, sales and query system. System administrator can input key information through the system and the user can query information through the query system.

(2) Data layer: The data layer uses a database to store information and send data to ONS database.

(3) Application layer: This layer includes people manage and query key information. When users of different roles query the information, they also return different information that the user needs.

RFID readers read the necessary information in the bleeding, slaughter, transportation, and sales departments, which use tag technology. Then, ONS database filter information and store information by using EPC technology. When the user wants to query related information, they can enter the relevant information in the query system to get the required traceability information by identifying the two-dimensional code.

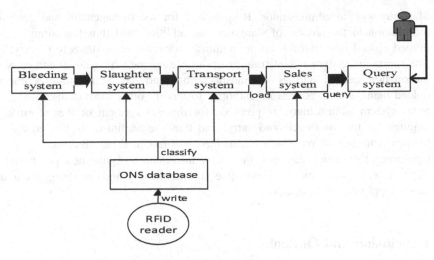

Fig. 4. System structure

The remote ONS server will decode the EPC code and return the corresponding information in the QR code. As shown in Fig. 5.

Fig. 5. QR code and result

2.3   Character Classification

Because the traceability system contains relatively many functions, it probably contains seven kinds of roles:

(1) System administrator: responsible for maintaining the operation of the entire traceability system and managing information of various roles;

(2) Production and aquaculture system administrators: For the information that needs to be entered in the production and breeding process, and the administrator's unified upload management, but no permission for other subsystems to be modified;

526   X. Yang et al.

(3) Slaughter system administrator: Responsible for the management and entry of information in the process of slaughter and addition, and thus the administrator unified upload management, but no authority for other subsystems to modify;

(4) Transportation system administrator: responsible for the management and entry of information needed during the transportation, and the administrator's unified upload management, but has no authority to modify other subsystems;

(5) Sales system administrator: responsible for the management of the information required for the sales cycle and entry, and thus the administrator unified upload management, but for other subsystems have not modified permissions;

(6) Consumer: Consumers can view the safety information of raw meat purchased;

(7) Supervisor: Supervisors are responsible for monitoring and inquiring about the entire supply chain information.

3 Conclusion and Outlook

Based on the traceability system technology that has been established at home and abroad, this system has added RFID and modern agricultural internet of things to this traceability system, resulting in a more efficient and convenient system. This traceability system provides a more complete data management platform for the meat supply chain. Raw meat has its own code using EPC coding technology. The system thus constructed ensures unique information and effective management of information. Finally, both consumers and supervisors can more efficiently and conveniently search for information they need by using this system that combined with encrypted two-dimensional code technology.

At present, it is impossible to provide a unified tracking and tracing system framework in the world, and this system is more complex, the system cost is high, and the operation requirements for the users are high. Moreover, our country's tracking in the field of food safety is still in its infancy. These are all important factors affecting the promotion of traceability systems. However, in order to monitor the meat supply chain more effectively and prevent safety issues from happening again, we still have to accelerate such system construction as much as possible.

References

1. Huang, C., Ma, B., Jiang, W., Dong, D., Ye, J., Zeng, Q.: Traceability design of cotton seed supply chain based on wireless radio frequency technology and EPC internet of things. Jiangsu Agric. Sci. **45**(23), 239–243 (2017)
2. Feng, W., Wang, L., Zhao, J., Ruan, H.: Research on agricultural development based on "Internet +". In: Li, D., Li, Z. (eds.) CCTA 2015. IAICT, vol. 479, pp. 563–569. Springer, Cham (2016). https://doi.org/10.1007/978-3-319-48354-2_58
3. Hongwen, B.: Construction of traceability system for facility vegetables based on agricultural Internet of Things. Northern Hortic. **15**, 224–226 (2014)
4. Lianmin, S., Zhifeng, C., Zhihua, G.: Application of Internet of Things in wisdom agriculture. J. Agric. Mech. Res. **35**(06), 250–252 (2013)

5. Bao, X.: Research on traceability system of pork food supply chain based on Internet of Things. Changsha University of Science and Technology (2013)
6. Hao, L., Gao Feng, X., Huanliang, X.X., Guanghong, Z.: Development of tracking system for pork tracking based on RFID/EPC Internet of Things. Food Ind. Sci. Technol. 33(16), 49–52 (2012)
7. Yujuan, L.: ONS architecture and security analysis in EPC Internet of Things. Inf. Netw. Secur. 12, 6–9 (2010)
8. Yi, C., Niu Nan, Q., Jianfeng, W.J.: Design and implementation of pork processing chain information traceability system based on RFID and barcode technology. Logistics Technol. 28(04), 127–129 (2009)
9. Qiaolian, S.: Comparison of RFID tags and barcodes. J. Acad. Libr. Inf. Sci. 27(01), 69–70 (2009)
10. Kai, L., Wei, L.: Research on product traceability system based on Internet of Things technology. J. Hubei Inst. Technol. 31(02), 27–30 (2015)
11. Bi, H.: Construction of traceability system for facility vegetables based on agricultural Internet of Things. Northern Hortic., 224–226 (2014)
12. Ren Shougang, X., Huanliang, L.A., Guanghong, Z.: Design and implementation of meat tracking and tracing system based on RFID/GIS Internet of Things. Chin. J. Agric. Eng. 26 (10), 229–235 (2010)
13. Xie, J., et al.: Research on pork production safety monitoring and traceability system. In: China Civil Engineering Society. Science and Technology, Engineering and Economic and Social Development - China the 5th Youth Academic Annual Conference of the Association for Science and Technology. China Civil Engineering Society: China Civil Engineering Society, February 2004
14. Luo, Q., Xiong, B., Geng, Z., Yang, L., Pan, J.: A study on pig slaughter traceability solution based on RFID. In: Li, D., Liu, Y., Chen, Y. (eds.) CCTA 2010. IAICT, vol. 346, pp. 710–720. Springer, Heidelberg (2011). https://doi.org/10.1007/978-3-642-18354-6_83
15. Musa, A., Dabo, A.A.A.: A review of RFID in supply chain management. Global J. Flex. Syst. Manag. 17(2), 189–228 (2016)

IOT Security

A Biometrics-Based Remote User Authentication Scheme Using Smart Cards

Jianming Cui[1], Rongquan Sui[1], Xiaojun Zhang[1(✉)], Hengzhong Li[1], and Ning Cao[2]

[1] Shandong University of Science and Technology,
Qingdao, Shandong, People's Republic of China
sdustcuijm@163.com
[2] University College Dublin, Belfield 4, Dublin, Ireland
ning.cao@ucd.ie

Abstract. Biometric technology is an important characteristic and a reliable authentication method, which can be used to verify the user's identity for its accessibility and uniqueness. In this paper, we analyze the existing protocols and find that they still have some security flaws. In order to effectively enhance the security, we present a biometrics-based remote user authentication scheme using smart cards to overcome those weaknesses. According to security and cost analysis, compared with other authentication schemes, the proposed scheme costs $21T_h$. However, it can implement more security goals and withstand different attacks, such as DoS attack, anonymity attack and leak of verifier attack.

Keywords: Biometrics-based · Remote user · Smart card
Authentication

1 Introduction

Biometric technology has the characteristics of universality, uniqueness, invariability and non-replication. Applying it to identity authentication protocols can effectively enhance the security. Thus, the biometric-based three-factor authentication protocol is more effective and secure. It can withstand the existing attacks, such as eavesdropping attacks, stolen authentication table attacks, password guessing attacks, and masquerade attacks. The biometric-based protocol has a better way to achieve secure and reliable identity authentication.

Since biometrics are introduced into remote authentication protocols, researchers have proposed many biometric-based three-factor remote authentication protocols [1–4]. Lee et al. [5] proposed a remote user authentication protocol based on fingerprints and smart cards. Their protocol is based on El-Gamal public-key encryption and does not rely on storing password tables to verify user's identity. In the login phase of the protocol, the user inserts the

© Springer Nature Switzerland AG 2018
X. Sun et al. (Eds.): ICCCS 2018, LNCS 11066, pp. 531–542, 2018.
https://doi.org/10.1007/978-3-030-00015-8_46

smart card into the card reader, enters the ID and password, and then imprints the fingerprint to the fingerprint input device. The user can access the server after the user's fingerprint is successfully verified. [6,7] also analyzed and improved the protocol. In 2010, Li and Hwang [8] proposed a remote user authentication protocol based on biometrics, smart card, one-way hash function, and random number. The protocol is also a light-weight authentication protocol and is more suitable for open networks, especially wireless communications. Das et al. claimed that Li-Hwang's scheme still have security flaws and presented an improved protocol [9]. Hsiang-Shih Improvement of the secure dynamic ID based remote user authentication scheme for multi-server environment [10]. Sood et al. found that their protocol could not resist replay attack, impersonation attack, stolen smart card attack and could not update password correctly [11]. Then Li et al. [12] pointed out the deficiencies and proposed an improved protocol. Xue et al. also presented an improved dynamic identity authentication for multi-server [13]. However, we find that they still can not withstand password guessing attack and other problems. He and Wang [14] proposed an efficient multi-server authentication scheme using biometrics-based smart card. Vanga et al. [15] analyzed their solutions and showed some design flaws in their solution, then proposed a new secure multi-server authentication protocol, which had more security functions based on biometric smart cards and ECC.

This paper proposes an authentication protocol in which the registration center does not participate in authentication. The registration center and the server trust with each other and share the master key. Users register in the registration center firstly and obtain the identity authentication information issued by the registration center. Users can use the information to log in to any server trusted by the registration center directly. The registration process does not require the participation of registration center.

The remaining of this paper is organized as follows. We propose a new three-factor remote authentication scheme in Sect. 2. Section 3 analyzes the security analysis of the proposed scheme. Section 4 compares the functionality features and computational cost of the proposed with several related schemes. Section 5 present our conclusions.

2   Proposed Authentication Protocol

The protocol has three parts: user (U_i), registration center (RC), and sever (S_j). The symbols used in this paper are described in Table 1. The protocol includes four phases: registration phase, login phase, authentication phase, and password change phase.

2.1   Registration Phase

The user sends his own *ID* and password, as well as his own biological information, to the registration center. Then the registration center stores the relevant

Table 1. Notations.

Symbols	Description
U_i	The i-th user
S_j	The j-th service providing server
RC	Registration center
ID_i	The identity of the user U_i
P_i	The password of the user U_i
B_i	The bioinformatics of user U_i
P_i	The password of the user U_i
SID_j	The identity of S_j
x	The master key selected by RC that shared with the server
y	One key shared by the RC, server, and user
N	The selected random value used to register
CID_i	The dynamic identity generated by U_i for authentication
SK	Session key shared by user U_i, sever S_j and RC
R_u, R_S, R_C	Random numbers chosen by user U_i, sever S_j and RC
$h(\cdot)$	One way hash function
$\oplus$	Bitwise exclusive-OR operation
$\parallel$	Bitwise concatenation operation

information into the smart card and then sends the smart card to the user via secure channels. The details as shown in Fig. 1.

The user U_i selects his own identity ID and password P_i, and collects his biological information B_i on a specific sensor. The smart card generates a random number N, then sends $\{ID_i, B_i, P_i, N\}$ to the RC, and RC performs the following steps:

(1) Calculate $RPW_i = h(N\|P_i)$, hide the user's password by introducing a random number N;
(2) Calculate $CID_i = h(N\|ID_i)$, hide the user's identity by introducing a random number N;
(3) Calculate $BPW_i = B_i \oplus h(RPW_i)$, hide the user's biological information in an XOR operation, so that the user's biological feature template can be extracted during the login phase;
(4) Calculate $e_i = h(CID_i\|x) \oplus RPW_i$, the intermediate variables used by the server to verify the user legality;
(5) Calculate $T_i = h(CID_i\|RPW_i)$, authenticate the legality of the user's identity and password locally;
(6) Calculate $H_i = h(T_i)$;
(7) RC will store $(BPW_i, H_i, e_i, h(\cdot), y, N)$ into the smart card;
(8) Send the smart card to the user U_i.

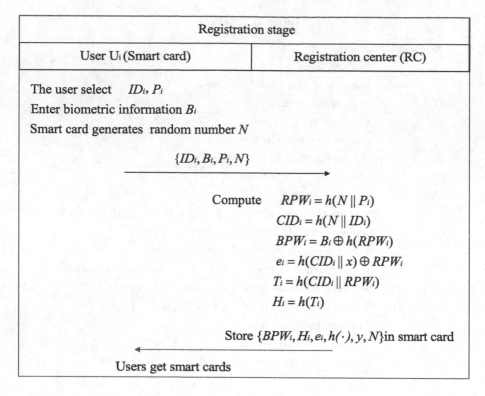

Fig. 1. Registration phase of the proposed protocol without RC's involvement.

2.2 Login Phase

When the user wants to login to a server, he first enters his own ID and password, then the smart card verifies the user's legality. If it is legal, the smart card will sample the user's biological information and perform related verification. If the verification is successful, the smart card sends the login message to the server, as shown in Fig. 2.

When users want to obtain the server data or services, they must login firstly. After the authentication passes, they can continue to communicate with each other. Proceeding as follows:

Step1: U_i enters the ID_i and password P_i, then the smart card performs the following steps:

(1) Calculate the user's dynamic identity $CID_i = h(N_i \| ID_i)$;
(2) Hide the user's password $RPW_i = h(N_i \| P_i)$;
(3) Calculate $T_i = h(CID_i \| RPW_i)$;
(4) Verify H_i whether or not equal to $h(T_i)$. If they are not equal, terminate the session; Otherwise, continue with the following steps.
(5) The smart card samples biological information B'_i of the user U_i;

(6) Calculate $B_i = RPW_i \oplus h(RPW_i)$, and verify whether B_i' match with B_i or not. If it has less match degree than the threshold, it is considered a illegal login, then terminate the session. If greater than or equal to the threshold, then the local login is successful.

Step2: The smart card generates a random number R_c and starts calculating the following.

(1) Compute $M_1 = e_i \oplus RPW_i$;
(2) Compute $M_2 = M_i \oplus R_c$;
(3) Compute $M_3 = h(y \| R_c)$;
(4) Compute $M_4 = RPW_i \oplus M_3$;
(5) Compute $M_5 = h(M_2 \| M_3 \| M_4)$, the server eventually verifies the user's legitimacy by M_5;
(6) Send $\{CID_i, M_2, M_4, M_5\}$ to server S_j.

2.3 Authentication Phase

When the server receives the login request, it starts to authenticate the legality of the user. If the server is legal, the relevant information is sent to the user for verifying the validity of the server, as shown in Fig. 2.

Step1: After the server S_i receives $\{CID_i, M_2, M_4, M_5\}$, performs the following calculations.

(1) Calculate $M_6 = h(CID_i \| x)$, M_6 should be equal to M_1 at the login phase.
(2) Calculate $M_7 = M_2 \oplus M_6$, M_7 should be equal to R_c at the login phase.
(3) Calculate $M_8 = h(y \| M_7)$, M_8 should be equal to M_3 at the login phase.
(4) Verify whether $h(M_2 \| M_8 \| M_4)$ is equal to M_5, if they are equal, continue with the following steps.

Step2: The server S_j generates a random number R_s, and S_j performs the following calculations:

(1) Compute $M_9 = M_4 \oplus M_8$;
(2) Compute $M_{10} = h(M_9 \| SID_j \| M_8 \| M_6)$;
(3) Compute $M_{11} = h(M_9 \| SID_j \| y) \oplus M_8 \oplus R_s$;
(4) Compute $M_{12} = h(M_6 \| M_9 \| R_s \| \mathrm{y})$;
(5) S_j sends information $\{M_{10}, M_{11}\}$ back to the smart card.

Step3: The smart card performs the following steps after receiving $\{M_{10}, M_{11}\}$:

(1) Verify whether $h(RPW_i \| SID_j \| M_3 \| M_1)$ is equal to M_{10}, if equal, continue the follow steps. And terminate the session if not;
(2) Compute $M_{13} = h(RPW_i \| SID_j \| y) \oplus M_3 \oplus M_{11}$;
(3) The smart card calculates the session key $SK = h(M_1 \| RPW_i \| R_c \| M_{13} \| \mathrm{y})$ and the server calculates the session key $SK = h(M_6 \| M_9 \| M_7 \| R_s \| \mathrm{y})$, (where $M_1 = M_6$, $RPW_i = M_9$, $R_c = M_7$, $M_{13} = R_s$).

Thus, the authentication phase is completed.

Login and authentication phase	
User U_i (Smart card)	Server S_j

User input ID_i, P_i
Smart card compute $CID_i = h(N \parallel ID_i)$
$\qquad\qquad\qquad RPW_i = h(N \parallel P_i)$
$\qquad\qquad\qquad T_i = h(CID_i \parallel RPW_i)$
Verify $\qquad\qquad H_i? = h(T_i)$
Input biological feature $B_i{}'$
Smart card compute $B_i = P_i \oplus h(RPW_i)$
Judging the matching threshold of B_i and $B_i{}'$
Smart card generates a random number R_c
Smart card compute $M_1 = e_i \oplus RPW_i$
$\qquad\qquad\qquad M_2 = M_1 \oplus R_c$
$\qquad\qquad\qquad M_3 = h(y \parallel R_c)$
$\qquad\qquad\qquad M_4 = RPW_i \oplus M_3$
$\qquad\qquad\qquad M_5 = h(M_2 \parallel M_3 \parallel M_4)$

$$\{CID_i, M_2, M_4, M_5\} \longrightarrow$$

$\qquad\qquad$ Compute $\quad M_6 = h(CID_i \parallel x)$
$\qquad\qquad\qquad\qquad\quad M_7 = M_2 \oplus M_6$
$\qquad\qquad\qquad\qquad\quad M_8 = h(y \parallel M_7)$
$\qquad\qquad$ Verify $\quad h(M_2 \parallel M_8 \parallel M_4)? = M_5$
$\qquad\qquad$ Server generates random number R_s
$\qquad\qquad$ Compute $\quad M_9 = M_4 \oplus M_8$
$\qquad\qquad\qquad\qquad\quad M_{10} = h(M_9 \parallel SID_j \parallel M_8 \parallel M_6)$
$\qquad\qquad\qquad\qquad\quad M_{11} = h(M_9 \parallel SID_j \parallel y) \oplus M_8 \oplus R_s$
$\qquad\qquad\qquad\qquad\quad M_{12} = h(M_6 \parallel M_9 \parallel R_s \parallel y)$

$$\longleftarrow \{M_{10}, M_{11}\}$$

Verify $\quad h(RPW_i \parallel SID_j \parallel M_3 \parallel M_1) = ? M_{10}$
Compute $\quad M_{13} = h(RPW_i \parallel SID_j \parallel y) \oplus M_3 \oplus M_{11}$

$SK = h(M_1 \parallel RPW_i \parallel R_c \parallel R_{13} \parallel y)$ $\qquad\qquad\qquad$ $SK = h(M_6 \parallel M_9 \parallel M_7 \parallel R_s \parallel y)$
$$\longleftarrow \qquad\qquad \longrightarrow$$

Fig. 2. Login and authentication phase of the proposed protocol with RC's involvement.

2.4 Password Change Phase

The user enters his own ID_i and password P_i, then the smart card starts computing the follows.

(1) Compute $RPW_i = h(N\|P_i)$, $CID_i = h(N\|ID_i)$, $T_i = h(CID_i\|RPW_i)$;
(2) Verify whether H_i is equal to $h(T_i)$, if not, terminate the session; Otherwise prompt the user enter new password P_i^{new};
(3) Compute $RPW_i^{new} = h(N\|P_i^{new})$, $T_i^{new} = h(CID_i\|RPW_i^{new})$;
(4) Compute $H_i^{new} = h(T_i^{new})$, $B_i = BPW_i \oplus h(RPW_i)$;
(5) Compute $RPW_i = B_i \oplus h(RPW_i^{new})$, $h(CID_i\|X_5) = e_i \oplus RPW_i$;
(6) Compute $e_i^{new} = h(CID_i\|X) \oplus RPW_i^{new}$;
(7) Replace the information $\{BPW_i, H_i, e_i, h(\cdot), y\}$ in the card with $\{BPW_i^{new}, H_i^{new}, e_i^{new}, h(\cdot), y\}$.

3 Security Analysis of the Improved Protocol

The improved protocol can resist attacks such as eavesdropping attack and stolen smart card attack, especially denial-of-service (DoS) attack and stolen authentication table attack. The detailed analysis is performed as follows.

3.1 Eavesdropping Attack

Suppose there is an attacker A, who eavesdrops on the information $\{CID_i, M_2, M_4, M_5\}$ and $\{M_{10}, M_{11}\}$ through public channels between users and servers by technical method. After the attacker obtains the data, he begins to attack the user's private information. Make the following calculations:

(1) Compute $CID_i = h(N\|ID_i)$, the attacker A does not know N. Even if the attacker A obtained N through other method, because the hash function is irreversible, so A is not possible to deduce the user ID_i;
(2) $M_2 = M_1 \oplus R_c$, where A does not know M_1 and R_c;
(3) $M_5 = h(M_2\|M_3\|M_4)$, $M_4 = RPW_i \oplus M_3$, where A does not know RPW_i and M_3;
(4) By $M_{10} = h(M_3\|SID_j\|M_8\|M_6)$, $M_{11} = h(M_9\|SID_j\|\text{y}) \oplus M_8 \oplus R_s$, because the attacker does not know M_3, M_8, M_6, M_9, y, and R_s, thus he cannot get any information that is useful to him. The proposed protocol can resist eavesdropping attack.

3.2 Stolen Smart Card Attack

If a legal user's smart card is obtained by attacker A, A can use differential power analysis to obtain $\{BPW_i, H_i, e_i, h(\cdot), y, N\}$ in the smart card, and can also eavesdrop on $\{CID_i, M_2, M_4, M_5\}$ and $\{M_{10}, M_{11}\}$ through insecure channels. Attacker A performs the following steps.

(1) By $CID_i = h(N\|ID_i)$, the attacker cannot compute out the user ID_i;

(2) By $BPW_i = B_i \oplus h(RPW_i)$, it can not obtain the biological feature information if the user's password is incorrect.

(3) By $e_i = h(CID_i \| X_s) \oplus RPW_i$, the attacker is even more unable to get any values.

Therefore, it is impossible for an attacker to carry out stolen smart card attack on this protocol.

3.3   Stolen Authentication Table Attack

Since the protocol stores the authentication table information (ID_i, M_7) in the server, it gives the attacker an opportunity to obtain valid information of the user. Assume that the attacker obtains the user's (ID_i, M_7) and analyzes the data in the smart card, and eavesdrops on the user's transmission information $\{M_{10}, M_{11}\}$ and $\{CID_i, M_2, M_4, M_5\}$ successfully, it should be noted that these two data are not the information of the most recent call. The attacker began to make the following calculations:

(1) By $e_i = h(CID_i \| x) \oplus RPW_i$, $M_1 = e_i \oplus RPW_i$ and $M_6 = h(CID_i \| x)$, it can get $M_1 = M_6$;

(2) Since $M_7 = M_2 \oplus M_6$ and $M_2 = M_1 \oplus R_c$, it can calculate $M_7 = R_c$. By this way, the attacker get M_1.

(3) According to $RPW_i = M_4 \oplus h(y \| R_c)$ and $R_s = h(RPW_i \| SID_i \| y) \oplus h(y \| R_c) \oplus M_{10}$, the attackers can get RPW_i and R_i of users.

(4) The attacker sends the intercepted login information $\{CID_i, M_2, M_4, M_5\}$, thus it can masquerade the legal user successfully.

However, the proposed protocol does not store the authentication table in the server, so the attacker cannot obtain R_c, thus cannot calculate out M_1. Therefore, stolen authentication table attacks cannot be achieved.

3.4   Password Guessing Attack

Although the password for this protocol is also memorable for users, we introduces the biological feature information. Suppose the attacker obtains the data $\{CID_i, M_2, M_4, M_5\}$ and $\{M_{10}, M_{11}\}$ in the public channel by eavesdropping technology, but the attacker cannot conjecture the user's password from the obtained data. The attacker can guess the user's password in an exhaustive way, even if the attacker passes the password verification but cannot pass the biometric verification. So it can resist the password guessing attack.

3.5   Forgery and Masquerade Attack

Assume that the server is secure, x is not leaked. Attacker A eavesdrops on the information $\{CID_i, M_2, M_4, M_5\}$ in an insecure channel, and the attacker uses the eavesdropping data to perform forgery and masquerade attacks.

Attacker A conducts a forgery attack and falsifies data $\{CID_i, M_{A2}, M_{A4}, M_{A5}\}$, where $M_2 = M_{A2}$, $M_4 = M_{A4}$, $M_5 = M_{A5}$.

Step1: The attacker sends the forged data to the server, and the server starts to calculate as follows.

(1) Calculate $M_{A6} = h(CID_i\|x)$, $M_{A7} = M_{A2} \oplus M_{A6}$, and $M_{A8} = h(y\|M_{A7})$.
(2) Check $h(M_{A2}\|M_{A8}\|M_{A4})? = M_{A5}$, if they are equal, the sever generates random number R_{As}. If not, the session should be terminated.
(3) $M_{A9} = M_{A4} \oplus M_{A8}$, $M_{A10} = h(M_{A9}\|SID_j\|M_{A8}\|M_{A6})$;
(4) $M_{A11} = h(M_{A9}\|SID_j\|y) \oplus M_{A8} \oplus R_{As}$, $M_{A12} = h(M_{A6}\|M_{A9}\|R_{As}\|y)$;
(5) The server sends $\{M_{10}, M_{11}\}$ to attacker A.

Step2: When attacker A receives the message $\{M_{10}, M_{11}\}$, he starts the following calculations.

(1) Attackers can skip validation calculations themselves;
(2) Calculate $M_{13} = h(RPW_i\|SID_j\|y) \oplus M_3 \oplus M_{11}$, but the attacker does not know y, RPW_i, and M_3. Thus he cannot calculate and the attack is terminated.

Attacker A performs a masquerade attack. First, the attacker imitates the user. To imitate the user, he needs to know the user's secret information. Even if the attacker obtains the data in the user's smart card through differential power analysis technology, but the user's information is encrypted and stored in the smart card. Therefore masquerade user attacks failed. When an attacker forgery a server attack, the attacker cannot continue because X_s cannot be acquired. The attacker will be forced to terminate.

3.6 Denial-of-Service Attack

Assume a malicious legal user continuously sends login request information to the server. His purpose is to cause the server to crash, then makes other users cannot use the server normally. However, because the proposed protocol adds local authentication, it will not be delivered to the server when the login request message is illegal. Therefore, the protocol in this paper can resist the DoS attacks.

3.7 Anonymity Attack

It is assumed that the attacker obtains $\{CID_i, M_2, M_4, M_5\}$ through a public channel through eavesdropping attacks. Since the proposed protocol in this paper used dynamic ID, each time the login CID_i is different. Thus the attacker cannot perform an anonymous attack on the user.

4 Functional and Computational Analysis

We analyze the functionality and computational complexity of proposed protocol with other related biological-based protocols. The comparisons are illuminated in Table 2. Let Yes denote the protocol has the function, and No indicates that the protocol does not have this function. Through analysis the protocols that based on biological information which RC does not participate in authentication of Das [9], Li [12], Li and Hwang [8] etc. It can be observed that their protocols has some flaws and cannot be used in the actual circumstances.

Table 2. Functional comparison between the proposed protocol and other related protocols.

Function	Proposed	Das [9]	Li [12]	Li and Hwang [8]
Computation cost	Low($21T_h$)	Low($18T_h$)	Low($15T_h$)	Low($10T_h$)
Resist eavesdropping attack	Yes	Yes	Yes	Yes
Resist stolen smart card attack	Yes	Yes	Yes	Yes
Resist stolen authentication table attack	Yes	No	No	No
Resist password guessing attack	Yes	Yes	Yes	Yes
Resist DoS attack	Yes	Yes	No	No
Resist masquerade attack	Yes	Yes	Yes	No
Resist anonymity attack	Yes	No	No	No
Correct password update	Yes	Yes	No	No
Correct mutual authentication	Yes	Yes	Yes	No
Generate session key	Yes	Yes	Yes	No

To compare the computational complexity among the proposed and other related protocols, let T_h denote the time required for one-way Hash operation. Because the computational complexity of XOR and concatenation operation in the protocol are very low, compared with hash operation, we can ignore them. From Table 3, it can be seen that the calculation costs of the protocol in the registration phase, login phase, and authentication phase are $6T_h$, $7T_h$ and $8T_h$, respectively. Although the computational complexity of the proposed protocol is higher than that of other protocols. However, as seen from Table 2, this protocol has all the listed functions, while other protocols only have parts of them.

Table 3. Performance comparison between the proposed protocol and other related protocols.

	Proposed	Das [9]	Li [12]	Li and Hwang [8]
Registration phase	$6T_h$	$4T_h$	$4T_h$	$3T_h$
Login phase	$7T_h$	$5T_h$	$4T_h$	$2T_h$
Authentication	$8T_h$	$9T_h$	$7T_h$	$5T_h$
Total	$21T_h$	$18T_h$	$15T_h$	$10T_h$

5 Conclusion

In this paper, we propose a three-factor authentication protocol based on biometric. Through the comparison of feature threshold, the improved protocol can implement biometric match and conceal the user biological data and avoid privacy leakage. Compared with other related protocols, the proposed scheme can resist DoS attack, anonymity attack, stolen smart card attack and so on with a light increase in computational complexity.

References

1. Lu, Y.-R., Li, L.-X., Peng, H.-P.: A biometrics and smart cards-based authentication scheme for multi-server environments. Secur. Commun. Netw. **8**(17), 3219–3228 (2015)
2. Moon, J., Choi, Y., Jung, J., Won, D.: An improvement of robust biometrics-based authentication and key agreement scheme for multi-server environments using smart cards. PloS One **10**(12), e0145263 (2015)
3. Wang, C., Zhang, X., Zheng, Z.: Cryptanalysis and improvement of a biomet ricbased multi-server authentication and key agreement scheme. PloS One **11**(2), e0149173 (2016)
4. Xie, Q., Tang, Z.-X.: Biometrics based authentication scheme for session initiation protocol. Springerplus **5**(1), 1045 (2016)
5. Lee, J.-K., Ryu, S.-R., Yoo, K.-Y.: Fingerprint-based remote user authentication scheme using smart cards. Electron. Lett. **38**(12), 554–555 (2002)
6. Khan, M.-K., Zhang, J.-S.: Improving the security of 'a exible biometrics remote user authentication scheme'. Comput. Stand. Interfaces **29**(1), 82–85 (2007)
7. Fan, C.-I., Lin, Y.-H.: Provably secure remote truly three-factor authentication scheme with privacy protection on biometrics. Trans. Inf. Forensics Secur. **4**(4), 933–945 (2009)
8. Li, C.-T., Hwang, M.-S.: An efficient biometrics-based remote user authentication scheme using smartcards. J. Netw. Comput. Appl. **33**(1), 1–5 (2010)
9. Das, A.-K.: Cryptanalysis and further improvement of a biometricbased remote user authentication scheme using smart cards. Int. J. Netw. Secur. Appl. **3**(2), 13–28 (2011)
10. Hsiang, H.-C.: Improvement of the secure dynamic ID based remote user authentication scheme for multi-server environment. Comput. Stand. Interfaces **31**(6), 1118–1123 (2009)

11. Sood, S.-K., Sarje, A.-K., Singh, K.: A secure dynamic identity based authentication protocol for multi-server architecture. J. Netw. Comput. Appl. **34**(2), 609–618 (2011)
12. Li, X., Niu, J.-W., Ma, J., Wang, W.-D., Liu, C.-L.: Cryptanalysis and improvement of a biometrics-based remote user authentication scheme using smart cards. J. Netw. Comput. Appl. **34**(1), 76–79 (2011)
13. Xue, K.-P., Hong, P.-L., Ma, C.-S.: A lightweight dynamic pseudonym identity based authentication and key agreement protocol without verification tables for multi-server architecture. J. Comput. Syst. Sci. **80**(1), 195–206 (2014)
14. He, D.-B., Wang, D.: Robust biometrics-based authentication scheme for multi-server environment. IEEE Syst. J. **9**(3), 816–823 (2015)
15. Odelu, V., Das, A.-K., Goswami, A.: A secure biometrics-based multi-server authentication protocol using smart cards. IEEE Trans. Inf. Forensics Secur. **10**(9), 1953–1966 (2015)

A BLF Generation Scheme with Clock Variance-Tolerance for Baseband Processor of EPC Gen2 UHF RFID Tag

Liangbo Xie$^{(\boxtimes)}$, Wei Nie, Xiaolong Yang, Yong Wang,
and Mu Zhou

School of Communication and Information Engineering, Chongqing University
of Posts and Telecommunications, Chongqing 400065, China
xie.liangbo@hotmail.com

Abstract. In this paper, a novel backscatter link frequency (BLF) generation scheme is presented. The accuracy of BLF required by EPC Class-1 Generation-2 (Gen2) is one of the critical issues in UHF RFID tag design. By analyzing the effects of division ratio and division error on the accuracy of BLF, a novel BLF generation scheme is proposed to reduce the BLF errors. Simulation results show that the BLF generated by the proposed scheme can satisfy the requirement of EPC Gen2 standard when the clock frequency is no less than 1.632 MHz, which significantly simplifies the design complexity of clock generator.

Keywords: UHF RFID · Low power · Backscatter link frequency

1 Introduction

Radio Frequency Identification (RFID) technology, as one of the key technologies of Internet of Things (IOTs), can identify objects by wireless communication. With the advantages of long communication range, high speed, multi objects identification and low cost, ultra-high frequency (UHF) RFID system has been wildly applied to systems of IOTs, such as logistics, traffic, anti-counterfeiting and trace [1–3].

The EPC Class-1 Generation-2 (Gen2) [4], which features high data-rate, large storage capacity, long operating range and moderate security, is the most popular UHF RFID standard, and has been absorbed as ISO/IEC 18000-6C by ISO. Many researches have been conducted to improve the performance of EPC Gen2 tags [4], and low power is often the first priority [5, 6]. However, the accuracy of backscatter link frequency (BLF) also plays an important role in tag design, because the reader cannot identify tags when the BLF of tags exceeds the frequency tolerance (FT) defined by EPC Gen2. Techniques proposed in [7, 8] obtain BLF by generating accurate clock frequency, which increase the design complexity of clock generator. BLF generation method by dividing the clock frequency is developed in [9], which uses (N + 0.5) divide ratio to reduce the BLF error. Unfortunately, when (N + 0.5) is less than 5.5, the duty-cycle of backscatter link data will larger than 55%, which exceeds the required range of 45%–55% by EPC Gen2.

© Springer Nature Switzerland AG 2018
X. Sun et al. (Eds.): ICCCS 2018, LNCS 11066, pp. 543–552, 2018.
https://doi.org/10.1007/978-3-030-00015-8_47

In this paper, a novel BLF generation scheme is developed. By analyzing the effects of division ratio and division error on the accuracy of BLF, a BLF generation scheme with large clock variation-tolerance is proposed, which not only meets the required BLF accuracy of EPC Gen2, but also simplifies the design complexity of clock generator.

2 Brief Review of EPC Gen2 Standard

In EPC Gen2 standard, the reader utilizes a Pulse Interval Encoding (PIE) format to communicate with the tag. Figure 1(a) shows the PIE format. The length of data-0 symbol is one Tari while that of data-1 ranges from between 1.5Tari and 2Tari, and it is determined by the reader. Here, Tari is the timing reference with typical values of 6.25 μs, 12.5 μs and 25 μs.

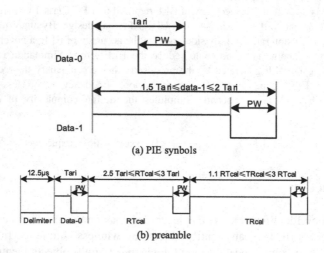

Fig. 1. Symbols defined in EPC Gen2 standard: (a) PIE; (b) preamble.

In EPC Gen2 standard, an inventory round is initiated by the *Query* command. The *Query* command is preceded by the preamble as shown in Fig. 1(b), in which RTcal and TRcal are reader-to-tag (R => T) calibration symbol and tag-to-reader (T => R) calibration symbol, respectively. The length of RTcal is the sum of data-0 symbol and data-1 symbol, and it is used to distinguish data-0 and data-1. When the symbol length is less than RTcal/2, it is interpreted as data-0, otherwise it is interpreted as data-1. The BLF is specified by TRcal symbol and the parameter DR in *Query* command. And BLF is defined as:

$$BLF = \frac{DR}{TRcal} \tag{1}$$

where DR has two values: 8 or 64/3. The error of BLF should be within the frequency tolerance (FT) required by EPC Gen2 as shown in Table 1.

Table 1. FT of BLF in EPC GEN2

DR	TRcal(μs)	BLF(kHz)	FT
64/3	33.3	640	±15%
	33.3 < TRcal < 66.7	320 < BLF < 640	±22%
	66.7	320	±10%
	66.7 < TRcal < 83.3	256 < BLF < 320	±12%
	83.3	256	±10%
	83.3 < TRcal $\leq$ 133.3	160 $\leq$ BLF < 256	±10%
	133.3 < TRcal $\leq$ 200	107 $\leq$ BLF < 160	±7%
	200 < TRcal $\leq$ 255	95 $\leq$ BLF < 107	±5%
8	17.2 $\leq$ TRcal < 25	320 < BLF $\leq$ 465	±19%
	25	320	±10%
	25 < TRcal < 31.25	256 < BLF < 320	±12%
	31.25	256	±10%
	31.25 < TRcal < 50	160 < BLF < 256	±10%
	50	160	±7%
	50 < TRcal $\leq$ 75	107 $\leq$ BLF < 160	±7%
	75 < TRcal $\leq$ 200	40 $\leq$ BLF < 107	±4%

3   BLF Generation Scheme

3.1   Error in BLF Generation

In digital domain, the length of TRcal is usually measured by counting the edges of clock. If the frequency of clock is f_{clk_sys}, then the count number N_{TRcal} of TRcal can be expressed as:

$$N_{TRcal} = f_{clk\_sys} \times TRcal \qquad (2)$$

Using Eqs. (1) and (2), the following equation can be arrived:

$$BLF = DR/(N_{TRcal}/f_{clk\_sys})$$
$$= \frac{f_{clk\_sys}}{(N_{TRcal}/DR)} = \frac{f_{clk\_sys}}{Div} \qquad (3)$$

where Div is the division ratio, and can be expressed as:

$$Div = \frac{N_{TRcal}}{DR} \qquad (4)$$

Usually, Div is obtained by right shift operation for low power consideration, then Eq. (4) can be rewritten as:

$$\begin{cases} R = \frac{N_{TRcal}}{64/3} = (3 \cdot N_{TRcal}) > > 6, & DR = 64/3 \\ R = \frac{N_{TRcal}}{8} = N_{TRcal} > > 3, & DR = 8 \end{cases} \qquad (5)$$

where R is the integral part of Div. Unfortunately, large error can be introduced when using right shift operation to calculate Div. Figure 2 illustrates how the error E is introduced by right shift operation when DR = 8. It is clear that BLF error occurs when $E \neq 0$. In [10], a fixed number is added to N_{TRcal} when calculating Div to reduce the BLF error. However, it is assumed that the frequency of clock is 1.28 MHz, and the variation of clock due to process, voltage and temperature variations is not taken into consideration.

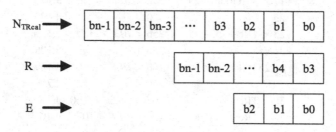

Fig. 2. Illustration of error due to right shift operation

3.2   Relationship Between BLF Error and Division Ratio

As analyzed above, the error of BLF is caused by right shift operation shown in Fig. 2. Supposing the ideal BLF demanded by reader is BLF_{ideal} and the clock is f_{clk_sys}, then Div can be expressed as:

$$Div = \frac{f_{clk\_sys}}{BLF_{ideal}} \qquad (6)$$

With rearrangement, we expressed Div as:

$$Div = R + \sigma \qquad (7)$$

where R is the integral part, σ is the fractional part. The proposed BLF generation scheme can be expressed as:

$$\begin{cases} R_{final} = R, \sigma < \sigma_{th}; \\ R_{final} = R + 1, \sigma \geq \sigma_{th}; \end{cases} \qquad (8)$$

R_{final} is the final division ratio for calculating BLF and σ_{th} is the threshold value for R_{final} calculation. Let error0 and error1 are the absolute errors of BLF corresponding to division ratio R and (R + 1), respectively. Using Eqs. (6) and (8), then BLF_{ideal} can be expressed as:

$$BLF_{ideal} = \frac{f_{clk\_sys}}{R} - error0 \tag{9}$$

$$BLF_{ideal} = \frac{f_{clk\_sys}}{R+1} + error1 \tag{10}$$

As can be seen from Table 1, only the relative error of BLF is concerned. Thus, $\varepsilon 0$ and $\varepsilon 1$ are defined as the relative errors of BLF for R and (R + 1), respectively. And the following expressions can be obtained by using Eqs. (6–10):

$$\varepsilon 0 = \frac{error0}{BLF_{ideal}} = \frac{\sigma}{R} \tag{11}$$

$$\varepsilon 1 = \frac{error1}{BLF_{ideal}} = \frac{1-\sigma}{R+1} \tag{12}$$

The relationship between $\varepsilon 0$, $\varepsilon 1$ and σ under different R are evaluated and the simulation results are illustrated in Fig. 3. It can be observed that $\varepsilon 0$ and $\varepsilon 1$ decrease when R increases under a certain σ. If we choose σ_{th} equal to the value of σ when $\varepsilon 0 = \varepsilon 1$, then the maximum relative error ε_{max} of BLF under a certain division ratio R can be obtained by the following equation:

$$\varepsilon_{max} = \varepsilon 0 = \frac{\sigma}{R} = \frac{1-\sigma}{R+1} = \varepsilon 1 \tag{13}$$

Solving the above equation, we can get:

$$\sigma_{th} = \frac{R}{2R+1} = 0.5 - \frac{0.5}{2R+1} \tag{14}$$

If R is known, σ_{th} can be calculated by Eq. (14), and then ε_{max} is obtained by Eq. (13). Thus, the BLF error ε can be expressed as:

$$\begin{cases} \varepsilon = \varepsilon 0, & \sigma < \sigma_{th}; \\ \varepsilon = \varepsilon 1, & \sigma \geq \sigma_{th}; \end{cases} \tag{15}$$

In other words, the BLF error ε has the maximum error defined by Eq. (13) under a certain R.

According to Table 1, the maximum absolute error of BLF is 15% when BLF is 640 kHz. From Fig. 3, it can be seen that the minimum division ratio R_{min} should be 3 to meet the FT requirement of BLF. As the maximum BLF is 640 kHz in EPC Gen2

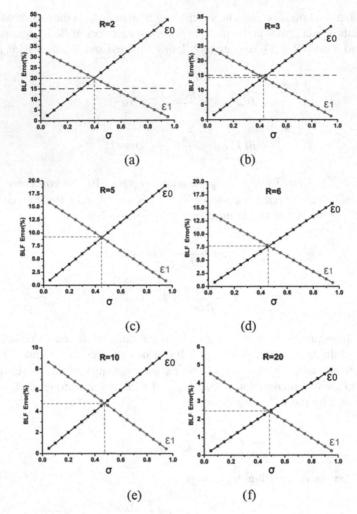

Fig. 3. BLF error with different σ: (a) R = 2; (b) R = 3; (c) R = 5; (d) R = 6; (e) R = 10; (f) R = 20

standard, thus the minimum clock frequency for the proposed scheme is f_{clk_sys} = $BLF_{max} \times R_{min} \times (1 - |FT|)$ = 640 kHz × 3 × (1 − 15%) = 1.632 MHz.

3.3 Proposed BLF Generation Scheme

From Eq. (14), it is clear that different R has different σ_{th}. If different R with its corresponding σ_{th} calculated by (14) is implemented, the design complexity is significantly increased. Fortunately, as can be seen from Eq. (13), BLF error reduces when R increases. Thus, if R_{min} = 3 meets FT requirement of BLF shown in Table 1, then the implementation of the BLF generation scheme would be significantly simplified. Two cases are considered:

(1) DR = 64/3

In this case, as $R_{min} = 3$, the corresponding $\sigma_{th\_ideal} = 0.428$. However, R is obtained by 6-bit right shift of $(3 \cdot N_{TRcal})$ as shown in Eq. (5). Thus, the actual σ_{th_actual} in digital circuit is:

$$\sigma_{th\_actual} = \frac{round(64 \times \sigma_{th\_ideal})}{64} = 0.422 \qquad (16)$$

With $\sigma_{th} = 0.422$, the relationship between BLF error ε and division ratio R is simulated and the results is shown in Fig. 4. The maximum BLF error is 14.7% which is less than 15% required by EPC Gen2 standard.

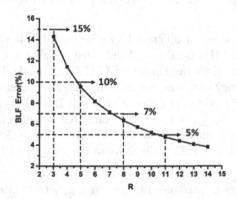

Fig. 4. BLF error with $\sigma_{th} = 0.422$ when DR = 64/3

(2) DR = 8

As Table 1 listed, the maximum BLF is 465 kHz when DR = 8. The minimum clock frequency is 1.632 MHz as discussed above. Thus, the minimum Div is equal to 1.632 MHz/465 kHz = 3.51. Then the minimum value of R may equal to 3 or 4, and the corresponding σ_{th_ideal} is 0.428 or 0.444 by applying Eq. (14). Similar to the scenario of DR = 64/3, σ_{th_ideal} cannot be obtained because of the right shift operation. Thus, the acutal σ_{th_actual} of DR = 8 is:

$$\sigma_{th\_actual} = \frac{round(8 \times \sigma_{th\_ideal})}{8} = 0.375 \text{ or } 0.5 \qquad (17)$$

The simulation results are shown in Fig. 5. As calculated above, Div = 3.51 when BLF = 465 kHz and $f_{clk\_sys} = 1.632$ MHz, and the fractional part σ of Div is 0.51. Thus, R_{final} is 4 regardless of $\sigma_{th\_actual} = 0.375$ or $\sigma_{th\_actual} = 0.5$. From Fig. 5, it is clearly noted that BLF error of $\sigma_{th\_actual} = 0.5$ is always less than that of $\sigma_{th\_actual} = 0.375$ when $R \geq 4$. So we choose $\sigma_{th} = 0.5$ when DR = 8.

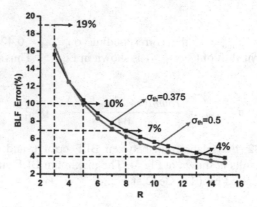

Fig. 5. BLF error with different σ_{th} when DR = 8

For FT inflection points of different BLF, the final division ratio R_{final} and BLF error at f_{clk_sys} = 1.632 MHz is calculated and listed in Table 2. It can be seen that the accuracy of BLF meets the requirements of EPC Gen2 standard. For a certain BLF, when the clock frequency increases, the division ratio also increases, so the BLF error will never exceeds the maximum BLF error shown in Table 2 except BLF = 640 kHz. That is because when f_{clk_sys} = 1.632 MHz and BLF = 640 kHz, the division ratio Div < 3, and the above simulation results are based on Div $\geq$ 3. However, the actual BLF will never exceeds FT of EPC Gen2 when f_{clk_sys} $\geq$ 1.632 MHz.

Table 2. Maximum BLF error (f_{clk_sys} = 1.632 MHz)

DR	BLF	R_{final}	$\|\varepsilon_{max}\|$[a]	$\|\varepsilon_{acutal}\|$[b]	|FT|
64/3	640 kHz	3	14.3%	15%	15%
	320 kHz	5	9.53%	2%	10%
	160 kHz	10	5.2%	2%	7%
	107 kHz	15	3.575	1.7%	5%
8	465 kHz	4	12.5%	12.2%	15%
	320 kHz	5	10%	2%	10%
	160 kHz	10	5%	2%	7%
	107 kHz	15	3.33%	1.7%	4%

(a) ε_{max} is the maximum BLF error under a certain R;

(b) ε_{actual} = 100% $\times$ (f_{clk_sys}/R_{final} − BLF)/ BLF.

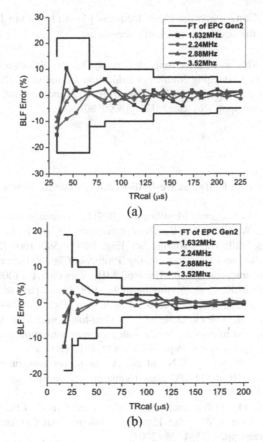

Fig. 6. Relationship of BLF error and TRcal over different clock frequencies: (a) DR = 64/3; (b) DR = 8.

4 Simulation Results

To validate the robustness of the proposed BLF generation scheme, we simulated the BLF error under different lengths of TRcal with different clock frequencies. Figure 6 shows the simulation results. It can be noted that the proposed BLF generation scheme can meet the FT requirement of EPC Gen2 in a large frequency range, which is an important improvement on tag design.

5 Conclusion

A novel BLF generation scheme for UHF RFID tag complying with EPC Gen2 standard is presented. By analyzing the effects of division ratio and division error on the accuracy of BLF, a BLF generation scheme with clock variance-tolerant is proposed. Simulation results show that the scheme can generate BLF satisfied the requirement of EPC Gen2 when the clock frequency is no less than 1.632 MHz, which significantly relaxes the accuracy of clock generator.

Acknowledgements. This work was supported partly by the Scientific and Technological Research Foundation of Chongqing Municipal Education Commission (No. KJ1704083), the National Natural Science Foundation of China (No. 61704015) and the Fundamental and Frontier Research Project of Chongqing (No. cstc2017jcyjAX0380).

References

1. Dolkin, D.: The RF in RFID Passive-UHF-RFID in Practice. Newnes, Amsterdam (The Netherlands) (2008)
2. Roberts, C.M.: Radio frequency identification (RFID). Comput. Secur. **25**, 18–26 (2006)
3. Ma, H., Wang, Y., Wang, K., Ma, Z.: The optimization for hyperbolic positioning of UHF passive RFID tags. IEEE Trans. Autom. Sci. Eng. **14**(4), 1590–1600 (2017)
4. EPCglobal: EPC Radion-Frequency Identity Protocols Class-1 Generation-2 UHF RFID Protocol for Communication at 860 MHz–960 MHz Version 1.1.2 (2008)
5. Yin, J., Yi, J., Law, M.K., et al.: A system-on-chip EPC Gen-2 passive UHF RFID tag with embedded temperature sensor. IEEE J. Solid-State Circ. **45**(11), 2404–2420 (2010)
6. Pillai, V., Heinrich, H., Dieska, D., et al.: An ultra-low-power long range battery/passive RFID tag for UHF and microwave bands with a current consumption of 700 nA at 1.5 V. IEEE Trans. Circ. Syst. I Regul. Pap. **54**(7), 1500–1512 (2007)
7. Chan, C.F., Pun, K.P., Leung, K.N., et al.: A low-power continuously-calibrated clock recovery circuit for UHF RFID EPC class-1 generation-2 transponders. IEEE J. Solid-State Circ. **45**(3), 587–599 (2010)
8. Najafi, V., Jenabi, M., Mohammadi, S., et al.: A dual mode EPC Gen 2 UHF RFID transponder in 0.18 μm CMOS. In: 15th IEEE International Conference on Electronics, Circuits and Systems, pp. 1135–1138 (2008)
9. Wang, Z., Mao, L., Chen, L., et al.: Design of a passive UHF RFID transponder featuring a variation-tolerant baseband processor. In: 2010 IEEE International Conference on RFID, pp. 61–68 (2010)
10. Luo, Q., Guo, L., Li, Q., et al.: A low-power dual-clock strategy for digital circuits of EPC Gen2 RFID tag. In: 2009 IEEE International Conference on RFID, pp. 7–14 (2009)

A Design of Mobile Phone Privacy Protection Based on Block Chain

Kun Yang[1,2], Mingzhe Liu[1,2(✉)], Yaming Yang[1,2], and Xin Jiang[1,2]

[1] State Key Laboratory of Geohazard Prevention and Geoenvironment Protection, Chengdu University of Technology, Chengdu 610059, China
2321567752@qq.com
[2] College of Nuclear Technology and Automation Engineering, Chengdu University of Technology, Chengdu 610059, China

Abstract. This paper introduces a platform development and implementation method which is based on block chain to protect mobile phone privacy. It is applied to collective maintenance, programmable, safety and reliability, and the requirements of personal privacy protection. The platform consists of the manufacturer node, market node, mobile phone node and user node, which is connected by a star topology construction. All nodes include data collection module, data storage module, target detection module and data application module, which is matched by the publish/subscribe mode. Each node will match a distributed storage database for storing various transaction data. The data storage module realizes the communication between nodes and completes the building of mobile phone protection platform. This method can solve the problems such as get the usage right by flashing root, user information leakage and so on. Finally, we give the application scenario of mobile phone protection platform, aiming at realizing the privacy protection on the block chain.

Keywords: Block chain · Privacy protection · Distributed storage
Decentralization

1 Introduction

Dorian S. Nakamoto put forward the concept of block chain for the first time in 2008, it has become a core component of electronic currency bitcoin in the following years [1]. As the basic and core technology for bitcoin transaction, block chain is a public ledger of all transactions which achieves decentralized Self-management by using Point-To-Point networks and distributed time stamping servers [2]. In 2012, Ripple System was released, making the first use of block chain technology for Cross-Border transfers [3]. In 2014, Austin Hill and Adam Baker began building block chain side chains [1]. Storj opens storage data services for customers with block chain technology [4]. Search engine DuckDuckGo accesses to the block chain query [4]. The Tilecoin team unveiled the first IoT lab device with integrated block chain [5]. How to apply block chain technology to the Internet of Things is still the focus of all walks of life in the society.

In general, block chain is a database composed of data layer, network layer, consensus layer, incentive layer, contract layer and application layer [6] which is maintained by decentralization and De-trust to achieve high reliability of the database. The base involves asymmetric encryption, time stamping, P2P, hash functions and distributed consensus techniques [4, 5].

Before the new node registers into the block chain, it needs to pass identity authentication and authorization. For a long time, due to the separation of data flow, processors, and consumers, data secondary transactions have no means of auditing, control, or Real-Time verification of the authenticity of authorizations [7]. Data transaction authorizations have remained on the paper protocol for a long time. Therefore, it has not made big progresses at the technical level.

It is feasible to use block chain technology for data transaction authorization because its transaction is transparent, safe, reliable, difficult to tamper with, and comes with a timestamp attribute [8]. In the process of data collection and processing, it is possible to synchronize the circulation and verification of the authorized documents so as to realize the purpose of Real-Time verification of the authenticity of authorization, secondary transaction auditing and control. Random authorization can also be performed through the central node. The new node sends out an authentication request, and the central node broadcasts to them according to the address information of the data processing node and the supervision node in the management data block chain. In the data processing node, a node is randomly authorized to generate a data block. Referring to POW and POS naming methods, this mechanism is tentatively called random authorization (RA) [8]. After the data block is generated, it is sent to the central node, data processing nodes, supervisory nodes and other nodes.

At present, the use of smart phones is more frequent, and its functions are no longer confined to communication. Instead, it is applied in various fields such as information storage, mobile payment and smart navigation. The security of smart phones is vital as it directly affects the security of user assets and private information.

From this perspective, in this paper, a mobile phone protection scheme based on block chain is proposed. We design block chain mobile phone protection platform in which phones can register and protect their privacy security in order to prevent leakage of user information once the phone is lost or stolen, resulting in the loss of property. Hash algorithm and timestamp technology are used to encrypt mobile phones. Block chain distributed storage technology [1] is used to store mobile phones, and database is used to achieve mutual communication between mobile phone nodes. Finally, Anti-Theft protection of smart phones is implemented to meet the requirements of high performance and high reliability.

The work of this paper is as follows:

1. We assign a database to each node in the block chain, keeping track of each transaction per node.
2. We proposed two methods for registered users to access the block chain mobile protection platform and view their protected status in real time.

3. We provide a variety of interfaces for the base of the platform, using the SDK to submit the transaction interface, through the handshake protocol to complete the transaction platform to achieve Real-Time mobile phone and platform communications.

2 Preliminaries

In this section, we will formally define some of the prerequisites for this mobile phone protection scheme based on block chain. Specifically, mobile phone manufacturer nodes, mobile phone market nodes, mobile phone nodes, and mobile phone user nodes need to be distributed to form the platform with a topology [9]. This contents build on a previous work in which we define detailed data collection, data storage, target detection and data application modules in each nodes. We will introduce four types of nodes in detail. Mobile phone manufacturer nodes store trading information about phone manufacturer. Mobile phone market nodes store trading information about phone market. Mobile phone nodes store trading information about mobile phone. Most transactions in mobile phone block chain are done with mobile phones. Mobile phone user nodes store trading information about mobile phone user. We also authenticate the mobile phone users who registered the platform. Completed registered mobile phone information and user information encryption to ensure the security of the user privacy. It further describes the cooperation between the protection platform with the 5G operators and app developers through the routing protocol. This cooperation protects its internal resources by terminating the lost mobile Internet services and application usage features.

2.1 The Four Modules in Nodes

We consider a protection platform in which the collaboration between nodes and information exchange are done on the underlying mesh routing network. Therefore, each node needs to collect data for each transaction, and distributed store [10] trading information in their own database. After completing the trading information storage, it also needs to achieve the target data detection and data application functions.

The data collection module is a communication module based on the remote data acquisition module platform. The communication chip and the memory chip are integrated on a circuit board. The data collection module has the functions of sending and receiving messages, voice calls and data transmission through the platform of the remote data acquisition module. The data collection module in the node is responsible for collecting all the real data information about mobile phones and users from all independent channels and collecting the data information of each transaction between the four types of nodes so as to record the data in each node.

The data storage module is responsible for the storage of mobile phones and user information. The module needs to confirm and verify the identity information of the user. Once authenticity verification is passed, user information is stored. Simultaneously, the data storage module forms the transaction block for each transaction between nodes through the relevant mining algorithm [11], so as to realize the distributed storage of the transaction information.

Regarding target detection module, when the mobile phone and user information is saved to the platform, target detection module through the target detection and information matching detects fast and efficiently the target cell phone (lost and unexpected mobile phone). Thus, the fastest protection of lost information and resources inside phones can be achieved.

The data application module can transmit information on lost mobile phones to the 5G operators and app developers through the server transmission to terminate the Internet access and app use functions of the lost mobile phones that protect the internal information and resources to minimize user losses. Through the storage of mobile phone and user information data, data mining [1], big data analysis [2], etc. can be distributed data stored within the database system to provide effective storage, indexing and query processing [1].

2.2 Encryption Keys

In the mobile phone protection platform, the protection of registered user information is crucial. Therefore, we use the hash algorithm [12] to digitally encrypt the identity information of the registered users who are authenticated by the identity. After encryption, a pair of keys is generated, which is the user's public key and private key. Users can use their own secrets key to login mobile protection platform.

We will also use asymmetric encryption (ECC) [13] to encrypt the user's mobile phone IMEI code, and only provide to its users to ensuring the security of mobile information. When the user's mobile phone is lost, the registrant directly provides encrypted data of the mobile phone IMEI code to the mobile phone platform. After the platform decrypts it, the IMEI code of the mobile phone is sent to the 5G operator and the app developer through the server, terminating the IMEI mobile phone's Internet access function and app use function.

3   Design Formulation

3.1   Platform Model

The mobile phone protection platform based on block chain consists of four types of nodes: manufacturer node, market node, mobile node and user node connected by topology structure. All four types of nodes include data collection module, data storage module, target detection module and data application module matched with each other in publish/subscribe [14] mode. Figure 1 shows the design model of a mobile phone protection platform.

(1) Manufacturer Node: the most basic information in the manufacturing process of mobile phones are all recorded to the node, including information such as manufacturer and cell phone models. The node saves the information to the database and sends it to other manufacturer nodes.

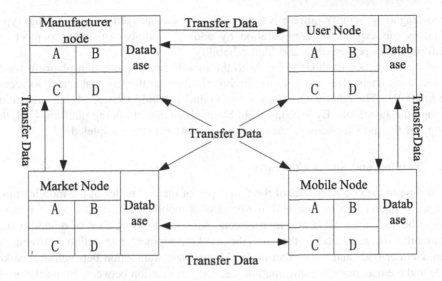

A Data Collection Module   B Data Storage Module

C Target Detection Module   D Data Application Module

Fig. 1. Platform model of four types of nodes.

(2) Market Node: The Market Node is responsible for recording every single circu-
    lation and transaction information that enters the market after each handset is
    manufactured. After the production of the mobile phone, it is recorded in every
    circulation in the market and protected at all times. Through the data collection
    module inside the market node, the information is collected in real time and stored
    in the database of the market node in a distributed manner.
(3) Mobile Node: The mobile node records the details of the mobile phone itself and
    internal resource information, including the configuration of the mobile phone, the
    app information of the mobile phone, and various account password information of
    the user registration app.
(4) User Node: The core node in the mobile phone protection platform is user node
    where records the user information registered with the platform, including the
    user's identity information, public or private key of registrant, identity encryption
    information and the mobile phone's internal information.

The mobile phone manufacturer node, the mobile phone market node, the mobile
phone node and the mobile phone user node establish a mobile phone protection
platform through a distributed arrangement, and connect their own database to store
user information, mobile phone information and transaction information. Therefore, the
four types of nodes between the database will also achieve communication, while
mining block chain algorithm to form a transaction block, stored in their own database.

According to the actual requirements, the decentralized management of these four types of nodes can expand the configuration by adding a number of nodes to meet the platform's high performance and high reliability.

We provide two methods to log in to the mobile phone protection platform based on the block chain. The first is to log in directly through the terminal server to access the http URL. The other is to complete the login by calling the underlying subroutine through the Java SDK. By learning Bubi block chain digital trading platform [15], the design of the mobile phone privacy protection platform was completed.

3.2   Trading and Smart Contracts

According to the characteristics of the four types of internal nodes of the mobile phone protection platform, combined with the process of mobile phone production to use, we divide the node transaction into four aspects. After establishing a set of reliability and profitability between nodes, they are the market shipment transaction between the manufacturer node and the market node, the purchase transaction between the market node and the user node, the information feedback transaction between the market node

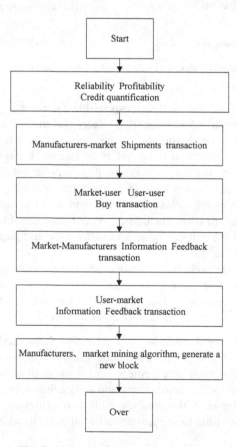

Fig. 2. Node trading inside the platform.

and the manufacturer node, and the information feedback transaction between the user node and the market node. For each transaction, four types of nodes will use hash mining algorithm to generate a new block, record the transaction data information. Specifically, the Intra-node transactions are shown in Fig. 2.

The market shipment transaction between the manufacturer node and the market node is the information flowed to the markets of various countries after the mobile phone is manufactured by the manufacturer, including the place, name and time of the inflow to the market; The purchase transaction between the market node and the user node is a process in which the user purchases the mobile phone from the mobile phone market after the mobile phone enters the market. The information needs to be recorded including the market name, the purchase time, and the model of the mobile phone.

Simultaneously, information feedback transactions exist between the user node and the market node, mainly for user feedback on the market of their own purchased mobile phones, including market mobile phone price/performance ratio, market mobile phone quality and mobile phone After-Sales service. There is also a feedback transaction between the market node and the manufacturer node. Market node feeds back sales information of different brands of mobile phones to respective manufacturers.

The P2P technology is used to communicate between the mobile phone manu-facturer node, the mobile phone market node, the mobile phone node and the mobile phone user node in the platform to further perform data transmission and transaction. Each transaction will generate a new transaction block through the mining algorithm to record the trading node's identity information and transaction information. The transaction block chain formation process is shown in Fig. 3.

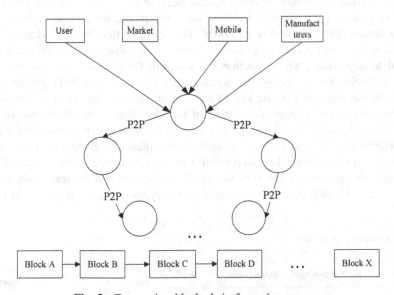

Fig. 3. Transaction block chain formation process.

Every block is connected according to its generation time to forms the block chain of mobile phone protection. Blocks are divided into block headers and block blocks. The block header encapsulates the version number of the current block [1], the target hash of the current block [1], the solution random number of the consensus process, Merkle [1] and the address value of previous block [1]; the block stores the number of transactions in the current block and all transaction records associated with the block.

3.3   Privacy Protection Process

A design of mobile phone privacy protection based on block chain, instead of relying on central institutions, we use cryptographic algorithms to establish trust between dishonest nodes. Therefore, Block chain technology could build a decentralization platform to protect mobile phone privacy. All transactions need to be exposed to all participating nodes which includes mobile phone manufacturer node, mobile phone market node, mobile phone node and mobile phone user node. As a result, the platform is unable to protect privacy in the form of central storage. The only way we can use is to encrypt node identity and transaction information by encryption algorithms. So, the Anonymity can be implemented. Then attackers couldn't find the real identity of the transaction parties.

In this scheme, we combine the secret key encryption algorithm with digital signature algorithm. Then we used it to protect the privacy information inside the mobile phone. Before transaction, asymmetric encryption algorithm (ECC) [16] is used to encrypt identifies of nodes in the whole network. The system assigns a unique pair of public and private keys to each node. Nodes use the public key to encrypt the message, and only the corresponding private key can decrypt [17]. After identity encryption, addresses generated by random numbers and asymmetric encryption algorithms are used to replace the real identity of nodes. This ensures that the real identity of the transaction node isn't published in the platform. At the same time, the private key can be used to sign your own transaction information. Other nodes can use the corresponding public key to verify the signature of the message. Both parties of the transaction use their own public key to sign the transaction information. Transaction message is processed to generate a string of numbers that cannot be forged by other nodes. The node that received the message verifies the digital signature using the public key corresponding to the digital signature in the platform. After the transaction is completed, a timestamp is added to prevent it from being tampered by an unauthorized node. Signature can ensure the authenticity of transactions and the legitimacy of node identities. Specifically, the transaction privacy encryption process is shown in Fig. 4:

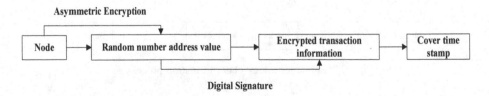

Fig. 4. Transaction privacy encryption process.

Nodes use random numbers and addresses generated by asymmetric encryption algorithms instead of their own identities. The private key is used to digitally sign the transaction information to protect the transaction information and node identity information. Through the combination of key encryption algorithm and digital signature algorithm is realized the protection of mobile phone privacy information.

4 Conclusions

This paper describes a design of mobile phone protection platform based on block chain. The four nodes of the mobile phone manufacturer node, the mobile phone market node, the mobile phone node and the mobile phone user node are arranged in a distributed manner, and the mobile phone protection platform is built and connected to the database for distributed storage. The asymmetric encryption algorithm (ECC) is used to encrypt the identity of the nodes within the platform to protect the node identity information. After encryption, each node is assigned a unique pair of keys. The node's private key is used to digitally sign its transaction information to enable protection of mobile transactions in the platform based on block chain. Through the design of mobile phone protection platform based on block chain, it solves the problem that the thief uses the brush method to obtain the right to use the mobile phone and leakage of user information, thereby achieving the protection of mobile phone privacy information.

References

1. Khan, M.A., Salah, K.: IoT security: review, blockchain solutions, and open challenges. Future Gener. Comput. Syst. **82**(2018), 395–411 (2017)
2. Xia, Q., Sifah, E.B., Asamoah, K.O., et al.: MeDShare: trust-less medical data sharing among cloud service providers via blockchain. IEEE Access **5**(99), 14757–14767 (2017)
3. Maccari, L., Facchi, N., Baldesi, L.: Optimized P2P streaming for wireless distributed networks. Pervasive Mob. Comput. **42**(2017), 335–350 (2017)
4. Hu, C.C., Lai, C.F., Hou, J.G.: Timely scheduling algorithm for P2P streaming over MANETs. Comput. Netw. **127**(2017), 56–67 (2017)
5. Xia, Q., Sifah, E., Smahi, A., Amofa, S., Xiaosong, Z.: BBDS: blockchain-based data sharing for electronic medical records in cloud environments. Information **8**(2), 44 (2017)
6. Michael, N., Peter, G., Oliver, H., Dirk, S.: Blockchain. Bus. Inf. Syst. Eng. **59**(3), 183–187 (2017)
7. Huang, H., Chen, X., Wu, Q., et al.: Bitcoin-based fair payments for outsourcing computations of fog devices. Future Gener. Comput. Syst. **78**(2018), 850–858 (2016)
8. Yuan, C., Xu, M.X., Si, X.M.: Research on a new signature scheme on blockchain. Secur. Commun. Netw. **2017**(2), 1–10 (2017)
9. Sullivan, C., Burger, E.: E-residency and blockchain. Comput. Law Secur. Rev. **33**(4), 470–481 (2017)
10. Yan, Z., Gan, G., Riad, K.: BC-PDS: protecting privacy and self-sovereignty through BlockChains for OpenPDS. In: 11th International Symposium on Service-Oriented System Engineering. IEEE Computer Society, San Francisco (2017)

11. Azaria, A., Ariel, E., Thiago, V., Andrew, Li.: MedRec: using blockchain for medical data access and permission management. In: 2nd International Conference on Open and Big Data. IEEE Computer Society, Vienna (2016)
12. Bozic, N., Pujolle, G., Secci, S.: A tutorial on blockchain and applications to secure network control-planes. In: 3rd Smart Cloud Networks and Systems, pp. 1–8. IEEE Computer Society, Dubai (2016)
13. Huh, S., Cho, S., Kim, S.: Managing IoT devices using blockchain platform. In: International Conference on Advanced Communications Technology, pp. 464–467. IEEE Computer Society, Bongpyeong-myeon, Korea (South) (2017)
14. Teslya, N., Ryabchikov, I.: Blockchain-based platform architecture for industrial IoT. In: Proceeding of the 21st Conference of FRUCT Association, pp. 321–329. IEEE Xplore, Helsinki (2017)
15. Hao, L., Lianming, Z., Wenhua, H.: Topology optimization algorithm based on resource sharing gravitation in P2P network. J. Chin. Comput. Syst. **38**, 87–91 (2017)
16. Dorri, A., Steger, M., Kanhere, S.S., et al.: BlockChain: a distributed solution to automotive security and privacy. IEEE Commun. Mag. **55**(12), 119–125 (2017)
17. Lei, A., Cruickshank, H., Cao, Y., et al.: Blockchain-based dynamic key management for heterogeneous intelligent transportation systems. IEEE Internet Things J. **4**(6), 1832–1843 (2017)

A Dominance-Based Constrained Optimization Evolutionary Algorithm for the 4-th Tensor Power Problem of Matrix Multiplication

Langping Tang[1(✉)], Yuren Zhou[2,3], and Zefeng Chen[2]

[1] School of Computer Science and Engineering,
South China University of Technology, Guangzhou 510006, China
`langping_tang@126.com`
[2] School of Data and Computer Science,
Sun Yat-sen University, Guangzhou 510006, China
[3] Guangzhou College of South China University of Technology,
Guangzhou 510800, China

Abstract. As one of the fundamental operations, matrix multiplication plays a significant role in mathematics, computer science and many other science fields. In Williams' research of studying matrix multiplication problem, she put emphasis on studying the even tensor powers of Coppersmith-Winograd approach, and then obtained improved upper bound for the matrix multiplication exponent. In fact, the program for calculating the so-called even tensor power is a constrained optimization problem with complicated constraints. In this paper, we focus on the 4-th tensor power problem of matrix multiplication. After converting this practical problem, we design a dominance-based constrained optimization evolutionary algorithm. Empirical results show that this algorithm can effectively solve the 4-th tensor power problem. What is more, the feasible solution obtained by this algorithm is better than the current known solution of the problem.

Keywords: Matrix multiplication · Tensor power
Constrained optimization · Evolutionary algorithm

1 Introduction

In many scientific and engineering disciplines, there exist a variety of constrained optimization problems (COPs for short). Without loss of generality, a standard COP can be formulated as the following minimization problem with n decision variables and m constraints:

Supported by the National Nature Science Foundation of China [grant numbers 61472143, 61773410, 61673403].

X. Sun et al. (Eds.): ICCCS 2018, LNCS 11066, pp. 563–575, 2018.
https://doi.org/10.1007/978-3-030-00015-8_49

$$\text{minimize } f(\mathbf{x})$$
$$\text{subject to } \mathbf{L} \leq \mathbf{x} \leq \mathbf{U}$$
$$g_j(\mathbf{x}) \leq 0, \ j = 1, 2, \cdots, q \tag{1}$$
$$h_j(\mathbf{x}) = 0, \ j = q+1, \cdots, m$$

where $\mathbf{L} = (l_1, l_2, \cdots, l_n) \in \mathbb{R}^n$ and $\mathbf{U} = (u_1, u_2, \cdots, u_n) \in \mathbb{R}^n$ represent the lower and upper bounds of $\mathbf{x} = (x_1, x_2, \cdots, x_n) \in \mathbb{R}^n$, respectively. q $(0 \leq q \leq m)$ is the number of inequality constraints, and $m - q$ is the number of equality constraints. The decision space $S \subseteq \mathbb{R}^n$ of $\mathbf{x}$ is an n-dimensional rectangle space determined by $\mathbf{L}$ and $\mathbf{U}$, and can be expressed as: $S = \{\mathbf{x} \in \mathbb{R}^n | \mathbf{L} \leq \mathbf{x} \leq \mathbf{U}\}$. The feasible region $\Omega \subseteq S$ of $\mathbf{x}$ is determined by all the inequality constraints and equality constraints (linear or nonlinear), and can be expressed as: $\Omega = \{\mathbf{x} \in S | g_j(\mathbf{x}) \leq 0, \ j = 1, 2, \cdots, q; h_j(\mathbf{x}) = 0, \ j = q+1, \cdots, m\}$.

In the past decade, a lot of researchers attempted to apply evolutionary algorithms (EAs) to solve COPs, and designed many constrained optimization evolutionary algorithms (COEAs for short) [5,10]. Since EAs belong to the unconstrained optimization methods, it is required to design an additional mechanism for dealing with constraints when applying EAs to solve COPs. To this aim, researchers have designed various kinds of constraint handling techniques [20]. Among these existing constraint handling techniques, one kind of classical method is employing multi-objective optimization to deal with constraints. The main idea of this kind of method is to transform the original constrained optimization problem to an unconstrained multi-objective optimization problem, and then utilize multi-objective evolutionary algorithm (MOEA) to solve the multi-objective optimization problem [4]. In this respect, there has been many researches, including the classical CW [3], ZW [24] and other algorithms. And it has been demonstrated that this kind of using multi-objective optimization technique to deal with constraints has the ability to solve COPs.

When applying COEA to solve a practical COP, we need to analyze the characteristic of the practical problem and then adopt related techniques to design an algorithm to solve this problem. In this paper, we mainly focus on how to apply EA to solve the classical matrix multiplication problem, which can be transformed to an optimization problem with complicated constraints. We firstly simplify and convert this practical problem based on the elaborate analysis of the problem characteristics. Then, we design a dominance-based constrained optimization evolutionary algorithm called D-COEA$_\omega$. Empirical results show that this algorithm can effectively solve the 4-th tensor power problem.

The rest of the paper is organized as follows. Section 2 briefly introduces the multi-objective optimization technique for handling constraints and the 4-th tensor power problem of matrix multiplication. Section 3 describes how to solve the 4-th tensor power problem, including the simplification and transformation of problem and the design of our proposed D-COEA$_\omega$ algorithm. Section 4 presents the experimental results and discussions, and Sect. 5 concludes the paper.

2   Preliminaries

2.1   Multi-objective Optimization Technique for Handling Constraints

In the kind of using multi-objective optimization technique to deal with constraints, we need to transform the original COP to an unconstrained multi-objective optimization problem, and then utilize MOEA to solve the multi-objective optimization problem. Thus, it is necessary to introduce the concrete transformation process. Considering the COP defined by Eq. (1), by the penalty function method, we can construct the penalty function of each constraint which can be expressed as follows:

$$G_j(\mathbf{x}) = \begin{cases} \max\{0, g_j(\mathbf{x})\}, 1 \le j \le q \\ |h_j(\mathbf{x})|, \qquad q+1 \le j \le m \end{cases} \tag{2}$$

The penalty function of each constraint represents the violation degree of an individual $\mathbf{x}$ in each constraint. By summing them, we can obtain the commonly used form of the degree of constraint violation, that is, $G(\mathbf{x}) = \sum_{j=1}^{m} G_j(\mathbf{x})$. It measures the distance of $\mathbf{x}$ to the feasible region. In fact, we use the degree of constraint violation to punish an infeasible solution and make the probability for this infeasible solution to survive into the next generation become less than that for a feasible solution. Thus, in this kind of using multi-objective optimization technique to deal with constraints, other than minimizing the original objective $f(\mathbf{x})$, we should also attempt to minimize the degree of constraint violation $G(\mathbf{x})$. On the basis of this consideration, we can transform a COP into an unconstrained bi-objective optimization problem:

$$\text{minimize } F(\mathbf{x}) = \left(f(\mathbf{x}), G(\mathbf{x})\right)^T \tag{3}$$
$$\text{subject to } \mathbf{L} \le \mathbf{x} \le \mathbf{U}$$

2.2   Matrix Multiplication Problem

As one of the fundamental operations, matrix multiplication plays a significant role in mathematics, computer science and many other science fields. Employing the matrix multiplication, people can efficiently conduct more advanced matrix operations (such as computing the determinant of a matrix, matrix inversion and matrix decomposition) and solve many computational problems [1]. Formally, the matrix multiplication can be expressed as the following process: given two matrices $A = (a_{ij})_{n \times p}$ and $B = (b_{jk})_{p \times m}$, the product of A and B is an $n \times m$ matrix $C = AB = (c_{ik})_{n \times m}$, whose element is given by $c_{ik} = \sum_{j=1}^{p} a_{ij}b_{jk}$ $(i = 1, 2, \ldots, n, k = 1, 2, \ldots, m)$.

Naively, the multiplication of two $n \times n$ matrices over a field requires $\mathcal{O}(n^3)$ arithmetic operations. In 1969, Strassen firstly presented a sub-cubic time algorithm for the matrix multiplication problem, which only needs $\mathcal{O}(n^{2.808})$ arithmetic operations [9,18]. Strassen's amazing work has attracted great attention, and made many researchers devote themselves to reducing the exponent of the matrix multiplication (denoted ω), which means that the arithmetic operations required by a matrix multiplication algorithm is $\mathcal{O}\left(n^{\omega}\right)$. In fact, many researchers hold the opinion that the true value of ω is 2, which means that there exists an optimal matrix multiplication algorithm with a time complexity of $\mathcal{O}\left(n^2\right)$. To this aim, different researchers attempted to analyze the matrix multiplication problem with different techniques and formed novel algorithms for matrix multiplication. In 1978, Pan proved $\omega < 2.796$ with the trilinear aggregation technology [11]. And in 1979, Bini *et al.* proved $\omega < 2.78$ by introducing of the concept of border rank [2]. In 1981, Schönhage generalized Bini *et al.*'s method and proved that $\omega < 2.548$ [14]. And he also proved $\omega < 2.522$ by combing his work and Pan's ideas. In 1982, Romani proved that $\omega < 2.517$ [12]. Almost in the same time, Coppersmith and Winograd obtained $\omega < 2.496$, which is the first result to break 2.5 [6]. Subsequently, in 1986, Strassen proved $\omega < 2.479$ by introducing his *laser* method [16,17]. In 1990, Coppersmith and Winograd further obtained a famous result $\omega < 2.376$ by combining Strassen's techniques with a new form of analysis [7]. Twenty years later, Stothers obtained that $\omega < 2.373$ in 2010 [15].

In 2012, Williams [21] started to more closely analyze the techniques behind the Coppersmith-Winograd approach, and in 2014 obtained that $\omega < 2.372873$ [22]. In her research, she put emphasis on studying the second, 4-th and 8-th tensor powers of Coppersmith-Winograd approach, and then obtained improved upper bound for the matrix multiplication exponent. In essence, in her analyses, the program for calculating the so-called even tensor power is a constrained optimization problem. Particularly, the constrained optimization problem corresponding to the 4-th tensor power can be formalized as follows:

$$
\begin{aligned}
&\textbf{minimize } f(\mathbf{x}) = 3\tau \\
&\textbf{subject to } \mathbf{x} = (q, \tau, a, b, c, d, e, f, g, h, i, j) \in \Omega
\end{aligned}
\tag{4}
$$

where the decision space $S \subseteq \Re^{12}$ is expressed as

$$
S = \left\{ \mathbf{x} \in \Re^{12} \,|\, q \geq 3, q \in Z; \; a, b, e, f, g, h, i, j \in [0,1]; \; c, d \geq 0; \tau > 0 \right\}
\tag{5}
$$

And the feasible region $\Omega \subseteq S$ is determined by the following four constraints:

$$
\begin{cases}
3a + 6(b + c + d) + 3(e + f) + 6(g + h) + 3(i + j) = 1 \\
(q + 2)^4 \prod_{I=0}^{8} A_I^{A_I} = V_{017}^{6b} V_{026}^{6c} V_{035}^{6d} V_{044}^{3e} V_{116}^{3f} V_{125}^{6g} V_{134}^{6h} V_{224}^{3i} V_{233}^{3j} \\
c = \frac{fej}{h^2} \\
d = \frac{egj}{hi}
\end{cases}
\tag{6}
$$

The above constraints involve several parameters. Among them, parameters A_I $(I = 0, 1, \cdots, 8)$ are related to variables $a, b, c, d, e, f, g, h, i, j$, and they can be expressed as follows:

$$
\begin{cases}
A_0 = 2a + 2b + 2c + 2d + e \\
A_1 = 2b + 2f + 2g + 2h \\
A_2 = 2c + 2g + 2i + j \\
A_3 = 2d + 2h + 2j \\
A_4 = 2e + 2h + i \\
A_5 = 2d + 2g \\
A_6 = 2c + f \\
A_7 = 2b \\
A_8 = a
\end{cases}
\tag{7}
$$

Parameters V_{ijk} $(i, j, k = 1, \cdots, 8)$ satisfying $i + j + k = 8$ are related to variables q and τ, and they are expressed as follows:

$$
\begin{cases}
V_{017} = (4q)^{\tau} \\
V_{026} = \left(4 + 6q^2\right)^{\tau} \\
V_{035} = \left(12q + 4q^3\right)^{\tau} \\
V_{044} = \left(6 + 12q^2 + q^4\right)^{\tau} \\
V_{116} = 2^{2/3}\left(8q^{3\tau}\left(q^{3\tau} + 2\right) + (2q)^{6\tau}\right)^{1/3} \\
V_{125} = 2^{2/3}\left(2\left(q^2 + 2\right)^{3\tau} + 4q^{3\tau}\left(q^{3\tau} + 2\right)\right)^{1/3}\left(\frac{4q^{3\tau}\left(q^{3\tau}+2\right)}{\left(q^2+2\right)^{3\tau}} + (2q)^{3\tau}\right)^{1/3} \\
V_{134} = 2^{2/3}\left((2q)^{3\tau} + 4q^{3\tau}\left(q^{3\tau} + 2\right)\right)^{1/3}\left(2 + 2(2q)^{3\tau} + \left(q^2 + 2\right)^{3\tau}\right)^{1/3} \\
V_{224} = \frac{\left(2\left(q^2+2\right)^{3\tau} + 4q^{3\tau}\left(q^{3\tau}+2\right)\right)^{2/3}\left(2 + 2(2q)^{3\tau} + \left(q^2+2\right)^{3\tau}\right)^{1/3}}{\left(q^2+2\right)^{\tau}} \\
V_{233} = \frac{\left(2\left(q^2+2\right)^{3\tau} + 4q^{3\tau}\left(q^{3\tau}+2\right)\right)^{1/3}\left((2q)^{3\tau} + 4q^{3\tau}\left(q^{3\tau}+2\right)\right)^{2/3}}{q^{\tau}\left(q^{3\tau}+2\right)^{1/3}}
\end{cases}
\tag{8}
$$

From τ-theorem, we can know that the relationship between the matrix multiplication exponent ω and τ is $\omega \leq 3\tau$ [14,22]. Thus, by means of minimizing 3τ (that is, solving the above constrained optimization problem), we can obtain the upper bound of ω. To this aim, Williams adopted the NLopt package [8] to solve this constrained optimization problem, and obtained $\omega \leq 2.3729268610$.

Hereinafter, for the sake of clarity, the constrained optimization problem corresponding to the 4-th tensor power is called the 4-th tensor power problem for short.

3 Solution to 4-th Tensor Power Problem

3.1 Simplification and Transformation of Problem

Considering the aforementioned 4-th tensor power problem, we firstly attempt to simplify this problem based on the elaborate analysis of the problem characteristics, and then transform it to an unconstrained bi-objective optimization problem.

Recall that c and d can be determined by e, f, g, h, i, j. Thus, we can reduce the number of decision variables from 12 to 10 by regarding c and d as parameters. Moreover, considering that the true range of the matrix multiplication exponent ω is $\omega \leq 3$, we shrink the range of τ by replacing $\tau > 0$ with $0 < \tau < 10$ (that is, adding a relatively relaxed upper bound for τ). Also, we take the logarithm of both sides of the second equation constraint in Eq. (6). In conclusion, the original problem can be simplified to the following problem:

$$
\begin{aligned}
&\text{minimize } f(\mathbf{x}) = 3\tau \\
&\text{subject to } \mathbf{x} = (q, \tau, a, b, e, f, g, h, i, j) \in \Omega
\end{aligned}
\tag{9}
$$

where the new decision space $S \subseteq \Re^{10}$ is expressed as

$$
S = \left\{ \mathbf{x} \in \mathbb{R}^{10} \,|\, q \geq 3,\, q \in \mathbb{Z};\, a, b, e, f, g, h, i, j \in [0, 1];\, 0 < \tau < 10 \right\}
\tag{10}
$$

And the new feasible region $\Omega \subseteq S$ is determined by the following two constraints:

$$
\begin{cases}
h_1(\mathbf{x}) = 3a + 6(b + c + d) + 3(e + f) + 6(g + h) + 3(i + j) - 1 = 0 \\
h_2(\mathbf{x}) = 4\ln(q + 2) + \sum_{I=0}^{8} A_I \cdot \ln A_I - 6b \cdot \ln V_{017} - 6c \cdot \ln V_{026} - \\
\qquad 6d \cdot \ln V_{035} - 3e \cdot \ln V_{044} - 3f \cdot \ln V_{116} - 6g \cdot \ln V_{125} - \\
\qquad 6h \cdot \ln V_{134} - 3i \cdot \ln V_{224} - 3j \cdot \ln V_{233} = 0
\end{cases}
\tag{11}
$$

By means of the penalty function method, we can further transform the problem to the following unconstrained bi-objective optimization problem:

$$
\begin{aligned}
&\text{minimize} \quad F(\mathbf{x}) = \Big(f(\mathbf{x}), G(\mathbf{x})\Big)^T \\
&\text{subject to } \mathbf{x} = (q, \tau, a, b, e, f, g, h, i, j) \in S
\end{aligned}
\tag{12}
$$

where $f(\mathbf{x}) = 3\tau$, $G(\mathbf{x}) = \sqrt{\sum_{j=1}^{2} G_j(\mathbf{x})^2} = \sqrt{|h_1(\mathbf{x})|^2 + |h_2(\mathbf{x})|^2}$. It should be noted that we do not adopt the commonly used form of the degree of constraint violation. The form used here (i.e., $G(\mathbf{x})$) is the square root of the quadratic sum of the degree of each constraint violation, which is conducive to the solving of the problem.

3.2   Proposed Algorithm: D-COEA$_\omega$

To solve the unconstrained bi-objective optimization problem (12) in the previous subsection, we design an algorithm called D-COEA$_\omega$, whose pseudo-code is given in Algorithm 1.

Similar to the multi-objective optimization based ZW algorithm [24] and CW algorithm [3], the framework of D-COEA$_\omega$ is also an improvement and of the so-called MGG model [13]. At the beginning, an initial population with size N is randomly generated. The procedures from Line 4 to Line 22 (that is, the process of generating the next population P_{t+1}) are repeated until the termination criterion is fulfilled.

First of all, to measure the relative quality of an individual in a population P with size N, we design a new indicator called D_RATIO. As for an individual

---

Algorithm 1. Framework of D-COEA$_\omega$

1: $P_0 \leftarrow$ InitializePopulation();
2: $t \leftarrow 0$;
3: **while** *termination criterion is not fulfilled* **do**
4:      $count \leftarrow 0$;
5:      $P_{t+1} \leftarrow \emptyset$;
6:      **while** $count < N$ **do**
7:           $P_{\text{parent}} \leftarrow$ RandomSelect$_\mu(P_t)$;
8:           $P_{\text{offspring}} \leftarrow$ Recombine$_\lambda(P_{\text{parent}})$;
9:           $\mathcal{F}_1 \leftarrow$ DDA-NS$_1(P_{\text{offspring}})$;
10:          **if**   there exist individuals satisfying $G_1(\mathbf{x}) = 0$ or $G_2(\mathbf{x}) = 0$ in $P_{\text{offspring}}$ **then**
11:               Select these individuals to constitute CV_0;
12:               $R_t \leftarrow \mathcal{F}_1 \cup CV_0$;
13:          **else**
14:               $R_t \leftarrow \mathcal{F}_1$;
15:          **end if**
16:          Calculate the values of D_RATIO for all the individuals in R_t;
17:          Add the best solution (in terms of D_RATIO) into P_{t+1};
18:          Select the solution with the minimum value of $G(\mathbf{x})$ from P_{t+1}, and add it into P_{t+1};
19:          $count \leftarrow count + 2$;
20:      **end while**
21:      Record the solution with the minimum value of $f(\mathbf{x})$ and its degree of constraint violation;
22:      $t \leftarrow t + 1$;
23: **end while**

$\mathbf{y}^i$ ($i \in \{1, 2, \cdots, N\}$), its indicator D_RATIO_i can be calculated as follows:

$$D\_RATIO_i = \frac{dom\_strength_i}{\sum_{i=1}^{N} dom\_strength_i} + C_1 \cdot \frac{sup\_num_i}{\sum_{i=1}^{N} sup\_num_i} - C_2 \cdot \frac{inf\_num_i}{\sum_{i=1}^{N} inf\_num_i} \tag{13}$$

where $C_1 \in [0,1]$ and $C_2 \in [0,1]$ are two user-defined weighting parameters. $dom\_strength_i$ represents the product of the number of objectives (m) and the number of the individuals dominated by $\mathbf{y}^i$ in P. sup_num_i represents the number of objectives on which $\mathbf{y}^i$ is superior to other individuals in P, while inf_num_i is the number of objectives on which $\mathbf{y}^i$ is inferior to other individuals in P. If an individual has a larger value of D_RATIO, then this individual is of better quality, and vice versa.

In the t-th generation, μ parents are randomly selected from P_t to constitute P_{parent}. Then, a recombination operator called simplex crossover operator (SPX for short) [19] is conducted on these μ parents to generate λ offspring, which constitute $P_{\text{offspring}}$. On the basis of the triple objectives $\left(f(\mathbf{x}), G_1(\mathbf{x}), G_2(\mathbf{x}) \right)^T$, the dominance degree approach for non-dominated sorting [23] is invoked to determine the first front $\mathcal{F}_1$ (that is, the non-dominated individuals in $P_{\text{offspring}}$).

If there exist individuals which satisfy $G_1(\mathbf{x}) = 0$ or $G_2(\mathbf{x}) = 0$ in $P_{\text{offspring}}$, then these individuals are taken out to constitute CV_0, and $\mathcal{F}_1$ and CV_0 are merged to form a new population R_t. In a sense, R_t can be viewed as a small population which is constituted by the elite individuals in $P_{\text{offspring}}$.

It should be noted that the key goal of constrained optimization is to seek for feasible solutions, that is, the solutions whose degree of constraint violation is 0. Thus, in the evolution process, we should not only make the value of $G(\mathbf{x})$ become smaller and smaller but also make it converge to 0. To this aim, each time we select two individuals from R_t and add them into the next population P_{t+1}. The selection rule for these two individuals is as follows:

1. On the basis of the triple objectives $\left(f(\mathbf{x}), G_1(\mathbf{x}), G_2(\mathbf{x})\right)^T$, the individual having the maximum value of D_RATIO is determined and added into P_{t+1}. If there exist several individuals having the maximum value of D_RATIO, then the one having the minimum value of $G(\mathbf{x})$ is selected from these individuals.
2. Select the individual having the minimum value of $G(\mathbf{x})$ from the remaining individuals in R_t, and add it into P_{t+1}.

The aforementioned operations, starting from randomly selecting μ parents, are repeated until the size of P_{t+1} reaches N. It should be noted that in each repetition, two individuals are added into P_{t+1}.

It is worth stressing that in every generation of the proposed D-COEA$_\omega$ algorithm, the solution with the minimum value of $f(\mathbf{x})$ and its degree of constraint violation are recorded. Further, when the termination criterion is fulfilled, the algorithm does not directly output the optimal solution in the last generation as the final result. In fact, the D-COEA$_\omega$ algorithm collects the solutions recorded in all generations, and screens out the feasible solutions (that is, the ones whose degree of constraint violation is 0) among them. Then, the solution having the minimum value of $f(\mathbf{x})$ is selected from the feasible solutions, and is output as the final result of algorithm. If all the solutions recorded in all generations are not feasible, then the algorithm outputs NULL.

4   Experimental Results and Discussions

In this section, we will present in detail the experimental results of the classical CW algorithm [3] and the proposed D-COEA$_\omega$ algorithm. In the experiments, each algorithm is run 10 times independently for each case. And the population in each case is randomly initialized with random seed.

4.1   Performance of CW Algorithm

Firstly, as a comparison with our proposed D-COEA$_\omega$ algorithm, we adopt the classical CW algorithm to solve the problem (12). The CW algorithm is a multi-objective optimization based constrained evolutionary algorithm proposed by

Cai and Wang [3], and is popular for solving constrained optimization problems. The degree of constraint violation used in CW is the commonly used form, that is, $G(\mathbf{x}) = \sum_{j=1}^{2} G_j(\mathbf{x}) = |h_1(\mathbf{x})| + |h_2(\mathbf{x})|$.

In the experiments, the related parameters in CW are set as suggested in the original literature [3]. The termination criterion of an algorithm is a predefined maximum function evaluations (*MaxGen* for short), and *MaxGen* is set to the default value 35000.

To investigate the performance of CW algorithm in different cases, we only change the value of two parameters including the expanding rate ε used in the simplex crossover operator and the population size N. Concretely, we set N to different values (i.e., $N = 50, 100, 150$), and set ε to two commonly used values (i.e., $s = 7, 8$). The experimental results are shown in Tables 1 and 2. It should be noted that $f(\mathbf{x})$ represents the objective function of the 4-th tensor power problem, and $G(\mathbf{x})$ is the degree of constraint violation.

Table 1. Results of CW algorithm on the 4-th tensor power problem ($\varepsilon = 7$)

	$f(\mathbf{x})$	$G(\mathbf{x})$	$f(\mathbf{x})$	$G(\mathbf{x})$	$f(\mathbf{x})$	$G(\mathbf{x})$
	$N = 50$		$N = 100$		$N = 150$	
1	0.0346571809	1.8177247290	0.0000000000	1.8357353693	2.3768536405	0.0000007150
2	0.0000000107	1.8357356681	2.3797605092	0.0000000618	0.0000000000	1.8357353693
3	2.2250989169	0.2101016907	0.0000000000	1.8357353693	0.0000000000	1.8357353693
4	0.3037787849	1.4650239889	2.3875643439	0.0000000719	0.0000000000	1.8357353693
5	1.6445169913	0.7953099790	1.5317433074	0.6089399198	0.0000000000	1.8357353693
6	0.0165164958	1.8149852563	0.0000000000	1.8357353693	0.0000000000	1.8357353693
7	**2.5714555039**	**0.0000000000**	0.0000000000	1.8357353693	0.0000000000	1.8357353693
8	1.5922361256	0.3162135927	0.0000000000	1.8357353693	0.0000000000	1.8357353693
9	2.0624361630	0.2626378405	0.0000000000	1.8357353693	0.0000000000	1.8357353693
10	0.0000000473	1.8384552577	1.9664741103	0.4378022626	0.0000000000	1.8357353693

Table 2. Results of CW algorithm on the 4-th tensor power problem ($\varepsilon = 8$)

	$f(\mathbf{x})$	$G(\mathbf{x})$	$f(\mathbf{x})$	$G(\mathbf{x})$	$f(\mathbf{x})$	$G(\mathbf{x})$
	$N = 50$		$N = 100$		$N = 150$	
1	2.4161447836	0.0001789758	0.0000000000	1.8357353693	0.0000000000	1.8357353693
2	2.4503836782	0.0000003907	2.4099609096	0.0000660420	0.0000000000	1.8357353693
3	2.3798215617	0.0000000014	0.0000000000	1.8357353693	0.0000000000	1.8357353693
4	1.3889305768	0.9385665383	0.0000000000	1.8357353693	0.0000000000	1.8357353693
5	2.3933073787	0.0000000089	0.0000000000	1.8357353693	0.0000000000	1.8357353693
6	**2.3863715925**	**0.0000000000**	0.0000000000	1.8357353693	0.0000000000	1.8357353693
7	0.0000000000	1.8357353693	0.0000000000	1.8357353693	0.0000000000	1.8357353693
8	0.0000000000	1.8357353693	0.0000000000	1.8357353693	0.0000000000	1.8357353693
9	0.0000000000	1.8357353693	0.0000000000	1.8357353693	0.0000000000	1.8357353693
10	2.4415493097	0.0000001038	0.0000000000	1.8357353693	0.0000000000	1.8357353693

In these two tables, if the algorithm can obtain a feasible solution (whose corresponding value of $G(\mathbf{x})$ is 0) in a run, then this solution is highlighted with bold font. As for $s = 7$, the CW algorithm can only find a feasible solution in the 7-th run of $N = 50$. And in terms of $s = 7$, the CW algorithm can only find a feasible solution in the 6-th run of $N = 50$. The results obtained in other cases are all infeasible. Thus, when solving the 4-th tensor power problem, the CW has a poor and unstable performance. In a whole, the best result obtained by CW algorithm is $\omega \leq 2.3863715925$, which is still worse than Williams' result $\omega \leq 2.3729268610$.

4.2   Performance of D-COEA$_\omega$ Algorithm

As for the proposed D-COEA$_\omega$ algorithm, the population size N and the maximum function evaluations $MaxGen$ are set to 300 and 1000, respectively. And the settings of other related parameters are as follows: $\mu = n + 1$, $\lambda = 30$, $\varepsilon = 7$.

When the values of the weighting parameters in D_RATIO are set to $C_1 = 0.8, C_2 = 0.2$, the results obtained by D-COEA$_\omega$ is shown in Table 3. It is worth noting that the $OptimalGen$ is the optimal generation, which means that D-COEA$_\omega$ algorithm obtains the optimal feasible solution in the $OptimalGen$-th generation.

As can be seen from Table 3, the proposed D-COEA$_\omega$ algorithm can obtain feasible solutions in all runs, which indicates that the D-COEA$_\omega$ algorithm owns a stable performance. Retrospecting the design idea of D-COEA$_\omega$, we know that D-COEA$_\omega$ records the solution with the minimum value of $f(\mathbf{x})$ and its degree of constraint violation in every generation, and outputs the optimal feasible solution among the solutions in all generations as the final result. Thus, if D-COEA$_\omega$ can output a solution, then this solution is certainly feasible.

Table 3. Results of D-COEA$_\omega$ algorithm on the 4-th tensor power problem ($C_1 = 0.8, C_2 = 0.2$)

	$f(\mathbf{x})$	$G(\mathbf{x})$	$OptimalGen$
1	**2.3729268609**	0.0000000000	530
2	2.3729268610	0.0000000000	988
3	**2.3729268608**	0.0000000000	490
4	**2.3729268607**	0.0000000000	560
5	**2.3729268608**	0.0000000000	465
6	2.3729268610	0.0000000000	981
7	**2.3729268609**	0.0000000000	501
8	**2.3729268609**	0.0000000000	522
9	2.3729268615	0.0000000000	991
10	2.3729268610	0.0000000000	985

Table 4. Comparison results of D-COEA$_\omega$ algorithm on the 4-th tensor power problem under different combinations of C_1, C_2

	Best	Median	Worst	$AverageOptimalGen$
0.8 + 0.2	**2.3729268607**	**2.3729268609**	2.3729268615	701
0.2 + 0.8	**2.3729268608**	**2.3729268608**	2.3729268624	678
0.2 + 0.2	**2.3729268608**	**2.3729268608**	2.3729268615	652
0.5 + 0.5	**2.3729268607**	**2.3729268608**	2.3729268846	608
0.8 + 0.8	**2.3729268607**	**2.3729268609**	2.3729268612	619
0 + 0	**2.3729268608**	2.3729268612	2.3729268625	803
1 + 1	**2.3729268607**	**2.3729268608**	2.3729268610	606
2 + 2	**2.3729268608**	**2.3729268608**	2.3729268610	597

Now, we change the values of C_1, C_2, and investigate the performance of D-COEA$_\omega$ under different combinations of C_1, C_2. As for each case (that is, a certain combination of C_1, C_2), we record the best, median and worst solution among the obtained optimal solutions in 10 runs. Besides, in each case, we also record the average of the values of $OptimalGen$ in 10 runs and denote this average value as $AverageOptimalGen$. The comparison results are shown in Table 4.

Focusing on Table 4, we can find that the value of $AverageOptimalGen$ in the case of $2 + 2$ is the least, which can represent the peak convergence rate of D-COEA$_\omega$. The value of $AverageOptimalGen$ in the case of $0 + 0$ is the largest, which indicates that the D-COEA$_\omega$ algorithm has a slow convergence rate when the values of the weighting parameters in D_RATIO are set to $C_1 = C_2 = 0$. It can be clearly seen that the D-COEA$_\omega$ algorithm can obtain feasible solutions with good quality under all different combinations of C_1, C_2. This phenomenon fully testifies to the strength of the proposed D-COEA$_\omega$ algorithm when solving the 4-th tensor power problem.

It is especially rewarding to note that in Tables 3 and 4, the obtained results better than Williams' result $\omega \leq 2.3729268610$ are highlighted with bold font. To conclude, the best result D-COEA$_\omega$ can obtain is corresponding to the case of $C_1 = 0.8, C_2 = 0.8$, and the values of all the variables (i.e., $\tau, q, a, b, c, d, e, f, g, h, i, j$) are as follows:

$$\tau = 0.790975620232833, q = 5, a = 0.000000140617757, b = 0.000017056451366,$$
$$c = 0.000495822752670, d = 0.004639814337209, e = 0.012488978678568,$$
$$f = 0.000677747997282, g = 0.009861949349570, h = 0.046296682217252,$$
$$i = 0.071989680046970, j = 0.125554135808253.$$

5   Conclusions

In this paper, we have proposed an algorithm called D-COEA$_\omega$ to solve the 4-th tensor power problem of matrix multiplication. Empirical results have demonstrated that the D-COEA$_\omega$ algorithm can effectively solve this complicated problem. What is more, the feasible solution obtained by this algorithm is better than the current known solution of the problem.

Recall that this paper mainly focuses on the 4-th tensor power problem. As can be known from Williams' analyses, we can obtain an improved upper bound of the matrix multiplication exponent based on the result of 8-th tensor power problem. Thus, in the future research, it is necessary to consider the issue of how to design new constrained optimization evolutionary algorithm to effectively solve 8-th tensor power problem, and investigate how to further improve the upper bound of the matrix multiplication exponent.

References

1. Aho, A.V., Hopcroft, J.E.: The Design and Analysis of Computer Algorithms. Addison-Wesley, Wokingham (1976)
2. Bini, D., Capovani, M., Romani, F., Lotti, G.: 0(n2.7799) complexity for n × n approximate matrix multiplication. Inf. Process. Lett. **8**, 234–235 (1979)
3. Cai, Z., Wang, Y.: A multiobjective optimization-based evolutionary algorithm for constrained optimization. IEEE Trans. Evol. Comput. **10**(6), 658–675 (2006)
4. Coello, C.A.C.: Treating constraints as objectives for single-objective evolutionary optimization. Eng. Optim. **32**(3), 275–308 (2000)
5. Coello, C.A.C.: Theoretical and numerical constraint-handling techniques used with evolutionary algorithms: a survey of the state of the art. Comput. Methods Appl. Mech. Eng. **191**(11–12), 1245–1287 (2002)
6. Coppersmith, D., Winograd, S.: On the asymptotic complexity of matrix multiplication. In: Proceedings of the 22nd Annual Symposium on Foundations of Computer Science, pp. 82–90 (1981)
7. Coppersmith, D., Winograd, S.: Matrix multiplication via arithmetic progressions. In: Proceedings of the Nineteenth Annual ACM Symposium on Theory of Computing, STOC 1987, pp. 1–6. ACM, New York (1987). https://doi.org/10.1145/28395.28396
8. Johnson, S.G.: The NLopt nonlinear-optimization package. http://ab-initio.mit.edu/nlopt
9. Laderman, J.D.: A noncommutative algorithm for multiplying 33 matrices using 23 multiplications. Bull. Am. Math. Soc. **82**(1976), 126–128 (1976)
10. Michalewicz, Z., Schoenauer, M., Schoenauer, M.: Evolutionary algorithms for constrained parameter optimization problems. Evol. Comput. **4**(1), 1–32 (1996)
11. Pan, V.Y.: Strassen's algorithm is not optimal. In: Proceedings of FOCS, vol. 19, pp. 166–176 (1978)
12. Romani, F.: Some properties of disjoint sums of tensors related to matrix multiplication. SIAM J. Comput. **11**(2), 263–267 (1982)
13. Satoh, H., Yamamura, M., Kobayashi, S.: Minimal generation gap model for gas considering both exploration and expolation. In: Proceedings of Fourth International Conference on Soft Computation, pp. 494–497 (1997)

14. Schönhage, A.: Partial and total matrix multiplication. SIAM J. Comput. **10**(3), 434–455 (1981). https://doi.org/10.1137/0210032
15. Stothers, A.J.: On the complexity of matrix multiplication (2010)
16. Strassen, V.: The asymptotic spectrum of tensors and the exponent of matrix multiplication. In: Proceedings of Annual Symposium on Foundations of Computer Science, pp. 49–54 (1986)
17. Strassen, V.: Relative bilinear complexity and matrix multiplication. Journal Fr Die Reine Und Angewandte Mathematik **1987**(375–376), 406–443 (1987)
18. Strassen, V.: Gaussian elimination is not optimal. Numerische Mathematik **13**(4), 354–356 (1969)
19. Tsutsui, S.: Multi-parent recombination with simplex crossover in real coded genetic algorithms. In: GECCO, pp. 657–664 (1999)
20. Venkatraman, S., Yen, G.G.: A generic framework for constrained optimization using genetic algorithms. IEEE Trans. Evol. Comput. **9**(4), 424–435 (2005)
21. Williams, V.V.: Multiplying matrices faster than Coppersmith-Winograd. In: Forty-Fourth ACM Symposium on Theory of Computing, pp. 887–898 (2012)
22. Williams, V.V.: Multiplying matrices in o(n2.373) time (2014). http://theory.stanford.edu/~virgi/matrixmult-f.pdf
23. Zhou, Y., Chen, Z., Zhang, J.: Ranking vectors by means of the dominance degree matrix. IEEE Trans. Evol. Comput. **21**(1), 34–51 (2017). https://doi.org/10.1109/TEVC.2016.2567648
24. Zhou, Y., Li, Y., He, J., Kang, L.: Multi-objective and MGG evolutionary algorithm for constrained optimization. In: The 2003 Congress on Evolutionary Computation, CEC 2003, vol. 1, pp. 1–5 (2004)

A Kind of Agricultural Content Networking Information Fusion Method Based on Ontology

Donghui Li[1], Cong Shen[1(✉)], Xiaopeng Dai[1], and Haiwen Chen[2]

[1] Hunan Agricultural University, Changsha, China
ml8374889745_1@126.com
[2] National University of Defense Technology, Changsha, China

Abstract. The rapid development of agricultural Internet of things is difficult to deal with a lot of information. This paper proposes a method based on ontology of agricultural network information fusion, from this point the basis of ontology and information fusion classification and methods, basic principle, technology in agricultural Internet information fusion as a foundation, in view of the agricultural Internet information uncertainty, heterogeneity and representation problem, put forward agricultural content networking information fusion method based on ontology. It provides theoretical support for the information processing of agricultural Internet of things.

Keywords: Ontology · Agricultural internet of things · Neural networks
Information fusion

1 Introduction

In the process of traditional agricultural production, raising management of all kinds of assignments and rely mainly on the manpower, workload is big, and easy to cause misjudgment and the management decision-making errors, the various inputs and the growth of crops or livestock demand does not match, imbalance, including time applying pesticide excessive, improper irrigation control, often overuse of chemical fertilizer, etc. This "misjudgment" and "mistake" not only increase agricultural inputs, but also may cause environmental pollution in the form of soil, degradation and eutrophication of water. In addition to the production habits, certain planting and breeding technologies, the key is the collection and processing of information such as breeding environment. The research and development application of Internet of things technology brings an opportunity for the development of agricultural informatization. The Internet of things is recognized as the world after computer, Internet and mobile communications, information industry and a new wave has been listed as one of the seven strategic industries in China, become a research hotspot in recent years. The efficient management of information of agricultural Internet of things is an effective way to renovate agricultural production mode, promote the construction of smart countryside, and promote the increase of farmers' production and income and improve the happiness index of life.

In the field of Agriculture, the United Nations Food and Agriculture Organization (FAO, Food and Agriculture Organization) has a lot of research on the agricultural

X. Sun et al. (Eds.): ICCCS 2018, LNCS 11066, pp. 576–588, 2018.
https://doi.org/10.1007/978-3-030-00015-8_50

ontology [2, 3]. In 2000, the FAO implemented the Agricultural Ontology Service plan (AOS) to establish the relevant standards for Agricultural information resources, and standardize Agricultural terminology in various languages. Moreover, the AOS international symposium has been held many times, so that the researchers of agricultural ontology can exchange and discuss together, and promote the integration and resource sharing of agricultural information systems in various countries of the world. At the same time, the FAO has developed various agricultural domain ontology, including fishery body, food safety ontology, antibacterial agent and so on. At home, the agricultural field also carried out some research on ontology knowledge service. Professor Qian of the Chinese academy of agricultural sciences first started the research on the theory of agricultural ontology. He first puts forward the concept of the agricultural ontology service, combined with China's national conditions in China is expounded the agricultural ontology service content and the organization form of [12], open the domestic agricultural ontology service in the new stage. Jing Li of the Chinese academy of sciences has designed and constructed a floral ontology retrieval system with a certain inference function [13]. Her first fused ontology in agricultural disciplines, the application research of agricultural ontology service, such as knowledge engineering, biological engineering, book information service in the field of ontology applied research provides exemplary role. In addition, Zhang Lu, China agricultural university, research on agricultural capital goods ontology [14], the Chinese academy of sciences Xu Yongdeng agricultural ontology construction process research given by the [15], for the agricultural domain ontology knowledge service provides a knowledge base.

Information fusion [17, 18] is a combination of multiple sources of information technology in order to get unified description results, is the sense of people or animals use a variety of access to information, and through the comprehensive analysis and understanding of the objective world a brain function simulation [8, 10]. The theory was originally put forward by the scholars (Camogolo) in 1959 the multi-source information integration theorem, namely: will all kinds of ways, at any time, any space information comprehensive analysis and processing as a whole, provides a basis for decision making and control [8]. In 1973, the United States, scientific research institutions in the study of sonar signal of target detection, the fusion of multiple independent signal, a single detection systems were obtained on enemy ships higher detection accuracy, promote the development of the theory of information fusion in military [10], in the late 1970s, the university of Connecticut Y Bar - professor Shalom in public for the first time in the literature and the basic methods of multi-sensor information fusion is given, namely: the Probabilistic Data Association Filter (Probabilistic Data Association Filter: PDAF [11]. Since the 1980s, the information fusion theory has been widely adopted in the tasks of target tracking, identification, situation assessment and threat estimation worldwide [4]. In 1998, the International Society of Information Fusion was founded by the International Society of Information Fusion (ISIF), which holds an annual International conference on Information Fusion to systematically summarize the research achievements in the field of Information Fusion. Since then, information fusion technology has been comprehensively developed as an independent subject and has been widely studied in various fields of military and civil [5–7, 9]. In China, the research on information fusion technology started late, and only began to be studied in the late 1980s. In the mid and late 1990s, some key technologies of information fusion were obtained. After entering the 21st century, information fusion technology to get the attention of many domestic universities and research institutes, and on the electromagnetic space, land, airborne, naval and air multi-source information fusion in the field of applications such as object orientation, tracking and recognition technology is a comprehensive research and development, but it is still in its infancy.

Based on the comprehensive elaboration, on the basis of ontology, through using the method of information fusion, the comprehensive processing of the data of agricultural iot, agricultural content networking information fusion method based on ontology, to a certain extent brought agriculture information processing is convenient.

2 Ontology

Ontology is a philosophical term derived from the Greek "onto" and "logia", namely "the theory of existence"; Ontology is the study of the existence of a discipline, can answer such as "what is existence", "what is the nature can explain the existence", "the nature of how to explain the existence of different" and so on.

In the field of information system, ontology is applied and developed. McCarthy, realize the philosophical ontology and the logic of artificial intelligence theory similarities and overlaps between build activities, is put forward based on the logical concept of smart systems must be "to list all the things exist, and build an ontology to describe our world" point of view, and the researchers respectively from different point of view put forward the different understanding of the ontology, the ontology is not a unified concept. Perez et al. analyzed the existing ontology with taxonomy, and concluded 5 basic modeling primitives, that is, a complete ontology should have 5 parts:

(1) classes or concepts, which refer to any transaction, such as job description, function, behavior, strategy, and reasoning process. On semantic, said it is a collection of objects, the definition generally adopts frame (frame) structure, including the name of the concept, with the rest of the concept of the relationship between the collection, as well as the description of the concept in nature language.

(2) relationship (relations): the interaction between concepts in the domain. In terms of semantics, there are four basic relationships: part-of, kind-of, instance-of, attribute-of, as shown in Table 1. Of course, in the actual modeling process, the relationship between concepts can be added to the specific situation in the field.

Table 1. Relations among concepts

Relationship name	Describe relations
Part-of	Represents the relationship between the parts of the concept and the whole
Kind-of	Represents the inheritance relationship between concepts
Instance-of	Represents the relationship between an instance of a concept and a concept. Like "Zhang San" and "student"
Attribute-of	A concept is an attribute of another concept. Such as "title" and "teacher"

(3) functions: a special kind of relationship.
(4) axioms: the theorem that represents the eternal truth and the accepted right.
(5) instance (instances): represents the element, which is semantically represented by an object.

Ontology is a kind of scientific thought, which is to use computer model and language to conduct domain knowledge representation and organization, and to combine information sharing technology to carry out knowledge service methodology. And ontology is through active participation and collaboration of experts in the field and build system of domain concepts, axiom and field collection, in the form of a computer can understand and language knowledge description and organization, the purpose of the building ontology knowledge reuse and knowledge sharing and knowledge service.

Agricultural ontology is the combination and application of ontology thought and methodology in the field of agriculture. Agricultural ontology, also known as the agricultural knowledge concept system, in today's Internet age for huge amounts of information and knowledge management system is becoming more and more important. Agricultural ontology is through agriculture and other related fields (e.g., agricultural products processing, economic management, etc.) of experts actively involved in and work together to build models and expressed as a machine can understand the formal language and the organization of agriculture of agricultural information integration.

3   The Theoretical Basis of Information Fusion

3.1   Type of Information Fusion

In multi-sensor data fusion system, data fusion can be divided into three levels according to different levels of data processing: data level fusion, feature level fusion, decision level fusion [19–21].

Data Level (pixel level) Fusion. At the lowest level of fusion, the sensor's observation data is directly integrated and processed, and then the feature extraction and decision making are made based on the result of fusion (Fig. 1).

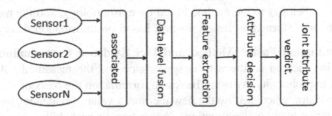

Fig. 1. Data level (pixel level) fusion

Feature Level Fusion. At the intermediate level, each sensor abstracts out its own feature vector, and then the fusion center completes the fusion process. It can be divided into two categories: target state and target feature information (Fig. 2).

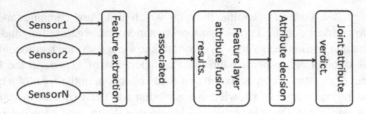

Fig. 2. Feature level fusion

Decision-Making Level Integration. At a high level of integration, each sensor makes decisions based on its own data, and then a local decision is made by the fusion center (Fig. 3).

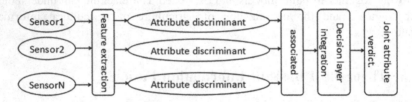

Fig. 3. Decision level fusion

3.2 Method of Information Fusion

There are many methods for information fusion from existing research and analysis, which can be divided into probabilistic statistical methods, epistemological methods and information based methods. Commonly used Bayesian estimation method, the combination of evidence theory to estimate method belongs to the information fusion method based on probability and statistics, the method based on expert system, such as knowledge rules belongs to the method based on epistemology, and the method based on neural network information fusion method based on information theory.

Bayesian Estimation Fusion Method and D-S Evidence Combination Method.
Bayesian fusion method is forecast the appearance and the measured values of estimated results in probability, by using Bayesian formula, on the basis of the given prior likelihood estimator, calculated by the new measured values (evidence), and reasoning forecast (posterior likelihood estimation). According to probability theory, Bayesian formula is expressed as:

If there are n incompatible A_1, A_2, ... A_n. The fully assumed domain of An, B represents the fact or event of a observed value (or the sensor measured here), then.

$$P(A_j|B) = \frac{P(B|A_j)P(A_j)}{\sum\limits_{i=1}^{n} P(B|A_i)P(A_i)} \tag{1}$$

The conditions that must be met are:

$$\sum_{j=1}^{n} P(A_j) = 1, \quad \sum_{i=1}^{n} P(B|A_i)P(A_i) = P(B) \tag{2}$$

Where, $P(A_j)$ represents the event $A_j (j = 1,2 \ldots N)$ probability of occurrence, that is, the probability of an event (assuming) A_j is presented as a prior probability of $P(A_j)$; $P(B)$ for observing the prior distribution of density, $P(B|A_i)$ as the conditions, under the assumption that the A_i is true for the probability of observed value B (evidence), $P(A_i|B)$ for the observation of conditions, according to the prior probability calculated assuming that A_j is really a posteriori probability.

For multi-source sensing information, the above Bayesian estimation formula and principle can be used to deduce and merge the obtained context and relevant information. Suppose the Internet of things USES n sensors, B_1, B_2, ..., B_n (homogeneous or heterogeneous information acquisition device) to build information acquisition and processing system, and the one who has a m judging property targets, namely the incompatibility of the formula (1) hypothesis (or thesis) A_1, A_2, ... A_m, then, based on Eqs. (1) and (2), calculate the maximum value of the joint probability at the time, which is the information and fusion result, when the joint probability is greater than that of a certain constant C; Otherwise, the sensor data source will be scanned again, and new observations will be formed, and the fusion calculation will be carried out according to the Bayesian formula.

It can be seen that the information fusion method based on Bayesian network has simple reasoning and strong reasoning ability. Which need a priori knowledge, however, this requires the active participation of relevant experts in the field of: in addition, when the observation value (sensor) any increase or decrease, need to recalculate the joint likelihood distribution function.

The evidence combination theory was first proposed by Dempster and expanded by his student Shafer, so it is also called the D-S evidence theory. Trust function, introduced the theory, to a certain extend, the Bayesian estimation method does not need to determine the probability of accurate, can distinguish between uncertainty and don't know, meet the weaker than probability of justice, for multi-sensor and platform, application of D-S evidence theory is helpful to the fuzziness and randomness of uncertainty information representation and reasoning. However, this method also has its obvious disadvantages: (1) it cannot solve the problem of evidence conflict, and it is difficult to focus on the weight because it cannot determine the size of the subset; (2) the combination of evidence will cause the growth of the focal element index, which leads to the large computation; (3) the conditions of evidence reasoning are harsh and require independent evidence.

The Fusion Method Based on Expert System and the Fusion Method Based on Neural Network. Expert system (Expert Systems) to imitate people's perception of multi-source information fusion system mechanism, from the eyes, ears, Canon. Son, hands and feet, sensory organs so as to obtain the data information of comprehensive physical identification and prediction, that is to say, this is a similar experts forecast and decision-making ability of information system. Expert systems generally pass If… Then…The generation of inference rules and patterns realize logical reasoning, information and integration. The fusion method based on expert system has the advantages of adaptability and flexibility, composite expert knowledge, long and short supply, stability and reliability. However, the expert system relies on knowledge representation, as the knowledge rule increases, the problem domain increases, the reasoning search becomes more difficult, and even the combination explosion; Therefore, it is difficult to design and develop the expert system for information fusion.

Neural network to simulate the biology information processing process and methods achieve information processing, its basic processing unit for neurons, the related knowledge on the connection weights between neurons layered said. Through the training of the neural network learning, and constantly modify the weights, progressively closer to the desired output and the output and optimize it, it can be said that the neural network learning process, is the organization of the neural network weights between neurons in the modification process. Unlike neural network information fusion system based on epistemology that need domain knowledge or to form certain rules, it does not rely on basic expert knowledge, using the training set data information network, application testing set for validation, the result of the fusion processing and then use trained neural network to deal with a lot of information fusion problem. The information fusion process based on neural network is as follows:

Step 1. Select appropriate neural network models based on the data information and system characteristics obtained, such as BP model, RBF model, ART model and Hopfield model; The most commonly used model is BP neural network, which can be logically divided into input layer, hidden layer and output layer. The establishment of a BP neural network includes the determination of the number of input layer neurons, the determination of the number of output neurons, the determination of the number of hidden layer neurons, and the selection of activation functions.

Step 2. Data information correlation, alignment and transformation, feature extraction. Data alignment and transformation is primarily for data preprocessing, to coordinate alignment calibration, timing, unified measurement units, such as operation, observation and the information associated with measured target classification operation, in order to effectively obtain eigenvector, sometimes still need to some kind of transformation of data information, such as fast Fourier transform (i.e., the observed signals do between the time domain a frequency domain transform). Then, the feature extraction is carried out on the data information of alignment and transformation to extract feature vectors.

Step 3. Normalization processing. The eigenvectors extracted from the previous step are normalized to make the input data information, mapping to [0,1] or smaller.

Step 4. Conduct neural network learning and testing. Neural network training process actually is a process of modifying connection weights between neurons, starting from the existing data information characteristics, connotation and law of learning which, continuously adjust and optimize the network connection weights, makes the configuration of the neural network and the actual situation constantly close to reflect the real situation, it is also a neural network is competent for the root causes of uncertainty reasoning and information fusion, especially when mixed with noise data in the data processing more showed the advantage of neural network.

Step 5. Use the neural network obtained in training for practical information and fusion. Neural network to simulate biological decision-making function, and make full use of in the application of self-learning and self-organization ability, according to the actual situation of constantly learning new knowledge, information fusion, optimize network structure, the cumulative value generally can improve the reliability of information and integration.

For agricultural Internet information fusion, neural network is one of the biggest advantages is the processing of uncertainty information fusion, the fusion of uncertainty information processing ability of expert system based on knowledge or rules such as information processing system is difficult to compare. Agriculture, for example, in the Internet of things, the pressure sensor applications broader sense (weight) of livestock and poultry, the sensor values (pressure) in addition to the affected by the target parameter m, tends to suffer from a temperature t, power source current fluctuation coefficient of target parameters, the influence of the pressure sensor output voltage U actually affected by these three parameters, can be said with a ternary function, namely, $U = f(m, t, a)$, in which t available measured temperature sensor, and current fluctuation coefficient of a sensor data from the current sensing. Therefore, the voltage value that best reflects the actual pressure should be fused by the data information obtained by the pressure sensor, the temperature sensor and the current sensor. Based on the information fusion method based on neural network, it is very effective to eliminate the uncertain influence of the non-target parameters in the process of Internet of things, such as sensor, etc.

Of course. the information fusion method based on neural network has its disadvantages. For example, its network structure is not easy to set up, which often leads to local extremum (optimal) problem. Its network parameters (such as initial offset value, learning speed, etc.) can easily cause problems such as too fast convergence when the setting is not suitable. In addition, it is difficult to obtain the extensive representative and typical training sets of neural networks.

To sum up, all kinds of information fusion each has his strong point, each has a number of shortcomings, the solution can have two kinds: one is to strengthen a certain algorithm to improve research, try to improve the algorithm, and avoid its shortcomings; Second, integrated the advantages of each algorithm, the combination of two or more than two algorithm used, foster strengths and circumvent weaknesses, promoting stability, real-time information, fusion, this approach is more commonly used.

4 Research on the Integration of Agricultural Internet of Things Based on Ontology

In terms of goods information coding, EPC (electronic item code) and UID (generic code) standards emphasize the unification of the information coding format, and follow certain communication protocols, but a given information, exactly how concepts or terms to express, these standards are not unified or imposed, which affect the Internet of things human, machine and a correct understanding, interaction and sharing of information. If the information is allowed to follow the common semantic rules in terms of expression, information sharing and system interoperability can be promoted.), on the other hand, OGC (development of geographic information alliance organization based on the W3C standards developed SWE iot standard solution (sensor networks), provides a distributed infrastructure services platform, to publish, discover and access sensor resources, but SWE lack definite concept model, it is difficult to realize the semantic understanding and interoperability, is unfavorable to the fusion of different granularity of time and space information, and help. Formal representation of ontology in the information, knowledge and promote information sharing and interoperability aspects advantage significantly, and USES ontology to describe and said agricultural network information, including the context of agricultural Internet access information and knowledge of related areas. It can be seen that ontology based information fusion research is the key link to improve the reliable perception ability and system intelligence level of agricultural Internet of things.

4.1 Ontology Based Information Fusion Method

There are three kinds of ontologies from information fusion participation: a single ontology based agricultural Internet information fusion method, multi-ontology-based agricultural Internet information, fusion method and hybrid method.

(1) the former is the use of a global ontology is formal and semantic information fusion to provide a common vocabulary (term) library, this method, all the information and the local ontology is related to the vocabulary.

(2) based on multi-ontological information and fusion method, the semantics of each sensor (data source) are described by its own ontology; Among various sensors (data sources) and no definition of common global words, in the information fusion, a combination of ontology mapping, etc. to complete different between heterogeneous sensor (data source)/semantic annotation, classification and terminology. Among them, the core is the ontology mapping, which is still based on the calculation of the similarity degree of the ontology, thus obtaining the aggregation and dispersion degree of ontology concept and other conditions of concern.

(3) hybrid method. Multiple ontologies are used to describe the information source semantics, but the information concept described by ontology is based on a global Shared vocabulary (term) library.

In general, the information fusion method based on single ontology is relatively simple, but often not easy to build the global ontology, especially the agricultural information in Internet of things is often with uncertainty, the more increased the difficulty of the global ontology construction. The disadvantage of the multi-ontology-based information fusion method is that there is no global vocabulary (term) library, which requires the mapping and operation of ontology. However, the advantages of this method are very convenient in the addition and removal of the sensor (information source). A hybrid approach is a tradeoff between the two approaches, but a global vocabulary (term) library is also needed. In general, for the Internet of things of agriculture, aiming at the characteristics of the information, in the three basic methods of information fusion method based on ontology is often the first choice, mainly through ontology mapping and ontology integration calculation with the model of transformation operations to achieve semantic fusion. Ontology mapping algorithm with two or more ontology for the input, find out the input ontology by calculation of the corresponding element-that is, the concept, the connection between the concept, attribute and instance-the semantic relationships between, including equivalent relation, similarity relation and opposite relationship, the relationship between the whole and part, etc. The purpose is to synthesize a new ontology by calculating the semantic relation between corresponding ontology elements by calculating the existing ontology (input quantity). Of course, the ontology mapping is often based on similarity mapping, which is mainly the calculation of the similarity of the ontology, which is a large calculation.

4.2 Information Fusion Based on Ontology and Neural Network

There are some defects in the existing algorithm of similarity calculation.

(1) large computation. If two noumenon Ontology1 and Ontology2 similarity, should calculate the similarity between each pair of concepts in the Ontology: suppose Ontology including x class (concept), Ontology2 contained in a class y (concept), must calculate x*y similarity, form x*y similar matrix. When programming implementation, some ontologies are not similar, that is, the similarity is 0, and time and space are wasted.

(2) the name of ontology can't just according to the similarity of concept similarity or just contact with attributes and concepts of joint distribution to determine, he should include the name of concept similarity, similarity of concept instance, the relationship between the concept similarity (such as is_Part_of relationship between parts and whole, genus relationship is_a or has_a), concept definition of similarity (synonyms, upper concept, a concept) comprehensive analysis.

Agriculture in the Internet of things, about agricultural information through the sensor, intelligent devices such as card reader to obtain or through Internet or other information facilities, including agricultural environment context information, domain knowledge concept, etc. After the access to information, and to transform the unit or analog to digital signal conversion, calibration, associations, such as pretreatment, and then build or integrate ontology, and deposited in the ontology library. Extracted from an ontology in ontology analysis, parsing in OWL ontology (where specific choose OWL DL- a language), extract the information, and the Class (concept, Class), attributes (including data object and attribute), the corresponding instance (also known as the individual, Individuals), and the corresponding metadata (including basic descriptive definition metadata, metadata, metadata, operation time/position management metadata types) structure types such as temporary storage of information, the similarity calculation needed to for information fusion; The process of ontology parsing can also be regarded as the feature extraction process in information fusion. For name of concept similarity, instance, similarity, the similarity relations, such as concept relations between parts and whole part-whole, inheritance relationship is_a or has_a) and after the definition of similarity calculation, the input of neural network, the result to input information as the neural network computing. Similarities are due to the above four aspects has contribution to the information fusion, but because of the influence of the uncertainty information and noise data, and the agricultural Internet information fusion to comprehensively consider the context information, and related fields of the concept of knowledge integration calculation, thus, the contribution ratio of actual difficulty with artificial or established algorithm, neural network information processing ability strong uncertainty and nonlinear calculation ability, the training by setting the network structure and optimize the network parameters, application described in Sect. 3.2.2 based on neural network information fusion, the basic process and algorithm, calculation, get the new ontology for storage or the new ontology elements (such as the concept, attribute and instance, etc.) is applied to specific issues.

This section proposes the combination of neural network information fusion method based on ontology and framework, and make full use of the semantic description of ontology technology in information expression, fully considered and combined with the neural network method in the uncertainty, incomplete information classification and processing advantages. Because of its openness, the information acquired by the agricultural Internet of things has significant heterogeneity and diversity of expression forms. At the same time because of the complexity of the environmental changes and iot information facilities physical properties limited, measured in terms of time and space limitations, agricultural Internet information with a certain degree of uncertainty and incomplete. Ontology has unique advantages in heterogeneous information description, promotion of information sharing and resource reuse and semantic interoperability. But because of ontology based on description logic, for its uncertainty information, and, with noise data, classification, performance is not strong, nonlinear reasoning and neural network in nonlinear classification, the uncertainty of the information and data information with noise data information processing ability. In a word, combining various methods and optimizing the utilization is the main characteristic of the proposed method and framework.

5   Conclusion

Around the agricultural Internet information fusion method, this paper starts with the basic principle of information fusion, should put forward according to the characteristics of the agricultural Internet information, research suitable information fusion method, based on the analysis summary information fusion method based on Bayesian network, information fusion method based on evidence theory and the information fusion method based on expert system and information fusion method based on neural network, on the basis of the advantages of ontology technology and neural network is put forward based on ontology and neural network of agricultural network information fusion method and framework.

Acknowledgments. The work described in this paper was partially supported by national key research and development project (Project No: SQ2017YFNC050022-06), Hunan education department scientific research project (Project No: 17K044; 17A092).

References

1. Zheng, J.-Y.: Research on Application Architecture and Key Technologies of Agricultural Internet of Things. China Academy of Agricultural Sciences (2016)
2. Rani, M., Dhar, A.K., Vyas, O.P.: Semi-automatic terminology ontology learning based on topic modeling. Eng. Appl. Artif. Intell. **63**, 108–125 (2017)
3. Ruy, F.B., Guizzardi, G., Falbo, R.A., et al.: From reference ontologies to ontology patterns and back. Data Knowl. Eng. **109**, 41–69 (2017)
4. Li, Liggins, M., Hall, D., Llinas, J.: Handbook of multisensor data fusion: theory and practice. Artech House Radar Libr. **39**(5), 180–184 (2008)
5. Milenkovic, A., Otto, C., et al.: Wireless sensor networks for personal health monitoring: issues and an implementation. Comput. Commun. **29**, 2521–2533 (2006)
6. Garcia, M., Sendra, S., Lloret, G., et al.: Monitoring and control sensor system for fish feeding in marine fish farms. IET Commun. **5**(12), 1682–1690 (2011)
7. Pirmez, L., Pinto, L.A.V., Souza, J.N.D., et al.: A localized algorithm for structural health monitoring using wireless sensor networks. Inf. Fusion **15**(1), 114–129 (2014)
8. Wang, R.: Information fusion. Science Press, Beijing (2007)
9. Zhang, N., Lin, C., Pang, X.-L., et al.: Study on time-frequency identification of weak signals of ships under complex sea conditions. J. Mil. Eng. **30**(6), 834–838 (2009)
10. Kang, J.: Research on Key Technologies Based on Multi-sensor Information Fusion. Harbin Engineering University (2013)
11. Bar-Shalom, Y., Tse, E.: Tracking in a cluttered environment with probabilistic data association. Automatica **11**(5), 451–460 (1975)
12. Qian, P., Meng, X., Zheng, Y.L., et al.: Preliminary study on Chinese agricultural ontology service. Agric. Netw. Inf. **2009**(8), 5–8 (2009)
13. Li, J., Meng, L.: Ontology theory and application research in agricultural literature retrieval system – a case study of the modeling of flower ontology. Mod. Book Inf. Technol. (3), 94–94 (2005)
14. Zhang, L., Kang, L., Cheng, X., et al.: Research on the classification system of agricultural commodities ontology. Agric. Netw. Inf. **2009**(8), 38–41 (2009)
15. Xu, Y., Gan, G., Niu, F.Q., et al.: Establishment of information collaborative service system for dairy farming based on process ontology. J. Agric. Eng. **26**(3), 227–232 (2010)
16. Palomares, I., Browne, F., Davis, P.: Multi-view fuzzy information fusion in collaborative filtering recommender systems: application to the urban resilience domain. Data Knowl. Eng. **2017**(113), 64–80 (2018)
17. Zhang, L., Wu, X., Zhu, H., et al.: Perceiving safety risk of buildings adjacent to tunneling excavation: an information fusion approach. Autom. Constr. **73**, 88–101 (2016)
18. Xu, W., Yu, J.: A Novel Approach to Information Fusion in Multi-source Datasets: A Granular Computing Viewpoint. Elsevier Science Inc. 2017

19. Pan, Q., Yu, X., Cheng, Y., et al.: Basic methods and progress of information fusion theory. Control Theory Appl. **29**(10), 599–615 (2012)
20. Stiller, C., León, F.P., Kruse, M.: Information fusion for automotive applications-an overview. Inf. Fusion **12**(4), 244–252 (2011)
21. Dasarathy, B. V.: Information fusion as a tool for forecasting/prediction - an overview. In: International Conference on Big Data and Smart Computing, pp. 532–538 (2016)

A Lightweight Graph-Based Model for Inter-networking Access Control

Zhongmiao Kang, Wenting Jiang$^{(\boxtimes)}$, and Yan Chen

Guangdong Power Grid Corporation, Guangzhou 510000, China
jiangwenting@gddd.csg.cn

Abstract. In classic operation systems, processes are assigned different privileges according to the resources. The enforcement of privilege differentiation on diverse processes indicates that strict security management on the individual process, whose emphasis on the restriction on respective process, however, may also overlook the security risk among the processes. Specifically, one process can invoke another one and establish a session, during which the privileges of invoked process may be passed to the invoking process (e.g., by the inter-processes requests). Thus, it may result in the abuse of privilege and resource leakage. Moreover, the inter-networking of the processes and their relations also complicate the tasks for the regulation on authorized privileges, and those can be obtained by inheritance. The management on the latter case (i.e., the inherited privileges) has not been well considered in the existing access control models, whose implementation also incur large overhead. In this paper, we propose a lightweight graph-based access control model to manage the privileges between the networked processes, which provides a general solution for the pervasive applicabilities such as process inter-invoking and network-based access control.

Keywords: Access control · Privilege management · Graph theory
Networking

1 Introduction

In computing, access control is a process for granting access and certain privileges for users (or processes that request for access permission) to systems. It determines whether users' attempting to do an operation is actually acting according to its authorized manner (e.g., can not access non-permitted information). Moreover, access control also associates and coexists with other security services (e.g., authorization, auditing) in a secure system and thus a successful access control model should be competent in preventing activities that could lead to security breach [1].

Traditional access control models are specifically focusing on the *direct* access control, i.e., if a user can be granted certain resources (and privileges) or not. For example, the role-based access control models define different privileged roles

© Springer Nature Switzerland AG 2018
X. Sun et al. (Eds.): ICCCS 2018, LNCS 11066, pp. 589–597, 2018.
https://doi.org/10.1007/978-3-030-00015-8_51

with corresponding privileges, for which each user will be granted selectively [2]. The assigned roles are assumed that they can only possess the exclusive privileges under the strict access control enforcement (i.e., cannot gain the out-of-role access permission). Those schemes have presented thorough analysis and built many sophisticated mechanisms on how to achieve secure access granting (e.g., attributed-based access control of encrypted data [3], sensor access control via operation bindings [4]). On the other hand, when it comes to the context of inter-networking model, the complexity and more open structure have impose constraints on these existing schemes, which may lack of concerns of the *indirect* security breach, i.e., the inherited privileges that can be gained without authorization.

The modern information networks have become more heterogeneous, which not only evolves the network structures, but also entails new security concerns. In an inter-networked model, there may be frequent interactions between the processes due to the tasks requiring collaborative efforts (e.g., a shopping App needs to cooperate with a transaction App for product payment). While these different processes possess different privileges (e.g., the transaction App can access the users' back account), unexpected security weakness may arise during the inter-processes interactions. For example, by invoking a process that have direct access to the sensory location information, an intended process may indirectly gain access to the sensitive information.

In this case, though existing schemes (e.g., [4]) have demonstrated proficiency in effectively discerning the abnormalities of some malicious operation requests (e.g., a message app requests for access to positioning sensor) and reject them instantly, the access to privacy-sensitive sensors may still be achieved by detouring methods (i.e., exploiting the intermediate parties with granted permission to bypass access control and attain sensitive information). The above scenarios present a critical challenge for the existing access control models and thus further analysis should be concerned.

In this paper, we examine the possibility to design a lightweight graph-based model specifically emphasizing on the inter-networking access control. The lightweight property is considered in order to perform efficient alarming on the access control decision (e.g., to enable human users to quickly track down the on-device Apps' abusing of privileges and resources). We design a graph-based model to accommodate the inter-networking structures. Specifically, the contributions of this paper are as follows:

1. We design a access control model in terms of graph theory, which is befitting for illustrating the complex relations of the inter-networking model.
2. We build a privilege management scheme for effectively detecting the abuse of privileges arisen from inter-processes invoking, providing supplementary efforts for addressing the deficiencies of the existing mechanisms.

The rest of the paper is organized as follows. Section 2 surveys related work. Section 3 formulates the research basis and challenges, and Sect. 4 elaborates on the proposed models. Extensive analysis of the proposed scheme is presented in Sect. 5 and we conclude the paper in Sect. 6.

2   Related Work

In [4], the authors proposed an access control model on the privacy-sensitive sensor permission on mobile devices. They proposed to use binding applications' operation requests to the associated user input events and how these events were explicitly obtained from the user), from which the users could verify whether the applications' operation requests were accorded with the users' expectations explicitly. The proposed mechanism in [4] had achieved satisfactory results from the experiments on 1000 android applications while four types of attacks that could get rid of their proposed access control restriction were also identified.

Attributed-based encryption (ABE) is a type of public-key encryption in which the secret key and ciphertext are dependent upon attributes. This features can be utilized for enabling access control model. Specifically, the study in [3] developed a new cryptosystem for fine-grained sharing of encrypted data called Key-Policy Attributed-Based Encryption (KP-ABE), to be applied for access control of encrypted data. The research into ABE had given rise to many access models based on different scenarios (e.g., cloud computing [5,6], web service [7,8]).

The popularity of HTML5-based mobile applications have triggered security concerns due to its wide adoption in various platforms. Thus, the authors in [9] proposed a fine-grained access control mechanism for the HTML5-based applications in Android system. For an application to access the system resources isolated in WebView, the JavaScript should be directed to the Java code in Android, which, unfortunately, breaks the default protection policy in the meanwhile. The scheme in [9] therefore introduced a access control model to target on the above security weakness based on the investigation over the existing mobile systems' access control mechanisms.

RBAC has remained a dominant form in access control models. Compared with the traditional RBAC that exploits features like static/dynamic separation of duty, the quantified approach that accommodates dynamism in access decisions based on the contexts had been proposed [10,11]. In [11], the difference between traditional constraint-based access control and the quantified risk-aware approaches in RBAC were analyzed, from which a framework for risk-awareness in RBAC models incorporating quantified-risks were built.

Online social networks (OSNs) have seen a rapid prevalence in recent years and that these platforms (e.g., Facebook) include many user-specific information (i.e., privacy-sensitive) pose challenges on the security management on these platforms [12]. Specifically, the study in [13] presented a semantic web-based access control mechanism on OSNs. The main idea of [13] was to encode social network-related information (e.g., user's profiles, relationships among users) by means of an ontology, based on which the access control model can be achieved and it is remarked that such mechanism was adaptable to various OSNs by modifying the ontology.

3   Problem Formulation

We have stated previously that how security breach may arise from the indirectly invoking of processes and, we use Fig. 1 to exemplify such concerns on the mobile applications in devices.

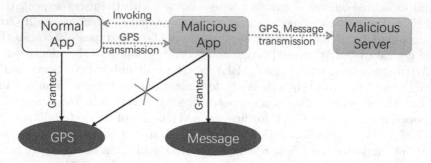

Fig. 1. An example on how a malicious app can stealthily access ungranted information by detouring methods

In Fig. 1, the malicious app cannot directly access to GPS data, which, however, could become available when the malware invokes and gains from the normal app that have granted permission to GPS data. Those GPS data transmitted from the normal app to the malicious app can be sent back to the server and be further exploited for malignant purpose.

The above threat model has formulated our research basis, to which we introduce our graph-based access control model that can visualize the inter-relation among the processes and the resource set (e.g., GPS data, message text), and unmask the indirect data-flow path(s) that would lead to the ungranted access permission. Below we give the definition of access control graph to better understand our graph-based scheme.

Definition 1. *Access Control Graph. It is a graph with direction. There exists directed edges between vertexes that represents calling relations. Each vertex links to a label that lists all resources that can be accessed, and corresponding privileges for each resource.*

4   Proposed Scheme

4.1   Basic Model

Figure 2 illustrates a simple access control graph, with which we can interpret the relation model lying in the inter-networking map. We can see from Fig. 2 that the processes (i.e., the vertexes) can access to the resource set by both *direct* and *indirect* means. It is realistic in some situations that a process may require

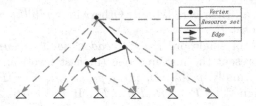

Fig. 2. An example of Access Control Graph. *Vertex* denotes processes (e.g., applications) that request access permission. *Resource set* is the system resource and *Edge* indicates calling relations between *Vertex* and *Resource set*.

indirect information from another process (e.g., a shopping app may request for GPS data), which, however, can not justify all of such cases. We remark the inter-processes interactions as the potential weakness that are vulnerable to intended attacks (e.g., see Fig. 1) and, our goal is to discover all of such *indirect* paths that may lead to the abuse of privileges (e.g., gain access without permission), and denote these ungranted privileges as privilege violation set.

The notations in the paper is listed in Table 1, where the expression of some notations are presented follows.

- $R = res[i], i \in \mathbb{N}^*$
- $P = pri[i], i = 1, 2, ..., |P|$
- $AC = \langle V, E \rangle$
- $e = \langle from, to \rangle, \forall e \in E$ and $from, to \in V$
- $v = [res[i], pri[i][k]], i \in \mathbb{N}^*$ and $k = 1, 2, ..., |P|$
- $link(v) = \{v' | e \in E, e.from = v, e.to = v'\}$

In the above, $pri[i]$ is a list of boolean values for privilege set, e.g., suppose privilege set is $[read, write, update, execute]$ where the privileges are independent and they can be expressed as $pri[i] = [1, 1, 0, 0]$. Formally, $pri[i][j] = 1 \vee 0$, $j = 1, 2, ..., |P|$, $P = P_1, P_2, ..., P_n$ is a designated privilege set. If the privilege

Table 1. Notations

Notation	Description
R	Resource set
P	Privilege set
E	Set of edges
e	A directed edge
V	Set of vertexes
v	A vertex, which indicates the resource it can directly access and its access privilege
AC	Access control graph
$link(v)$	All vertexes linked to v as destinations

includes $P_k, k \in [1, n]$, then $pri[i][k] = 1$. Otherwise, $pri[i][k] = 0$. $|P| = n$ is the number of items in set P.

If privileges are of single order, e.g., $read \subset write \subset update \subset execute$, then $pri[i]$ can represent the maximal one (highest level) among these single-order privileges. Formally, $pri[i] = \max(p_1, p_2, ..., p_n)$, $n = |P|$, $p_i \in \mathbb{N}^*$ is the privilege level assigned to $P = P_1, P_2, ..., P_n$. If $P_1 \subset P_2 \subset ... \subset P_n$, then $p_1 < p_2 < ... < p_n$.

$\forall e_i, e_j \in E$, $i \neq j$, if $e_i.to = e_j.from$, then $e_k.from = e_i.from$, $e_k.to = e_j.to$, and add e_k into E. For example, in Fig. 2, an edge between two distant $Vertexs$ that do not have direct connection can be constructed. In other words, we can establish a virtually *new and direct* path to represent the indirect path between two distant vertexes that can interact with each other (e.g., accessing the information on the other vertex).

Least Privilege Principle:

1. $\forall v \in V$, if $\exists i, j \in \mathbb{N}^*$ such that $\forall v_1, v_2 \in link(v)$, $v_1.res[i] = v_2.res[j]$, then let $pri = v_1.pri[i][k] \wedge v_2.pri[j][k]$, $k = 1, 2, ..., |P|$, or $pri = \min(v_1.pri[i], v_2.pri[j])$, and add $[v_1.res[i], pri]$ into v.
2. $\forall v \in V$, if $\exists i, j \in \mathbb{N}^*$ such that $\forall v_1 \in link(v)$, $v_1.res[i] = v.res[j]$, then let $pri = v_1.pri[i][k] \wedge v.pri[j][k]$, $k = 1, 2, ..., |P|$, or $pri = \min(v_1.pri[i], v.pri[j])$, and modify $[res[i], pri[i]]$ to $[res[i], pri]$ for v.

To evaluate whether $v \in V$ transgresses its granted privileges (i.e., gain unauthorized access permission), we need to find out all the resource accessibility that are not directly authorized to v, which we remark as privilege violation set as they can be accessed by non-explicit requests and may subsequently lead to privilege abuse. On detecting the privilege violation set, they should be prompted out explicitly to the users, who can determine if they should reject such operation request (i.e., the circumvention of access control would be deterred as these stealthy activities will be disclosed).

4.2   Algorithm Description

We next present our algorithms to achieve the above graph-based access control model.

Algorithm 1 is a graph-based recursive algorithm that can obtain all of the *accessible* resources of v, accessed by both direct and indirect path. In Algorithm 1, $v.res, v.pri$ denotes the resources v can access and the corresponding privileges. $visit[i] = 0, i = 1, 2, ..., |V|$, $visit$ is a dictionary to denote whether a vertex has been visited.

On computing $v.res, v.pri$ for v, the privilege violation set for process v can be derived from Eq. 1:

$$set_{vio} = v_{all} - v_{org} \tag{1}$$

where set_{vio} is the privilege violation set for v, v_{all} represent all of the accessible resources/privileges of v from Algorithm 1 and v_{org} denote the resources/privileges that are directly granted to v.

Data: $AC, v, visit[]$
Result: $v.res, v.pri[i]$ for v
1 **for** *each v' in $link(v)$* **do**
2 | **if** $visit[v'] \neq 1$ **then**
3 | | $visit[v'] = 1$; /* denote the current vertex v' has been visited */
4 | | /* add all of those resources and their corresponding privileges belonged to $v' \in link(v)$ to v */
5 | | $v.res$ adds $\bigcup_1^{|R|} res[i]$;
6 | | $v.pri$ adds $\bigcup_1^{|P|} pri[i]$;
7 | | Iterate algorithm using v' as parameter;
8 | **end**
9 **end**
10 **return** *result*;

Algorithm 1. Compute all of the accessible resources and corresponding privileges that v possess

Apart from the above manner, a more direct way to discover the privilege violation set can be achieved by the following algorithm. Algorithm 2 illustrates how to compute all of the resources that a process can access by *indirect* paths (i.e., privilege violation set) and they need to be disclosed. $visit[i] = 0, i = 1, 2, ..., |V|$, $visit$ is a dictionary to denote whether a vertex has been visited.

Data: $v, link(v), visit[]$
Result: Privilege violation set set_{vio}
1 **for** *each $v' \in link(v)$* **do**
2 | **if** $visit[v'] \neq 1$ **then**
3 | | $visit[v'] = 1$; /* denote the current vertex v' has been visited */
4 | | /* add those belong to v' but not include in v into violation set */
5 | | /* $\forall v \in Vertex, v = [v.res, v.pri]$ */
6 | | set_{vio} adds $v' - v$;
7 | | Iterate algorithm using $v', link(v')$ as parameters;
8 | **end**
9 **end**
10 **return** *result*;

Algorithm 2. Compute the privilege violation set set_{vio} for v.

In both of above ways, if the output result (set_{vio}) is not empty, there exist ungranted privilege for the process v. In this case, those ungranted privileges should be explicitly alarmed to the users (or administrators) and then corresponding measures can be taken. For example, if a user notices that a game application attempts to access the GPS data by invoking the map app, he/she can reject this permission (and the game application will be deemed as suspected malware).

Based on the above, our proposed scheme can contribute to targeting efforts for the existing access control mechanisms and, with combination of existing models (e.g., [4,9]) the malicious attempts to access stealthy information by *both* direct and indirect paths will be frustrated, thus fulfilling a secure access control model as envisioned in [1].

5   Analysis

In this section, we conduct the theoretic analysis of the proposed model.

Lemma 1. *All of the resources and privileges that can be accessed by indirect paths can be disclosed.*

Proof. By Algorithm 2 we can obtain all of the indirectly accessed resources and their corresponding privileges by iterative searching.

Theorem 1. *Our model is secure against security breach from inter-processes invoking.*

Proof. The risk from inter-processes invoking comes from the resource/privileges transmission between processes. Lemma 1 proves our model to be capable search out all of these resource/privileges, which will be alarmed to be users (or administrators) and they can take certain responsive measures, e.g., explicitly reject the permission.

Remark 1. The mechanism on whether to authorize access permission to processes is not within consideration.

Proposition 1. *The model is lightweight.*

Proof. Straightforward.   □

6   Conclusion

In this paper, we propose a lightweight graph-based model for inter-networking access control. This model is from the observation on the privilege misuse due to the invoking between different processes. Certainly, this model is general and can be applied in inter-networking style access control, which is a novel powerful enhancement for role-based access control, as the model is graph-based.

Acknowledgement. This work was supported by the science and technology project of Guangdong Power Grid Co., Ltd, (036000KK52170002).

References

1. Sandhu, R.S., Samarati, P.: Access control: principle and practice. IEEE Commun. Mag. **32**(9), 40–48 (1994)
2. Sandhu, R.S., Coyne, E.J., Feinstein, H.L., Youman, C.E.: Role-based access control models. Computer **29**(2), 38–47 (1996)
3. Goyal, V., Pandey, O., Sahai, A., Waters, B.: Attribute-based encryption for fine-grained access control of encrypted data. In: Proceedings of the 13th ACM Conference on Computer and Communications Security, pp. 89–98. ACM (2006)
4. Petracca, G., Reineh, A.-A., Sun, Y., Grossklags, J., Jaeger, T.: AWare: preventing abuse of privacy-sensitive sensors via operation bindings. In: 26th USENIX Security Symposium (USENIX Security 17), pp. 379–396. USENIX Association, Vancouver, BC (2017)
5. Yu, S., Wang, C., Ren, K., Lou, W.: Achieving secure, scalable, and fine-grained data access control in cloud computing. In: 2010 Proceedings IEEE INFOCOM, pp. 1–9. IEEE (2010)
6. Wang, G., Liu, Q., Wu, J.: Hierarchical attribute-based encryption for fine-grained access control in cloud storage services. In: Proceedings of the 17th ACM Conference on Computer and Communications Security, pp. 735–737. ACM (2010)
7. Yuan, E., Tong, J.: Attributed based access control (ABAC) for web services. In: 2005 IEEE International Conference on Web Services, ICWS 2005, Proceedings. IEEE (2005)
8. Shen, H.-B., Hong, F.: An attribute-based access control model for web services. In: 2006 Seventh International Conference on Parallel and Distributed Computing, Applications and Technologies, PDCAT 2006, pp. 74–79. IEEE (2006)
9. Jin, X., Wang, L., Luo, T., Du, W.: Fine-grained access control for HTML5-based mobile applications in Android. In: Desmedt, Y. (ed.) ISC 2013. LNCS, vol. 7807, pp. 309–318. Springer, Cham (2015). https://doi.org/10.1007/978-3-319-27659-5_22
10. Cheng, P.-C., Rohatgi, P., Keser, C., Karger, P.A., Wagner, G.M., Reninger, A.S.: Fuzzy multi-level security: an experiment on quantified risk-adaptive access control. In: 2007 IEEE Symposium on Security and Privacy, SP 2007, pp. 222–230. IEEE (2007)
11. Bijon, K.Z., Krishnan, R., Sandhu, R.: A framework for risk-aware role based access control. In: 2013 IEEE Conference on Communications and Network Security (CNS), pp. 462–469. IEEE (2013)
12. Hu, H., Ahn, G.-J., Jorgensen, J.: Multiparty access control for online social networks: model and mechanisms. IEEE Trans. Knowl. Data Eng. **25**(7), 1614–1627 (2013)
13. Carminati, B., Ferrari, E., Heatherly, R., Kantarcioglu, M., Thuraisingham, B.: Semantic web-based social network access control. Comput. Secur. **30**(2), 108–115 (2011)

A Method for Energy Consumption Audit and Intelligent Decision of Green Buildings

Jinlong Chen[1,2,3], Mengke Jiang[1], Kun Xie[1], Zhen Guo[2], Hang Pan[2],
and Xianjun Chen[1(✉)]

[1] Guangxi Key Laboratory of Cryptography and Information Security,
Guilin University of Electronic Technology, Guilin, Guangxi 541004, China
hingini@126.com
[2] Guangxi Cooperative Innovation Center of Cloud Computing and Big Data,
Guilin University of Electronic Technology, 541004 Guilin, Guangxi, China
[3] Key Laboratory of Intelligent Processing of Computer Image and Graphics,
Guilin University of Electronic Technology, 541004 Guilin, Guangxi, China

Abstract. According to the problem that the traditional building energy audit analysis and research methods are too single, which is not applicable to the analysis of specific survey objects such as campus buildings, this article has made an audit of water, electricity and gas energy consumption for campus buildings and put forward a new research program for water and electricity consumption. Compared with the traditional method, the research on electric energy consumption has improved the traditional formula and come up with a new research model for electric energy consumption in campus buildings. And the research on water energy consumption has added the analysis of daily water consumption per person, so the overall data will be accurate to the individual and make the results more accurate. Proved by the experiments, the improved model proposed in this paper can predict the energy consumption of the investigated objects more accurately.

Keywords: Building energy efficiency · Energy audit
Energy saving measures · Campus buildings

1 Introduction

1.1 Background and Research Status at Home and Abroad

At present, China is in a period of rapid development, the potential for building energy conservation is the greatest. In the 1990s, Canada conducted a random inspection of 60% of its domestic residential buildings, through the calculation of energy consumption and energy structure at the end of the building, Canada's energy consumption trend formula was proposed [1]. Generally, most of the domestic audit methods use the total annual building consumption compared with the same type of building energy consumption, or analyze the energy consumption peak of the whole year to take energy-saving measures [2]. In the face of specific audit objects, there always have a large deviation. National Ministry of Construction Science and Technology Division of the Ministry of Construction commissioned scientific research units to compile the

© Springer Nature Switzerland AG 2018
X. Sun et al. (Eds.): ICCCS 2018, LNCS 11066, pp. 598–607, 2018.
https://doi.org/10.1007/978-3-030-00015-8_52

"State organ office buildings and large public buildings energy audit guidelines", which provides the audit methods for fieldwork [3]. But the "Guidelines" are not fully applicable to special buildings such as campus buildings.

1.2   Research Process

(1) Analyze the advantages and disadvantages of traditional research methods for building energy consumption.
(2) Energy audit analysis of campus buildings.
(3) Propose an improved model for the study of subjects.
(4) Simulate energy consumption data and make decision potential analysis.

2   Energy Audit and Analysis

According to the survey, the building energy consumption model of the campus is as follows. This paper will analyze the energy consumption audit of the target from the following aspects (Fig. 1).

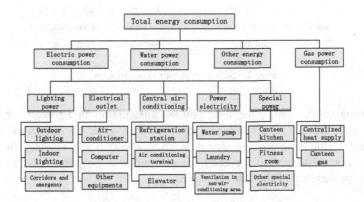

Fig. 1. Total energy consumption model

2.1   Electrical Energy Consumption Analysis

Lighting and Socket Use. According to "State organ office buildings and large public buildings energy audit guidelines". The total power of the equipment is multiplied by the estimated time to obtain the total energy dissipation of the equipment.

$$E_L = \sum_{i=1}^{k} N_i W_i T_i \tag{1}$$

Where: E_L is the total energy consumption of k equipment in the building; K is a total k equipment in a single building; N_i is the number of installations; W_i is the standard power of the equipment; Ti is the operating time of the equipment.

According to the survey respondents, the number of large power consumption equipment such as central air-conditioning is negligible. Instead, the central air-conditioners is replaced by a large number of fans and split type air conditioners, so the lighting and socket equipment also applies to this formula. Schools have uncertainty due to holidays. The uncertainty of the school has formed the unconformity of the opening time of the same equipment and the random characteristics of the number of opening devices. Figure 2 shows the power consumption level of main buildings in the campus.

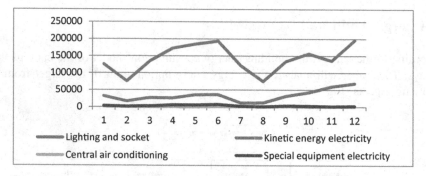

Fig. 2. Sub-item power consumption

According to the figure, the total power consumption in February and August showed a huge decline. If we still use the existing models for energy consumption analysis there would be a huge deviation. According to the original formula, an improved calculation method for energy consumption is proposed, this paper introduces open probability of the i-th equipment:

$$\begin{cases} \sum_{i=1}^{k} P_{is}N_iW_iT_{is} & n = 1, 4, 5 \ldots \\ \sum_{i=1}^{k} P_{ij}N_iW_iT_{ij} & n = 2, 3, 7, 8 \end{cases} \tag{2}$$

Where: P_{is}, P_{ij} is the open probability for i equipment in the unit time after statistics, and the calculation formula is:

$$P_{is,ij} = N_s \div N_k \tag{3}$$

Where: N_s is the actual number of open devices in the month; T_{is} is the average daily open time of a normal monthly i-device; T_{ij} is the average daily opening time of i equipment for a special month (winter vacation and summer vacation). The formula for T_{is}, T_{ij} is:

$$T_{is,ij} = \frac{\sum_{i=1}^{k} N_c T_c}{N_m} \qquad (4)$$

Where: m represents the number of statistics by time; N_c indicates the number of equipment turned on per unit time; T_c indicates the total running time of the equipment during the N_c period; N_m is the total number of open equipment; n is the month judgment parameter.

Introduced annual operating days coefficient:

$$E = AEL|_{n=1,4,5...} + BEL|_{n=2,3,7,8} \qquad (5)$$

Where: E is the total energy consumption of k types of equipment in the revised building; A is the number of normal equipment operating days; B is the number of equipment operating days for a special month.

Dynamic Power Consumption. The main power consumption part of the Jinjiling Campus includes elevators, water pumps, non-air-conditioned area ventilation (fans, exhaust fans), etc. In addition to elevator equipment, energy consumption of other power equipment can be calculated from the above formula, due to the uncertain frequency and intensity of use of elevators, elevators should be calculated separately.

The elevator energy consumption can be calculated according to the following formula:

$$E_D = (K_1 \times K_2 \times K_3 \times H \times F \times P)/(V \times 3600) + E_s \qquad (6)$$

Where: E_D is the total energy consumption of a single elevator; K_1 is the coefficient of the drive system, taking the exchange system coefficient $K_1 = 1.6$; K_2 represents the average running distance coefficient, when single ladder or two and more than two layers, $K_2 = 0.5$, three elevators and above $K_2 = 0.3$; K_3 represents the average load factor, the value 0.35; H represents the maximum operating distance (the unit is meter); F indicates the number of starts; P represents elevator rated power; V represents the speed of the elevator (the unit is m/s); E_s indicates the total energy in standby for one month (the unit is kw/h).

Model Validation. This section selects a student dormitory in Jinjiling Campus to conduct the verification and evaluation of the model. Due to the large variety of devices but the vast majority are low-power devices, only the main energy-consuming devices in the building is calculated. So only the main power have been calculated.

According to the statistical analysis of the opening of the lights throughout the year as shown below (Fig. 3):

The fans and other power devices are similar to lighting devices and such devices have obvious seasonal characteristics. The same statistics are required for detailed analysis (Fig. 4).

The use of computers, hair dryers and other equipment is less affected by environmental factors and seasonal characteristics are not obvious. Detailed statistics can be obtained by visiting the survey. The annual energy consumption of the building is

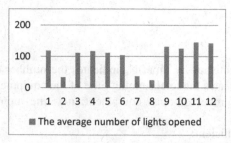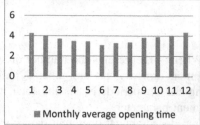

Fig. 3. The average monthly lighting situation

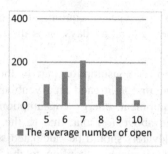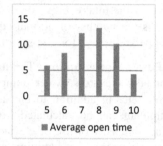

Fig. 4. Fan open situation

compared with the actual energy consumption according to the above formula. The comparison is shown in Fig. 5.

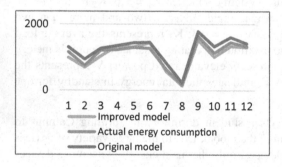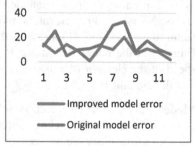

Fig. 5. Model error analysis

It can be seen from the figure that the energy consumption curve calculated from the improved statistical model is closer to the actual energy consumption curve. The original energy consumption calculation model results in the calculation of energy consumption generally high due to the calculation of the number of equipment installations, and the deviation is more pronounced in particular months. The main reasons for the error are the following: when modeling, the average usage time and average usage probability of each outlet device are counted. Other high-powered devices with indefinite switching time and short duration cannot be effectively tracked. According to past experience, this energy consumption usually accounts for about 5% of the total electricity consumption. Calculation method based on monthly energy consumption calibration model:

$$S_m = |E_s - E_a| \div E_a \tag{7}$$

Annual average energy consumption calibration model calculation method:

$$S_y = \sqrt{\frac{1}{12}\sum_{i=1}^{12}\left(S_{mi} - \frac{1}{12}\sum_{i=1}^{12}S_{mi}\right)^2} \tag{8}$$

Where: S_{mi} is the month-by-month error of month i. The monthly maximum error of the original model is 33%, and the minimum error is 5%. Annual average energy consumption error is 8.8%. The monthly maximum error of the improved model is 20.2%, the minimum error is 0.9%, and the average annual energy consumption error is 5.152%. The experimental results show that the improved model can truly reflect the overall energy consumption level of the building, and has better accuracy than the traditional model.

2.2   Water Power

The Research Method of Traditional Water Energy Consumption. Nowadays, most of the domestic papers only simply collecting the data in the study of energy consumption of building water. They compare the water consumption of different seasons in different regions of the same type of building, and draw simple energy-saving suggestions [4].

Taking the annual water consumption of this research object in 2017 as an example (data from the Green Campus Resource Platform of Guilin University of Electronic Technology), and getting the following figure.

Advantages: Intuitive, easy to find the overall problems of water consumption.

Disadvantages: Only macro data and it is no easy to propose more detailed energy-saving advices.

Improved Research Method. From the traditional search method it can be seen intuitively that the comparison between the two parts. But in order to make a more detailed and targeted decision-making program, that requires a deeper analysis data (Fig. 6).

This paper proposes to consider the indicator of per capita water consumption in campuses in order to analyze from another point of view to get the more powerful energy-saving desions. Daily per capita water consumption is calculated as follows (the unit is L/person·day).

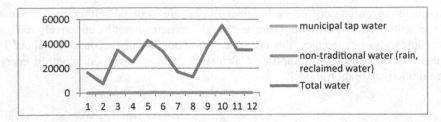

Fig. 6. Annual water energy consumption of jinjiling campus in 2017

$$Daily\ per\ capita\ water\ consumption = Total\ use\ of\ domestic\ water / (The\ number\ of \atop people\ who\ use\ the\ water * The\ number\ of\ days) * 1000 \tag{9}$$

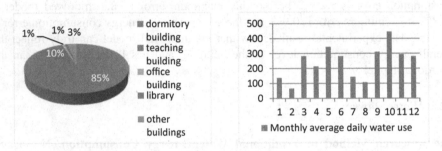

Fig. 7. Analysis of water consumption in buildings and per capita water consumption

The water statistics as shown in Fig. 7.

The number of teachers and students in Jinjiling Campus is approximately 4,000. The annual water consumption in 2017 is 353,893 (t). According to the above formula, the daily water consumption per capita is 242 L/person·day. The following figure shows the comparison of per capita water consumption in each month of the year.

The urban residents' water consumption standard was obtained from the Standard for Urban Residents' Living Water Consumption. The survey object belongs to Guangxi, and the water consumption standard is 150–220 (L/person·day). Based on this, compared with the above figure, it is found that in addition to January, February, April, July and August, all other months exceeded the water standard. Especially in October, the daily per capita water consumption was as high as nearly 440 (L/person·day), the wastage was serious.

Brief Summary. The generally traditional research on water energy consumption only counts the total water consumption of the building. There is only macro feelings and it can not be objectively evaluated. Using the improved water energy assessment method can not only analyze the data based on the total building energy consumption, but also compare the daily water consumption per capita with national standards to see if there is potential for energy saving and energy saving potential, so we can formulate a reasonable decision-making program and make more efficient energy-saving processing.

2.3 Gas

The survey is located in Guilin, Guangxi, and there is no heating equipment. Therefore, the gas consumption is mainly for hot baths in winter and gas for canteens.

Centralized Heat Supply. The centralized heating on campus is mainly reflected in the use of hot water in the dormitory. The statistics on the central heating data in the dormitory area are as follows (unit: cubic meter):

December, January and February are in winter, and the gas consumption volume reaches a peak, the bathing time is correspondingly increased because of the low temperature, so the air volume is increased a lot. Besides, the meals are getting cold quicker than the other seasons, and the amount of gas used is also increased (Fig. 8).

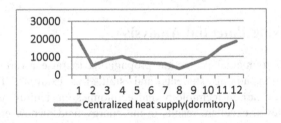

Fig. 8. Gas consumption statistics

Canteen Gas. The number of diners in the campus cafeteria is relatively fixed, the staff base is large and so does the daily gas consumption. This article uses the gas quota method to calculate the student cafeteria gas consumption, the formula is as follows [5]:

$$Q = Q_n Nq/H_1 t \tag{10}$$

Where: Q represents Calculated flow in student cafeteria (m^3/h); Q_n represents Air quota for student cafeteria (kJ/kg of food); N represents number of people in the restaurant (person); q represents Quantitative food per person per meal (kg food/person); H_1 represents low calorific value of gas (kJ/m^3); t represents time required to make N_q kg of food (hours).

The school canteen can be eaten by about 800 people. The City Gas Planning Reference provides gas quota of 8374 to 10467 kJ/kg of grain, generally take Q_n = 10467 kJ/kg of grain, and take an average of 0.2 kilograms of food per person per meal, the low calorific value of 15382.4 kJ/m^3, and it will take 3 h to make a 900 people staple. The calculated gas consumption in the cafeteria should be around Q = 10467*800*0.2/15382.4/3 = 36.3 (m^3/h).

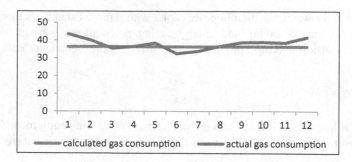

Fig. 9. Comparison of actual gas consumption and calculated gas consumption

According to the actual data, make the following table (Fig. 9):

From the above figure, we can learn that the actual gas consumption fluctuates near the calculated gas volume, and the gas consumption in June and July are both low than the others, while the gas consumption in winter is significantly higher than the average value.

3 Energy-Saving Potential Analysis

1. Strengthen environmental protection propaganda to raise awareness of environmental protection among students and staff. For example: Beijing Jiaotong University's low-carbon technology and economics curriculum and related materials have achieved excellent results in the energy field of new energy, renewable energy and so on [6].
2. According to on-site investigations found that the surveyed building in the old transmission system, the new cable should be replaced as soon as possible. The hallway lights are always on. It is recommended to change to an induction lighting system. In addition, it is recommended that incandescent the lamps which are at a large number replaced with more energy-saving fluorescent lamps. There are also some other unattended equipment have unnecessary power consumption. It is recommended to use high-tech means, such as automatic power control systems for intelligent power distribution and monitoring of abnormal power consumption.

4 Conclusion

This paper analyses the use of water energy, electric energy and gas energy consumption, and proposes an improved research method for electric energy and water energy consumption by conducting an energy audit and model evaluation for a university in Guilin, Guangxi. Compared with the traditional method of simply analyzing the building as a whole, the method proposed could show the energy consumption more clearly. And through experimental verification, the experimental results show that the new model has higher accuracy than the traditional methods and can achieve better energy-saving analysis and decision-making.

Acknowledgments. This research work is supported by the grant of Guangxi science and technology development project (No: 1598018-6), the grant of Guangxi Cooperative Innovation Center of Cloud Computing and Big Data of Guilin University of Electronic Technology (No: YD16E11), the grant of Guangxi Key Laboratory of Cryptography & Information Security of Guilin University of Electronic Technology (No: GCIS201601), the grant of Guangxi Colleges and Universities Key Laboratory of Intelligent Processing of Computer Images and Graphics of Guilin University of Electronic Technology (No: GIIP201602), and the grant of Innovation Project of GUET Graduate Education (2017YJCX55).

References

1. Fang, Z.: A Study on the Statistics of Energy Consumption of Various Kinds of Public Buildings, Analysis of Influencing Factors and Auditing Methods of Building Energy. Tongji University (2008)
2. Zhou, L.P., Liu, Z.X., Gao, J.: Analysis of building energy consumption audit and energy saving measures in a large hospital in shanghai. industrial. Building **38**(6), 9–11 (2008)
3. Wan, L.D.: Research on Energy Audit Method and Energy Saving Reform Project of Office Buildings. Huazhong University of Science and Technology (2016)
4. Wang, J.F.: Analysis on energy consumption characteristics of public buildings in Xiamen. Build. Energ. Effi. **12** (2012)
5. Wu, Y.: The selection of commercial drink user gas consumption and gas meter. Appl. Energy Technol. (3) (2002)
6. Huang, C.Y.: Research on Energy Saving and Emission Reduction in Colleges and Universities. Guangxi Normal University (2015)

A Mixed Mobile Charging Strategy in Rechargeable Wireless Sensor Networks

Yang Yang[✉], Xiang yang Gong, Xuesong Qiu,
Zhipeng Gao, and Haitao Yu

State Key Laboratory of Networking and Switching Technology,
Beijing University of Posts and Telecommunications, Beijing 100876, China
{yyang,xsqiu,gaozhipeng}@bupt.edu.cn,
{1203398121,1341067360}@qq.com

Abstract. Based on the mobile charging scheduling strategy, the Mobile Charger (MC) complements the power supply for the sensor nodes. We proposed a Mixed Charging Schedule Algorithm (MCS) based on the periodic charging scheme and the on-demand charging scheme. We add a node's rate grouping mechanism to determine which nodes need to be recharged based on a dynamic threshold mechanism. Based on the periodic charging loops and the service station deployment mechanism, a charging loop is constructed according to guide the MC to wirelessly charge the sensor nodes. The proposed algorithm reduces the power consumption of the sensor network, improves the efficiency of MC mobile billing, and ensures the normal operation of the network.

Keywords: Rechargeable wireless sensor network · On-demand
Mixed charging strategy · Service station · Pre-charging

1 Introduction

Sensor nodes in the wireless sensor networks (WSNs) are mostly powered by batteries with very limited energy, which require frequent battery replacement during long operating hours to maintain their uninterrupted work. This situation not only greatly increases the maintenance cost of the WSNs, but also seriously affects the further application of the WSNs. In order to solve the energy bottleneck problem of the WSNs, many experts have done a lot of research.

However, in the process of mobile charging scheduling in the WRSNs, due to the limited energy of the MC and the sensor nodes, it is very important to adopt appropriate scheduling strategies in mobile charging tasks of the wireless sensor network. Firstly, we must ensure that each sensor node receives the charging service of the MC before its energy is exhausted. Secondly, on the basis of ensuring the normal operation of the WRSNs, we need to design a reasonable charging strategy to reduce the energy consumption of the sensor network and the latency of the sensor nodes.

We propose a Mixed Charging Scheduling (MCS) Algorithm based on the periodic charging scheme and the on-demand charging scheme, which is able to guide each round of the mobile charging scheduling of the WSNs. Based on the dynamic threshold mechanism, node rate grouping mechanism is added to determine the nodes to be charged. On the basis of the periodic charging loops and the service station deployment mechanism, a charging loop is constructed according to guide the MC to wirelessly charge sensor nodes. The algorithm aims to reduce the total consumption of sensor network as much as possible and improve the efficiency of MC mobile charging.

In the paper, we briefly discuss related works in Sect. 2. The mixed charging scheduling algorithm is proposed in Sect. 3, and Sect. 4 is the experimental results and comparative analysis. Section 5 concludes the paper.

2 Related Works

Some current charging schemes are based on the expansions of the single MC charging scheme. The main researches are to optimize the charging efficiency of MC or to reduce the charging cost of MC. The concept of the renewable energy cycle (RNC) has been defined by Xie et al. [1]. They explore how to plan the charging timing and the charging path of the single MC scheme, trying to minimize the moving time of the MC in the charging cycle. In medium and large WRSNs, Lu et al. have put forward the charging strategy of the multiple mobile charging equipment MCs working together [2]. The charging scheme of MC generally converts MC's charging path problem into the TSP problem or the vehicle routing problem (VRP) and solves the problem based on the existing heuristic algorithm or greedy algorithm. By calculating and establishing the minimum encircling area and its overlapped parts, we can find the best location to allow MC to perform the single to multi charging in order to reduce the waiting delay of the sensors [3]. However, the scheme with MC's limited and insufficient charging capacity generally assumes that MC cannot complete the energy supplement task covering all the sensor nodes in one charging scheduling, and can only choose part nodes for charging services according to the scheduling strategies. Li et al. have researched how to jointly optimize the charging path and the charging time of MC under the condition that the charging capacity of MC is limited [4], in order to maximize the charging efficiency of MC.

Liang et al. have researched the charging path planning of the multi-MC problem [5]. In order to ensure that each MC can independently charge every node on each subtree, we get the minimum number of MC needed by WSNs. Guo et al. have researched the problem of combining wireless charging with mobile data collection [6]. The selection problem of MC's residence point is transformed into the utility maximization problem of the WSNs under the constraints of the node's maximum electric quantity and MC's residence time, and a distributed algorithm is proposed to solve the maximum residence time of MC at each residence point.

According to the charging cycle, the periodic charging scheme refers that in each round of charging, and the selection of nodes need to be recharged and the charging order of MC are all fixed [7]. In the paper [8], researchers have divided the periodic activity of the MC into two stages: MC firstly follows the working status of the planned moving path and provides the billing service for the target node; and then the resting state in which MC rests in the service station as well as waiting for the next round of charging scheduling. In the on-demand charging scheme, the sensor nodes with the highest priority are selected to receive charging services in each round of charging scheduling [9]. The problem of the on-demand charging is often defined as the scheduling problem, and the most intuitive scheduling scheme is the FCFS (First-Come First-Served). However, the FCFS scheme ignores the moving distance of MC, which will lead to MC's constant back and forth movement.

3 Mixed Charging Scheduling Algorithm

3.1 Variables Definition and Algorithm Flow

We proposed the Mixed Charging Scheduling Algorithm (MCS) based on the periodic charging scheme and the on-demand charging scheme is designed. The variables and symbols used in the MCS algorithm are shown in Table 1.

Table 1. Variables and symbols.

Variables and symbols	Description	Variables and symbols	Description
A	The Test Zone(m*m)	$d_{i,j}$	The Distance between Sensor Node N_i and Sensor Node N_j (m)
Γ	The Expected Life Cycle of the WRSN (s)	S	The Service Station Node
$M = \{N_1, N_2 \ldots N_n\}$	The Set of the Sensor Network Nodes	L_S	The Location of S
N_i	The Sensor Node	MC	The Mobile Charger
E_i	The Remaining Electric Quantity of the Sensor Node (J)	E_S	The Maximum Electric Quantity of All the Sensor Nodes (J)
V_i	The Energy Consumption Rate of the Sensor Node (W)	E_M	The Maximum Electric Quantity of the MC (J)
T_i	The Remaining Operating Time of the Sensor Node (s)	η	The Charging Efficiency of the MC
φ	The Threshold (Remaining Operating Time) (s)	q_c	The Charging Power of the MC(W)
α	The Grouping Coefficient		

The detailed descriptions of the algorithm flow of the MCS are as follows:

1. The deployment of the service station. Finish the initialization work after deploying the set of all the sensor nodes $M = \{N_1, N_2, \ldots\ldots, N_m\}$ according to demand. Then try to run the sensor network and count the energy consumption rate and the deployment coordinates of each sensor node. On this basis, a weighted operation is carried out to get the best deployment coordinates of the service station.

2. The grouping of the sensor nodes. After the initialization of the sensor network or the completion of a cycle's charging task of the MC, sensor nodes are dynamically grouped, nodes with similar energy consumption rate V_i are divided into one group, and the groups are used as the scheduling unit of the initial mobile charging. Meanwhile, for different groups corresponded by different grouping coefficient α, the mobile charging efficiencies are simulated and the optimal solution of α is determined by comparison.

3. The presupposition of the charging threshold (remaining operating time φ). After the initialization of the sensor network or the completion of a cycle's charging task of the MC, the charging threshold is calculated. According to the grouping situation, we calculate the minimum remaining operating time of the last node T_i in different loop circuits of different groups, and take the maximum value as the charging threshold φ of the current sensor network by comparison.

4. Construct the charging loop circuit. According to the threshold set in step 3, when a node's remaining operating time $T_i \leq \varphi$, it will send a charging request to the MC, and all the sensor nodes in its group are all included in the charging sequence. Meanwhile, some pre-charging nodes are brought in and the charging sequence is updated. According to the charging sequence, we construct the shortest Hamilton loop with the service station S as the start and the stop point that covers all the nodes in the charging sequence, and take it as the moving path of MC's charging service.

5. Calculate the charging amount. According to the charging loop circuit constructed in step 4, calculate the maximum T_0 which satisfies all the nodes' waiting delay and MC' s limited electric quantity range. It can be obtained that the charging amount for each node N_i is $E_i = T_0 \times V_i$. Thus, the MC will carry out charging services to each node according to the planned charging loop circuit and the charging amount. The MC returns to the service station S to rest and replenish its own power, as well as waiting for the next round of charging scheduling after it completes the current charging task for all the nodes need to be recharged. Thus, the WRSNs complete a complete mobile charging scheduling based on the MCS algorithm.

3.2 The Deployment of the Service Station

The service station S is served as the start and the end point of each round of the charging service, its location will greatly affects the moving distance of the MC, and then affects the energy consumption of the MC. In the general mobile charging strategy, the service station is generally deployed in the marginal area far away from the center of the sensor network. The charging frequency of the sensor nodes with higher energy consumption rate is far higher than that of the other sensor nodes with lower energy consumption. An intuitive idea is to make the deployment location of the service station S close to these high power consumption nodes, which can shorten the total moving distance of the MC in each round of charging scheduling, and further reduce the energy consumed by MC's movement.

In the WRSNs, we deployed m sensor nodes, and endow weight $\varepsilon_i(1 \leq i \leq m)$ to each sensor node N_i to indicate its charging frequency. That is, the higher the energy consumption rate, the higher the weight ε of the node. So,

$$\varepsilon_i = \frac{V_i}{\sum_{i=1}^{m} V_i} \tag{1}$$

Where V_i represents the energy consumption rate of the sensor node N_i, the weight ω of all the sensor nodes can be obtained accordingly. The coordinates of the service station S can be set to the weighted average of all the sensor nodes' coordinates:

$$L_S = \sum_{i=1}^{m} (\varepsilon_i \times l_i) = \sum_{i=1}^{m} \frac{V_i \times l_i}{\sum_{i=1}^{m} V_i} \tag{2}$$

Where $l_i(1 \leq i \leq m)$ and L_S are two-dimensional vectors that represent the coordinates of the node N_i and the service station S respectively. As a result, the service station is bound to be deployed in the most centralized location of the WRSNs' power consumption (such as convergence nodes and routing nodes). Therefore, we calculate the best deployment location of the service station S. When the WRSNs have a dynamic change, for example, a new sensor node joins or a sensor node gets out of the network, we can re-calculate and update the deployment location of the service station.

3.3   Grouping Mechanism and the Grouping Coefficient

The sensor nodes can report the remaining electric quantity with the collected data to the control center of the base station. In the applications of the actual sensor network, the sensor nodes upload the data about each 10 s or so, and the instantaneous energy consumption rate of the sensor nodes can be obtained accordingly. Assuming that V_{max} and V_{min} are the maximum and minimum of energy consumption in the entire network sensor nodes, the total number of groups can be ordered as follows:

$$m = \lceil log_\alpha(V_{max} - V_{min}) \rceil \tag{3}$$

Among them, $\lceil x \rceil$ represents the smallest integer larger than x, the grouping coefficient α is a number that is larger than 1 as the entry parameter. The number of groups can be adjusted according to the changes in the entry parameter α, and then the rate gradient equation can be constructed to obtain the upper limit of each group:

$$y = \frac{V_{max} - V_{min}}{m^2} x^2 + \frac{2(V_{max} - V_{min})}{m} x + V_{min} \tag{4}$$

Among them, $x = [1, 2, \ldots, m]$ corresponds to the m groups, y corresponds to the upper limit of each group. We can get m intervals in ascending order of the energy consumption rate, that is, m groups. For example, the upper and lower limits of the n group in the rate groups are ($\frac{[2m(n-1)-(n-1)^2]V_{max}+[(n-1)-m]^2V_{min}}{m^2}$, $\frac{(2mn-n^2)V_{max}+(m-n)^2V_{min}}{m^2}$]).

Each sensor node can be put into the corresponding group according to its energy consumption rate. i.e., assuming $V_{max} = 7$, $V_{min} = 2$, and $\alpha = 2$, the node's rate can be divided into 3 groups, which can be obtained by $m = 3$. [2, 4.78], [4.78, 6.44] and (6.44, 7] are the scope of the 3 groups. The grouping with the smallest moving distance is used as the best grouping and its corresponding value of α is the optimal value of α. The specific process is:

(1) In a charging cycle of the pre-operation (MC's battery can finish any round of charging scheduling), the total moving distance of the MC for each charging is:

$$D_{M,1} = \sum_{i=1}^{n} d_{i-1,i} + d_{n,0} \tag{5}$$

$d_{i-1,i}$ represents the linear distance between the sensor node N_{n-1} and the sensor node N_n. When i = 1, $d_{0,1}$ represents the distance between the service station S and the first node needs to be recharged. $d_{n,0}$ represents the linear distance between the last node needs to be recharged in the charging sequence and the service station S.

(2) According to Formula (5), the total moving distance of the MC in a charging cycle with k charging rounds which can be obtained as follows:

$$D_{M,k} = \sum_{j=1}^{k} D_{Mj} = \sum_{j=1}^{k} \left(\sum_{i=1}^{n} d_{i-1,i} + d_{n,0} \right) \tag{6}$$

Thus the average moving distance of the MC in each charging round of a charging cycle can be obtained as follows:

$$D_M = \frac{D_{M,k}}{k} = \frac{\sum_{j=1}^{k} \left(\sum_{i=1}^{n} d_{i-1,i} + d_{n,0} \right)}{k} \tag{7}$$

(3) The grouping with the minimum D_M is the optimal grouping, the corresponding value of α is used as the optimal grouping coefficient of the sensor network. At this time, the minimum MC's average moving distance of each round for mobile charging, i.e. the minimum cost of MC's charging can be reached.

After experiment demonstrating, when $\alpha = 1.2$, namely, when all sensor nodes are divided into 7 groups according to the energy consumption rate, the current mobile charging performance is the best. At this time, the moving distance of MC's charging task is relatively shorter, the energy consumption of the MC is relatively lower, and the overall nodes' waiting delay is lower.

3.4   The Presupposition of the Charging Threshold

In each charging schedule, the MC only selects nodes with the remaining electric quantity and other information below the charging threshold to perform charging services. The paper proposes to select a remaining operating time T_i as the threshold φ of the mobile charging strategy for the sensor network to select the nodes need to be recharged. Only when the remaining operating time of the sensor node is lower than the charging threshold, the nodes send charging request and get energy supplement given by the MC as the target nodes. The selection rules of the charging threshold φ are as follows:

(1) According to the grouping situation in Sect. 3.3, nodes of the longest charging loop circuit constructed by the Dijkstra algorithm are selected as the nodes need to be recharged. Calculate the longest waiting time of the last node needs to be recharged N_n in the charging loop circuit, and set it as $T_{n,1}$. Assuming that the initial threshold of the sensor network is φ_0, when the remaining operating time of nodes in the group is lower than the charging threshold φ_0, the MC starts from the service station S and perform charging services to each sensor node according to the constructed charging loop circuit. Meanwhile, the greedy mechanism is taken in the charging process. That is, for each node, the MC moves to the next node only if the current node is fully charged. So MC's service time for the node needs to be recharged N_i is as follows:

$$t_i = \frac{E_s - E_i}{q_c \times \eta} \quad (1 \le i \le n) \tag{8}$$

E_s represents the maximum electric quantity of the node, E_i represents the current electric quantity of the node N_i, q_c represents the charging power of the MC, η represents the charging efficiency of the MC.

(2) According to Formula (8), the time required for the MC to complete the charging service for a node is t_i, so in the progress of completing the charging task for the former $n - 1$ nodes by the MC, the needed waiting time for the last node needs to be recharged in the charging sequence N_n can be obtained as follows:

$$T_{n,1} = \frac{\sum_{i=1}^{n} d_{i-1,i}}{V} + \sum_{i=1}^{n-1} \frac{E_s - E_i}{q_c \times \eta} \tag{9}$$

Where, $d_{i-1,i}$ represents the distance between the node N_{i-1} and the node N_i. It represents the distance between the service station S and the first node needs to be recharged when $i = 0$. So $\frac{\sum_{i=1}^{n} d_{i-1,i}}{V}$ is the moving time required for the MC to start from the service station S to the last rechargeable node N_n. In the Formula (9), the longest waiting time of the last node needs to be recharged in the charging sequence N_n is $T_{n,1}$. So, if N_n's remaining operating time $T_n \ge T_{n,1}$ when the MC starts its mobile charging, the node N_n will not be "dead" because of the exhaustion of energy. Therefore, $T_{n,1}$ can be used as the threshold to satisfy the charging loop circuit.

(3) Similarly, the group of nodes with the maximum energy consumption rate is selected as the nodes need to be recharged to construct a loop circuit. And based on Formulas (8) and (9), the waiting time of the last node needs to be recharged in the charging loop circuit $T_{n,2}$ can be obtained. In order to guarantee all the nodes are not "dead" in every charging round in the process of mobile charging, we select the larger value of $T_{n,1}$ and $T_{n,2}$ as the charging threshold, which is

$$\varphi = \max\{T_{n,1}, T_{n,2}\} \tag{10}$$

The MC only selects the nodes whose remaining operating time is lower than the charging threshold φ as the nodes to be recharged at each time of charging.

3.5 The Pre-charging Mechanism

Assuming that the sensor node uploads the remaining electric quantity E_i every 10 s, the real-time energy consumption rate of the node can be obtained according to the remaining electric quantity of the two uploads as follows:

$$V_i = \frac{E_{i,1} - E_{i,2}}{10} \tag{11}$$

Where, $E_{i,1}$ and $E_{i,2}$ are two contiguous remaining electric quantity values respectively. According to Formula (11), the current energy consumption rate of each sensor node can be updated, and on this basis, the remaining operating time of the node is:

$$T_i = \frac{E_i}{V_i} \tag{12}$$

When a node's remaining electric quantity falls below the threshold, $T_i \leq \varphi$, the node and other nodes in this group are all included in the charging sequence, which means the groups are served as the charging scheduling unit. After the charging groups are obtained, continuously include the nodes with the remaining operating time of $[\varphi, 2\varphi]$ to the charging sequence. When the MC goes through a node in the process of moving to the next node after completing the energy supplement of one node, include the node N_i in the loop sequence. We use the Dijkstra algorithm to construct the shortest Hamiltonian loop that covers all nodes in the charging sequence. Therefore, the path for the MC to perform the charging task can be obtained.

3.6 The Calculation of the Charging Amount

Each round of the charging scheduling strategy is required to meet the energy constraint of the MC. Assuming that the total energy of the MC is E_M, a part of which is used as MC's moving waste, and the remaining part can be used to charge the sensor nodes. According to the constructed charging loop circuit, the MC starts from the service station, moves a full circle according to the charging loop circuit and returns to the service station with an energy consumption of $q_m \times \left(\left(\sum_{i=1}^{n} \frac{d_{i-1,i}}{V} \right) + \frac{d_{n,0}}{V} \right)$. So the energy that can be used for nodes' electric quantity supplement is as follows:

$$E_{M,c} = E_M - q_m \times \left(\left(\sum_{i=1}^{n} \frac{d_{i-1,i}}{V} \right) + \frac{d_{n,0}}{V} \right) \tag{13}$$

Where, q_m represents the energy the MC needed for every meter when the MC moves, $d_{i,j}$ represents the linear distance between the node N_i and the node N_j. In this way, the energy consumption of the MC to carry out a mobile charging service along the charging loop circuit can be obtained. The remaining energy $E_{M,c}$ is used to charge nodes need to be recharged. So T_0 needs to meet the following constraints:

$$\frac{d_{i-1,i}}{V} + \sum_{j=1}^{i-1} \frac{d_{j-1,j}}{V} + \frac{T_0 \times V_j - E_j}{q_c \times \eta} \leq T_i (1 \leq i \leq n) \tag{14}$$

$$\sum_{i=1}^{n} \frac{T_0 \times V_i - E_i}{\eta} \leq E_{M,c} \tag{15}$$

To ensure the survival of the last node of the charging loop circuit, the MC must arrive before the energy of the node run out and charge the node to satisfy the waiting delay of all the nodes need to be recharged, that is, the Formula (14) must be satisfied. Meanwhile, the energy required by the MC to charge all the nodes must be less than $E_{M,c}$, so that the MC can have enough energy to return to the service station S after completing the charging service. That is, the electric quantity of the node can be replenished to $E_i = T_0 \times V_i$.

4   Experimental Analysis

4.1   The Environment of the Experiments

We design a monitoring area of 100 m * 100 m with 40 sensor nodes, a service station, a base station and a MC with a moving speed of 0.5 m/s randomly deployed. The experimental simulation scene is shown in Fig. 1. The comparing algorithm is TADP algorithm [10]. The energy consumption rate V_i of the node Ni in the network is a random floating number between 0.05 W and 0.15 W. The maximum electric quantity of the sensor nodes and the MC is 3240 kJ and 32400 kJ respectively. MC's moving speed is 0.5 m/s, the moving energy consumption is 10 J/m, the charging power is 10 W. Assuming that MC's charging efficiency is 1.

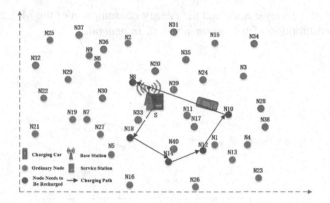

Fig. 1. The experimental charging network model of the MCS

4.2 Node's Waiting Delay

As shown in Fig. 2, within the 6 continuous operating cycles, the overall waiting delay of each operating cycle using the TADP algorithm are 237.63 Min, 210.62 Min, 211.80 Min, 225.48 Min, 210.30 Min and 225.92 Min respectively. And the average waiting delay for each cycle is 220.29 Min. The overall waiting delay of each operating cycle using MCS are 176.93 Min, 194.50 Min, 176.93 Min, 217.40 Min, 173.44 Min and 204.00 Min respectively. And the average waiting delay for each cycle is 190.54 Min. The overall delay of sensor nodes using MCS is always lower than that of the TADP algorithm, which means that the charging performance based on the MCS algorithm is relatively better, and the efficiency is increased by about 13.51%.

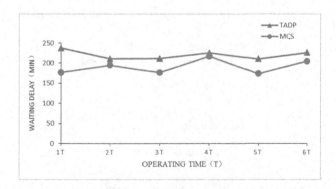

Fig. 2. Comparison on node's waiting delay

4.3 MC's Moving Distance

As shown in Fig. 3, the MC's average moving distance of each cycle is 2127.97 m. Compared with the TADP algorithm, it is reduced by about 19.06%. It can be seen that the MCS algorithm can greatly reduce the MC's moving distance, thus reducing the waiting delay of the sensor node and the energy consumption of the MC, and reducing the energy consumption of the sensor network in general.

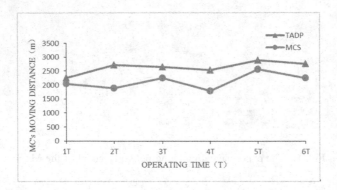

Fig. 3. Comparison on MC's moving distance

4.4   Ratio of MC's Resting Time

In Fig. 4, the ratio of MC's resting time in each cycle using TADP are 46.50%, 45.81%, 46.04%, 46.41%, 45.54% and 45.90% respectively. The average ratio of the resting time of each cycle is 46.03%. The average resting time of each cycle is 379.86Min, and the average ratio of the resting time of each cycle is 47.96%, about 1.93% higher than that of the TADP algorithm. It shows that the charging efficiency of the MC is improved increasing the ratio of the resting time of the MC.

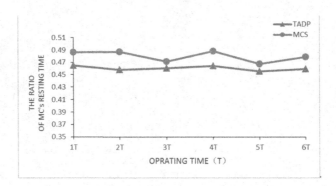

Fig. 4. Comparison on the ratio of MC's resting time

4.5   MC's Service Time

In Fig. 5, the average service time of each cycle using TADP is 435.72 Min, however MCS is 412.20 Min, about 5.40% lower than that of the TADP algorithm.

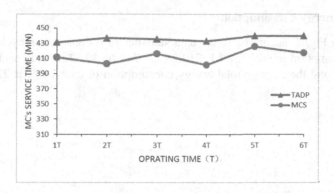

Fig. 5. Comparison on the MC's service time

At the same time, during the working state of the MC, the higher the ratio of MC's moving time consuming to the service time, the higher the MC's mobile charging price, the worse the planning of the mobile charging scheduling path, the lower the charging efficiency. That is, it will take a longer time and a longer moving distance for MC's mobile charging services to the same set of the nodes need to be recharged.

In Fig. 6, the average moving time of the MC in each cycle is 87.63 Min and the average ratio of MC's moving time consuming to the service time is 20.10%. The moving time of the MC in each cycle using MCS are 67.87 Min, 62.84 Min, 75.02 Min, 59.51 Min, 85.27 Min and 75.07 Min respectively. And the average moving time of each cycle is 70.93 Min. The ratio of MC's moving time consuming to the service time are 16.50%, 15.61%, 18.04%, 14.83%, 20.06% and 20.18% respectively, and the average is 17.17%, about 2.93% lower than that of the TADP algorithm.

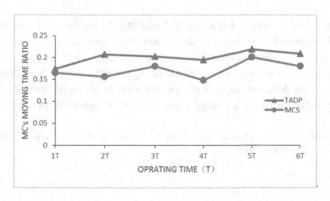

Fig. 6. Comparison on the MC's moving time ratio

4.6   The Energy Consumption

As shown in Fig. 7, according to the data statistics of 6 consecutive cycles, the total energy consumption are 220.38 kJ, 219.58 kJ, 217.66 kJ, 222.46 kJ and 221.93 kJ respectively, and the average total energy consumption of each cycle is 219.66 kJ.

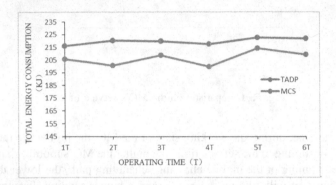

Fig. 7. Comparison on total energy consumption of the sensor network

The total energy consumption of the sensor network in 6 consecutive cycles using the MCS algorithm are 205.59 kJ, 200.82 kJ, 208.58 kJ, 199.72 kJ, 214.30 kJ and 209.19 kJ respectively, and the average total energy consumption of each cycle is 206.37 kJ, about 6.05% lower than that of the TADP algorithm.

5   Conclusion

The paper proposes a Mixed Charging Scheduling Algorithm (MCS), in which put forward the deployment of the service station and the grouping mechanism of the nodes to group all sensor nodes according to the energy consumption rate, and make the grouping of nodes as the unit of the mobile charging scheduling. It is determined that MCS algorithm has different degrees of optimization in terms of waiting time delay of node, moving distance of MC, energy consumption of sensor network.

Acknowledgments. This work was supported by National Science and Technology Pillar Program Project (2015BAI11B01).

References

1. Xie, L., Shi, Y., Hou, Y.T., et al.: On renewable sensor networks with wireless energy transfer: the multi-node case. In: INFOCOM, pp. 1350–1358 (2011)
2. Lu, S., Wu, J., Zhang, S.: Collaborative mobile charging for sensor networks. In: International Conference on Mobile Ad hoc and Sensor Systems, pp. 84–92 (2013)
3. Chai, B., Deng, R., Shi, Z., et al.: Energy-efficient power allocation in cognitive sensor networks: a coupled constraint game approach. Wirel. Netw. **21**(5), 1577–1589 (2015)
4. Li, K., Luan, H., Shen, C.C.L.: Qi-ferry: energy-constrained wireless charging in wireless sensor networks. In: Wireless Communications and Networking Conference, pp. 2515–2520 (2012)
5. Liang, W., Xu, W., Ren, X., et al.: Maintaining sensor networks perpetually via wireless recharging mobile vehicles. In: Local Computer Networks, pp. 270–278 (2014)
6. Guo, S., Wang, C., Yang, Y.: Mobile data gathering with wireless energy replenishment in rechargeable sensor networks. In: INFOCOM, pp. 1932–1940 (2013)
7. Shi, Y., Xie, L., Hou, Y.T., et al.: On renewable sensor networks with wireless energy transfer. In: INFOCOM, pp. 1350–1358 (2012)
8. He, L., Gu, Y., Pan, J., et al.: On-demand charging in wireless sensor networks: theories and applications. In: International Conference on Mobile Ad-Hoc and Sensor Systems, pp. 28–36 (2013)
9. Lin, C., Xue, B., Wang, Z., et al.: DWDP: a double warning thresholds with double preemptive scheduling scheme for wireless rechargeable sensor networks. In: International Conference on High Performance Computing and Communications, pp. 503–508 (2015)
10. Lin, C., Wang, Z., Han, D., et al.: TADP: enabling temporal and distantial priority scheduling for on-demand charging architecture in wireless rechargeable sensor networks. J. Syst. Archit. **70**, 26–38 (2016)

A Multi-controller Load Balancing Strategy for Software Defined WiFi Networks

Sohaib Manzoor[✉], Xiaojun Hei, and Wenqing Cheng

School of Electronic Information and Communications,
Huazhong University of Science and Technology, Wuhan 430074, China
{sohaibmanzoor,heixj,chengwq}@hust.edu.cn

Abstract. Software Defined WiFi networks (SD-WiFi) support scalable network control functions, flexible resource allocation and changes in traffic. But the load balancing in SD-WiFi is challenging due to involvement of numerous users in the network. In this paper, we propose an efficient algorithm approach to achieve load balancing in SD-WiFi architecture. The user generated traffic arrives at WiFi access points (APs), which is classified into high prioritized (HP) flows and low prioritized (LP) flows, based on flow size and delay constraint values using support vector machine (SVM). Controllers are organized as two-tier: global controller (GC) and local controllers (LC). Markov Chain Model (MCM) is employed with two transition states as overloaded and underloaded in GC to predict future load of LCs based on the current load. The optimal underloaded LC for flow migration is selected by using Type-2 Fuzzy based Particle Swarm Optimization (TFPSO) algorithm. We conducted extensive simulation experiments to evaluate the performance of the proposed scheme using OMNeT++ simulator. The proposed scheme outperforms flow stealer scheme by a 33% increase in throughput and 70% in workload performance. In comparison to MPSO-CO scheme the proposed scheme exhibits better latency results.

Keywords: WiFi · SDN · Load balancing · Multi-controllers

1 Introduction

Software Defined Network (SDN) is a new emerging network platform which provides flexibility to program a network through a centralized and decoupled architecture. SDN serves as a solution for managing the network with more flexibility and network visibility to achieve better resource utilization and high performance [1]. In SDN, load balancing is achieved by migrating switches from controller using greedy efficiency-aware switch migration algorithm [2]. Load balancing is an important subject in high density software defined WiFi networks [3]. Prioritizing flows and controller cluster management helps achieving dynamic two-tier load balancing in software defined WiFi networks [4]. Load balancing

© Springer Nature Switzerland AG 2018
X. Sun et al. (Eds.): ICCCS 2018, LNCS 11066, pp. 622–633, 2018.
https://doi.org/10.1007/978-3-030-00015-8_54

in WiFi network is performed by transferring traffic between WiFi and WiMAX network [5]. The handover process is performed by the following process: (i) bandwidth reservation in Access Point (AP) and base station (BS) (ii) admission control at AP and BS and (iii) class aware load balancing. In SDN based wireless networks, the network devices such as accessing devices and forwarding devices are simplified and behave in accordance to the rules scheduled by centralized controller [6].

In SD-WiFi network load balancing is performed by incorporating Access Network Discovery and Selection Functions (ANDSF) to select proper APs for incoming packets [7]. An SDN based load balancing algorithm is proposed for load balancing in wireless networks [8]. The advantage of SDN controller's view is taken to select optimal neighboring BS in BSs list for handover. A wildcard method based on the SDN protocol is presented in [9] for server load balancing. The wildcard method is improved by incorporating SDN open flow rules to assign priorities for load balancing.

In this paper, we propose an efficient algorithm approach to achieve load balancing in SD-WiFi architecture. In our multi-controller SDN architecture the GC is responsible for taking decisions that require network-wide knowledge and pass instructions to LCs. The WiFi APs differentiate the traffic flows generated from user devices into two classes including HP flows and LP flows using support vector machine, a machine learning approach. HP flows are more delay sensitive, so they are forwarded to a switch earlier. Upon a new flow arrival at the switch, this switch inspects the first flow request and queries the GC for computing the corresponding flow policies. This global controller dispatches the requests to local controllers based on their load values for flow processing. The load of each LC is calculated. Markov Chain Model (MCM) decides whether a LC will remain in underloaded or overloaded state in the future. If the LC is forecasted as overloaded then the flow migration process is initiated by the GC. The LC to transfer the flows is decided by Type-2 Fuzzy based Particle Swarm Optimization (TFPSO) algorithm. Once the appropriate LC is chosen by the GC, the flows are forwarded to it for computation of the flow policies which are then deployed back to the switch to achieve high request processing at a reduced response time.

The rest of this paper is organized as follows: In Sect. 2 we describe the details of the proposed efficient algorithm approach to achieve load balancing in SD-WiFi. Then in Sect. 3 we report the simulation results for evaluating the performance of the proposed scheme. In Sect. 4 we summarize the related work on the load balancing issue in SD-WiFi. Finally we Conclude this paper in Sect. 5.

2   Method

2.1   Overview

In this section, we discuss the proposed SD-WiFi architecture which consists of three modules, the first module performs flow classification at the data plane, the second module contains the multi-controller arrangement of local and global controllers at the control plane and the third module supports the load balancing algorithms at the application plane, as shown in Fig. 1. Flow requests are generated from access networks (i.e., wireless local area networks (WLAN) and smart home networks), which are then classified with priority by the WiFi APs using SVM. The requests are then forwarded to the controller via Open-Flow switches for further processing. MCM predicts the future load of a LC and TFPSO determines the optimal underloaded LC for migration.

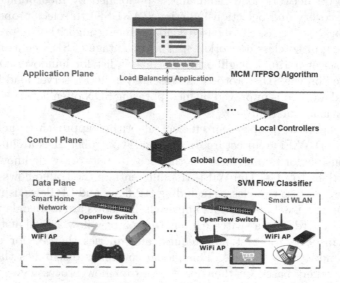

Fig. 1. The proposed software defined WiFi network architecture with multi-controller load balancing strategy.

SVM Flow Classifier. To help achieve load balancing at the data plane, we classify the incoming flow requests into two types. SVM classifier which is an efficient binary classifier is used to find the type of incoming flows based on flow size and delay constraint.

SVM is a supervised approach which uses training data to categorize incoming flow requests by determining optimal hyperplane. In SVM classifier, flows are represented by support vectors in which each point can be laid on hyperplane. If we have n training observations $(\boldsymbol{x}_1, ..., \boldsymbol{x}_n) \in \mathbb{R}^p$, where $\mathbb{R}^p$ is the real valued $\mathcal{P}$ dimensional space, and n class labels $y_1, ..., y_n \in \{-1, 1\}$, support vector machine tends to build an optimal hyperplane boundary subject to the constraints given in Eq. 1,

$$y_i \left(\boldsymbol{b} \cdot \boldsymbol{x} + b_0 \right) \geq M(1 - \epsilon_i), \quad \forall i = 1, ..., n \tag{1}$$

where y_i represent either HP i^{th} flow or LP i^{th} flow, $\boldsymbol{x}$ represent the flow size and delay constraint values, $(\boldsymbol{b} \cdot \boldsymbol{x} + b_0)$ defines an affine hyperplane, M represents the maximum possible margin between two flows, ϵ_i are the slack variables used to handle the non separable cases.

The flows having a small size and low deadline are classified as HP flows and flows having a large size and high deadline are classified as LP flows. Based on the flow type, WiFi APs forward the flows to the GC through OpenFlow switches.

Load Balancing. A Markov chain model is used in GC to predict the future load of LCs using the overload and underload states. If an LC is identified as overloaded, GC initiates the flow migration process. Fig. 2 shows the transition states of LCs using MCM model.

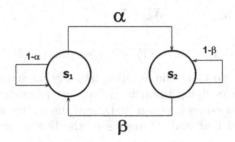

Fig. 2. Markov Chain Model

In Fig. 2, α represent the probability of a LC to become overloaded state (S_2) and β represents the probability of an LC to become underloaded state (S_1) at next state. The transition probability of LC to become S_2 state from S_1 is determined as,

$$P(S_1, S_2) = P(S_1/S_2) P(S_2) \qquad (2)$$

Transmission matrix is constructed using transition probability and given as,

$$T = \begin{bmatrix} (1-\alpha) & \alpha \\ \beta & (1-\beta) \end{bmatrix}$$

Transition matrix is filled by the current load status values of the LC. These probability values help in determining the future load of an LC which is calculated as follow,

$$L_F(LC) = Current\ load\ on\ LC * Transition\ matrix \qquad (3)$$

Where $L_F(LC)$ represent future load of LC. The current load of LC is computed using the number of flows in controller at time t and it is given as,

$$L = \frac{\sum_{i=1}^{n} S_i(T)}{T} \qquad (4)$$

Where i represents the switch and n represents the number of switches, T denotes time instant and $S_i(T)$ represent amount of flows received from i^{th} switch by an LC.

If an LC is predicted as overloaded from 3, then GC migrates the flows from overloaded LC to underloaded LC. The destination LC for migration is selected using novel TFPSO algorithm. In TFPSO, initially the PSO algorithm is started. The algorithm takes every LC as a particle i with position X_i and these particles pass through search space to find the optima with velocity V_i. The position of the particle is updated after every cycle with a new position and velocity values represented as primes in Eqs. 5 and 6.

$$X_i' = X_i + V_i' \tag{5}$$

$$V_i' = \omega V_i + c_1 \text{rand}\,()\,(Y_i - X_i) + c_2 \text{rand}\,()\,(Y^* - X_i) \tag{6}$$

Where c_1 and c_2 represent the learning factors that represent the weight of velocity of the particles flying towards global best position, $rand()$ is random function with uniform values between $[0, 1]$, w is the inertia weight, Y_i represent the previous personal best and Y^* represent the best present solution among all Y_i.

Type-2 fuzzy logic helps in computing the fitness of each LCs. The fuzzy logic system consists of fuzzifier, rule base, inference machine and a defuzzifier giving a crisp output value. Load, available memory and CPU are taken as membership functions. Type 2 fuzzy set is fed into inference model which combine fuzzy set and rule base. It takes multiple membership functions as input and gives single output. The rule base consist of M rules and l^{th} rule is given as,

$$R^l : IF x_1 is \widetilde{F_1^l} and \ldots and x_p is \widetilde{F_p^l} \; THEN \; y \; is \; \widetilde{G^l} \tag{7}$$

Where $x = (x_1, x_2, x_3, \ldots, x_p)$ represent input membership functions and $\widetilde{F^l} = (\widetilde{F_1^l}, \widetilde{F_2^l}, \widetilde{F_3^l}, \ldots \widetilde{F_p^l})$ represent type 2 fuzzy set of x and $\widetilde{G^l}$ represent crisp output value for input membership function in l^{th} rule.

The output defuzzified values for each LC is updated as a fitness value in the PSO algorithm. The pbest and gbest values are updated at each iteration using fuzzy set and optimal LC is selected based on gbest value. As per our proposed work the defuzzified value is high for an LC which has a small amount of load, large memory and CPU.

Algorithm 1 explains the process of our proposed load balancing method. The optimal selection of an LC helps to prevent a specific LC from overloading.

Algorithm 1. The Proposed Load Balancing Algorithm

1: Receive all flows from users
2: **for** *all flows* **do**
3:    Initialize flow size, delay constraint.
4:    Feed flows into SVM classifier
5:    Classify flows into HP and LP
6:    Send flows to GC through switches based on priority
7: **end for**
8: Assign flows to LCs
9: **for** *all LCs* **do**
10:    Compute current load on LCs using eqn 4
11:    Compute probability of state transition for each LC using eqn 2
12:    Construct transmission matrix
13:    Compute future load using eqn 3
14: **end for**
15: **if** *LC is overloaded* **then**
16:    Migrate flows from that LC
17:    Initialize all particles with fitness value
18:    Initialize pbest & gbest values
19:    **for** *all particles* **do**
20:       Compute fitness value for each particle using fuzzy logic
21:       Update pbest & gbest in each iteration
22:       If maximum epochs meet
23:       Stop.
24:    **end for**
25: **else**
26:    repeat the process;
27: **end if**

---

3 Performance Evaluation

In this section we report the simulation setup and the parameters adjusted to evaluate the performance of the proposed scheme.

3.1 Simulation Setup

We have used OpenFlow to implement the simulation model of the software defined WiFi networks for the proposed load balancing algorithm. The proposed SD-WiFi architecture consists of mobile users, WiFi APs, OpenFlow switches, and controllers. POX is used as an SDN controller and the load balancing algorithm is designed in C++. The simulation setup is depicted in Fig. 3.

Finally, all our experiments are performed on a HP PC with windows 10 OS, a core i7 2.4 GHz CPU and 16 GB of RAM. Table 1 show the key simulation parameters used for the proposed SD-WiFi architecture.

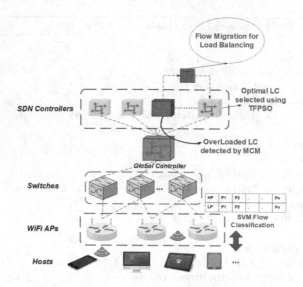

Fig. 3. Simulation topology

Table 1. Simulation parameters

Parameters	Value	
Number of controllers	Global Controller	1
	Local controllers	4
Number of OpenFlow switches	3	
Number of WiFi access points	3	
Number of users	40	
Number of CPU	4	
Memory	16 GB	
Hard disk	500 GB	
Connection speed	300 Mbps	
Flow size	100 Bytes	
Flow request interval	0.001 s	
Flow table size	1000 Entries	
Flow timeout	0.2 s	
Transmission range	1000*1000 m	
Simulation time	200 s	

3.2 Comparative Results

In this section we compare our proposed load balancing method based on a novel TFPSO algorithm, with existing research works [10,11], on load balancing to show the efficiency of our proposed work.

Throughput. Figure 4 shows the improved throughput performance achieved by the TFPSO method. Our results are compared to the flow stealer method.

A light weight load balancing method for multiple SDN controllers named as flow stealer was proposed for load balancing [11]. In this method the load was balanced by idle controllers which shared workloads temporarily from overloaded controllers. This method failed to balance the load, if the idle node became busy as opposed to our proposed scheme where an optimal underloaded LC is selected prior to a specific controller getting overloaded.

The TFPSO method achieves throughput about 5000 responses/s which is significantly greater than the flow stealer method.

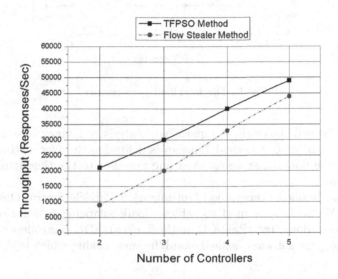

Fig. 4. The throughput performance.

Work Load. Figure 5 depicts the work handled by the controllers in a given period of time.

In [11] the work load for controllers was measured under burst traffic for different time durations. Best work load performance was achieved when the time duration of burst traffic was short. After the burst traffic a certain controller gets overloaded and when the flow steal event is initiated the workload decreases linearly. In comparison to this method, the TFPSO method shows constant behavior in the work load pattern as the flows are shifted prior to the controller getting overloaded.

At 12 s the flows handled by the controller in the flow stealer method are 4500 in comparison to under 1000 flows handled by the controller under the TFPSO method. This shows a better workload performance by our proposed load balancing algorithm.

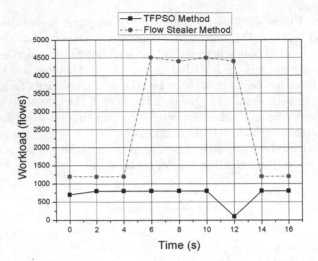

Fig. 5. The workload performance.

Latency. Figure 6 shows the comparative analysis of latency of our proposed scheme to the MPSO-CO method. Latency is defined as the average time between the start of the flow transmission from one end-user to the time it reaches the other end user

In [10] a Modified Constrained Optimization Particle Swarm Optimization algorithm (MPSO-CO) is used to achieve load balancing in software defined cloud/fog networking. In MPSO-CO method, cloud, SDN controllers and fog are integrated to form software defined cloud/fog networking which is then applied

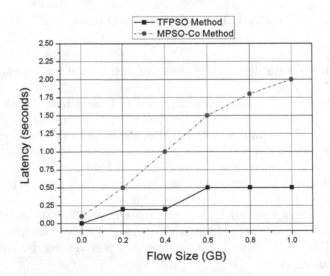

Fig. 6. Comparative analysis of latency.

to IoV. The cloud server computation system is enhanced when the load is high or a controller gets overloaded.

The latency curve for TFPSO shows better performance in comparison to the MPSO-CO method as the controllers are prevented from going into the overloaded state, which implies fast flow processing and response time. Our proposed work maintains latency within 0.5 s upto a flow size of about 1 GB.

4 Related Work

Load balancing was performed using a Genetic Algorithm in an SDN controller [12]. GA performs selection, mutation and cross over processes for load balancing in SDN. In this method all switches were ranked according to their load and a switch with the largest load was assigned to a controller with the least load. The switches were assigned based only on the load and other parameters were not considered which increased the execution time. The initialization of GA is complex due to many parameters such as mutation rate, cross over rate etc. which need to be initialized. Our proposed scheme takes into account other parameters apart from load such as available memory and CPU. Finite State Machine (FSM) and policy was introduced for load balancing based on SDN [13]. In FSM state of each controller was related to a policy which decides the packet forwarding in network. In this method the load of each controller is not determined for load balancing. A Collaborative platform based on restless framework was used to balance the load among controllers in a distributed SDN network [14]. The platform uses the data collecting algorithm to collect the controllers load information. Load was balanced by migration of the control permission of the switch among distributed controllers. In migration process, load was considered only in source controller, as apposed to our proposed method where the load on destination controller was also considered. In dense Wireless Local Area Network (WLAN), load balancing among APs was performed by a semi-matching based load balancing scheme [15] which runs in centralized controller. The controller determined the load distribution among APs according to collected Channel Busy Time Ratio (CBTR) information of entire network. The problem was modeled as a weighted bipartite graph matching problem and semi-matched APs for overloaded APs were found that maximize the total weight of weighted bipartite graph. The computational complexity is increased due to several model calculations. In our proposed scheme PSO is used which has a limited number of parameters to tune.

In [16] SDN based WiFi network controllers and APs were organized into a two-tier architecture to allow the controller to evaluate the degree of load balancing among APs. The load balancing was performed at AP side and controller side by using openflow extension messages. The Controller receives reports from an AP such as capacity, load and association table. The associated client stations are de associated using Last In First Out (LIFO) which increases the waiting time for first requested user since user priorities are not considered. The TFPSO method process flows on the base of their nature, HP flows sensitive to delay are

S. Manzoor et al.

processed first. AP load balancing scheme based handover in SDN based WiFi networks was proposed in [17] which involves two processes including a load balancing and hand over process. Load balancing was achieved by incorporating three modules in the network as follows: (i) load control module (ii) Metric monitoring module and (iii) Decision conversion module. If an AP was overloaded then the station in that AP was transferred to a neighboring AP by an SDN controller. But this method does not consider load of a neighboring AP, so there are chances of that AP becoming overloaded as opposed to our proposed scheme where the load of the destination controller is also measured. SDN based load balancing for LTE network was proposed in [18]. In this method when a new flow was received at the switch it informs the controller by sending PACKET_IN message. The new flow rules were installed by the controller whenever a flow was received at the switch. The load of the gateway was calculated using static information about traffic per volume which was determined by OpenFlow switches. In this method one controller is employed which is insufficient for numerous packets from users. Our proposed scheme takes into account the scalability issues and hence has introduced multi controllers.

5 Conclusion

In this paper, we have proposed a novel multi-controller load balancing algorithm to balance load efficiently in SD-WiFi. We have designed an SDN architecture with multiple controllers and balance the load among those controllers. Initially we have classified the incoming flow requests into HP and LP flows at WiFi APs using an SVM approach. The GC is responsible for monitoring all LCs and predicting future load of LCs using an MCM model. The flows in an overloaded LC are migrated to another LC which is selected by a TFPSO algorithm to balance load. TFPSO ensures load balancing in a migrated LC by selecting optimal LC with consideration of load, memory and CPU. Our simulation results have shown that the proposed scheme has higher throughput by 33% and higher workload performance by 70% than the flow stealer approach. Our scheme outperforms the MPSO-CO method by achieving better latency results. Our proposed scheme can be applied to real time applications running on cloud-based software defined WiFi network frameworks with heavy loading to achieve improved QoS.

Acknowledgment. This work was supported in part by the National Natural Science Foundation of China (No. 61370231).

References

1. Rawat, D.B., Reddy, S.R.: Software defined networking architecture, security and energy efficiency: a survey. IEEE Commun. Surv. Tutor. **19**(1), 325–346 (2017). https://doi.org/10.1109/COMST.2016.2618874
2. Wang, C., Hu, B., Chen, S., Li, D., Liu, B.: A switch migration-based decision-making scheme for balancing load in SDN. IEEE Access **5**, 4537–4544 (2017)

3. Chen, Z., Manzoor, S., Gao, Y., Hei, X.: Achieving load balancing in high-density software defined WiFi networks. In: International Conference on Frontiers of Information Technology (FIT), December 2017
4. Manzoor, S., Hei, X., Cheng, W.: Towards dynamic two-tier load balancing for software defined WiFi networks. In: International Conference on Communication and Information Systems (ICCIS), November 2017
5. Sarma, A., Chakraborty, S., Nandi, S.: Deciding handover points based on context-aware load balancing in a WiFi-WiMAX heterogeneous network environment. IEEE Trans. Veh. Technol. **65**(1), 348–357 (2016)
6. Yang, M., Li, Y., Jin, D., Zeng, L., Wu, X., Vasilakos, A.V.: Software-defined and virtualized future mobile and wireless networks: a survey. Mob. Netw. Appl. **20**(1), 4–18 (2015)
7. Yang, S.N., Ke, C.H., Lin, Y.B., Gan, C.H.: Mobility management through access network discovery and selection function for load balancing and power saving in software-defined networking environment. EURASIP J. Wirel. Commun. Netw. **2016**(1), 204 (2016)
8. Duan, X., Akhtar, A.M., Wang, X.: Software-defined networking-based resource management: data offloading with load balancing in 5G HetNet. EURASIP J. Wirel. Commun. Netw. **2015**(1), 1–13 (2015)
9. Lin, T.L., Kuo, C.H., Chang, H.Y., Chang, W.K., Lin, Y.Y.: A parameterized wildcard method based on sdn for server load balancing. In: 2016 International Conference on Networking and Network Applications (NaNA), pp. 383–386. IEEE (2016)
10. He, X., Ren, Z., Shi, C., Fang, J.: A novel load balancing strategy of software-defined cloud/fog networking in the internet of vehicles. China Commun. **13**(2), 140–149 (2016)
11. Song, P., Liu, Y., Liu, T., Qian, D.: Flow stealer: lightweight load balancing by stealing flows in distributed SDN controllers. Sci. China Inf. Sci. **60**(3) (2017)
12. Kang, S.B., Kwon, G.I.: Load balancing of software-defined network controller using genetic algorithm (2016)
13. Zhou, Y., Ruan, L., Xiao, L., Liu, R.: A method for load balancing based on software defined network. Adv. Sci. Technol. Lett. **45**, 43–48 (2014)
14. Zhong, H., Sheng, J., Cui, J., Xu, Y.: SCPLBS: a smart cooperative platform for load balancing and security on SDN distributed controllers. In: 2017 3rd IEEE International Conference on Cybernetics (CYBCONF), pp. 1–6. IEEE (2017)
15. Lei, T., Wen, X., Lu, Z., Li, Y.: A semi-matching based load balancing scheme for dense IEEE 802.11 WLANs. IEEE Access **5**, 15332–15339 (2017)
16. Lin, Y.D., Wang, C.C., Lu, Y.J., Lai, Y.C., Yang, H.C.: Two-tier dynamic load balancing in SDN-enabled Wi-Fi networks. Wirel. Netw., 1–13 (2017)
17. Kiran, N., Changchuan, Y., Akram, Z.: AP load balance based handover in software defined WiFi systems. In: 2016 IEEE International Conference on Network Infrastructure and Digital Content (IC-NIDC), pp. 6–11. IEEE (2016)
18. Adalian, N., Ajaeiya, G., Dawy, Z., Elhajj, I.H., Kayssi, A., Chehab, A.: Load balancing in LTE core networks using SDN. In: IEEE International Multidisciplinary Conference on Engineering Technology (IMCET), pp. 213–217. IEEE (2016)

A Novel Golden Models-Free Hardware Trojan Detection Technique Using Unsupervised Clustering Analysis

Rongzhen Bian, Mingfu Xue$^{(\boxtimes)}$, and Jian Wang

College of Computer Science and Technology, Nanjing University of Aeronautics
and Astronautics, Nanjing 210016, China
mingfu.xue@nuaa.edu.cn

Abstract. Recently, hardware Trojan has become a major threat for integrated circuits. Most of the existing hardware Trojan detection works require golden chips or golden models for reference. However, a golden chip is extremely difficult to obtain or even does not exist. In this paper, we propose a novel hardware Trojan detection technique using unsupervised clustering techniques. The unsupervised clustering technique can obtain the structure information of the set of unlabeled ICs, and then distinguishes the suspicious ICs from the ICs under test. We formulate the unsupervised hardware Trojan detection problem into two types of detection models: partitioning-based and density-based detection model. We also propose a novel metric to determine the labels of the clusters. Compared with the state-of-the-art detection methods, the proposed technique can work in an unsupervised scenario with no need of ICs' prior information. It does not require fabricated golden chips or golden models. We perform simulation evaluation on ISCAS89 benchmarks and FPGA evaluation on Trust-HUB benchmarks. Both evaluation results show that the proposed technique can detect infected ICs in the unsupervised scenario with a good accuracy.

Keywords: Hardware security · Hardware Trojan detection
Partitioning-based clustering · Density-based clustering

1 Introduction

In recent years, the malicious alteration of integrated circuits (ICs), also referred as hardware Trojan, has become an emerging security problem in the IC industry. The existing non-invasive hardware Trojan detection methods can be divided into three categories: logic testing [1,2], side-channel analysis [3–5], and design-for-security approaches [6,7]. However, most of the existing works require golden chips to provide reference for hardware Trojan detection.

Recently, there are a few machine learning based hardware Trojan detection methods. In [8], the proposed method can facilitate the reverse engineering-based destructive hardware Trojan detection. However, it requires golden chips

© Springer Nature Switzerland AG 2018
X. Sun et al. (Eds.): ICCCS 2018, LNCS 11066, pp. 634–646, 2018.
https://doi.org/10.1007/978-3-030-00015-8_55

for training. The method proposed in [9] does not need golden chips. It uses real-time Trojan behaviors to adaptively train the machine learning algorithm. However, the Trojans are mostly keeping stealthy and will not generate attack behaviors. An enhanced classification-based golden chips-free hardware Trojan detection method is proposed in [10]. It can eliminate the need of golden chips but still needs golden models.

There are few works exploiting clustering techniques for hardware Trojan detection which can eliminate the need of golden models. Authors in [11] present an information-theoretic approach which evaluates the statistical correlation between the signals in a design. Then, a clustering algorithm is used to explore how this estimation can be reveal the Trojan logic. Using an unsupervised clustering analysis, authors in [12] show that the controllability and observability features of the Trojan gates have remarkable inter-cluster distance from the genuine gates in a Trojan-inserted circuit. Authors in [13] propose an anomaly detection based procedure to identify suspicious signals which may be a part of a Trojan in a netlist. However, all of the above works are focusing on the gate-level or register-transfer level (RTL) of the IC designs which can not be used for detection of hardware Trojans inserted in the fabrication stage.

In this paper, we propose a novel hardware Trojan detection technique using unsupervised clustering analysis. The contributions of this paper are summarized as follows:

1. The proposed technique works in an unsupervised scenario and does not need golden chips or golden models. It can detect the Trojans inserted in the fabrication stage with no need of the ICs' prior information.
2. We formulate the unsupervised hardware Trojan detection problem into two types of detection models: partitioning-based detection model and density-based detection model.
3. In the partitioning-based detection model, we propose a metric, called cluster labeling index CMI, to determine the labels of the clusters.
4. In the density-based detection model, we analyze the parameter selection for better detection performance since this model is affected by the parameters.
5. We preform simulation evaluation on ISCAS89 benchmarks under different process variations (PV) sets. We also perform FPGA evaluation on Trust-HUB benchmarks. Both of the evaluation results show that the proposed technique can achieve a decent performance.

2 Preliminary of the Clustering Techniques

2.1 Partitioning-Based Clustering Technique

There are many types of partitioning-based clustering algorithms. A typical partitioning-based clustering algorithm is hierarchical clustering [14]. Hierarchical clustering algorithms are either top-down or bottom-up. In this paper, we use a bottom-up hierarchical clustering algorithm for partitioning-based hardware Trojan detection. The exploited algorithm is hierarchical agglomerative clustering (HAC).

The procedure of a simple HAC is shown in Algorithm 1. In the algorithm, A is a list which stores the clustering results. I is an array used to record activated clusters. The algorithm first computes the $N \times N$ similarity matrix E, then it executes $N - 1$ steps to merge the most similar clusters. In each iteration, the most similar two clusters are merged into one cluster. Then it updates value of the rows and columns of the merged cluster in E [14]. At last, the clustering result is stored in A. The corresponding value of the pre-merger clusters in I is set to be 0. It means that the pre-merger clusters are no longer activated clusters.

Algorithm 1. SIMPLE-HAC$(d_1, ..., d_N)$ [14]

1: **for** $n = 1$ to N **do**
2:    **for** $i = 1$ to N **do**
3:       $E[n][i] = SIM(d_n, d_i)$
4:       $I[n] = 1$ (activate clusters)
5:    **end for**
6: **end for**
7: initialize list A
8: **for** $r = 1$ to $N - 1$ **do**
9:    $< i, m > = \arg\max_{\{<i,m>: i \neq m \wedge I[i]=1 \wedge I[m]=1\}} E[i][m]$
10:   $A[< i, m >]$ (store the merged cluster)
11:   **for** $j = 1$ to N **do**
12:      $E[i][j] = SIM(i, m, j)$
13:      $E[j][i] = SIM(i, m, j)$
14:   **end for**
15:   $I[m] = 0$ (deactivate clusters)
16: **end for**
17: **return** A

2.2 Density-Based Clustering Technique

Density-based methods assume that the points belonging to each cluster are drawn from a specific probability distribution [15]. The overall distribution of the data is assumed to be a mixture of several kinds of distributions. The density-based clustering technique we used is the DBSCAN (Density Based Spatial Clustering of Applications with Noise) algorithm. It can discover arbitrary shapes of clusters in a spatial database efficiently [15].

We will present the basic version of the DBSCAN algorithm, it does not consider the data types of clustering data and the information of clusters. Therefore the algorithm can be modified and recapitulated in Algorithm 2. There are two important notions in the algorithm, *ε-fields of a point* and *density-reachable*, which can be defined as follows [15], where D is the clustering data set:

Definition 1 (ε-field of a point). *The ε-field of a point p is denoted as $N_\varepsilon(p)$. p and q are two points in the clustering data set D. $N_\varepsilon(p)$ is defined by $N_\varepsilon(p) =$*

$\{q \in D | dist(p,q) \leq \varepsilon\}$, where $dist(p,q)$ indicates the distance from point p to point q.

Definition 2 (density-reachable). *For a given parameter ε, there is a chain of points $p_1,...,p_l$, in which $p_1 = q$, $p_l = p$. If the distance of two connected points meet the condition $dist(p_\tau, p_{\tau+1}) \leq \varepsilon$, we can consider that the point p is density-reachable from the point q.*

Algorithm 2. DBSCAN

Input: $SOP, \varepsilon, MinPts$
Output: SOP
  $ClID = nextID(NOISE)$
  for $count = 1$ to $SOP.size$ **do**
    $P = SOP.get(count)$
    if $P.ClID = num(SOP)$ **then**
      if $ExtendCluster(SOP, P, ClID, \varepsilon, MinPts)$ **then**
        $ClusterID = nextID(ClID)$
      end if
    end if
  end for

---

3 Proposed Partitioning-Based and Density-Based Hardware Trojan Detection Techniques

3.1 Problem Formulation

In general, the simulated ICs which pass pre-silicon detection or through strict design process can be assumed as Trojan-free ICs. If the ICs under test do not have the label information, i.e., Trojan-free or Trojan-inserted, they are treated as unlabeled ICs. Otherwise, the ICs are treated as labeled ICs. We formulate the unsupervised hardware Trojan detection problem into two models as follows:

Definition 3 (Partitioning-based hardware Trojan detection model). *Given M fabricated ICs, denoted as $IC_t(1 \leq t \leq M)$, each IC has a few features. The ICs can be denoted as points in the high-dimensional feature space. The problem is to divide these points into two clusters. A metric, called cluster labeling index CMI, is proposed to figure out which cluster is genuine.*

Definition 4 (Density-based hardware Trojan detection model). *Given M fabricated ICs, denoted as $IC_t(1 \leq t \leq M)$, each IC has a few features. The ICs can be denoted as points in the high-dimensional feature space. The problem is to merge these points into one cluster based on the density of the IC sets. The anomalous points which can not be merged into the cluster are considered as Trojan-inserted ICs.*

3.2 Partitioning-Based Hardware Trojan Detection Method

The proposed partitioning-based detection method is shown in Fig. 1. We propose a heuristic method to divide the clustering data set into two mutual independent clusters. Then, we propose a cluster labeling index CMI (refer to Sect. 4 for details) to determine which cluster is genuine. The steps of the proposed heuristic method are as follows:

1. Collect data from ICs under test to constitute the clustering data set U.
2. Set up parameter $s = 2$.
3. Randomly choose s points as initial center point of each cluster, separately.
4. Compute the distances from center points to each point. Merge the points into the closest cluster based on the calculated distances.
5. Update center points based on the clustering results of the previous steps.
6. Repeat step 4 and step 5 until the results of clustering are becoming stable.
7. Calculate the cluster labeling index CMI for each cluster.
8. Determine the label of the two clusters based on the cluster labeling index CMI.

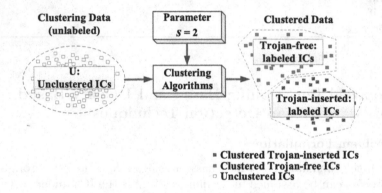

Fig. 1. Overall flow of the partitioning-based hardware Trojan detection method

in which, the input of the detection method is a batch of unlabeled ICs (U). The parameter s indicates the desired number of clusters. The ICs under test can be Trojan-free or Trojan-inserted. Therefore, s is set to be 2. At the first iteration, the exploited clustering technique randomly chooses two points as the initial center point of each cluster. Then it calculates the distances from each point to the two center points. Every point is merged into the closest cluster based on the calculated distances. After each iteration, the clustering technique updates the center point of the two clusters and repeats the previous process. The proposed technique terminates when the results of clustering are becoming stable.

There are many representative partitioning-based clustering algorithms. We will formulate different algorithms and figure out which one is more suitable to address the partitioning-based hardware Trojan detection problem.

3.3 Density-Based Hardware Trojan Detection Method

The proposed density-based detection method is shown in Fig. 2. Based on the analysis of the density of the IC set under test, this method separates the anomalous ICs from the IC set. Without the impacts of hardware Trojans [16], the genuine ICs are more congregated. Therefore, it is possible to merge genuine ICs into a cluster. The ICs which can not be merged into the cluster are represented as anomalous ICs. They will be considered as the Trojan-inserted ICs. Considering the impact of noises, we use the DBSCAN algorithm in this method. The DBSCAN algorithm is more robust than other density-based clustering algorithms under noises. The proposed heuristic method for the density-based detection model is shown as follows:

1. Collect data from ICs under test to constitute the clustering data set U.
2. Set up parameters ε and $MinPts$.
3. Input the clustering data set and parameters to the DBSCAN algorithm.
4. Adjust parameters ε and $MinPts$ to form a boundary, which can divide the clustering data into one cluster.
5. Repeat step 3 and step 4, until it obtains the desired structure of the cluster.

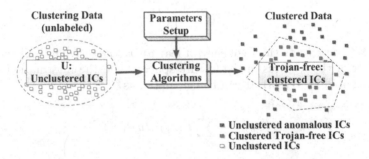

Fig. 2. Overall flow of the density-based hardware Trojan detection method

For a pair of parameters $(\varepsilon, MinPts)$, at first, the exploited clustering technique finds out the ε-field (defined in Sect. 2.2) of each point. There are two kinds of points in a ε-field, points inside of the ε-field (core points) and points on the border (border points). Then it determines the set of core points. Initially, the set of core points contains lots of points. During iterations, the set of core points shrinks gradually. After that, it chooses a core point as the seed to find out all density-reachable (defined in Sect. 2.2) points. Finally, it merges the core points and its density-reachable points into a cluster. The clustered points would be removed from the set of core points. The above process will be repeated until the set of core points is empty. The exploited algorithm will form a boundary based on the density of the IC set under test. The ICs which drop into the boundary will be considered as Trojan-free ICs. On the contrary, the ICs which can not drop into the boundary will be considered as Trojan-inserted ICs.

4   The Proposed Cluster Labeling Index CMI and Parameter Selection

In the partitioning-based detection model, s is the critical parameter. Besides, other parameters do not affect the performance of the detection model. The parameter s indicates the desired number of clusters. The ICs under test can be Trojan-free or Trojan-inserted. Therefore, the parameter s could be set to be 2.

Since people do not have any prior information of the ICs under test, another problem is that how to determine the labels (Trojan-free or Trojan-inserted) of the two clusters. As mentioned above, the genuine cluster is more congregated. It means the average mutual information of the genuine cluster is greater. Therefore, we propose a cluster labeling index CMI based on mutual information to determine the labels of the two clusters. The two clusters are denoted by C_1 and C_2. The ICs in a certain cluster C is denoted by G. We suppose that each IC has z features, denoted as $x_\ell (1 \leq \ell \leq z)$. In order to calculate the CMI of a certain cluster C, we first calculate a probability of ICs' features. The probability indicates the frequency that the feature x_ℓ appears in the feature space of the cluster C. The probability of each feature is denoted by $P(x_\ell)$ and can be calculated as

$$P(x_\ell) = \frac{CNT_\ell}{|X|} \tag{1}$$

where CNT_ℓ represents the frequency of feature x_ℓ, $x_\ell \in G$, and $|X|$ represents the number of the features in the feature space. Then the information entropy of G_θ is denoted by $H(G_\theta)$. It can be calculated as

$$H(G_\theta) = -\sum_{\ell=1}^{N} P(x_\ell) \cdot ln P(x_\ell) \tag{2}$$

where $G_\theta \in C$. After that, the mutual information (MI) of two ICs can be calculated as follows:

$$MI(G_\theta, G_\delta) = H(G_\theta | G_\delta) + H(G_\delta | G_\theta) \tag{3}$$

where $G_\theta, G_\delta \in C$. Finally, the proposed metric CMI is calculated as

$$CMI(C) = \frac{1}{|C|} \sum_{1 \leq \theta \leq \delta \leq |C|} MI(G_\theta, G_\delta) \tag{4}$$

where $|C|$ represents the number of ICs. Compared to the cluster of Trojan-inserted ICs, the cluster of genuine ICs would have a larger CMI.

In the density-based detection model, the performance of the model depends on the parameters $(\varepsilon, MinPts)$. The algorithm DBSCAN provides a distance function k-dist to form a graph of the clustering results, represented as k-dist graph. For $k > 5$, the results of k-dist graphs do not significantly differ from the 5-dist graph. Besides, for $k > 5$, the presented k-dist graphs need more computation. Therefore the parameter $MinPts$ can be set to be 5 for all data sets. The parameter ε is used to find out other density-reachable points for a specific point. Then these points are merged into a cluster. ε can not be too small, otherwise all points are recognized as anomalous points. ε also can not be too large, otherwise all data points will be merged into the same cluster.

5 Experiment Evaluation

5.1 Simulation Evaluation of ISCAS89 Benchmarks

We evaluate the proposed technique on ISCAS89 benchmark circuits with different levels of PV. Trojans are inserted in benchmark circuits for test. The two basic Trojans are a 4-bit comparator and a 3-bit counter. Other Trojans are obtained by adding several logic gates each time on these two basic Trojans. The sizes of these Trojans are varying from 0.005% to 0.2% of the original design. The designs are synthesized with Synopsys Design Compiler with 65 nm technology. The process variations are set to be 10%, 15% and 20%. We apply HSPICE to perform the Monte Carlo Simulation to obtain the power traces of each IC. For each benchmark, the clustering data set U consists of 50 Trojan-free ICs and 50 Trojan-inserted ICs.

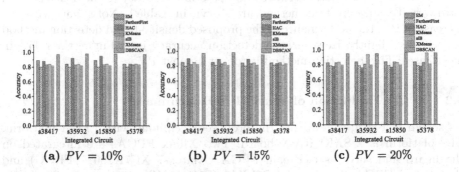

Fig. 3. Comparison of two detection methods under different PV sets

As shown in Fig. 3, we compare the detection accuracy of the two proposed detection methods. The accuracy represents the rate of ICs the algorithm correctly clustered among all the ICs under test. The detection accuracy of most of the clustering algorithms is above 80%. For each benchmark circuit, the first six algorithms are used in the partitioning-based hardware Trojan detection method. The DBSCAN algorithm is used in the density-based hardware Trojan detection method. For the partitioning-based method, we find out that the accuracy of the HAC algorithm is higher than the others in most cases. Besides, with the increase of PV, the performance of the proposed partitioning-based detection method is decreased. It is clear that the density-based method obtains a better performance under all PV sets.

Table 1. Detailed parameter settings and detection accuracy of the density-based detection method under different PV sets

Algorithm	Benchmarks	PV = 10%		PV = 15%		PV = 20%	
		ε	Accuracy	ε	Accuracy	ε	Accuracy
DBSCAN	s38417	2.1	93.00%	3.55	93.00%	4.45	92.00%
		2.2	97.00%	3.57	97.00%	4.65	95.00%
		2.3	95.00%	3.8	96.00%	4.85	89.00%
	s35932	3.05	96.00%	3.55	95.00%	5.2	90.00%
		3.1	98.00%	3.75	98.00%	5.3	95.00%
		3.2	96.00%	3.8	97.00%	5.4	88.00%
	s15850	2.2	84.00%	3.63	92.00%	4.57	94.00%
		2.25	98.00%	3.8	96.00%	4.67	96.00%
		2.3	97.00%	3.9	93.00%	4.77	95.00%
	s5378	2.95	95.00%	4.4	93.00%	5.15	92.00%
		3.05	97.00%	4.5	96.00%	5.25	96.00%
		3.15	95.00%	4.6	95.00%	5.35	90.00%

The detailed parameter settings and detection accuracy of the density-based hardware Trojan detection method are shown in Table 1. Note that, with the increase of PV, the performance of the proposed density-based detection method is decreased slightly. However, the detection accuracy is still more than 95% in most cases. This detection method is robust against PV.

5.2   FPGA Evaluation of Trust-Hub Benchmarks

As shown in Fig. 4, we evaluate the proposed technique with FPGA platform. The platform is a SAKURA-X board. Two Xilinx FPGAs are integrated on the board and serve as the main FPGA (Kintex-7 XC7K160T-1FBGC) and the control FPGA (Spartan-6 XC6LX45-2FGG484C), respectively. The main FPGA is in charge of carrying out operations and running benchmark circuits. The control FPGA provides the digital stimuli for the main FPGA and controls its operating conditions. The SMA-BNC cable is connected to the measurement point (J19) to obtain the power consumption waveform. Then the signals are captured by a Keysight InfiniiVision DSOX3102A oscilloscope and transferred to the computer for further analysis.

The benchmark circuit is Advanced Encryption Standard (AES) [17]. The Trojans are supplied from the Trust-HUB online repository [18]. According to the study in [19], some of the Trojans will be removed during the synthesis process. Therefore we exclude these Trojan benchmarks from our experiment. The remaining benchmarks are used in the experiment, which are AES-T100, AES-T200, AES-T400, AES-T700, AES-T800, AES-T900, AES-T1200, and AES-T1700. These 8 Trojans would not be removed during the synthesis process.

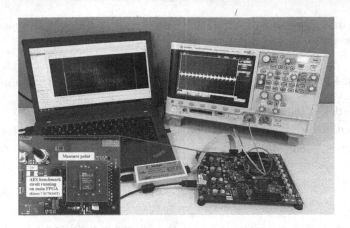

Fig. 4. Experiment platform

According to the implementation utilization report of the Vivado Design Suite, we record and report the number of LUTs and registers utilized by Trojans, and we calculate the area overhead of the Trojan circuits, as shown in Table 2.

Table 2. Hardware overhead

Benchmarks	LUTs	Registers	Trojan_LUTs	Trojan_Registers
AES	1822	2692	0	0
AES-T100	1824	2776	5(0.27%)	84(3.12%)
AES-T200	1824	2776	5(0.27%)	84(3.12%)
AES-T400	1978	2848	158(8.67%)	156(5.79%)
AES-T700	1827	2776	6(0.33%)	84(3.12%)
AES-T800	1828	2777	9(0.49%)	85(3.16%)
AES-T900	2117	2776	299(16.41%)	84(3.12%)
AES-T1200	2111	2776	290(15.92%)	84(3.12%)
AES-T1700	2138	2846	317(17.40%)	154(5.72%)

For each Trojan-inserted benchmark, 20 traces are collected from real experiments without triggering Trojans. The clustering data set U consists of 160 genuine traces and 160 Trojan-inserted traces. In these benchmark circuits, AES-T100 and AES-T200 are always-on Trojans, while the rest six Trojans are triggered with various conditions. The FPGA evaluation results are shown in Table 3 and Table 4. It is obvious that the sIB algorithm's detection accuracy in FPGA evaluation is much lower than its detection accuracy in simulation evaluation. Because the sIB algorithm is more vulnerable to noise and process variations. The detection accuracy of the remaining clustering techniques in both detection methods is in a range of 83%−88.75%. Considering that this is an unsupervised detection scenario, it is an ideal result.

Table 3. FPGA evaluation results of the partitioning-based detection method

Scenarios	Partitioning-based					
Algorithms	EM	FarthestFirst	HAC	KMeans	sIB	XMeans
Accuracy	84.25%	83.63%	86.63%	83.80%	52.81%	83.12%

Table 4. FPGA evaluation results of the density-based detection method

Scenarios	Algorithms	Parameter settings and detection accuracy					
Density-based	DBSCAN	$MinPts$	140	140	140	140	140
		ε	11.33	11.35	11.40	11.43	11.45
		Accuracy	85.63%	88.75%	87.50%	86.88%	85.63%

6   Conclusions

This paper proposes a novel golden-models free hardware Trojan detection technique. The proposed technique can work in an unsupervised scenario with no need of ICs' prior information. We formulate the unsupervised Trojan detection problem into two types of detection models. Moreover, we propose a novel metric to determine the labels of the clusters. Experiment results on both EDA simulation and FPGA evaluation show that the proposed technique under both models can obtain a decent performance. This technique can be applied in the practical unsupervised detection scenarios without increasing hardware overhead.

Acknowledgments. This work is supported by the National Natural Science Foundation of China (No. 61602241), the Natural Science Foundation of Jiangsu Province (No. BK20150758), the CCF-Venustech Hongyan Research Plan (No. CCF-VenustechRP2016005), the CCF-NSFocus Kunpeng Foundation (No. CCF-NSFocus2017003), the Postdoctoral Science Foundation of China (No. 2014M561644), the Postdoctoral Science Foundation of Jiangsu Province (No. 1402034C), and the Fundamental Research Funds for the Central Universities (No. NS2016096).

References

1. Chakraborty, R.S., Wolff, F., Paul, S., Papachristou, C., Bhunia, S.: *MERO*: a statistical approach for hardware Trojan detection. In: Clavier, C., Gaj, K. (eds.) CHES 2009. LNCS, vol. 5747, pp. 396–410. Springer, Heidelberg (2009). https://doi.org/10.1007/978-3-642-04138-9_28
2. Xue, M., Hu, A., Huang, Y., Li, G.: Monte Carlo based test pattern generation for hardware Trojan detection. In: IEEE International Conference on Dependable, Autonomic and Secure Computing (DASC), pp. 131–136 (2013)
3. Nowroz, A.N., Hu, K., Koushanfar, F., Reda, S.: Novel techniques for high-sensitivity hardware Trojan detection using thermal and power maps. IEEE Trans. Comput. Aided Des. Integr. Circ. Syst. **33**(12), 1792–1805 (2014)
4. Xue, M., Liu, W., Hu, A., Wang, Y.: Detecting hardware Trojan through time domain constrained estimator based unified subspace technique. IEICE Trans. Inf. Syst. **97**(3), 606–609 (2014)
5. Xue, M., Hu, A., Li, G.: Detecting hardware Trojan through heuristic partition and activity driven test pattern generation. In: Communications Security Conference (CSC), pp. 1–6. IET (2014)
6. Xiao, K., Forte, D., Tehranipoor, M.: A novel built-in self-authentication technique to prevent inserting hardware Trojans. IEEE Trans. Comput. Aided Des. Integr. Circ. Syst. **33**(12), 1778–1791 (2014)
7. Xue, M., Wang, J., Wang, Y., Hu, A.: Security against hardware Trojan attacks through a novel Chaos FSM and delay chains array PUF based design obfuscation scheme. In: Huang, Z., Sun, X., Luo, J., Wang, J. (eds.) ICCCS 2015. LNCS, vol. 9483, pp. 14–24. Springer, Cham (2015). https://doi.org/10.1007/978-3-319-27051-7_2
8. Bao, C., Forte, D., Srivastava, A.: On reverse engineering-based hardware Trojan detection. IEEE Trans. Comput. Aided Des. Integr. Circ. Syst. **35**(1), 49–57 (2016)
9. Kulkarni, A., Pino, Y., Mohsenin, T.: Adaptive real-time Trojan detection framework through machine learning. In: IEEE International Symposium on Hardware Oriented Security and Trust (HOST), pp. 120–123 (2016)
10. Xue, M., Wang, J., Hu, A.: An enhanced classification-based golden chips-free hardware Trojan detection technique. In: IEEE Asian Hardware-Oriented Security and Trust (AsianHOST), pp. 1–6 (2016)
11. Çakir, B., Malik, S.: Hardware Trojan detection for gate-level ICs using signal correlation based clustering. In: Proceedings of the Design, Automation and Test in Europe Conference and Exhibition (DATE), pp. 471–476 (2015)
12. Salmani, H.: COTD: reference-free hardware Trojan detection and recovery based on controllability and observability in gate-level netlist. IEEE Trans. Inf. Forensics Secur. **12**(2), 338–350 (2017)
13. Ba, P.S., Dupuis, S., Flottes, M.L., Natale, G.D., Rouzeyre, B.: Using outliers to detect stealthy hardware Trojan triggering?. In: IEEE International Verification and Security Workshop, pp. 1–6 (2016)
14. Zepeda-Mendoza, M.L., Resendis-Antonio, O.: Hierarchical agglomerative clustering. In: Encyclopedia of Systems Biology. pp. 886–887. Springer, New York (2013)
15. Ester, M., Kriegel, H.P., Xu, X.: A density-based algorithm for discovering clusters in large spatial databases with noise. In: International Conference on Knowledge Discovery and Data Mining, pp. 226–231. AAAI Press (1996)
16. Ngo, X.T., Najm, Z., Bhasin, S., Guilley, S., Danger, J.L.: Method taking into account process dispersion to detect hardware Trojan Horse by side-channel analysis. J. Cryptogr. Eng. **6**(3), 239–247 (2016)

17. Daemen, J., Rijmen, V.: The design of Rijndael: AES-the advanced encryption standard. Springer, Heidelberg (2013). https://doi.org/10.1007/978-3-662-04722-4
18. Trust-HUB. http://www.trust-hub.org/
19. Reece, T., Robinson, W.H.: Analysis of data-leak hardware Trojans in AES cryptographic circuits. In: IEEE International Conference on Technologies for Homeland Security (HST), pp. 467–472 (2013)

A Novel Part-Based Model
for Fine-Grained Vehicle Recognition

Ye Zhou$^{(\boxtimes)}$, Jiabin Yuan, and Xuwei Tang

College of Computer Science and Technology,
Nanjing University of Aeronautics and Astronautics, Nanjing, China
{aye,jbyuan,xuweitang}@nuaa.edu.cn

Abstract. In recent years, fine-grained vehicle recognition has been one
of the essential tasks in Intelligent Traffic System (ITS) and has a multitude of applications, such as highway toll, parking intelligent management and vehicle safety monitoring. Fine-grained vehicle recognition is
a challenging problem because of small inter-class distance and substantial sub-classes. To tackle this task, we propose a part-based model for
fine-grained vehicle recognition in a weakly unsupervised manner. We
also provide a part location method that locates the discriminative parts
based on saliency maps which can be easily obtained by a single back-
propagation pass. The advantage of the method is that the resolution of
saliency maps is the same as the resolution of input images. Thus, we
can locate discriminative parts efficiently and accurately. Additionally,
we combine the whole-level features and part-level features and improve
the accuracy of recognition up to 98.41% over 281 vehicle models in the
large-scale dataset CompCars.

Keywords: Fine-grained vehicle recognition
Convolutional neural network · ITS · Saliency maps
Weakly unsupervised learning

1 Introduction

Nowadays, video cameras have been extensively deployed for traffic surveillance.
This has greatly promoted the research of fine-grained vehicle recognition, which
is critical to Intelligent Traffic System. Fine-grained vehicle recognition has a
multitude of applications, such as highway toll, parking intelligent management
and vehicle safety monitoring. Furthermore, the results of vehicle recognition can
be used as key clues to search the target vehicle in traffic surveillance images,
when the license plate of the vehicle is faked.

The main challenges of fine-grained vehicle recognition are as followed: (1)
Small inter-class distance. Different fine-grained classes are highly similar in
appearance which is hard to distinguish the subtle difference. (2) Substantial
sub-classes. Some classes of vehicle have many sub-classes, i.e., Audi Q3, Audi
Q5 and Audi Q7. As pointed out by Luo et al. in [1], fine-grained images have

© Springer Nature Switzerland AG 2018
X. Sun et al. (Eds.): ICCCS 2018, LNCS 11066, pp. 647–658, 2018.
https://doi.org/10.1007/978-3-030-00015-8_56

small signal-to-noise ratios and information containing sufficient discrimination tend to exist only in small parts. Therefore, it is important to find out and utilize these discriminative parts.

In order to make full use of part information, many classification methods were heavily dependent on artificial annotations, including bounding box and part location. However, the cost of artificial annotations is so high that practicality of these methods is limited. More and more researches try to extract features from images automatically. Zhang [2] and Psyllos [3] used SIFT features to recognize the manufacture and model of a vehicle. Petrovic [4] et al. extracted many features, such as Harris corner response, edge orientation and locally normalized gradients from vehicle images to classify vehicle types. Zhang [5] combined the Gabor transform features and PHOG feature to recognize vehicle. However, the methods mentioned above are based on the artificial features. Due to the limited ability to describe the artificial features, the classification performance doesn't work well.

Recently, the great success of deep learning, especially convolutional neural networks (CNN), has aroused great interest of researchers in it. Donahue et al. [6] analyzed convolutional network models trained on ImageNet datasets and found that the features extracted from convolutional networks had stronger semantic characteristics and better discrimination than artificial features. Liu [7] reported a hierarchical joint CNN-based model to learn the multi-grained feature representations. Gao and Lee [8] proposed a framework which needed the binary image of detected of ROI and entrusted CNN to do feature extraction. In Fang's work [9], he detected discriminative regions based on feature maps extracted by CNN. And a mapping from feature maps to the input image is also established. However, it is difficult to accurately locate the region in the input image because the resolution of the feature map is quite different from that of the input image.

Inspired by these works, in this paper, we propose a novel part-based model for fine-grained vehicle recognition which can detect discriminative parts automatically. The framework of our model is illustrated in Fig. 1. There are three procedures: *part location, feature extraction* and *classification*. In *part location*, we locate discriminative parts based on the saliency map generated by back propagation. The whole image and parts are extracted feature by CNN in *feature extraction*. In *classification*, an one-against-all SVM is applied for classification.

The contribution of our work are summarized as follows:

- We present a part location method that locates the discriminative parts based on saliency maps which can be easily obtained by a single back-propagation pass. The advantage of the method is that the resolution of saliency maps is the same as the resolution of input images.
- We combine the whole-level features and part-level features by a linearity weighted method and we get a set of best weights to make the final feature most reliable.

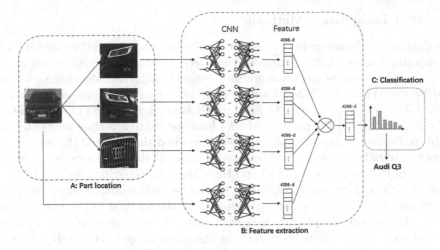

Fig. 1. The framework of our method

The remainder of this paper is organized as follows. Section 2 discusses related work. Section 3 details our overall framework based on the proposed method. Experimental results are reported in Sect. 4. Finally, we summarize the whole paper in Sect. 5.

2   Related Work

2.1   CNN

CNN is a special feedforward neural network model with a deep structure, which consists of Input Layer, Convolution Layer, Pooling Layer, Fully-connected Layer and Output Layer. Figure 2 shows a simple structure of CNN.

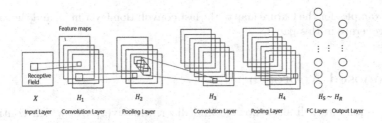

Fig. 2. A simple structure of CNN

In contrast to vision methods, which explicitly encode images into explicit feature expression, CNN is able to learn features automatically based on large-scale training data. With the development of GPU and parallel computing, there is a big advancement for big data processing capability, which also accelerates the development of CNN.

2.2 Part Localization Methods

The difficulty with fine-grained vehicle recognition is the small difference between the categories. Detecting the image and extracting features from important parts are the basic process of most fine-grained image classification algorithms. Zhang et al. proposed Part R- CNN [10] which used R-CNN to detect images and locate parts. Wei et al. [11] proposed to learn part-based segmentation model by FCN [12] and transformed the problem of part localization to a n-class segmentation problem. Besides, Fang et al. [9] proposed a method that located the important regions automatically based on the feature maps of the last convolution layer. The size of feature maps is 13 * 13 and the size of the input images is 227 * 227. Thus, it is difficult to accurately locate the region in the input image. The part localization method in this paper is inspired by the method in [9], but the size of the saliency map we generate is the same as the size of input image. Thus, it is easier to locate discriminative parts in the input images accurately. Figure 3 shows examples for the feature map of the last convolution layer in [9] and the saliency map we generate in this paper.

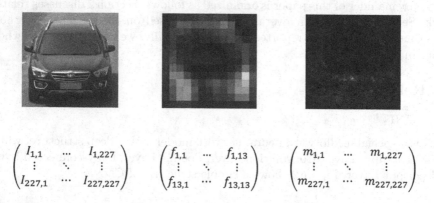

$$\begin{pmatrix} I_{1,1} & \cdots & I_{1,227} \\ \vdots & \ddots & \vdots \\ I_{227,1} & \cdots & I_{227,227} \end{pmatrix} \quad \begin{pmatrix} f_{1,1} & \cdots & f_{1,13} \\ \vdots & \ddots & \vdots \\ f_{13,1} & \cdots & f_{13,13} \end{pmatrix} \quad \begin{pmatrix} m_{1,1} & \cdots & m_{1,227} \\ \vdots & \ddots & \vdots \\ m_{227,1} & \cdots & m_{227,227} \end{pmatrix}$$

Fig. 3. Examples for the feature map of the last convolution layer in [9] and the saliency map we generate in this paper.

3 Proposed Approach

In this section, we will show how to find discriminative parts which contribute to image recognition in an unsupervised way given a set of training images of an object class and how to recognize vehicle based on the parts we find. Most of our innovations is that we can locate the useful parts which contribute more for recognition automatically by a single back-propagation pass. The process of part location is illustrated in Fig. 4.

First, we use gradient visualization method [13] to generate saliency maps. We find that only parts of the image contribute to the image classification. Then, we generate the average saliency map of the entire training set. We create binary

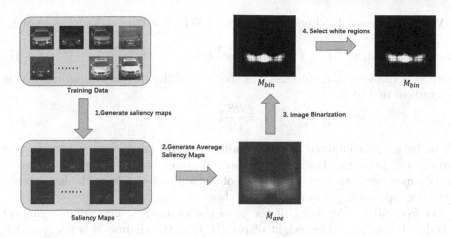

Fig. 4. Overview of part location

saliency map by a thresholding method. Based on the binary saliency map, we can locate the informative regions.

After part location, we feed these parts into CNN model and force the CNN model to focus on the key regions of the image, thereby improving the performance of fine-grained image recognition. The CNN model in this paper is shown in Fig. 5.

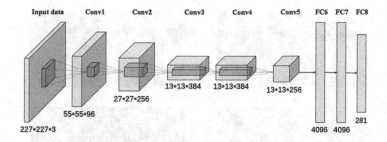

Fig. 5. Architecture of the CNN model in our paper

3.1 Saliency Map Generation

As shown in the Fig. 4, the first step in *part location* is to create saliency maps. We consider CNN as a black box. Now, let function $S(I, c)$ be the score of the class c, computed by the classification layer of the CNN for an image I. It should be noted that I is represented in the 3-dim vector(height m * width n * channel d).

As mentioned earlier, the key to fine-grained image classification is to find discriminative parts of the image. More specifically, given an image I_0 and a class c_0, we need to rank the pixels of I_0 according to their impact on the score $S(I_0, c_0)$.

We take a first order Taylor expansion of $S(I, c)$ in the neighbourhood of I_0:

$$S(I, c) \approx w^T I + b, \tag{1}$$

where w is the weight vector and b is the bias of the model. Numerically, w is the gradient of I at I_0:

$$w = \left. \frac{\partial S}{\partial I} \right|_{I_0}. \tag{2}$$

w can be easily computed by performing a single pass of back propagation through the network. The intuition behind using gradient magnitudes as a saliency measure is that the magnitude of elements of w defines the importance of the corresponding pixels of I for the class c.

Let $h(i, j, d)$ be the index of the w in the channel d. The saliency map of I_0 is denoted as M_{I_0}. The weight of pixel(i, j) in the channel d is $w_{h(i,j,d)}$. We use $\left| w_{h(i,j,d)} \right|$ as the measure of the saliency of pixel(i, j) in I_0 and take the maximum magnitude of w across all colour channels:

$$pixel(i, j) \ in \ M_{I_0} = \max_d \left| w_{h(i,j,d)} \right|, \tag{3}$$

where $1 \leq i \leq m$, $1 \leq j \leq n$. It is obvious that the shape of M_{I_0} is the same as the shape of I_0 and all the value is non-negative.

We visualize the saliency map for some images. The results are shown in Fig. 6.

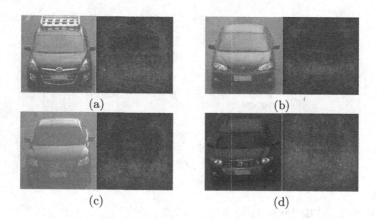

(a)   (b)

(c)   (d)

Fig. 6. Original images and its saliency maps

Saliency maps tell us how much each pixel in the I affects its class score and show the location of the target in image. The pixels with lighter color are considered to contribute more for class recognition.

3.2   Locate Regions Based on Saliency Map

Now, we simply calculate the average value of saliency maps of all images in training set to achieve the average saliency map:

$$M_{ave} = \frac{\sum\limits_{i=1}^{N} M_{I_i}}{N}, \tag{4}$$

where N is the amount of the training set, I_i is the saliency map of image for its category. The average saliency maps of entire training set M_{ave} is shown in Fig. 4. M_{ave} indicates which regions have more influence on the final prediction. The regions with brighter color are considered to be more discriminative.

Inspired by OSTU method [14], we divide the pixels in M_{ave} into class C_0 (target) and C_1 (background) by a threshold T. We would like to find an optimal threshold T^* to make C_0 and C_1 have the biggest difference. Let $N_0(T)$ and $N_1(T)$ respectively be the amount of pixels in C_0 and C_1 and N be the amount of pixels in M_{ave}. Then, let $w_0(T)$ and $w_1(T)$ be the probabilities of class occurrence:

$$w_0(T) = \frac{N_0(T)}{N}, \tag{5}$$

$$w_1(T) = \frac{N_1(T)}{N}. \tag{6}$$

Let $\mu_0(T)$ and $\mu_1(T)$ respectively be the mean of pixels in C_0 and C_1, then the mean of pixels in M_{ave} is μ:

$$\mu = w_0(T) * \mu_0(T) + w_1(T) * \mu_1(T). \tag{7}$$

The between-class variance at threshold T is denoted as:

$$\sigma^2(T) = w_0(T) * (\mu_0(T) - \mu)^2 + w_1(T) * (\mu_1(T) - \mu)^2. \tag{8}$$

By (7) and (8), we can get that:

$$\sigma^2(T) = w_0(T) * w_1(T) * (\mu_0(T) - \mu_1(T))^2. \tag{9}$$

The optimal threshold T^* that maximizes $\sigma^2(T)$ is:

$$\sigma^2(T^*) = \max_{p_{min} \leq T \leq p_{max}} \{\sigma^2(T)\}, \tag{10}$$

where p_{min} is the min pixel in M_{ave} and p_{max} is the maximum pixel in M_{ave}.

In M_{ave}, p_{min} is 0.0019 and p_{max} is 0.18298. We search a list value of T to find the optimal threshold T^*. The results of $\sigma^2(T)$ of different T are illustrated on Fig. 7. From Fig. 7, we can see that the target and background have the biggest difference when $T = 0.10$. After T^* is found, we can get the binary saliency map M_{bin} by thresholding method. M_{bin} is shown in Fig. 4. The regions with white

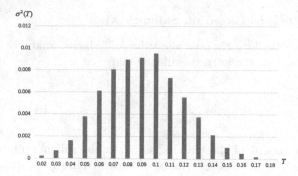

Fig. 7. The results of $\sigma^2(T)$ of different T

color are considered to be more discriminative. We choose tight rectangular to block the regions with white color. Figure 8 shows the rectangular we select. We select points (47,143) and (82,175) for rectangular A, points (87,148) and (148,179) for rectangular B, points (150,145) and (183,178) for rectangular C. When given an image, the position of discriminative parts is corresponding to the position of rectangular in Fig. 8. Figure 9 shows the process of locating parts according to the rectangular.

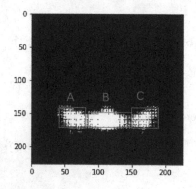

Fig. 8. The tight rectangular are selected to block white color regions

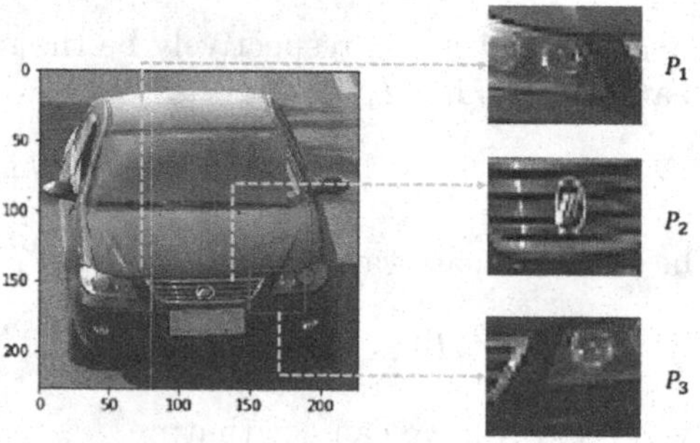

Fig. 9. The process of locating parts according to position of the rectangular in Fig. 8

3.3   Part-Based Classification

It is shown in Fig. 9, we can get three discriminative parts P_1, P_2 and P_3 for each input image I. These regions will be regarded as the new input images and be trained by the CNN model again. It is noted that each region is resized into $227 * 227$ before fed into CNN model. Depicted in Fig. 5, the output of FC7 is a 4096 dimensional feature vector. So, we get such vectors from the whole and parts for input I. Let f_0 be the feature vector from whole image and f_i be the feature vector from part P_i, $i \in \{1, 2, 3\}$. We concatenate these vectors to a 4096 dimensions vector f by a linearity weighted method:

$$f = W_0 f_0 + W_1 f_1 + W_2 f_2 + W_3 f_3, \tag{11}$$

where $0 \leq W_0, W_1, W_2, W_3 \leq 1$ and $W_0 + W_1 + W_2 + W_3 = 1$. Then, f is utilized as the input to train the one-against-all (OAA) SVM model. Assume we have L different categories. OAA will train one classifier per category in total L classifiers. For category i, it will assume i-labels as positive and the rest as negative. In the test stage, each SVM model takes on each test example and calculate the output probability of each category. The model which has the highest probability will be regarded as the corresponding category.

4 Experiment

4.1 Dataset Description and Processing

We use the surveillance-nature data captured in the front of view in the Comp-Cars [15] dataset to train our CNN model. There are 44481 images of 281 vehicle models. The dataset is split into two parts for model training and testing. The training set contains 281 vehicle models with a total of 31148 images and the testing set contains 281 vehicle models with 13333 images. In order to compute features by CNN, we firstly convert the images to a fixed $227 * 227$ pixel size, as well as the detected informative parts.

4.2 Pre-train CNN

We pre-train our CNN model using ImageNet [16] to extract deep convolutional features. Then, we fine-tune the pre-trained CNN model so as to adapt to our specific dataset and generate more features. For CompCars [15], the dimension of FC8 is set to 281. Since we use a smaller target database to fine-tune the pre-trained CNN model, the initial learning rate is set to 0.001 and reduce it by a factor 10 when there is no change in the loss anymore.

4.3 Results and Analysis

In this part, we will show the results of our experiments on the CompCars [15]. As is demonstrated in Fig. 10, the data in each category are not distributed uniformly, we use an average accuracy to evaluate our models performance:

$$\text{Average accuracy} = \frac{\sum_{i=1}^{N} \frac{p_i}{c_i}}{C}, \tag{12}$$

where C represents the amount of categories, p_i represents the number of correct prediction on i-th category and c_i is the amount of samples of i-th category. *Sklearn.svm.LinearSVC* is used in our experiments. In order to prevent

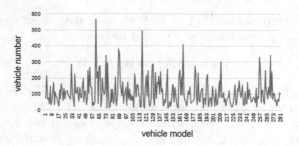

Fig. 10. Vehicle numbers of 281 models

Table 1. Results of the representative experiments.

Row	W_0	W_1	W_2	W_3	Average accuracy
1	1	0	0	0	73.79%
2	0	1	0	0	94.46%
3	0	0	1	0	95.67%
4	0	0	0	1	94.37%
5	0.5	0.5	0	0	93.27%
6	0.5	0	0.5	0	94.17%
7	0.5	0	0	0.5	94.13%
8	0.25	0.25	0.25	0.25	97.16%
9	**0.1**	**0.2**	**0.6**	**0.1**	**98.41%**

the overfitting problem, we use 10-fold cross-validation in every experiment. We conduct 120 times experiments. Table 1 shows the results of the representative experiments.

We achieve 73.79% for the whole vehicle image. The accuracies in row 2 to 4 are much higher than 73.79%, which indicates that the regions located by our method are informative. The results in row 5 to 8 reveal that feature of part P_2 achieves better performance than the feature of P_1 and P_3. The accuracy in row 8 indicates that when we utilize both the whole and subtle local feature we can achieve much better performance. When $W_0 = 0.1, W_1 = 0.2, W_2 = 0.6, W_3 = 0.1$, we achieve the best performance 98.41% as shown in row 9.

We also compare with other methods. For fair consideration, we implement their methods on the CompCars. The comparison results are shown in Table 2.

The comparison results show that our methods achieve 98.41%, better than the results of previous method. Method [8] generated parts just based on the binary maps of original images without analyzing pixels impact on category recognition. Method [5] is not adapted to large-scale dataset. Method [7] used a region proposal method and CaffeNet to learn features. The structure of CaffeNet is deeper than the structure of CNN model in this paper, but the accuracy in [7]

Table 2. The comparison results on the dataset in [15].

Methods	Average accuracy
Gao [8]	79.31%
Zhang [5]	84.57%
Liu [7]	95%
Fang [9]	98.29
Ours	**98.41%**

is lower than the accuracy of our method, which indicates that the regions we locate are more discriminative. Our approach improves the result of [9] by 0.12%. The underlying reason is that we concatenate the feature of whole image and parts by linearity weighted method. And by conducting many times experiments, we find a set of best weights to make the final feature most reliable.

5   Conclusion

In this paper, we propose a part-based model for fine-grained vehicle recognition in a weakly unsupervised manner. We present a part location method that locates the discriminative parts based on saliency maps which can be easily obtained by a single back-propagation pass. The advantage of the method is that the resolution of saliency maps is the same as the resolution of input images. Thus, we can locate discriminative parts efficiently and accurately. We combine the whole-level features and part-level features and improve the accuracy of recognition up to 98.41%. The researches in this paper hold great significance for Intelligent Traffic System. In the future, we intend to solve the problem of vehicle recognition in different viewpoints, which is a more challenge problem.

Acknowledgments. This work was supported by Research and Industrialization for Intelligent Video Processing Technology based on GPUs Parallel Computing of the Science and Technology Supported Program of Jiangsu Province (BY2016003-11) and the Application platform and Industrialization for efficient cloud computing for Big data of the Science and Technology Supported Program of Jiangsu Province (BA2015052).

References

1. Luo, J., Wu, J.: A survey on fine-grained image categorization using deep convolutional features. Zidonghua Xuebao/acta Automatica Sinica **43**(8), 1306–1318 (2010)
2. Zhang, S., Zhan, Z.: Research on vehicle classification system based on SIFT features and support vector machine. Comput. Knowl. Technol. **8**(17), 4277–4280 (2012)
3. Psyllos, A.P.: Anagnostopoulos: vehicle logo recognition using a sift-based enhanced matching scheme. IEEE Trans. Intell. Transp. Syst. **11**(2), 322–328 (2010)

4. Petrovi, C.V.: Analysis of features for rigid structure vehicle type recognition. In: British Machine Vision Conference, pp. 587–596 (2004)
5. Zhang, B.: Reliable classification of vehicle types based on cascade classifier ensembles. IEEE Trans. Intell. Transp. Syst. **14**(1), 322–332 (2013)
6. Donahue, J., Jia, Y., Vinyals, O.: Decaf: a deep convolutional activation feature for generic visual recognition. In: International Conference on Machine Learning, pp. 647–655 (2014)
7. Liu, M., Yu, C., Ling, H., Lei, J.: Hierarchical joint CNN-based models for fine-grained cars recognition. In: International Conference on Cloud Computing and Security, pp. 337–347 (2016)
8. Gao, Y., Lee, H.J.: Vehicle make recognition based on convolutional neural network. In: 2015 2nd International Conference on Information Science and Security (ICISS), pp. 1–4. IEEE (2015)
9. Fang, J., Zhou, Y., Yu, Y., Du, S.: Fine-grained vehicle model recognition using a coarse-to-fine convolutional neural network architecture. IEEE Trans. Intell. Transp. Syst. **18**(7), 1782–1792 (2017)
10. Zhang, N., Donahue, J., Girshick, R., Darrell, T.: Part-based R-CNNs for fine-grained category detection. In: Fleet, D., Pajdla, T., Schiele, B., Tuytelaars, T. (eds.) ECCV 2014. LNCS, vol. 8689, pp. 834–849. Springer, Cham (2014). https://doi.org/10.1007/978-3-319-10590-1_54
11. Wei, X.S., Xie, C.W.: Mask-CNN: localizing parts and selecting descriptors for fine-grained bird species categorization. Pattern Recognit. **76**, 704–714 (2018)
12. Shelhamer, E., Long, J., Darrell, T.: Fully convolutional networks for semantic segmentation. IEEE Trans. Pattern Anal. Mach. Intell. **39**(4), 640 (2017)
13. Simonyan, K., Vedaldi, A., Zisserman, A.: Deep inside convolutional networks: visualising image classification models and saliency maps. arXiv preprint arXiv:1312.6034 (2013)
14. Otsu, N.: A threshold selection method from gray-level histograms. IEEE Trans. Syst. Man Cybern. **9**(1), 62–66 (1979)
15. Yang, L., Luo, P., Chen, C.L., Tang, X.: A large-scale car dataset for fine-grained categorization and verification. In: Computer Vision and Pattern Recognition, pp. 3973–3981 (2015)
16. Deng, J., Dong, W., Socher, R., Li, L.J., Li, K., Li, F.: Imagenet: a large-scale hierarchical image database. In: IEEE Conference on Computer Vision and Pattern Recognition, CVPR 2009, pp. 248–255 (2009)

A Novel Photovoltaic Cell Simulator for Green Internet of Things

Zhe Wang⑩, Weidong Yi, Yongrui Chen(✉), and Ming Li

University of Chinese Academy of Sciences, 100049 Beijing, China
chenyr@ucas.ac.cn

Abstract. This paper designs and implements a new type of photovoltaic cell simulator based on LabVIEW platform, which is used to simulate the output I-V characteristics of photovoltaic cells. The main contribution of this work is the implementation of the point-by-point comparison algorithm, which is used to control the power supply of a photovoltaic cell to follow a given I-V output curve on the LabVIEW platform. The experimental results show that the photovoltaic cell simulator can achieve 96% accuracy, and can be used as a reliable tool for the simulation of the MPPT (Maximum Power Point Tracking) algorithm and the analysis of power supplies of sensor nodes in green internet of things.

Keywords: Photovoltaic cell simulator
Point-by-point difference comparison algorithm · LabVIEW
Programmable power supply

1 Introduction

The explosive expansion of Internet of Things (IoT) leads to a large amount of energy consumptions. To ease the burden of the energy demands from interconnecting all kinds of things, the greenness of IoT is crucial for the success of IoT. Green IoT means saving the energy consumption, reducing the environment pollution as well as resource waste. Besides improving the energy efficiency of IoT devices, it's also a vital research area on how to power IoT devices with green energy resources instead of traditional ways.

Solar energy is a clean and inexhaustible energy source. Therefore, using photovoltaic (PV) cells to power IoT devices is one of the effective ways to achieve the Green IoT. As for the appliance of PV cells, one of the most important considerations is how to ensure the optimal utilization of solar energy. Due to its high cost, and the varying output characteristic of PV cells which is greatly affected by environment conditions (e.g., temperature, illumination and weather), the process of developing a solar powering system based on PV cells will be expensive and slow. Therefore, by emulating the PV output characteristics with a PV cell simulator, it will be much more convenient for the development and test for PV systems.

Ishaque [4] established a PV system simulation model with dual diodes, the model can combine the MPPT algorithm with the actual electronic power converter circuit on MATLAB Simulink. However, the interaction of the photovoltaic cell model proposed

© Springer Nature Switzerland AG 2018
X. Sun et al. (Eds.): ICCCS 2018, LNCS 11066, pp. 659–670, 2018.
https://doi.org/10.1007/978-3-030-00015-8_57

in this article for MPPT was only performed in the simulation, and the practically available photovoltaic cell simulator was not made. Deng [5] designed a digital photovoltaic array simulator based on the ARM control, and the main circuit is BUCK circuit. The simulator could well fit the solar cell output curve. Whereas, this design only considers the simulation of photovoltaic arrays under standard conditions (S = 1000 W/m^2, T = 25 °C) and cannot simulate the output of photovoltaic arrays in other environmental conditions. Unlu and Camur [6] proposed a relatively simple and low-cost photovoltaic simulator that consist of a DC power supply and a power diode to establish the relationship between the output current and the light intensity of the photovoltaic cells work in. The simulator obtains the I-V curve of the photovoltaic cell under the desired light intensity by adjusting the output value of the DC power supply. At the same time, due to the fact that the design of the current cannot be adjusted to a very precise degree, it is difficult to obtain the photovoltaic cell I-V characteristics under exact light intensity and temperature. Hassan Hosseini [7] designed a photovoltaic cell simulator using two microprocessors to control a DC/DC converter, this design is high-precision and no power limitation, but it is complicated in model and slow in operation.

LabVIEW is a graphical programming language. Over the years, an increasing number of projects using LabVIEW to test and simulate photovoltaic cell system. Han [12] proposed a photovoltaic cell simulator based on LabVIEW. The hardware devices this simulator used include power amplifier circuits, signal conditioning circuits and data acquisition cards. Liu [13] used LabVIEW and Simulink hybrid programming to implement the modeling and simulation of photovoltaic system and provided basis for in-depth research on other aspects of photovoltaic power generation systems. However, it is only a simulation system and cannot be used as a photovoltaic cell simulator which could replace a photovoltaic cell to research. Jaya et al. [14] established a mathematical model for photovoltaic cells using LabVIEW, coupled with a DAQ PCI-6251 acquisition card and NI-ELVIS virtual instrument to implement a photovoltaic simulator for testing photovoltaic cell MPPT algorithms, cause a high cost to implement this simulator.

According to previous experience, this paper adopts the improved mathematical model of solar cell single-diode circuit and uses the point-by-point difference comparison algorithm so that the output converge at the static working point of the load. Using LabVIEW to control programmable power supply to output photovoltaic cells I-V characteristics curve by implementing point-by-point difference comparison algorithm. The point-by-point difference comparison algorithm is simple in calculation and fast in speed, it is appropriate as a photovoltaic simulator algorithm. The proposed photovoltaic cell simulator does not require additional hardware circuit design nor complex software programs. Cost-saving, simple in structure and fast algorithm are the features of the proposed photovoltaic cell simulator.

2   Mathematical Model of Photovoltaic Cells

To design a photovoltaic cells simulator, selecting the appropriate mathematical model for photovoltaic cells is a significant part. The equivalent circuit of the photovoltaic cell is shown in Fig. 1. On the base of this equivalent circuit, the I-V algebraic relationship of the photovoltaic cell can be given by formula (1).

$$I = I_{pv} - I_0 \left\{ \exp\left[\frac{q(V + IR_S)}{AKT}\right] - 1 \right\} - \frac{V + IR_s}{R_{sh}} \tag{1}$$

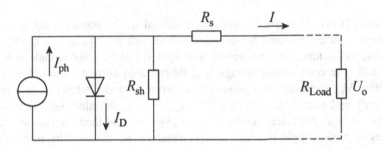

Fig. 1. Photovoltaic cell equivalent circuit

Among them, I_{pv} is the photogenic current, which is proportional to the amount of sunlight irradiance in the environment. R_{sh} is the equivalent parallel resistance, and the main reason for its formation is the leakage resistance of the P-N junction corresponding to the leakage current. R_s is the equivalent series resistance and is mainly formed by the PV panel's bulk resistance, the surface resistance, the electrode conductor resistance, and the contact resistance between the electrode and the silicon surface. I and V are the output current and voltage of photovoltaic cells. I_0 is the reverse saturation current of P-N junction. A is the p-n junction curve parameter. T is the absolute temperature and K is the Boltzmann constant (1.38×10^{-23} J/K).

As shown above, it is tough to obtain the definite value of each parameter in formula (1), means adopting formula (1) to establishing mathematical model of PV is very difficult. Therefore, a simplified PV cell mathematical model which is suitable for engineering applications needs to be established according to a sequence of translation from formula (1).

Ignore $\frac{V + IR_s}{R_{sh}}$, since it is usually much smaller than the photocurrent. When setting $I_{pv} = I_{sc}$, R_s is usually much smaller than the forward conduction resistance of the diode, so formula (1) can be simplified as:

$$I = I_{sc} \left\{ 1 - C_1 \left[\exp\left(\frac{V}{C_2 V_{oc}}\right) - 1 \right] \right\} \tag{2}$$

At the maximum power point, $V = V_m$, $I = I_m$, taken into formula (2) and the -1 term in (2) could be ignored, so the expression about C_1 can be obtained:

$$C_1 = \left(1 - \frac{I_m}{I_{sc}}\right)\exp\left(-\frac{V_m}{C_2 V_{oc}}\right) \tag{3}$$

Again, under the open-circuit condition, $I = 0$, $V = V_{oc}$, and formula (3) is taken into formula (2), the expression for C_2 can be obtained:

$$C_2 = \left(\frac{V_m}{V_{oc}} - 1\right) * \left[\ln\left(1 - \frac{I_m}{I_{oc}}\right)\right]^{-1} \tag{4}$$

Formula (2) (3) (4) is the PV cell mathematical model equation set used in this paper. The parameters required for this photovoltaic cell model are V_{oc}, I_{sc}, V_m, I_m for photovoltaic cells, ambient temperature and light intensity. Photovoltaic cell manufacturers will give open circuit voltage V_{oc}, short circuit current I_{sc}, maximum power point voltage V_m, and maximum power point current I_m under reference light intensity (1000 W/m^2) and temperature(25 °C). V'_{oc}, I'_{sc}, V'_m, I'_m in other light intensity and specific temperature are calculated by formula (5)–(10), and then the Photovoltaic cell IV Curves in specific light intensity and temperature are obtained by inserting those parameters to Eqs. (2)–(4). The variables in this mathematical model are temperature T and light intensity S.

$$\Delta T = T - T_{ref} \tag{5}$$

$$\Delta S = \frac{S}{S_{ref}} - 1 \tag{6}$$

$$I'_{sc} = I_{sc}\frac{S}{S_{ref}}(1 + a\Delta T) \tag{7}$$

$$V'_{oc} = V_{oc}(1 - c\Delta T)\ln(1 + b\Delta S) \tag{8}$$

$$I'_m = I_m\frac{S}{S_{ref}}(1 + a\Delta T) \tag{9}$$

$$V'_m = V_m(1 - c\Delta T)\ln(1 + b\Delta S) \tag{10}$$

Among them,

$$a = 0.0025/°C$$
$$b = 0.5$$
$$c = 0.00288/°C$$

Figures 2 and 3 are the I-V curves of photovoltaic cells at different temperatures and different light intensities obtained by using MATLAB according to the above-mentioned mathematical model of photovoltaic cells.

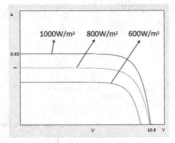

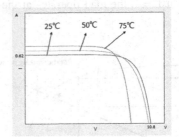

Fig. 2. I-V characteristics under different light intensities

Fig. 3. I-V characteristics under different temperatures

3 Determination of Static Working Point

For a fixed photovoltaic cell, its output I-V curve is also fixed at a certain light intensity and temperature, and the output power is shifted between $0-P_m$. The specific operating point of the photovoltaic cell is determined according to the load characteristics. The intersection of the characteristic curve of the solar cell and the load characteristic is the working point of the load, also called the static working point. Determining the static operating point is a very important part of the photovoltaic cell simulator.

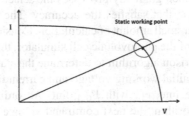

Fig. 4. Static working point

When the simulator is driving the load, the output voltage or current needs to be adjusted so that the operating point of the load is on the output I-V curve of the simulated solar cell. When taking the load voltage V as the reference, the mathematical model of the photovoltaic cell is used to calculate $I' = F(V)$. F is the mathematical model of the photovoltaic cell, and the load current is I at this time. As shown in Figs. 4, 5 and 6, the adjustment load operating point is divided into three situations:

1. When $I' > I$, the output voltage V should be increased;
2. When $I' < I$, the output voltage should be reduced;
3. When $I' = I$, the load operates at the static operating point.

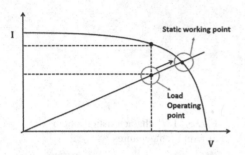

Fig. 5. Work point adjustment 1   **Fig. 6.** Work point adjustment 2

$I' = I$, i.e. $F(V) = I$, at which point the load operating point lies at the intersection of its load characteristic curve and the I-V curve of the photovoltaic cell. Determining the direction of adjusting the operating point and adjusting the voltage step size are all performed by the iterative algorithm.

The numerical iterative algorithm is a successive approximation method, the approximate process of this algorithm is giving an initial value first, according to a certain rule, and then repeating recursive and taking iterative calculation, so that the middle value of each calculation is gradually approaching a stable value. The point-by-point difference comparison algorithm is a successive approximation algorithm that first provides an iterative initial value, and then gradually processes the selected initial value of the iteration into an iterative value that satisfies the accuracy. The point-by-point difference comparison algorithm has a small amount of calculation. Considering the requirements of the real-time performance of the photovoltaic cell simulator, this article selects the point-by-point difference comparison algorithm to determine the static operating point.

First at all, detect the initial working voltage and current of the load: I_0, V_0, current I_0 and PV cell I-V curve intersect with P_0 point. According to the point-by-point difference comparison algorithm, the next command voltage should be:

$$V_1 = V_0 + K[F(I_0) - V_0]$$

$K[F(I_0) - V_0]$ is the iteration step length and $V = F(I)$ is the photovoltaic cell mathematical model. In this paper, in order to facilitate the calculation, using K as the iteration step and $\text{sign}[F(I_0) - V_0]$ as the iteration direction, the next command voltage should be:

$$V_1 = V_0 + K\text{sign}[F(I_0) - V_0]$$

The load current at V_1 is detected as I_1, the current I_1 intersects with the photovoltaic cell I-V curve at point P_1, and the next command voltage is:

$$V_2 = V_1 + K\mathrm{sign}[F(I_1) - V_1]$$

In this order, the command voltages are V_0, V_1, V_2,..., V_n, and the corresponding load currents intersect with the photovoltaic cells' I-V curve sequentially at P_0, P_1, P_2, ..., P_n, and finally converge to the static operating point. The algorithm principle is shown in Fig. 7 and the flow is shown in Fig. 8.

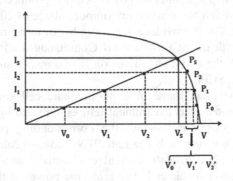

Fig. 7. The working principle of point-by-point difference comparison algorithm

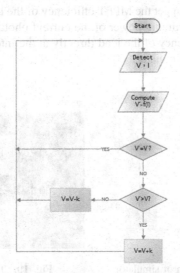

Fig. 8. The flow chart of point-by-point difference comparison algorithm

4 Implementation and Verification of Simulator

4.1 Implementation of Simulator

Proposed simulator is implemented through program programmable power supply APS-1102 which controlled by LabVIEW. LabVIEW has two interfaces, the program panel and the front panel. The program panel edits the calculation steps and the front panel displays various types of controls, like data input and display controls and so on. Using LabVIEW programming is not only convenient and concise but also has a good user interface.

The APS-1102 is a programmable power supply produced by the Good Will Instrument Company, which has a maximum output voltage of 200 V and a maximum output capability of 1 kVA. It provides a large number of measurement functions. The APS-1102 complies with the SCPI (Standard Commands for Programmable Instruments) standard. Install the USBTMC driver on the computer and then communicate with the APS-1102 via SCPI.

Figure 9 shows the basic frame of a photovoltaic cell simulator. User inputs photovoltaic cell parameters, sets the ambient temperature and light intensity, and the programmable power supply can output the corresponding photovoltaic cell I-V characteristic curve to drive the load. The LabVIEW program calculates the maximum power of the photovoltaic cell in the current environment according to the mathematical model of the photovoltaic cell. The real-time power of the load is calculated according to the current voltage and current of the load detected by programmable power supply. The real-time power of the load divide the maximum output of the photovoltaic cell, and we can get the MPPT efficiency of the load. As shown in Fig. 10, the user can acquire the maximum power of the current photovoltaic cell, the operating power and the MPPT efficiency of the load directly at the interface. Figure 10 shows a real shot of the entire PV simulator.

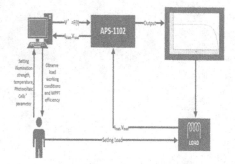

Fig. 9. The frame diagram of simulator

Fig. 10. The photo of simulator

4.2   Verification of the Simulator

In order to verify the reliability and effectiveness of the photovoltaic cell simulator and ensure that the photovoltaic cell simulator can work accurately, three sets of experiments were designed.

Experiment Setup

The first experiment is to compare the actual current of the photovoltaic cell simulator with theoretical current under the same voltage. The second experiment is the comparison of the current, voltage and power of the photovoltaic cell and the photovoltaic simulator under the same load. The third experiment is to test the working condition of the circuit board with MPPT algorithm under the photovoltaic cell simulator. The fourth experiment is to test the output change of the photovoltaic cell simulator when the load, light intensity, and temperature changed.

In the second experiment, the output of the photovoltaic cell and the photovoltaic cell simulator in the same light environment is tested, but it is difficult to obtain a regular light intensity in a natural light source environment to measure the output of the photovoltaic cell under different light intensities. The spectrum of a xenon lamp is similar to sunlight. Using a xenon lamp to simulate a sun light source, adjusting the power of the xenon lamp can obtain different light intensities. Therefore, using a xenon lamp to build a simulated solar light environment. As shown in Fig. 12, the left side is a power controller and the right side is a xenon lamp.

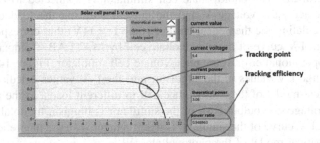

Fig. 11. MPPT tracking display

The xenon lamp is placed on the top of the test bench, and a space of $60 * 35 * 40$ cm^3 is surrounded by four movable aluminum plates. The power controller controls the power of the xenon lamp to simulate the change of the light intensity of the solar light source. At the same time, a wider range of the light intensity can be obtained by disassembling or installing the four aluminum plates. The TES-1333R is a record-type solar energy meter that can measure the solar power at different azimuths and angles, it used to measure the light intensity in the simulated solar light environment. Figure 13 shows that the photovoltaic cell was tested under a simulated solar light source environment.

XHH3-9 is the production type of the actual photovoltaic cell used in this paper. At a temperature of 25 °C and an illumination of 1000 W/m^2, this photovoltaic cell's open circuit voltage $V_{oc} = 10.85$ V, the short circuit current $I_{sc} = 0.38$ A, and the maximum power point voltage $V_m = 9$ V, current $I_m = 0.34$ A.

Fig. 12. Simulated solar light experimental environment

Fig. 13. Photovoltaic cell was tested under a simulated solar light environment

In the third experiment, the power management module based on the TI charge management chip BQ24650 developed by the laboratory was used. The MPPT algorithm used in this power management module is the [10] P&O perturbation algorithm. Test the MPPT efficiency of the power management module under the photovoltaic cell simulator.

Experimental Results

The first experiment: The photovoltaic cell simulator is connected to the load with different resistances, the voltage V and the current I during the load operation are measured. Calculating the theoretical current value $I' = F(V)$ that corresponds voltage V on the output I-V curve of the photovoltaic cell by MATLAB. Comparing I and I', calculate the operational error of the photovoltaic cell simulator. Figure 14 is the result that compares the I-V values of the simulator and the I'-V values calculated by using the mathematical model of the photovoltaic cell in different loads. In the area near the open circuit voltage, the output error of the simulator is biggish, the total error is 5%, and the output I-V curve of the simulator is in agreement with the theoretical I-V curve of the mathematical model of the photovoltaic cell.

The second experiment:Actual photovoltaic cell XHH3-9 and photovoltaic cell simulator were respectively connected to the same load, and the relative errors of the output voltage, current, and power of the load under the photovoltaic cell and the simulator under different illumination intensities were measured. The relative error is defined as the difference between the V, I, and P values of the photovoltaic cell and the simulator and then divided by the value of the photovoltaic cell. The test results are shown in Fig. 15. The errors of voltage and current between Photovoltaic cell and photovoltaic cell simulator is less than 4% at different light intensities and same load.

The third experiment:The simulator connected the BQ24650 power management board with the P&O disturbance MPPT algorithm. The simulator output can be traced to the vicinity of the MPP, and the tracking efficiency is about 95%, which is in line with the efficiency of the P&O disturbance MPPT algorithm tracking. Figure 11 is the

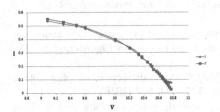

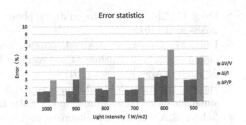

Fig. 14. Comparison between simulator measurements and theoretical calculations

Fig. 15. The relative error of V, I, P between photovoltaic battery and simulator

work display interface of the photovoltaic cell simulator connected to the power management module containing the MPPT algorithm.

The four test results of the above for simulator can indicate that the photovoltaic cell simulator is working correct and reliable, and can replace the photovoltaic cell as an effective tool for the development of photovoltaic system and the research of MPPT algorithm.

5 Conclusion

Using PV cells to power IoT devices is an effective strategy of Green IoT. To facilitate the research of photovoltaic cells, this paper proposed a novel photovoltaic cell simulator by implementing the point-by-point difference comparison algorithm to control the programmable power supply on the LabVIEW platform. The experimental verification shows that the photovoltaic cell simulator can output the I-V curve that satisfies the characteristics of the PV cell. The error of current value between the simulator output and the theoretic value of photovoltaic cell mathematical model at the same voltage is 5%. Under the same load, the deviation of the current and voltage between the PV simulator and actual PV cell is less than 4%. The simulator output changes rapidly in the wake of different load and external environment, additional, the operation and test of MPPT algorithm could be carried out. The proposed simulator can replace actual PV cells to develop photovoltaic cell system and can be used as a reliable tool for the research of the Green IoT node which powered by PV cells.

References

1. Chouder, A., et al.: Modeling and simulation of a grid connected PV system based on the evaluation of main PV module parameters. Simul. Model. Pract. Theory **20**, 46–58 (2012)
2. Riordan, H.: The origins of the PN junction. IEEE Spectr. **34**, 46–51 (1997)
3. Tan, Y.T.: A model of PV generation suitable for stability analysis. IEEE Trans. Energy Convers. **19**(4), 748–754 (2004)
4. Ishaque, K., Salam, Z.: Accurate MATLAB simulink PV system simulator based on a two-diode model. J. Power Electron. **11**(2), 179–187 (2011)

5. Deng, C., Liu, X.: ARM-based digital photovoltaic cell simulator. Power Technol. **139**(12), 2688–2691 (2015)
6. Unlu, M., Camur, S.: A simple photovoltaic simulator based on a one-diode equivalent circuit mode. In: International Conference on Electrical and Electronics Engineering, pp. 33–36. United Arab Emirates (2017)
7. Hassan Hosseini, S.M., Keymanesh, A.A.: Design and construction of photovoltaic simulator based on dual-diode mode. Solar Energy **137**, 594–607 (2016)
8. Salam, R.A., et al.: Development of a simple low-scale solar simulator and its light distribution. In: 2016 International Conference on Instrumentation, Control and Automation (ICA), pp. 29–31. Institut Teknologi Bandung (ITB), Bandung (2016)
9. Shinde, U.K., et al.: Dual mode controller-based solar photovoltaic simulator for true PV characteristics. Can. J. Electr. Comput. Eng. **40**(3), 237–245 (2017)
10. Paz, F., Ordonez, M.: Zero-oscillation adaptive-step solar maximum power point tracking for rapid irradiance tracking and steady-state losses minimization. In: 2013 IEEE International Symposium on Power Electronics for Distributed Generation Systems (PEDG), pp. 1–6 (2013)
11. Nzimako, O., Wierckx, R.: Modeling and simulation of a grid-integrated photovoltaic system using a real-time digital simulator. IEEE Trans. Ind. Appl. **53**(2), 1326–1336 (2017)
12. Han, X.: Design of photovoltaic cell simulator based on PXI and LabVIEW. East Chin. Electr. Power **40**(5), 882–884 (2012)
13. Liu, Y.: Simulation of photovoltaic power generation system based on LabVIEW and simulink mixed programming. Power Technol. **40**(10), 1987–1989 (2016)
14. Agrawal, J.H., et al.: Photovoltaic simulator developed in LabVIEW for evaluation of MPPT techniques. In: 2016 International Conference on Electrical, Electronics, and Optimization Techniques, Chennai, India, pp. 1142–1147 (2016)

A Review of Privacy-Preserving Machine Learning Classification

Andy Wang[1], Chen Wang[1], Meng Bi[1,3], and Jian Xu[1,2(✉)]

[1] Software College, Northeastern University, Shenyang 110169, China
xuj@mail.neu.edu.cn
[2] State Key Laboratory of Information Security (Institute of Information Engineering, The Chinese Academy of Sciences), Beijing 100093, China
[3] Shenyang University of Technology, Shenyang 110023, China

Abstract. Machine Learning (ML) Classification has already become one of the most commonly used techniques in many areas such as banking, medicine, spam detection and data mining applications. Often, the training of models require massive data which may contain sensitive information and the classification phase may expose the train models and the inputs from the users. Neither the models nor the train datasets and inputs should expose private information. Addressing this goal, several schemes have been proposed for privacy preserving classification. In this paper, we review those privacy preserving techiniques which applied for different machine learning classification algorithms. These algorithms conclude k-NN, SVM, Bayesian, neural networks, decision tree and etc. we sum up the comparison protocols. Finally, this work comes up with some correlative problems which are worthy to study in the future.

Keywords: Machine learning · Privacy preserving · Classification Comparison protocol

1 Introduction

In recent years, machine learning (ML) classification is widely concerned and has led to great success in variety of applications, including spam detection [1], abnormal behavior detection, face recognition, picture classification [2], autopilot and more areas which is associates with our daily life. These shows that ML classification will gradually penetrate into all areas of our lives and become a key technology to facilitate our lives and promote social progress.

ML classification has include two stage, depicted in Fig. 1. One is the training phase during which the algorithm trains a large amount of labeled examples to get model w. These datasets almost sensitive and private which are collected from different data owners. Another is testing phase that uses the model w to test an new comming feature vector x and then output a label c which is the most posibility it belongings to.

Supported by Fundamental Research Funds for the Central Universities (N171704005) and Shenyang Science and Technology Plan Projects (18-013-0-01).

© Springer Nature Switzerland AG 2018
X. Sun et al. (Eds.): ICCCS 2018, LNCS 11066, pp. 671–682, 2018.
https://doi.org/10.1007/978-3-030-00015-8_58

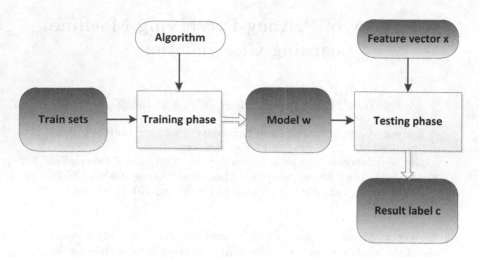

Fig. 1. Machine learning classification Model. Each shaded box means private data that should not be exposed. non-shaded box indicates an algorithm, each rectangle indicates an processing phase, single arrows means inputs and double arrows indicates outputs.

Desipite tremendous advantages that ML classification offers, privacy and security issues in the training and testing phase can present an obstacle to data owners to outsource their data to train centers. For instance, as reported in Kaufman et al. [3] about 90% of respondents has privacy concerns when considering contribution to biobanks. Hence, researchers have developed techniques to protect the privacy and confidentiality of the data, training and testing phase.

There are reviews and introductions to privacy preserving techniques aimed at different ML classification algorithms and each with different data distribution (Fang 2015 [4]; Bharath 2015 [5]; Barthe 2016 [6]; Dou 2018 [7]). The aim of this paper is to provide ML classification learners with sufficient knowledge to become involved in developing privacy-preserving techniques to ML classification. As part of this effort we introduce three main privacy preserving techniques and sum up some comparison protocols which is the basic and necessary operation used in training and testing phase. In the end of this paper we present some correlative problems that can be considered in the future.

In Sect. 2 reviews three kinds of ML techniques which have been successfully implemented for different algorithms by researhers. Section 3 lists up some comparison protocols. Section 4 prospects the next research trend of privacy-preserving ML classification.

2   Privacy Preserving Techniques

This section reviews the main privacy preserving techniques with an emphasis on their applications for different algorithms and insufficient that each techniques have.

2.1 Differential Privacy

Differential privacy [8–11] is emerging as a gold standard in data privacy. Its definition was first proposed in CynthiaDwork's ICALP paper [12]. It can be achieved by adding randomized noise to aggregate data to protect individual entries without significantly altering. The differential privacy algorithm guarantees that the personal data an attacker can acquire is almost the same as the data they obtained from a dataset without this person's record.

Differential privacy has several properties that make it especially useful in many applications:

(1) *Composability.* It means if each component in a mechanism is differential privacy then the composition of them is the same.
(2) *Deal with large datasets.* It means differential privacy works well on big datasets, where the presence or absence of an individual has limited affect.
(3) *Group privacy.* If datasets contain correlated inputs such as the records contributed by the same user, it can implie smooth degradation.
(4) *The Robustness of side information.* The auxiliary information gets by the adversary can not threat the individuals privacy.

Abadi et al. [13] use the property (1)(3)(4) developed privacy-preserving deep neural networks ML scheme. They designed new mini-batch stochastic gradient descent (SGD) algorithm to improve the computational efficiency of differentially private training and use non-convex objectives, several layers, and many parameters to train models while keep modest privacy loss. They use two datasets MNIST and CIFAR-10 to do the experiment on the TensorFlow [14] software library. As their approach applies directly to gradient computations, so it can be used in other optimization methods, such as SVRG [15], AdaGrad [16]. Although the training of deep neural networks with differential privacy achieved well, the accuracy should be improved for larger datasets not only for MNIST and CIFAR-10.

Gaboardi et al. [6] make use of the property (1) and (2) designed a framework, PrivInfer, achieving differentially private Bayesian inference. PrivInfer is composed of two parts: PCF, a probabilistic functional language and a relational higher-order type system which is used for verify differential privacy for programs wriiten in PCF. The framework has three advantages, it enables to write functional programs such as data analysis for Bayesian inference and also permits adding noise to them in different ways using different metrics. Moreover, it allows to infer f-divergences for Bayesian inference.

Other works [10,17,18] also use property (2) to design privacy-preserving ML techniques with the help of machine learning community and the differential privacy community.

Although differential privacy has been well applied in ML classification, it can not guarantee the semantic security of data and also the accuracy of classification result is poor. So there appears another privacy preserving technique which we called homomorphic encryption.

2.2 Homomorphic Encryption

Data privacy issues can hinder statistical analysis and data acquisition and application of ML algorithms. Traditional encryption methods can ensure the long-term storage of information security, but when the data is analyzed, it needs to be decrypted first.

Rivest et al. [19] first proposed an idea in 1978: it is possible to design an encryption scheme that can support a limited number of mathematical operations on undecrypted data. And later they proposed one homomorphic encryption, RSA [20] which is only support multiplication operation. Other homomorphic encryptions are showed in Table 1.

Table 1. Type of homomorphic encryption

Number	Homomorphic encryption	Operation support	Year
1	RSA [20]	Multiplication	1978
2	Goldwasser-Macali (GM) [21]	Addition	1982
3	ElGamal [22]	Multiplication	1985
3	Paillier [23]	Addition	1999

From Table 1 we can see that they only support addition or multiplication, and with the times of addition or multiplication increase the noise is becoming more which may led to wrong decryption, such that they only support limited addition or multiplication. It was not until 2009 that Gentry et al. [24] proposed an encryption scheme that theoretically supports arbitrary operations which is called fully homomorphic encryption scheme (FHE). This scheme allows a mathematical operation such as addition and multiplication to be performed directly on a ciphertext. The result is encrypted, and the decrypted result is consist with the result of the execution on the plaintext. Aslett et al. [25] proposed that "Although homomorphic encryption schemes theoretically guarantee arbitrary computations, the actual constraints mean that many current algorithms cannot achieve this". This has motivated scholars to study customization machine learning algorithms and putting it into practical interest.

Yu et al. [26] proposed a privacy-preserving SVM on horizontally partitioned data by using nonlinear kernels, and also considered the vertically partitioned data in [27]; however, they only focus on the data represented by binary feature vectors. Laur et al. [28] designed kernelized SVM, which outputs encrypted kernel value, classifier or classifications. However, all the above mehods are limited to the distributed model as showed in Fig. 2 where users hold the data in plaintext locally. Fang et al. [4] implemented Outsourced SVM classification on outsourced model as showed in Fig. 3 where data outsourced, centralized and encrypted; they implemented three protocols that's KernelMatrixProtocol, SVMModelSetup, SVMClassification among one querier, one cloud and one data owner who all semi-honest. Moreover achived from training to classification phase over FHE data. But, in the above phase the data owners and the querier should online all the time.

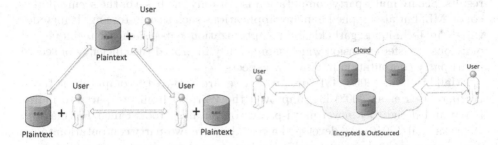

Fig. 2. Distributed model   **Fig. 3.** Outsourced model

Bharath et al. [5] implemented k-Nearest neighbor classificaion over semantically secure encrypted relational data. They use an Somewhat Homomorphic Encryption (SFHE) Paillier to encrypt the data and also outsource them to the cloud, at the same time data owners send the secret key to another cloud, the two clouds are semi-honest and not collusion. They designed some subprotocols such as Secure Multiplication (SM) Protocol, Secure Squared Euclidean Distance (SSED) Protocol, Secure Minimum (SMIN) Protocol and etc., through call the subprotocols in the main protocol to accomplish the classification. It's worhty to mention that they encrypted the class label which is never done and the data owners and the querier are offline after uploading the private data, as they have two clouds, the computational works all done by them. However, if the two cloud are collusion, the classification will not secure anymore.

Li et al. [29] proposed multi-key privacy-perserving deep learning on outsourced encrypted data, focusing on multi-key problems. In compare with above only have one key scheme, this is more practical in real world. Each data owners encrypted data with their own keys, guaranteed all operations including intermediate results is secure and reduced the computational and communication costs by only decrypt operation needs the communication among data owners.

2.3   Secure Muti-party Computation

The number of sensitive data that are digitally recorded is rapidly increasing. In payments, transportation, navigation, shopping, and health, people now rely more on digital services than ever before. Apart from outsourced data to cloud, there are numerous situations where multiparties would like to share data for a common goal. The collection of safe multi-party computation has become an important scientific issue.

The existing solution is basically about a two-party set of security calculations. The concept of two-party Secure Function Evaluation(SFE) was mention in 1982 by Yao [30]. In the setting of secure multi-party computation, two or more paties with encrypted inputs hope to calculate some joint function of their private inputs without explose any information about their inputs beyond the outputs and the processing, and also need to get correct encrypted or unenrypted results. Secure multi-party computation is not only the basic of the secure protocol on ML, but also applied in many applications such as coin-tossing. It includes three core techniques: garbeld circuits optimization, cut-and-choose techique and oblivious transfer extension which significantly improved the efficiency of secure multi-party computation in different aspects.

Malkhi et al. (2004) [31] designed a secure two-party computation tools, Fairplay. Ben et al.(2008) [32] improved the Fairplay from two-party to multi-party and designed a novel mutli-party computation tools called Fairplaymp. Henecka et al. (2010) [33] developed a genral secure two-party computation tools, Tasty, using garbled circuits, and it implemented the exchange among plaintext, homomorphic value and garbled value. These tools all support general functions, which are addtion, multiplication. Bost et al. (2015) [34] designed a novel secure two-party computation framework and use it to develop a series of secure two-party protocols for basic operations such as addition, dot product, comparison and with the help of modular sequential composition technique successfully implemented three machine learning classification: hyperplane decisions, naive Bayes and binary decision trees. Compare with Fairplaymp and Tasty it's more efficient when applying in machine learning classification. However, they only implemented the testing phase.

The above researchs almost interaction among parties who either data owners or querier, with the advent of cloud computing, there are also some attempts to outsource a part of the multi-party computation which based on secret sharing to the cloud servers to mitigate the computation costs.

Jakobsen et al. [35] researched oursource the gate circuit calculation interaction protocol, which is one part of the secure multi-party computation protocol and participates by n parties, to m cloud servers. In their settings, the servers can not be trusted, but at least one server be honest; the inputs from the parties is secret at the same time everyone can get the correct results which only known by themselves even the untrusted cloud can not tamper them. Through outsourced this they minimize the communication complexity of parties which only need to upload inputs and download outputs. Asharov et al. [36] implemented secure multi-party computing protocol based on homomorphic encryption in cloud, where the homomorphic private keys are shared to all parties through threshold fully homomorphic encryption (TFHE) avoiding the collusion of clouds.

3   Comparison Protocols

Resent advances in Homomorphic Encryption promise to enable secure ML classification on encrypted data, whereby a limited set of operations can be carried out without the need to first decrypt. However, the comparison operation is not directly supported by homomorphic encryption and it's an essential part of implementing a ML classifier model on a ciphertext domain, so researchers starts to design comparison protocols based on homomorphic encrypted datasets. In this section we will review some comparison protocols of Table 2, which are called in the training and testing phase.

Table 2. Summary of comparison protocols

Number	Encryption scheme	Participants
1	Somewhat Homomorphic Encryption (SWHE)	One-party
2	Paillier & Quadratic Residuosity (QR)	Two-party
3	Paillier	Two-party

3.1 Comparison with SWHE Encrypted Inputs

Jiang et al. [37] implemented a comparison protocol based on SWHE encrypted inputs. It's corresponding to Row 1. In their settings, they divide a compare computation operation into three relationships: $L(A > B)$, $M(A < B)$ and $G(A = B)$, where A and B are inputs of n bits integers. They combine the Digital Value Comparator and SWHE scheme to construct an Multi-bit ciphertext numerical comparator. The idea is as follows:

User Inputs:

$E(A)$, $E(B)$, where $A = A_0 A_1 A_2 A_3 (A_i \in 0, 1)$, $B = B_0 B_1 B_2 B_3 (B_i \in 0, 1)$, E means SWHE encryption.

Server:

$$
\begin{aligned}
E(M) =& E(A_3 \odot B_3)E(\overline{A}_2 B_2) + E((A_3 \odot B_3)(A_2 \odot B_2))E(\overline{A}_1)E(B_1) \\
&+ E((A_3 \odot B_3)(A_2 \odot B_2)(A_1 \odot B_1))E(\overline{A}_0)E(B_0) \\
E(G) =& E(A_3 \odot B_3)E(A_2 \odot B_2)E(A_1 \odot B_1)E(A_0 \odot B_0) \\
E(L) =& E(\overline{M + G})
\end{aligned}
$$

Through the homomorphic evaluation they can computation $E(M), E(G)$ and $E(L)$. It's clear to know that $E(L) = E(1)(E(A > B)), E(M) = E(1)(E(A < B))$ and $E(G) = E(1)(E(A = B))$, if $E(M) = E(1)$, then $A < B$, if $E(L) = E(1)$, then $A > B$ and if $E(G) = E(1)$ then $A = B$.

Only server knows the compare result which is encrypted form so that this comparison protocol is suitable for the decision tree classification developed in [38], where the comparison result is directly participate in add and multiplication without decrypt in the middle process.

3.2 Comparison with Two Encryption Scheme

Bost et al. [34] implemented five types comparison protocols by slightly modify the Veugen's [39] protocol. Compare with Veugen's their protocols settings are more flexible: it's able to choose which party owned the inputs, which party owned the outputs, and outputs also have two forms: encrypt or unencrypt. They use two homomorphic encryption scheme which is showed in Table 2, the idea of it is compute $x = 2^l + b - a$ where a and b are both encrypted and l bits integers, then check the $l + 1$-th bit of x. If it is 1, it means that $b \geq a$, else $b < a$.

Table 3. The key setup of five comparison protocols

Type	Input A	Input B	Output A	Output B
1	PK_P, PK_{QR}, a	SK_P, SK_{QR}, b	$[a < b]$	-
2	$PK_P, SK_{QR}, [[a]], [[b]]$	SK_P, PK_{QR}	-	$[a \leq b]$
3	$PK_P, SK_{QR}, [[a]], [[b]]$	SK_P, PK_{QR}	$a < b$	$[a \leq b]$
4	$PK_P, PK_{QR}, [[a]], [[b]]$	SK_P, SK_{QR}	$[a \leq b]$	-
5	$PK_P, PK_{QR}, [[a]], [[b]]$	SK_P, SK_{QR}	$[a \leq b]$	$a < b$

As showed in Table 3, type1 is used to compare two unencrypted inputs, which is called in later four protocols; the result of this protocol is encrypted. Apart from helping instruct the later protocols, it also can be used alone.

To demonstrate these protocols, Bost et al. use them to construct a series of ML classifiers such as adaboost, linear classification, face recognition. Although they can be used to construct so many classifiers, it's worthy to mention that when use it with other general protocols should by careful about the encryption keys setup as shown in Table 3, where PK_P and SK_P indicates the public and private key of Paillier, PK_{QR} and SK_{QR} indicates the public and private key of QR, $[[a]]$ means the Encrypted data which encrypted by PK_P.

3.3   Comparison with One Homomorphic Encryption

Samanthula et al. [5] implemented a comparison protocol, SIMN, with data encrypted by Paillier. The main idea is that for P_1 who hold the encrypted inputs, randomly choose a function F, eithor $u < v$ or $u > v$, $u = (u_1, u_2, .., u_l)$, v is the same, and only known by P_1, then with the help of P_2, P_1 starts to compare $[u_i]$ and $[v_i]$ for $1 \leq i \leq l$, the idea is $min(u, v)_i = (1 - \alpha) * u_i + \alpha * v_i$. If $u_i \geq v_i$, then the result $min_i = 1$, else $min_i = 0$. Finally, they will gets the value $min(u, v)$. For instance, $u = 55 = (110111)_2$ and $v = 58 = (111010)_2$ then $u_1 = 1$, $v_1 = 1$, $u_1 = v_1, min\{u, v\}_1 = 1$, the result $min\{u, v\} = (110111)_2$. The details you can see paper [5].

The protocol of this section is different from above protocols, it's result are not $E(1)$ or $E(0)$, it's the min value of two encrypted inputs. so when use this SMIN protocol to construct a protocol such as SMINn which is used to compute the min value among n inputs, it's more safer than above protocols. It guarantees all the processing is under encrypted data and no need to decyrpt anymore, which is convenient for both parties have not own private keys.

4   Conclusion

This paper has provide a review of privacy-preserving ML classification techniques which applied for different ML classification algorithms. It also introduces the comparison protocols and demonstrates the aspects they suits.

For three privacy preserving techniques, Differential privacy are often combined with database query and is suitable to deal with big datasets. But the main technique of it is to add randomly noise to data to keep the distribution of noised datasets are similar with the real datasets, so that people can get the prediction they want and also keep the personal data privacy. However, the adding of noise with data has led to decrease of classification accuracy. Researchers can study how to reduce the noise affects on the data, once reduced the noise's affects on classification, differential privacy will be more practical.

Homormorhpic encryption has been used in many privacy-preserving ML classification. With it people initially train datasets based on distributed model which data stored locally, only when traing phase starts can they use Homormorhpic encryption to encrypt data and compute a joint function with other users. However, this model ML classification based has high performance requirments for users equipment. For intance, smart mobile phones may not have enough capacity to support this computation. With time goes by, the cloud computing has appeared which enable people outsource their both storage and computation to the cloud. Then the secure ML classification scheme over outsourced model has been developed which people can encrypted their personal data first and then outsource it to the cloud, even the cloud is untrusted. At first, ML classification works only rely on one cloud, the data owners and querier should online all the time. Then it deveopled to two clouds, one is used for store encrypted data, another is used for store private key. But the premise is that the two cloud servers are not collusion.

This paper studies and analyzes the related works, and considers that there are several development trends in the privacy preserving ML classification:

(1) Reduce noise interference with data classification and improve the accuracy of classification resuls;
(2) Once the cloud server collusived, the cloud-based ML classification will not be safe, therefore, it is an urgent problem to design an anti-collusion cloud-based ML security classification;
(3) Altough many techniques have been developed to construct a privacy preserveing decision tree classification, it's just for a binary decision tree, for general decision there is no constrcution. Moreover, the focus of attention is on the testing phase, and little works have been done on training phase. Hence, it's great opportunity for researchers do some research on the training phase of security decision tree classification, and even develop a complete system for decision tree. Designeing a scheme for general secure decision tree is also a good function.

Acknowledgements. Supported by the National Natural Science Foundation of China (61872069), Fundamental Research Funds for the Central Universities (N171704005) and Shenyang Science and Technology Plan Projects (18-013-0-01).

References

1. Drucker, H., Wu, D., Vapnik, V.N.: Support vector machines for spam categorization. IEEE Trans. Neural Netw. **10**(5), 1048–54 (1999)
2. Krizhevsky, A., Sutskever, I., Hinton, G.E.: Imagenet classification with deep convolutional neural networks. In: Advances in Neural Information Processing Systems, vol. 2, pp. 1097–1105, Lake Tahoe, NV, United states (2012)
3. Kaufman, D.J., Murphy-Bollinger, J., Scott, J., Hudson, K.L.: Public opinion about the importance of privacy in biobank research. Am. J. Hum. Genet. **85**(5), 643–654 (2009)
4. Liu, F., Ng, W.K., Zhang, W.: Encrypted SVM for outsourced data mining. In: IEEE International Conference on Cloud Computing, pp. 1085–1092 (2015)
5. Samanthula, B.K., Elmehdwi, Y., Jiang, W.: k-nearest neighbor classification over semantically secure encrypted relational data. IEEE Trans. Knowl. Data Eng. **27**(5), 1261–1273 (2015)
6. Barthe, G., et al.: Differentially private Bayesian programming. In: ACM SIGSAC Conference on Computer and Communications Security, pp. 68–79 (2016)
7. Dou, J.W., Liu, X.H., Zhou, S.F., Li, S.D.: Efficient secure multi-party computation protocol and application over set (2018)
8. Dwork, C., Roth, A.: The algorithmic foundations of differential privacy. Found. Trends Theor. Comput. Sci. **9**(3–4), 211–407 (2014). http://dx.doi.org/10.1561/0400000042
9. Dwork, C.: Differential privacy: a survey of results. In: Agrawal, M., Du, D., Duan, Z., Li, A. (eds.) TAMC 2008. LNCS, vol. 4978, pp. 1–19. Springer, Heidelberg (2008). https://doi.org/10.1007/978-3-540-79228-4_1
10. Dwork, C., Rothblum, G.N., Vadhan, S.: Boosting and differential privacy, pp. 51–60, Las Vegas, NV, United states (2010). http://dx.doi.org/10.1109/FOCS.2010.12
11. Dwork, C., McSherry, F., Nissim, K., Smith, A.: Calibrating noise to sensitivity in private data analysis. In: Halevi, S., Rabin, T. (eds.) TCC 2006. LNCS, vol. 3876, pp. 265–284. Springer, Heidelberg (2006). https://doi.org/10.1007/11681878_14
12. Dwork, C.: Differential privacy. In: Bugliesi, M., Preneel, B., Sassone, V., Wegener, I. (eds.) ICALP 2006. LNCS, vol. 4052, pp. 1–12. Springer, Heidelberg (2006). https://doi.org/10.1007/11787006_1
13. Abadi, M., et al.: Deep learning with differential privacy. In: Proceedings of the ACM Conference on Computer and Communications Security, vol. 24–28, pp. 308–318, Vienna, Austria (2016)
14. Abadi, M., Agarwal, A., Barham, P., Brevdo, E., et al.: Tensorflow: large-scale machine learning on heterogeneous distributed systems (2016)
15. Johnson, R., Zhang, T.: Accelerating stochastic gradient descent using predictive variance reduction. In: Advances in Neural Information Processing Systems, pp. 315–323, Lake Tahoe, NV, United states (2013)
16. Duchi, J., Hazan, E., Singer, Y.: Adaptive subgradient methods for online learning and stochastic optimization. J. Mach. Learn. Res. **12**, 2121–2159 (2011)

17. Chaudhuri, K., Monteleoni, C., Sarwate, A.D.: Differentially private empirical risk minimization. J. Mach. Learn. Res. **12**, 1069–1109 (2011)
18. Hardt, M., Ligett, K., McSherry, F.: A simple and practical algorithm for differentially private data release. In: Conference on Neural Information Processing Systems 2012, NIPS 2012, vol. 3, pp. 2339–2347, Lake Tahoe, NV, United states (2012)
19. Rivest, R.L., Adleman, L., Dertouzos, M.L.: On data banks and privacy homomorphisms. In: Foundations of Secure Computation, pp. 169–179 (1978)
20. Rivest, R., Shamir, A., Adleman, L.M.: A method for obtaining digital signatures and public-key cryptosystems. Commun. ACM **21**(2), 120–126 (1978)
21. Goldwasser, S., Micali, S.: Probabilistic encryption & how to play mental poker keeping secret all partial information. In: Fourteenth ACM Symposium on Theory of Computing, pp. 365–377 (1982)
22. ElGamal, T.: A public key cryptosystem and a signature scheme based on discrete logarithms. IEEE Trans. Inf. Theory **31**, 469–472 (1985)
23. Paillier, P.: Public-key cryptosystems based on composite degree residuosity classes. In: Stern, J. (ed.) EUROCRYPT 1999. LNCS, vol. 1592, pp. 223–238. Springer, Heidelberg (1999). https://doi.org/10.1007/3-540-48910-X_16
24. Gentry, C.: A fully homomorphic encryption scheme. Stanford University (2009). http://crypto.stanford.edu/craig
25. Aslett, L., Esperanca, P., Holmes, C.: A review of homomorphic encryption and software tools for encrypted statistical machine learning. Computer Science (2015)
26. Yu, H., Jiang, X., Vaidya, J.: Privacy-preserving SVM using nonlinear kernels on horizontally partitioned data. In: ACM Symposium on Applied Computing, pp. 603–610 (2006)
27. Yu, H., Vaidya, J., Jiang, X.: Privacy-preserving SVM classification on vertically partitioned data. In: Pacific-Asia Conference on Advances in Knowledge Discovery and Data Mining, pp. 647–656 (2006)
28. Laur, S., Lipmaa, H.: Cryptographically private support vector machines. In: ACM SIGKDD International Conference on Knowledge Discovery and Data Mining, pp. 618–624 (2006)
29. Li, P., Li, J., Huang, Z., Li, T., Gao, C.Z., Yiu, S.M., Chen, K.: Multi-key privacy-preserving deep learning in cloud computing. Futur. Gener. Comput. Syst. **74**, 76–85 (2017)
30. Yao, A.C.: Protocols for secure computations. In: Symposium on Foundations of Computer Science, pp. 160–164 (1982)
31. Malkhi, D., Nisan, N., Pinkas, B., Sella, Y.: Fairplay-a secure two-party computation system. In: Conference on USENIX Security Symposium, pp. 287–302 (2004)
32. Ben-David, A., Nisan, N., Pinkast, B.: Fairplaymp - a system for secure multi-party computation, pp. 257–266, Alexandria, VA, United states (2008)
33. Henecka, W., Kogl, S., Sadeghi, A.R., Schneider, T., Wehrenberg, I.: Tasty: tool for automating secure two-party computations, pp. 451–462, Chicago, IL, United states (2010)
34. Bost, R., Popa, R.A., Tu, S., Goldwasser, S.: Machine learning classification over encrypted data. In: Network and Distributed System Security Symposium (2015)
35. Jakobsen, T.P., Nielsen, J.B., Orlandi, C.: A framework for outsourcing of secure computation. In: 2014 ACM Cloud Computing Security Workshop, CCS 2014, pp. 81–92, Scottsdale, AZ, United states (2014). https://doi.org/10.1145/2664168.266417

36. Asharov, G., Jain, A., López-Alt, A., Tromer, E., Vaikuntanathan, V., Wichs, D.: Multiparty computation with low communication, computation and interaction via threshold FHE. In: Pointcheval, D., Johansson, T. (eds.) EUROCRYPT 2012. LNCS, vol. 7237, pp. 483–501. Springer, Heidelberg (2012). https://doi.org/10.1007/978-3-642-29011-4_29

37. Jiang, L.Z., Xu, C.X., Wang, X.F., Chem, K.F., Wang, B.C.: The application of (fully) homomorphic encryption on ciphertext-based computational model. J. Cryptogr. (6) (2017)

38. Tai, R.K.H., Ma, J.P.K., Zhao, Y., Chow, S.S.M.: Privacy-preserving decision trees evaluation via linear functions. In: Foley, S.N., Gollmann, D., Snekkenes, E. (eds.) ESORICS 2017. LNCS, vol. 10493, pp. 494–512. Springer, Cham (2017). https://doi.org/10.1007/978-3-319-66399-9_27

39. Veugen, T.: Comparing encrypted data (2011). http://siplab.tudelft.nl/sites/default/files/Comparing%20encrypted%20data.pdf

A Self-organizing LSTM-Based Approach to PM2.5 Forecast

Xiaodong Liu[1], Qi Liu[1(✉)], Yanyun Zou[2], and Guizhi Wang[3]

[1] School of Computing, Edinburgh Napier University, Edinburgh, UK
q.liu@napier.ac.uk
[2] School of Computer and Software, Nanjing University of Information Science
and Technology, Nanjing, China
[3] School of Mathematics and Statistics, Nanjing University of Information
Science and Technology, Nanjing 210044, Jiangsu, China

Abstract. Nanjing has been listed as the one of the worst performers across China with respect to the high level of haze-fog, which impacts people's health greatly. For the severe condition of haze-fog, $PM_{2.5}$ is the main cause element of haze-fog pollution in China. So it's necessary to forecast $PM_{2.5}$ concentration accurately. In this paper, an artificial intelligence method is employed to forecast $PM_{2.5}$ in Nanjing. At the data pre-processing stage, the main factors among the air pollutants (O3, NO2, SO2, CO, etc.) as well as meteorological parameters (pressure, wind direction, temperature, etc.) that affect $PM_{2.5}$ are selected, and these factors of previous hours are as input data to predict $PM_{2.5}$ concentration of next hours. Considering the air pollutants and meteorological data are typical time series data, a special recurrent neural network, which is called long short term memory (LSTM) network, is applied in this paper. To determine the amount of nodes in the hidden layer, a self-organizing method is used to automatically adjust the hidden nodes during the training phase. Finally, the $PM_{2.5}$ concentrations of the next 1 h, 4 h, 8 h, and 12 h are predicted separately by using the self-organizing LSTM network based approach. The experimental result has been validated and compared to other algorithms, which reflects the proposed method performs best.

Keywords: Haze-fog · $PM_{2.5}$ forecasting · Selecting main factors
Time series data · LSTM network · Self-organizing algorithm

1 Introduction

Haze-fog is not only related to meteorological conditions, but also has a non-negligible relationship with human activities. Once the emission exceeds the atmospheric circulation capacity and carrying capacity, the concentration of fine particles will be getting to high. As a result, it is easy to have a large range of haze-fog. The greatest impact of haze-fog is the human health, it's easy to affect the respiratory tract of the body and causes various diseases. In Nanjing, there are many sources of pollution such as building construction, vehicle exhaust, coal power generation and so on. And because Nanjing is a downwind area, the pollution in the upwind area will be imported into

© Springer Nature Switzerland AG 2018
X. Sun et al. (Eds.): ICCCS 2018, LNCS 11066, pp. 683–693, 2018.
https://doi.org/10.1007/978-3-030-00015-8_59

Nanjing. As a result, Nanjing is one of the most air polluted cities. So this study aims to forecast $PM_{2.5}$ concentration of Nanjing.

The early $PM_{2.5}$ prediction methods were mainly based on the original statistical methods. Fuller et al. [1] use the average of the pollutants of API, and statistics the linear relationship between the factors and the $PM_{2.5}$ and PM_{10}, so as to realize the forecasting of $PM_{2.5}$. At the same time, this linear method is also used for the prediction of other air pollutants. Combined with the local climate, API air pollution can be predicted through empirical judgement and linear regression. Jian et al. [2] find the correlation between meteorological factors, that is, the humidity is positively related to haze-fog, and the wind speed is negatively related to haze-fog. It is proved that auto-regressive integrated moving average (ARIMA) model can effectively explore the relationship between haze and meteorological factors. Kibria et al. [3] use naive Bayes to integrate the distribution of $PM_{2.5}$ in space. Dong et al. [4] use the mathematical model based on the hidden Markov function to predict the $PM_{2.5}$ concentration. The prediction results show that the predicted value of $PM_{2.5}$ can fit the real value better.

To improve the accuracy of prediction, artificial neural network (ANN) has been widely used in this field. Zhu et al. [5] put forward an improved BP neural network algorithm, combining the auto-regressive and moving average (ARMA) model with BP neural network to predict $PM_{2.5}$ concentration. Venkadesha et al. [6] combine genetic algorithm and BP neural network to fuse multiple time domain meteorological factors, and determine the duration and resolution of prior input data, and improve the accuracy of prediction. Zheng Haiming et al. [7] use the radial basis function (RBF) neural network to predict the concentration of $PM_{2.5}$. The results show that the prediction accuracy is better than BP neural network. Mishra et al. [8] combine the Principle Component Analysis (PCA) and artificial neural network to get the correlation between meteorology and air pollutants variables, so as to predict the concentration of NO_2 in the air. Mishra et al. [9] use non-meteorological parameters (CO, O_3, NO_2, SO_2, $PM_{2.5}$) and meteorological parameters to make the fusion analysis combining artificial intelligence to forecast haze-fog, it is concluded that compared with the artificial neural network and multilayer perceptron model, NF model based on the artificial intelligence can better predict the urban haze-fog events in Delhi, India. Neto et al. [10] use artificial neural networks to recursively analyse residual residuals to find current patterns, so the accuracy of predicting the concentration of $PM_{2.5}$ and PM_{10} is improved. Shanshan Zhou et al. [11] use recurrent neural network (RNN) to predict $PM_{2.5}$ concentration. Compared with fuzzy neural network (FNN) and RBF feed-forward neural network, the experimental results show that RNN is outstanding. Bun et al. [12] put forward a new training method for automatic encoder, which is designed for time series prediction, to enhance the deep recurrent neural network (DRNN). The experiment shows that DRNN is better than the typical and most advanced automatic coder training method used in the time series prediction. Liu et al. [13] use the comprehensive prediction model to forecast the $PM_{2.5}$ concentration using the autoregressive moving average (ARIMA), artificial neural network (ANNs) model and exponential smoothing method (ESM).

Although the above literatures can achieve good prediction results, air pollutants and meteorological data are typical time series data. It is difficult to reflect the correlation between data and time. In addition, how to decide the number of hidden nodes is still a major challenge for researchers.

2 Basic Knowledge

2.1 Time Series Prediction

Meteorological data are typical time series data. Time series prediction is a prediction that extends to the future according to the historical data of the past. According to the process and regularity of the time series data, it establishes a mathematical model that is more accurate to reflect dynamic dependency relations. Then after the learning historical data period, this model can make a prediction of the trend of time series development.

The general steps of the time series prediction are as follows:

(1) After the collected historical data are reorganized, the time series data are formed after necessary pre-processing (noise reduction, removal of singularity, etc.). According to the composition and different influence factors of the time series, they're usually divided into four categories:

Long-term trend: the tendency to maintain steady growth or decline within a period of time is known as a long-term trend. For example, the recent growth in the price of bitcoin, or the declining price of electronic consumer goods.

Seasonal variation: the time series changes obviously according to the change of the four seasons. For example, the four seasons of sunspots, the company's sales volume changes within one year and the rainfall trend in this paper. And the time interval of the change is not fixed, it can be a month, a quarter, or even a day.

Cyclical change: cyclical change often appears inseparable with long-term trend. For example, the process of the replacement of the ancient Chinese dynasties usually includes the stages of recovery, prosperity, flourishing age, decline, and destruction.

Irregular change: irregular change refers to the part of random changes of the time series, and there is no law to follow between these data. It's often impossible to use mathematical models to fit their changes.

(2) Time series analysis. The formation of continuous values in time series is closely related to a number of factors, and it is usually not the result of only one factor. Therefore, when new time series data are obtained, it is usually necessary to analyse the interaction between their internal factors, and then get the implied features in the data.

(3) Characterizing the characteristics of extraction. According to the long-term trend, seasonal variation and cyclic variation of the time series, the approximate mathematical models are selected to characterize them.

(4) The training and prediction of the model. The correctness of the mathematical model is verified by historical time series, and the model is properly adjusted. After reaching the error requirement of the model, it can be used to predict the time series.

2.2   Long Short Term Memory Network (LSTM)

The input of recurrent neural network (RNN) hidden layer overlay the original data information as time goes by, which leads to the loss of contextual information. Therefore, in practical applications, the range of contextual information that general recurrent neural network structure can use is limited, resulting in gradient vanishing problem. To solve this problem, LSTM network is brought up. LSTM is very popular at the moment. It is not essentially different from the general RNN structure, but uses a different node, called "memory block" to replace a hidden layer node of general RNN.

Figure 1 shows the architecture of the memory block. There are three gates in the block. When the outside wants to write to memory cell, it must go through an input gate. Only when the input gate is opened, memory gate can be written. The input gate is opened or closed, which is learned by neural network itself. In the same way, there is an output gate, which is also learned by neural network. There is also a forget gate to decide when to forget the contents of memory cell, and the condition of opening or closing is also learned by neural network itself. Z, Z_i, Z_f, Z_o are scalers, which are derived from the inner product of input vectors and weight vectors adding to the bias. Weight vectors and bias are learned by gradient descent from training data. The function f often chooses sigmoid function, because the output value is between 0 and 1, which can indicate the opening degree of the gates (0 is closing; 1 is opening). When $f(Z_i) = 1$, $g(Z)$ can be input. Instead, $f(Z_i) = 0$ is equivalent to no input. Similarly, $f(Z_o)$ controls the output of value. $f(Z_f) = 1$ is equivalent to remember the previous value C in memory cell; when $f(Z_f) = 0$, it is equivalent to forget value C. The values in the memory cell are updated by the formula in Fig. 2.

So the LSTM memory block can be seen as special neuron (4 inputs, 1 output), and 4 inputs refers to the signal that the outside wants to put into the memory cell as welas three control gates signal.

3   Self-organizing Algorithm

3.1   Sensitivity Analysis

In this paper, the amount of hidden nodes in LSTM network is adjusted by a self-organizing algorithm [14] during training phase. In this algorithm, a crucial method, sensitivity analysis (SA), is adopted to calculate how important the hidden nodes are. Sensitivity analysis is always used to judge the degree of dependence between output and input. So it's feasible to add or delete hidden nodes according to sensitivity analysis.

Before knowing the working mechanism of SA, it's necessary to understand the internal feedback dynamic characteristics of LSTM network. Figure 2 displays decomposition of network. It's divided into two parts. The first part is the self-circulatory part of hidden layer nodes. And the second part is a direct relationship between hidden layer nodes and output layer nodes.

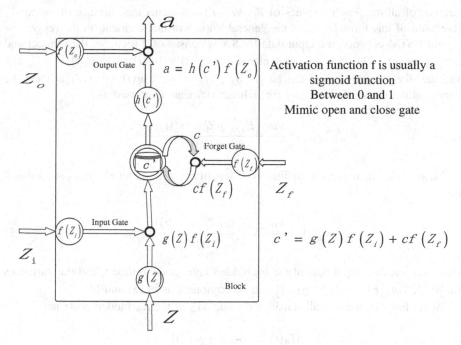

Fig. 1. Structure of memory block

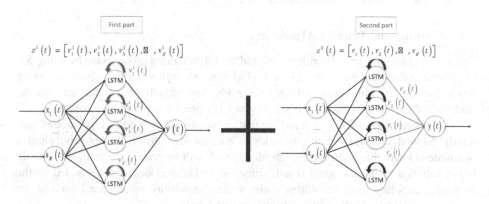

Fig. 2. Decomposition of LSTM network

The numerical calculation method adopted by this paper is as follows

$$S_h = \frac{Var[E(Y|Z_h)]}{Var(Y)}, \quad h = (1, 2, \cdots, H) \tag{1}$$

where Z_h represents h_{th} input factor, Y is equal to the output of this model. $E(Y|Z_h)$ is the expected variance under the condition of output Y. And $Var[E(Y|Z_h)]$ is the variance of all the feasible values of Z_h. $Var(Y)$ represents the variance of output Y. The result of this formula, S_h, is the general impact of that element on the reply.

For LSTM network, the input data for SA is consist of 2 sections: the indirect and direct elements. The indirect input element is $z_1(t) = \left[v_1^1(t), v_2^1(t), v_3^1(t), \cdots, v_H^1(t)\right]$. And the direct input element can be get by $z^2(t) = [v_1(t), v_2(t), \cdots, v_H(t)]$. Then the numerical definition of sensitivity for indirect elements is revised as:

$$S_h^1(t) = \frac{Var_h\left[E\left(y(t)|Z_h^1 = v_h^1(t)\right)\right]}{Var(y(t))}, \tag{2}$$

Meanwhile, the numerical definition of sensitivity with direct elements is modified as:

$$S_h^2(t) = \frac{Var_h\left[E\left(y(t)|Z_h^2 = v_h(t)\right)\right]}{Var[y(t)]}, \tag{3}$$

where $v_h(t)$ is the output data of the h_{th} hidden layer node at time t, and the variances $Var[y(t)]$, $Var_h\left[E\left(y(t)|Z_h^2 = v_h(t)\right)\right]$ can be computed as in (3) and (4).

According (2), the overall sensitivity value ST_h of the h_{th} hidden node is:

$$ST_h(t) = \alpha S_h^1(t) + \beta S_h^2(t), \tag{4}$$

where α and β are the judgment constants, $\alpha \in [0, 0.2]$, $\beta \in [0.5, 0.8]$.

3.2 Growing and Pruning Algorithm

The growing and pruning algorithm is to add or delete hidden layer nodes by using SA to achieve self-organizing ability of the LSTM network during training phase. By using this algorithm, the number of hidden layer nodes can be adjusted to the best. So the structure of the network is able to satisfy the high precision prediction condition.

The general idea of this method is: first, generate some hidden layer nodes randomly. Second, calculate sensitivity index of each node. Third, if the sensitivity index of a node is lower than a certain threshold, the node will be pruned; instead, if the result is not satisfied to get the ideal result, some new hidden nodes will be added to the network, according to those hidden nodes whose sensitivity values are large. At the same time, associated connection weights are updated.

Growing Step. At time t, if there are H nodes in the hidden layer, the RMSE for the neural network is $E(t) > \delta(t)\left(\delta(t) = t^{-0.65}\right)$, so it suggests that the learning process is not able to get the ideal result and a new hidden node is needed for the current construction. The final sensitivity value is

$$ST_h(t) = max\{ST_j(t)\}, j = 1, 2, \cdots, H \tag{5}$$

$$e(t) = y_d(t) - y(t)$$

h is the node, which has the largest overall sensitivity value.

Pruning Step. Like the above step, at time t, if the overall sensitivity index is $ST_h < \tau$ (τ is the pruning threshold), then the hth node needs to be deleted. And the weights of the hth node are updated as well. Experiment

4 Experiment

4.1 Data Pre-processing

To predict PM2.5 concentration, this study uses hourly files from the ground automatic station in Nanjing, which include meteorological data as well as air pollutants. Raw data contains 30 factors, such as O_3, NO_2, CO, SO_2, pressure, relative humidity, temperature and so on. However, there are some missing values and outliers, this paper uses the average value of neighbour data to replace these values. Then, after the standardization, in order to select the main factors with respect to $PM_{2.5}$ concentration, a selection method called Mutual Information (MI) is adopted. This method can calculate that whether there is a relationship between the two variables X and Y, as well as the strength of the relationship. As a result, the MI values of these factors are over 2.5: O_3, NO_2, $PM_{2.5}$, pressure, wind direction of the instant maximum wind speed, temperature, wind direction of maximum wind speed, horizontal visibility, body temperature. Figure 3 shows the distribution of these factors.

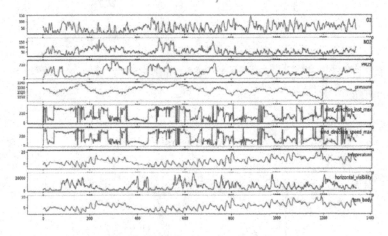

Fig. 3. Distribution of main factors

4.2 Experimental Results

According to the self-organizing algorithm, the number of hidden layer nodes is 30. And training dataset and test dataset are set to be 1200 h and 141 h separately. The epochs are equal to 50 times.

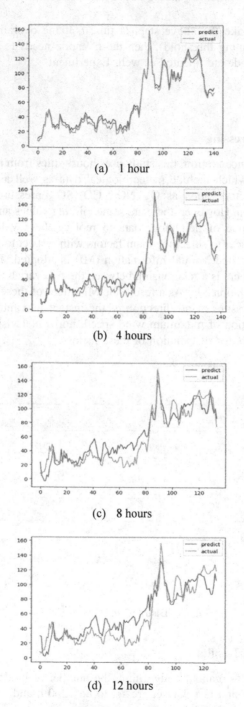

(a)   1 hour

(b)   4 hours

(c)   8 hours

(d)   12 hours

Fig. 4. Actual and predict PM$_{2.5}$ concentration for the evaluation dataset for one-, four-, eight-, and twelve-hour

This experiment uses self-organizing LSTM network to predict the PM2.5 concentration of next 1 h, 4 h, 8 h and 12 h. Figure 4 displays the curves of actual value and predict value. The X-axis is the quantity of the test samples, and the Y-axis is the concentration value of $PM_{2.5}$. From these four pictures, we can see that the fitting degree of one-hour prediction is the highest, then that of four hours prediction is lower. And, the fitting precision of eight hours and twelve hours decreases gradually. We can draw conclusion that with the increase of time domain, the prediction precision is reduced. So this method has advantages in nowcasting.

And Table 1 shows the comparison between SO-LSTM (self-organizing LSTM) and the algorithm in [6]. The evaluation parameter is coefficient of determination (R^2).

Table 1. The comparison between SO-LSTM and GA-ANN

Algorithms	Hours			
	1	4	8	12
GA-ANN	0.992	0.965	0.935	0.915
SO-LSTM	**0.999**	**0.991**	**0.937**	**0.918**

From this table, it's obvious that the SO-LSTM shows a higher coefficient of determination from 1 h to 12 h than GA-ANN.

Table 2 shows the performance of MLR, ANN, NF [9] and SO-LSTM in the case of predicting the PM2.5 concentration after 39 h.

Table 2. The comparison between SO-LSTM and other algorithms

	MLR	ANN	NF	SO-LSTM
R^2	0.51	0.53	0.72	**0.79**

From Table 2, we can see that SO-LSTM performs the best.

5 Conclusion and Future Work

In this paper, a self-organizing LSTM network is employed to predict $PM_{2.5}$ concentration.

First, by using the mutual information algorithm, nine main factors (O_3, NO_2, $PM_{2.5}$, pressure, wind direction of the instant maximum wind speed, temperature, wind direction of maximum wind speed, horizontal visibility, and body temperature) that affect $PM_{2.5}$ in Nanjing are as input data. Because these data are typical time series data, recurrent LSTM network is suitable to apply in this case for its memory capability.

Then, to determine the number of hidden nodes of this network, a self-organizing algorithm called grow-prune is adopted. This method can add or delete nodes during training phase. And in this paper, the number of hidden nodes is determined to be 30.

Finally, after training and test steps, the model is built to predict $PM_{2.5}$. According to the experimental results, the SO-LSTM model performs better than MLR, ANN, NF, GA-ANN. The accuracy is improved.

With time interval growth, the accuracy of prediction is getting lower. For future work, we intend to further improve on the accuracy of long-term forecasting with more excellent pre-training methods.

Acknowledgements. This work was supported by Major Program of the National Social Science Fund of China (Grant No. 17ZDA092). It has also received funding from the European Union's Horizon 2020 research and innovation programme under the Marie Sklodowska-Curie grant agreement No. 701697.

References

1. Fuller, G.W., Carslaw, D.C., Lodge, H.W.: An empirical approach for the prediction of daily mean PM_{10} concentrations. Atmos. Environ. **36**(9), 1431–1441 (2002)
2. Jian, L., Zhao, Y., Zhu, Y.P., Zhan, M.B., Bertolatti, D.: An application of ARIMA model to predict submicron particle concentrations from meteorological factors at a busy roadside in Hangzhou. China. Sci. Total Environ. **426**(2), 336–345 (2012)
3. Kibria, B.M.G., Sun, L., Zike, J.V.: Bayesian spatial prediction of random space-time field with application to mapping $PM_{2.5}$ exposure. J. Am. Stat. Assoc. **97**(457), 112–124 (2002)
4. Dong, M., Yang, D., Kuang, Y.: $PM_{2.5}$ concentration Prediction using hidden semi-Markov model-based time series data mining. Expert Syst. Appl. **36**(5), 9046–9055 (2009)
5. Zhu, H., Lu, X.: The prediction of $PM_{2.5}$ value based on ARMA and improved BP neural network model. In: 2016 International Conference on Intelligent Networking and Collaborative Systems (ICINCS), pp. 515–517 (2016)
6. Venkadesh, S., Hoogenboom, G., Potter, W.: A genetic algorithm to refine input data selection for air temperature prediction using artificial neural networks. Appl. Soft Comput. **13**(5), 2253–2260 (2013)
7. Zheng, H., Shang, X.: Study on prediction of atmospheric $PM_{2.5}$ based on RBF neural network. In: 2013 Fourth International Conference on Digital Manufacturing & Automation (ICDMA), pp. 1287–1289 (2013)
8. Mishra, D., Goyal, P.: Development of artificial intelligence based NO_2, forecasting models at Taj Mahal, Agra. Atmos. Pollut. Res. **6**(1), 99–106 (2015)
9. Mishra, D., Goyal, P., Upadhyay, A.: Artificial intelligence based approach to forecast PM 2.5, during haze episodes: a case study of Delhi, India. Atmos. Environ. **102**, 239–248 (2015)
10. Neto, P., Cavalcanti, G., Madeiro, F.: An approach to improve the performance of PM forecasters. PLoS ONE **10**(9), 1–23 (2015)
11. Zhou, S., Li, W., Qiao, J.: Prediction of $PM_{2.5}$ concentration based on recurrent fuzzy neural network. In: Proceedings of the 36th Chinese Control Conference (PCCC), pp. 3920–3924 (2017)

12. Bun, T., Komei, S., Koji, Z.: Dynamically pre-trained deep recurrent neural networks using environmental monitoring data for predicting $PM_{2.5}$. Neural Comput. Appl. **27**(6), 1553–1566 (2016)
13. Liu, D.J., Li, L.: Application study of comprehensive forecasting model based on entropy weighting method on trend of $PM_{2.5}$ concentration in Guangzhou, China. Int. J. Environ. Res. Pub. Health **12**(6), 7085–7099 (2015)
14. Han, H., Li, Y., Guo, Y., Qiao, J.: A soft computing method to predict sludge volume index based on a recurrent self-organizing neural network. Appl. Soft Comput. **38**(C), 477–486 (2016)

A Three-Factor Remote Authentication Scheme for Multi-server Environment

Jianming Cui[1], Chen Chen[1], Xiaojun Zhang[1(✉)], Yihui Liu[1], and Ning Cao[2]

[1] Shandong University of Science and Technology,
Qingdao, Shandong, People's Republic of China
sdustcuijm@163.com
[2] University College Dublin, Belfield 4, Dublin, Ireland
ning.cao@ucd.ie

Abstract. In this paper, we investigate Chen et al. biometrics-based remote user authentication scheme and find that it cannot validate the correctness of the password, complete the storage and verification of the password, and vulnerable to anonymity attacks, smart card stolen attacks and forgery attacks. To remedy these flaws, we propose an improved three-factor remote authentication scheme based on smart cards. It can implement mutual authentication and generate session keys to effectively improve security in multi-server environments. The proposed scheme can resist smart card attack, anonymity attack, forgery attack and other attacks. In addition, the proposed scheme costs $5T_h$ more compare to Chen et al. work and less computation complexity compared with other schemes.

Keywords: Three-factor · Multi-server · Biometrics · Forgery attack

1 Introduction

With the development of fingerprint identification technology, iris recognition, voice recognition technology, and biometric technology have been applied to many fields. One of the important areas is identity authentication protocol. The three-factor authentication protocol verifies the identity of the user through three factors (what you know, what you have, who you are), and utilizes the unique feature of biometric information to enhance the security of the authentication protocol. When a user logins to a server, he must provide the biometric information, password and identity. If the biometric information does not match the preset threshold of registered biometric information, the server will not provide services to the user. Since the biometric is applied to the authentication protocol, great efforts have been made on the three-factor authentication protocols [1–4]. Li et al. [5] presented a remote password authentication scheme for multi-server architecture using neural networks. The scheme does not require duplication registration and suit to multi-server environments. However, users need to store a large number of public parameters to complete the verification, which makes the

© Springer Nature Switzerland AG 2018
X. Sun et al. (Eds.): ICCCS 2018, LNCS 11066, pp. 694–705, 2018.
https://doi.org/10.1007/978-3-030-00015-8_60

protocol requires high storage space and calculations. Later, Tsaur et al. [6] proposed an authentication protocol using Lagrange polynomials and RSA encryption methods, which also has high computational complexity. Juang [7] brought the hash function into the authentication protocol for multi-server environments, which effectively reduce the amount of computation. However, Chang et al. [8] found that the sensitive information stored in the smart card of Juang's protocol can be easily extracted which may cause safety problems. Therefore, they proposed a new authentication protocol, but it still cannot resist internal attacks, impersonation attack and etc. Tsai also proposed an authentication protocol [9] for the multi-server environment that did not require verification table, which is applicable to distributed networks and uses a one-way hash function and random number. Tsaur et al. [10] found the protocol proposed by Tsai is vulnerable to man-in-middle attacks and then proposed a two-factor authentication protocol using smart card for multi-server environment which can self-validating the time-stamping. Wang et al. [11] found that the Tsai et al. protocol was not resistant to server simulation attacks and then proposed an improved protocol that could compensate for the Tsai et al. protocol. Chen et al. [12] analyzed Wang et al. protocol and proposed a three-factor authentication protocol based on smart card in multi-server environment. However, we find that chen's protocol is vulnerable to anonymity attacks, stolen smart card attacks, and anonymity attacks. Therfore, this paper proposes a three-factor authentication protocol with low computational complexity and can achieve more security goals.

2   Analysis of Chen et al. Protocol

Chen et al. protocol can be found in [12], we mainly analyze the security in this section as follows. The symbols used are described in Table 1.

(1) Unable to verify password
    During the registration phase of Chen et al. protocol, RC stores the encrypted value C_i, the system parameter g, and the one-way hash function $h(\cdot)$, where $C_i = RU_i \oplus h(PW_i) = h(UID_i \parallel x) \oplus h(PW_i)$. Only C_i contains the password information. We cannot obtain RU_i without knowing the password, which means it cannot verify the correctness of the user's password only through C_i.

(2) Fingerprint storage and verification
    In the registration phase, after RC sends the smart card to the user U_i, he needs to input the fingerprint into the smart card through the fingerprint input device. In the login and password change phase, the user enters the fingerprint for matching verification. For it needs to match fingerprint completely, it is unpractical to implement based on the existing fingerprint identification technology.

Table 1. Notations.

Name	Description
U_i	The i-th user
RC	Registration Center
S_j	The j-th service providing server
UID_i	The identity of U_i
PW_i	The password of the user U_i
SID_j	The identity of S_j
g	The generator of Z_q^*, q is a large prime
x	The master key selected by RC that shared with the server
y	One key shared by the RC, server, and user
$h(\cdot)$	One way hash function
$\oplus$	Bitwise exclusive-OR operation
$\parallel$	Bitwise concatenation operation

(3) Stolen smart card attack

After receiving the smart card, the user sets a PIN code to protect it. The protocol does not encrypt the PIN code for storage. Once the smart card is stolen, attackers can perform differential energy analysis and simple energy analysis, and get the information stored in the smart card. That is, the attacker can get the PIN code, so that he has the ability to unlock the smart card.

(4) Anonymity attack

During the login phase, the user transmits its identity UID_i in plaintext over a public channel. By analyzing the Chen et al. scheme, an attacker can intercept the login time and regularity of the user U_i by monitoring the communication between the user and the server, thereby realizing the anonymity attack.

(5) Eavesdropping attack

If an attacker steals a smart card, the sensitive value g stored in the smart card by using the DPA and SPA methods. When user U_i logins to server S_j, he will send $\{UID_i, M_1, g^{r_u}, T_i\}$ over a public channel. After the server S_j receives the login message, it will send $\{UID_i, M_1, g^{r_u}, T_i, SID_i, M_2, g^{r_s}, T_j\}$ to RC via a public channel. After the server S_j completes identity authentication, it will send $\{M_4, g^{r_s}, T_j\}$ to U_i through the secure channel. Through monitoring messages between the user and the server or messages between the server and the registration center, an attacker can get two important values: g^{r_u} and g^{r_s} which make the attacker can obtain the session key $SK = (g^{r_u})^{r_s}$ of the communication, so this protocol can not resist eavesdropping attack.

3 The Three-Factor Authentication Scheme Proposed in This Paper

In order to make up for the inadequacies of the aforementioned protocols, this paper proposes an improved authentication protocol. The proposed protocol implements local authentication by storing the encrypted value of the user's password and removes the PIN unlocking process for the local authentication of the user's password is the same as the PIN-unlocking smart card. The PIN code not only increases the complexity of the authentication protocol, but also needs users to remember some extra login information. The proposed protocol in this paper represents a reasonable biological information verification link based on the current fingerprint identification technology, so that the protocol achieves a security goal of non-repudiation. In addition, the new protocol protects against stolen smart card attacks and anonymity attacks by encrypting information stored in smart cards. By adding an effective anti-anonymity attack method, the problem which the protocol is vulnerable to anonymity attacks is completely solved.

The proposed protocol in this paper has three participants: users, servers, and registration centers. The protocol contains registration phase, login phase, identity authentication phase, and password change phases. In order to facilitate comparative analysis, symbols and related parameters of the proposed protocol remain the same as Chen's work. The following section will detail the implementation of each phase.

3.1 Registration Phase

The registration phase is divided into two parts: server registration and user registration, as shown in Fig. 1.

As a legitimate server, it needs to submit its identity SID_j to the registration center. Then the registration center calculates the encrypted value $RS_j = h(SID_j \| y)$, and stores $\{RS_j, g, h()\}$ into the server through a secure channel, where g is a system parameter.

As a legitimate user, you need to submit the user identity UID_i and password PW_i to the registration center and enter the fingerprint when registration. The registration center extracts the digitized fingerprint feature F_i. Then, the registration center performs the following steps:

Step 1. Registration Center calculates two hash values of the password, $P_i = h(h(PW_i))$, identity encryption value $D_i = UID_i \oplus h(PW_i)$, User's encrypted value $RU_i = h(UID_i \| x)$, and $C_i = RU_i \oplus h(PW_i)$, system parameter encryption value $G_i = g \oplus h(PW_i)$, and fingerprint feature encryption value $V_i = F_i \oplus h(PW_i)$.

Step 2. The smart card generates a random number b, the registration center calculates $B_i = UID_i \oplus b$, then $Z_i = h(B_i \oplus z)$, where z is the key of registration center.

Step 3. The registration center stores $\{P_i, D_i, C_i, G_i, V_i, Z_i, B_i, h()\}$ into the smart card, and sends the smart card to the user through secure channel.

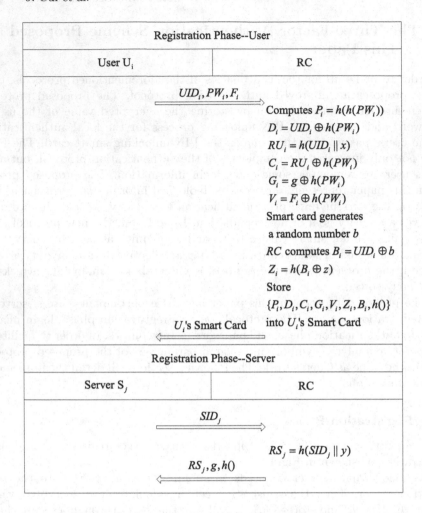

Fig. 1. Registration phase of the improved protocol.

3.2 Login Phase

To login the server, user needs to insert a smart card into the reader and then enters the password, PW_i^*. The smart card verifies whether the user's password is correct or not by determining the equation $P_i = h(h(PW_i^*))$. Only if the password is entered correctly, the smart card will hint user to enter the fingerprint then extract its feature value F_i^*. The smart card retrieves the registered fingerprint feature value by calculation $F_i = V_i \oplus h(PW_i^*)$, and checks the matching degree of F_i^* with F_i. If the matching degree of the two does not exceed the set threshold (the threshold can be set according to the requirement of security), the login is terminated, and if the threshold is exceeded, then it can be considered as the user's login. The smart card continues to generate random numbers r_u and b_{new}, and retrieves the user identity

$UID_i = D_i \oplus h(PW_i^*)$, calculates $B_{new} = UID_i \oplus b_{new}$ and $Q_i = B_{new} \oplus Z_i$. Then the smart card retrieves $RU_i = C_i \oplus h(PW_i^*)$ and calculates the user authentication message $M_1 = h(RU_i \| g^{r_u} \| SID_j \| T_i)$. Finally, the smart card will sent $\{Q_i, B_i, b_{new}, M_1, g^{r_u}, T_i\}$ to the server to complete the login process. The steps as shown in Fig. 2.

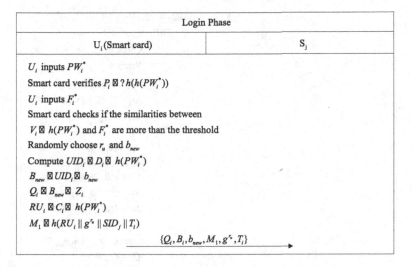

Fig. 2. Registration phase of the improved protocol.

3.3   Identity Authentication Phase

At the authentication phase, the server and the user will implement bidirectional authentication of the identity with participations of the registration center, and generate a session key, as shown in Fig. 3. The detailed description of this stage is as follows.

Step 1. After the server receives the user's login request information $\{Q_i, B_i, b_{new}, M_1, g^{r_u}, T_i\}$, it will verify the validity of its timestamp T_i. If the timestamp is not within the service time range, the server terminates communication; otherwise, the following steps are continued.

Step 2. The server generates random number $r_s \in Z_q^*$, and calculates $M_2 = h(RS_j \| g^{r_s} \| UID_i \| T_j)$, where T_j is the server-side timestamp represents the current time. Then, the server forwards the login request information $\{Q_i, B_i, b_{new}, M_1, g^{r_u}, T_i\}$ sent by the smart card to the registration center, and sends the verification information $\{SID_j, M_2, g^{r_s}, T_j\}$ of the server to the registration center at the same time.

Step 3. After the registration center receives $\{Q_i, B_i, b_{new}, M_1, g^{r_u}, T_i\}$ and $\{SID_j, M_2, g^{r_s}, T_j\}$, it will first verify T_i and T_j. If they are valid, it will verify whether the identity of the server and the user is valid. If the server and the user is legal. The registration center will send the identity authentication message to

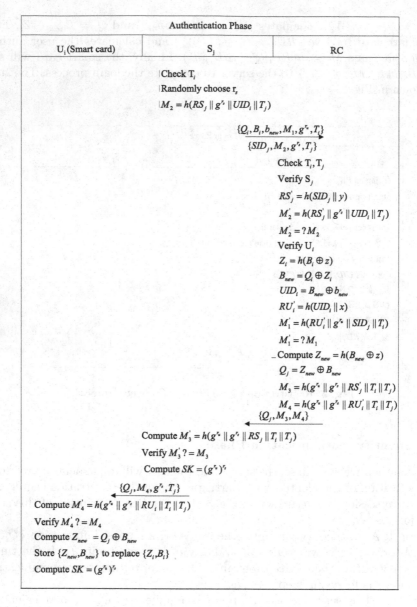

Fig. 3. Registration phase of the improved protocol.

the server, the server and the user can complete authentication based on this authentication message. The substeps below for details.

Step 3-1. The registration center calculates $RS'_j = h(SID_j\|y)$ and $M'_2 = h(RS'_j\|g^{r_s}\|UID_i\|T_j)$, then checks whether the equation $M'_2 = M_2$ is true. If it is true, it proves that the message sent by the server contains the key information of y, which proves the validity of the server. If the equation is not established, the registration center terminates the session.

Step 3-2. The registration center calculates $Z_i = h(B_i \oplus z)$ and $B_{new} = Q_i \oplus Z_i$, and restores the user identity $UID_i = B_{new} \oplus b_{new}$, calculates $RU'_i = h(UID_i \| x)$ and $M'_1 = h(RU'_i \| g^{r_u} \| SID_j \| T_i)$, checking whether M'_1 is equal to M_1, if equal, it can prove the user's identity is legal. If not, the registration center informs the server that the user is illegal.

Step 3-3. After the identities of the server and the user have been verified, the registration center calculates $Z_{new} = h(B_{new} \oplus z)$ and $Q_j = Z_{new} \oplus B_{new}$, and sends the message for the user and the server to complete the authentication $M_3 = h(g^{r_u} \| g^{r_s} \| RS'_j \| T_i \| T_j)$ and $M_4 = h(g^{r_u} \| g^{r_s} \| RU'_i \| T_i \| T_j)$. And send $\{Q_j, M_3, M_4\}$ to the server.

Step 4. After the server receives $\{Q_j, M_3, M_4\}$, it calculates $M'_3 = h(g^{r_u} \| g^{r_s} \| RS_j \| T_i \| T_j)$, and verifies whether M'_3 is equal to M_3. If they are equal, it proves that the message from the login process is actually sent by the registration center, and it is actually sent after the registration center has verified the user information, that is, the server has completed the authentication of the user at this time. The server calculates the session key $SK = (g^{r_u})^{r_s}$ for this service, and sends $\{Q_j, M_4, g^{r_s}, T_j\}$ to the user.

Step 5. After the user receives the feedback information $\{Q_j, M_4, g^{r_s}, T_j\}$ sent back from the server, it calculates the identity authentication message $M'_4 = h(g^{r_u} \| g^{r_s} \| RU_i \| T_i \| T_j)$, and verifies whether it is equal to M_4 that sent by the server. If it is equal. M_4 is verified, and the registration center will calculate this value after authenticate the validity of the server. So the user also completed the authentication of the server. Finally, the user calculates the same session key $SK = (g^{r_u})^{r_s}$ as the server. At this point, the authentication phase is completed.

3.4 Password Change Phase

The password change phase is similar to the login phase, as shown in Fig. 4.

When the user wants to change the password, he first inserts the smart card into the card reader, enters the previous password PW^*_i, the smart card calculates $P^*_i = h(h(PW^*_i))$, and judges P^*_i whether or not equals to P_i. If they are equal, the password is correct. The smart card returns a response signal to prompt the user to enter a fingerprint. After the user enters the fingerprint, the smart card extracts the feature value F^*_i, and checks the matching degree of $V_i \oplus h(PW^*_i)$ and F^*_i whether or not meets the security requirement. If the fingerprint verification passes, the smart card prompts the user to enter a new password PW_{new}, and recalculates the password's two hash values $P_{new} = h(h(PW_{new}))$ and the values that have been encrypted with the password hash $D_{new} = D_i \oplus h(PW^*_i) \oplus h(PW_{new})$, $C_{new} = C_i \oplus h(PW^*_i) \oplus h(PW_{new})$, $G_{new} = G_i \oplus h(PW^*_i) \oplus h(PW_{new})$, and $V_{new} = V_i \oplus h(PW^*_i) \oplus h(PW_{new})$. Finally, store $\{P_{new}, D_{new}, C_{new}, G_{new}, V_{new}\}$ to replace $\{P_i, D_i, C_i, G_i, V_i\}$, so far complete the password change.

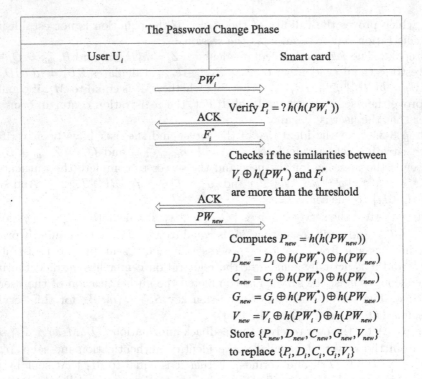

The Password Change Phase

User U_i	Smart card

PW_i^* →

← ACK   Verify $P_i = ? h(h(PW_i^*))$

F_i^* →

Checks if the similarities between
$V_i \oplus h(PW_i^*)$ and F_i^*
are more than the threshold

← ACK

PW_{new} →

Computes $P_{new} = h(h(PW_{new}))$
$D_{new} = D_i \oplus h(PW_i^*) \oplus h(PW_{new})$
$C_{new} = C_i \oplus h(PW_i^*) \oplus h(PW_{new})$
$G_{new} = G_i \oplus h(PW_i^*) \oplus h(PW_{new})$
$V_{new} = V_i \oplus h(PW_i^*) \oplus h(PW_{new})$
Store $\{P_{new}, D_{new}, C_{new}, G_{new}, V_{new}\}$
to replace $\{P_i, D_i, C_i, G_i, V_i\}$

Fig. 4. Registration phase of the improved protocol.

4   Security Analysis

This section will address the security flaws of the Chen et al. protocol and introduce the proposed method of the three-factor authentication protocol by our work.

(1) Verify password correctness
This protocol stores $P_i = h(h(PW_i))$ in the smart card. After the user enters the password, the smart card will calculate the two hash values of the password, and verify it whether or not equal to P_i, thus that the correctness of the password can be verified locally. This compensates for the inability of the Chen's protocol to verify the correctness of the password.

(2) Fingerprint storage and verification
In the registration stage, according to the fingerprint identification technology, fingerprints are collected and feature points are extracted, and the digitized feature points are encrypted and stored in a smart card. In the login or password change phase, the smart card matches the feature points of the newly entered fingerprint of the user with the fingerprint sampled in the registration phase. If the matching degree exceeds the predetermined threshold, the fingerprint entered passes the verification.

This process can effectively verify the validity of the user's identity and can play a non-repudiation function.

(3) Stolen smart card attack

In the protocol proposed by Chen, after the smart card was stolen, the attacker could obtain the PIN code and system parameters g from the smart card to implement further attacks. In this paper, the improved protocol $\{P_i, D_i, C_i, G_i, V_i, Z_i, B_i, h()\}$ is stored in the smart card. In addition to the hash function, other information is an encrypted value. Even if the attacker steals it, it will not reveal sensitive information, from this point, we achieve the goal of resisting stolen smart card attacks.

(4) Anonymity attacks

The improved protocol integrates the anti-anonymity attack method into a three-factor authentication protocol. The keys z and encryption values Z_i in the protocol correspond to the y and Y_i of the methods. As we mentioned before, the three-factor protocol completes user authentication at the registry, the registry does not need to share the key z with the server. Combining the specific characteristic of the three-factor identity protocol, the work of the server in the anti-anonymity attack method is completed by the registration center in the three-factor protocol.

(5) Eavesdropping attack

For the protocol of Chen et al., an attacker can obtain $\{g, g^{r_u}, g^{r_s}\}$ by means of attack, then calculates the session key $SK = (g^{r_u})^{r_s}$ for eavesdropping attacks. In the improved protocol, we encrypt the system parameters g that originally stored in the smart card. Thus the attacker's access is blocked, and the computing session key must completely obtain $\{g, g^{r_u}, g^{r_s}\}$. If the system parameters g is missing, the attacker can not calculate the session key. To this extent, the protocol is improved to resist eavesdropping attacks.

5   Performance Analysis

This section evaluates the computational complexity and security of the three-factor authentication protocol proposed in this paper. Table 2 compares the computational complexity of the proposed protocol with other existing protocols proposed by Hsiang et al. [13], Liao et al. [14], Li et al. [15], and Chen et al. Where T_h represents the time required for a hash operation. Because the amount of computation is mainly caused by hash operation, other operations are ignored here. From the comparison of the amount of calculation, it can be seen that the computational complexity of the proposed protocol is relatively less compare with the same types of protocol.

From Table 3, it can be seen that the proposed can be more secure than other schemes. It can be seen that the proposed performs are better in terms of security than other protocols. Combining the comparison results in Tables 2 and 3, it can be considered that the proposed protocol adds three hash operations in one login process, which makes up for the three security issues of the Chen et al. protocol. And compared with similar protocols, the improved protocol has a lower computational complexity, and it accomplishes more security goals.

Table 2. Comparison on computation cost of the three-factor schemes

Phases	Proposed	Hsiang and Shih	Liao and Wang	Li et al.	Chen et al.
Login	$3T_h$	$7T_h$	$6T_h$	$6T_h$	$2T_h$
Session key generation phase	$11T_h$	$15T_h$	$9T_h$	$20T_h$	$9T_h$
Password change phase	$4T_h$	$4T_h$	$4T_h$	$6T_h$	$2T_h$
Sum	$18T_h$	$26T_h$	$19T_h$	$32T_h$	$13T_h$

Table 3. Comparison on safety of the three-factor schemes

Safety goal	Proposed	Hsiang and Shih	Liao and Wang	Li et al.	Chen et al.
Users anonymity	Yes	Yes	Yes	No	No
Forward and backward security	Yes	No	No	Yes	Yes
Change password	Yes	Yes	Yes	Yes	Yes
Bidirectional verification	Yes	No	No	Yes	Yes
Resist Dos attacks	Yes	Yes	Yes	Yes	Yes
Resist verification table attack	Yes	Yes	Yes	Yes	Yes
Resist password leak attack	Yes	Yes	Yes	Yes	Yes
Resist stolen smart card attack	Yes	Yes	Yes	Yes	No
Resist impersonation attack	Yes	No	Yes	No	Yes
Resist replay attack	Yes	Yes	Yes	Yes	Yes
Resist hacking attack	Yes	Yes	Yes	Yes	No
Resist impersonation attack	Yes	Yes	Yes	Yes	Yes
Resist insider attack	Yes	Yes	No	Yes	Yes

6   Conclusion

This paper mainly focuses on three-factor authentication protocols based on smart cards, passwords and biometric information in a multi-server environment. We analyzes the protocols proposed by Chen et al. and find that the Chen et al. protocol cannot verify the correctness of passwords, and it is vulnerable to anonymity attacks, stolen smart card attacks and masquerade attacks. To overcome these weaknesses, this paper presents an improvement authentication protocol and analyzes the security of the proposed protocol. Compared the new protocol with the related protocols, it can be observed that the proposed can achieve more safety goals with a lower computational complexity.

References

1. Jiang, Q., Khan, M.K., Lu, X.: A privacy preserving three-factor authentication protocol for e-Health clouds. J. Supercomput. **72**(10), 3826–3849 (2016)
2. Wei, F., Wei, Y., Ma, C.: Attack on an ID-based authenticated group key exchange protocol with identifying malicious participants. Int. J. Netw. Secur. **18**(2), 393–396 (2016)
3. Jangirala, S., Mukhopadhyay, S., Das, A.K.: A multi-server environment with secure and efficient remote user authentication scheme based on dynamic ID using smart cards. Wireless Pers. Commun. **95**(3), 1–33 (2017)

4. Baruah, K.C., Banerjee, S., Dutta, M.H.P.: An improved biometric-based multi-server authentication scheme using smart card. Int. J. Secur. Appl. **9**(1), 397–408 (2016)
5. Li, L., Lin, I., Hwang, M.: A remote password authentication scheme for multi-server architecture using neural networks. IEEE Trans. Neural Network **12**(6), 1498–1504 (2001)
6. Tsaur, W.-J., Wu, C.-C., Lee, W.-B.: A smart card-based remote scheme for password authentication in multi-server Internet services. Comput. Stand. Interfaces **27**(1), 39–51 (2004)
7. Juang, W.-S.: Efficient multi-server password authenticated key agreement using smart cards. IEEE Trans. Consum. Electron. **50**(1), 251–255 (2004)
8. Chang, C.C., Lee, J.S.: An efficient and secure multi-server password authentication scheme using smart cards. In: International Conference on Cyberworlds, pp. 417–422. IEEE Computer Society (2004)
9. Tsai, J.-L.: Efficient multi-server authentication scheme based on one-way hash function without verification table. Comput. Secur. **27**(3–4), 115–121 (2008)
10. Tsaur, W.J., Li, J.H., Lee, W.B.: An efficient and secure multi-server authentication scheme with key agreement. J. Syst. Softw. **85**(4), 876–882 (2012)
11. Wang, R.-C., Juang, W.-S., Lei, C.-L.: User authentication scheme with privacy-preservation for multi-server environment. IEEE Commun. Lett. **13**(2), 157–159 (2009)
12. Chen, T.-Y., Lee, C.-C., Hwang, M.-S., Jan, J.-K.: Towards secure and efficient user authentication scheme using smart card for multi-server environments. J. Supercomput. **66**(2), 1008–1032 (2013)
13. Hsiang, H.-C., Shih, W.-K.: Improvement of the secure dynamic ID based remote user authentication scheme for multi-server environment. Comput. Stan. Interfaces **31**(6), 1118–1123 (2009)
14. Liao, Y.-P., Wang, S.-S.: A secure dynamic ID based remote user authentication scheme for multi-server environment. Comput. Stand. Interfaces **31**(1), 24–29 (2009)
15. Li, X., Xiong, Y.-P., Ma, J., Wang, W.-D.: An efficient and security dynamic identity based authentication protocol for multi-server architecture using smart cards. J. Netw. Comput. Appl. **35**(2), 763–769 (2012)

A VANET Anonymous Authentication Mechanism for Multi-level Application Scenarios

Xiaoliang Wang[1(✉)], Jianming Jiang[1,2], Baowei Wang[3],
and Zhihua Xia[3]

[1] Department of Computer Science and Engineering,
Hunan University of Science and Technology, Xiangtan 411201, China
fengwxl@163.com
[2] School of Engineering and IT, University of New South Wales,
NSW Sydney, Australia
[3] Nanjing University of Information Science and Technology,
Nanjing 210044, China

Abstract. Vehicular Ad-hoc Network (VANET) is a rapid developing application of the Internet of Things, which has totally difference with the conventional traffic network. On one hand, a VANET needs to provide end-to-end verification that has been widely concerned by researchers. On the other hand, the privacy is also very important in a VANET. Because of the openness of VANETs, conventional security measures do not effectively guarantee vehicle's privacy. In other words, there is an urgent requirement for new security schemes to guarantee vehicular privacy in VANETs. Therefore, ensuring anonymity and authentication is a double requirement in VANETs. The both requirements seem contradictory but have to coexist. However, effective technology is few in literature and the existing anonymous authentication schemes cannot provide reverse trace mechanism when anonymity abuse happens. At the same time, these existing researches are limited to the application layer without considering the particularity of the perception layer and network layer. Without the support of the lower layer, the upper layer cannot achieve real security. Our aim is to build a lightweight anonymous authentication security system under the privacy preserving which considers the limitation of bottom layer devices and anonymity abuse problem.

Keywords: VANET · Privacy preserving · Authentication · Anonymity abuse

1 Introduction

VANET is a kind of intelligent transportation network. By a variety of sensing equipments of On Board Units (OBUs) in vehicles such as sensors, radio frequency identification (RFID) tags, global positioning systems and other devices, the inter-vehicle communications or communications with roadside infrastructure can be achieved. In VANETs, there are plenty of different applications and these applications have different requirements from the bottom layer to the top layer.

© Springer Nature Switzerland AG 2018
X. Sun et al. (Eds.): ICCCS 2018, LNCS 11066, pp. 706–717, 2018.
https://doi.org/10.1007/978-3-030-00015-8_61

Because of the use of electronic equipment and the openness of VANET, the security of the bottom layer of the VANET causes users' concerns [1]. Conventional methods often use symmetric or asymmetric key systems to guarantee the security of a system. However, symmetric key system is able to suit the limitation of bottom hardware but does not meet the high security requirements. An heavy-weight asymmetric key system is able to meet the high security requirements but not satisfy the low cost of the hardware of OBUs [2]. So in the perception layer, such a resource constrained but open environment, unilateral emphasis on the high security of encryption algorithm or unilateral emphasis on hardware resource constraints is an unwise choice. There should be a balance between high security and hardware overhead.

In addition, in the application layer of a VANET, the privacy and authentication requirements of vehicles are different in different scenarios. The existing security protocols do not address this issue. In practice, the privacy rights of vehicles are not the same. In normal driving, the system respects vehicle's privacy rights and can provide a lot of privacy rights to vehicular identity information, data transmission and location positioning. When verifying the identity information on OBU, coarse-grained authentication could be provided between vehicles and roadside units (RSU), which we call "generic certification" involving the entities of OBUs and RSUs. When a vehicle commits anonymity abuse such as escaping from traffic accidents, spreading false traffic information, issuing false certificate or launching malicious attacks to other vehicles under the protection of the anonymity, system will take the fine-grained authentication to track the anonymous vehicle, which we call "confirmed certification" between the entities of the authority and the anonymity abuse vehicle.

In this paper, a lightweight VANET anonymous authentication scheme for multi-level requirements is proposed. The scheme will uses the alias and the cryptographic algorithm based on the elliptic curve to realize multi-level anonymity, hierarchical authentication and implementing tracking requirements under anonymity abuse. Its advantages are as follows. (1) Two equilibrium points are proposed. One is the balance between the hardware limitation and the high security performance. The other is the balance between the privacy and authentication. The hierarchical verification including "generic certification" and "confirmed certification" is proposed. (2) Lightweight and center-less verification method between strange vehicles is proposed. (3) Scalable key management is designed.

2 Related Work

Some researchers pay attention on privacy preserving and propose a number of anonymous authentication schemes. Among them, because of the anonymity of group signature, some researchers choose group signature to design anonymous authentication schemes. Sun et al. [3] and Guo et al. [4] use Boneh's group signature scheme for vehicular communication early. Considering the high cost and hidden danger of group signature, later researchers improved it. However, Calandriello et al. [5] pointed out that the inherent computation cost and signature length of group signature is much larger than that of the general PKI digital signature algorithm like the elliptic curve digital signature algorithm (ECDSA). Therefore, other researchers turn to the ring signature scheme. Ring signature is a simplified group signature scheme, which has an anonymous character because the signature is made up of a ring. For example, literature [29] implements an effective privacy protection and authentication mechanism by using a ring signature scheme with non bilinear pairings. It abandons the complex operation of bilinear to reduce the computing overhead in the process of signature generation. Besides, some researchers focus on anonymous authentication based on identity based signature (IBS) such as Sun [6], ACPN [7], Jinila [8], He [9], WCCV [10]. Among them, Sun et al. [6] are the earlier researchers in this field. They use zero knowledge proof and threshold secret sharing algorithm to design an anonymous authentication scheme based on identity signature. In order to achieve the authentication function under conditional privacy protection, He et al. [11] designs an anonymous authentication algorithm based on identity signature using elliptic curve algorithm without bilinear operation, which is of higher security and less computation. WCCV [10] points out the anonymous authentication scheme with a trusted third party has disadvantage that is easily compromised by adversaries, so it proposes an anonymous authentication scheme without trusted center based on bilinear mapping and the Diffe-Hellman hypothesis.

Other anonymous authentication mechanisms are committed to using such auxiliary technologies as kana, Mix sharing and batch processing technology to achieve or optimize anonymous authentication process. VSPN [12] uses bilinear mapping and proxy re-encryption to design a pseudonym mechanism for vehicular self organizing networks. Berg et al. [13] propose an vehicle-based certificate-selection method for the privacy preserving of vehicles. In their method, a vehicle can detect and use the certificates in use by neighboring vehicles to secure its own communication and also verify the certificates possessed by their own. It allows a vehicle to hide its privacy in its region without increasing an attacker's ability to evade exposure. K-anonymity means that only if the information of k − 1 entities is disclosed at the same time, it is possible to deduce who is the Kth entity. Literature [14] proposes an authentication algorithm based on K anonymous with P perception, which takes K entities as an anonymous whole in the information interaction of a region, and the authority can optimize those queries to track a specific entity if necessary. However, this scheme does not take into account the problem of anonymity abuse. Candido [15] is also based on the K anonymous algorithm, but it takes into account the tracking problem after anonymity abuse happens. By the theoretical analysis and the experiments of NS2, SUMO and other simulation tools, the effectiveness of the scheme in anonymity abuse tracking is proved. LESPP [16] can quickly generate and verify MAC signature by using lightweight symmetric key system and MAC mechanism. The memory cost of this scheme is low, but it does not consider the single point failure of the third party authentication center. 2FLIP [17] takes advantage of the Hashi signature and MAC information of multiple lightweight terminals. By the distributed processing of trusted nodes, it can quickly issue and verify a signature. At the same time it has non-repudiation of signature so that the abusers can be tracked when anonymity abuse happens. Some researchers like to apply batch technology to reduce the overhead in the process of anonymous authentication. For example, literature [18] designs an anonymous authentication algorithm based on identity encryption. The use of a small fixed number of pairing computations and point multiplication operation of relatively small overhead makes it beyond the limitation of the number of authentication data packets. At the same time, it uses the batch mode to realize the quick authentication between vehicles, vehicles and roadside units. The [19] uses the same batch concept to optimize redundant certificate revocation list (CRL) in the process of anonymous authentication and certificate renewal process. Moreover, batch authentication process is applied to not only anonymous identity batch but also anonymous information and it significantly reduces the system overhead.

3 Preliminaries

In 1987, Montgomery put forward the Montgomery type elliptic curve [20] that is a new type of elliptic curve. It has been attracted more attention in the cryptography field because it has more advantages than the Weierstrass elliptic curve has. Compared with the Weierstrass elliptic curve, its advantages exist in next aspects: Firstly, Montgomery type elliptic curve has faster computing speed than Weierstrass elliptic curve because its multiplication operation does not need to calculate the value of Y; Secondly, it has better immunity to simple energy and time attack.

The mapping coordinate equation of Montgomery type elliptic curve in E/Fp is: $By^2 = x^3 + Ax^2 + x$, which can be transformed from some Weierstrass elliptic curves, but not all Weierstrass elliptic curves. The basic conditions of Montgomery type elliptic curve are as follows.

(1) $x^3 + ax^2 + b = 0$ should have at least one root in F_p;
(2) $3a^2 + a = 0$ has two residue roots on F_p, in which the α is a root of the $x^3 + ax^2 + b$ in the F_p.

Modular addition formula of Montgomery elliptic curve (affine coordinates): $P \neq \pm Q$.

Assume $P = (x1, y1)$, $Q = (x2, y2)$ is the point of the elliptic curve in E(k), the point addition and the multiplication of the Montgomery elliptic curve are as follows. The value of $P + Q = (x_3, y_3)$ is as follows.

$$\Delta = \frac{y_2 - y_1}{x_2 - x_1}$$

$$x_3 = B\Delta^2 - A - x_1 - x_2$$

$$y_3 = \Delta(x_1 - x_2) - y_1$$

The point multiplication equation is as follows.

$$\Delta = \frac{3x_1^2 + 2Ax_1 + 1}{2By_1}$$

$$x_3 = B\Delta^2 - A - 2x_1$$

$$y_3 = \Delta(x_1 - x_3) - y_1$$

Improved ECDSA algorithm based on Montgormery type elliptic curve was proposed by Wang et al. [21], which uses binary shift NAF coding algorithm to avoid most of the inverse modular operation in the projective coordinates, and uses the point addition and the point multiplication operation without calculating the value of y.

The point addition equation is as follows.

$$X_{m-n} = Z_{m-n}[(X_m - Z_m)(X_n + Z_n) + (X_m + Z_m)(X_n - Z_n)]^2$$

$$Z_{m+n} = X_{m-n}[(X_m - Z_m)(X_n + Z_n) - (X_m + Z_m)(X_n - Z_n)]^2$$

The point multiplication equation is as follows.

$$4X_n Z_n = (X_n + Z_n)^2 - (X_n - Z_n)^2$$

$$X_{2n} = (X_n + Z_n)^2 (X_n - Z_n)^2$$

$$Z_{2n} = (4X_n Z_n)[(X_n - Z_n)^2 + ((A+2)/4)(4X_n Z_n)]$$

The calculation of the coordinates (X, Z) in the projective plane of point multiplication dP of the point $P = (x, y)$ is as follows:

(1) $i \leftarrow |d| - 1$
(2) Calculate integers:

$$X_1 \leftarrow x$$

$$Z_1 \leftarrow 1$$

$$T_1 \leftarrow (X_1 + Z_1)^2 - (X_1 - Z_1)^2$$

$$X_2 \leftarrow (X_1 + Z_1)^2 (X_1 - Z_1)^2$$

$$Z_2 \leftarrow T_1((X_1 - Z_1)^2 + ((A+2)/4)T_1$$

(3) If $i = 0$, go to (12), otherwise execute (4).
(4) $i \leftarrow i - 1$
(5) If $d_i = 0$, execute (6), otherwise go to (9).
(6) Calculate integers:

$$T_1 \leftarrow X_2$$

$$X_2 \leftarrow [(T_1 - Z_2)(X_1 + Z_1) + (T_1 + Z_2)(X_1 - Z_1)]^2$$

$$Z_2 \leftarrow x[(T_1 - Z_2)(X_1 + Z_1) - (T_1 + Z_2)(X_1 - Z_1)]^2$$

(7) Calculate integers:

$$T_1 \leftarrow X_2$$

$$T_2 \leftarrow (T_1 + Z_1)^2 - (T_1 - Z_1)^2$$

$$X_1 \leftarrow (T_1 + Z_1)^2 (T_1 - Z_1)^2$$

$$Z_1 \leftarrow T_2((T_1 - Z_1)^2 + ((A+2)/4)T_2$$

(8) Go to (3)
(9) Calculate integer:

$$T_1 \leftarrow X_1$$

$$X_1 \leftarrow [(X_2 - Z_2)(T_1 + Z_1) + (X_2 + Z_2)(T_1 - Z_1)]^2$$

$$Z_1 \leftarrow x[(X_2 - Z_2)(T_1 + Z_1) - (X_2 + Z_2)(T_1 - Z_1)]^2$$

(10) Calculate integers:

$$T_1 \leftarrow X_2$$

$$T_2 \leftarrow (T_1 + Z_2)^2 - (T_1 - Z_2)^2$$

$$X_1 \leftarrow (T_1 + Z_2)^2 (T_1 - Z_2)^2$$

$$Z_2 \leftarrow T_2((T_1 - Z_2)^2 + ((A+2)/4)T_2$$

(11) Go to (3).
(12) Output integer X_1 and Z_1 as the X and Z corresponding to dP.

4 Our Proposal

4.1 The Formation of Aliases

The perception layer constructs the identity information of OBU. The conventional OBU identity is arranged by manufactures. Once the identity information is installed on the vehicle, it will be bound with vehicle identification number (VIN), license plate number and so on, so in this scheme we use OBU identity as vehicular identity information. The identity information exists as two forms in order to realize the different application requirements under the different scenarios. One is the real sequence code of the OBU device, and the other is the alias corresponding to the real sequence code of the OBU device. After obfuscation or intercepting process, system calculates a hash value of OBU identity using the hash function with key K_{OBU}. The hash value works as an alias for this OBU. Because the alias is bound with the real vehicle identity, it can be used for qualification authentication between strange vehicles after authority signing. On the same time, the K_{OBU} will be transmitted through subliminal channel of signing, so that the authority can use it for the abuser tracking once anonymity abuse happens.

4.2 Register and Signing

In above process, user identity is divided into two forms and real vehicular identity is concealed and the alias represents the user's real identity. Vehicles will use the signed alias to complete mutual authentication between strangers, which makes the stranger vehicles believe the partners from the trusted party, but do not know the real identity of the partner vehicle. The detailed procedure is as follows. The system uses the dynamic grouping management strategy based on geographical location and time concept [22] to elect the local certificate authority (CA) for every region. In registration stage, a vehicle registers at its local CA with the assistance of nearby RSUs and its identity information (including the OBU alias, real sequence code of OBU and other information) is sent to the local CA.

To reduce the overhead of key management such as storage, computation and communication, this scheme adopts the idea of combined public key cryptography (CPK) based on Montgomery elliptic curve [23] to generate public/private key pair for these CAs. The scheme will construct the public/private key matrix based on the mathematical principle of elliptic curve discrete logarithm, and map the identities of CAs to matrix row and column coordinate sequence through hash process. By selection and combination of the elements of the matrix, system can generate a huge number of the private keys for CAs, which lightens the burden of key management, makes key generation and distribution scalable. At the same time, plus using the geographic location based dynamic packet management policy, vehicle nodes can calculate the public key of a certain CA if they know the geographic information of the CA, so that lightweight quick verification can be easily realized.

The methods used in the scheme are as follows. The domain parameters of elliptic curve is denoted as D: $D = (F, a, b, P)$, where F is the finite field $GF(p^n)$, $a, b \in GF(p^n)$, p represents a base point, $\#E(GF(PN))$ is the order of point of

Montgomery elliptic curve. h() represents the hash function. A CA uses the private key that the system generates using CPK based on Montgomery elliptic curve as its private key to sign the alias of the vehicle as a credential for the vehicle access to the VANET network.

Compare with the conventional signature system based on elliptic curve whose signature verification signature time is two times longer than signing [21], the use of Montgomery type elliptic curve will distinctly decrease the computational complexity of scalar multiplication, which greatly shorten the authentication time between strange vehicles and make quick-authentication true. After a vehicle registers at its CA, the CA will sign the alias of the registered vehicle. The signing process is as follows.

(1) The CA generates a random numbers K, d_{CA} in the interval $[1, n - 1]$, where d_{CA} is the projection of its private key in the interval $[1, n - 1]$.

2) The CA calculates $kG = (x, y)$ and $R = x \bmod p_1^n$, G is a point of $GF(p^n)$, where y not to be computed due to the use of Montgomery elliptic curve.

3) The CA calculates $E = h(m)$, m is an integer representing the alias information of the signed vehicle, $h(m)$ is a hash fuction result.

4) The CA calculates $s = k^{-1}(E + d_{CA}) \bmod n$.

Then CA sends (R, s) as the signature of the alias to the registered vehicle, which will be taken as a credential for the verification between stranger vehicles.

4.3   The Construction of the Subliminal Channel

At the same time of signing, the CA will hide the $Encrypted_{K_{CA}}(K_{OBU})$ in the signature base on ECC. The key is to find a subliminal channel based on the above elliptic curve digital signature algorithm. In 1993, Simmons's article [24] about "The Prisoners" problem and the subliminal channel was firstly proposed. He noted that if a prison guard could not control the choice of random number, the sender could select a specific "random number" to transmit secret as a subliminal channel. Therefore, as long as there exists random number selection in the process of signature, it is possible to have a subliminal channel, and the signer can skillfully use it as the transmission of secret information.

When CA wants to use the subliminal channel in the signature to transfer OBU Key, it encrypts the K_{OBU} using its public key K_{CA} and gets the $Encrypted_{K_{CA}}(K_{OBU})$, then replace the above random integer K with the $Encrypted_{K_{CA}}(K_{OBU})$. This process does not affect the encryption and signature operation so it will not affect the next authentication of the signature. It is noteworthy that we assume that only the authority and local CAs know the existing of these subliminal channels (most of the information hiding algorithms are based on this similar hypothesis). The other CAs do not know the private key of the local CA, so they are unable to obtain the hash key K_{OBU}.

In order to prevent the failure of single point and causing attack, after the signing stage the local CA do not keep the vehicle's identity information. In the future, if the local CA will not get the signature submitted by the victim vehicle after anonymity abuse, because the identity information of the vehicle is not kept locally, CA cannot misuse the subliminal channel.

4.4 Generic Certification Between Strange Vehicles

After receiving the local CA signature, a vehicle can use the signature as a mutual authentication certificate between strange vehicles. If a vehicle provides an invalid digital signature, the bidirectional authentication process is interrupted. Only if the signature is valid, the both start to communicate with each other.

When communication with strange vehicles for the first time, a vehicle needs to verify the alias of the corresponding vehicle signed by its CA. The steps are as follows:

(1) The vehicle verifies whether R, s of corresponding vehicle is an integer of the interval $[1, n - 1]$. If fail, it discards the signature and stops communicate with corresponding vehicle. If successful, the both enter the next bidirectional authentication.
(2) Calculate $e = h(m)$;
(3) Calculate $w = s^{-1} \bmod p_1^n$;
(4) Calculate $u_1 = ew \bmod p_1^n$, $u_2 = rw \bmod p_1^n$;
(5) Calculate $a = (u_1 + u_2 K_{CA}) \bmod p_1^n$, K_{CA} is the public key of CA,
(6) Computing the point multiplication of $a \times G$ using Montgomery type elliptic curve.
(7) Calculate $v = xR \bmod \bmod p_1^n$. Only when $v = r$ it accepts the signatures and trust the identity of unfamiliar vehicles.

4.5 Confirmed Certification

When anonymity abuse happens the victim vehicle will submit the signature certificate that the abuse provided in the generic certification stage to its local CA. Then the CA checks who is the signer of the signature and then forwards the signature certificate to the signing CA. The signing CA will calculate $Encrypted_{K_{CA}}(K_{OBU}) = k^{-1}(e + d_{CA})$ $\bmod p_1^n$ in order to recover the $Encrypted_{K_{CA}}(K_{OBU})$ information hidden in the subliminal channel of the signature. Because ordinary vehicles do not know the existence of the subliminal channel, they cannot know the secret. For the other CAs do not know the private key d_{CA} of the signing CA, nor can they reveal the real identity of the vehicle (OBU's real serial number). At the same time, because the identity information of a vehicle is not saved in the signing CA after signing stage, it is impossible that the signing CA fork a signature to a certain innocent vehicle, which prevents the tracking abuse.

5 Security and Performance Analysis

5.1 Security

In this scheme, the security of the signature is based on the elliptic curve discrete logarithm problem. The computational complexity of elliptic curve discrete logarithm problem (ECDLP) is completely exponential. It is not feasible for attackers to decode private keys d_{CA} through public keys K_{CA}, which can meet the security requirements for VANETs. The bidirectional authentication method proposed in this scheme can also resist the attack of the middleman. The security of the alias is based on the security of chosen hash function. At present, the method of MD5 with salt can keep the high security.

5.2 Computing Overhead

Vehicular authentication and re-authentication process repeatedly uses the encryption, decryption and digital signature algorithm. In these processes, scalar point multiplication is the main computing overhead. In the traditional ECDSA algorithm, when calculating $(x, y) = (u_1 G + u_2 K)$ [25], system firstly calculates the result of the point multiple of $u_1 G$ and $u_2 K$ respectively, then calculates the point addition of $u_1 G + u_2 K$, and finally performs the verification operation. Therefore, the time used to verify a signature is 2 times than the time used for signing. Our scheme does not calculate the point multiple of $u_1 G$ and $u_2 K$ and uses Montgomery curve fast multiplication calculation to calculate $a = (u_1 + u_2 K_{CA}) \mod p_1^n$ with modular operation instead of $(x, y) = (u_1 G + u_2 K)$ operation, which hugely lighten the authentication overhead. By experimental simulation, we find although the somewhat increase of transmission capacity (about 10bit transmission capacity), but lighten the verification overhead of the signature from the original 2 times reduced to 1.2 times of the signing overhead. The computational complexity is $(6|d| - 3)M + (4|d| - 2)S$, where M denotes mulplication operation, S denotes square operation.

5.3 Storage Overhead

This scheme adopts the concept of CPK algorithm based on ECC of Montgomery curve, so a large number of public/private key pairs can be combined from a small matrix, which achieves large-scale key management. The system only needs to save the information of the elliptic curve public key matrix, without the need to save a large number of key information that saves the storage space. For normal CA nodes, they only need to save their own public/private key pair. The public key of other nodes can be gotten by querying the public key matrix and performance addition operation to the public key factor.

5.4 Center-Less Authentication

In the scheme, when verifying the CA signature of a strange partner, the vehicle can calculate the combined public key CPK of the CA according to the identity of the CA and key matrix, so it can achieve a simple and efficient authentication process without the participation of the third party, which achieves center-less authentication.

5.5 The Embedding and Extracting Time Overhead of the Subliminal Channel

From the simulation results, we find the time overhead of signing is 0.01 s, the time overhead of signing with subliminal information embedded is 0.02 s, the mutual verifying time overhead is 0.012 s, and the extraction time overhead of hidden information is 0.1 s. With the number of nodes from 1 to 200, the time cost of the signing, the signing with subliminal information embedding, and the information extraction from a subliminal channel grows linearly, the time cost of the mutual verification grows polynomially.

6 Conclusions

This paper proposes a lightweight VANET anonymous authentication scheme for multi-level application requirements. The scheme designs multi-level certification for different application scenarios under privacy preservation. Firstly, it proposes an algorithm for the "generic certification", which guarantees that all aliases of vehicles in the VANET can be verified quickly. Secondly, it proposes an algorithm based on subliminal channel for the "confirmed certification", which provides the tracking function when anonymity abuse happens. At the same time, the authentication scheme based on Montgomery curve ECC addresses both the hardware limitations of the bottom layer devices and the lightweight and fast authentication requirement of the upper layer.

References

1. Cheng, W., Cheng, X., Song, M., Chen, B., Zhao, W.W.: On the design and deployment of RFID assisted navigation systems for VANETs. IEEE Trans. Parallel Distrib. Syst. **23**, 1267–1274 (2012)
2. Mojtaba, A., Wan, H.H., Mazdak, Z., Sasan, K., Eghbal, G.: Implementation and evaluation of lightweight encryption algorithms suitable for RFID. J. Next Gener. Inf. Technol. **4**, 65–77 (2013)
3. Sun, X., Lin, X., Ho, P.H.: Secure vehicular communications based on group signature and id-based signature scheme. In: IEEE International Conference on Communications, pp. 1539–1545. IEEE Press, New York (2007)
4. Guo, J., Baugh, J.P., Wang, S.: A group signature based secure and privacy-preserving vehicular communication framework. In: Mobile Networking for Vehicular Environments, pp. 103–108 (2007)
5. Calandriello, G., Papadimitratos, P., Hubaux, J.P., Lioy, A.: Efficient and robust pseudonymous authentication in VANET. In: International Workshop on Vehicular Ad Hoc Networks, Vanet 2007, Montréal, Québec, Canada, September, pp. 19–28 (2007)
6. Sun, J., Zhang, C., Zhang, Y., Fang, Y.: An identity-based security system for user privacy in vehicular ad hoc networks. IEEE Trans. Parallel Distrib. Syst. **21**, 1227–1239 (2010)
7. Li, J., Lu, H., Guizani, M.: ACPN: a novel authentication framework with conditional privacy-preservation and non-repudiation for VANETs. IEEE Trans. Parallel Distrib. Syst. **26**, 938–948 (2015)
8. Bevish, J.Y.: An efficient authentication scheme for VANET using Cha Cheon's ID based signatures. Indian J. Appl. Res. **4**, 106–109 (2014)
9. He, D., Zeadally, S., Xu, B., Huang, X.: An efficient identity-based conditional privacy-preserving authentication scheme for vehicular ad hoc networks. IEEE Trans. Inf. Forensics Secur. **10**, 2681–2691 (2015)

10. Wang, X., Li, S., Zhao, S., Xia, Z., Bai, L.: A vehicular ad hoc network privacy protection scheme without a trusted third party. Int. J. Distrib. Sens. Netw. **13**, 1–10 (2017)
11. He, D.B., Zeadally, S., Xu, B.W., Huang, X.Y.: An efficient identity-based conditional privacy-preserving authentication scheme for vehicular ad hoc networks. IEEE Trans. Inf. Forensic Secur. **10**, 2681–2691 (2015)
12. Chim, T.W., Yiu, S.M., Hui, L.C.K., Li, V.O.K.: VSPN: VANET-based secure and privacy-preserving navigation. IEEE Trans. Comput. **63**, 510–524 (2014)
13. Berg, E.V.D., Zhang, T., Pietrowicz, S.: Blend-in: a privacy-enhancing certificate-selection method for vehicular communication. IEEE Trans. Veh. Technol. **58**, 5190–5199 (2009)
14. Chen, J., Xu, H., Zhu, L.: Query-aware location privacy model based on p-sensitive and k-anonymity for road networks. Internet Things **2012**, 157–165 (2012)
15. Caballero-Gil, C., Molina-Gil, J., Hernandez-Serrano, J., Leon, O., Soriano-Ibanez, M.: Providing k-anonymity and revocation in ubiquitous VANETs. Ad Hoc Netw. **36**, 482–494 (2016)
16. Wang, M.Z., Liu, D., Zhu, L.H., Xu, Y.J., Wang, F.: LESPP: lightweight and efficient strong privacy preserving authentication scheme for secure VANET communication. Computing **98**, 685–708 (2016)
17. Wang, F., Xu, Y.J., Zhang, H.W., Zhang, Y.J., Zhu, L.H.: 2FLIP: a two-factor lightweight privacy-preserving authentication scheme for VANET. IEEE Trans. Veh. Technol. **65**, 896–911 (2016)
18. Tzeng, S.F., Horng, S.J., Li, T.R., Wang, X., Huang, P.H., Khan, M.K.: Enhancing security and privacy for identity-based batch verification scheme in VANETs. IEEE Trans. Veh. Technol. **66**, 3235–3248 (2017)
19. Vijayakumar, P., Chang, V., Deborah, L.J., Balusamy, B., Shynu, P.G.: Computationally efficient privacy preserving anonymous mutual and batch authentication schemes for vehicular ad hoc networks. Futur. Gener. Comp. Syst. **78**, 943–955 (2018)
20. Montgomery, P.L.: Modular multiplication without trial division. Math. Comput. **44**, 519–521 (1985)
21. Chao, W., Xiang-yong, S., Zhi-hua, N.: The research of the promotion for ECDSA algorithm based on Montgomery-form ECC. J. Commun. **31**, 9–13 (2010)
22. Pathak, V., Yao, D., Iftode, L.: Securing location aware services over VANET using geographical secure path routing. In: IEEE International Conference on Vehicular Electronics and Safety, pp. 346–353. IEEE Press, New York (2010)
23. Chao, W., Guang-yue, H., Huan-guo, Z.: Lightweight security architecture design for wireless sensor network. J. Commun. **33**, 30–35 (2012)
24. Simmons G.J.: The prisoners' problem and the subliminal channel. In: Chaum D. (ed.) Advances in Cryptology. Springer, Boston (1984). https://doi.org/10.1007/978-1-4684-4730-9_5
25. Wang, H., Li, B., Yu, W.: Montgomery algorithm on elliptic curves over finite fields of character three. J. Commun. **29**, 25–28 (2008)

Author Index

Printed in the United States
By Bookmasters